WHAT's APP ENED? Or WHAT THE F... WAS ALL THAT ABOUT?

An Observational and Experiential Commentary on Life from 1950 to 2025, as seen through the eyes of a proud Lancastrian.

By

James Briggs

MAPLE
PUBLISHERS

WHAT's APP ENED? Or WHAT THE F... WAS ALL THAT ABOUT?

Author: James Briggs

Copyright © 2026 James Briggs

The right of James Briggs to be identified as author of this work has been asserted by the author in accordance with section 77 and 78 of the Copyright, Designs and Patents Act 1988.

First Published in 2026

ISBN 978-1-83538-859-4 (Paperback)
   978-1-83538-860-0 (E-Book)

Book Cover Design and Layout by:
   White Magic Studios
   www.whitemagicstudios.co.uk

Published by:
   Maple Publishers
   Fairbourne Drive, Atterbury,
   Milton Keynes,
   MK10 9RG, UK
   www.maplepublishers.com

A CIP catalogue record for this title is available from the British Library.

All rights reserved. No part of this book may be reproduced or translated in any form or by any means, electronic or mechanical, including photocopying, recording or by any information storage and retrieval system without written permission from the author.

This book is a memoir. It reflects the author's recollections of experiences over time. Some names and characteristics have been changed, some events have been compressed, and some dialogues have been recreated, and the Publisher hereby disclaims any responsibility for them.

This work is dedicated to:

- Joan O'Hara and Verna Dale Howarth for pointing me in the right direction, away from being another wayward teenager.
- Dee, for always remaining true and loyal when at times I didn't deserve it.
- My parents, brothers and sisters for giving me an identity.
- My partners and friends, true and transient, who gave substance to the day-to-day reality of my life.
- To the children, young and old, who entered my life, both in a teaching and non-educational context, and made it such a rich tapestry. Finally,
- To the good people who fight and stand up against the smug, arrogant, greedy, power – crazed individuals who roam the planet and put pounds before people and profits before pain. Without you my journey would never have taken the course it did and been as fruitful as it was.

Thank you.

My own disclaimer:

I am aware of slander-spoken, and libel-written. I am also aware that the truth is frequently overlooked or misinterpreted in case it might offend but I refuse to change facts to fiction, recant names, times, dates and places, just in case the truth offends or upsets. How can a piece of literature based on the personal experiences of someone's life and substantiated by the facts and research be subject to litigation? It's an insult to the people who have inspired me to then use fictitious names and recant the real perpetrators just to hide the reality.

Contents

1. **SETTING THE SCENE.** 7
   - 'Know Thyself' 11
   - Life: The Meaning of.... 12
   - Dreams and Aspirations. 15

   The Bah Bah, Woof Woof, Instant Gratification, Easily Disposable Society. 18

2. **DYSFUNCTIONAL FAMILIES AND CHILDHOOD RECOLLECTIONS: 0-16yrs.** 111
   - My Family: More the Merrier. 112
   - More Childhood Nostalgia. 129
   - What has happened to family values? 137
   - Early Childhood Educational and Religious Influences. 139
   - Early Sporting Prowess and the Therapy of Exercise. 140
   - North Chadderton Secondary Modern School: Hormones, Rejection 147
   - My First Love and Leaving Home. 147
   - Chadderton and Lancashire Schoolboys. 150
   - Manchester United FC and Oldham Athletic FC. 151

3. **CONNECTING WITH THE ADULT WORLD: 16-21years.** 159
   - Norweb. 159
   - The Education Department and School of Education, Manchester University: 161
   - Meeting Atlas and Anita. 161
   - TV, Radio, Music, DJ's, Films, Musicals and the Theatre. 170
   - Crossing Over to the Other side: 176
   - Mather Teacher Training College, Manchester University, 18-21yrs. 176

4. **THE PRIMARY TEACHING YEARS, 1971 to 1987: 21-37 years,** 193
   - Mather Street Infant and Junior School, 1971-76. 193
   - Independence: Carnarvon Castle, Meals on Wheels, Les Dawson and George Dews FC. 199
   - Our First Home, Financial and Family Planning and Living within Your Means. .. 203
   - Whitegate End Primary School, 1976-1979. 207
   - Blackshaw Lane Infant and Junior School, 1979-1987, ... 212
   - My B.Ed. Honours Degree. 224
   - Alandale Drive, Jim's Gym Club and It's a Knockout. 226

5. **A Change of Direction: 1988 onwards.** 233
   - Ashton Private Clinic. 233

- The Northern Institute of Massage, (NIM), and the Northern School of Osteopathy, (NSO)..................233
- Sheila Carter, Alan Ayckbourn, Sir Andrew Lloyd Webber, John Denver and Marianne Jepson's School of Dance and Drama. 240
- Writing and becoming a published author. 247
- National Coaching Foundation/Sports Coach UK, 1991 to 2003..................250
- Simply the Best: NW Counties, Junior Rugby League U15s, Tour to Fiji, New Zealand and Australia, 1993..................253
- Sport, the FA, FATOI's, Positive Discrimination, Disillusionment, Bullshit and Balderdash. 256
- The Society of Sports Therapists. 277
- My First Clinic: Eaves Lane and the Crown Prosecution Service. 280
- University of North London-BSc Sports Science and Sports Therapy, 1996-1997. 284
- Arnside Close, Hoghton, Preston, Sunseekers and Asking Prices. 289
- Claughton Avenue, ...292
- Teesside University. 293
- University of Central Lancashire: Final Straws and Camel's Backs. 301
- UCLAN, Voluntarily Revisited: The School of Medicine. 304

6. **PERSONAL STUFF.** **307**
   - Marriage and Children..................307
   - Friends, Acquaintances, Colleagues and Significant Others. 318
   - Relationships and their Baggage – Struggling with Rejection. 324
   - Personality Studies Re-visited: The Link, Lancashire Dining Club and the Last Chance Saloon..................333
   - Warners For Adults. 338

7. **RETIREMENT, VOLUNTARY WORK AND BUCKET LISTS: 56+years.** **340**
   - My Travel Log and Bucket List: Being chased by 4 ton of rhino on Safari. 342
   - My Retired Job Portfolio and Job Seekers' Allowance: 56 plus years. 353
   - CTS Travel and Transport. 358
   - The Ranger Service: 2007-2012..................360
   - St. Catherine's Hospice, 2009-2015. 366
   - Penwortham Racing Park: 2012 plus, Which Tribe Do You Belong To? Tickle-tackle and Playground Syndrome..................368

8. **THE END IS IN SIGHT:** **386**
   - Funerals, Death, Hindsight, Regrets and the Euthanasia Debate..................386

1.
SETTING THE SCENE.

In the late 1960s, during my teacher training at Mather College, Manchester University, I was informed that Homo Sapiens, (Latin: wise man), was the highest form of intelligence in the animal kingdom. Was there a female equivalent or in today's politically incorrect world, as I call it, is the term, 'wise man,' still permitted or does it have to be wise person? Years later, I seriously questioned that assertion as the questions, reservations and doubts started to emerge. During the writing of this book these are there for all to see, providing a continuous train of thought and perhaps some kind of reason as to why certain things happened or in many cases didn't happen. When you initially train as a Primary school teacher, choosing biology and physical education as your main subjects, with a whole raft of other 'ologies to take on board and on a regular basis update your pedagogical skills and the theoretical knowledge that underpins such, as part of your on-going professional development, to be confronted, over the past 30 plus years, with a society that has assigned much of what you have learned and experienced to be good practice, to the trash can and to then be patronised and condescended to by others who do not possess your knowledge, skill, expertise and experience because you dare to question and ask why, has been disconcerting to say the least. Under human stewardship, the world appears to be out of control. You have only to see how the UK and USA have become vindictive, divisive and dangerously divided countries mainly caused by individuals who have been tasked with caring for the populace. **"Government of the people, by the people, for the people shall not perish from the earth."** (Lincoln A, Gettysburg Address). How did a hairless primate evolve into a species that's created nuclear and chemical weapons of mass destruction that any power crazed crackpot with money can buy? Scientists claim to have proven that God doesn't exist, but we still allow religious fanatics to govern us and terrorise the planet. Supposed 'wise man', is destroying the ecosystems and social fabric of society in its pursuit of greed, power and wealth. Global warming is dismissed by many, especially if it interferes with this pursuit of power and wealth. Politicians arrange expensive global summits to con the people into thinking they actually care about its significance, whilst actually doing nothing of significance. It would appear they are not bothered about being shamed by well intentioned, articulate, well informed, honest teenagers around the world, after all what do they know? In my humble opinion, it would appear far more than many patronising politicians and adults. **Don't forget, power you can take but respect you have to earn. Power + Greed are a toxic cocktail.** Social media tycoons, who are responsible for building the technology and the subsequent positive or negative consequences of such, appear to have no conscience whatsoever. Maintaining absolute faith that the technology and connectivity is always going to turn out for the best, no matter how much this is proven **not** to be the case. And the answer to all this mayhem seems to be that we need to be less homophobic, more politically correct and watch Celebrity Big Brother. **I also started to challenge the view, held by many, that progress was in essence a good thing.** If true, why in 2025 do some people hate, maim and even want to kill another just because of their accent, race, colour, creed, political persuasion, or to which tribe they belonged? Is it insecurity and paranoia? Why are people discriminated against purely and simply because they don't fit into someone else's box? To me that's social grading and racial profiling at its worst. Which I thought we'd seen the last of with Adolf Hitler and the Klu Klux Clan but no, over the years there has been a steady stream of personnel filling the vacancies some of whom again have been put in place by so called intelligent people. Who says the witch trials in the 17th century are a thing of the past when 'Fake News', conspiracy theories and trolling abound in the 21st century? Scientists and academics get caught up in the statistics but human behaviour can't easily be broken down into bell curves and graphs. The questions seem endless. **"Why does a well-spoken university graduate studying urban preservation fly a passenger plane into a skyscraper, killing thousands of people? Why does a boy, barely into his teens, spray a schoolyard with bullets, or a teenage mother give birth in a toilet and leave the baby in a wastepaper bin? What makes a privileged child warp into a monster? We try to blame it on traumatic childhoods or abusive parents or environmental lead. No one knows where these creatures come from. Yet every generation, every society produces them."** (Gerritsen T, 2008. Keeping the Dead, PB, p348).

Why do so called intelligent people choose a lifestyle that has a massive impact on not only their own and their families' lives but also on society as a whole? In simplicity the answer would appear to be, **"You've got to know people – what frightens them, how they think, what they cling to when they're in trouble. You've got to watch and listen. People reveal themselves in a thousand different ways. In the clothes they wear, their shoes, their hands, their voices, the pauses and hesitations, the tics and gestures."** (Rowbotham M, 2008, Shatter, PB, p15).

And whilst many would say they agree with such sentiments, somehow, for many, this compassion doesn't appear to realise itself in everyday life, because, **"Human life spans are not predictable. Don't ever make the mistake of measuring someone by the length of their life. Measure them by the difference they made to the world."** (James P, 2014. Want You Dead, PB, 93:381). Sadly, in 2025 and especially in the world of politics and religion, trying to define and measure difference, is dependent on which tribe you belonged to. Is covering yourself in tattoos a way of denoting which tribe a person belonged to? In the 50s, 60s and 70s it was mainly the male armed forces and sailors who had them. By trying to recall and find answers, I was well aware that everything in life was a matter of perception and that the memories can become amplified and distorted. **"Someone once said that memories are photographs on the wrong side of your eyes."** (Booth S, Blood On The Tongue, 2003, 3:51). **"Memory is a jangle of neurons rinsed in amino acids which are transformed by new experiences and represent the reconstruction of an event in the mind."** (Case J, 2001. Trance State, PB, p 94, 224-225). However, in reality, memory plays strange tricks. We often remember things the way we would have liked them to be. So it is foolish to try and rekindle what has gone because it's never the same. Also, **"When you looked back at a life, you used a magnifying glass. Everything was bigger, amplified. A college tryst could become the love of a lifetime in memory."** (Connolly M, 2016. The Wrong Side of Goodbye, PB. 3:34).

So, the challenge for me, and to use the words of my fellow Lancastrian Eric Sykes, **"Browsing through the library of my mind, how much could I remember, how much had I forgotten? Could I access the inaccessible?"** (Sykes E, 2007, 'If I Don't Write it Nobody Else Will', PB, p 243). Memory comes in beats and flashes. It has also been said, **"....nothing was ever forgotten, but merely filed in an inaccessible corner of the memory. He had never been sure what the difference was between forgetting and being unable to remember ......"** (Bruce A, 2010. The Siren, PB, 40:229). Also, **you can't un-know and un-see things that you have learnt, heard and seen in your life. "You can't unring a bell."** (Coben H, 2007, The Woods, 7:74). At the end of the day perhaps there is only so much nostalgia one can draw from, before the well becomes dry. The mind creating false recollections, layer by layer, until the memories drift beyond reality. Also, I tried not to think of change as good, or bad, just inevitable, painful but necessary. For me, writing and putting into print my thoughts is a salve. Unfortunately, the salve has a limited shelf life before its healing power starts to fade. So, you keep writing hoping to eventually eliminate the demons. Unfortunately, the demons are real people and the news keeps repeating itself.

IF POSSIBLE, WHAT I REALLY WANTED TO FIND OUT WAS:

WHO decided and at what point did society embrace the changes in the name of progress? Or as Rudyard Kipling wrote, **"I keep 6 honest serving men. They taught me all I knew. Their names being What and Why and When and How and Where and Who."**

HOW did life and society arrive at such a point becoming subservient, corrupt, proselytised, venal, weak, greedy, materialistic, dissatisfied, irresponsible and yet, arrogant? No one is accountable anymore because there is no effective deterrent.

WHY is the creation of a fairer society that promotes a decent work ethic and values, where the bad people get punished and the good get rewarded, still considered a pipe dream 75 years after I was born? Is it because that's what you do? Nearly everyone does it. It's called progress because we are supposedly the highest form of intelligence on the planet. Or is it just, like sheep, we follow the rest, taking the line of least resistance, with very little thought as to the consequences for themselves or society as a whole. Hence the Bah, Bah, Woof Woof, Instant Gratification, Easily Disposable Society tag, or in simplicity the M Society of Me, Myself and I, Money, Money, Money. Today for many, me comes first all the time, very rarely, if ever, are these people prepared to sacrifice personal gain for the greater good. What of the future? Finally, before setting off on my journey to try and find some answers I would like to quote W Shakespeare, **"If you want to be a writer**

speak to others and for others. Speak first for yourself. Search within, consider the contents of your own soul, use humility and humanity, be honest with yourself then whatever you write, all is true." (Film, All is True, 2018).

James Briggs: The Seeker Of Truth.

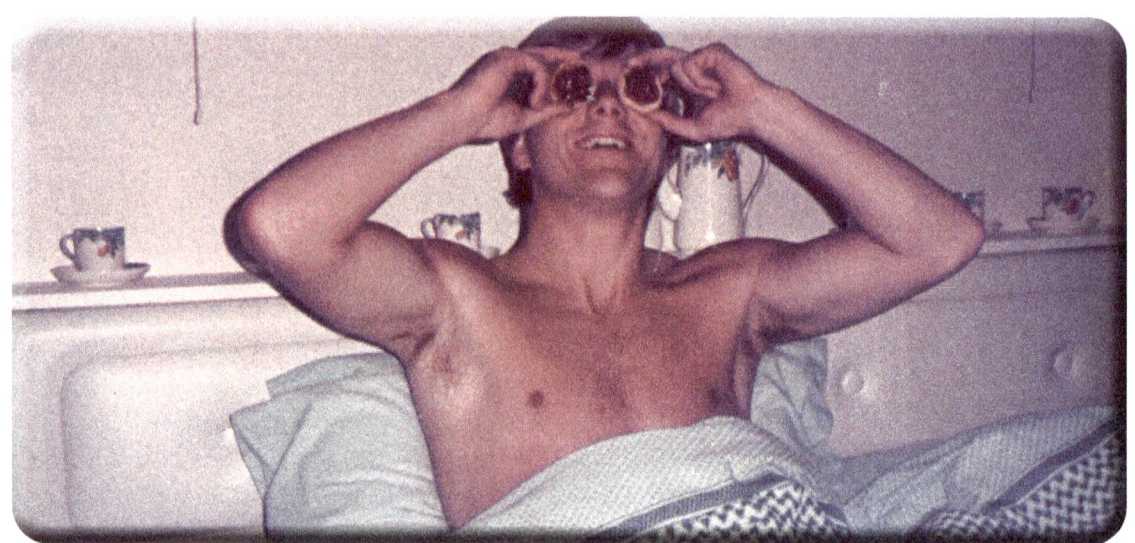

'Know Thyself'

Inscription on the Temple of Apollo, at Delphi. This is the first signpost on my journey. As you grow and develop unless you regularly engage in introspection and self-analysis, effective communication can be flawed. How can you empathise, sympathise, compromise and relate to others unless you know, understand and accept yourself, warts and all? As for me I'm, **"....like Tigger, bouncing around being loveable, and being bloody irritating at the same time."** (Keane J, 2012. Nameless, 89:339). And my closest friends would say, **"You know your trouble?..........You think too much. Analyse too much. Agonise too much."** (Keane J, 2009. Scarlet Woman, PB, 36:369). And as a result, **"You let things bruise your soul and question what's wrong with humanity."** (Robotham M, 2013. Watching You, PB, p143).

Does that mean I'm nosey or that I just have a healthy curiosity? Is the reason I have frequently found myself alone because of, **my honesty and, at times, lack of diplomacy?** When I think I'm just an old man with opinions and prejudices. **But what is honesty but wisdom smuggled in simplicity and what is diplomacy but insincerity in disguise?**

As you go through life you realise many people, for many reasons, have great difficulty accepting you for who you are, and need to put you in a box as soon as possible. From the day you are born you are labelled, put in a box and assigned to a tribe. 'Oh, isn't he /she a little cutie?' I hear you say. Or as one of my relations once said to me when describing a new born, "She looks like a bulldog that's been stung by a bee." As you grow and develop the labels, boxes and tribes change with each passing phase of the journey, the people you encounter and the places that are frequented. When you are single, with no children, and the aging process is in evidence, you see the world from a different perspective. There's only you and so therefore you don't have any distractions to observe things on a daily basis - the good, the bad and the ugly. During the following pages I'll let the reader decide which of these observations and opinions they concur or disagree with. I'll also consider why people need to put you in a box not long after meeting you for the very first time and why we all end up belonging to various tribes during our lives. So much so that as I got older, I started to consider, **"to have something missing from his brain: some vital piece of social equipment which should have told him when he was boring people or that they didn't wish to speak to him."** (Harris R, 2013, An Officer and a Spy, 4:62). Or was I becoming paranoid?

But first let's consider society in the year 2025 to see if I can identify significant moments in my life when such changes, subtle or obvious, slow or rapid, good or bad, occurred, before looking back to see if further changes were being instigated much earlier. In 2005 the book, 'Talk to the Hand', by Lynne Truss, was published. An expression, I am led to believe, originated on the Jerry Springer TV Show. **"Talk to the hand because the face is not listening."** As I didn't read the book until I'd almost finished writing my manuscript, I realised that she talked about many of the topics I was discussing but did so almost 20 years previously. Interesting.

Life: The Meaning of....

"**What happened? Life happened.**" (Rankin I, 2009. Doors Open, PB. 16:172). "**Being alive and living are two distinct things …..The former was strictly biological; and the latter was everything else.**" (Baldacci D, 2022, Dream Town, PB, 79:541).

This topic is a book in itself as most people have an opinion on the meaning of life and conversely, death, because life attracts idealists but as it goes on, develops realists. What biologists call 'life,' fatalists call, 'the luck of the draw,' and clergymen, 'the ways of the Lord.' So here is a small selection of views on life with the ones on death being included, not surprisingly, at the end in the final chapters. **But remember there are very few absolutes in life. Nothing is certain, apart from, 'a closed mind,' change and of course death. The thing about life is that just when you think you are in control someone runs a red light.**

"**I couldn't live without trying and I did that and everything worked out. You think you want something and along the way realise you needed something else. Life's a struggle with little beautiful surprises that make you want to carry on through all the shit until the next beautiful surprise.**" (Brent D, Life on the Road, film 2016, starring Ricky Gervais).

The playwright, Alan Bennett said that life was like a tin of sardines with all of us looking for the key. Keeping on a foodie theme,

"**Life is like a shit sandwich. The more bread you've got, the less shit you have to eat.**"

(Cole M, 1992. Dangerous Lady, PB, 19:324).

But in 75 years I've **NEVER** met anyone, irrespective of which end of the socio-economic spectrum they belong to, who was skipping and dancing through life telling everyone this is a wonderful experience, long may it continue because time and experience can change a person's perspective on life. And many only realise how precious it is, when it's coming to an end.

"**But that's life, isn't it? Sometimes you are the dog: sometimes you're the lamppost.**"

(Steadman C, 2018. Something in the Water, 9:69).

The Danish philosopher, Soren Kierkegaard, stated,

"**Life is not a problem to be solved but a reality to be experienced.**"

Walters M, 2008. The Chameleon's Shadow, PB, p206.

Sheer determination and will can bring you the good things in life but it doesn't guarantee it will keep away the horrors.

"**As you get older the regrets pile on you.**" (Baldacci D, 2012. The Innocent, PB, p 520).

"**There are various theories as to why the years seem to pass faster as you get older. The most popular is also the most obvious. As you get older, each year is a smaller percentage of your life. If you are 10 years old, a year is 10%. If you are 50 years old a year is 2%. But she had read a theory that spurned that explanation. The theory states that time passes faster if we are in a set routine, when we aren't learning anything new, when we stay stuck in a life pattern. The key to making life slowdown is to have new experiences …… If you want to make the days last, do something different.**" (Coben H, 2017, Don't Let Go. PB, 22:245).

"**Life is temporary, transient, moments in time that could end, change in the blink of an eye, today, tomorrow, next week, a year, 50 years, for better or worse.**" (Goss A, 2008. Dark Side, p 596).

"Life by definition is temporary and always changing." (Nesbo J, 2017. The Thirst, PB, 30:442).

"Life is random and fucked up and arbitrary." (Quick M, 2008. The Silver Linings Playbook, P 274).

For me life was very simple but living it appeared to be the problem. It appeared to be about replicating, duplicating and creating variations on a theme of what others had done previously. It is said that age was a fact of life, whilst aging was a state of mind but in actual fact it is soon realised that it was about a whole raft of factors, genetics, nutrition, diet, lifestyle and personal habits etc. So, is it just a peaks and troughs, roller coaster ride in the exploration of emotions and senses, interspersed with periods of active tasks that society expected you to perform?

But remember there are,

"... simple and complex emotions.....Be aware that it is very difficult to sustain a particular emotion for a long time......... Linked to this is the phenomenon that opposite emotions often come in sequence. So, if you experience a period of great happiness, it is likely to be followed by some sort of comedown, possibly even depression. People very rarely live, 'happily ever after'

(Macdonald H, 2000. The Mind Game, p215 &83).

Newton's Law states that for every action there is an equal and opposite reaction.

"Being alive is the easy bit though, isn't it? It's feeling alive that's the hard part."

(Billingham M, 2007. Death Message, PB, 8:105).

"Not dying isn't the same as being alive. You're only alive when you're surviving. And you only survive when there's a risk. There's something that you can lose. The more you risk losing the more you are alive." (Deaver J, 2020, The Never Game, PB, 72:413).

"Life is what it is,....You take it as it comes. It gave no quarter, spared no feelings, limited no pain. Put no ceiling on happiness." (Baldacci D, 2012. The Innocent, PB, p589-90).

"Life seemed to be one continuous accident. Birth where, when, and to whom – is just an accident of faith, a genetic lottery. Win that lottery and you're born in a first-world country with opportunities in life and a life expectancy of seventy-eight years or more. Lose, and you're born in a third world country with no opportunities and a life expectancy of forty-eight years or less. Death – early, late, natural, violent – no matter your station in life, death would come to you. Would it come at age five, thirty-five or seventy-five? Would it come by crime or disease or old age? Was that destiny or luck? God's will or man's mistake? In the end it didn't really matter. It's what happens between birth and death that matters.....Do we matter? Or are we just matter?" (Giminez M, 2013. Con Law, p189-90).

"In order to be great, in fact in order to achieve anything in this life, the first rule is you have to survive." (Martini S, 2001. The Jury, PB, p214).

Or as David Baldacci in his book, The Escape, 2014, would say,

"What's a life without disappointment?" 34:293.

With Chris Evans, the radio DJ and television presenter, in his third autobiography saying,

"Life is not only what happens when we get here. It's also how we get here...Life shouldn't be about survival it should be about enjoyment." (Evans C, 2015. Call the Midlife, HB, p311).

Were we put on this earth just to re-produce believing the rest to be a pastime to fill the void? **Don't** forget that if you don't produce, belong to a tribe, or believe, you are stigmatised. We are also reminded about the importance of our lives by Scott Turrow when we are informed that,

"Our place on earth is leased not owned." (Turrow S, 2003. Reversible Errors, PB. 23:307). Life is a constant reminder that every day, without notice, it can be snatched away from even the fittest and healthiest. Possessions and people were two things that people carried with them throughout life, and the more they carried the slower the journey. After all what is the point of having loads of money to live off if you've nothing to live for? Is losing your life not as bad as losing your will to live? Not ignoring the fact that as you go through life you always have more past than future and the gap becomes greater with each passing moment. David Frost, the TV and media personality, told his three sons **not to spend their lives doing things they didn't like doing, but to channel their energies into doing what they liked.** As the highest form of intelligence on the planet you would have thought that this was not only a good piece of fatherly advice but also a relatively easy path to take. After all, **as we grow and develop, is life not all about having freedom of choice? So why is it many, who are classed as the highest form of intelligence in the animal kingdom, live unquestionably by dogma, obligation or religious protocol, and are not very good at making informed decisions, which admittedly for some is restricted, whilst being brilliant at blaming everyone but themselves for the ones they make.** For some it could be argued that life doesn't move on, and such people commit the biggest crime by being afraid of living it. But I digress and will continue to do so during the writing of these memoirs. So, there you have it, the meaning of life. But no matter how people view their lives, during the journey, **"Life is too difficult to travel alone."** (Townsend S, 2012. The Woman Who Went to Bed for a Year, PB, p 346).

Also, **"Life's short. Never miss a chance to say hello to somebody, never miss a chance to say goodbye."** (Deaver J, 2020. The Never Game, PB, 73:423).

Not forgetting, **"Life is more fun if you can treat it as a series of impulses."** Bryson B, 1992. Neither Here nor There, 13:386.

Noel Edmonds, the radio and television celebrity, who after 50 years in the entertainment industry left the UK to start a new life with his wife Liz in New Zealand. During a documentary, 'Noel Edmonds' Kiwi Adventure,' shown on ITV in June 2025, he talks at length about his thoughts on life, which I found interesting and fascinating.

In simplicity, **you arrive, you exist, you depart,** so,

TRY TO LIVE LIFE WITH DIGNITY AND DIE WITH DIGNITY.

NIL CARBORUNDUM ILLIGITIMI – Don't let the bastards grind you down.

CARPE DIEM – Seize the moment, and

NUNC AUT NUQUAM – You never know until you try, are sentiments that people may want to consider during life's trials and tribulations.

Finally, I cannot end this section without referring to Diana Morgan's thoughts on the meaning of life, extolled during, Cunk on Life, BBC2, 30/12/24. I defy you not to have a good old 'belly laugh' as she discusses with a variety of facial expressions, interesting observations and thoughtful questions, with various personalities, the, at times, absurdity of the subject. Also, The Grumpy Old Git's Guide to Life, by Geoff Tibballs, 2011, will hopefully add to the merriment.

Dreams and Aspirations.

What do I want from life?

Where do I want to be?

What are my long term aims, short term objectives?

"If you don't know where you are going, you are likely to end up some place else and not even know it." Major RG, 1962. Preparing Instructional Objectives.

When you realise you have an active, fertile imagination and view things, on one hand, from an amusing perspective, but on the other, an angry man and then become, amongst other things, an orator, writer, teacher and senior lecturer, it can open up a vista of endless possibilities. As will be discovered, I could have been many things to many people, so read on and all will be revealed. I might not fully subscribe to, 'Blood is thicker than water,' but I do believe that, 'the pen is mightier than the sword'.

<u>Always believe.</u>

Always believe that the best is in store.

Never let hope lag behind…

Always believe that you'll find more and more-

That life will be good, and time kind.

Make the most of the first times because their can only be one.   Source unknown.

Probability: likely to happen or be true.

Possibility: capable of existing or happening or being done.

As a child having had unpleasant, recurring dreams of either being trapped in the box room at Parkway, which was full of snakes, or experiencing that my tongue, swelled to the extent that it filled my mouth and I couldn't speak, (no comment), I, like many, became fascinated with dreams and nightmares. Fortunately, as soon as I opened my eyes the bad dream had gone, only for it to return at a later date during another sleep. Also, as a youngster I would often dream of being a multitude of other beings to escape reality only to find out as I got older that dreams where an integral part of everyone's life. As a young student I'd been informed that everyone only actually slept for 3 to 4 hours and the rest of the time was actually spent dreaming. But if we accept the expression, 'I was only dreaming', why do we never hear of anyone nightmaring? Napoleon, Winston Churchill and Margaret Thatcher were renowned for needing very little sleep, so when did they dream? On the other hand, the musician Mark Knopfler, of Dire Straits fame, spent his life writing music/songs trying to make his dreams come true. As a young student, at Mather Teacher Training College, Manchester, 1968-1971, I was encouraged to read many books in my pursuit of knowledge. One of the earliest books that I skimmed and scanned was, 'Conscious and Unconscious Interpretation of Dreams,' by Eysenck. I was no wiser after the exercise but being very organised and practical and not really a romantic, in the true sense of the word, sentimental yes, I became a dreamer, with aspirations. Sadly, because of the 3-tier class system that pervaded society at that time and therefore my social status, these initially were not very ambitious but nevertheless gave me something to think about, or should I say dream about? This characteristic was pointed out very succinctly by Mr. Stuart Ford, a teaching colleague and friend, in my 30s when he told me one day that I lived in a dream world. My reply being that to take away my dreams was to effectively resign me to a life of boredom. As my life experiences, knowledge, skill and expertise increased, I realised dreams and aspirations could be limitless and ever changing. Over time I also started to consider the possibility that people who got bored mustn't dream very much, or have few, if any, aspirations and worked very hard at being negative. So, when in my 60s I was accused of having become boring, I was surprised, to say the least. If true, how had this come about? Was I in denial, or was it just that I had stopped dreaming? Had I grown out of my dreams? Had I stopped aspiring? As the following pages will show certain people not only helped me realise some of my dreams and aspirations, but also raised the bar as to what I could achieve. Hopefully, during my literal journey, I will also find answers as to how I became boring and isolated. In the meantime,

Keep Dreaming.
Keep dreaming though useless it appears
And failure dogs you down the years
In spite of heartaches and tears
Keep dreaming.
You think that your chance has faded now.
You see no fruit upon the bough, but your luck will change somewhere, somehow.
Keep dreaming.
The prize is still there for you to win
Don't give up and don't give in.
Keep dreaming.
The thing you banked on in the end
May pay a golden dividend
Just around tomorrow's bend.
Keep dreaming. Patience Strong.

Not forgetting that,

'**Success is the ability to go from one failure to another, with no loss of enthusiasm**'.
Winston Churchill.
Or is it?
"**Success is not getting what you want – it is wanting what you have.**"
(James P, 2020, I Follow You, 23:99).

As I see it, dreams are just twisted versions of memories and so I've often wondered if identical twins have the same dreams, aspirations and eventually memories? To find, via a little research, Twin Brains and Twin Dreams, Psychology Today, June 2001, that they do share the same dreaming process. Interesting.

"**The key to making your dreams a reality is to ignore your nightmare so you can focus on that dream.**" (Will I Am, The Voice, 30/01/2020).

Finally, according to the Oxford Popular Dictionary and Thesaurus, irony is the expression of meaning, by the use of words normally conveying the opposite, apparent perversity of fate or circumstances. Regarding life, **it would appear that when you need anything, life offers/gives you everything and when you need something, life deprives you.**

The Bah Bah, Woof Woof, Instant Gratification, Easily Disposable Society.

In the early 1990s I coined the term, the bah, bah, instant gratification, easily disposable society. Later I added woof, woof. We now live in a world where people are so proselytised and brainwashed, that they actually believe they are being governed and guided when in actual fact they are being insulted and herded like sheep. With many preferring the company of pets rather than humans. For years now, large portions of this so-called intelligent life form started to just embrace and follow the latest trend that the food, fashion, financial, sporting, media, technology, political and advertising industry had spun with not the slightest doubt or question that it was beneficial financially, socially, intellectually or healthily. Which is called, adopting the line of least resistance, and is clearly evident when the use of information technology is considered. "**Most people were perfectly fine with being sheep their whole lives.**" (Baldacci D, 2008. The Whole Truth, PB, 27:147). "**They're sheep led by the nose.**" (Woodruff W, 2006. Nab End and Beyond, PB, 17:298). Unfortunately, the problem with instant gratification is that it's not long before the person needs another fix.

"**The click and buy mentality has led to the production of misery and monsters.**" (Truss L, 2005, Talk to the Hand, P85).

Humans think they are the pinnacle of evolution but history shows they have got so much wrong. "We used to build civilisations. Now we build shopping malls." (Bryson B, 1992. Neither Here Nor There, 10:360).

"**We are going down a very dark and dangerous path being influenced by people we shouldn't really be influenced by.**" Sean Pertwee, actor in the Night Caller, July, 2024. Via anti-social media, which with its lies, abuse and harassment has led to a breakdown of social cohesion and created an **M WORLD of ME, ME, ME, MONEY, MONEY, MONEY.** What has happened to the expression, 'We want to create a better future for our children', when the word children has become almost extinct, and that children are now seen as baby goats, abandoned and are the central core of many acrimonious relationships and court cases?

Every child grows up asking why, why, why to a myriad different things. This phase in a child's development is designed to give meaning to actions so that the child acquires a moral compass. Later, when hormones reign supreme, most teenagers, don't need to ask why because they think they know everything there is to know about life. As I grew and hopefully matured, I realised how immature and ignorant I was at 16. Unfortunately, I now seem to be surrounded by many twenty, thirty, forty plus year olds who still hadn't matured and still considered they, and only they, were the centre of the universe and didn't need to ask for reassurance as to the accuracy of their pontifications, bullshit, lies, deceit, insincerity and daily actions. With some bankers, religious leaders, royalists, journalists and politicians actually earning a living from this arrogance. But as Dean Spamley, in the film of the same name in 2008, reminds us, **"Only the closed mind is certain."** In recent times certain high-profile figures actually believed they could walk on water and of course if, during the act, they sank, they would accuse someone of trying to drown them and dispense with their services. The resulting media intrusion to report what actually happened being labelled, 'Fake News.' This expression later being used by others to silence, beat, torture and imprison any citizen who opposed a war against innocent people. In March, 2022, a law criminalising the spreading of, 'Fake News,' was passed in Russia. Is this known as a dictatorship as opposed to a democracy? Ever since I was introduced into the world of academia, at the age of 18 and research, introspection, self-analysis and reflection, my life started to take on a more significant meaning. Writing, in much the same way as reading, exercise and music, became a therapy. But writing could also be a chore. Reading became an escape, a possible solution or explanation. I am very proud of my achievements and would never apologise for acquiring knowledge, skills, expertise and experience, but the fact was, that at times, I found it very difficult to reconcile such with the realities of life. Being told that this or that was a fact, or that the overwhelming statistical/research evidence could make you arrive at a fairly definitive, but not absolute conclusion, caused me, over the years, untold heartache and confusion. Hence the term professional student, as I was constantly searching for the truth, or meaning of life in a society full of love, lies, indifference, greed and cruelty. Which, no doubt, earned me a smart-arse reputation. During my 30s I became increasingly more interested in the Behavioural Sciences as I discovered humans were a melting pot of behaviours, some genetic and some acquired. Enter the nature, nurture debate. So, when a course assignment involved writing an essay on the effects personality could have on learning, my curiosity was further ignited. Later I was to relate all this interest in human behaviour to not only health and illness, but also day to day life itself when I carved out a career in Osteopathy and Sports Therapy. **"Human beings were just endlessly fascinating to him…"** (Connolly J, 2009. The Lovers, PB, 14:179). By then I seriously started to question what I had put in my essays as an 18 to 21 year-old student teacher. I also realised that I had never actually voted in a General Election. Why, I wasn't sure but as my story unfolds all will be revealed. By the time I was 40, I stopped buying newspapers and tried to avoid watching the news as it was anything but. The topics always being the same and to all intents and purposes, the outcomes to the stories didn't change much. Politics, religion, banking scandals, the Monarchy, trouble in the Middle East, Russia, Northern Ireland, and yet another sporting scandal involving drugs, racism, sexism, child abuse and financial irregularities, blah, blah. **I became bored with hearing the same old mantra of, 'We need another public enquiry so this never happens again'. Well, not until the next time, which it invariably did. THE ONLY THING WE LEARN FROM HISTORY IS THAT WE NEVER LEARN FROM HISTORY.** During the writing of this book you will hear this said many times. To be honest the rest of the animal kingdom seemed to me to be far more stable without all this so-called higher intelligence and technology. In terms of child rearing many so-called lower forms of intelligence appeared to be far more committed to the task than humans, who wanted to abdicate their responsibilities asap.

"We get pleasure from eating fat, from having power over others, from beating up people who don't belong to our group, from killing animals, from gossiping, from belittling our rivals, from

accumulating possessions. WHY?" (Macdonald H, 2000. The Mind Game, PB, p 395). Four true, real-life dramas shown on TV in June and July, 2017, 'Little Boy Blue', 'Three Girls,' 'Murdered for being different,' and 'The Walk In,' October, 2022, illustrated just how far down the social degenerative pole, society had slipped. But I suspect many watching these true dramatisations would be guilty of, **'I look but I don't see, I hear but I don't listen'. "Stupid, isn't it, the games we play? The conventions that tie us together. The rules that make us do things we don't want to do; talking to people we despise, shacked up with people we don't love, sleeping with people we don't fancy any more, or who we suspect don't fancy us."** (Billington M, 2012. Rush of Blood, p 395). In 2000, Robert D Putman in, Bowling Alone, talks about, BRIDGING (inclusive) and BONDING (exclusive), in relation to **'social capital' or, as I call it, belonging to a tribe.** The former being people who adapt and compromise, whilst the latter tribe are identified by desires and connection, and are people who locate one another on the internet and watch people getting kicked on their smartphones. Why do we find moderation difficult? Obesity or Anorexia. Social drinker or Alcohol dependent. Tech savvy or Tech junkie/zombie. Thrill seekers, addicts and adrenaline junkies choose to live on the edge, wanting to conscientiously go beyond what is considered safe. Why do selfish nicotine junkies who smoke before, during and after pregnancy, become horrified when their children become asthmatics and develop associated respiratory medical conditions? Surely it can't be ignorance, so is it arrogance? On the same theme another issue I have is regarding nicotine junkies, disguised as so-called pet lovers who, because of their selfish and delusional behaviour, apart from upsetting the neighbours with their dog's constant barking, try to poison their dogs with passive smoking. As nicotine junkies, are they aware that they are subjecting their pets to respiratory problems, certain allergies, nasal and lung cancer, as a result of the dog having to breathe in all the carcinogenic pollutants that existed in their property? (Source: Royal College of Nurses and PETMD, Coates D J. Risks of Second-Hand Smoke for Dogs and Cats). Are these people also aware that cruelty to animals is punishable by an unlimited fine and/or 5 years in prison? Since starting writing this book, this has risen to 5 years from 3 years. But why are there such people? Should these so-called pet lovers be reported to the RSPCA for not providing a 'suitable home' for their pets because it is full of toxic, chemical fumes? The evidence gathered from the Royal College of Veterinary Surgeons and the Royal College of Nursing on the effects of second-hand smoke linked to pet deaths and illnesses is becoming just as significant as the effects that passive smoking has on humans. The charge labelled against people who **knowingly** try to poison another living being is murder. Is it because some people think they are superior to others and only certain behavioural traits, rules and regulations apply to them? Is it because of upbringing, money, size of house, choice of car, size of private parts, are they born that way or do they acquire the attitude over time? The genotype/phenotype, individualism versus collectivism debate rages on. Or are these people simply in denial? Personally speaking, I have always found these people extremely insecure because at the end of the day, if they are lucky, they have two arms, two legs and a bit in the middle and sitting astride the porcelain are like everyone else. I have labelled these people as having, **'playground syndrome'**. My house is bigger and cost more money than your house. Our car's better and cost more money than your car. Our garden furniture cost over £1,000 and you only paid £75 from Aldi. You get the idea? The individualism versus collectivism debate, is another key factor in trying to understand why there are such people. Individualism being about expressing a person's sense of identity and who they are as an individual, says Jay Van Bavel, an associate Professor of Psychology at New York University, with these types of people tending to reject rules, or appeals for altruism, whereas collectivists are more likely to do what is best for the group. According to Michael Saunders, expert at the Policy Institute at Kings

College, London, this became very apparent during the Covid pandemic when wearing a mask, to protect others was accepted by the collectivists but the individualists adopted an attitude bordering on couldn't care less. As for the injections some postulated farcical theories to justify non-take-up. I was informed that one resident on Penwortham Residential Park where I live, died of Covid because it was alleged a member of her family told her she didn't need to have the vaccinations.

Returning to the themes of **highest forms of intelligence**, informed decisions, choices, blame and life, which as the author Peter James reminds us, people may choose not to join in as, **'Life is not compulsory'**. I appeared to be surrounded by people who were obsessed with/dependent on/ addicted to alcohol; were even more seriously addicted to modern technology with their pecking, scrolling, tapping, swiping and trolling; thought it was a good idea to punish everyone within earshot by giving them a 24/7 update of their insecure lives; had mortgages they couldn't afford; debt they couldn't pay off; a partner with whom they had very little in common and considered cheating on; children they wanted to not only rename as baby goats, but also such children to be given away at the earliest opportunity, so a speedy return to the work place could be organised so the next 'sickie' could be planned. They chose a job they 'fucking hated', their words not mine, and the only things they seemed good and happy with was moaning, groaning and winging about politicians, that they had helped put in power, and interfering in other peoples' lives because it distracted them from their own shortcomings. Although what other people think of you should be none of your business. Just as what is every body's business is nobody's business. At the age of 52 researching my PgCLTHE, which allowed me to become a Fellow of the Higher Education Academy, my original belief that Homo Sapiens was the highest form of intelligence in the animal kingdom was well and truly shattered, and the human race was in serious trouble. The song, Oh La, La, with the catchy sing along line, 'Wish that I knew what I know now, when I was younger', encapsulated my thoughts. **It has not been easy watching society come apart at the seams by trying to implode and self-destruct.** An assertion that became yet another thread that would permeate through this piece of writing.

On the question of who decided and when society would change from doing this to doing that, and this is now a no, no and should never be mentioned and the resultant reasons that many would give for such changes, is an interesting one. Mainly because the reasons given are that it was progress and therefore it must be good. Twenty years ago, Truss wrote, **"This is an age of lazy, moral relativism combined with aggressive social insolence ....and even to distrust points of actual law without having the shadow of a leg to stand on."** L Truss, Talk to the Hand, 2005, P6.

For many years I have asked myself the same question, time and time again, **why have many of the topics over the past 30 plus years become such contentious issues for discussion? And of course, it is very difficult to compartmentalise such, as they are all so interrelated. Human behaviour is not an exact science.** I am not trying to play down the significance of many issues that are now considered contentious but it's as though topics such as child and partner abuse, funny, queer folk, serial killers, terrorists, another sporting scandal, paedophilia, drugs sex and rock and roll, etc. etc., have suddenly appeared on the scene and become major subjects of interest. This has tended to be associated with the rise in television infamy, so called reality television fame, littered with wannabes and the disclosure of the sordid activities of the rich, powerful and famous. As a child growing up in the 50s and 60s **I WAS NOT AWARE OF** homosexuals or lesbians. **I NEVER HEARD** of any child at Primary or Secondary school being abducted and abused. Abused yes, as the board duster or chalk flew across the classroom, but abducted no. When I taught in Primary Schools, in the 70's and 80's, I only came across one child with asthma and one with dyslexia, whom I recognised and managed to get specialist help for. So, it was not that people were not aware of such, 'Way Back Then.' Didn't such illnesses exist in the 50s, 60s and 70s? Today we mustn't let our children walk to school because it's too dangerous. Didn't bad people exist when I was growing up and **walking to school,** with thousands of other children? When I entered the teaching profession, working initially in primary schools, these issues were not front-page headlines or a TV documentary. But in latter years, that's what they have become. **The rise and significance of many issues highlighted and discussed in this text were just not issues during the first 30 plus years of my life.** It could be argued that during the first 20 to 35 years of my life, society didn't question or was it that society was naive as to what was going on around them? Please don't say **it's because society is far more tolerant today because this book shows that is certainly NOT the case. It could also be argued that society is now far more educated, but just because a person has a piece of paper to say they have completed a course of study, which involves large swathes of the population, doesn't mean they qualify as having common sense or that they are using their new found knowledge to its greatest effect.** 'I look but I don't see; I hear but I don't listen', springs to mind.

Paedophilia, Funny, Queer Folk and Weirdos.

The terms funny, queer folk and weirdos are terms that I grew up with, and have been part of my life since I was a young child. These people, who freely walked the streets with everyone else, were just considered different. Little knowing that Eugenics in the early 1900s, which originated in the UK and was later taken up by Adolf Hitler to ethnically cleanse the German population, was still around in 2025 masquerading as 'Wanting to Make This Country Great Again', via sexism, racism etc. With many wanting the UK and USA to be populated ONLY BY WHITE SUPREMISTS. As mentioned at secondary school I was not aware of the terms lesbian or homosexual, let alone all the raft of gender titles that now pervade our lives. I was only aware of one pupil that was effeminate and carried a hammer in the inside pocket of his three-quarter length coat, much later realising he may have had some kind of mental illness. Not that being effeminate and carrying a hammer are necessarily interrelated. There was another pupil who I heard about that broke into Chadderton morgue to stick nails into dead bodies. He certainly could be classed as, 'a weirdo'. Can I still use such a term now or has it been given some new 'super-doopa' title? But these were the only two. Today they would be peak time documentaries on TV. Unfortunately, today being a queer person and a weirdo seems to be a life, career choice for some and 'outing' a passport to greater and better things. Normal walking gait patterns are being superseded by mincing, and all forms of bastardised gait patterns, not to mention language. We now have gender issues when using pronouns. How silly is this pretentious world becoming? **As a biologist, I'm struggling to differentiate the genuine from the false and ridiculous.** The Catholic and Church of England seem to be locked in a competition of who has the most paedophiles and abusers. Whilst male football still leads the way for sexism, racism and child abuse in sport. But as soon as such issues are raised, the wagons are circled and mission statements abound. However, it would appear that as I was growing up, society was awash with paedophiles in sport and the entertainment industry. Chris Denning, Jimmy Saville, Jonathan King, Stuart Hall, Rolf Harris, Gary Glitter, Tam Paton and Barry Bennison to name just a few. **Many being ignored whilst carrying out their crimes in full view of the public, and being protected by the rich, titled and privileged hierarchy because of their high profile, celebrity status, just so they could be associated with them. So, what has changed?**

ICs, ISTs and ISMs - Sexism, Racism and Political Correctness. "You can't say anything these days for fear of being lynched." (Day E, 2021. Magpie, 21:195). The biggest problem with today's society and the speed at which things have changed is that now I cannot open my mouth and utter a word, without being accused of some heinous crime and given a label of one description or another. I believe in America they now have, Sensitivity Councillors, but that shouldn't come as a surprise because even before Trump appeared on the scene, to alter the democratic landscape, they enjoyed having their own therapists to deal with the trials and tribulations of life. Jon Sopel's book, 'If Only They Didn't Speak English', is a fascinating read of the idiosyncrasies of the American species and for me, along with my trips to the USA, gave me some answers to the many questions as to these particular people. I often wonder who analyses the head shrinks and life coaches? **What's 'Appened** to a sense of humour, light hearted banter, common sense and having a laugh? Pierce Morgan, not the most popular of individuals, in his book, Wake Up, in 2022, called for a return to liberalism, where free speech was king. **Honesty now seems to have become a crime.** Spending most of my career as a teacher and then senior lecturer, who communicated, I often wonder how the communicator today goes about their job. Since entering the teaching profession, full time, at the age of 21, in 1971, I have always known the odds were always stacked against the teacher in favour of the pupils. Books such as, The Teacher and the Law and The Law and the Teacher succinctly outlined this fact. So how teachers carry out their daily roles with their hands and feet tied behind their backs, gagged and blindfolded, whilst little Johnny creates havoc, I'm not quite sure. **Luckily, I don't and have never involved myself in anti –social media and so cannot be trolled or subjected to whatever happens to people who decide to spew out their daily 'news' for all the synthetic world to digest. TROLLING is a modern-day version of the Pendle and Salem witch trials during the 17th century. David Baddiel, Trolls Not The Dolls, recently shown on Sky Arts, 23/11/24, waxes lyrical, and not so lyrical, about this toxic activity. Who decided free speech was a thing of the past? Who decided that bastardised English and text speak was now legal tender? Can a dog still be a man's best friend or is that sexist? Can you still be blackmailed or give someone a black look, or is that now racist? Can you still have a best man at a wedding? If a coloured person gives a white person a black look, are they now guilty of being racist and homophobic? Should Blackpool and Blackburn be labelled as racist places to visit because they refer to colour? Are we still allowed to blush, go red with rage and become green with envy? Is there still such a thing as a blackhole in the universe or, as Dianna Morgan asks, does it now have to be a hole of colour? Can Muslims have Christian names or is it politically incorrect to ask?** As a biological agnostic, atheist and nihilist who feels very strongly that politics, religion, finance and greed are the root of much that is wrong and corrupt in life, I make no apologies for making references that have a materialistic, political or religious bias. For me in today's politically incorrect world, being racist and sexist could just simply be that you're honest and **society isn't comfortable with honesty,** especially if it challenges power, authority and belief. It could also be argued that just because your opinion differs from another who is the guilty party? **During the writing of this book, I've tried answers to the many questions related to WHO, WHY AND WHEN with limited success but still the sheep follow without question. Honesty being wisdom smuggled in simplicity.** The academics will argue, via the application of academic rigour, that all views must in some way be racist, sexist, political or religious, and as I am very proud to now be an academic myself, I cannot help but justify my views, opinions, perceptions and beliefs objectively by including other people's views, perceptions, beliefs and research. Not only to try and produce balanced arguments, but also because I'm verbose by nature and others can sometimes say things far more succinctly than I can. **Why is biological fact challenged just because a member**

of the species doesn't want it to be so? To repeat, WHO, but more importantly, WHERE are these people and WHAT are their qualifications and experiences that allow them such liberties? Have they nothing better to do than to try to seek fast tracked, fame and fortune? The only absolutes in life are death and change.

Gender neutrality is un-biological and a falsehood **unless ALL MY BIOLOGICAL TRAINING AND QUALIFICATIONS are to be assigned to the trash can.** Why have teachers historically planned lessons on differences between genders to now be told that is no longer relevant? **SAYS WHO?** Female species are different to males in so many different ways. One minute you are female and the next minute you are not. How can you suddenly become gender neutral and adjust your DNA profile other than via surgery or in the head? **What is non binary, gender neutrality? What is cisgender?** Just Google and all will be revealed. But who or what is Google and what qualifications and experiences does it have to qualify as the fountain of all knowledge? When I've attended University, in my many different roles, I've never heard or seen him or her on campus. Should we not just refer directly to the person who wrote the computer programme? As Sherlock Holmes reminded us, it's a big mistake to theorize before one has the data, because one begins to twist fact to suit theories, instead of theories to suit fact. In early 2024 'a lady' announced that it had taken her 30 years to realise she was **ABRUSEXUAL** because her sexuality fluctuated and changed. One minute she was a female, the next a male. I would love to ask her/him which days she had a vagina and which days he had a penis. **Binary** notation is related to ones and noughts identified by punched holes in paper or card, which was used by the first computers but now it denotes gender. But I suppose, if you can mis-use a term and it gets you noticed, go for it!

Ageism is prejudice on the grounds of age. Something I have personally experienced, especially since retirement in 2006. The pages in this manuscript devoted to such, go into detail of the implications of this disgraceful discrimination of the elderly. But where this idea that once you have reached a certain age, you cease to exist and have very little, if anything, to offer society other than to become a cash cow or babysitter, came from I have yet to find out. It does, however, afford the less informed of the species the opportunity to patronise and be condescending to others who have far more knowledge, skills, expertise and experience that they could only dream about. On a factual level as we get older, we are adding more years of disability and expressions such as, 'prolonging life,' used by those with an invested interest in doing so, usually aren't specific as to what this involves. Enter the euthanasia debate.

Sexism is the assumption that a person's abilities and social functions are pre-determined by sex. Or should that be gender? Positive discrimination against women is cited in the belief that in the macho culture of "….**Anything to imply that the reason for a woman's advancement has nothing to do with merit."** (Paterson J &Ellis D, 2019. Unsolved, 53:200). With many not realising they're innately sexist. Perhaps the 'Hollywood Tape', presented during Trump's Presidency, may offer an insight why this was so. The film Bombshell, 2019, was a true story of 3 female Fox News reporters who exposed sexual harassment by a media mogul. This topic, along with chauvinism, is greatly interlinked with the discussion on Homophobia and is yet another recurring theme throughout this book. **"She reached up on tiptoe and kissed him on the cheek. Thank you, Archer. For what? For being a nice guy. They are a lot rarer than you think, as every woman out there can tell you."** (Baldacci D, 2022. Dream Town, PB, 63:432). Hollow pledges by politicians won't stop the malignant misogyny that is now endemic in society. Positive discrimination against men is usually based on the assumption that, 'all men are bastards.' No comment. ""**Men are pigs but so are adolescents…Nature demands that**

males between the ages of, say, 14 and 17, become walking hormonal erections." (Coben H, 2007, The Woods,26:275).

Racism is the belief in the superiority of a particular race and it is true that certain races have a specific somatotype, temperament, and have certain skill sets and so, therefore they may be better suited to certain jobs or sports etc. **And so, by definition are superior.** But historically it has been easy to categorise others because it suited someone's agenda, sometimes purely and simply on colour and 'I don't like them'. But at the time, mainly through ignorance, they totally chose to ignore the factual evidence and research. Whether or not they were aware of such is again open to debate. Why has the treatment of the coloured person who is seen by many as an inferior being and second-class citizen, been allowed to prosper in a world that professes progress, tolerance, compassion, integration and intelligence? Is it because these arrogant, delusional, white supremist, racists lack empathy, tolerance understanding, compassion and sympathy under the guise of being patriotic. Alex Scott, the ex-Arsenal and England footballer, during the television programme, 'Who Do You Think You Are?' in 2024, said, **"Ownership of someone's life is so wrong."** This was with reference to coloured people being held accountable and scrutinised by white supremists who believe they are omnipotent and perfect and only whites should 'rule the world'. Irrespective of the fact that there is very little evidence, if any, to support their claims. The Chinese have an area of the brain that is more developed, that can make them more creative and artistic than others. Generally speaking, West Indian males have certain biological, physiological and psychological advantages over their white English counterparts that historically has proven beneficial, in say, cricket and athletics, which has created a production-line of fast bowlers and athletes. Momentarily ignoring the issue of drugs in sport, lean muscle mass, ratio of fast twitch to slow twitch muscle fibres, large bones to assist leverage and a more, 'laid back temperament', to control aggression etc are just some of the differences. In terms of 'work ethic' it is accepted that certain migrant workers have a more positive work ethic than their English counterparts. **Understanding the Perception of the "Migrant Work Ethic".** (*Work, Employment and Society*, Dawson, C, Veliziotis, M, & Hopkins, B. 2018, *32*(5), 811-830). **"I went and stood at the base of the cathedral and gazed up at it for a long time, impressed by its sheer mass..........You can understand how it took 700 years to build – and that was with German workers. In Britain, they will still be digging the foundations."** (Bryson B, 1992. Neither Here Nor There, 7: 335-6). But still there are many that want to get rid of all these bloody foreigners. Why? To create an all-white, British Eutopia? Sieg Heil, Mein Herr. Who says Hitler lost the war? He's still around but he's just been re-branded. Eugenics is alive and well. The film, Just Mercy: Brian Stevenson, 2020, was about racist murders via the judicial system in Alabama, **where a black person could be electrocuted for just breathing.** Malcolm Gladwell in his book Blink, 2006, says that there is a fundamental unconscious racism in society as a whole. To demonise immigrants is dangerous rhetoric. So, we can ask the question, how many so called law enforcement agencies reflect and exacerbate existing bias and exercise discriminatory intent regarding race, colour and political persuasion? The Romans fed Christians to the lions. The Nazis gassed the Jews and today we wear white pointy hats, persecute, ridicule and try to eliminate black people and immigrants per se. And we call it progress, or should that be lack of understanding? John Grisham's book, Sooley, 2021, was about a 17-year-old Sudanese boy who moves to America to try and become a professional basketball player but more so to escape the corruption, persecution, ridicule, harassment, abuse, genocide and natural disasters that were everyday occurrences in his village. But that is of little interest to the super intelligent racist, who sees these people of, 'inferior intelligence', as scroungers and people to be sent back to where they came from.

Homophobia and being homophobic is the fear of homosexuality. **The emphasis here is on fear NOT fact.** Being gay is still considered a disease that many feel should be extinguished. Defining one's sexuality in some cultures, religions and social groups is considered an illness, both physiological and psychological, worse than cancer, and needs to be excised immediately. Sexism, racism, bigotry and misogyny are present in all walks of life, especially male sports and the police force. Ruth Bader Ginsburg , a Jewish American gender rights lawyer of her generation, who was appointed to the Supreme Court by 96 votes to 3, 1993-2020, and played brilliantly by Felicity Jones in the 2018 film, On the Basis of Sex, would probably not be surprised that men's football is still one of the leading Premier league sports in 2025, in discrimination against women and blacks, in spite of what they would have you believe and see. **A Karen Carney documentary, shown on ITV1, 30/11/24, 'The State of It', and kneeling down before a football match isn't going to eradicate a lifetime of discrimination. CULTURE BEING THE MOST DIFFICULT TO CHANGE AND CAN TAKE MANY YEARS.** It is interesting, not only for me but others, how the racist, bigotry, chauvinistic, sexist debate has raised some interesting and at times, amusing analogies. Why do some men choose a social lifestyle that ensures they end up looking like a pregnant woman? Why do some supposedly 'macho' men choose to wear jewellery and makeup, with a little 'bun 'on their heads? Are trans genders and cross dressers homophobic and sexist? Why do white supremists go on holiday to get a dark coloured tan? Do they know that if they achieve their aims, they could be shot just for being coloured? On 11/4/2024 BBC4 screened, 'I am not your Negro', which was about 3 high profile figures, James Baldwin, Medgar Evans and Martin Luther King Junior who were shot because they weren't white. **"It is interesting that the alpha male needs to feel the weight of his own superiority and masculinity when he is with a woman. Otherwise, what would prevent him from marrying someone just like him – another man?"** (Girls of Riyadh, Alanea R, 2005, 45-248). Sadly, this weight is sometimes found in the fist. This book, which was officially banned in Saudi Arabia, is, **"One of those rare books with the power to shake up an entrenched society."** (LA Times). **If the power of the pen and language is not mightier than the sword, why was it banned?** For me it was a brilliant portrayal of the differences that exist between different cultures. Issues such as intolerance, family traditions, racism, moral values, self-respect and the hypocrisy that permeates all cultures. It identifies why integration is difficult when the parties involved come from different backgrounds. Sadly, it will take more than a book to change mentality. Why should Muslim girls go out with the alcohol obsessed, scantily clad, tattooed, botoxed, foul mouthed, English girls, with low moral values, just to fit in by belonging to someone else's tribe? Whilst I am all in favour of equality, the problem as I see it, is that many British women now behave like men have always behaved. I have been brought up to respect women but have found it difficult for a long time now to do so, with certain elements of their gender. In the equality debate is it now acceptable for a man and woman to fight, with no rules or restrictions, or would one or the other, or both be accused of abuse? It's a good job I'm not on anti-social media otherwise I would be trolled and cyber bullied for the rest of my living days for asking such questions and being honest. Also historically, well certainly in my life time, the so-called highest form of intelligence in the animal kingdom has **REFUSED TO ACCEPT THE FACTS that one cap does not fit all. And people talk about progress, becoming more tolerant and developing nations. Deeds are measured by the intentions behind them. If only those who find**

fault sorted out their own shit before they started agitating others to join their fight. I repeat, 'What is every body's business is nobody's business'.

Before moving temporarily on from the battle of the sexes debate, I must include two quotes one from Eleanor Roosevelt, **"A woman is like a tea bag. You never know how strong she is until she's dropped into hot water."** Love it, but now I will probably be accused of another ic, ist or ism. But as Catherine Tate would say, 'Am I bovvered?' And the other by Mae West, who in 1933 famously said, **"Men are all alike, married or single, it's their game. I 'appens to be smart enough to play it their way."** (Dirty Blonde, Sky Arts 19/8/24). Which for the time was a revelation that a woman could be intelligent, insightful, financially independent and a self-governing individual. There are numerous examples, as with all the ics, ists and isms referred to, of this attitude towards women throughout this book especially when we consider politics, religion, entertainment, the police force and sport. **White Supremacy, which is closely related to racism,** is based on the mis-guided assumption, **NOT FACT,** that white people are superior to coloured people. It can also be extended to include being homophobic. Frighteningly, events in America during 2020, have seen the re-emergence of white SUPREMISTS wanting to murder fellow Americans. Fuelled, it was alleged, by the childish, petulant President in office at that time. **"Today Donald is much as he was as a three-year-old: incapable of growing, learning or evolving, unable to regulate his emotions, moderate his responses or take in and synthesise information."** (Trump M, 2020, Too Much and Never Enough. How my family created the world's most dangerous man). Who has since been given a mandate to continue in his quest to emulate Putin by becoming a dictator, so he can eliminate people who upset him in the style of the Egyptian plagues and Shakespearean tragedies. This mandate being given by so called intelligent people who, **"still confuse his arrogance for strength; his false bravado for accomplishment and his superficial interest in them for charisma."** Trump M, 2022. Too Much But Never Enough, 2:44. This issue being addressed by Thom Hartmann when he talks about why Republicans worship Trump as their sick and twisted role model, (NY Times, 19/20th July 2025). A person who has risen from humorous obscurity to becoming the next world dictator with his toxic masculinity and ideology of power, by dominating, controlling and mesmerising a cult of foolish, unquestioning and dangerous followers, who fail to realise that if he is deprived of his dominance and control, he would be left with nothing. Graydon Carter, a well-respected Canadian author in his book, 'When The Going Was Good', referred to Trump, when he was growing up, as **dopey**. As he has yet to be significantly punished for his selfishness, obstinacy and cruelty, the events surrounding his existence have given me more than enough food for thought to question so called human intelligence, or lack of it, and provide further evidence as to how far down the greasy pole society has slipped in the year 2025. Over time his actions and behaviours can be related to other historical events where a direct comparison can be made with the Pendle and Salem witch trials, 1612 – 1690's, in which visual Spectres, Q Anon and Conspiracy Theories abounded and even Trump himself announced that he was being witch hunted, purely and simply because he was being confronted with the facts, figures and truthful evidence, and was being asked pertinent questions related to his behaviour. Or is that just, 'fake news'? This term is now part of the American and Russian narrative. For Trump 'Fake News' is news that shows him in a bad light. But many books written about Trump, especially the ones written by Bob Woodward, of Watergate fame, such as, Rage, 2020, Fear and Peril; and Michael Wolff, Trump's biographer, are anything but 'Fake News.' On the 6th January, 2021, Donald Trump was impeached for inciting a riot at the White House only for him to be acquitted later, and I believe all charges against the perpetrators were given a pardon by the President himself. As Cilla Black, the late singer and television host would say, Surprise, Surprise. Nearer to home The Dalton Report, in the 1970s, highlighted a deep seated, cultural bias against West Indians by the English white population. In October 2023, Lenny Henry's drama, Three Little Birds, was screened on ITV and was based on his personal experiences upon coming to Britain. The Mangrove 9 case, which was shown on BBC 1, in November 2020, as part of a series of plays about the West Indian community in the 1970s, by Steve McQueen, highlighted the racist, sexist bigotry that was systemic in the British Police force at that time and was further highlighted in, Three Little Birds. **As an aside, the word WOGS, is derived from Egyptian men working on the Suez Canal project and stands for, Working on Government Service, and has nothing to do with colour.** The Hillsborough football disaster in 1989, which saw the death of 97 Liverpool supporters, showed the lengths that the police and judicial system would go to deflect criticism away from their incompetence, intolerance and discrimination. With several police officers involved in the numerous enquiries over 20 plus years, being promoted for their ineptitude. On the 13/4/2022 ITV screened, 'New Worlds Collide: The Manchester Bombings'. Reporting on the public enquiry into the disaster where many lost their lives, it highlighted, yet again, how the powers that be, 'circled the wagons', and went into self-preservation mode by lying and was yet another example of how this so called highest form of intelligence finds it difficult to accept responsibility for its actions, has trouble being honest, even when such actions result in death.

I REPEAT CULTURE IS THE MOST DIFFICULT TO CHANGE AND CAN TAKE YEARS AND YEARS.

As for changing mind sets in many cases these are unachievable. "It is easy to hate gays and blacks, or Jews, or Arabs. It was more difficult to hate individuals." (Coben H, 2007, The Woods, 7:74).

Further to the issues of sexism, racism, misogyny and sexual harassment, and as an introduction for issues covered in the next section, an ITV Inside Story, 9/2/23, Women and The Police, further highlighted the fact that the Boys Club Culture, toxic masculinity, misconduct and potential criminal behaviour were rife in certain Police Forces. During 2013 to 2022, 18,000 cases were reviewed finding systemic bias in relation to colour minority, ethnic groups and women. It also highlighted, yet again, how a culture of, 'Circling the Wagons', whilst trotting out **meaningless mission statements,** existed to try and hide the truth. Dame Cressida Dick, the then Metropolitan Police Commissioner, actually went on record to try and, 'shut down the narrative', by referring to the officers cited as just, 'one bad apple'. If they were bad apples, what fruit was she? Highlighting the fact that exploitation of privilege and position by senior officers was common. The higher the rank the greater the exploitation. As one example of many depressing facts and figures quoted in the programme was the case of prolific sex offender David Carrick, nicknamed Bastard Dave by his colleagues, one of the worst sex offenders in modern history, was never reported by his colleagues, because they feared recrimination by the powers that be. Not surprisingly, if the accuser happened to be a female officer, then her position became untenable. One such officer waited years until she was due for retirement, before reluctantly becoming a whistleblower. We will return to what will become another re-occurring theme of whistleblowing during the remainder of this book. To keep the toxic culture of misogyny, racism, sexism and homophobia in the public's mind David Carrick's name once again reared its ugly head when he was mentioned in a Channel 5 TV programme on 13/10/23, Wayne Couzens: Killer in Plain Sight, who kidnapped, raped and murdered 33-year-old Sarah Everard in 2021. Carrick and Couzens both worked in the Parliamentary Diplomatic unit protecting politicians. How ironic is that as we have yet to fully consider what misdemeanours they got up to? Again, the statistics quoted in the programme were, in my humble opinion, disgraceful. In the last 5 years 2715 Police Officers and staff had been reported for sexual offences. Many abuses involved their own spouses who felt they couldn't report the crimes to the police knowing that **their complaints would fall on deaf, male ears.** Also, during the past 5 years 1,694 police officers and staff were reported for domestic abuse and 78% of those were still serving officers. In the last 6 years, 259 Police Officers and staff had received multiple allegations of a sexual offence with 2 having faced more than 15. During the programme, another name was also thrown into the mix, Stephen Mitchell. What I was asking myself whilst researching and watching such programmes was, how many female police officers and staff had committed such crimes, relative to the men, whilst carrying out their duties? Apart from Dame Cressida Dick who appeared to have a closed mind regarding her male officers, I never found one female name accused of such abuses of power. In 2023/4 Channel 4 screened, 'To catch a Copper', which took 4 years in the making, cited David Lovell, amongst others, who after 17 years of being a sex predator was dismissed from the force. Up until then, he enjoyed his life of luxury on a full pension, supported by the CPS who despite numerous allegations kept coming up with pathetic criteria as to why he shouldn't or couldn't have his penis removed. When he was dismissed, was he given a golden handshake and all his pension rights upheld? How can a corrupt society, in the guise of a police force, compensate **ALL** the victims who suffered, amongst other things, mental and psychological turmoil because of these men? Some women actually not wanting to pursue their careers in the force, knowing their cries for help and protection would be ignored. After all they are only females according to the boys. Unless of course, they are a non- binary, gender neutral or abrusexual. Stop it, Jim, this is serious crime reporting. I'm sorry to bore the reader with yet more statistics and to cause shock/horror but as a result of the programme, it was reported that 5,178 complaints were made against just one, Avon and Somerset Police Officers and Special Constables. I couldn't be bothered to research how many others there are because I was too depressed and getting bored. Of those 4,175 were dismissed and only 3 convicted of criminal offences. **And who says crime doesn't pay, when many of the perpetrators come from law enforcement agencies?** On the 25th November, 2024, the main news item was related to drug barons controlling the prisons, with Prison Officers smuggling mobiles into prisons in exchange for cash. Unfortunately, as this book tries to show, it's always the low life and dross that get the attention and who give the rest a bad name. Not forgetting that in my dedications on page 2 of this book, one is dedicated to the good people who fight and stand up to and against the smug, arrogant greedy, power-crazed individuals who roam the planet. The novel, The Midnight Club, by James Patterson, is an interesting read and please don't say it's only fiction. Will Harper's Law eliminate the scum in society responsible for police officer Andrew Harper's death? **I THINK NOT.** On the issues of racism and privilege, Peggy McIntosh, a feminist scholar, in an article that first appeared in the HuffPost, described white privilege as an, **"invisible weightless, knapsack of special provisions, maps, passports codebooks, visas, clothes, tools and blank cheques."** And says, whilst a start, it was not enough for white people to merely acknowledge their privilege, only positive action would help dismantle the bias against black populations. She pointed out that the problem was that many white people didn't acknowledge that they were privileged because they didn't understand it. Thinking that it was about wealth and an, 'easy life'. Finally, on the question of sexism, 'Honour Killings', are, for me, one of the worst forms of sexism that can be identified. The intransigent arrogance of the individuals involved, who, like suicide bombers, hide behind the racist card when their atrocities are highlighted, is what can make people racist. This blind obedience to religious doctrine is why it is so dangerous. Even when related to the, common man, or should that now be common person? "**It is amazing how the so- called enemies of the state – whether they be anarchists, jihadis or revolutionary communists - all use the laws of the state they're so keen to overthrow, for protection the minute their so-called rights are breached.**" Kernick,S, 2016. The Witness, PB,4:14. "**Some people may argue that atheism is too much trouble by putting so much energy into something you can't absolutely know. Maybe there is a God, and he's a terrific guy-or girl, or hermaphrodite, or whatever people want to believe. What annoys and upsets me is when people think that by believing in a certain God gives them a licence to crap on other people, by maiming or even killing them – Christian, Protestant, Catholic, Muslim, blah, blah, blah, it makes no difference. Some would actually have us believe that all that is good in life is God's will and the rest is someone else's fault. The old pictures of the clan lynchings in America, show supposedly upright white folks, dressed in their Sunday best straight from church, with their good day's work hanging from some tree.**"

Wikipedia: Atheism and Religion.

Materialism, Greed, Lies, Deceit, Corruption, Denial and Self Delusion.

"**Life gets by on 90% truth and 10% deception. And not all of those lies are bad. Sometimes honesty derails a train bound for important destinations.**" (Deaver J, 2022, Hunting Time, 89:382). "**Humans being all about self-delusion.**" (Coben H, 2008. Hold Tight, PB, p364).
 "**People's capacity for self-delusion was pretty much unlimited.**" (McDermid V,2020. Still Life, 53:475). "**Eastern philosophy begins and ends with personal responsibility. What we do as individuals, has an immediate effect on anything and everything around us. That's it, period. Whereas, in the West, it doesn't suit our culture for that to be the case. We are brainwashed into passing the buck. We are brainwashed into believing that we can buy, steal, beg, borrow, or lie our way out of the vast majority of life's sticky situations, personal conflicts or physical and mental dilemmas. It's always easier to hand responsibility to other people.**" (Evans C, 2015. Call The Midlife, p101). **Greed is always at the core of human nature.**" (Patterson J and Roughan H, 2009. Sail, PB, p360). "**Life was about money, no one was immune from it.**" (Bruce A, 2011. The Siren, PB, p12). Money that was now readily available in the credit card Nirvana of the 21st century with Spike Milligan remarking that, "**Money can't buy you happiness …..But it does bring you a more pleasant form of misery.**" Can it buy you respect, love, guaranteed good health, admiration and acceptance? False acceptance, probably, but for the rest I think not. Returning to the theme of sickies for many, life was about lies and deceit with the reasons, depending on the research, being numerous. "**So, FA is a notorious liar? No, he lies out of necessity, not from predisposition or inclination.**" (Nesbo J. 2005. The Son, PB, 26:351). Everyone lies, evades or holds back the full truth. It's one of the traits bestowed upon junkies, addicts and alcoholics, but one doesn't have to be one to lie. Lies they told themselves, because they were in denial, and lies they told other people, either to distract from their own problems or to inflate their own egos. Kevin Spacey and Russel Brand are just two examples of such people. 'Under The Spotlight', C4 in 2024. We are all guilty at one time or another of using, 'author's licence' and exaggerating. People lie on their resumes. We all have to live with self-justification. Sometimes people lie to spare someone pain, or at least that's what they tell themselves, or because they are scared or nervous, or they have something to hide, i.e. a petty crime, drunk driving, speeding, using their mobile whilst driving, parking in the wrong place, having a disability parking badge that they have 'borrowed' because they couldn't be arsed to walk 200 metres, etc. They lie because they don't want to get involved, or they don't want to face reality. They lie to hide a personality defect. Some people lie,

because they just can't help themselves and each time they are successful it gives them encouragement to do it again. **This is known as Neural Adaptation.**

"**Everybody lies. Husband to wife, colleague to colleague, doctor to patient. A good many of these liars do what they do for very good reasons. Some of them have the best intentions, being able to lie is what 'perverts us'. Lying is what makes us human.**" (Billingham M, 2012. Rush of Blood, 107-9). Don't forget research is related to a hypothesis and therefore bias can be an issue. What is, however, factual is that lying is proof of cognitive development and that children can start at the age of 2 or 3. By 4 years children grasp the concept of lying to avoid punishment, (Serota K, Levine Timothy R, Boster Franklin J, 2010. Human Communication Research). Do people manipulate and exaggerate the truth? Of course they do. Of course, the hypochondriacs and habitual liars will deny this. Sometimes the exaggeration is to give more gravitas to the story. Fitzpatrick's Law highlights the fact that: '**The science doesn't lie, people do.**' Some would argue, "**Truth is a moveable feast.**" (Rowbotham M, 2013. Say You're Sorry, PB. 6:69). Can wear several coats and according to Kierkegaard, "**Truth always rests with the minority.**" Simply because there are too many tributaries of possibility, (capable of being done), probability, (likelihood), and inference, (opinion). Bob Woodward and Carl Bernstein, the journalists who provided the evidence which led to the Nixon Watergate Scandal in the 1970s, talk about the, "**Best possible attainable versions of the truth.**" (Nixon to Trump, BBC2 18/5/23, The Amol Royan interview). Sometimes the differences between lies and truth are related to pre-conceptions and biases, amply demonstrated in the Louise Woodward nanny case in 1997 and that, "**Truth is an overrated quality. Lies make a dull world more interesting. They take things in unexpected directions. They add complications and layers of texture.**" (30:293). "**One of the most important things to realize about systems of animal communication is that they are not systems for the dissemination of the truth. An animal may be selected to convey correct information, misinformation, or both.**" Referring to the work of the biologist Robert Trivers R, Social Evolution, in 1985 this quote comes from, Macdonald H, 2000. The Mind Game, Part Two. In January, 1991, Trivers in his article, 'Deceit and Self Deception: The relationship between Communication and Consciousness,' argued that our flair for self-deception dates back to prehistoric times when we first formed into tribes. There is ample evidence that the average person thinks he or she is more skilful, beautiful and kinder than others because deception and self-deceit require the same skill sets. These people are not delusional. The best liars are those people who are good at lying to themselves, being deceitful and cheating. People such as Ghislaine Maxwell, Jeffrey Epstein, Boris Johnson, Prince Andrew, King Charles and Donald Trump to name but a few. Have **you** ever peeked at the answers to a puzzle? I have. Pub quizzes are now about how fast a person can find the answer on a smartphone and NOT ABOUT a person's general knowledge recall. Is this why they are labelled smart? As we are being bullied and coerced into owning a smartphone why not call these quizzes, **F1 Smartphone Races?** Mark Twain wrote, "**When a person cannot deceive himself, how is he going to deceive other people?**" "**That's the problem, when you can't admit you have a problem, you stop controlling it, it starts controlling you.**" (Diamond K, 2016. PB, 5:54). For Donald Trump, lying has become a psychosis as he sees his flexibility of beliefs as a strength not as confusion. "**In the absence of cold hard facts, imagination expanded, 'to fill the space.' It created truths of its own.**" (Billingham M, 2011. The Burning Girl, 25:356). Psychiatrists would say a person's state of mind/memory hinges on the ability to compromise between what is worth remembering and what is best forgotten; between what can be controlled and what cannot; between what is a truth and what is a lie. Aggression being engaged when lying is profitable. Whilst children initially lie to avoid punishment, there is an argument that as we get older, we get better at it. Why? Well, as we shall discover, for a whole multitude of reasons based on a person's general personality type. One reason is to feel better about ourselves as we learn to get away with more. In other words, we've evolved into liars. **In the year 2025, many are walking around with knives in their backs, with the perpetrators sometimes being family members and friends. "We all presented one face to the world, and kept another hidden."** (Connolly J, 2009. Lovers, PB, 19:242). **In its extreme this is known as Borderline Personality and has become more evident with the advent and rise of what I call anti-social media, because these devices take out the physical, human contact of communication, as the user does not have to look a person in the eyes. Neither can the delivery of the words, and the accompanying body language be analysed. The problem with anti-social media and artificial intelligence is that it has degraded the truth by flooding the media with lies, 'fake news,' and disinformation, interspersed with a smattering of truth. So that trying to distinguish between what is false and what is real is challenging. This has led to a climate of poisonous and political hate, rioting, racial and social polarisation.** Seen by some as a passport to greater and better things. Mind you if you are a very wealthy child by the age of 9, because your father was a billionaire, who was responsible for your deprived up bringing but who covered up all your failures, of which there were many, you can have a distorted view of life and will do and say anything to get your own way. And if unsuccessful, will have a temper tantrum. Jon Sopel in his book, 'If Only they didn't Speak English,' calls Donald Trump, Mr Angry. A man who doesn't know the truth is an idiot, but a man who knows the truth and calls it a lie, is a crook. Such people act as a catalyst to delegitimize or undermine established fact-based journalism and get elected on tall stories, lies, deceit, 'fake news' and falsehoods. During the past 30 plus years, democracy has again been put under threat with fanaticism, fascism, racism, narcissism, misogyny and misinformation in all their many guises. Also, it has seen the emergence, or re-emergence, of unprincipled characters who have risen to power, some would argue by questionable means, who are after their own wellbeing rather than what is best for the populace. Trump and Musk being two prime examples, (6/2/25, Can Elon Musk Rule the World?) **What is the agenda of social media influencers and what's their knowledge, skill, expertise, experience and qualifications to bestow upon themselves such an impressive title?** Certainly not, in many cases to improve the nation's moral status with many of these individuals barely out of childhood. Every generation has had its share of playground bullying but **my generation was never cyber stalked, cyber bullied or trolled, let alone be guided by influencers. Yet another example of how society is losing its ability to think for itself.** In 2025 we now have, Social Media Murders, as a title for a television programme on ITVX. **Cyber-lying** being a 21st century strategy for ruining a person's life/career. Which begs the question do lies have a shelf life after which they are forgotten? History has shown that this is not the case. Once a person has been character assassinated, the label tends to stay with that person for the rest of their lives. **TROLLING, A LICENSE TO INSIGHT SUICIDE,** and to re-iterate, is the modern-day equivalent of the witch trials in the UK and America during the 17th century. David Baddiel, 'Trolls Not The Dolls', Sky Arts, 23/11/24, discusses the cesspit of social media. **"They set up blogs and tweets. They paid search engines so that when you perform a search on these guys, your viral feeds get seen first and foremost – right at the top of the page. This is like viral marketing – but is designed to destroy rather than build up."** Coben H, 2011. Caught, 23:218. According to Jeffrey Deaver in his book, Roadside Crosses, 2009, **blogs are now the mushrooms of the internet. They are sprouting up everywhere. Blogs alongside online content, games, social networking sites are dictating most peoples' lives.** This conversation about blogs and tweets is discussed later in this chapter when I consider modern technology. Anti-social media, in all its many guises, which propagates rumour, has motivated and persuaded so called intelligent people to become divisive and intensely hateful, so much so that there has been a swing away from democracy where democracy itself, the press, the academics and the state itself have become the enemy, and political espionage and sabotage are the name of the game. On the 6th January, 2021 Americans were incited via, some would argue, the use of incendiary language, to storm the Congress Building, which is testimony to this. **Why does society find honesty a difficult trait to accept? Why can't we just be honest with each other and deal with our own problems instead of sticking our noses into other peoples' business? Which is usually done to deflect from our own problems.** Personally speaking, a lot of people would be far better off if they stopped lying. **These days it appears that very few people accept responsibility for anything. Very few apologise. Very few resign, unless threatened with castration or are given a generous, golden handshake. It's always someone else's fault. We have become masters of passing the buck. Or should that now be, mistresses of passing the doe? Incidentally, in conflicts can the barricades still be manned or do they now have to be womaned as well?** Referring to the work of Albert Mehrabian, in the 1970s, but which is even more relevant today, the words, worth 7%, the delivery of the words, such as pitch, speed and the number of pauses, 38%, and the body language accompanying them, gestures, glances, breathing etc. 55%, can be better disguised, when there is no face-to-face interaction. These three components form the basis of a truthful communication. With the last two being the basis of what interviewers and interrogators are most interested in, as they are far more revealing than the words themselves. With the advent of anti-social media lying is now just part and parcel of everyday life, as there is no face-to-face interaction. The telephone being a poor means of communication, as it has no room for eye movement, body language and nuance. Charles Darwin introduced the world to **Kinesics** and we now have Doctors in **Emotional Intelligence,** which is about **Repressed Emotion coming to the surface in the form of body motion. Linguists, using Voice Biometrics,** analyse the words, their delivery, messages and hidden meanings. Into the mix we can add **Psychological Profilers** to study body language. Raised eyebrows, or eyebrows drawn upwards causing short lines across the forehead, eyes wide, pauses and mouth open in response to questions, touching or scratching of the nose, can all be tells for someone lying. With reference to the nose when you lie, a rush of adrenaline to the capillaries in the nose cause it to itch. The gripping of the hands, flipping the hair and a rising pitch in the voice denote fear and anxiety. Below consciousness, responses such as shoulder raising and pulling lips sideways are only activated to denote fear and anxiety. Arm and leg crossing being defensive gestures that can signify discomfort. With conscious responses such as smiling being easy actions to manipulate to hide a lie. **Response Latency**, such as flow issues with stuttering, false starts and moving from thoughts to facts, unnecessary digressions, rambling and over generalised statements, eyes closed, blinks, the head and body moving backwards are all indicative of avoiding a threat such as probing difficult questions. **PEOPLE IN POWER, ESPECIALLY ECONOMIC POWER, were the worst culprits. The REALITY PARADIGM of these people is that they basically believe that their behaviour is NOT wrong.** The Paula Vennels and the Post Office hierarchy during its historic scandal, and Ghislaine Maxwell, who was found guilty of 5 out of 6 charges, including sex trafficking, which gave her a 20-year custodial sentence; Prince Andrew, Trump, Al Fayed, Putin and Epstein are just a few examples of such personalities. In 2023 when Trump found himself in court defending a sexual assault charge, it was reported that that he said he couldn't possibly be guilty as she wasn't his type. In April, 2024, Democracy on Trial, screened on PBS America, looked at the criminal cases against Mr Trump and included the Stormy Daniels debacle, where Trump and his team systematically tried to destroy her credibility with fake news, lies and innuendo just because he couldn't face the truth and reality of his actions. On May 30th 2024, Trump was convicted in New York of 34 felony counts of falsifying business records in order to conceal a $130,000 hush money payment to adult film star Stormy Daniels. Mary L Trump, with a PhD in Clinical Psychology and with first-hand experience of his behaviours, is more than an expert, credible witness to detail his many disorders. As early as page 13, she writes that, **"Donald's pathologies are so complex, and his behaviours so often inexplicable, that coming up with an accurate and comprehensive diagnosis would require a full battery of psychological and neurophysiological tests that he'd never sit for. So, we would never know how he would thrive, or even survive, on his own in the real world."** But this still did not stop her listing what she believed the conditions he suffered from, enveloping them in the phrase, **"He Is Frankenstein without conscience."** (P19). **"With Donald the story mattered more than the truth, which was easily sacrificed, especially if a lie made the story sound better."** (1:7). On the 17/9/24 C4 screened, Trump Heist: The President Who Wouldn't Lose, which provided further evidence of how dangerous he was, because as a narcissist his ego wouldn't /couldn't accept he was a loser, which for him was worse than being a black homosexual. My research has discovered that he even lied and cheated whilst playing golf with Tiger Woods. Mary Trump stated that if he was to become President again in 2025, he would continue to try and turn America into his Russia, with him being the Oligarch who would continue to crush and eliminate his enemies. This was after he had pulled America out of NATO. On the 9/9/2024 C4 screened, Trump: Should We Be Scared? The programme provided even more evidence and scenarios, based on the court rulings, Trump versus The Supreme Court, which would give the President unrestrained power and theoretically, total immunity for his actions, so he could carry out his duties unhindered because whatever sentence Judge Merchan handed down, Trump would appeal. But without going into a discussion involving, What If's, after all this is my autobiography; since winning the election in November 2024, he has already started to announce who his 'yes people' are, who he intends to surround himself with. Robert Reich, Professor of Public Policy at Berkley saying that Trump's picks for his 2025 administration were not loyalists but subservient hacks or a coalition of creeps, who found him rather than the other way around, who would be more loyal to him than the nation. These people are helping him to turn America into a chaotic, dysfunctional, police state with their servile deference, fawning adulation and total submission. On 9/3/25 the Guardian published an article, 'Sycophancy and Toadying are de riguer in Trump's court of self-aggrandizement.' Fear being the other side of the coin. It outlined how Trump's concentric rings of court required different rings of servility. Comparing one level to Hitler's governing style. The New York Mayor once quipped, **"I wouldn't believe Donald Trump if his tongue were notarized."** Trump's repetitive compulsion to create disorder allows him to present himself as a would be master. He cares less for alliances and diplomacy, preferring instead to victimise and self-promote. He bans the traditional White House press pool, in favour of his own press office. Although historically, the relationship between the press and politicians has frequently been likened to that of dogs and lampposts. He rewards his followers, irrespective of their crimes, with pardons and promotions, including 1,583 people involved in the January 6th 2021, acts of violence and vandalism. But for me what was more frightening was the acceptance by, 'his supporters,' that, 'he is the man for the job.' Could his so-called popularity also have something to do with the suggestion by Alec Baldwin, the American actor, in an article in the Independent, Nov. 2024, that generally Americans were uninformed and had little or no knowledge of current affairs or what's going on around them? To repeat, Jon Sopel's, 'If Only They Didn't Speak English', 2017, is a brilliant read on the subject. In a democracy, people have choices but Trump's idea of a democracy is based on a dictator's model of don't oppose me or there will be consequences. With 30 million followers on Twitter initially, he will character assassinate you and if that doesn't work well…..On the question of intelligence, or lack of it, is the fact that many believe most of the malicious twitter trolling he promotes as the truth to get his own way. Sopel, 9:317 quotes ex-President Obama on the subject. **"If we are not serious about facts and what's true and what's not, if we can't discriminate between serious arguments and propaganda, then we have problems…In an age where there is so much misinformation, and it's packaged very well, and it looks the same when you see it on a Facebook page or you turn on your television, where some over-zealousness on the part of a US official is equated with constant and severe repression elsewhere, if everyone seems to be the same and no distinctions are made, then we don't know what to protect."** Incidentally, Mr Putin has a very low opinion of Mr Trump, as do certain members of his family, who think **"he is a clown,"** (Mary L Trump, 'Too Much and Never Enough', p9). This impulsive, impetuous behaviour, further highlighted in another Jon Sopel book, 'A Year at The Circus', 2019, is, in my humble opinion, far superior to any Monty Python comedy sketch. The words hilarious, incredulous and frightening, immediately spring to mind, as he frequently tweeted, using the Contagion Theory, whilst watching television. Which, according to many, is his favourite way of spending his time during the day. According to David Aaronovitch, Voodoo Histories, Conspiracy Theories are formulated by the politically defeated, and taken up by the socially defeated. If more insight is needed Michael Wolff's, 'Fire and Fury', 'Inside the Trump White House', is another interesting read. Incidentally Wolff, Trump's biographer, says that, in relation to Jeffrey Epstein, **"There is far more to their relationship than a few words and images."** On July 19th/20th 2025, the New York Times stated that Trump sent Epstein birthday cards and hosted a party featuring, 'young women,' where Epstein was the only other guest.

In 2024 Trump invited Elon Musk into his inner sanctum, Musk seeing it as an ideal opportunity to seize even more power. It is claimed, for Musk it was not about the money. This was a man who bought Twitter for billions way over the odds, so that only his views were advocated as the truth, whilst claiming to be a free speech advocate but who denigrated his opponents. In Trump, he had found a soul mate or vice versa. In June 2025, they spectacularly fell out in a barrage of 'mud-slinging' with Musk aligning Trump with the convicted sex offender Epstein. The truth for Musk is to be racist, misogynistic, anti-semitic and promote misinformation. **With his money and social media platform, Musk is accountable to no one.** His success has also encouraged him to feel confident to not only interfere in the US narrative, but also the UK, German, Australian and Italian political arena. His attacks on Starmer, a human rights lawyer, and Jess Phillips, a tireless campaigner against sexual abuse, are but two examples. His delusional views even extend to campaigning for the release of Tommy Robinson, an opportunist grifter, who has also been labelled a hooligan and thug who was jailed for contempt of court. How far down 'the greasy pole' has society in the UK and USA slipped, and **can we really claim to be the highest form of intelligence in the animal kingdom by believing all the lies and bullshit, and promoting such behaviour associated with people such as Boris Johnson and Donald Trump?** How long does it take a First World Country to become a Third World one? Well, overnight in the case of the USA when in 2005, Hurricane Katrina reduced great swathes of it to rubble; and in terms of credibility, Trump's reign and his behaviour is making the rest of the world question its position as a world leader. With MSNBC columnist, Michael Cohen, reporting on the 20th July 2025, that in his opinion, Trump was in 'Cognitive Decline.' In the case of the UK, reading this book should give people enough food for thought.

In March 2023 and April 2024, TV programmes such as Glitter: The Popstar Paedophile, were about Mr Gadd, aka Gary Glitter who was eventually jailed for 14 years for gross indecency and sexual acts on children as young as 6, mentioned that Jimmy Saville was one of his best mates. And if the younger generation were not aware of what Mr Saville got up to in his lifetime the TV drama, The Reckoning, shown on BBC in October, 2023, gave the viewer an insight. Mr Saville being brilliantly portrayed by Steve Coogan. Again, what makes me angry is that how many people in power, which included Royalty and politicians, were quite happy to be associated with the paedophiles. Hindsight is a wonderful thing and we now know why one of Gary Glitter's hit songs was entitled, 'Do you want to be in my gang?' As previously mentioned, **Kinesic Analysis** is not an absolute science but does help in identifying truth from fiction. Firstly, there is a need to **establish a base line of behaviours** that indicate the subject is telling the truth. There is what is known as the construct side of the brain related to constructing a story, that people use to avoid telling the truth. This is also related to eye movements. So, by starting off with several questions that are known facts such as name, date of birth, etc whilst watching eye movement gives the interrogator a clue as to which side of the brain the eyes move towards to tell the truth. Also, by observing, 'blocking gestures,' where the subject puts their hands, where they look, and how often, do they swallow or clear their throats, how often do they interject with an Uhm or hesitations, tap their feet or slouch, or sit forward, all help to establish this base line of behaviour. . Once established, any deviations from the norm in speech patterns or gestures can be identified when the interview or interrogation become more probing. **"It is the instinctual interpretation of voice and personality, that we form our judgement of others."** (Connolly M, 2013, The Gods of Guilt, 2013, 29:282). So, when people tell you that they are definitely not racist or sexist and don't look you in the eye, or blush, whilst uttering such words, which don't forget are only a small percentage of the message; you can presume, with a certain degree of accuracy, that they are. Just as, 'it all depends', is usually a pre-cursor to lying. Also, don't forget they are just words, it's the actions that give credibility to the words. Also, if not guilty who are they trying to convince with the words? **"Nothing is so tiring as excavating nuggets of meaning from mountains of words."** Sir Henry Evans. In analysing if a person is lying or not, one might consider **WHY? What is their motive to lie?** Also, a **person's general personality,** based on the **Myers-Briggs** personality type indicator, Introvert –Extrovert, shy-gregarious etc. can be used but what is more significant is **WHAT Kind of a Liar's Personality** do they have? **Manipulators, or High Machiavellians** who see absolutely nothing wrong with lying, and using deceit to achieve their goals in love, politics, business and crime. **In recent times, residents on Penwortham Residential Park have experienced such.** They are rarely moved by human connections, whether romantic, social or professional. They even approach confrontation with equanimity, which makes them very efficient but potentially dangerous. In the higher echelons of power these abound. **Social liars**, lie to entertain; **Adaptors**, are basically insecure, who lie to make positive impressions; and **Actors** lie for control as they inherit a character. A modern-day expression that is touted about regularly on television is, **'OWN IT.'** As an avid reader and watcher of real-life crime dramas on television, these behaviours are there for all to see or read about. Returning to the thoughts of Sir Henry Evans, Seymour adds, **"but it was his practice to examine the face rather than merely listen to the words. Words can be delivered to sound more palatable, but actions are the biggest telltale give-aways."** (Seymour G, 2009. The Collaborator, PB, 3:78). **"Lying triggers emotions. Fredrik was good at lying with his choice of words, logic and body language. But his voice was the one emotion he couldn't control... So, he started nodding as if he didn't know... And he shook his head when I asked him if he knew."** (Nesbo J, 2005. The Son, 26:352-353). In the famous Prince Andrew, Jeffrey

Epstein television interview, on 17th November 2019, how many times did Andrew nod or shake his head when confronted with the facts? **This has led to corruption becoming one of the new growth industries** as people consciously or unconsciously edit the negatives. Many terms and meaningless phrases, which in essence could be classed as **instinctive lies,** are now just trotted out because that's what everyone does. **"I'll see you later,"** or, **"I'll catch you later,"** said every total stranger I happened to exchange a few sentences with. No, you won't, I'll never, ever see you again in my whole life. I've more chance of winning the lottery, or the football pools, than I have of seeing you later. Perhaps they were asking me out on a date and I didn't realise it. Or perhaps we were having a race, or they thought I was a fish to be caught. **"It's alright for you,"** is a phrase that, as I became more successful and less tolerant to society's selfishness, refusing steadfastly to join the blame culture that had certainly become entrenched into society, became a stimulus for me to switch off from and out of conversations. Not easy for a person with a reputation for being a chatter-box and making people's ears bleed. When uttering the phrase, the implication was that **it was MY FAULT they had a partner they had serious issues with, but with whom they had produced x number of children. Not forgetting a mortgage, they couldn't afford or being in a job they, 'fucking hated'.** Actually, the fact of the matter is that, for some, making decisions that are different from others is unacceptable, especially if it puts them in a better situation. And of course, when that happens, **individuals and society can always go into default mode and blame immigration, colour and race. Heaven forbid, they accept responsibility for their own, at times, poor decision making or chauvinist, misogynist, narcissistic, sexist, racist bigotry. With institutions, when called to account for their lies and deceit, churning out their mission statements, which are the theoretical models of what they should be doing, but at times bear little or no resemblance to what they are actually doing. During May 2021, that great British institution, known as the BBC, was berated for not being totally honest regarding the Bashir, Lady Diana interview shown just before her death.** Which brings us neatly, or at least I think so, to:

Politics, Power, the Police, the Monarchy, Finance and Religion.

During my Continuing Professional Development, I studied the pros and cons of the different styles of management from autocratic, democratic to laissez-faire and this, together with my personal experiences, helped me to develop my own leadership style. I also realised that people can abdicate or delegate responsibility to achieve their aims. These criteria all being very much related to personality which, as mentioned, is not a fixed entity, but can fluctuate according to circumstance. As I got older, I realised this behaviour was not only relevant to education but all walks of life. **"I hate this world sometimes. The fact that it's so full of wicked, greedy, selfish people."** (Kernick S, 2001. Payback, PB p395). To me they are a toxic addition to society. **"She was privy to their secret societies-the police, business, the government, the military, organized crime. For years men had controlled the white houses, pentagons, palaces, bordellos. The bottom line was always the same. They were in it for the power, the visceral thrill; because of some lurid and primal fascination with violence."** (Patterson J, 1989, The Midnight Club, 42:158). **"The deck is stacked against the little guy in this country. Businesses have no moral centre and will rob, cheat, and steal their way to maximise profits at the expense of the consumers. Higher education is reserved for the elite who can afford the ridiculous tuition. The criminal justice system will give liberal breaks to affluent white people, but trample the rights of minorities and poor and disenfranchised. In every way, big and small, the powerful keep their power, and the rich keep the poor down."** (Patterson J & Ellis G, 2019, Unsolved, PB, 16-62). **"The laws of the super rich, people who think they are above ordinary laws."**

(Patterson J, 1989, The Midnight Club, 69:258). **Absolute power corrupts absolutely, "because people with money, power and privilege, which always surrounded and nourished them, like amniotic fluid."** (Burns C, 2017, The Visitors, P62). Margaret Thatcher reminded us that meritocracy was related to work ethic and achieving your aims through hard graft and a strong work ethic, but she personally had to tolerate so many MEN who didn't even earn their place but who bluffed and blagged their way through life because they just knew someone, who knew someone, who knew someone! They were also given so many chances which in her experience were not afforded to the female species. The BBC2 programme shown on 3/4/25, Mhairi Black: Being Me Again, was about the ex-SNP MP's time in Parliament and its toxic, chauvinistic environment. Watching it, I felt so sad that this young, vibrant, intelligent, gay, young lady, who was diagnosed with several behavioural conditions, was character assassinated because she received more votes in an election than the males in opposition. To counteract my sadness, I felt proud of myself for never voting. Once I'd started to not only acquire knowledge, but also experience life in all its guises, I understood what she meant as there were people with elite privilege, power, position, wealth, prestige and authority, who in simplicity, went through life doing what they wanted to do, irrespective of the consequences of their actions, with apparently no moral compass or conscience whatsoever. So, the expression, **actions have consequences,** doesn't seem to bother these people who appear not to heed or need council as they firmly believe only, they and they alone are right. These people appear to have two antagonistic, disparate personas as they drifted from one to the other with relative ease depending on the circumstance. One minute turning on the charm, and pontificating as to how much charity work they were involved in, and the next, inflicting untold harm, psychologically, physically or otherwise on those who didn't believe the lies and bullshit. **It also became clear to me that they did so, because there was no effective deterrent stopping them.** Unfortunately, they are found in all walks of life and society harbours such people. Even voting for them in election campaigns. The Pew Research Centre reported that in 1958 about 78% of Americans trusted Federal Government but by 2017 this was down to 19%. David Frost when interviewing the disgraced ex-President Nixon asked, **"Has there ever been an honest government?"** Ronald Reagan once said that the most terrifying words in the English Language are, **'I am from Government and I'm here to help.'** The threat of jail time would appear not to cause these people to lose too much sleep. Just as finding a Premier league male footballer, who was on at least £550,000+ a week, a few pounds, plus a few penalty points on his licence, for using his mobile phone, whilst drink driving, was like stealing an old penny from my piggy bank. **I have also become bored with listening to mission statements and hearing that yet another public enquiry was going to be set up so that it never happened again.**

Returning to the Whistleblower theme, the film of the same name shown in 2010, was a true story of a Nebraska police lady, Kathryn Bolkovac, who outed the United Nations for covering up a sex trafficking scandal. Human trafficking being one of the fastest growing criminal activities with an estimated 2.5 million people being trafficked around the world. The film asked the question, 'What price a peace keeping force?' The film highlighted the fact that when billions of pounds are at stake the, 'Powers That Be,' aren't interested in earning respect, ONLY MONEY. Even if it's at the cost of many, many, innocent lives. As far as I'm aware, to date no one involved in the cover up has faced criminal charges in their home country. The US State Dept to this day continues to do business with private contractors like the one outed. Contracts worth billions of pounds in Iraq and Afghanistan are still being sanctioned. As for Kathryn Bolkovac, who now lives in the Netherlands, since bringing the scandal to the UN attention, has been unable to regain employment in the international community.

To add more fuel to the fire, in the film Dark Waters, based on yet another true story, starring Mark Ruffalo, as Rob Bilott, a corporate lawyer, and his wife, played by Anne Hathaway, fought the chemical giant DU Pont, who he was initially employed to defend. Discovering multiple misdemeanours, both civil and legal, as well as a raft of just downright lies, he showed that the unregulated chemical PFOA, which was related to the famous TEFLON brand, was responsible for being found in the blood of virtually every living creature on the planet with the potential to cause a whole raft of cancers, neurological issues, birth deformities and death. The company eventually settled 3,535 cases, for $670.7 million, which was considered, 'chicken feed,' for a company that made billions of pounds profit. Over the years, the Lancashire towns of Oldham and Rochdale, have been the subject of many high-profile cases involving child abuse and human trafficking. From 2003, street grooming involving young vulnerable children as young as 13, were manipulated and coerced into having sex with Pakistani adults. And although the so-called protective services including the police and CPS were aware of this nationwide scandal, nothing was ever done until years later, in case it offended the Pakistani community, who obviously went into default mode and played their race card. **If a black person gives a white person a black look is that racist?** Maggie Oliver, a senior Police Officer, voluntarily resigned in protest and Sara Robinson, a Social Services Officer, who dealt with child abuse cases was harassed and eventually made redundant for speaking out. The TV programme 3 Girls, shown in March 2025, charted this public scandal resulting in **NO POLICE OFFICER HAVING TO FACE DISCIPLINARY ACTION. No surprise there then. And people chastise me for not voting, watching the news or reading newspapers and can't understand why I get angry and depressed. "The war had taught me to distrust political myths and grand panaceas."** Woodruff W, Beyond Nab End, 2006, PB, 15:722. I've already alluded to the fact that I have never voted in a General Election and have only ever voted once in 75 years of my life, and that was in the Royton bye- election in the 1980s. Whilst Mr Woodruff can identify where his distrust of politicians originated, but where my apathy for politics and religion came from, I am not sure, there must be an, 'ology reason' and I'm sure some person will happily give me an ic, ist or ism title, but it's been with me since I was old enough to vote, or not, as in my case. As I've got older and increased my knowledge, I am quite proud of the fact that I have, on more than one occasion, stood up for what I believed in and tried to do something about it, no matter how insignificant others may have viewed my actions. By not voting I haven't suffered any major attacks of scurvy, rickets, sexually transmitted disease or a desire to sign up for the Big Brother House, Love Island or retreat into the jungle and eat frogs. In fact, I've felt quite proud that I hadn't joined the millions who vote, elect the next Government and spend the next 4 years winging, moaning, and groaning about their chosen one, even if some of them had no sooner moved in, than they had to move out. If you were asked to compile a Top 10 of **'questionable British politicians'** in terms of their honesty, lies, deceit, integrity etc. where would you place, Foot, Archer, Portillo, Brown, Wilson, Blair, Thatcher, Johnson, Cameron, Farage and any others you would like to throw in the mix? Any American readers could compile their own list of politicians. To help in the decision-making process I have included some, 'Food for Thought,' during the writing of this book. Many years ago, a fellow, female student on my osteopathy course berated me for not voting, citing the suffragette movement, which Dr Nick Edwards informs us is not a condition of the bowels but an historic moment in history to give women the vote, and she thought it was disgraceful that I didn't vote. **Quite frankly I'd never given much credence as to who was in power. They were all the same colour to me, wore the same two faces, theoretically had the same pocket money to spend, and caused the same havoc and mayhem under the guise of running the country.** Many so-called leaders have great difficulty organising and running their own lives, let alone a country with over 64 million inhabitants. A politician's default mode appears to be disgraced, at some time in their tenure, for lies, greed and mis-management of either sex or money. Many politicians in my lifetime both in the UK and America have had many books written about their many alleged indiscretions. That man Trump, long before his liason with Musk, learnt his craft from not only his father Fred but also from the National Enquirer journalist, David Decker who in 2018 was granted immunity from federal prosecutors, for admitting illegal payments were made to influence the 2016 Presidential Election. **(Scandalous: The Tabloid that Changed America, BBC4, 7/2/23).** Enter Roger Stone, Trump's Republican friend and political fixer for over 30 years who has been described as, 'a serial liar, self-promoter, thug and bully'. BBC4 30/7/24, A Storm Untold. Then we have the Nixon, Watergate Affair, 1973, where Nixon resigned rather than be impeached. 50 years later this debate has resurfaced regarding Mr Trump. Then we have the Clinton, Monica Lewinsky scandal, 1998; the Jeffrey Epstein/Ghislaine Maxwell, sex trafficking scandal and Max Clifford, the alleged rapist and paedophile, all of whom either had their own financial power base or had political friends in high office. As previously mentioned in 2019, Harvey Weinstein, the film mogul, was eventually found guilty of sex abuse. Not forgetting the fact that over the years the Royal Family has not been without its scandals and controversies. My mother loved anything royal, and used to get frustrated with me if I didn't reciprocate her enthusiasm. Where this negativity towards the Royal Family came from, I'm unsure but over time I started to align them with politicians in the column of don't believe a word they say. Prince Charles, now King Charles, was allegedly having an affair with Camilla, now Queen Camilla, before, during and whilst married to Princess Diana. Both Charles and Camilla were not actually inconsolable after Diana's death. It has been alleged that Trump and Epstein competed to see who could sleep with Diana first. How much truth there is in the theory that the driver of Diana's car was blinded by 'Shark's eye' depends on who you talk to. King Charles, whilst President of the Royal Ballet School in Richmond found himself involved in the BBC documentary, 11/9/23, 'The Dark Side of Ballet Schools', when the Royal Ballet School was involved in accusations of body shaming, intimidatory and cruel behaviour leaving some students, 'broken', as they became anorexic, addicted, depressed and suicidal. Another school, Elmhurst in Birmingham, of which Camilla was a Patron, was another school accused of such appalling emotional, physical and psychological abuse of dancers under their control. After attendance at Elmhurst, one boy committed suicide at the age of 21. At the same time Camilla was seen fraternising on television with Rolf Harris, the convicted paedophile. Not forgetting King Charles's association with Jimmy Saville and the religious paedophile Stephen Ball. Then there's Prince Andrew, the late Queen's blue-eyed boy, being a close friend of Epstein and Ghislaine Maxwell, who was also involved in having sex with underage girls, so much so that the Queen was left with very little option but to strip him of his all his Royal titles, and his royalty money. Virginia Robers-Giuffre, an underage teenager, was actually flown to London to meet Andrew. Something he pathetically denied during the infamous TV interview. But then paid £12m to settle the sex abuse claims, as well as incredibly claiming he was not friends with Epstein or Ghislaine Maxwell despite being shown numerous photographs of himself with them. At the age of 41, Giuffre committed suicide as a result of being involved in the sex trafficking and sexual abuse scandal, with amongst others, a member of the Royal family. Where was Andrew now getting his money from? Was it from his Pitch @ the Palace scheme which was using tax payer's money but from which he claimed 2% of all monies raised, claiming it was for expenses. He also sold his Sunningdale Park property for £3m over the asking price, to the son of a Tunisian despot. In December 2024, it was brought to light that he'd been involved with an alleged Chinese spy, Tengbo Yang, who actually attended Andrew's birthday party, despite being banned from Britain in 2023. Two television documentaries shown on Channel 5 on 16/5/2025: Fergie Where did all the money go? and, The Banishing of Prince Andrew, highlighted what certain members of the Royal Family get up to in their spare time. With sex and money addictions being at the forefront of their activities. These are all further examples of the lengths politicians and people with privilege, money and power will go to keep such power and protect their unrestrained behaviour with lies, deceit, corruption and arrogance in order to pervert the course of justice. Was the Royal family involved, with its press attaché, in a campaign to discredit Prince Harry and Meghan because they wouldn't ignore what was happening behind closed doors? Or was it just the fact that Harry strongly objected to his father disrespecting his mother by marrying Camilla? The revelations, including suggested racism by Charles as he allegedly questioned the colour of Harry and Megan's offspring, presented to the world, via the Oprah Winfrey interview, and in Harry's writings; gave the general public an insight into the 'mind-set' of British Royalty, who definitely belong to an elite, privileged tribe. And if one only believes half of what was disclosed then the expression, 'What goes on behind closed doors', or in this case should that be, 'What goes on under the crown', no one knows? Personally, I know who I believe. On the 24/11/24 Channel 4 screened, Queen Camilla: The Wicked Stepmother, examining claims that her transformation destroyed her relationship with Prince Harry. I like the word transformation as it is open to many interpretations, especially in relation to the Royal Family, with its alien attempts to try and be more relatable to the 'common man', sorry, and woman. Robert Maxwell, Ghislaine's father, was quoted as saying, **"By having lived in it, I have influenced my children in the right direction and I will have left the world in a slightly better place."** How arrogantly delusional is that considering all the skulduggery that Mr Maxwell himself was involved in? Or perhaps he wasn't delusional as such behaviour was acceptable in, 'his world or his tribe'. What I cannot do, and have not done for many years, is have any respect whatsoever for a Royal family that exploits its position. Why has Andrew never been held accountable in a court of law for his actions? Did he feel guilty that Victoria Giuffre committed suicide after he'd had sex with her? His punishment to date being to have been stripped of his Royal titles and being asked to move out of his £30m mansion and move into Harry and Megan's smaller home, after they had been asked to vacate the premises by Harry's father, which may have been one of the many reasons as to why Harry and Megan moved to California. Was this also the catalyst to pave the way to a television programme in October 2024, in which Prince William informed us that, 'We can end homelessness'. Which could be seen by the populace as a wonderful intention if it wasn't for the fact that on 2/11/24, C4 screened a Dispatches programme, The King, The Prince and Their Secret Millions, highlighting the fact that as the Duchy of Lancaster and the Duchy of Cornwall, William and Charles, as landlords, were making money by using tax payers' money to amass a property portfolio worth millions, £20 million profit in 2023 to be precise, but didn't pay any corporation tax or capital gains tax. Perhaps William intended to house all the homeless in his and his father's properties. Obviously, Camilla had to get in on the act. Why has Sarah Ferguson who was addicted to spending money that was not hers or that she never had, never made to pay off her debts, which would have then made her homeless? But fear not, William, Charles and Camilla could have re-housed her. The Rise and Fall of the house of York, by Andrew Lownie, 2025, answers some of these questions. Then there was Charles Haughey, the Northern Island politician, 1979-1992, being referred as a, **"former gun runner, bribe taker, and friend to Mugabe, Castro, Gaddafi."** (Nally J, 2015. Alone with the Dead, PB,21:180). **"That's the thing about politics, when one dickhead leaves the scene, half a dozen rush in to fill the vacancy."** (Barclay L, 2011. 'Never Look Away', p28-29). Into the melting pot, we can add the fact that politicians Blair and Bush allegedly lied about weapons of mass destruction, of which there weren't any, to instigate an illegal war on Iraq, but were never tried for war crimes because the trial against the whistleblower, Catherine Teresa Gunn, and covered in the film, Official Secrets, screened in 2019, was dropped because if she was successful in proving her case, Blair and Bush would have been put on trial. Blair being rewarded for his dishonesty with a knighthood, despite a 1.2M signature petition to later have it removed. The aftermath of the war, which he helped to instigate, being a civil war between the Kurds, Shias and Sunnis. Leaving the country in a far worse situation than it was before Blair and Nixon Intervened. So, I suppose Boris Johnson's, 'partying', during the pandemic lockdown in 2021-22, could be considered relatively insignificant in that no one, as far as I am aware, was killed. Impregnated yes, killed, no. **The brilliant comedy, Yes Minister, first screened on British Television in 1980, was nearer to the truth than many viewers at the time realised. It also frequently used the word CHILDREN as the word had not yet been superseded by KIDS/baby goats.**

Pragmatism never took the bull by the horns and solved any problem. For me honesty for many politicians and people in power, in positions of privilege, was something they considered to make them appear almost caring. It was also a way of protecting themselves and their position by feigning they were doing it because it was **in the public interest, or was it, in the interests of the public? The two phrases meaning different things, and, as all journalists know, these two phrases are greatly intertwined to allow journalistic licence to print anything they so desire, truth or otherwise. I have personally been accused of being patronising, when I questioned and pointed out a few relevant facts to a local journalist, Catherine Musgrove, about an article she had written pertaining to and used as evidence in a Tribunal case that our Resident's Association was involved in. Lack of 'Due Diligence' being one such accusation. I think Catherine was confusing patronising with honesty. The judge eventually ruled in the resident's favour in both the first and second tier cases, and refused the appeals of the site owner. Although her article included inaccuracies she still stood by what she had written because it was about a millionaire site owner, Alfie Best, with a questionable reputation, who had access to a legal team used to fighting defamation cases. To be fair, she did revisit her article and accepted she was misled, but overlooked her lack of due diligence. But that was after the fact. As mentioned, the term, fake news and Contagion theories abound to cover a multitude of alleged sins.** A good old smear campaign, with a smattering of truth, sometimes obtained via illegal phone hacking, hidden amongst the disinformation, usually does the trick. As long as it sells newspapers, or grabs the headlines, that's all that matters. After all, who, apart from the odd rich and famous celebrity, is going to take the time and trouble, or indeed have the money to risk the flawed, judicial system, to authenticate the print or the tweet? As long as the waters are muddied and discoloured sufficiently- job done. **Most people are aware of the part the press played in the life of Princess Diana and in 2020, the target being Prince Harry and Megan. Add to that, today's use of information technology which has become a far more potent, dangerous weapon, should be a red flag to any so-called intelligent individual. But unfortunately, over the years many so called intelligent individuals have become colour blind.** The Capture, BBC 1, August/September 2022, was a drama all about how data can be used to virtually transform and destroy peoples' lives. **But these colour blind, drug addicted, so called intelligent life forms are so immersed in tapping, clicking and swiping, they appear totally and utterly oblivious as to what is happening in the, 'real world'.** Whilst on a very personal level, and on the subject of colour and mudded waters, Clifford Taylor, a church going mason and headteacher, who was allowed to be in the teaching profession at the same time as my good self, was appointed even though there was more than a strong rumour going around at the time that the masons had been more than a little evident when it came to offering him his headship. Don't get me wrong, I am more than aware of the good work that the masons do as I had friends belonging to one lodge or another, it just wasn't my thing. **I am however, intrigued, if not a little worried, about this black balling business. In today's politically in-correct world was the term still in use? Is it now off-white balling?** Taylor eventually left Blackshaw Lane Primary as he was proving too much of an embarrassment. Was this to avoid too many awkward questions from parents, press and Joe public after I had voluntarily resigned in protest. He became not only an embarrassment, but also a liability because he wasn't aware of how ineffective he was, and because he had friends literally in high places, he felt safe and secure. When the shit eventually hit the fan, he blamed the masons for putting him in such a stressful position. Hilarious, if it wasn't so true. I resigned as his deputy, after fighting for several years to have him removed. Personally, I was character assassinated, subjected to psychological and emotional pressures, became isolated from my colleagues and as a result my marriage was put under tremendous strain, just because I wouldn't keep quiet, and accept the situation. An educational advisor, who at the time was very worried about what effect the Taylor debacle may have had on, and ultimately reflect upon, his tenure, tried to placate me in my pursuit of justice, by telling me that the Taylor case was not uncommon. Up until then, I genuinely believed in teacher quality and the honourable profession. **What a pompous, patronising arse. But then again, the advisor also went to church on Sundays and it was alleged, belonged to the brotherhood tribe.** Ann Williams a parent fought for 25 plus years to get justice for those affected by the Hillsborough disaster, so my struggle was relatively minimal. My fight for honesty was at a time when Christine Keeler, Mandy Rice Davies, John Profumo and Kim Philby were in the news and spies and double agents were under everyone's bed. Well, not literally, and at least not mine. **During the ensuing years I soon realised that greed and corruption was no respecter of race, colour, creed or political persuasion and existed in all walks of life from sport, entertainment, education, politics, royalty, policing, religion, banking, and that included the Post Office, and NHS.**

The Post Office scandal, screened by Panorama on 25/4/22, and made into an ITV drama, November, 2023, Mr Bates v The Post Office was yet another example of greed, lies and deceit at the highest level of people in power. **It was an expose of the most widespread miscarriage of justice in British legal history, and the devastating effect it had on those involved. Resulting in yes, you've guessed it, another public enquiry so it never happens again, until next time. Paid for by Joe Public NOT the Post Office or Fujitsu.** At the time of including this scandal into this book, **NOT ONE PERSON WHO WAS RESPONSIBLE FOR RUINING AT LEAST 3,500 SUB POST OFFICIALS' LIVES, WITH AT LEAST 60 DYING BEFORE JUSTICE PARTLY PREVAILED, WITH AT LEAST 4 OF THOSE TAKING THEIR OWN LIVES, HAS BEEN PUT ON TRIAL FOR WHAT THEY DID. Power and the people who have it, will fight tooth and nail and do ANYTHING to hang on to it.** Paula Vennells, the CEO of the Post Office, from 2012 to 2019, received a £389,000 bonus and in 2019 a CBE from the government for her part in the scandal. Which in my opinion was equivalent to giving Sadaam Hussain and Vladimir Putin the Nobel Peace Prize. And only after a 1 million plus signed a petition to strip her of the title, did she eventually capitulate, unlike Tony Blair, and agreed to hand back her 'gong'. Not to mention other members of the PO Board and government officials who were aware of what was going on, but did nothing. Upon leaving the Post Office Paula Vennells decided to hide behind a lectern as an Anglican priest from where she could denounce her culpability in the horrendous crimes against humanity. No surprise there then, and **yet** another example of how politics and religion sit hand in glove with hypocrisy. Mr Bates who for over 20 years led the campaign against the Post office, refused to accept his OBE. As for Fujitsu, which developed the Horizon system at the centre of the scandal, which incidentally was introduced by Tony Blair, made over £950M profit and was paid £3.5M for its work with the PO. Not forgetting that it was rewarded for its lack of accountability with a £48M contract to run the Police National Computer, which at least put them nearer to their fellow criminals. **"The reality is that when the public come knocking on the doors of this chamber seeking justice, the Government only ever answer when they have no other option left......because this place never changes."** (Stephen Fry, Daily Express, 11/1/24). I suppose the PO scandal could be a classic example of the Nietzschean philosophy /core belief that the weak were always going to be devoured by the strong. I say could, because in this example the weak were anything but, as they decided to take on the hierarchy, even though it cost them dearly. Since the television drama, the floodgates have been opened with, in February 2024, two true dramas hitting our screens, 'Breathtaking,' about the disgraceful treatment of NHS staff during the Pandemic and 'The Way,' about the closure of Port Talbot steel works with an estimated loss of 3.000 jobs. Incidentally, as this book highlights, 'Breathtaking' is the latest in a long line of NHS scandals.

As a young man entering into the world of social gatherings, dinner parties and cream teas I was informed that to bring politics and religion into the conversation was not a good idea. As I grew older, and acquired more experience of life I realised why this advice was well grounded in truth, as the clash of secular ideologies could lead to war. **As a humanist, who mainly believes in things that I can see and touch from experience and feelings, I strongly dislike religion and its fanaticism. Over the years I've found it hard to accept that so called intelligent people can be so proselytised, indoctrinated and subservient. RELIGION IS ALL ABOUT BLIND OBEDIENCE, PATRONAGE, CONTROL AND MANIPULATION. Or as Dianna Morgan says, "formalized grovelling, known as worship." Is that why Trump pretends to be religious, as he sees it as a massive vote getter because in America atheism is seen by many as being on a par with child molesters, estate agents and rapists?** (Sopel J, If Only They Didn't Speak English, 2017, 5:174.) **Religious people are dutiful, resigned, and unquestioningly do as they are told. "What makes anyone religious? Fear of death, ignorance, lack of imagination. Take your pick."** (Tsiolkas C, 2008. The Slap, PB, p268). One resident on our Residential Park informed me that we would all be better off living our lives as Jesus intended. This being a resident, who asked me to stop sending her a Christmas card as she was a non-believer and was always complaining about her lot in life, such as ongoing back problems and not being able to retire. Obviously, her life style was being ignored by her Jesus. The freedom to think for oneself is a precious freedom. So, to be told by 'another', **"that hatred is evil and love is good; that tolerance is preferable to intolerance; and that to help the poor is right; and that to ignore the misery of the poor is wrong,"** (Woodruff W, 2006, Beyond Nab End, 7:554), insults my intelligence. As Marx pointed out organised religion of any kind was, **"the opium of the masses."**

"Faith is such an odd thing", said Jack, "People say they just know things, but you can't know what can't be proved, you can only believe." (French N, 2017. Saturday Requiem, PB, 14:123). When people pray, all they are doing is working on the statistical chance, probability, possibility theorem, and has nothing to do with some divine deity. Faith is about what you have or don't have, not just something you choose when convenient. **"Finding God seemed to mean that her parents had lost touch with everything else."** (Griffiths C, 2022.The Locked Room, PB, 1:4). **"Thou shalt not steal, but it's OK to cheat on your taxes. Love thy neighbour, as long as they believe in the same

God that you do and are not gay." (Billingham M, 2017. Love Like Blood, PB, 46:332). I'd like to add to that, and doesn't have a different coloured skin to you. **Faith is also about what you think and feel, NOT what you know as the truth.** In other words, the ability to manipulate common sense to accept something intellect rejects. It's the same model of intellect, that historically dictatorships, disguised as world leaders, have used throughout time. In other words, the concept of higher reasoning without any obligation to discharge the burden of proof. And because Trump probably doesn't understand the concept of higher reasoning, or the burden of proof, he cannot be questioned about it, labelling it as, 'Fake News'. The Bible being an historical story book with not one reference that states that its contents are in fact true, with actual, empirical, or any form of evidence, for that matter. **"There's nothing whatsoever literal within the Bible. It's a tale riddled with inconsistencies and the only way they can be explained is through the use of faith." "Each gospel was a murky mixture of fact, rumour, legend, myth that had been subjected to countless translations, edits and redactions."** The Templar Legacy, 2006, P77. Billy Connolly used such a fact as part of his standup routines citing biblical stories that he stated were based on no factual, truthful evidence whatsoever. Also, if GOD is so wonderful why does he allow a mother to be butchered in front of her young child? I often wonder what criteria is used to award theology degrees and what reference material is quoted to support the stories in the Bible. John Grisham in his book, The Testament, 1999, 130:266 writes, **"He is omnipotent but you have to go to Him, in prayer, in the spirit of forgiveness, and your sins will be forgiven. Your slate will be wiped clean. Your addictions will be taken away. The Lord will forgive all your transgressions and you will become a new believer in Christ."** Is that why there is so much depravity, greed, power, hunger etc. in religion because any transgression can easily be dismissed by just having a quick word with the boss? Whilst Karen Slaughter, 2011, Blindsighted, PB, 28:370, reminds us, **"The good thing about the Bible, Sara, is that it's open to interpretation."** Expressions such as, 'It's God's will,' 'Allah will guide us', *'Inshallah',* 'If Allah wills', are trotted out twenty-four seven every time there is an atrocity. Historically, religion appears to give people justification for what they do no matter how extreme. **Also, the hypocrisy of religion is that it is supposed to teach tolerance, not force people to commit suicide if they dare to challenge its power and put non-believers into coffins or wheelchairs.** In the modern anti –social, synth world, now known as cyber- trolling everything and everyone is fair game, so look out, Jim. The fact that religious zealots, if not blowing themselves up, will actually maim and murder, if society dares to question their actions and beliefs, has just become an integral part of life with its own label, **TERRORISM, social or otherwise.** Honour killings, highlighted in the docudrama, Honour, shown on ITV television in September, 2020, are, for me, the worst form of sexism there is, but appears to be tolerated and accepted as a part of certain religions. The intransigent arrogance of the people involved who, like suicide bombers, hide behind the racist card whenever their atrocities are highlighted. **"Do we actually have any idea how many people over the ages have actually lost their lives as a result of religious strife?"** Martini S, 2001. The Jury, PB p212. In November 2024, the Israeli leader Benjamen Netanyahu and his former Defence Minister, Yoav Gallant, together with the Hamas leader Mohammed Deif, had arrest warrants issued against them for war crimes against humanity. I accept some people may need ritual and belief to get through the day, and without ignoring the fact that certain doctrines have at their heart a genuine desire by most of their followers to do good, but these appear to be immersed in the dross. The comedy TV programme, 'Every One Else Burns', Feb, 2023/November 2024, was a subtle dig at the ridiculousness of pursuing any particular religious doctrine, in the belief it will in some way make you happier and superior to others. Of recent time, Rebecca Vardy, who gained notoriety for her failed court case against Colette

Rooney, pointed out the negative impact that religion can have on children in the television programme, Rebecca Vardy: Jehovah's Witnesses and Me, C4 16/5/23. Whilst in November 2024, Colette decided to enter the jungle to perhaps rebrand her celebrity status/image by sharing her personal space with snakes. Probably because her husband's managerial career was not doing too well? The fictional novel, Exile by RN Patterson, 2007, is an excellent read on the complexities, realities and impact that religion has on people's lives. Dave Allen, the Irish comedian, spent his career in the 60s, 70s and 80s highlighting the destructive power of the Catholic church, received death threats for his so-called comedic blasphemy. **The church, like most powerful institutions, doesn't like any hidden agendas becoming public.** In later years Ricky Gervais, in interviews and standup, questioned the absurdity of God but was trolled for his views and was assigned his place in hell. The film Spotlight, in 2015, **was based on a true story** involving the Boston Globe newspaper and how it uncovered the massive scandal into cases of widespread, systemic, child sex abuse and its cover up, not only by the Massachusetts, Catholic Archdiocese, but by lawyers and politicians who lined their own pockets, initially within Boston but then worldwide. The result of which was that one of the main culprits for the cover up, Cardinal Law, resigned only to be later re-assigned by the church to not only the highest-ranking RC church in Vatican City, Rome but also the world. On the 27/9/19, BBC television screened, 'Inside the Vatican', and highlighted a report, from Pennsylvania, that named 300 sexually abusive priests, in the State, with over 1,000 victims. Not to be outdone the Church of England championed Bishop Peter Ball as their answer to Cardinal Law. In January 2020, BBC 2 screened a two-part documentary, Exposed: The Church's Darkest Secret, charting the history of Bishop Peter Ball, Bishop of East Sussex, 1977 and Bishop of Gloucester, 1992, as a sexual predator and child abuser, under the guise of doing, 'God's work and Active Ministry'. It showed that not only was he a paedophile but also, he ran a network of abusers, priest Roy Cotton and priest Colin Pritchard, to name but two of his flock, during his time in Sussex. Despite on-going police investigations, dating back to Neil Todd in the 1970s, who was one of the first people to raise concern as to Ball's behaviour whilst living with Peter Ball, as he trained to be a priest, until he was eventually charged in March 2014, the most Ball received was a police caution. This was because Ball had, 'friends in high places', including the Archbishop of Canterbury, Cardinal George Carey, and a raft of Bishops in Gloucester and Sussex. As previously alluded to, Prince Charles, now King Charles, who was a, 'good friend', of the infamous paedophile, Jimmy Saville, **(Saville: Portrait of a Predator, ITV, October, 2021),** allowed Ball and his brother to rent a house on his Highgrove Estate in which he lived for 14 years. Charles eventually became a King, but there were many unanswered questions as to his credibility to hold such an office. Many MPs, including Tim Renton and Margaret Thatcher, withheld vital information from the police, not least by not disclosing letters of complaints against Ball for 15 years. If that wasn't enough, pressure was exerted on the Crown Prosecution Service whenever charges were proposed. Of course, when eventually the actual truth emerged, all of these people were suddenly struck with amnesia, and a deep sense of remorse, whilst still attempting to distort the facts. Sadly, Neil Todd, who was not only being sexually abused but was also being psychologically and emotionally abused by the church, as they carried out a relentless character assassination of anyone who dared to challenge their power and authority, committed suicide before Ball was held to account. Cardinal George Carey was eventually forced out of office in 2017 but as far as I'm aware, is still a member of the House of Lords. Some authors actually risk hell and damnation, whatever that is, by making light of such atrocities in the form of a joke. **"A paediatrician, a lawyer and a priest were on the Titanic when it started to go down. The paediatrician says, 'Save the children'. The lawyer says, 'Fuck the children!' And the priest says, 'Do we have time'?** (Slaughter

K, 2011. Blindsighted, 4:31). The idea that a 'religious person' who supposedly devotes their life to preaching the gospel could commit such acts of crime is shocking to the non-believers. **But why?** The only difference between these people and the rest of society is a dog collar. Harlan Coben in his book, The Match, 2022, suggests that many, many people could be potential criminals because like many addictions, people don't become addicts until they have tried the drug/fix and get a taste for it. John Smyth, a distinguished barrister and friend of the Archbishop of Canterbury, Justin Welby, got the taste because over a 40-year period he groomed and exploited as many as 130 young men and boys, and then savagely beat them in the UK, Zimbabwe and South Africa. In 2017 Channel 4 revealed that he was carrying out his sadistic behaviour at Christian summer camps, Universities and Winchester College. His sojourn abroad being sponsored by Susie Colman and the Church of England. When the shit hit the fan, triggered by Andrew Morse's first suicide attempt; the Keith Makin Report, 2024 and the book, Bleeding For Jesus, by Andrew Greystone, revealed all. Welby, not surprisingly, went into shut down mode with denial, deceit, lies and transient memory loss. Claiming he personally didn't do anything wrong, not realising that was the main reason he was guilty because he did nothing to stop the abuse. Initially he refused to resign until I suspect, and only history will prove my suspicions, he was offered some deal by the powers that be, to do so. Perhaps he was asked to join Paula Vennels behind her lectern, or he was head hunted by Donald Trump to be part of his inner sanctum as he'd amply demonstrated he possessed all the qualities Trump admired, such as lying, deceit, dishonesty etc. No doubt, there will be a television drama and film deal being negotiated as I write this. Farcically days before taking over from Welsby, the Archbishop of York faced calls to quit whilst Bishop of Chelmsford, Stephen Cottrell, let priest David Tudor stay in post after Tudor was barred by the C of E from being left alone with children. In June 2025, Cottrell confirmed that the Bishop of Liverpool, John Penumbalath, had resigned over sexual misconduct allegations. Perhaps Cottrell was Penumbalath's sponsor. Other clergymen were cited in the Makin Report. To date, Justin Welby is still being allowed to reside at Lambeth Palace. **Is it me or is there a pattern emerging here where all the religious factions in society are trying to outdo each other for, 'Abusers of the Century'? There you are, my title for the forthcoming film, what do you think? But I suspect I will not be around to see it as I probably have a contract out on my life already, not to mention the trollers hoping to tap and peck my life away.** On the 7th December, 2020, a BBC television programme, 'The School That Chains Boys', was an undercover documentary on Islamic schools, known as Hadwas (Khalwas or Madrasas?). These places, that had been in existence hundreds of years, were held in high esteem, and were places parents could send their children, to memorise the Koran and receive education, which one day would lead to their off-springs becoming Sheikhs. The reality being that these children were abused psychologically, emotionally and physically chained up, raped and brutally beaten by the very people who were supposed to be looking after them. I, once frustratingly and impetuously, slapped a very naughty child on his legs and immediately regretted my actions as the school had a non-corporal punishment policy. I received a bollocking, sorry, severe telling off, from the Head. But everything is relative I suppose. Of course, as with most institutions with a historical power base, they avoided prosecution by weak kneed politicians, who probably feared for their own lives. **Because the Church is run on a centuries old system of power and patronage, religious people are dutiful, resigned and unquestioningly do as they are told, whilst many of their 'leaders' are basking in relative wealth, knowing their 'flock' don't even earn minimum wage.** Who pays for the upkeep of the beautiful adorned churches in Malta? I presume it's in the belief that it somehow makes them superior to non-believers, who are meanwhile getting on with living in the blood and guts of the real world. In the real world being guilty of a crime could result in a 5 to 20 year sentence or the rest of that person's life in prison whereas in the Church it could result in just being given a caution, leading ultimately to promotion. 'Forgive me father I have sinned,' results in confession, an act of contrition, a few Hail Marys and Our Fathers, and don't forget a quick fiddle with the rosary beads. Better the beads than a youngster, I say. In the real world the punishment is meant to act as a deterrent but in the religious world the 'penance' appears to give the impression that such behaviour can be deterred by following a set protocol, all under the guise of compassion, forgiveness and tolerance. How can peoples' lives, which are generally so materialistic, pay homage to a non-materialistic presence? According to Richard North Patterson, God is only an idea and that the problem with religion is that it takes metaphor as fact, i.e. Adam and Eve. **"The notion of any kind of a God is laughable when I see what happens to good people all the time."** Pobi R, 2013. River of the Dead, PB 8:41. Referring to the great plague that swept across Europe, Bill Bryson writes, **"I don't know about you, but if I lived in an age when God was zinging every third person in my town with suppurating buboes, I don't think I'd look at Him as being on my side."** Neither Here Nor There, 1992, 17:437. However, with regard to hidden agendas some would argue, **"It has served us well this myth of Christ."** (Berry S, The Templar, 2006). And that has always been the problem. The hypocrisy of the TV programme, 'Songs of Praise', and people wanting to be married or to have their children christened in church when they are non-attenders, and possibly non-believers, beggars belief. Yes, I did get married in church but once someone asked me why, I realised that I hadn't a clue, or had I become a sheep? No, I'm not going to blame Dee my wife. In 2015, Steve Coogan in his autobiography, 'Easily Distracted', who himself was brought up as Catholic, was frequently furious with the dogma of the church, citing women bringing condoms from Northern Ireland by train who were arrested. He further vents his anger at religion when he played the journalist Martin Sixsmith, alongside Dame Judy Dench in the brilliant film, Philomena. The film further highlighted the hypocrisy of the Roman Catholic church and the, at times, evil intent with which it goes about its business. In January, 2021 a news item on television, highlighted the results of an investigation that had taken 5 years to compile, about intolerance, unspeakable cruelty and neglect towards unmarried mothers and their children, in Irish Catholic Care Homes, between 1922 and 1998. With over 9,000 cases being reported with an appalling level of infant mortality, with many persons buried in some kind of sewage system, Tuam Maternity Home, in Galway, being cited as one such establishment. Society is spun the idea by our political and religious leaders that there are noble causes to justify their actions. Government would rather let innocent people be bombed, shot at, lose their limbs in IED attacks, whilst they sit at home fiddling their expenses, buying second homes, having affairs and eating canapés, all in the name of fighting global terrorism. Whilst allowing parasitic lawyers to benefit from such rhetoric. For what? Democracy, freedom, sacrifice and human rights, so that people who don't believe in making the streets of Britain safer for future generations can go about their business, knowing they cannot be deported because of infringement of civil liberties or human rights. And although there has been religious conflict for centuries, **what have the interventions in Northern Island, Vietnam, Afghanistan, the Falklands and the Middle East achieved? Certainly not stability and a more harmonious world.** After the American and English intervention, Iraq was left in a worse state than before they invaded. (Once Upon a Time in Iraq, BBC, July, 2020). **I dread to think what Brexit will do in the long term to the stability of the UK, if the racist, sexist, white supremist, misogynistic, chauvinist, bigots get their way. In August 2024, more racist, child killings were reported in the Lancashire town of Bolton.** I've already drawn attention to the true television drama, 'The Walk In', shown during October 2022. The books, Sniper One, written in

2007, by Sergeant Dan Mills, an Englishman, and American Sniper, 2014, written by Chris Kyle, the latter being made into a sanitized film version of the real events, starring Bradley Cooper, **were true stories written by the central characters** about their tours of duty in the Middle East, and were classic examples of the destructive influence on people's lives that politicians and religious zealots can have. **"But that's politics for you: a bunch of game players sitting around congratulating each other in safety while real lives are getting screwed up."** It also highlighted the injustices and frustrations for the troops in the front line of battle. **"They hated us because we weren't Muslim. They wanted to kill us …because we practised a different religion than they did…The fanatics we fought valued nothing but their *twisted interpretation* of religion. And half the time they just *claimed* they valued religion – most didn't even pray….Many of the insurgents were cowards."** (5:94). **"Terrorism isn't merely a tactic of the enemy; it's the root of their ideology. They believe in destruction."** (Patterson J & Roughan H, 2019, Killer Instinct, 3:18). According to Adam Smith, economist and philosopher, the irony of Islamic terrorism against the West is how much it is dependent on a capitalistic principle of supply and demand if the question is asked, **are martyrs a dying breed?** Knowing the American troops were bound by ROE (rules of engagement) and court-martials, where civilians, women and children could not be shot at, the insurgents would hide behind, and were prepared to sacrifice their own women and children to save their own lives. A more recent event can be found regarding, 'The Chennai Six', who were 6 ex British servicemen, one being an ex-paratrooper, named Nick Dunn, who on the 11th January, 2016, after already spending more than 2 years on bail or in horribly, horrendous conditions in Indian jails, was given a 5 years prison sentence, by a 60 year old judge, who saw taking bribes as part of his job, with not one single piece of evidence as to Dunn's guilt. Dunn had served his country in 2 war zones Afghanistan and Iraq and almost died after being blown up in a convoy attack. This very high-profile case involved at least three British foreign secretaries, three Prime Ministers and exposed the corrupt and disgraceful Indian sham of a judicial system, with almost total and utter disregard for justice. The events of which were documented in a book, written by Mick Dunn upon his eventual release. A book that did nothing for my blood pressure or stress levels at it made me so angry upon reading it. **"David Cameron, Prime Minister at the time of our arrest, at first, seemed more worried about kissing Prime Minister's Modi's arse than the fate of six of his citizens."** The reason given for Cameron's indifference to Mr Dunn's plight being, that there was an enormous trade deal with India in the offing and no one wanted to rock the boat. **"When he was asked about the case by one of his fellow Tory MPs in the House of Commons he promised, 'to leave no stone unturned', in the effort to get us released. It is fair to say that he left a lot of stones unturned. What did he do for us? Nothing, as far I could tell. He was all mouth. Since Boris Johnson has become Prime Minister, a job he has always wanted, I have never believed a single word he said about anything."** Dunn N, 2020, Surviving Hell, PB, 20:50. In 2021, during the pandemic, 'Partygate', was further evidence of Johnson's inability to tell the truth. But this almost pales into insignificance compared to 'Pussygate', a tape released by the Washington Post about Donald Trump's sexist behaviour where he boasts of being able to do what he liked to women because he was famous. Followed closely by, 'Sharpie Gate', known as the 'Trump Heist', regarding the election process. It's as though Trump and Johnson had become kindred spirits as, like spoiled, naughty children, they both craved the limelight and attention. Only when a 136,000-signature petition was handed in to Downing Street, years after the six were incarcerated, was the government shamed into doing anything. As an aside, but on a personal note, it is interesting that both Cameron and Johnson were involved in the debacle known as Brexit. With the Chennai 6 case demonstrating how powerless the UK had become as a nation. Liz Truss in

October, 2022, definitely cemented our position as a serious contender for the laughing stock of the world. As far back as 2003, Ben Elton, under the guise of a fictional novel, High Society, was pointing out the reality of power, greed and corruption in the UK. Later in his life, his standup routines included many of the topics covered in this chapter. In June 2023 Johnson resigned for, **'Deliberately misleading Parliament.' SHOCK, HORROR!** How will the British populace get over it? Well, they could always follow what the Americans do and re-elect him. **"I don't know if I trust first impressions very much anymore, ... People are becoming too slick nowadays. There are too many good actors in the world."** (Patterson J, 1989, The Midnight Club, 25:93). It would appear that for some politics was just a stepping stone for greater and better things financially, in the public speaking and entertainment world. Do you not agree, Mr Blair? Not long after, on the 27th June, 2023, a television documentary, 'Boris, The Lord and The Russian Spy', revealed that whilst he was the Prime Minister he ignored and overruled, the intelligence services in Canada and the UK to award Evgeny Lebedev, his 'good pal', who was the son of an ex KGB agent, a peerage, and by doing so, he was putting himself not only in a compromising position, but also was putting the country at risk. It also was no surprise to me, after Partygate, that he frequently attended parties given by Lebedev. How much has changed since the days of Kim Philby, Donald Maclean, Guy Burgess and Anthony Blunt? Perhaps the answer may involve further reference to Partygate. And whilst not directly related to spying, it does consider how nothing changes in politics. The Sue Gray Report, reported on 3/10/23, Channel 4, was as a result of the Daily Mirror reporter Pippa Crerar breaking the first newspaper story, whilst Paul Brand ran the first ITV report. **It identified 14 lockdown parties with Boris Johnson denying there were any.** At the time the average fixed penalty court fine for breaking Covid lockdown protocols and rules was £6,000, but could be as high as £15,000. There were over 115,000 residents found guilty of such. **Number 10, Downing Street received 126. Boris Johnson, Carrie Johnson and Rishi Sunak each paid £50.** March 2024, 'The Rise and Fall of Boris Johnson', was shown on C4 and the only statistic missing from the programme was, how many times Boris's pecker rose and fell whilst he was in office. On the 22/2/23, a one-off documentary about Nazanin Zagari –Ratcliffe, a British, Iranian charity worker, showed that she was arrested at Tehran airport in 2016 and was accused of spying by the Iranian Revolutionary Guard. Separated from her daughter when she was only 21 months old, she was initially put in solitary confinement for 9 months, and imprisoned for 6 years purely and simply, because the British Government refused to pay £300M, an outstanding debt related to the Chieftain tank. At the time there were some £5,000M worth of contracts with Iran. But when the Shah's regime fell, the contracts were cancelled. 5 Foreign secretaries and 5 Prime Ministers including, Boris Johnson, repeatedly lied about their inability to do what they had been elected to do by the populace, which was to govern and look after the people of the UK. Boris Johnson repeatedly tried to deflect her case away from being connected to the unpaid debt. The Foreign Office also forced Nazanin to sign a false confession to appease the Iranian Revolutionary Guard before they would release her. The programme ended with a UK government statement that demonstrated how delusional they were, by stating they had worked tirelessly to end Nazanin's unfair, disgraceful and scandalous detention. What really happened was they worked tirelessly not to upset the Iranians. **And I repeat people ask me why I don't vote and question people's intelligence.** The film, The Post, in 2017, featuring Meryl Streep and Tom Hanks, was yet another true expose about a government cover up of the Vietnam War secrets in 1971. Another example of hypocrisy, and the evil of politics and religious zealots is by reference to the docufilm, Looming Tower, shown on BBC2 TV, in June 2019, about the background leading up to the 9/11 disaster in America. It is also interesting to consider the dichotomy that exists between organised crime, and the threat of terrorism. This is not to denigrate or belittle significant events in history but the death toll of the Twin Towers event in New York, in 2001, yielded 3,000 bodies, whilst in the same year, in the same city, 30,000 men, women and children died from narcotics related illnesses, gang wars and overdosing, (Seymour G, 2013.The Outsiders, PB 5:112). The number of Americans killed since 9/11 by terrorism, is less than 100 whereas the number killed by everyday gun violence is in the tens of thousands. This is supposedly a First World country, which historically appears to not want to address the issue of common-sense related gun safety. On Christmas day 2015, more people died from gun homicides in the USA than those who died in the UK throughout all of 2013, (Sopel J, If Only They Didn't Speak English, 2017, 6:189). But the rest of society isn't blameless in its hypocrisy. **"We embrace diversity but engage in white flight. We want to hug minorities because it makes us feel good. We want to revel in those differences and yet the very act, the recognition of differences, separates us."** (Martini S, 2001. The Jury, PB p213) In January /February, 2014, the BBC four part series, 'Inside the Commons,' further cemented my beliefs as to the behaviour of politicians, who have been tasked with governing the country. Many can't govern themselves let alone a country.

"In an age of scientific enlightenment and technological miracles, we judge our leaders on their physical stature and television presence and we select fools and the false priests of corruption to govern us." (Martini S, 2001. The Jury, PB p213)

"He was what she termed an 'educated villain'....rich , educated men who pulled off brilliant scams, scams that were never allowed to get into the newspapers or come to prosecution because the firms involved would lose their credibility on the Stock Market, with disastrous economic and political results. Instead, the wrongdoers were given enormous golden handshakes and a big party as a leaving present. And their pictures appeared in papers with the sob story: 'Ill health brings the head of So and So Corporation's career to an end.' 'I want to spend more time with my wife and family,' was another favourite excuse. It was not only big businessmen who were involved in these things, but politicians, judges....just about every profession had its fair share of con men." Cole M, 1992, Dangerous Lady, p374. Don't forget Joss Ackland in the film, 'White Mischief', 1987, reminded us that a banker was a man who lent you his umbrella when the sun was shining, then asked for it back as soon as it started raining. In 2020, the script would probably have to be re-written with man being replaced by person for fear of being accused of sexism. On the 15th September, 2015 I watched Daniel Radcliffe, of Harry Potter fame, play Rock Star games co-founder and the Grand Theft Auto video game creator Sam Houser, defending the fact that his games did not make some people violent. The BBC film was called, The Gamechanger, and his opponent was a lawyer called Jack Thomson, played by Bill Paxton. The film documented the background to **this true, very high-profile court case in America, where a coloured, video games junkie had shot many, many police officers after being arrested for stealing a car and copying the violence he had seen whilst watching videos.** Houser, representing the greed in society, got a slap on the wrist, with his video games making billions of dollars, whilst the lawyer, representing the honest, common man, was ruined in every sense of the word, after being subjected to a relentless smear campaign, to assassinate his character, instigated by the video creators. Although 'fictional' the book, Roadside Crosses, by Jeffrey Deaver, 2010, was a brilliant and well researched book, detailing the dangers and side effects of using anti-social media as a tool of communication. TV programmes such as Panorama and Dispatches regularly and depressingly report on everyday news worthy items including fraud and corruption in the UK, related to tax avoidance, educational grants and social housing etc. One such Panorama programme on the 6/11/2017 entitled,

'Britain's off-shore secrets exposed', was yet another example of how the rich and famous avoided paying billions of pounds of tax, resulting in the financial and social mayhem we see today, just so these people could drink champagne 24/7. The programme had documented evidence, known as the Paradise Papers, and involved, amongst others, a company called Appleby, of corruption at the highest level that was endemic in these strata of society. I know that I am not alone in being annoyed, angry and frustrated when finding out about such injustices in life, and on a personal note, such injustices ultimately lead me to resign from certain relatively high-profile positions because I refused to kowtow to the pressure of brushing questionable practices under the carpet. **I think it was Schultz who said that the world's a whore house. All we had to do was work out our place in it. Everyone was ruining someone for something.** As a biologist, I am aware that within the species there are many, many, types. Why do some people feel the need to ignore that fact, and try to make people into something they are not genetically wired to be, no matter how many excuses are made. Why does society try to change biological fact? Real evil doesn't announce its presence. **"Shit doesn't change its stink it only breaks down into nothing."** (Coben H, 2010. Play Dead, PB, p87). The fictional works of Linwood Barclay, Martina Cole, Mandasue Heller, Jo Nesbo, Kimberley Chambers, Jesse Keane, Michael Robotham, Jeffrey Deaver and Mark Billigham are just a few of the fabulously, well researched insights into today's society, its people, their personalities, their lives and the lengths they will go to create a persona that is the total antithesis to reality, and please don't try to tell me it's all just fiction as the author has probably based the characters on real life individuals, circumstances, incidents and research. On a lighter note, the writings of Matt Dunn and Sue Townsend, the latter being famous for creating Adrian Mole, managed to highlight the foibles of human nature whilst giving the reader a belly laugh in the process. 'The Woman Who Went to Bed for a Year', was one of the funniest books I have read, as it encapsulated the various idiosyncrasies of human behaviour and societal conditioning. The £1.7 Billion Fraud, shown on BBC4, 2/3/2015, was about the Japanese company Olympus, and highlighted how greed and arrogance, in the financial and political sectors, was endemic, and for many was a way of life. In the same year the film, The Big Short, which highlighted the events leading up to, and after the banking crises that brought the world to its financial knees in 2008, was further evidence of how politics and finance were still very much sleeping in the same bed. And whilst such greed and arrogance claimed to affect all walks of life, the most vulnerable in society seemed to suffer the biggest losses. In 2019, the shambles referred to as Brexit, was further evidence, if any was needed, of the diabolical state of not only politics in the UK but also at times, its bigoted, racist, misogynistic, sexist, chauvinistic populace, masquerading as intelligent people. Finally, when all this shit keeps cropping up on a regular basis the old cricketing joke springs to mind. When a batsman was asked if he was alright after he had repeatedly been struck by short pitched deliveries from a fast bowler his reply was, I'm OK, because by now I'm getting used to it. Sadly, and annoyingly today's shit can have more devastating consequences than a bang on a crash helmet.

Ageism and the Elderly: What the fuck is an app?

Does everything become irritable with age? Do memory foam products suffer from memory loss as they get older? ITV's Tonight: Ripping Off The Elderly, 21/3/24 highlighted the fact that last year £500 million was stolen from the over 65s by family, friends and people in trust. In 2024, the Labour Prime Minister, Mr Starmer, decided to take away the Winter fuel allowance from thousands of elderly pensioners, who had paid class one and two stamps all their working lives, and were entitled to it because power you can take and he wanted to prove that was true. Or was it to pay for yet another hair brained scheme he and his cronies had dreamt up? If after receiving such benefits the pensioners wanted to give it to a deserving cause who the fuck is a Mr Starmer to say no, we'll stop you doing that by saying you don't need it. Perhaps he was unaware how long he would be in situ and wanted, like most politicians, to make an impression. Way back in 2002, the film, 'Mrs Caldicot's, Cabbage War', whilst advertised as a comedy but was anything, but as it illustrated, very succinctly, how society viewed and treated the elderly. The reference to cabbage being the staple diet served to such people in a so-called care home because it ensured better profits for the owners. Ricky Gervais after writing Derek, about life in a retirement home in 2012, said that no one cared about old folks in the UK, with all their wealth of experience, knowledge, skill and expertise, which he found really weird. 11 years later in September 2021, C4 screened Help, starring Jodie Comer and Stephen Graham, about life in a Liverpool care home when Covid struck. Sheila Hancock in the BBC play, 'The 6th Commandment', shown in July 2023, when visiting a care home, said, **"You can never go home because it's been sold to pay for the prison. No escape but feet first.....They want to control us-the elderly, lock us up, rinse us for revenue."** Entering the world of politics, priorities and profits it again emphasised how the elderly were not considered high priority in terms of help and resources to deal with the pandemic, resulting in a much higher mortality rate compared to the rest of society. In our society and culture is there a correlation between aging and social alienation, castigation, castration, isolation and rejection? Yes, because people with less experience, and dare I say intelligence, do not like to be questioned or challenged about their opinions or motives, by people who they perceive as past their sell by date, after all what do they know? I am personally subjected to such and am summarily dismissed for writing and discussing the contents of this book. As Dean Spanley, starring Sam Neill, said in the film with the same name in 2011, **"Only the closed mind is certain."** But, **"Young people who dismissed the elderly overlooked one important thing. The older you were, the less you cared. That was the one great liberating thing about old age. Really you didn't care anymore. You were free."** (James P, 2013. Dead Man's Time, p480). Whilst I don't totally agree with these sentiments I understand the implications. **"And of course they thought he was stupid because that's what the young think. They couldn't see past the trembling hands, defective hearing and battered eyesight. They interpreted slowing of thought as a decline in intelligence. This is paid up lip service to the idea of experience, but that's all it was because secretly they believed all their bright idea were new ones."** (Paterson J and Holmes A, 2018, Revenge, PB, 53:286). Another film, 'Song for Maria,' in 2012, was another poignant reminder of society's view of the elderly and dying, which was at odds with how the elderly perceived themselves. Historically, but more so today, many youngsters and many not so young actually believe that elderly people are born old, grumpy, with lots of money, a generous pension and were a sub species removed from their world. Mind you if they spend most of their lives in the synthetic world of their smartphones, computers and game consoles it's easy to see why. Or as Simon Callow, the actor, in an interview for TV Choice, p9, 16-23rd July, 2016, said, **"Older people are ignored,"** he says, **"We live in a society where people hardly ever see each other at all. It is as if you don't exist. Most people are on mobile phones, so they don't see anybody and nobody listens to each other."** What's happened to mano mono-eyeball to eyeball? On the 7/3/24 BBC screened a programme, 'On Line Britain: Who's Being Left Behind?' It informed the viewer that over 40% of over 65s' didn't use the internet at all, and that 10 million adults in the UK lacked basic skills to access the internet. Tom Allen, the comedian, when interviewed about an upcoming TV programme he was involved in, 'Tom Allen, Goes to Town', shown on C4, on 30th December, 2020, said, **"Instead of staring at our phones, to actually look up and see all the history and the brilliant people around us is a really good thing."**

In the Pixar film, Inside Out, 2015, when all the modern electronic communication technology, and social media paraphernalia breaks down, the children, in desperation, ask their parents how are they ever going to survive, to which their parents replied, that perhaps they might have to resort to talking to one another. I'll return to the topic of communication later but in the meantime, **"the abandonment of respect for the aged was an indication of moral emptiness and materialism."** (Tsiolkas C, 2008 The Slap, PB, p334). Kathy Burke, the actress now re-branded an actor, by whom I ask myself, in the C4 television programme, Growing Up, shown on the 8/3/2023, wanted answers to questions about what was going on in society. She asked Rani A Harves, Professor of Sociology at Greenwich University, why it was that the thoughts and opinions of the elderly weren't as valid as the young. It would appear it's all to do with the values and principles of the society and in a capitalistic system your value is based on you being a worker, a producer and a consumer. As a retired person these elements have changed and so therefore the value to society is reduced and youth is valued over experience and the elderly become invisible. But unless society can put a materialistic value on experience, which can't be bought on the internet, Amazon or E Bay, this argument can't stand up to academic rigour. Also, when you retire you don't immediately expire. **The interesting dichotomy that has now come to be is that whilst great swathes of the younger generation have dismissed and relegated the elderly because they are past their sell by date, only to be used as cash cows and/or as a babysitting service, the elderly have decided to dismiss the younger generation because they don't live in the real world but in the world of a smartphone.**

On the question of the generation gap, which will be revisited when retirement is considered, many questions remain unanswered. Should each generation expect the next generation to behave the way they have? Change, as an absolute, is inevitable and so we need to consider how people perceive such change. Do they accept, reject, modify or rebel against it? If we accept everyone is an individual and cannot be expected to conform, that would appear to be an answer but as I go to great lengths to show in this book today's society has difficulty in accepting such and also finds great difficulty in compromise. **What is peculiar and specific to today's social media, zombie like generation is to consider with so much choice how much is the brain adapting to this?** 1 in 5 youngsters now suffer from mental health issues because they worry if they are making the right choices from all these options. The inflicted pressure to be liked and popular, I am told is tremendous. The aptly named, age old expression that, ignorance was bliss, springs to mind. Would not engaging so much with the anti-social media help because **when I was growing up and even when I entered the teaching profession, mental health issues caused by the telephone was certainly NOT an issue. In fact, running to the nearest red telephone box was considered healthy. Who decided that the elderly should be rewarded with the torture and indignity of losing not only their money but also their minds?** But this closed mind mentality permeates much of what is wrong with certain aspects of society today where many don't give a dam about other people's back catalogue, stories, arguments or points of view. Great swathes of the populace, the sexists, racists, bigots, misogynists, zealots and ideologists seem incapable of compassion. Add to that greed and power and you have an unpalatable cocktail. Upon semi-retirement at 56, I, and many others I have spoken to, certainly felt the full force of leaving the socially acceptable bubble of the workplace, to the unacceptable bubble of retirement. No mortgage, no managers, no morons, no health and safety; no addendums to a memorandum; no moaning work force, and no full-time work. The under 50s society's covert alienation and body language was telling me that I had passed my sell by date and I had no definitive purpose in my existence other than to quietly keep in the background, until it was time to read my will, when I would suddenly become a person of interest once more. Such was the shock as to how I was treated upon retirement that I've devoted a whole chapter to it. Ricky Gervais said it was the arrogance of youth but, **"all youth is not necessarily fire proof,"** (Sykes E, 2007 If I Don't Write it Nobody Else Will, P89), stating that one thing was for certain, age and aging was going to happen to everyone. **"Even the chunks of muscle marinated in steroids to be found in the gym or guarding the doors to a night club,"** (Hosp D, 2007. Innocence, p354), eventually end up either as a piece of rotting fat and flesh in a casket or a pile of ashes in an urn. No amount of drugs, deceit, denial, lies, greed, arrogance, insincerity, money, fame and fortune would alter that. In the noughties the TV programme, 'Little Britain', created Brian, played by Matt Lucas and his carer, played by David Walliams. Brian was a supposedly disabled, wheelchair bound person, but who in actual fact had all his faculties, was physically fit and a fraud because he could climb trees unaided, and do all kinds of physical stunts. The joke was he used his supposed disposition to embrace the deceit that was becoming endemic amongst certain groups in society. He made the phrase, **"Yea, I know,"** famous. Although as far as I'm aware, teenagers, including myself, have been using that phrase as long as I can remember. With some even using it as their mantra, when asked to consider an alternative to their closed minds. Teenagers are always looking for a cause to champion and a tribe to join. Muslins looki to Jihad and non-Muslims join the army. Whilst funny, was 'Little Britain' an acknowledgement of a society that actually believed its own press? A society that was becoming honed on greed, lies, deceit and self-delusion with everyone having a right, but was weak on the responsibility. A society keen on stealing, or 'borrowing,' blue, disabled, parking badges just so they didn't have to walk more than a few metres to enter a property. A society on auto pilot that regularly uses the term, 'It's alright for you'. Do these people have any idea what it's like to go through the later stages of your life, proud of your achievements and the sacrifices made, to realise those achievements to then be patronised and greeted on a regular basis with, 'It's alright for you?' Purely and simply because of jealousy and because of their membership to the bah, bah, woof, woof, instant gratification, easily disposable society. In Harlan Coben's book, The Match, 2022, he quotes from Hamilton, 1:8. **"Quiet, I'm older than you and I'm about to drop some knowledge on you. …The ugliest truth is better than the ugliest lie."** In 2020/21 a certain elderly gentleman, Captain Tom Moore, carried the flag for the elderly and zimmer frame fraternity, by raising over £38million for the NHS during the Covid pandemic. Well done, Tom. I wish I could say the same about others in your family. I would like to end this section on the generation gap, aging and ageism by quoting Dame Judy Dench from the film Notes on a Scandal, which was about teaching. **"In the old days we confiscated cigarettes and .., now it's knives and crack cocaine and they call it progress."**

If Baby Goats Can Eat and Travel Free, What About the Children?

The word **children** is fast becoming almost extinct and obsolete in the English language, being superseded with the term **KIDS, that apparently many do not know, according to the Oxford English Dictionary, are baby goats**. How long before UNICEF becomes UNIKEF? In the film, The Witches, 2020, there is reference to characters being referred to as kids but are corrected by informing the culprit that they were children NOT baby goats. Childhood memories could now be re-gendered to kidhood memories. With today kids, baby goats, being a multi-million-pound industry, have a whole range of products specifically targeted at them. I wonder who did the market testing and research to decide on what number sun factor cream was necessary for a 1-year-old baby goat as opposed to a one-year-old child? What would happen if a member of the public was to take 2 baby goats on leads, into their local travel agent, and then restaurant, armed with an Oxford English Dictionary, a television crew, lawyer and press for company, and claim free holidays and meals. Why do travel companies offer free holidays to baby goats knowing they can't, without going into quarantine, get a passport and sit next to a human being on a plane, or restaurants, offering free meals to baby goats, knowing they would contravene Health and Safety? Is that not a contravention of trades' descriptions or fit for purpose? Ask the lawyer- what do I know? Well in actual fact I have and the response was, "Interesting." It would also be interesting to see the industries response if I asked why they were purposely trying to mislead the public? **Why don't they just advertise their freebies for children?** Perhaps writing kids is cheaper because there are less letters. But when this is brought to their attention they could always go into default mode and quote a mission statement or blame immigrants. Or to be more up to date blame it on the Pandemic or Brexit.

Family Planning, Self Respect, Children, Child Minding and Parenting.

Sadly today, where family or financial planning does not appear to be high on the agenda and yet another word, virgin, is slowly leaving the English language, other than as a consumer, travel brand, courting and the quest to become an adult, in the sexual sense, has become fast tracked, and have become another instant gratification, easily disposable must have. Enter the sociologists, psychologists and all the other 'ologists to continue the debate. In simplicity, sex today is probably the result of too much alcohol for both parties, and in some cases the participants cannot even recall each other's names, let alone achieve an erection. **What has happened to courting? What has happened to self-respect? What has happened to subtlety? What has happened to being intrigued?** These days many barely teenage females walk around nearly naked leaving very little to the imagination. Today family planning for some females is to possess an open house vagina, surrounded by tattoes, that must be regularly serviced so they can tell their mates about their latest conquest. Now you've done it Mr Briggs, life imprisonment at least or stoned to death outside your mansion by those having a sickie, suffering from stress because they have been trolled. The first time I came across a family of 5 children, 4 of which had different fathers, was on teaching practice in Beswick, Manchester, in 1969, when I was 19 years of age. Such was the rarity of this that our tutor, Chris Walker, asked us to research how many other similar families in the school there were? There were 3. I wonder what results similar research in 2025 would yield? As for single parent families they only entered my professional life when I was teaching full time in Primary Education during the 70s and 80s. Again, I wonder what the statistics on single parent families would yield in 2025? **Incidentally parenting is not about numbers or gender but quality.** Sadly, it doesn't please me to say that single parenting and multiple fathers are part of my extended family. **The nature–nurture debaters argue that for every foul-mouthed slob of a child you'd find a foul-mouthed slob of an adult somewhere in their daily lives. Does this apply to baby goats? After all children don't come out of the womb binge drinking, effing and jeffing, homeless, begging, beating up old ladies, stealing some one's pension or disabled parking badge, with an attitude that says, 'the world owes me'. That has to be learned from 'significant others' mainly in the guise of ADULTS.** "People weren't even getting married any more, and if they had children, they soon abandoned them to the street, to the internet." (Patterson J, 2012. I, Michael Bennett, PB p404).

To the list we could add childminder, crèche or the in-laws. **It's not rocket science to see why society was in moral decay, with children having more labels and acronyms attached to them than days of the week.** When I was teaching in Primary Education, 1971-1989, dyslexia and asthma was as bad as it got. Personally, I've never had too many issues with children, even when hormones kicked in, but I've had lots of issues, and still have, with so called intelligent adults. Yes, I was aware that research evidence indicated that peer pressure was far stronger than parental guidance, police threats and teacher education, but that was once the child had started to attend school. **What about the earlier years? The first 5 years of a child's life, which was a must-read book by J. K. Lovell, not Rowlings, at my teacher training college in 1968,** being the template for future mayhem, madness, melancholy and merriment? **A VITAL foundation for life.** Just as a foundation is a vital stage in the house building process. It is the time when the parents, along with significant others, can provide a loving, caring, secure, stimulating, environment in which the child can grow and develop physically, linguistically, spiritually, emotionally, morally and intellectually into an independent, responsible young adult. **Incidentally babysitting and parenting are NOT the same thing. In today's society, several hours after the umbilicus has been severed these so-called parents discuss who is going to look after IT and what arguments, or what lies they were going to give for the decisions they made regarding parenting?** That's if both parents were still speaking to each other. **Your parents, my parents, child minder, crèche-what's best? WE** can't possibly look after **IT** because we have to get back to our very important role in life, of making money and collecting material possessions so we can eat and drink ourselves to excess, become obese, get type 2 diabetes, sclerosis of the liver and possibly an early grave. Why? Well obviously, to give our child a better life than we had, and not because we want to carry on with the life style we had before pregnancy, and so we can totally ignore the fact that children will change our lives. "He'd forgotten how completely kids nuked your careful adult delusions." (Deaver J, 1992, Shallow Graves, 12:170). **In truth these loving, caring, adoring parents, like sheep, have decided to follow the flock by deciding they were only going to change their lifestyle slightly by having to arrange ownership during the working week.** Oh, and if asked, the reply was that they felt very guilty at having to return to work. **No, you aren't, you don't have to if you'd family planned, saved and financially planned for the child's arrival. There are choices in life and don't forget it's not compulsory.** Unfortunately, in today's internet bubble, choice doesn't necessarily equate to free will or more happiness. In January/ February 2023 there was a 6-part television programme on motherhood that outlined the problem of wanting a career but also wanting to be a parent. During my 35 years as an educator, I came across and was guided by many terms and expressions one such being, **'If ever you have children, first you give them roots, then you give them wings.'** In today's world, some children are given wings first so they can fly off to the crèche or childminder. At teacher training college I learnt about **the moral pinnacle** with grandparents, at the apex, passing on their knowledge, skills, expertise and experience to morally guide their children, give them the courage and attitude, and the resources they needed to fight their own battles and make valued judgements for themselves who in turn, at the appropriate time, passed these on to their children, so on and so forth. Children being at the base, hence the expression, 'Children should be seen not heard.' **In today's world this analogy has been turned on its head, with children with very little experience, knowledge, skills, expertise or moral compass at the apex are given independence not long after leaving the womb. If they shout, the relevant adult jumps.** Or as one of my young cousins patronisingly informed me, "**What my children want, my children get. You need to accept change, Uncle James."** Who decided and when this change in hierarchy took place I have yet to specifically find out, other than to relate to an approximate time span, i.e. over the past 30 plus years. Also, on the question of change its today's generation who are resistant. Just try taking their smartphones off them and you run the risk of physical harm. Or just ask them to 'hand over' their smartphones, laptops and gaming devices for a week or two, to avoid the temptation, to see if they could cope without having a nervous breakdown. But as they are addicted to their mobiles, they will fight to protect their fix. In December 2024, Emma and Matt Willis were involved in the C4 programme, The School That Banned Smartphones. Whilst I believe many viewers were shocked by the programme, although many programmes had previously warned the populace as to the dangers of modern technology, such as sleep deprivation, mood swings, depression, suicidal thoughts and actions, anxiety, concentration, the inability to communicate face to face, depression, etc. Plus, the fact that these devices were changing the fundamental nature of what it is to be a child. Not to mention what it is to be a so-called responsible adult, I was not in the least bit surprised with the programme content, as I had been writing about the subject for many years. I also was sceptical as to how many adults, apart from Matt and Emma would do anything about it. After all we are dealing with addicts here who are prone to cheating and telling lies.

On April 5th 2018, an article appeared in the Dominion Post, New Zealand, entitled, **'What future tyrants we create by giving kids a sense of entitlement', by Rosemary McCloud.** The article, whilst sadly using the term kids in the title, pointed out that so many parents now brought their children up to be entitled, to run riot in restaurants, shout and show off at the movies, demand the latest toy and sulk until they got it. **Children who run their parents have become, in some people's eyes, children being brought up properly.** These children became bullies and parents rather than deal with them, made excuses for them. Parents, through laziness, misguided loyalty and for the lack of an agreed code, maintain that their children must never be hindered, rebuked, inconvenienced, ignored, and no hand must ever be raised against them. These future tyrants are being created so they could attack ambulance workers on the job or have their ambulances trashed. Whilst car chases are called 'police car chases', **NOT** 'lout car chases'. I came out of the me, myself and I zone in my mid-20s, and started to embrace my adult responsibilities. The questions asked at the time were, 'Do you delegate, empower or abdicate your responsibilities?' And although these were related to management issues, it was argued that managing life was just as relevant and that managing your children was absolutely vital to the future development of the species. What my children want, my children get is another way of abdicating responsibility by saying that was a bad thing to do, but he's not a bad boy for doing it.

"My mother did what so many mothers did in the fifties and sixties – she brought us up full time, an operation which included decorating, curtain making, accounting, shopping, cooking, sewing, knitting, dressmaking, and every other aspect of housekeeping. There were one or two mothers in the street who worked, in shops and factories, but in our hearts, we knew that it wasn't right. A mum was meant to be at home when you wanted her." (Titchmarsh A, 2002, Trowel and Error, 3:16). **"Hers was the hardest job-housewife, mother and emotional dartboard."** (Boy George, Take it Like a Man, 1995, 2:22). Having spent most of my working life being in the company of women I don't consider myself a male chauvinist, **but, ladies, realistically you can't have it all. If you want equality, a career and children all at the same time then this needs serious consideration, not just a few too many drinks.** But what is the message from many parents to these wonderful, new anatomical creations, who after all didn't ask to be born? **We don't want you. We are going to give you away. To be honest you're an inconvenience.** No, not adoption as such, just temporary re-housing. You defecate, diarrhoretic void, cry, scream and demand our undivided attention, 24-7. But don't worry we'll give you the name of some wannabe or celebrity before abandoning you. We'll also say impressive things like, 'We love you and you are the centre of our universe.' To prove it we'll put a sweat band around your head with a flower on to make you look cute, and put your picture daily on every social networking site we can find, which hopefully will divert attention away from the fact that actually someone else, who should now be labelled a baby goat herder, is going to be tasked with your upbringing. Mummy and daddy's way of thinking being that a £100 pair of trainers at 3 years of age, or a 48-inch colour television in the bedroom to replace the chiming mobile hanging over the cot, was a positive way to demonstrate to society that their children were loved and well looked after. Or as Alan Bennet, in Talking Heads, puts it, **"Ornamenting your kiddies like Christmas trees."** Or that paying someone £150 plus a week to look after your little offspring showed that **you definitely cared.** Not forgetting the trip to foreign parts, as soon as the umbilical cord was severed. Sitting still on mummy and daddy's/boyfriend's/sperm/egg donor's knee for at least 4 hours, without crying and disturbing other passengers, in an aeroplane that puts tremendous pressure on your ear drums and makes you scream. Then on to a beach where the temperature will be at least 30 degrees centigrade, years and years before the child's thermo regulatory mechanisms have developed to cope with such. All under the guise of, we want them to have what we never had. What a slap in the face to their own parents whom they were now asking to baby sit for them. The implication being that their parents didn't give them anything when they brought them up. Hard faced bas...... How much does a profusion of hugs, cuddles, kisses, social correction, moral and ethical guidance and positive attention cost? Many of today's parents believe that food, fashion and materialistic rewards are adequate substitutes for correction, love and affection. Unfortunately, in a materialistic society the base line measure is money. **Is it not a truism that the best thing that you can give your children, to show you love them is, TIME NOT TRINKETS?** Studies have shown, (Cohen et al, 2015), that hugging can cure depression, reduce stress and boost the body's immune system, so why not start early to avoid such ailments later in life. Not taking their children to the nearest pub not long after they are born, because mummy and daddy need a drink, because they can't cope and besides that's what they did before bringing a child into the world. **For me there are now very few places that adults can go for, 'me time' without being confronted by someone else's, 'little darlins'.** I accept the argument that others involved in the process bring an extra dimension to the child's upbringing and, in certain cases, are perhaps more suited to the job than the parents themselves. **Also, life is about choice but for me this is one choice that is so important, because its success or failure transcends beyond just having sex.** Our choices and actions have consequences, good and bad, as people are architects of their own fate. **For me, it's the fact that many child producers don't even want to try and be part of the child development process, that makes me angry.** And the reply to such accusations is, 'What do you know, you've never had children?' Did my wife and I family and financially plan-YES, but sadly life doesn't always turn out the way you hoped it would. Also, these people want me to accept that by a female opening her legs, and becoming pregnant by allowing some male to give her his sperm and then giving their children away, as soon as you can instantly makes them the fountain of knowledge on all things related to parenting. Also, whilst I accept that the experience of producing a child is a unique, and arguably, priceless sound theory underpins all good practice. "Kate found it extraordinary how much ownership strangers felt they had over her uterus. People she had only just met would imagine they knew her age, her sexual proclivities and her maternal urges. There was an assumption, implicit in the question, that all women should want to have children and that those who didn't were somehow lacking. It used to infuriate her." (Day E, 2021, Magpie, p200). This issue of people putting you in a box and giving you a label transcends many areas, many of which will be highlighted in this text. I could be found guilty of such, but hopefully, the reader will appreciate it's just to show that there are very few absolutes in life. Many years ago, after my wife and I had separated, I went out with a young lady, Debs, who had a son

Ross, and she openly admitted she wanted to give him at least the first few years of his life before he went to school, by being a stay-at-home mum. She only worked part-time on Saturdays, selling bacon on Hyde market, when her son was either with his dad or grandparents. I know she was sometimes stigmatised for not going out to work full time, and labelled one of those single parents who live on handouts from the government. I had a lot of respect for her. I also have a great niece, Laura, who proudly calls herself a stay-at-home mum and she has 6 children. But I've no doubt she is also stigmatised for not being a sheep and following the trend. Sadly, in recent times though, she has started to patronise Uncle James who is trying to give her a moral compass to help her deal with her role as a responsible adult, and not succumb to the pressures of today's me, myself and I world. I know it never entered my brothers' or sisters' thought processes to ask my mother to look after their children whilst they went back to work. It just wasn't an option. **YOUR CHILDREN, YOUR RESPONSIBILTY was the mantra. What is more important than spending a few years to lay the foundation of your child's future? It shouldn't be viewed solely as a financial exercise and if this INVOLVES MISSING OUT ON A FEW HOLIDAYS AND BOTTLES OF WINE FOR A FEW YEARS, which many wouldn't be able to afford if the credit card companies weren't so greedy, out of a possible life expectancy of 80 plus years, so parents can save and plan accordingly, so be it.** I repeat, **whatever happened to family planning? For me, plastic love and materialistic parenting are at the root of many of society's social problems. Today, for many, but not all, trying to emotionally and psychologically blackmail one, but preferably both of the parents, into doing most of the child rearing job, appears to be the name of the game.** The thinking being that they are far more experienced at it than we are, and to be honest we can't be arsed to learn. Perhaps the thinking at the time was that if they could get both parents involved, it would reduce the costs even more. Throw in a little housework twice a week, paid for of course, would help granny and grandad survive in such a harsh financial climate. I have purposely not named the mother I'm referring to in case she tries to troll me, hoping I'll commit suicide, after reading her foul abuse. But wait a minute, aren't my generation always being told, on a daily basis, that we are the financially blessed generation with our generous pensions and don't need handouts. I have personally been told that it was wrong of me to accept my winter fuel allowance because I didn't need the money. In 2024, the newly elected labour government jumped onto this idea not long after coming into power. And who says politicians can't think for themselves? I now sit with my hat and gloves on watching television, with icicles hanging from my nose. The term cash cows is very prevalent these days because many children spend many hours planning how to spend their parents' hard earned cash once they're gone. **Yes, you do Julie B.** As mentioned, my wife and I saved up for several years to help pay for our wedding, and for the deposit and associated costs for a mortgage to buy our first house. At the age of 16, before I met my future wife, I took out an endowment policy, with the money I'd saved from delivering newspapers, running errands and expenses paid for playing on one of the teams at Oldham Athletic FC. Thirty shillings or a pound as I recall, in preparation for taking out an endowment mortgage when, at some time in the future, I bought a house. Our family planning, although unsuccessful as Dee and I didn't produce any children, was always based on one parent staying at home for at least the first few years of our offspring's life. Nowadays, many couples bleat on about not being able to afford to buy, but that's because for many it's considered beneath themselves to buy a two up, two down terrace, with no furniture and go without a car and all the trimmings especially if mummy and daddy can help buy that brand new, fully furnished semi-detached, just advertised in the local paper. **What's happened to living within one's means, by working at the marriage by, 'begging, stealing and borrowing', painting and decorating, gardening, saving for a table and a few chairs,** whilst missing out on a few holidays or not regularly visiting the pub to show off your latest acquisition? No wonder they get bored and separate within 55 hours to 72 days, (Elle, Aug, 2019), of their expensive wedding. It appears that many couples want the expensive wedding day but not the day-to-day routine of married life that follows. **Just as with their children they don't appear to place much emphasis on laying a foundation. Hence the instant gratification, easily disposable name tag.** Or is it simply because these intelligent life forms are aware that being a stay-at-home mother is equivalent to working 98 hrs a week unpaid, which is equivalent to 2.5 full time paid jobs? (A survey commissioned by the American juice brand Welch in March, 2018). Elderly family members should not be considered as cash cows and should not be made to feel the lowest form of life because they have refused to look after their grandchildren, whilst their own children go back to their very important lives of making money, eating and drinking to excess. How could certain elements in society, who we are led to believe are the highest form of intelligence in the animal kingdom, do that to our aging population, one of the most vulnerable groups in society? Linwood Barclay reminds us that as we get older, we learn to multi grieve, **not** multi task. Elderly people have done their bit for society and now that they were becoming more vulnerable and frail, they should be enjoying their retirement, not being made to feel guilty by refusing to look after the dark destroyer that can reduce the most child proof home to a scene from a Sam Peckinpah movie in 30 seconds. To re-iterate, **because that's what people do now. Nearly everyone does it. It's called progress because we are the highest form of intelligence on the planet. Or is it just, like sheep, we follow.** Unfortunately, such a mentality ensures that many end up in places and situations they don't want to be. Which gives them another reason to moan, groan and complain. **To repeat, for many years I have wondered where the evidence is that supports the belief that to have sex, resulting in pregnancy, and as soon as possible giving the child away, instantly makes those involved great parents? That's if they stay together. And people who also have sex and want children, but for one reason or another don't conceive, don't know what they are talking about, shouldn't have an informed opinion and, by inference, would not make good parents and are told, 'It's alright for you…shut up'?** Why are couples who decide, for one reason or another, stigmatised, by people who incidentally give their children away not long after the umbilical cord is cut, for not wanting children? **To re-iterate, life is all about choice.** As my mother used to frequently ask me as she was subjected to this ever-changing world, that she found great difficulty in understanding, **"James, why do they have children when it's blatantly obvious they don't want to accept the responsibility for their upbringing?"** My reply delivered with a straight face being, "Mum, it's called progress and must have something to do with social engineering and a total breakdown of agreed values in society." **As for myself as I got older, I became bored with being told I was just a grumpy old man, to accept the progress and stop living in the past. In other words, join the sheep. Bah, Bah.** In Chapter 6 under, Personal Stuff, I revisit the topic of children and parenting.

Social Drugs, Self Induced Illness and the NHS.

When I was a child, smoking and drinking amongst adult males was very prevalent and under-age drinking appeared to be, a rite of passage into adulthood, because society didn't know any different. In my mid teen years underage drinking was the next milestone to overcome. I also grew up near a tobacco factory and with a father who smoked and was alcohol dependent, this dependency eventually turned him yellow and killed him in his 60s. Obesity was a word that rarely, if ever, reared its ugly head on our council estate, because frequently there were only two tins of baked beans and one loaf of bread in the pantry to share amongst many. Today, with greater choice, better technological advances and health and hygiene education, the epidemiologists are informing society that humans are living 15 plus years longer but because many of its social habits it would appear many do not want to live longer. These habits can not only reduce a person's quality of life but also considerably reduce life expectancy. As a result of ALL the medical evidence, smoking is now considered both dangerous and stupid. Not to say excessively rude. **"Smokers light small poisonous fires twenty –forty times a day."** (Truss L, 2005. Talk To The Hand, p186-188. Hazards of Smoking and the Benefits of Cessation, Prabhit Jha, 2020. Found in Lancet under, Studies of current drinkers, Angela Wood and Stephen Kuptage et al, 2018, are but a few of the studies referred to). **Why do so many so-called intelligent life forms want to embrace such outcomes and want to kill themselves many years earlier than would otherwise be the case? And in certain cases, the dying and deaths not being very pleasant experiences.** The fact is that in a democracy people can't be told what to do and so such people will not so politely tell you to go away. Now they even have a whole raft of must not mention terms, ics, ists and isms, to hide behind as soon as ANY TRUTHS ARE EXTOLLED. Why have terms such as obesity and anorexia when body shaming is not allowed? Just as they will if, in your humble opinion you suggest they accept some personal responsibility for their appearance, lifestyle and their responsibilities. Even when it can be shown that such choices can have massive economic, financial and sociological consequences, impacting on the fabric of society and its health, in not only the family home but also in the workplace. Also, who should pick up the tab for their actions and why is the topic constantly, 'swept under the carpet'? **Are people born obese, attracted to junk food, addicted to alcohol, addicted to smartphones, actively looking for stress, nicotine junkies?** In the vast majority of cases the answer is NO. In September, 2023, 8 disposable vapes were discarded every second, that's 5 million a week. Many by teenagers wanting to, 'look cool', and to increase their chances of wanting to get lung cancer. Obviously, another, 'must have'. **To repeat, so called intelligent people have choices of how to conduct themselves in life.** Sadly, for me is that since retirement I have become more aware of the number of health care professionals who are overweight. **Crazy, isn't it, the games we play?** People who don't exercise, drink, smoke and eat junk food to excess do so because that is their choice, whilst knowingly increasing their risk of peripheral vascular disease, stroke, heart attack, clogged arteries, type 2 diabetes, obesity, cell necrosis, COPD, upper lung tract infections, cirrhosis of the liver, cancer etc. The effects of alcohol, of a given quantity on a specific body mass, showed that it undermined mental capacity, dulled reactions and shrank peripheral vision. Not to mention its effect on the immune system by reducing the number of Special Main line Lymphocytes and T cells, which protect us against a whole host of infections. (The Truth About Boosting Your Immune System, shown on BBC TV, 6/01/21.) **What I find fascinating is that if we are the highest form of intelligence in the animal kingdom, why are these people, who at times are arrogant about their invincibility, surprised when they get what they have been striving for all their lives?** What's more when these adults get their self-induced illnesses, society is asked to feel sorry for them? Enter the world of **Compassion Fatigue,** which is all to do with losing the ability to care. A condition I have partially suffered from as I've got older. A topic that can be applied to many things associated with life in 2025. Instead of asking for our compassion and sympathy should we not be celebrating their success? Should we not be rejoicing because they have achieved their goals? Many years ago, the NHS announced that carrying out operative back procedures, that cost thousands and thousands of pounds, on overweight/obese people was, to put it bluntly, a waste of public money. Until the cause of people's illnesses was addressed, success rates were always going to be low to say the least. "Doctor, I keep getting these headaches," "Well stop banging your head against a brick wall." But as soon as the politicians realised this topic was a mine-field and not a vote getter, and **putting self-**

induced illness to the back of the NHS queue became a non-starter. But we need to ask, **do these, at times arrogant, people care? I think not.** In that case should we not reciprocate such apathy when they develop self-induced illnesses and are looking to fellow man, for a sympathetic, hug and a cuddle, not to mention a transplant? **"If you don't look after your health, you can't expect free access to healthcare." Is this wrong? What are the economic arguments?** Young Economist Winner, Averill L, 2017. This excellent article highlighted the complicated issue of **self-induced illness,** which isn't something new but is somewhat of a political hot potato, as it costs the NHS billions of pounds a year.

"£5.2 billion per year was spent by the NHS on surgery and other treatments directly related to smoking", (S Allender et al, 2009). "In November 2014, the McKinley Global Institute published an essay estimating that obesity and overweight related illness, including type 2 diabetes, cost the NHS £6 billion in 2017", (R Dobbs et al, 2014). "These two figures add up to around 10% of the NHS budget of £122.6 billion for 2016/17." (Averill L).

In April, 2021, an ITV television Tonight documentary, 'Giving Up Sugar for Good,' updated the figures related to overweight and in particular obesity, by stating that obesity and overweight accounted for almost 70% of men and slightly less for women in the UK. With, according to Professor Jason Halford, one of the highest rates of obesity in Europe. Costing the NHS around £10 billion, a tenth of the annual budget, on treating complications caused by diabetes. Complications such as damaged retinas/blindness, lungs, kidneys and heart. In 2020, the UK consumed over 3 million tons of sugary foods, a rise of 3.5% in just 5 years. It was also interesting to note that as a result of the Covid 19, 90% of deaths occurred in countries with high obesity rates, and that having a Body Mass Index, (BMI), of 35-40 increased a person's chances of dying by 40% and a BMI over 40 increased that risk to 90%. **"Perhaps getting drunk was something for the weak, a crutch for people who were not strong enough to live their own lives, to stand on their own two feet. Drinking was running away from something."** (Slaughter K, 2011. Blindsighted, PB, 6:58).

"Drink is a convenient way to anaesthetise the masses." (Nail J, 2004. A Northern Soul, HB, 10:210). This observation is often portrayed in many television programmes as a way of life by showing people, upon returning home or back to base, immediately pouring themselves an alcoholic beverage. Something my partners and I have very rarely, if ever, done. Make a cup of tea or coffee, 'a brew', yes, but never, 'a stiff drink'. Some people seem incapable of making good, long- or short-term decisions, stumbling from one crisis to the next, I call it, **'The Soap Syndrome',** as many wanted to act out in real life what they saw on their televisions, smart phones and laptops. They viewed happy people with scepticism, and people who actually enjoyed going to work were considered weird. In much the same way as people who didn't drink alcohol to excess, couldn't possibly be having fun. Who decided that for the vast majority of the younger and not so young generation, the only way to have a good night out was to be drunk before leaving home, be sick in the pub/club/ taxi/ street, have a fight/ sex (you choose, maybe both), have a donner, that's the meat version, not the female singing Summers version, on second thoughts, perhaps both? According to a BBC Panorama documentary in January, 2015, alcohol related illness cost the NHS £3.5 billion per annum. It was reported by NHS Digital in 2018, that alcohol deaths in the UK had reached a record high of nearly 6,000, and that the UK was facing an addiction crisis. Again, the question is raised, **"Why would so-called intelligent animals want to destroy their liver and kidneys before they had reached early retirement? Is it because most addicts suffer from 'Impulse Control Disorder' and just can't help themselves?"** Research being done in the 2020s is that there is an area of the brain related to the topic and is trying to find out why

so many addicts relapse. In 2019, the Organisation for Economic Co-operation and Development, (OECD), found in their study of 36 nations, that the Brits were drinking far more than the rest of the Western World. Equivalent to 108 bottles of wine, or 427 pints of 4% strength beer, to be precise. Having a father dependent on alcohol certainly was the initial, childhood in-print on my negativity to all things connected to it. Was society hard wired and dependent on the drug yet in denial as to the damage or hurt it could cause? Many years previously Bertrand Russell remarked that drinking was temporary suicide. Moderation was seen as weak, whilst excess was considered, 'cool'. Reality showing that everyone's life was addicted to some form of social drug. **I repeat can these highest forms of intelligence not function without such dependencies/addictions?** In my opinion the answer is NO. Or if they could it would be with great difficulty, as the culprits would be alienated from society. Just organise a party where there is no alcohol, never mind sex, drugs or rock and roll and see how many attend.

"Britain is a country in love with alcohol. In fact, not to drink makes you weird and a killjoy." (Louise Mensch, 2013, writer and former Tory MP). **Or is it just because human beings are not hard wired for self-denial and that is why diets or abstinence rarely work in the long run?** On more than one occasion, whilst on my many travels around the globe, I have been asked, whilst just making polite conversations, what was it about the Brits and their obsession with alcohol? When was drinking out of bottles, obviously filled with alcohol, rather than glass tumblers specifically designed for such, that cats and dogs had urinated on whilst waiting in the warehouse or in the back of the pub to be brought onto the shelves, that's the bottles not the cats and dogs, introduced and why? Was it a cost cutting measure, or to make the drinker look, 'cool'? Or perhaps by limiting the choice of glass, for the idiots who liked to 'glass people' after a few beers, it was considered a good move to fight anti-social behaviour.

Add to the societal pressures brought about by self-induced illness we only need to look at the NHS itself to see why, in my personal opinion, in its present format and with the never-ending racist issues that pervade this country, it ultimately cannot survive. On the 24/6/24 the TV programme, New: Undercover A&E, NHS in Crisis, was further evidence, if any more was needed of the state of the NHS. Patients being left in chairs and on trolleys in corridors for up to 48 hours! As a little aside, how many people actually read the leaflets they get with the NHS drugs? In January, 2024, I was given a prescription of Quinine Sulphate 300mg tablets and under 4. Side effects there were many, but I was drawn to the last one, DEATH. Followed by: If these occur treatment should be stopped and a doctor contacted straight away. No comment.

Question: How many healthcare workers are overweight, alcohol dependent nicotine junkies? The Nursing Times /BMJ suggest that between 2008 and 2012, 25% of nurses were obese. With Kapta Nilan et al, 2019, citing 31% of males and 17% of females dependent on alcohol and nicotine. Is the Health Service so desperate to recruit that job specifications are left open ended. I am not suggesting such people are not good at what they do but, do as I say not do as I do springs to mind. On the 5th July 1948, the NHS was born and within a month, 98% of the population had received their NHS cards. A great many of the NHS workers and support staff were coloured, migrant, 'foreigners', from the West Indies, India and Africa. History has subsequently shown that that not only did these migrants, and subsequently their relatives and offsprings, work in the NHS but they also helped the British economy to reach dizzy heights by being an integral part of the British work force in other industries, such as transport and the postal services. During the Pandemic the Brits overtly applauded the work ethic of these NHS workers. **SO, WHAT's HAPPENED?** On the 31st July, 2020, Britain withdrew from the European Union because it wanted more autonomy and wanted to be a great nation again by, **GETTING RID OF ALL THESE BLOODY FOREIGNERS. Did the Brexit vote further demonstrate the intelligence, or lack of, in the British public because it believed all the lies pedalled by Boris Johnson and his cronies? Did these people know that St George was half Turkish and half Palestinian?** Many migrants move to escape lives of unspeakable danger, persecution, oppression and hardship. Relating back to ics, ists and isms, McCarthyism originated when paranoia about communism was rife in the USA and was related to fear and intolerance, where evidence was scant and authoritarianism rife. It is synonymous with the making of wild, unsubstantiated accusations to attack the character of your opponents. In 2025 Trump wants to, 'show immigrants the door', ignoring the fact that 40% of Americas 'Fortune 500' companies were founded by immigrants, (Sopel J, 2017/18, If Only They Didn't Speak English, 3:112). In relation to the UK, immigration was one of the big issues related to the Brexit vote, to which I have made more than a passing reference . To be treated like a piece of dog dirt, just because you are not a white supremist must be soul destroying. But let's move on and consider if the NHS is still fit for purpose? On the 18th October, 2021, a Channel 4, Dispatches, a television documentary entitled, 'Clapped Out: Is the NHS Broken?' highlighted the depressing state of the NHS and its 'systemic failings' over the last 30 years, whilst hiding under the guise of, it's a system envied by the rest of the world, when in actual fact in comparison to many other countries, it fares very poorly and it certainly isn't envied. But before looking at what the programme found, let's consider one more fact. **"Do they know that they've spent more money on developing Viagra than they have on research into Alzheimer's?"** (Billingham M, Buried, 2006, 21:429).

Long Term Staff Shortages. The latest figure being about 100,000, with chronic shortages even in training, and the ratio of doctors to patient in the UK being the lowest in 20 European countries, citing Essex as having 1 GP to 3,000 patients. All of which impacts on issues such as stress, reduced concentration, time off work, job satisfaction and staff retention. So, for me it is not surprising that recruitment is a big issue. Who would want to work in such an environment? But unperturbed, my Health Centre has recently, in Nov. 2024, started advertising for more money, sorry I meant patients.

Patient Outcomes.

With urgent cases, pre-covid, taking up to 7 months before intervention with thousands not getting diagnosis and treatment within the 6 to 8 weeks they were supposed to, 40 % of cancer patients **NOT** being diagnosed until the patient was at a more advanced stage, have massive implications for successful outcomes. Not to mention the financial implications. That's over 118,000 cases per annum. Closely aligned to outcomes was **Primary Care, which in the NHS is insufficient to meet demand.** The Netherlands is regularly top in health care league tables because it has, 'a multi-disciplinary, patient centred health care system', **not** a target centred system such as the NHS, **where the NHS sees itself as more important than the patient and where a generic diagnosis and a prescription is deemed enough to satisfy the time target allocated per patient by medical centres.** Everyone suffers from age ism and some form of arthrosis in their lives. There are over 200 types, with osteo and rheumatoid being the main ones. Juvenile arthritis is the childhood form. But it's your age and arthritis that are considered as adequate diagnosis for many doctors. With 26 bones in your foot what does, 'you've broken your foot,' mean? A patient centred approach means it takes as long as it takes to address a patient's health care issues, leading to quicker and more accurate diagnosis and treatment; less re-admits and visits to A& E, as well as far greater satisfactory patient outcomes.

Medical, Clinical Error, that destroys people's lives with a culture that covers them up. A culture where numbers matter much more than people. A culture where whistle blowers are castigated and sometimes 'blacklisted'. A culture that sees the NHS as a sacred cow above criticism that must not be criticised for fear of reprisal. During the Covid pandemic, the message was that the NHS must be protected rather than the public. A culture where the patient had to do as they are told rather than a service for the patient. A culture that when its failings are highlighted the, 'wagons are circled', by the pen-pushers and bureaucrats and the mission statements, with a few facts, are trotted out, without anything actually being done to address such issues. A culture where the person under investigation, carries on working with all the inherent dangers that this implies whilst the 'victims' are subjected to intense psychological and emotional scrutiny. A culture that instead of accepting liability, as is the case in Scandinavia, which adopts a no blame attitude, but accepts that mistakes happen, owns up, pays up and moves on, costs the NHS billions of pounds a year in compensation. In Scandinavia, the compensation bill is miniscule compared to the NHS, where there are 10,000 new claims annually. In March 2021, medical claims against the NH Trusts cost £83 billion, more than half the NHS England budget. In 2020, 354 events were reported, where 142 operative procedures were carried out on the wrong side of the body. In the past 30 years, there have been over 30 reports of systemic failings in the NHS. Many of which re-iterated what had already been highlighted in previous enquiries. Reports such as 'The Bristol Enquiry', and the 'Morecambe Bay Enquiry' in 2020, looked at a range of issues including the death of 11 babies, but as a result of the lack of transparency and the fact that most, if not all, of the recommendations were **NOT ACTED UPON,** the same issues kept re-occurring. The latest reports in Shrewsbury and Telford tell the same story. On the 30/1/2023 Panorama screened, 'Forgotten Heroes of Covid', and was yet another example of how 'the shirts', who held the purse strings of the NHS, treated the workers saving lives during the pandemic as, 'Collateral Damage', though these shirts did join in the applause once a week for such workers, as it would be seen as though they cared. These front-line workers who were not only twice as much at risk than the rest were subjected to, but also were subjected to being at double the risk of dying. Why? They were not provided with safe and effective protective wear and when many of those on the front line complained, their justifiable complaints were not noted in case the statistics caused alarm to an already frightened nation. The programme quoted tens of thousands of front-line workers who were now fighting compensation claims because they contracted Covid as a result of cost cutting measures taking priority over saving lives. Many of these heath workers lost their jobs, and have had their contracts altered purely and simply because adequate care and attention to their illnesses was absent. Problems such as deafness and lung, respiratory conditions being just some of the reported illnesses. In May 2023, there was going to be a far-reaching public enquiry because the results of previous ones had **NEVER** seen the light of day. But I suspect that not one single 'shirt', administrator or politician will take responsibility or will be held accountable for their actions. Also, in early 2023 it was reported that the NHS had not hit any of its A&E targets in over a decade. In August 2023 the latest NHS scandal involved neo natal nurse, Lucy Letby, who was accused of murdering babies whilst NHS managers ignored the 'red flags', whilst going about their daily duties. In July 2025, 3 bosses from Lucy Letby's hospital were arrested on suspicion of gross negligent manslaughter. **In June 2025, the new Chief Executive of NHSE, Sir Tim Mackay, in a damning criticism of NHS working practices, said that patients were seen as an inconvenience in a system that contained too many fossilised ways of working. Sorry to be boring but have we not heard similar stories before in the judicial system, police, entertainment, banking, religion, politics, education, sport and not forgetting the postal service, where we need a public enquiry so**

this never happens again? You don't need a psychiatric assessment to see why many elderly people, like myself, become depressed and at times suicidal. My final references about lies, deceit greed, corruption, drugs, microbiological invention etc in the NHS are Michael Connolly's book, 'Chasing the Dime', in 2002 and the television dramas shown in May 2023, Malpractice, and February, 2024, Breathtaking, about what was actually going on in the NHS during Covid 19 and **NOT** what we were told. **Perhaps the next big epidemic that the NHS might have to deal with, if it still exists, is the operative extraction of knives from people's backs and dealing with an epidemic of deniability within management teams.**

Insecurity, Image and Somatotypes: Anorexia versus Obesity.

In June 2021, a survey, reported in the Edinburgh News, involving 2,000, 18–25-year-olds, found that young adults spent one and a half hours a day, equivalent to 26 days per annum, worrying about their appearance and in some cases this was because of their attendance at Ballet Schools, where Charles and Camilla are/were Patrons. This worry being instigated by so called intelligent, responsible adults working in such prestigious establishments. When I was a young lad, Barbie doll and Ken were toys to play with. Now today's younger generation are being bullied, manipulated and coerced, with very little resistance I might add, to become clones of them. All in the name of beauty, or should I say insecurity**. Society now has social influencers so it doesn't have to think for itself.** But as been shown, 'Be careful what you wish for'. I thought a selfie was an image of what someone naturally looked like. What is it called if the image of that same person has been pumped full of sh.., nipped, tucked and air-brushed and had their features re-constructed, via the surgeon's knife, just so they can get on certain TV programmes? Again, answers on a postcard please? **"Your lust for things, for objects, for trinkets will be the death of you all! You've abandoned true values and in doing that lost your precious "control", that happens when you don't use your data wisely. You have rejected the love of families and friends for the addiction of belongings. You must own more and more and more until, soon, your possessions will possess YOU..."** (Deaver J, 2017. The Steel Kiss, PB p248). World Cancer Research informs us that being overweight or obese increases our risk OF AT LEAST 13 CANCERS not to mention diabetes. Drinking too much alcohol increases the risk of AT LEAST 7 CANCERS. Eating fast and other processed food can promote weight gain. In the 50s the tobacco industry did everything it could to avoid telling the truth about smoking. We are now informed the Ultra Processing Billion Pound Industry is doing the same thing. On the 28/11/24 BBC screened, 'Irresponsible, Why we can't stop eating', to highlight how the food giants were spending a fortune to produce **BIASED research , paid for by themselves, to show their food didn't cause obesity when in actual fact it did.** "So many people sacrifice their health to gain wealth and later in life they spend their wealth trying to fix their health." (James P, 2020, I Follow You, PB, 7:22). But don't forget Midas died of starvation and we all know what he wished for, don't we? Or do we? In June, 2019, the BBC screened a futuristic drama, starring Emma Thompson and Anne Read highlighting some of the dangers I've highlighted in this chapter and who was to blame. I remember lecturing to students at the University of North London, in 1996, and telling them that in many aspects of life, the Brits were getting like the Americans. In the year 2025, I can safely say we are just as bad as them, citing obesity, litigation and who we elect as our leader as examples. **Like sheep we follow. If it's not wanting to starve ourselves to fit into a size 1, it's let's choose an eating disorder so we can attract attention.** Finally, it's not just the ladies who are guilty of insecurity. Many years ago, Winston Churchill informed us, '**A man should smell of himself'**. So could it be that humans are hard wired **NOT** to do moderation? **"How did emaciation become so cool?" (Grisham J, 1999, The Testament, PB, 48:435). **When did bald become the new lush?** Kellerman J, 2008, Bones, 21:256

Work Ethic, Apathy, Sickies and the Evolution of Homo Erectus Slack Arse. Many in employment now consider **a sickie** as four weeks extra holidays a year. To that we could add, **'a swipey', 'scrolly' and 'tappy',** as to date I am not yet aware of any research into how much time is spent doing these activities, during work hours, on issues **NOT** related to work. **In relation to Brexit, it's ironic that the white British are the sickie champions of Europe.** Research in February, 2020, highlighting the fact that in 2019, 8.6 million people, 'pulled a sickie', For this fifth of the population, a modern mathematical equation being that a few weeks of attending work equated to a day's sickie. **The term obviously being introduced to cater for the changing face and pathetic, work ethic of certain elements within the workforce and junk food, binge drinking society, who have found coping with work, just too much to bear.** And we then ask, why is obesity, with its health-related problems, such an issue? In a report by Diabetes UK in 2019 obesity in the UK had almost doubled in 20 years to affect 13million people, which was just under 13% of the population. During the same period the proportion of people over 16 with a BMI of a least 30 had increased from 18% to 29%. Were these people born obese with BMIs over 35? **How can we continue to pretend we are intelligent?** It has become all too easy to latch onto a label to give credence and credibility to our own failings, shortcomings and personality disorders. **But who introduced the term, sickie and when did it become part of the public's lexicon?** As of yet I haven't found out, other than it's an American slang term for a sick person, who is emotionally disturbed and sadistic. No comment. We now have a National Sickie Day, or Duvet Day, as some call it. **If supposedly intelligent why is society promoting being a lazy, bone-idle, shiftless sod? Could it be because people like Cheryl Lloyd from the Midlands, who works just two hours daily and this together with her benefits gives her an income of close to £46K. (Birmingham Live, Annabel Bogdi, 23/3/25).** And the government is wondering why, post Pandemic, people are reluctant to return to full time work away from home. Many but not all of my generation planned for retirement, but many of today's youngsters now spend time at and away from work planning for a 'sickie' and what benefits they can claim during their comfort breaks. As my sojourn into human behaviour and my knowledge into most things educational, medical and behavioural increased, I became more aware of the changes taking place in society. In relation to sickies I came to the conclusion that visits to the medical profession, where GPs are allocated 10-15minute slots, were akin to a game of expectation, satisfaction and disappointment. When visiting the doctor, a person required the doctor to, 'play the game', and give them a label/diagnosis and then a remedy/prescription to give credibility to their 'sickie'. Better still, a sick note or fit note if the patient can highlight enough, 'red flags'. Society being very suspicious of a Monday morning upset tummy, but was far more prepared to accept absence from work as a result of, 'ulcerative colitis', with a 'slipped disc' being far more serious than backache. Incidentally discs don't slip. They may bulge, prolapse, herniate or rupture, but not slip. Also, osteopaths and chiropractors don't put back slipped discs. But I digress. If receiving neither a diagnosis nor prescription, the doctor was deemed to have failed in, 'playing the game', and is therefore labelled, useless. The fact that unless the doctor has a fairly accurate diagnosis, they cannot safely prescribe is irrelevant to the other participants in the game. The doctor may also feel that the body's natural healing rhythms will do the trick, as all drugs have side effects, that could lead to death, and so bed rest and plenty of fluids are prescribed. But many patients feel cheated and disappointed, and in certain cases they choose to make up their own diagnosis. When running my clinic in the 1990s I consulted with several patients with various ailments that they said the doctor had diagnosed, such as sciatica of the shoulder or slipped disc of the elbow. Interesting, had some new ailments suddenly arrived on the scene? The pub on a Saturday night used to be a wonderful place for illness diagnosis and problem solving, hence the Glaswegian term, **'a bag of shite on a Saturday night'**, but unfortunately as social habits have changed, many drinking establishments have either shut their doors or become marginalised because of race, colour or political persuasion. Now the go to for illness diagnosis is the internet. On the 16/11/23 a Tonight, television programme, Britain: On the Sick, tried to give an overview of the situation but for me it again raised more unanswered questions, because people are not found in books. What's happened to Job Satisfaction I asked? As mentioned, **when I retired in 2006, I'd only had a week off work for 10 years, to deal with appendicitis. Surely that deserves some kind of ic, ist or ism, or a television programme where I am labelled weird or exceptional.** The programme apart from quoting some alarming statistics regarding the impact this malady was having on the Economy, Health and Wellbeing of society came up with phrases such as, 'Unable to work', but didn't define unable. Other questions such as, Has Society lost its appetite for work? Do employers really care about its workforce? Using the Pandemic as one reason, why some started to question their VALUE. Of course, the word stress kept rearing its ugly head **but it never mentioned the phrase, self-induced illness,** which I found interesting. **Before moving on may I again emphasise that my views are not intended to denigrate people with genuine physical disabilities, psychological and/or emotional issues, or those on long term sickness benefits, such as Long Covid sufferers, with up to 25% of them out of the work force.** These people being considered by some as not relevant, not supported, undesirable and a drain on society, when, as I see it, what they need at the very least is understanding, empathy, moral support and an accurate diagnosis. But this antagonism towards its work force where employees feel undervalued, underappreciated and in need of moral support was highlighted in the programme as being very relevant, when talking about the NHS and Prison Service. Some in the latter now finding it more rewarding by smuggling mobiles into prisons at £2,000 a pop. It could have included other professions such as Education but didn't. In relation to the NHS in 2022, 27 million days were 'taken off' which equated to 75,000 full time staff. Whilst in 2023, 7.2 million people were on the waiting list for operative procedures. The occupational phenomena, known as Burn Out and Unmanaged Stress, being cited as the biggest reasons for these statistics. Regarding the Prison Service, Mark Fairhurst, a serving prison officer in Liverpool and Chair of the Prison Officers Union, said the problems identified in the prison service was the **BIGGEST CRISIS in not only the Prison service itself but also in many other walks of life, adding 'over the past 30 years'. So, it's not only me that had identified the past 30 years as the time when 'things' started to change and, in many cases not for the better.** In 2021, a prison inspection at Wandsworth found that 30% of the work force were either off sick or just didn't turn up. As an aside, the trend Post Pandemic appears to be in many areas of the work force, and in particular those who are in employment is to **STRIKE**. Interesting. **And of course, the powers that be contributed to the programme by quoting, as usual, mission statements and statistics, to try and give the impression that the situation wasn't as bad as it was being painted and all issues were being addressed,** but as soon as the face of any politician appeared on screen, I decided to take such reassurances with a pinch of salt. Throwing money at personal attitudes and a culture of bullying and not caring, aligned with a history of mis-management, isn't a solution or a remedy. **Mind sets take time to change and in many cases are unachievable.** It's all about human behaviour. Returning to the Tonight programme it was pointed out that pre-Pandemic the number of people out of work was declining but since then the number has risen by 400,000, and now stands at

2.5 million people not working because of poor health, whilst asking the question, was society becoming less healthy? What I found astonishing, was the absence in the programme of any mention of the introduction of, as I call it, anti-social technology and gaming. To that we can add 'junk food,' sugar dependency, an obsession with alcohol as further reasons for this trend to being unhealthy, with the cost in lost taxes and benefits to these 'economically inactive' people being £15.7 billion. Since the Pandemic the number out of work has increased by 18% in the last 2 years; activity levels have declined by 300,000, whilst the number of sick/fit notes has risen by 0.5 million in the last year. Because of these trends, life expectancy in some parts of the country has decreased. In relation to the Private and Public sectors, 6 days per annum were 'sickie' related in the former whilst 10.5 days p.a. were related to the latter. Enough of the stats let's return to my favourite topic of human behaviour. Can you imagine if the medical profession en bloc decided one day to adopt the attitude of should we say, the least enthusiastic workers in society, and decide, 'Forget it, I can't be arsed to go in to work today, I've saved enough lives and performed enough lifesaving operations this week, I'm tired and stressed and people are, 'Doin my head in', I'll throw a sickie, Will you phone in, love, and tell them I've got anthrax?' Watching programmes on TV, where surgeons at Royal Papworth and Addenbrook hospitals, to name but two, are in theatre anything up to 18 hours performing lifesaving operative procedures, and 24 hours in A&E, apart from being fascinated and educated, both at the same time, I can't help but get annoyed that these people don't get paid £550,000 a week, plus perks, like someone who's chosen instead to kick a football, spit, swear, abuse the referee, dive about like Primary school children 'play acting', just because someone has taken the ball off them. **What a crazy world we now live in, where self-delusion, greed, insincerity, lying and jealousy abounds.** Biologists discuss, Natural Selection, which isn't influenced by emotions, and in simplicity is all to do with eliminating weak links with only the strong surviving. Only those positively contributing, as opposed to those always taking, being allowed to stay. Obviously, it doesn't consider birth defects and disabilities brought about by genetics or some unknown factors, and so therefore it is flawed. In the USA, individuals are expected to accept responsibility for their own wellbeing whereas in the UK the individual EXPECTS others to take on that role on their behalf. One of the reasons given for Trump's popularity is based on his statements of intent but being Trump he gives very little thought as to HOW he realistically intends to achieve his aims. As a result of progress, we now have cloning and so the topic of Eugenics has re-entered the scene. **"The so called science of improving the human race through controlled breeding that would eliminate undesirable attributes."** (Connolly M, 2016. The Wrong Side of Goodbye, PB, 2:23). When one considers all the greed, hate and evil in the world, at first, this science might appear to be something that should be thought of as more than a passing fantasy, but again the problem would be on agreeing on a definition of, 'undesirable'. History showing that not only has every generation had its share of despots, crooks and villains, but also attempts to ethnic cleanse the population have been based on very spurious definitions of undesirable by such despots, crooks and villains. Also, it could be argued that belonging to a particular tribe and the hatred this historically has engendered, is just another form of cleansing. **Is trolling now a form of cleansing? Also, what is the difference between the Nazis wanting to gas the Jews to produce a blue eyed, Aryan race and the homophobic, sexist, racist, chauvinist, bigots wanting to eliminate all coloured people, homosexuals and lesbians to win the Brexit vote, under the guise of white supremacy? In my opinion, there is no difference and I'm surrounded by such people.** In 1934, all grievances were blamed on the Jews and as time has moved on, these grievances have been blamed on either the Germans or the immigrants. Some of these people arguing that being a sperm or egg donor was enough of a contribution for a life living off the state, entitling them to free this and that, with many, many rights but no responsibilities. These people probably being responsible for Brexit claiming that migrants were doing what some of the locals had been doing for years, namely living off state handouts, having paid very little into the tax and National Insurance pot. Whilst politicians, to get the vote, claimed that most people actually wanted to work if they could, whilst at the same time giving them carte blanche to sit at home all day and viewed the right to malinger as some kind of social reform. **How would these so called higher intelligent life forms survive lower down in the animal kingdom? Answer, they wouldn't** so why was I informed at Teacher Training College in 1968, that we are the highest form of intelligence? The reasons given being, because we can tolerate, compare, contrast, empathise and show compassion, which other species cannot do. Whether or not we actually exercise these qualities in everyday life is very much open to discussion. Enter a new species, referred to as, **Homo Erectus Slack Arse.**

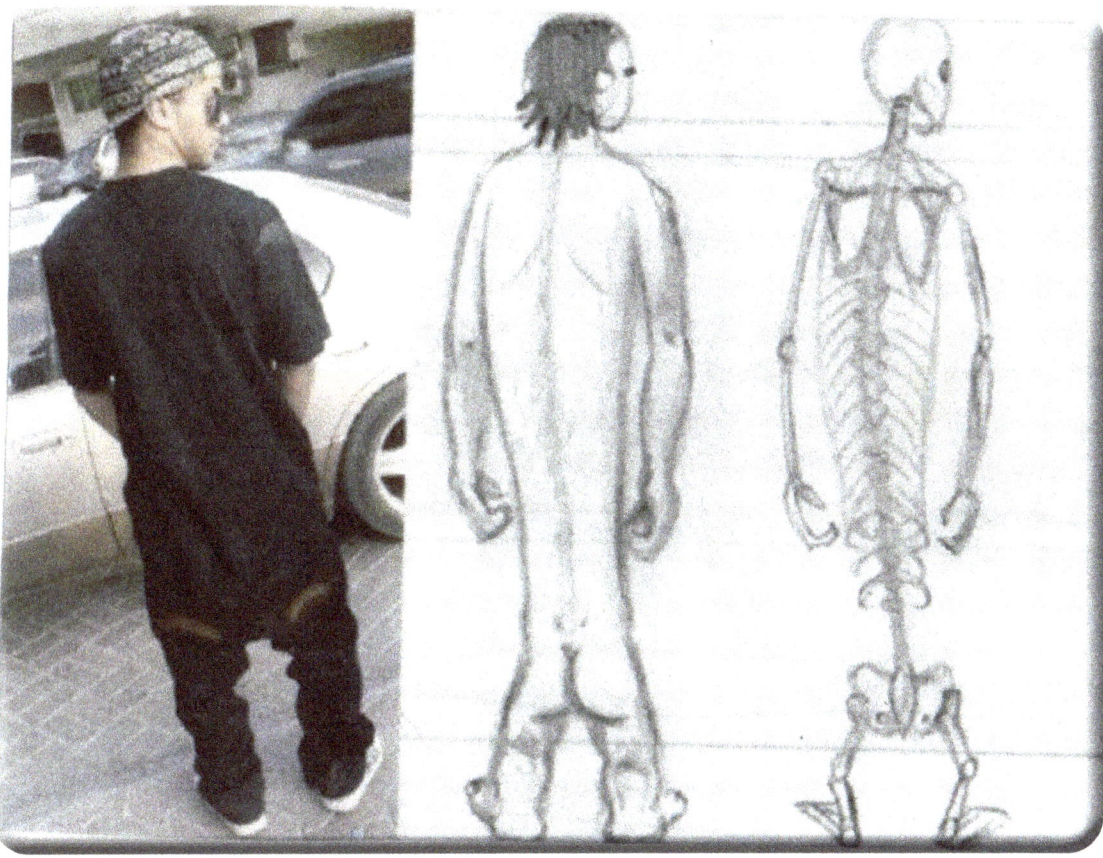

These new creatures have been created by natural genetic downward evolution through constant, spineless posturing and spasmodic upper limb gestures, which new research has shown to cause shorter legs and an inability to ambulate other than in an awkward, shuffling gait, comparable to the 'hormonal swagger'. Their antalgic gait being produced to create the delusional impression of supremacy and arrogance. The 'drag crutch' shape also seems to affect brain function, which is only three quarters the size of humans, so don't expect eye contact or intelligent verbal communication. I am led to believe there are 6,207 different languages with these new species, creating yet another which appears to have, **"a total vocabulary of about two dozen varying grunts,"** (Alison B, 2010. Cambridge Blue, PB p26). Each one denoting potential to attend university, as long as they could pay, or helping them to become possible rap artists. History has shown that this species receives mostly food stamps, state handouts and full government care. Unfortunately, they are highly fertile and are sometimes referred to as floaters as they are not easy to flush away. I also think it is highly unlikely that these new breeds realise that their fashion sense came from American death row prisoners, who were not allowed to wear belts to remove the temptation of suicide. It is rumoured that these new breeds, led by populist jingoism, xenophobia, social grading and racial profiling, claimed that immigration and crowding from growing populations of minorities, who sapped the infrastructure and lived off the dole, were partly responsible for Brexit in 2016. They argued that getting rid of all these 'foreigners', who had invaded the UK, would create a greater patriotic Britain. The actual reality is, that many of these migrants propped up the economy and saved lives by working in the NHS and so unfortunately for many of the sexist, racist, bigots if their wishes came true, they would have no excuses NOT to work, and would then be put in the invidious position they had **NEVER EXPERIENCED** in their lives, **HAVING TO WORK FULL TIME.** Their early life journey of negotiating their school truancy year to arrive at their unemployment, benefit destination was now under threat Yet another brilliantly, brutally honest TV programme in November 2017 entitled, 'British Workers Wanted', showed the difficulties a recruitment agency in Bognor Regis had in trying to overcome the pathetic work ethic of many of the white English with regard to getting them into work. Many employers actually stating on camera, that they would always prefer to hire Eastern European labour, as opposed to their white English counterparts. Why? To quote from Hamilton, **"Immigrants get the job done."** Through my experiences my sympathies started to lie very much with those, and there were many, who didn't fall into the generic cesspit of apathy, who had to put up with and tolerate such morons every day. For one who had been taught and tutored to believe in the quality of teaching and education, this lowering of standards and attitude led me to eventually resign from several high-profile posts in education. From an anthropological perspective, I started to consider whether Natural Selection was kicking in and that two opposing cultures were being established. Not the age old, have and have-nots, but the followers, the sheep and the independents who didn't want to go down the path of least resistance. Those who didn't know any different or adopted the attitude, if you can't beat them join them, and those who were hanging on grimly in the hope that ethics, morals, and common sense would return to the table for discussion. Sadly, I feared the latter were living in false hope, as the rot became institutionalised and self-discipline was abandoned. **"Self-discipline …the strength to abstain from or even turn away from a desire. It was the rejection of short-term gratification."** (Bruce A, 2010. The Calling, PB, p258). **Returning to Brexit, which occurred on 23rd June 2016, does this country actually believe it can survive on its own, once we've got rid of all these foreigners because the rest of the world appears to be laughing at us?** Could one of the reasons be that post Pandemic and as the country was settling into a life of post Brexit, in the summer of 2022, the country was in chaos because trains and planes were cancelled due to, wait for it, 'a shortage of staff', and everyone, apart from the intelligent ones, couldn't understand why prices were rising faster than people on Viagra. Strict limits were being imposed on the time Brits could spend in the EU. There were chaotic scenes at ports never designed to house a hard EU external frontier. There are fewer and higher fares on most forms of transport. Roaming charges for mobile users in Europe have been re-introduced. It is now more difficult and expensive to take pets abroad. Inbound tourism has been damaged by banning more than 200 million EU citizens who have national identity cards but not passports. The European Health card has ceased to be valid in the Schengen areas of Norway, Iceland and Liechenstein. **But hey, we now get cheaper alcohol and tobacco – result.** And the government's response to all this is to re-introduce the 'iconic blue passport', which they could have done any time when the UK was in the EU. Unfortunately, the GB passport is now far less powerful than a European Document in the access it confers to the holder. (I am indebted to Simon Calder of the Independent, for highlighting these facts in his weekly travel column). Let's continue, oh yes, and after working from home for many, many months let's go on strike as soon as we are asked to return to work, that's if we still have a job to go to. It's also ironic that a country that constantly harps on about foreigners, allowed a foreigner, Rupert Murdoch, to engineer Brexit because without him the UK would still be in Europe. (The Rise of the Murdoch Empire, BBC 2, 2020). It's also ironic that historically the white English in discovering so called new lands, force marched the indigenous Indians onto reservations, decimated the local population with bloodshed, not to mention measles, typhoid, smallpox, tuberculosis, and dysentery, introduced them to alcohol which brought about alcoholism, diabetes and suicide, branded them savages, and couldn't understand why they weren't grateful. **Don't forget we are the highest form of intelligence in the animal kingdom.** Putting aside the nation's obsession with alcohol, suspect work ethic, (**Imposter Syndrome relates to not being competent**), being top of the European league for time off work due to, 'a sickie', a country with one of the highest rates of obesity, questionable parenting skills, with a question mark over our financial and political masters, what else can we have a claim to fame for? In summer, if the sun shines for a few days, we panic by painting railway lines in case they buckle, change working hours to compensate for the rise in temperatures, close schools, one of the reasons given is that they don't have enough drinking water, suggest we don't go outside in case we suffer from being burnt alive, and it is suggested we drink litres and litres of water to stop us becoming raisins. Not tap water, **ONLY bottled** because it is far healthier than tap. **SAYS WHO, GIVE ME THE EVIDENCE?** The choice being hyper or hypothermia, maybe both. And of course, the nation is put on a hosepipe ban within weeks because there is a dangerous water shortage. Don't forget we are actually surrounded by water. Or if we have a few tropical storms our dams overflow and we have to evacuate a whole town. **"Snowflake Britain Shuts Down: SE and London's lightly dusted trains are delayed, children's football matches cancelled, and Christmas light switch–ons abandoned as winter officially begins with -12 chills."** (Duell M, Daily Mail, 1/2/23). Sometimes we shut down a whole city, i.e. Liverpool, cut down on flights at the airports, even before the Pandemic, and send the workforce home early. Well at least those that are not already at home on a sickie, as it is deemed a National Disaster. **We can't cope.** We run out of grit and salt to make the roads and pavements safer because we haven't stockpiled enough. Why? Because it's more important to ensure the shareholders get their dividends and bonuses, so we must make a profit. But fear not we'll have a public enquiry so this **never** happens again. **Well, not until next time at least.** Meanwhile the rest of Europe is in the middle of a heatwave and continues to accept holiday makers, and Canada has record snowfalls and ten-foot snow drifts but everyone turns up for work. B**ut we are so arrogant we don't give a damn because we are the highest form of intelligence in the animal kingdom and we won the men's World Cup in 1966, and our National sport of men's football, when not being accused of paedophilia, chauvinism, racism and sexism, sets a terrible example to growing impressionable minds. Not forgetting BREXIT and TROLLING, mandates to carry out hate crimes.** And I haven't, as yet, mentioned a certain Nigel Farage who decided to spend time in the USA befriending Donald Trump, so he could fine tune his skills on how to mislead the populace in case he decided he would **'have a go'** at being a Prime Minister.

Job Descriptions, Specifications and Responsibilities.

If washing up is a household chore what does washing down entail?

When did an office block become a human capital management facility? When did a shelf stacker in a store become an ambient replenishment operative, and removal men become relocation specialists? When did a window cleaner become a vision technician? When did a car mechanic become a vehicle technician? When did cleaners become floor sanitation operatives or environmental technicians? A caretaker /janitor become a hygiene maintenance co-ordinator? When did a library become an information resource facility? When did librarians become information management specialists? Was being an AVA technician not a fancy enough title that someone decided to rename them advanced technological facilitators? When did butty makers become sandwich artists working in Subway? When did nurses become triaged or trained, care investigators and a midwife become a birth technician? When did personnel become human resources and staff development officers become corporate strategy executives or internal operative consultants? When did goths become emos and vice versa, or police informants and snouts, become CHISs, covert, human information sources? When did police officers become homicidal perpetration and prevention officers, and distribution centres, fulfilment centres? When did a crack pipe not become something a plumber fixed? When did bin men, sorry that's now sexist and should be bin people or personnel, become refuse disposal operatives and a miner a subterranean mineral extractor? When did morticians become anatomical pathology technicians? When did a joint stop being a piece of meat? When did a wife become a domestic duties operative? I wonder what fancy title a ring doffer, tin basher and centre lathe turner, jobs my parents did, would be given in 2025? What are gynaecologists and embalmers now known as? Answers on a postcard please. Do we still send postcards anymore, whilst on holiday? Recently I noted a business advertised as, **Drainage and Sewage Rehabilitation**. How do you rehabilitate sewage or should I say, shit? When I was in the workforce, job advertisements stated specifically what the employer was looking for in the candidates. But now I suspect that whatever is put in such adverts, employers will be accused of a multitude of ics, ists and isms. Also whilst I try not to criticise anyone who works in the health care sector, unless it's warranted, since retirement, in 2006, I've frequently wondered what the job title, job description and job specification was to secure a position as a health care professional in the NHS, when I see the number of over-weight, over- stressed, smoking, alcohol and coffee, chocolate dependent personnel, who are tasked with advising the public on healthy lifestyles? When did obesity become the new cancer, and sugar the new default food? Do job descriptions and specifications in 2025 state that the working day **must** include spending most of it with a smartphone, surgically attached or glued to a person's ear/hand? And that person **must** pace up and down whist executing such an exercise. At least we must accept that they are carrying out their daily dose of exercise whilst realising this behaviour is to denote serious importance to the phone call. How many manual workers, all wearing high viz jackets, using their mobile phones, with not a spade in sight, looking down a hole in the road, does it take to lay a few pipes? In November, 2023, I passed 7 hard hatted, high viz workers on Riverside, supposedly working on the Flood Defence Scheme, with not a spade in sight, or a wave for that matter.

Reality Television.

How does one define reality? History shows the original Bedlam hospital in London was a place where society at that time could visit, for a fee, to view the mentally disturbed inmates under the guise of entertainment. From 2000, under the title of reality television, which for me is a misnomer as it has very little to do with real, hardworking, conscientious, people, we now have a whole raft of television programmes giving us an insight into the many facets of human behaviour. Made in Chelsea, Love Island, Big Brother and Towie to name but a few. Some people I have spoken to say they watch, reality

Television to avoid reality, which should tell us something about today's world. **"I've always wanted to be..........,"** said the latest contestant on the latest reality TV programme, accompanied by the obligatory sob story and tears of early child abuse/neglect and missed opportunity. Or, as Jimmy Nail, actor and musician, calls them, **"today's 15-minute fame seekers."** (Nail J, 2004. A Northern Soul, HB, 9:173.) Admittedly there are always exceptions and genuine cases but these are in a minority, so why couldn't the rest just be honest and say they couldn't be troubled to try and get a, 'proper job', or attend a dance, drama college, when they were younger, which would have taught and developed their singing, dancing and drama skills. The people in these establishments, whilst sharing their knowledge, experience, skills and expertise, would have been equally honest, and wished them luck in their possible success in the cut throat world called show business. Or again as Mr Nail puts it, **"the flaky, here today, gone tomorrow world of entertainment."** (Nail J, 2004. A Northern Soul, HB, 23:391.) Very few contestants /participants come out unscathed without being mocked or ridiculed, or made to look bad, heartbroken or deranged. Harlan Coban referred to these people as, 'Car Wrecks',(The Watch, 2022, 15:180.) On the other hand, a few come out as wealthy heroes. But as Tina Turner sang during the film Thunderdome, 'We don't need another hero.' But to be fair, viewers, young and old, may view these programmes as educational, forming the opinion that they either want to be like them, using them as role models, or come to the conclusion that they never want to be a wannabe. So, it could be argued they serve a purpose appealing to the voyeuristic nature of people's personality, But, **"Wasn't plucking unknown young people, often overly emotional and volatile people, and throwing their gas-soaked bodies into this famed tinderbox of a show asking for trouble?"** On the 20/3/23 ITV 2 screened, Revenge Porn: Georgia V Bear, which dealt with Reality star Georgia Harrison's successful court case against Stephen Bear for revenge porn which was an offence that sent him to prison. Having worked for several years in Marianne Jepson's Dance Drama College, I personally witnessed some precocious talent that genuinely did want to make a career by entertaining people, and were not afraid to work hard to achieve their dreams. If TV wants to find the next star just scour these colleges and institutions, without putting people on TV just to ridicule them, which was the case in early additions of X Factor, which was introduced in 2004. However, Susan Boyle soon put a stop to that nonsense. It must be soul destroying for these students, in colleges and higher education, to see someone fast tracked to so called fame, without any training, soul searching, hard work or back catalogue whatsoever. Just because some TV producer wanted to make a name for themselves, or celebrity judge, who incidentally had no significant history of acting, dancing or singing expertise whatsoever, deems that this person is just what we are looking for, and smugly announces, with an accompanying wink, "That's a yes from me." This said person having Max Clifford, the convicted rapist and paedophile as a, 'best mate'. long before Botox entered his life. Was it Andy Warhol that said we are all entitled to five minutes of fame? I can accept that, why lie and cry just to secure the vote and obscure the fact some of these wannabes just want to be rich and famous as quickly as possible, with very little effort. Of recent times I have been informed that some person I'd never heard the name of, was now a high profile 'celebrity', earning a great deal of money, purely and simply because they had been on a reality TV programme, effing and jeffing; walking around naked; had been nipped and tucked; had great difficulty speaking English, via meaningful sentences and was prepared to have sex with anyone who had a pulse. **How real are these plastic, demi-gods?** It has also become the norm to accept these people as real, based on a demographic stereotype. In much the same way as southerners and northerners view each other in the UK. Known as the North –South divide. In comparing the UK with America, with regard to the North and South, totally opposite view points exist. In the UK, it is generally considered that a person being born 'Up

North' is perceived by certain southerners as someone who wears a flat cap, has at least one pole cat down their trousers, talks with a broad accent, whatever that means, and is considered, 'thick as pig shit'. Where as in America, generally speaking, Southerners are perceived as slow and not very quick witted. That's without entering into the disgraceful treatment of Southern black people, which is where the UK and USA worlds unite. Do Northerners perceive Southerners as 'posh folk'? What does the reader think? Back to reality television, could we compare some of these shows to the Muppet Show, which was extremely popular in 1976, and Spitting Image, 1984, that made 'stars' out of its puppet characters? Not forgetting that in 2017, Donald Trump was the first reality TV star to become President of the USA. And there are many that question if the guy is for real? Margaret Thatcher once said, 'My generation was about doing, today's about being.' Speaking personally, my generation experienced, 'the finer things in life', at a time when we appreciated them. Many in today's society experience too much too soon and don't appreciate things the way we did. Do I watch some of these talent identification programmes? Initially yes, but soon realised the format was not for me. My choice. I will now only watch such programmes if the judging panel has the necessary knowledge, skill, expertise and experience to pass judgement on the contestants and, if asked, could demonstrate after their critique, i.e. Strictly Come Dancing and The Voice. Such programmes can and do discover some brilliant talent, hiding amongst the dross. **I would love to see a contestant ask Simon Cowell to come up on stage and demonstrate. It will never happen.** Is the TV programme Gogglebox typical of family life in the 21st century or is the reason some of these people are all together in one room, watching television, so they themselves can become fast tracked TV celebrities, or are being paid as celebrities? Returning to the issue of kids, perhaps I could enter baby goats into the TV programme, 'The Voice: Baby Goats'. Or 'Baby Goats in Need Week', showing distressing scenes of baby goats. Can these so-called reality shows/programmes come under the heading progress, because we are the highest form of intelligence in the animal kingdom, or are they just a return to the Bedlam days? **Shouldn't reality television** either be **re-named Fantasy Television** or just be about exposing the reality of people such as Jimmy Saville, Rolf Harris, Stuart Hall, Harvey Weinstein, Geoffrey Epstein, Ghislaine Maxwell, Max Clifford, Donald Trump, Mr Putin, Alfie Best and the like? Exposing the reality of who they really are as opposed to the public persona they try to portray through falsehoods, bribes, intimidation, threats and using the Contagion Theory to create fake news, rather than having programmes on television giving free publicity to the sex mad, alcoholic dependent, insecure wannabes.

Education: Bums on Seats Doesn't Equate to Quality of Education.

Education can sometimes fall into the misguided, ignorant thought process that works on a hierarchical assumption that the cleverest, most qualified teachers work with the eldest, more able pupils, whilst the less able, qualified teachers worked with the youngest, 'slower 'pupils'. The fact that teachers choose to work with a particular age range, or in a particular branch of education, is borne out of many reasons but having taught in Infant, Junior, a little Secondary, Further and Higher Education, I have come across many people with this belief. Where it stems from, I am not sure other than the fact that most people have been to school. But in my experience, for some, it is borne out of insecurity. So, without going into an academic debate, I will temporarily conclude this topic by stating that, in my humble opinion, many senior and principal lecturers would not survive, by that I mean possible nervous breakdowns, if they had to teach in an infant school, especially in 2025. NO INFANTS DON'T SPEND ALL DAY JUST PLAYING IN THE SAND PIT AND BAKING CAKES, ITS CALLED STRUCTURED PLAY. This not being the case, if the opposite was to happen. I can vividly recall having a discussion with a very insecure lecturer who vehemently believed that his 12 months post graduate training in teaching preparation, which involved preparing power points and a little teaching practice, was far superior to my 3 years teaching certificate from Mather College, Manchester University, in the 60s and 70s. Without wanting to earn brownie points, but having tutored and mentored a mature student on one of these courses I know where my vote goes. The move towards Post Graduate Teacher Training having more to do with finance and box ticking than quality control. So, "What's new pussycat?" sang Mr Tom Jones. Whenever politicians, whose turn it was on the revolving merry go round of job allocations, known as a cabinet reshuffle, are tasked with having a go at being an Education Minister, but who had NEVER TAUGHT and had NO QUALIFICATIONS OR EXPERIENCE OF TEACHING, other than to possibly have attended an elite, private school, I wonder how they go about their role? **The problem with teaching has always been the same, everyone who had been to school was an expert.** Once in situ, the minister actually believing that to solve society's ills, laziness and moral turpitude, because so many lacked basic numeracy and literacy skills, was to frequently take a cheap shot at education, citing poor teaching and a boring curriculum. In 2024, a report by the National Foundation for Educational Research suggested there was a substantial risk to the quality of children's education because of the critical state of teacher supply in England and that radical and ambitious action was needed to improve recruitment and retention. This was 6 years after the Guardian newspaper, in November 2019, highlighted a poll by the National Association of Education Union, which reported on the increasing numbers of teachers fleeing the UK to work abroad. With 1 in 5 (15%) expecting to quit in less than 2 years and 2 in 5 in the next 5 years, citing excessive workloads, stress, lack of support from LEAs and society in general, lack of work life balance, funding cuts, a dread of Ofsted, obsession with paperwork, excessive accountability, out of control children bringing weapons and drugs to school, high staff turnover….the list goes on. Not least the fact that in 2023, 4 in 10 schools were considered structurally unsafe because of 'crumbling concrete'. Moving abroad, teachers, on the whole, have very few, if any, of these problems and are appreciated and generally treated with respect and are trusted, as professionals, to get on with the job they are trained and qualified to do. **The problem is societal, and to task teachers with trying to solve its problems is ludicrous and soul destroying, no matter how much money you pay them. Teachers are educators, NOT social workers, full time child minders or prison officers.** Have these people passing judgment never heard the term educability, or the expression, 'You can lead a horse to water but you can't make it drink'? **The extremely significant, 1870 William Foster Education Act, 'Education For All', was opposed on the grounds that to educate the masses would make them discontent with their station in life. Up until then, rudimentary education was only available, via the church, or for the privileged few. HOW PROPHETIC WAS THAT OPPOSITION?** Before moving on I'd like to add that today for many, but not all, with a degree, has made them believe they are, 'the fountain of ALL knowledge', and pontificate on a whole raft of subjects they have very little, if any, experience of. Yeah I know, so like ye know wot like I'm sayin, babes. I passed my 3-year Teacher's Certificate with not a smartphone , computer or printer within, 'a million miles'. Totally ignorant as what google, cutting and pasting was all about.

    In 2025, it appears that everyone, including the pet dog, has 3 dozen, A star pluses and a degree. But then again if you lower the bar often enough everyone is a high flyer. But what is the value and significance of a pass mark of 40% other than to presume the candidate MAY NOT KNOW the other 60%?

Unfortunately, **many of these graduates appear to be depressed and suffering from stress. This, 'It's alright for you', depressive, lugubrious malady abounded. Some people are only capable of communication and having a good time under the influence of alcohol, nicotine, barbiturates or tranquilizers. For great swathes of the population drugs, per se, have been too easily available for too long and are now considered a necessity rather than a recreational pleasure. Are peoples' lives so empty that they can't face the world or enjoy themselves without a fix? Like sheep they followed, or is it because we are the highest form of intelligence?**

"In 20 years, we'll be a nation of prescription drug addicts and the NHS will be on its knees trying to pay for a sick nation's candy." (Jewell L, 2019. The Family Upstairs, PB, 14:95). Watch this space. **Since the introduction of the National Curriculum and Ofsted Inspections, teaching has definitely become less child centred and more to do with ticking boxes, achieving targets and financial management. In my day it was all about the process and developing individuality, which was difficult when you had 40 children in your class.** Ruth Perry, 53, a Headteacher at Caversham Primary School in Reading committed suicide in November 2022, after her school Ofsted report left her destroyed and humiliated. **Are higher educational institutions now guilty of trade descriptions where bums on seats take priority over quality of education. Should they be re-named financial institutions? Are Universities Racist? Well yes, according to a BBC 3 documentary shown in April, 2021. "Universities are businesses, which means that they are really interested in their public appearance and what they look like to other people."** In other words, along with politics, religion, healthcare, and any power-based institution, at the merest hint of scandal, in this case racist and sexist complaints not being taken seriously in case it damaged the reputation of the University, the wagons will be circled and bog standard mission statements are reeled out which at times do not stand up to scrutiny. **It is blatantly obvious to me that whichever area of education one visits today, the end product is more important than the process.** I don't blame the educators, they, like robots, are just doing what they have been programmed to do and individuality seems to have been discouraged. Fast tracking is the name of the game for training, whenever there is a shortage of personnel. During my 35 years in education and being involved in training and Continuing Professional Training, **I was NEVER aware of fast track training. CPD, yes, but fast tracking, no.** But if you gave a funny handshake and attended church that was another matter. If the pupils are not going to be tested on it, then don't bother? **What has happened to the 'Hidden Curriculum'? Working in Universities, as a Senior Lecturer and examiner, I soon realised that the name of the game was bums on seats and pass rates.** The more students that could be signed up, the more money could be generated. Also, the more student pass rates, the better the academic profile to attract more students. On more than one occasion, it was pointed out to me that without the money the students generated, I wouldn't earn the astronomical sums of money that I did. When I informed the patronising official that I would resign at the end of the semester, if my boss could 'get rid of' x number of students, who were struggling and in reality, shouldn't have been offered places, the conversation ground to a halt. Eventually the only protest I could make was to resign. Which definitely put the cat amongst the pigeons, as upon resignation the person resigning had to give their reasons. And if those reasons could be proven then awkward questions would need to be answered. Time to circle the wagons again, folks. When Covid -19 entered the scene, it posed an interesting situation that was reported in the Guardian newspaper, 16/10/20, **"The fear that was now gripping universities: will students come back in January? Like many academics, Ben believes the fear of scaring students off, or having to give them refunds, has** trumped safety concerns in a marketised, higher education system where Universities compete against each other to put bums on seats." On the 27th July, 2023, Rishi Sunak, said that too many people were getting degrees which couldn't get them a job. **Shock, horror, could this be true?** As a Sports Therapy lecturer was this topic ever discussed? Yes. Had Mr, here today gone tomorrow, Sunak, actually realised what was happening in the country that he and his cronies had been given a mandate to govern? Whatever next? Has the Society of Sports Therapist got a record of how many students actually gained meaningful, full-time employment in sport after qualification? See Chapter 5.

The Dog Mafia and Playground Syndrome.

Continuing on these themes, initially highlighted earlier when discussing thrill seekers, addicts and adrenaline junkies, and raised again in Chapter 7, I don't recall growing up surrounded by other people's pets. Having a goldfish that had been won at the annual wakes fair, maybe, and I recall sharing kitchen space with a cat, and we once had a tortoise and rabbit, but that was all. In simplicity the Briggs family, and many families living at the time, didn't want another mouth competing for the beans on toast on Saturday evening. No matter what valid reasons the animal lovers gave to persuade families to have a pet. On our housing estate my mate Peter Fletcher had a dog that used to terrorise the postman. My sister, Marlene, after she had left home and lived with Raymond's mother, had an Alsatian. I can also recall helping my sister Lilian and brother Jack deliver newspapers, as it gave me an opportunity to visit private, 'posh houses', not council ones like ours. One bungalow our Jack had to deliver to was at the end of Parkway where a large Alsatian dog used to sprawl across the front porch right in front of the letter box. To try and move the mutt, we used to throw a stone to the end of the garden and once the dog set off to try and retrieve the stone, we would sprint to try and deliver the papers before it returned to rip off our limbs. 'The Hound of the Baskervilles', by Arthur Conan Doyle was a black and white film, that was compulsive viewing in those days. I am also convinced that fear, of not wanting to be devoured by the dog, helped my brother and me to become very fast athletes. **But when the significance of families having a myriad of pets became an issue, I'm not sure but I suppose it was round about the time when jealousy and insecurity of 'not having or owning' reared its, at times, quite pathetic head.** In my younger days, this was known as wanting to be like the Joneses but who the Joneses were and where they lived I had no idea. **Since then, I've decided to include woof, woof in the term to describe today's society,** as it was now choosing to not only avoid eye to eye contact with fellow humans, because of its addiction to anti-social media, but was also choosing to have relationships with dogs rather than humans. It's as though they have transferred their love, interests and attention away from humans to pets, especially dogs. Rat dogs, dressed in the latest Armani creation can now be seen peeping from a handbag, or at the end of a piece of string. At times there are 2 or 3 dogs pulling on the leash, comparable to huskies in Alaska, shitting and barking at every conceivable opportunity. With **Synchronised Barking,** between households, becoming the latest trend. Upon moving to Park Rd. in 2012, I nicknamed these people, **'the dog mafia',** because they seemed to be taking over from the humans. Society intimating that you needed to own at least one dog to be part of the 'in crowd'. 'We're in with the in crowd', sang Dobie Gray in 1964.' Again, the issue of which tribe do you belong to becomes an issue? Every day I was seeing people taking their mobiles for 'walkies', with their pet dogs and the children just being taken along for security and fresh air. Beggar's dogs were becoming obligatory as a sympathy vote for many, who chose to sit on the pavement hoping for contributions from Jo Public. But surely if you're homeless and haven't any money for food, why collude with another animal to share the spoils? Just as if you are in the disadvantaged, lower, social strata, with many children, and financially finding it difficult to survive, you should not decide to have a dog or two, with all the extra expense this entails. Living on Penwortham Residential Park, has been, at times, like living in a dog compound, or next to Battersea Dogs Home, as there appeared to be more dogs than people, and where many owners had substituted talking to 'the wall', or their partner, with talking to their dogs as though they were human, calling them our children. Or should that now be baby goats? I know the animal rights activists will quote, 'a dog is a man's best friend', which today is probably an unacceptable, sexist expression, but for a single, lonely person, I totally understand the companionship argument, but for people in relationships, I wonder. **'The dog mafia',** could be seen and heard on a daily basis huddled together outside various properties, putting the world to right, or was that deciding who the next victim was to knife in the back? I found this both hilarious, but very sad as some had human partners at home, in much the same way as Shirley Valentine, in the film of the same name, starring Pauline Collins and Bernard Hill, who played her husband. But then again you can be lonely in a crowded room. Of course you had your quota of insecure residents who suffered from, **'playground syndrome'.** I've been asked on several occasions, since finding myself alone and depressed, did I fancy getting a dog for company so I could join the dog mafia tribe. Perhaps I'd been missing something all those years but I'd always preferred the company of humans, especially the female gender. Is that too honest or am I going to be accused of an ic, ist or ism? But I do now realise that if you don't have humans in your locker, then to turn to a dog's companionship can offer an alternative to contemplating suicide. I am also aware that there are many people, even those in relationships, who shy away from human company, preferring the company of animals instead. A certain member of my extended family could fall into that bracket. But what the hell do I know about relationships? It takes all kinds. In my defence, my last relationship, not long after moving into Penwortham Residential Park, was with a lady called Denise who was a dog lover and used to look after a friend's German sheep dog, Fritz. I have many photographs of Fritz and I, sharing each other's company. Obviously, this will come as a shock to those who instantly labelled me a pet hater. But hey, what's honesty and the truth compared to a smattering of 'tittle–tackle' and fake news? Perhaps these people have already decided I'm also homosexual because I'm a man living on my own. Unfortunately, as I prefer face to face communication and a lady's company and don't spend every hour, every day, feeding my smartphone, drug addiction, and reading what people think of me, I'll never know.

Modern Technology, Anti-social Media, Social Engineering, Communication and the Like button.

On the question of intelligence, in the 60s and 70s, if the Government had decided that everyone had to have a device so they could be tracked and monitored 24-7, there would have been outrage on so many levels. Not least that humans don't like being told what to do, preferring instead to be sheep and following, or by showing initiative and coming up with their own ideas, be they good, bad or indifferent. So, in the late 80s they decided to have a mobile phone surgically attached to their person. 'Sisters are Doing it for themselves', sang the Eurythmics in 1985. **"Who would use cell phones after what happened to Osama Bin Laden in Afghanistan?"** (Gladwell M, 2005. Blink, The Power of Thinking without Thinking, 4:109). **Or for that matter Caroline Flack? Why is trolling now a perfectly acceptable form of initiating suicide? And I'm not talking about trolling for prostitutes in Hollywood. Why is rudeness now perfectly acceptable? "In today's world being RUDE by ignoring people, by invading their personal space, by texting and phoning etc. is seen as being diligent and efficient."** (Truss L, 2005. Talking to the Hand, p98). In, 'The Brass Verdict', by Michael

Connolly, 2019, one female judge found any lawyer using their mobile in court 100 dollars. Interesting. If you have a visitor to your home, you can now leave the television on without even turning down the volume; peck, scroll and swipe and text whilst someone is talking to you, and read so you don't have to verbalise your thoughts. **Why do we crave the like button or feel the need to emoji the world? A selfie is a reflection of what has happened to society, that appears to have acquired permanent visual memory loss, as to what they actually looked like. Look at me, me, me me. Oh, are there other people around, I hadn't noticed. VANITY V INSANITY.** Behaviour associated with a three-year-old can be applied when discussing IDs and EGOs. The problem with anti-social media is that many now don't know how to personally interact with others, so they can empathise, socialise, sympathise and connect. They're losing their ability to retain these behaviours, traits and attributes. In 1979, Cliff Richards sang, 'It's So Funny How We Don't Talk Anymore'. Perhaps he should consider re-issuing it. **It is also frightening to consider that children and their 'minders/parents' are now equally entitled to accuse each other of being drug addicts, who on a daily basis break the rules/ law to feed their addictions. "Social media has polluted our culture."** (Stephen Fry, interview with LS Elliot, 30/1/23) Virtually all of the moral values and standards I had been brought up with as a child, in the 1950s, were rapidly being eroded by society. Or to coin a modernism, **vapourised.** This was before the internet highway, cyber space, cyber-lying, bullying, trolling, roofing, doxxing, viral marketing, google, tablets, wi-fi's, i-pods, instagrams, twitter, snapchat, chit chat, zoom, facebook and artificial intelligence, blah de blah, entered our lives and literally messed everything up. I've already alluded to a television programme screened on 7/3/24, On Line Britain: Who's Getting Left Behind? And quoted some of the statistics from the programme in relation to the elderly but what was just as interesting was that the viewer was informed, that by 2025 landlines were going to be phased out despite the fact that over 40% of over 65s were not using the internet. Forgive me, but I thought we lived in a democracy with freedom of speech, but it would appear Big Brother is making decisions for vast swathes of the populace with no mandate to do so. **It's nothing to do with me being opposed to change or modern technology, but the fact that others are making decisions for me and my generation on a whole raft of subjects. "People were spending less time in the real world and more in the virtual so much so that the dividing line between able and disabling was blurring."** (Deaver J, 2008. The Broken Window, p13). **As the power and positivity of modern technology is appreciated, more and more people are becoming concerned, to say the least, as to its dangers, especially its effects on children's and people's health and welfare. But when these are pointed out, great swathes of the mainly, but not exclusively, younger generation are choosing to ignore them. Why is this so? Is it because of their addictions and arrogance they have become deaf, dumb, blind and stupid?** In December 2022, on Channel 4, 'I am Ruth', starring Kate Winslett, was screened to highlight the endemic health crisis that was affecting young people consumed by the pressures of social media. On 11/12/24, C4 screened, Swiped: The School that Banned Smartphones, because of all the issues related to their use. But still they peck, scroll and swipe, why? To try and answer my own questions, let's return to a Michael Rowbotham quote given at the beginning of this chapter on page 7, **"You've got to know people - what frightens them, how they think, what they cling to when they're in trouble............"** But herein lies the problem and why I've always been fascinated with human behaviour and why **I seriously question that Homo Sapiens is supposedly the highest form of intelligence in the animal kingdom. Because in that quote is the word frighten, but being a drug addict and law breaker doesn't seem to bother these people.** Would adopting a system as is the case in the pharmaceutical industry, help where when dispensing a product, a leaflet is enclosed pointing out how it should be used and not used regarding say dosage etc; the contra-indications to its use; the side effects and its dangers etc? But how many people actually read these leaflets that are enclosed in their daily doses of drugs? Personally speaking, if we took serious note of **ALL** the side effects that our daily dose of drugs prescribed to us by the local GP, we would never touch the product. So, what I consider a sensible idea would probably have minimal effect as people wouldn't or couldn't internalise what they read. **Most people want instant results not lifelong changes to their daily routines.** Having said all that let's continue the journey by re-visiting some issues already mentioned by adding extra layers and textures to the debate.

In 1985 the first mobile network was launched in Britain and by 2011 our lives were being lived out on line with 100 million tweets a day. What is the number in 2025? I don't know and quite frankly, I don't care. It was William Gibson who termed the phrase, 'living in cyberspace'? "Pouring inanities into mobiles, lacking sense and showing no signs of actually being alive, as to what was actually going on around you has become the norm. Civilisation, with its so called blessings and labour-saving devices, had not contributed all that much to human happiness." (Yorke M, 1996. PB, p210). The expression, 'You're doin my hed in', is now part and parcel of everyday language. That's when people can be bothered to open their mouths to speak. Also, why parcels should now enter the conversation I have no idea. I find the Yorke quote fascinating and it relates to what I call the, **'Moan, Groan Zone'**. In fact, certain technologies have transformed great swathes of the population into robots because they affect emotional detachment and relationships. When television first emerged and then slowly became established in many peoples' lives, watching TV was a family, societal, bonding pastime, with personal verbal interaction, where families watched one programme because choice was limited. But now with recording devices, watching on demand or via streaming, laptops, tablets, computers and Youtube etc., where family members have their own medium, the activity has become entirely solitary with very little, if any, verbal interaction whatsoever, and is only punctuated by the constant pecking, swiping, scrolling and texting. Is this a form of multi-tasking? Please don't point me to the TV programme Gogglebox as being typical of family life because as I've mentioned, many will have an ulterior motive for being on television. **So why are parents surprised with their children's lack of social and communication skills? And even more so that their child is being cyber bullied or trolled. I repeat, my generation was never cyber bullied or trolled.** In February 2024, ITV screened, 'Laura Whitmore Investigates', stating that cyber stalking was up by 30% with disproportionately more women than men being affected. It's not rocket science. **Just as if you allow your barely teenage daughter to dress and act like a hooker, why are parents surprised if she attracts sexual attention and becomes pregnant shortly after puberty? After all what are hormones for?** Well, I suppose one of the uses is that distracted parents can blame their abdication on them. Why were certain members of a little, mixed-up pop group upset when they were being, 'trolled', because they had pumped their body, especially their lips with sh..., so they looked like a suction pad, and then put the results of their actions on every available, anti-social media site they could find? Some having to, 'take time away from the limelight', because of the resultant stress and abuse on-line, or is that honesty? Well obviously, so they could have a television programme made about them entitled, 'Me, me, me and me'. I have recently, upon renewing my phone and internet package, decided to only use my smartphone, purely and simply on financial grounds. My mobile is switched on for my convenience, my choice, and although castigated by certain members of my family, I'm totally ignorant of what people could potentially call me. Also, I've never been in a rush, or that insecure, to inform society what I was up to 24/7. It's called privacy and not wanting to be an insecure attention seeker. **Again, I repeat, I cannot understand why people crave what people say about them on anti-social media and then get upset if they say horrible things. DON'T READ IT, SWITCH IT OFF.** Progressive evolution is an interesting topic to consider, because it inevitably rolls on but one must seriously question **WHY? also WHO decided on these changes and did they ever consider what the impact of such changes may have on society?** Diana Morgan during 'Cunk on Life', BBC2, 30/12/24, bluntly said that if Artificial Intelligence is so good at mimicking humans we might as well, "fucking kill ourselves." We now have computers to navigate for us, shop for us, think for us. Social influencers, with very little significant experience of life, are being allowed to affect our behaviour by telling us what to do, etc. which is dulling our own senses. **"Whoever thought that computers would do away with paperwork was sadly mistaken. There was as much paper piled up on desks as there ever had been. The only difference was that now most of it was printed out by a computer."** (Billingham M, 2011. Lazybones, PB, 24:368).

In February, 2004, Mark Zuckerberg introduced social media to the masses via Facebook. **In 2020 it made £8M. profit and is now just considered as a money-making service, irrespective of what others may want you to believe.** It was also the year that **'fake news' entered the public lexicon, with hate and fear getting the biggest reactions. Mr Trump achieved, and still achieves his goals based on these and other reactions.** The result of which polarised content and pushed people apart. An injustice shouldn't just go away because someone with power, in politics or with money decides it. Social media is an invisible cyberspace world of open-source, at times, artificial information that people get lost in. And where other people, good and bad, can go cyber fishing for tit-bits of information to troll or sell to unscrupulous others. Sometimes it could be an internet 'bot' masquerading as a person. Information laundering is a text book component of disinformation, which is spreading fake information on line, but it has to come from a reliable source, which is then adopted by the mainstream sites in an attempt to legitimise it. The key phrase being, reliable source. Deep Seek is a Chinese AI chat box that excessively collects personal data to subvert. In 2006, Tweeting and Twitter entered the scene and in 2007 the first I-phone appeared, with flick and squeeze becoming the biggest, addictive hooks. Unfortunately, both didn't help matters, **with trolling and cyber bullying becoming a public past-time, with many of today's generation thinking it's 'cool'. Where a paediatrician could be trolled or cyber bullied because some illiterate idiot wasn't very good at spelling or was a dysfunctional wordsmith. Before then, social interaction meant being with actual human beings.** But the advent of the selfie, and its accessory the selfie- stick, in 2014, ensured social interaction was becoming a thing of the past, being superseded by people becoming, according to Truss, more self-important, solipsistic and rude, (p27).The principle of self-interest being taken to its ultimate destination. In 2012, Tinder with its 57million, swipe right for approval and left for no, thank you, also meant we didn't have to leave home searching for Mr or Miss. Right. **Unfortunately, the digital age was reducing our memory span to 8 seconds.** (The Knowledge, ITV, 14/4/17), and the Sat Nav, in May 2000, meant we didn't have to attend geography lessons to learn how to be able to read a map or to know where anyone lived in the world, or how to get to where they lived. **"Whatever the truth is it's complicated, and complicated is not what our information –overload society is good at grasping, because they would have to focus for longer than 5 seconds, which most folks can't do anymore."** (Baldacci D, 2014. The Escape, PB, 40:336). Every generation is getting to run faster but so-called progress is ensuring we don't even need to run at all, or for that matter leave home to get our exercise. Many jumping into the nearest car to take a 100-metre journey to drive to the local Spar or the pub. Obviously just to use our Sat Nav because we haven't a clue where our local Spar was. The latter trip being known as drink driving and the former being a lazy bastard. A journey, even at the age of 75, I can jog in just over 2 minutes or walk in 5. Do we need our arms when all we actually need are a proboscis to scroll, peck, swipe and tap the buttons, preferably the like button? These last two scenarios are not meant as a slight on disabled people, but a reference to so-called able bodied individuals. Isn't it great that society has all these wonderful labour-saving devices, which means we don't have to leave home, and we can now embrace, **OBESITY AND LAZINESS ON A SCALE NEVER BEFORE SEEN IN MY LIFETIME?**

In 1999, the late David Bowie was interviewed by Jeremy Paxton on BBC's Newsnight saying, **"I think we are on the cusp of something exhilarating, yet terrifying."** To which Paxton replied, **"It's just a tool, isn't it?" "No, it's an alien life form,"** said with tongue in cheek and laughing. **"The state of context and content is going to be so different to anything we can envisage at the moment. When interplay between the user and provider will be so in simpatico, it is going to crash our ideas of what mediums are all about."** How prophetic was that? If still alive Mr Bowie would be smiling and saying, **"what did I tell you?"** He might even burst into song with, **'Ch, Ch, Ch, Changes.'** All the undesirable elements of modern technology are there for all to see, addiction, greed, bullying, backstabbing, telling lies, laziness, hate, anger, revenge, control, paranoia, cowardice, humiliation, need I go on? All done under the guise, if someone so wished, of anonymity. **Addiction, in smart phone terms is the loss of reality between the real world and the synthetic, (Synth). "Sitting at screens and clicking buttons is very bad training for a life in the real world because, when we step outdoors and discover other people's lives, they can't just be deleted with a one strike command or dragged to the trash can."** (Truss p83). Pierce Morgan in his book, Wake Up, 2022, pleads for a return to liberalism or as I call it sensibility.

Who decided these so-called intelligent life forms, with their 10 A star pluses at A Level, only needed to communicate, I use that term loosely, via text speak, or using Neolithic grunting man linguistics? When did Neolithic grunting, text speak and behaviour be considered a passport to better things. Whilst attending Secondary School, in the 1960s young girls used to learn, 'shorthand', to prepare them for office- work. Now in 2025 we have, **'short mouth/breath verbalisation'**. In 2011, I received a hand written reply to a wedding invitation **from an infant teacher** which started, **'Thank U 4 your reply'**. I suppose we should have been impressed that it was hand written. In blogs and bulletin boards its now unconventional, creative and cool amongst the youngsters to misspell, abbreviate and make up words - IMHO – in my humble opinion or FOAD – fuck off and die. Or could it be that their standard of English Grammar is so poor it hides such a fact. **"The writer who neglects spelling and punctuation is quite arrogantly dumping a lot of avoidable work onto the reader. Just as the rise of the internet sealed the doom of grammar, so modern communication technology contributes to the end of manners."** (Truss p23). **"Consideration is the ability to imagine being someone other than oneself, and that's a bit of a lost cause."** (Truss p119). Many years ago in the late 1980s, not long after I had left Primary Education and was running my Osteopathy/Sports Therapy clinic, a secondary school teacher friend, Jo H, who incidentally used to blame everything on Margaret Thatcher, and I do mean everything, used to wonder how long it would be before her knowledge, skills and expertise and experience as an English language teacher would be considered redundant, because she was trying to educate a generation into grammar, syntax, capital letters and full stops, but where the communication currency was text speak, with a lazy clientele that refused to talk face to face, or on the phone, and pronounce words correctly but was more than happy to use text speak and bastardise the English language. Whilst rudely ignoring others, because pecking, tapping, scrolling and swiping was **MORE IMPORTANT** than eye to eye verbalisation. What's happened to words being legal tender? When did the letters RTY become a double EE so that party becomes pa ee? Why? Was it losing its ability to verbally communicate? How long will it be before text-speak books become the norm? Wordsmiths, such as the late Ronnie Barker, who appreciated the interplay between delivery, intonation and emphasis must be turning in his grave, if that was possible. We appear to have progressed from ancient Egyptian hieroglyphics to emojis, which were introduced in 2011. How progressive is that? Recently I have discovered,' **woke ideology'**, which as far as I'm aware, works on the premise that you have to speak a certain way to reflect reality or you are a bad person, (BBN News, 26/2/24). One of my roles as a Primary school teacher was to teach children to read, write, and communicate using the English language. To teach the TH blend involved asking the children to stick out their tongues and then retract it quickly with an out breath. This differed from the letter F, which involved flicking the bottom lip against the upper teeth on the out breath. With only **laziness** or a genuine physical disability, such as a genuine, speech impediment, preventing such exercises from being successful. When I was a young man all commentators and interviewers spoke, 'Queen's English', irrespective of dialects, regional accents and genuine speech impediments, and that was why they were given the job. And that was why they had regional newsreaders. Should that now be known as King's English? **So, when did it become acceptable to have commentators and interviewers, who are remunerated very well for, I would think, their communication acumen, bastardise the English language?** I pick up this theme later in Chapter 5 when discussing, Sports Punditry and Commentating. When did through become frew, three become free, which totally alters its definition, think become fink, truth become truf, together become togevah, brother become bruva and corner become corna? When did it become acceptable for people whose job was communication to lazily not pronounce the endings of words? When did going become goin, running become runnin, bowling become bowlin, etc? When did isn't it become init? And if this language is now acceptable why, asks my secondary school teacher friend Jo, do we still have English language teachers and offer degree courses in English? Why are nursery/infant teachers wasting their time teaching children to speak correctly? As a child, mum frequently used to tell me to speak correctly and she was, no disrespect, an academic. <u>I also found, when I temporarily returned to full time, main stream education but this time in higher education, that some students, irrespective of race, colour, creed, regional accents, gender or political persuasion couldn't communicate without using the words right, LIKE, uh, cool, ok, yeh, every other word, in every sentence which made half the language of description redundant. LIKE, you know, so yeh, right, LIKE, right, yeh, LIKE what LIKE I'm saying, LIKE, yeh, babe, cool.</u> The like button was influencing how young people communicated.

In 2021 a leading academic was pilloried and given an ic, ist or ism label on television for pointing out this lazy trend of not speaking English correctly that had now pervaded society, when all he was doing was, like me, being honest at what he perceived as a lowering of standards. I think in modern day parlance, he was accused of 'dissing' people. But this was not surprising as, **"Abuse was the weapon of the weak."** (Truss p150). **"Under attack the individual personality wastes no time in bolstering its defences. It circles the wagons and starts firing. Not a second is allowed for self-examination."** (Truss p135). **"We have become TEFLON PEOPLE where criticism cannot stick."** (Truss p130). Put another way, having rights but no responsibilities. And this book gives many examples of this behaviour in all walks of life when talking about greedy people with wealth, position and power. But now this behaviour has become commonplace, irrespective of such. **What is now the criteria that is asked for to apply for a job involving COMMUNICATION, or is it now not acceptable to stipulate? SAYS WHO, I ASK? Do people entering the acting/drama world now have to learn a whole new way of speaking, other than delivery, dialect and accents? What has happened to communicating face to face, via complete, descriptive and meaningful sentences?** Is Shakespeare now redundant in favour of text speak? Let's not forget I'm a proud Lancastrian, with what some would class as a broad Northern accent. Returning to pronunciation of word endings, even if attempts at meaningful syntax is achieved, for some the inclusion of extra words at the end of a sentence is now deemed an integral part of communication. Right, amazing, brilliant, cool, tremendous and super being some of the favourites. **"I'll come and explain everything to you in a minute, right, amazing." Or, "I just want to examine you if that's alright? I thought you'd be interested to see the x-ray, right, cool, OK, brilliant."** (TV programme, 24 Hours in A&E, March 2021.) In 2000, in her book, 'The Civility Glut', Barbara Ehrenreich asked where had the custom of adding extra words to the end of statements come from? Answers on a postcard please for those who know what one of them is.

But if you are, **"alone in front of a computer, TV or mobile screen, part of a global generation too over stimulated and self-obsessed to muster any idealism or sense of greater purpose."** (Hall MR, 2011, The Redeemed, C9, p150), what can you expect? **Many now believe that if it can't be found on their smartphone it's not real and doesn't exist. For many of today's generation life was a video game.** Is it called a smartphone, because it has a whole raft of University qualifications and a lifetime of real-life experiences to share with the tapper/rapper, scroller and swiper? Is an app a genuine University qualification, or just a money generating device? What are these people pouring profanities into, whilst staring at their mobiles for long periods of time, searching for? You see these people going to work, jockeying for position, minus the whip, with their obligatory, take-away caffeine fixes in one hand and a smartphone in the other. The former being held higher than the latter, with hip height for the mobile and shoulder height for the coffee. They walk across the road without looking and of course blame the drivers if there's a possibility, they could become another traffic statistic to claim compensation. Parents ignore their children, sorry baby goats, who can, if allowed, are out of sight, between 4 to 10 hours daily, playing on-line, role playing games in their bedroom because mummy and daddy are too busy on **anti-social media.** Convincing themselves that no harm is being done as 'the kids' are just 'playing games', by possibly face timing their 10-year-old boyfriend until midnight, in their bedroom, only pausing to go to the toilet and to be fed. It's also keeping them quiet which more importantly means it doesn't interrupt their own addictions. **Total Immersion Pods,** which originated in Japan were seen as a logical development in a country known for hikikomori, 'withdrawal'. And whilst it has been shown that such engagements could have some physical and mental benefits for some children with Attention Deficit problems, Aspergers and in some cases children with vertigo and vision issues by improving cognition, special awareness, faster response times and visualisation, **but these were far outweighed by the negatives.** As the pods provided everything a child needed for a digital experience, they created a lifestyle where children, mainly boys, sat for hours and hours in dark, private spaces, completely sealed off from the real world, playing computer games. Evidence has shown that many of these boys became reclusive, had difficulty in face-to-face communication, were overweight, unfit and had behaviour issues. This leading to potential diabetes and heart problems. (Deaver J, 2020, The New Game, 58:352-353). **Research by neuroscientists at Harvard University, in 2014,** and Oxford University, in 2018, found that social media and video games were giving children possible mental disorders and emotional immaturity, with behavioural habits of a 3-year-old, who was constantly looking for distractions and left them with poor communication skills. Yes, smiled mummy and daddy something else we can, 'claim for', and hide the fact we are abdicating our responsibilities. Whilst couples out for dinner sit at their tables totally and utterly devoid of eye-to-eye contact and verbal conversation.

"If she had to listen to one more mobile – phone – obsessed wanker telling anyone who'd listen about the ever so important meeting he/she was having…., she would kill before the night was out." (Heller M, 2005. The Charmer, PB, 3:32). It would appear that great swathes of the population want to listen to a domestic dispute being relayed via a blue tooth ear piece. A**s a child, people who walked through the streets talking inanely to themselves, were considered mentally ill and were to be avoided, for fear of abuse, and usually ended up in a white, straight jacket being taken to the local psychiatric unit, for examination, assessment and evaluation.** Eric Sykes, the author, scriptwriter, comedian and actor, in his autobiography waxed lyrical about the bottom block of Boundary Park Hospital, Royton, Oldham, where these types of people ended up. Between 2000 and 2003, one of the first, 'Reality' television programmes, Trigger Happy, featured Dom Joly, a comedian, later to be nicknamed, 'the big phone guy', walking around town centres, whilst being secretly filmed, shouting inanely into a huge, DIY made mobile phone. The programme, which captured on film, people's reaction, was hilarious, as many tried their best to avoid this obviously deranged, mentally ill person. Today, some 20 years later, we now talk to Alexa and Eliza and we are bombarded with these intrusions into our personal space and nobody bats an eyelid. What bats have to do with eyelids I don't know? **I suppose we can say 2000 was the year mentally deranged hilarity became reality.** When I'm using the internet to do my research for this book and planning my holidays, I don't walk around Preston telling everyone that I'm going to Rio de Janeiro to impress whoever wants to listen. With such trends, can we predict a rapid fall in the population as a vibrating mobile becomes the substitute for contact sex, with the total elimination of an exchange of body fluids? Is Anne Summer's business under threat? Don't laugh there are many that can't go to bed without their smartphones. Perhaps they are smart because they can vibrate and if strategically placed can ensure the users don't have to burn unnecessary calories to orgasm? With tapping and pecking now being a substitute for foreplay. A two-part Panorama TV programme, Smartphones, The Dark Side and The Secrets of Silicon Valley, screened during July 2018, informed us that one third of adults check their phones in the night. I know homicide detectives are disturbed 24/7 when another body has been found, or a hospital consultant might be contacted in a life threatening emergency, but what about the rest of society? This excellent programme also provided the behavioural science and psychological evidence **showing how social engineering was taking place and that for many smart phones had become more addictive than crack cocaine. In fact, it was stated that giving a child a smart phone was equivalent to giving them a gram of cocaine. I have already alluded to the C4 television programme shown in December, 2024, Swiped: The School That banned Smartphones and the reaction of the children both visually and verbally was interesting to say the least. Also, I was interested in the statement, "It feels like they are safer in the home but they're not because they've got every stranger in the world in the palm of their hands."** In July 2023 an on-line, MSE forum canvassed opinion from a cross section of over 2,763 people as to what age they thought children should be given a mobile phone, the range being from under 5 to over 17 years. It found that 27.17% thought 11years, whilst 27.9% thought they were too young for a phone without actually specifying what too young was. Personally, I wondered how many respondents actually lied to give the impression of being responsible parents because in my experience most, if not all, pre-adolescent children had a mobile, starting at age 5. The true Channel 4 series, The Girl from Plainsville, shown in July, 2023, highlighted the dangers of texting between vulnerable teenagers. And if any more disturbing evidence was needed, Can We Live Without Our Phones? Panorama, 2/9/24, provided it. On the 7/12/2021, Channel 4, broadcast the programme, The Cult Conspiracy: QAnon, which looked at how society was being manipulated because of the Conspiracy Theory, fake news, talk of rigged elections and unmitigated use of social media so that no one had any idea what to believe anymore. Does this sound familiar? **"Stacey hated people who abused digital systems. It affronted her that they had totally undermined the fundamental beauty and purity of the internet. They'd corrupted the most revolutionary invention of the twentieth century and turned it into an engine for triviality, for vitriol, for scamming and for undermining the very fabric of democracy."** (McDermid V, 2017. Insidious Intent, PB, 48:268-9). **"And because data collected by the Internet Community overseas was largely unregulated, there was a massive collection of content and metadata, including e-mail addresses of the sender and receiver, video, audio and photos. So anytime you sent data over the Internet, people you never intended to receive this information would in fact get it…..It was right there for the taking because pretty much anyone was connected to the digital universe, somehow."** (Baldacci D, 2014, The Escape, 152-155). **"Data is the new oxygen."** (Deaver J, 2020, The New Game, 50:256). For the sweet toothed hackers this was like candy in a sweet shop. In April, 2020, the National Cyber Security Centre was launched to enable the public to report suspicious e-mails. **Since then, 21 million reports have been made and 235,000 malicious websites have been removed.** On the 13/12/2021 BBC 2 screened, Social Media, Anger and Us, which stated that **social platforms had now become very, very dangerous places to be part of.** The toxic world of blogging and social media trolling was leading to real life anger, hatred and rage, involving knifing and torching homes and cars. **According to Dreamworks, trolls loved to hug, sing and dance and spread a happy culture.** Can't people see the irony? **WORDS HAVE CONSEQUENCES. "We are living in a world where laptop and the phone and media allows you to say whatever you want without any recrimination, and you have no idea what that comment could do to someone – it could push someone over the edge to do something…."** Amanda Abington speaking on radio and then on television, shortly after leaving Strictly Come Dancing in October 2023 for, 'personal reasons', received hate mail and death threats for giving her reasons for leaving the show. I only need to mention the late Caroline Flack, who sadly took her own life because she foolishly read what people said about her. **The culture we now live in has been brought about by motivating a culture of VINDICTIVENESS, POISON and HATE. Today's society has even made it creditable by giving such activity a name, TROLLING, 'A LICENCE TO INCITE SUICIDE', just because the cowards haven't the courage, or is that lack of communication skills, to look someone in the eyes and justify why they have such views?** Hate is what is driving not only politics and religion these days, but also certain elements of society, by overriding democratic choice, labelled Conspiracy Theory. A certain newspaper mogul's legacy being seen by many, especially the more senior members of society, as one of evil because he was seen promoting and accepting a culture of untruths. Hiding the truth by propagating rumours and obfuscation. The term **Artificial Intelligence** has now entered the public lexicon. This has led to a change in the way people get information and form opinions. It has also led in some quarters, especially amongst certain politicians, to an absolute disregard for democracy and the 'free press', which are seen as the enemy, leading to political espionage and sabotage to undermine the electoral process. Jon Sopel in his book, A Year at The Circus, asks the question, 'Who is the biggest cyber bully in America today?' (5:172). Oh, come on, this is not a question on Mastermind. It has led to the rise of unprincipled people who are only after their own wellbeing rather than what is best for the populace and society they live in. The problem is that many people feel protected on line and in the synth world because they can hide under a screen name but ignore the fact that every single piece of data they post, or someone else posts about them, truth or lie, is there forever. Fake news and disinformation have become rife, and the quest for the truth has become very challenging. So-called intelligent people tend not to question the accuracy or authenticity of blogs, especially if it suits their agenda. There is very little accountability on line. **GREAT SWATHES OF THE POPULATION HAVE BECOME TECHNO ADDICTED ZOMBIES DEVOID OF CONSCIENCE.** Watching all these programmes, apart from being alarmed, but not surprised, I immediately thought back to the 1950s when the tobacco industry was blatantly targeting youngsters knowing that if they got them hooked, dare I say addicted, on the nicotine, they had a customer for life? For young people social media was now their life, with 'apps' attached to smart phones being able to identify how often and how long the mobile is engaged. **With British teenagers checking their phones up to 90 times a day and spending on average 18 hours a week on them. With some adults spending a minimum of five and a half hours daily on their phones, whilst receiving 117 hits to satisfy their craving.** I suspect this is far more time than they spend engaging with their partners and children physically, emotionally and conversationally. **Social media, especially Facebook and Twitter, are now being referred to as habit forming technology, with gimmicky apps on smartphones being designed to affect behaviour by subtly persuading the user to engage in their use up to 30% more than necessary and that by keeping the user hooked, by selling them so called free-time, this time could then be sold to advertisers. Once again money rears its ugly head.** Once 'hooked' people's thinking could then be affected if advertisers could provide exciting things to click on, being known as, **'click bait'.** By **data mining** and identifying which type of thought processes the user adopts, one type being the hunch, guess, gut or I just know type, as opposed to the analytical, numbers and probability ones, Facebook, Twitter, Google and YouTube can act as conduits for these specific adverts. Referring to the work of BF Skinner, in the 1950s, it can be shown how neurosciences could affect behaviour by **CONDITIONING rats to run around in mazes. By making the technology user friendly and giving rewards, behaviour could be modified, now known as addicting.** The key being to only reward periodically, so the user would seek it more often. **The like button, the emblem of social media, instagram and twitter was an example of this and is related to behaviour such as acceptance and a desire to belong, which is a core social motive. The like button can now accurately predict personality and intimate traits. Not to mention its effect on speech.** Psychometrics being the science of predicting psychological traits such as personality. This being a far more sophisticated and, dare I say, covert way to predict personality than my first introduction into the subject in 1968, which consisted of filling out questionnaires on pieces of paper. **People's self-esteem can be affected as the smart phone user becomes addicted to the feedback. Loneliness and insecurity make the mobile a form of comforter in much the same way as a child needs their favourite dummy, cuddly toy, comforter, blanket, or 'gummy', to go to bed. A US study in 2016 found that a person on an average touches his/her mobile 2,617 times a day. CRAZY. A Dispatches, TV programme shown on the 16/11/20 said that 91% of the people in the UK were on line daily for 9+ hours.** This can be compared to gambling, which also uses unpredictable rewards, which drives motivation and affects the dopamine system. Mobiles like slot machines, with their pings, tunes, colours, especially red which relates to importance, and flashing images can drive compulsive behaviour. Tapping, pecking, scrolling and swiping are all related to this compulsion to stay engaged in case the user misses the reward because they don't give the brain time to catch up with the impulses to make the user stop. Every time a phone 'goes off', the stress level, triggered by the stress hormone from the adrenal gland, rises making the user feel anxious and in need of their next fix. **Like other addictions, smart phone technology is designed for the reward to make the user feel wanted, appreciated, joyous, delighted and belonging to a large audience.** And again, like other addictions, the withdrawal characteristics can have consequences such as irritability, confusion, distraction etc. which can lead to eating and stress disorders, depression and **sometimes suicidal tendencies.** Sadly, as mentioned, Caroline Flack, the TV personality, in February 2020, found to her cost, that entering the intangible world of cyberspace, cyber bulling and trolling, where geeks and uber geeks roamed, tapping, scrolling, swiping and trawling and crawling through other people's secrets, given away freely I might add, and then if they so wished, destroy their lives by assassination, or emptying their bank account. Or at the flick of a button steal their identity. **AND WE PRETEND TO BE INTELLIGENT BY IGNORING SUCH FACTS.** Sadly, Caroline chose to read what everyone said about her on, 'anti-social media', and with more than a little help from the 'responsible press', both of whom decided she was fair game after an altercation with her boyfriend, eventually decided to take her own life. Now a row with your boyfriend is considered a newsworthy item. **What the f... is going on?** Paul Macloud, a Capitol Hill Reporter, points out that at first, Twitter, for many, seemed a great idea but it would appear to have turned into hell. **A quarter of British children have had some negative experiences from social media. Of course, the people making billions from the sale of such devices, deny they are habit forming and addictive, just as the tobacco industry did in the 1950s, which employed scientists, on non-disclosure contracts, to shred all the evidence showing nicotine was addictive. Because if that was the case, they could be sued. But all that should have changed when Francis Haugen, a former Facebook employee, became a whistleblower. Claiming, in front of a US Senate committee, that Facebook and Instagram put their astronomical profits before people's welfare, especially children. Claiming children and young adults were suffering from not only eating disorders, but also harming themselves, with some actually resorting to suicide because of Instagram. Citing influencer Lauren Black, who admitted to having screen time on an average of 13 hours daily. Via the research, it is claimed the main aim of modern technology is to get people's time and attention, which can have massive social implications. Not forgetting a vast money-making device. As a result of TV programmes such as The Tik Tok Effect,5/9/24, The Instagram Effect 21/9/23,BBC 3, and Tik Tok: Murder Gone Viral, 20/4/24, the questions now being asked are, 'Are we going to let Algorithms rule us or are we going to rule Algorithms'? At the time of screening Algorithms were easily winning the battle. For me, such programmes further highlighted the fact that today's society had definitely become the Bah, Bah, Instant Gratification, Easily Disposable Society. And unfortunately, I see no evidence of a change back to normality. Why pay for a trip into outer space when many people are so far out there already, and cannot return to earth and reality. Or perhaps they don't want to return to reality.** Smartphones and consoles appear to be the most popular platforms, as opposed to computers, whilst action/adventure, shooters, sports and social being the most popular gaming categories. Another Panorama, TV documentary, 'Is Tik Tok Safe'? shown on 2/11/20, pointed out that it was a totally inappropriate environment for children stating, **"Many parents are unaware of how many users are groomed on line and if they are they don't think it will happen to them."** A Channel 4 documentary, 15/02/21, 'Under Cover Police: Hunting Paedophiles', highlighted the fact that because of children's ease of access to information technology, the number of sex offences against children had doubled in the last 5 years. Today, 'go and play in your bedroom', can mean something totally different to my time as a child, when the only danger to playing in a bedroom was frostbite or electrocution if you stuck your finger in the light bulb connector. In January, 2024, the television programme 'Tik Tok Murder Gone Viral', was yet another example of how anti-social media, via Instagram and Tik Tok was showing how such platforms can lead to the murder of two individuals –in this case being cremated alive in their own car. The perpetrators of the crime being, 'social media influencers' with thousands of followers, or should I say sheep. **But don't worry folks it's called PROGRESS. To re-iterate I question how so-called intelligent people can continue to behave in such a way even after being informed of the potentially frightening dangers and consequences. The amount of data some supposedly intelligent people, post on-line, borders on hilariously, ridiculous.** The author Jeffrey Deaver, in his book Roadside Crosses, 2009, page 69, introduced me to the terms, escribitionist – a term for blogging about oneself. Dooced- a term for getting fired because of what a person had posted on a blog. Why are so called intelligent people obsessed/addicted to spewing their personal bile on facebook and twitter etc. to people they have never met? WHY are they suicidal when they are trolled because THEY THEMSELVES HAVE PROVIDED THE PHOTOGRAPHS AND INFORMATION TO ALLOW SUCH ACTIVITY? Sadly, it's not always the obsessive, attention seekers who suffer.

Is human intelligence being relegated and becoming a thing of the past?

I eventually arrived at the conclusion that to be acceptable in today's society and to ensure I didn't become stigmatised and didn't need to converse with fellow human beings, all I needed was a computer, which would provide content, games, social networking sites and blogs. Previously mentioned as, 'the mushrooms of the internet', a website, (the venue), some blog software, at least two dogs, preferably small, yappy ones, a cigarette dangling from my mouth and a take-away cup of coffee or alcohol, to take with me on my travels. With the technology I would have a platform from where I could pontificate about a whole raft of stuff which would be seen all around the world. Providing an intoxicating sense of power. Unfortunately, such power would be stolen not earned, rumour would be accepted as truth, lives and reputations could be destroyed. But where is the responsibility, the conscience and the consequence? I ask the question, **How has social media in all its many guises improved the quality of people's lives** when trolling is part of the public lexicon? **Can becoming an addict be considered as improving someone's life?** Would Vardy and Rooney say, without any hesitation, after their £1.8 million trial that they were both in a much happier place than before they started tapping, scrolling and swiping? Financially maybe, but does the money stop people from getting depressed, paranoid and calmer? I wonder why, apart from the obvious, in November 2024, Collette decided to go into the jungle to share her personal space with snakes? Not long after, her husband was informed that maybe management was not for him. **Perhaps if society got back to face to face conversations and honesty, perhaps there would be less knives in people's backs and people could actually see the colour of someone's eyes instead of just noticing, if they could be bothered to look up from their phones, the bald patches on their heads.** Nurture seems to be winning the Nature-Nurture debate. The advent of personalised, electrical equipment was ensuring human facial contact, to communicate, was becoming a dying art form. **For me, the social networking was creating anti-social behaviour as many now refused eye contact and social interaction, losing the ability to verbally communicate cocooned in their internet, ethereal bubble,** although, for some that had nothing to do with advancements in information technology. Sue Townsend referring to these people as **attention whores,** 'The Woman Who Went to Bed for a Year', 2012, p 266. For years when I lectured and tutored in London, I, being a friendly, nosy Northener, desperately tried making eye contact on the London Underground, with very limited success, as many people just looked down at the floor. I was, being, **"starved of normal communication".** (Booth S, 2007. One Last Breath, p488). Now such people have a smartphone to look down on which makes personal, eye to eye, interaction almost impossible. Sheryl Crow, the singer and songwriter, during a live performance, Live at the Capitol Theatre, between tracks suggested to the audience that, **"tomorrow everyone throw away their cell phones and go roller skating."** Whilst this received a loud cheer and applause I wondered how many would actually take her advice and if asked why not, what lies they would come up with to justify their non-compliance. **"As far as I'm aware the only time there is a mass consensus of opinion to switch off the mobile is the Jewish Sabbath."** (Jon Sopel, A Year at The Circus, 2019, p17). As previously mentioned, Albert Mehrabian identified the impact of a message as being 7 % from the words, 38% from para-language and 55% from body language with all three of these elements having to correlate to make the receiver believe the giver. Applying such findings to certain members of today's highest forms of intelligence could prove extremely challenging, as they refuse eye contact and direct verbalisation. **Do they still have face to face, direct contact interviews, or do the participants just sit opposite each other sending text answers to the text questions? After the pandemic, patients were given a choice of a face-to-face or a telephone appointment with your GP. Knowing that many people lie how can you accurately, differentially diagnose over the phone? YOU CAN'T. When I was recently asked why I wanted a face-to-face appointment, I wanted to inform the receptionist that I needed the doctor to insert his/her finger up my anus to check my prostate, and that was impossible over the phone, but I didn't for fear of recrimination, as my medical practice doesn't tolerate abuse of its staff. What's ironic is that sticking one's finger up another person's jacksy is deemed acceptable but being honest during a telephone conversation isn't.** In fact, I surmise, not that I was old enough to have first-hand experience, that Stone Age man probably had more relevant communication skills, a more appropriate gait and was more civilised towards his fellow species, than many on Church Street, in Preston, at the weekend. Not that Preston is any different from any other town/city in the UK. **How far has society developed for the better, since Germaine Greer introduced, "The Female Eunuch," to the world? Some arguing the only thing that female emancipation and feminism created was a generation of sexually active, celebrity mad, half naked, binge drinking wannabes.** Oh, dear Jim, another ic, ist or ism label. But for me the interesting thing about female emancipation is the role conflict it has created amongst men and women, especially the alpha males. The kind of work that men do has changed dramatically. Their fathers and grandfathers did hard manual labour which, at times, was brutal and exploitive but it gave man an identity. Now there are a lot of men who feel they have lost their identity and so, shouting at women makes them feel better. They feel threatened when they latch on to the fact that some women are developing skills in various areas, and are afraid of any moves towards independency from their partners and wives. The rise of women's football is testament to this. Many male footballers are not happy bunnies. **Don't forget that historically, 'a woman's place was in bed with a chain around her neck long enough to reach the oven'.** Their words not mine. I take up this conversation when I talk about my experiences of playing, teaching, coaching, writing about, treating and rehabilitation in sport. Conversely, women should and hopefully, are realising that their relationship with a man should not just be about needs, especially money and especially, his money. This shift in needs is about the need to share. To share the domestic responsibility, his share of the development of their children, the acceptance that both have a need to appreciate their individual significances. Historically a woman had to have a man to make her feel this sense of importance. This dynamic is now rapidly changing. Another question that intelligent Homo Sapiens should consider, but I suspect will choose to ignore, just as it does Global warming and Greta Thunberg, and asked during the Channel 4, Dispatches programme, shown on 16/11/20 was, "Is Your online Habit Killing The Planet?" This was also very relevant to the impact that Covid-19 was having with people having to isolate, giving them virtual carte blanche to feed their drug addiction, with a 40% surge in IT usage during lock down. Both adults and children on the programme admitted that they were on their mobiles daily between 9 to 10 hours, playing games on face book etc., that was not work related. I myself am not blameless but my time on my computer, during Covid, was spent writing this book and planning my next travel excursion, but my time on my mobile was almost negligible, compared to many, and **I'm still alive!** I used to have a landline with an answer phone but recently have switched to just having a smartphone. But my choice to not have it switched on 24-7 causes many problems as some members of my family get angry with me because they cannot instantly speak to me. They will later inform they tried to phone me earlier, but didn't leave a message so I could ring them back when convenient. The inference being that I'm psychic and should know they rang. Please don't ask why I don't spend my day taking my mobile when I go to the toilet or to bed? Unless of course I need an extra vibrator. It's called choice and not wanting to be a sheep. In December 2021, I missed a dental appointment because when I arrived at the dental practice it was no longer there and had moved to another part of Leyland. When I phoned to ask why they had not informed me of their move, I was told it was because they didn't have a mobile number for me. When I pointed out that they had always contacted me via e-mail or my land line, or as a last resort left a message on my answer phone, they said they had not yet got all of their systems up and running. I would have loved to have seen their faces if I suggested they could have sent me a letter via Royal Mail. **I've no doubt there's now a term for people who don't use a smartphone 24-7, so individuals and institutions can castigate them. My response being, get lost and sort out your own shit.**

Back to the TV programme that pointed out with reference to, 'The Cloud', that at the end of 2019, there were 8 million data collecting centres in the world and that some centres in China were as big as 64 football pitches. With the energy used to power these, capable of powering 4 countries in Africa for a whole year. So much for the carbon footprint and global warming. The programme tried to ascertain how long it would be before demand outstripped production. Having mentioned Greta Thunberg, the documentary, 'I am Greta', screened on BBC 1 on 6/1/21, highlighted the fact that there were more than 200 murders, equating to 4 murders a week, of climate activists in 2008. **Don't ask me why as I've long ago given up on trying to find out why so-called intelligent life forms behave the way they do.** From 2022-24 the government decided to give people financial help to deal with the 'Energy Crisis' that they had helped create. **How long before will it be before help is needed to deal with society's addiction to the modern technology?** I am led to believe that there is now an app for people with internet addiction. No comment.

Finally, when I was teaching at Blackshaw Lane Primary in the 1980s we had to prepare for the introduction of computers and calculators into the curriculum. We were not sent on any courses to help with the transition, unless we paid for them ourselves, so it was a case of the blind leading the blind. We were also informed that initially we would have 1 computer per class. I had 40 pupils in my class at the time. Any extra computers would have to be bought out of school funds. **Yet another mind blowing, well thought out, educational initiative to set the world alight by some insignificant** politician, who had never taught in their lives. Our first task was to assess the educational suitability of the software, in this case floppy discs, **to be used to complement normal class lessons. I emphasise the word complement as opposed to, not take over, from working out a solution by thinking and calculation.** In much the same way, television programmes had to be relevant to class topics when a thematic approach was adopted, and not just something for the children to watch, so teacher could have a break from actual face to face teaching. **Any game that was considered just an exercise in tapping the keys to keep the children quiet was NOT acceptable.** It was also decided that calculators would **ONLY** be used to check answers once the pupils had worked out the sum/problem mentally or mechanically. NOT as a lazy way to find the answer. **Are the same strict criteria applied today as to the suitability of the software in both school and home?** As I don't teach anymore, I can't give an accurate, answer as to the situation in educational establishments today, but suspect the answer is NO, as SATS etc are seen to be all about end products ticking boxes, with processes NOT being high priority. As for in the home, I've already pointed out that in the vast majority of households, this certainly doesn't appear to be the case. I remember attending a conference in Manchester, not long after computers and calculators had been introduced, that had as its guest speaker some 'educational, big wig' from London, who we knew would not be around after the next election and he wasn't. When he asked the audience, what impact computers and calculators were having on teaching and the curriculum in Primary schools, one Primary School headteacher said that physically they had proved a huge success as most of the pupils in her school could now rhythmically, elevate and depress their shoulders alternatively, whilst tapping out a beat with their fingers and thumbs. As for improving their language and number skills, the impact had been zero. I can still hear the rapturous round of applause from the audience that was obviously not appreciated by the speaker. Could this tapping out a beat lead to a future as a rap artist? As the Olympics continues to try and appeal to a younger audience, as people's fingers skate over their screens at Olympic speed, could tapping, swiping and scrolling be considered as the next inclusion into the Olympic programme, along with synchronised dog barking? **"She is tapping away as if she were some kind of piano prodigy performing at the Royal Albert Hall."** (Bussi M, 2017. Don't Let Go, 14:90). Quite recently, I was awoken by my radio alarm by a news item that the Government was going to issue guidelines to schools to ban mobiles in schools. Shutting doors and horses bolting sprung to mind. And I've also mentioned that now we show television programmes related to such. Anyhow back to the news item which ended with some person saying it was, **"a non solution to a non problem."** No comment.

Being a Modern-Day Fashionista. When did wearing a 'hoodie' become a licence to mug, rape and plunder? Who decided and when did wearing a 'hoodie' become necessary when the sun was shining and it was 25 degrees centigrade? Who decided it was, 'cool', to ride your younger siblings' bike that was far too small for you, so you had transport to be involved in, 'the drug run'? And to repeat, 'Who decided bald was the new lush? When did a myriad body tattoos become a fashion accessory for people who were not in the navy or the armed forces'? Referring back to my first thirty years of existence people who wore 'beanies' to cover their heads, especially in restaurants or just indoors, did so because they had lost their hair, due to some illness or because they had or were having some aggressive invasive therapy. Sometimes, though it was just because they had head lice or nits. Do they still have 'nit inspectors' in schools in 2025? Today, these are worn as a fashion statement as it is seen as a measure of a person's trendiness or masculinity, or to show they batted for the other side, all in the name of progress. Can I say that? Too late, more castigation, Jim, for being honest. In the noughties, contestants on television shows started arriving on set wearing flat caps or an assortment of head gear, being quite happy to give the impression they had head lice or were recovering from chemotherapy. No disrespect to Amy Dowden of Strictly fame, or the genuine cases undergoing or having undergone therapy. Surely, such head apparel wasn't worn because the contestant was cold. Had a shaved head ousted the 'comb-over', to hide the beginning of baldness. Or was it to convey a visual message of pseudo macho toughness? When I was younger, men and women were proud of their hairstyles, be they bee-hive, Beatles, Stones or DAs, but today if hair is not hidden under a cap or hat, it's shaved off. The only exception being to have a nice little, 'bun', sitting atop the head, held together with an elastic band that had probably been discarded, by the post person doing their rounds. Fashion has gone in such a radical direction, it has become difficult to distinguish the whores from the rest and the boys from the girls. Is it to promote gender neutrality and less homophobia, or is it in the name of progress to gain more attention? Have I just instantly, been found guilty of another 'ism, ist or an ic'? This is getting too silly Mr Briggs, just accept without question and join the flock/tribe. Would you like to be trolled so you can contemplate suicide? I accept people have choice but I'm curious to know **who decided and when,** that leaving the house in a pair of jeans, that had been slashed and ripped by a sharp instrument, and ruined, sorry distressed, by having bleach spilled on them, and cost relatively a lot of money, was the height of fashion? Recently I threw away a pair of very old denim jeans that had become worn near the left pocket, and frayed around the ankles. I could hear my mother saying, "James, you can't go out looking like that, people will think you're a homeless tramp." Little knowing that those tatty jeans are now the height of fashion and are worth over 5 times what I originally paid for them. E bay here I come. How can so-called, highly qualified, professional people, turn up to work as mentors or teachers, who want to influence the next generation, wearing jeans and trainers? Do as I say not do as I do springs to mind. In 40 years of working, 35 years of which was teaching students, be they 5 or 55, **I NEVER arrived at work, school, college or university in jeans, ripped or otherwise.** I considered myself a role model, so set the standard I expected my students to follow. Teaching is more than just imparting knowledge, it's very much about the hidden curriculum. I also love the irony of the aging, sexist, male chauvinist, who walks around proudly displaying his beer belly, trying to look pregnant, like a woman, with a few 'tats', earrings, plenty of bling and the odd 'bun', here and there, in a track suit and trainers, trying to convince the populace they were 21 again and a local stud. But obviously I'm once again labelled sexist, racist and homophobic, when I think all I'm doing is just reporting what I see. **Homophobia becoming the antithesis to biological fact, with minority marginalisation superseding the majority.** When did quoting a person's vital statistics become sexist? When did children become a commodity instead of someone to be loved, protected and educated? When did it become fashionable **not** to wear socks, so that your feet stank and you became more susceptible to blisters, infections, fungal and viral problems? When did the behavioural default mechanism, for some males, involve mincing and being effeminate in posture, gait, dress and speech, just to gain attention or was it to secure a job on TV? Actors can do all of those things, if the role demanded it. **WHAT HAS HAPPENED TO FREE SPEECH? Perhaps because of so called progress, we don't live in a democracy and like in Russia, if you say something someone else doesn't like, no matter how true, you are severely, and I do mean severely, castigated. Russia going one better than trolling with actual murder. That man Trump has just been given another 4 years to try and fully emulate Putin.** When did mainly female insecurity become a multi-billion-pound industry? Who decided beauty was to be a certain size, or a double D cup, or to be anorexic to become a model, or something that could only be acquired via Botox or plastic surgery? At what point in evolutionary progress, was it necessary to go for a jog, in the middle of winter, with a bottle of water in hand, a mini television strapped to your biceps /triceps to test blood pressure, body mass index, heart rate, calories used, speed, cholesterol level, SA, testosterone and oestrogen levels, every 5 minutes? Obviously, it must have something to do with Health and Safety and to ensure the person is adequately hydrated and have a meaningful experience. That's if use of water hasn't been banned, because we have had a week of hot weather. Don't forget the smart phone, in case you wanted to find out which way to go, needed to take a selfie, or received a totally, insignificant text, after 10 metres, that **must** be replied to. I've **NEVER in 75 years**, gone out for a run or walk, loaded down, with such paraphernalia, sometimes without my watch. I own up to wearing a sweat band around my wrists, and the only worry I had was, where was the nearest toilet? **Who decided and conned these so-called intelligent life forms, into paying for bottled water, when the tap water in the UK was perfectly fit for purpose, and in some cases was more nutritionally beneficial?** I've travelled the world visiting countries where the poverty was heartbreaking and the sanitisation was horrendous, such as Soweto in South Africa and the Favellas in Rio de Janerio, and so followed the advice about not drinking the tap water. But I'm not aware that advice to, **'only drink bottled water'**, is given to visitors to the UK. In Zurich, there are hundreds of public water fountains and drinking kiosks scattered throughout the city for the populace to use **free of charge.** Do people buy bottled water thinking it will make them healthier, wealthier or wiser? To me, it just ensures the water distribution companies are laughing all the way to the bank. I've been thinking of labelling my water butt in my garden as being full of spring water from Preston, so I can bottle and sell it. Don't forget if you can't beat them, join them.

Driving and A Licence to Kill.

"A drug driver who hit a nursery worker at over 60 mph whilst on her phone has been spared jail." (McGuiness R., 18/7/2021). The 31-year-old driver was travelling at 63 mph in a 30mph zone, was 3 times over the legal drug limit, and went through a give way junction before hitting her victim. The 29-year-old victim was out for a jog. After the incident, the jogger spent 12 weeks in hospital, 3 in intensive care in a coma with a fractured skull and also suffered a fractured ankle. Although the driver was initially sentenced to 2 years in prison, this was suspended, probably because the jails were full or he/she cried uncontrollably, but was nevertheless told to complete 120 hours of unpaid work, possibly as a driver for some delivery company, and had to undergo 25 days of rehabilitation. What a deterrent! If her work ethic was as negative as her driving, I pity the poor sod who supervised his/her work and rehab. When I semi retired in 2006, I worked part time for several years doing traffic surveys for CTS Traffic and witnessed first-hand certain drivers' mentality, or should I say lack of? In several years I very rarely, saw drivers stop at red traffic lights that had just changed. The amber signal being a stimulus for some drivers to put more weight on the accelerator pedal. The most miscreants I personally counted as an enumerator was 6 drivers going through a red light on Barbra Castle Way, in Blackburn, the last one, a black 4x4, causing a multiple car incident. Who said counting vehicles was boring? Doing a survey with several of my colleagues on the A62 in Huddersfield, I witnessed a truck driver pull up at traffic lights using his mobile, his radio blaring out with a drink in his left hand. He then proceeded to open out a newspaper across the steering wheel and eat a sandwich. As a child I grew up on a Council Estate in the 50s when automobiles were a scarcity and owning a car was considered to be only in the domain of the privileged, rich and famous. Having a car was something to aspire to and only rarely impacted on my life. My earliest recollection of travelling in a car, apart from my older brother Barry taking me for rides, was as a teenager and was related to a girl named Hazel, whose parents owned an ice blue, Ford Popular. One Sunday, they took Hazel and me to Southport for, 'a ride out'. In the 60s such a journey was considered a highlight of the year. Such was the absence of cars on our Council estate that sitting cross-legged in the road as a child, bursting tar bubbles, was a pastime. As I became a teenager crossing the road was also a game, under the guise of a dare, called 'Chicken' that was a 'rite of passage', in order to be part of a gang/tribe. This initiation in 2025, in certain tribes has moved on, from bursting tar bubbles or playing dare to shooting or stabbing a fellow human being, whilst hiding under a hoodie. This even starting in pre-pubescent years. **It's called progress.** But even in the 50s and 60s danger on the roads was always lurking just around the corner, even with a scarcity of cars. A neighbour of ours on Parkway, one night ran straight under a car whilst playing, 'Knock a door run away', and was killed a few days before bonfire night. **At the age of 18, when studying personality, I was informed that two things could drastically alter a person's personality, alcohol and seating the person behind the wheel of a car and asking them to drive.** I'm pleased to say, when I was 21, I passed my driving test first time and years after that, became a member of The Guild of Experienced Motorists. Oo, get you, smarty pants. As mentioned upon retirement, I found myself doing traffic surveys for CTS Traffic and Transport, as well as surveys for IPSOS Moray. Not forgetting my lifetime's interest in human behaviour I, like thousands of others, have certain issues regarding drivers, both male and female. I remember being part of a survey in 2007, which involved asking the public to give as many reasons as they could think of, as quickly and spontaneously as possible, of things that annoyed them about drivers and driving. The list included: not using indicators, driving too close to the car in front, driving too fast, staying in the middle lane on the motorway, excessive use of the horn, etc, the list went on and on. Everyone taking part in the survey, even the 'non-drivers', had at least three responses. But what was interesting for me was the final question which asked the respondent, **"Do you or do you know of anyone driving who does any of the things you have mentioned?"** I was not surprised that all but a small percentage lied. Not guilty, M'Lord. Because if I was to believe them where were all these 'bad drivers' they had just alluded to? Being in denial, passing the buck and lying are things that immediately sprung to mind. **I also wonder if the drink drivers, or the Lewis Hamilton impersonators of this world, ever consider the stupidity or should I say criminality of their actions, or do they wait until they have either put someone in a wheelchair or ended another person's life, before remorse kicks in? Is remorse still part of such people's psyche?** A Panorama television programme, on the 17/1/22, 'Britain's Killer Roads', highlighted the statistics and issues involved but at the end of the day, driving too fast and without due care and attention was at the root of the problem. Not forgetting a person's lack of intelligence or moral code. Upon moving to Penwortham Residential Park in 2012, where the speed limit was supposedly 10 mph, but unfortunately there were no speed bumps or non-smiley emojis to deter the petrol heads. Where many residents were over 55, and many had issues related to physical mobility and could not suddenly jump out the way of a passing vehicle, the issues of driving too fast and road rage came closer to home. There are drivers who live or visit the Park who think they are Formula 1 drivers. One day I was sitting reading outside my property when an HGV driver drove into the park, stopped outside my property and asked for directions. Within several minutes there were at least 6 vehicles sounding their horns and shouting at the driver to move. And who says stress doesn't kill, or was that arrogant impatience? I've often wondered if these petrol heads, drink drivers, delivery drivers, or the Lewis Hamilton impersonators on the park, who numbered more than a few, such as **taxi drivers, care/social workers, Amazon drivers or drivers delivering lifesaving drugs,** ever consider that they might, at the very least, put someone in a wheelchair as a result of their lack of time management skills, impatient, selfish arrogance? Of course, whenever the issue was raised it wasn't an issue that concerned them personally, as they were all perfectly safe drivers, with very important jobs to do and musn't be delayed. **Not forgetting that life is habit and for many some people's habits are normal for them, irrespective of the laws of the land, and it's the rest of the species that have the problem.** More lies and denial. Were these drivers also part of the ever-growing tide of motorists who were trying to make indicators obsolete? When the insurance companies tried to make a stand against this anti-social behaviour and unquestioning acceptance of, 'well that's the way it is- **it's progress'**, they suggested the term car accident was considered completely misleading, because most involved substance abuse, alcohol, speeding, using a mobile or driving without due care and attention – all illegal acts. Most often than not, innocent people were the victims, sometimes being murdered or putting them permanently in a wheel chair, by selfish people who thought nothing of committing criminal behaviour, in their pursuit of speed, just to prove to anyone who was interested that they, **"Had a foot twice the atomic weight of lead."** (Reichs K, 2010. Spider Bones, PB, 9:80) and could press their foot down on the accelerator pedal harder and faster than anyone else. **Wow, now that is something that one should be proud of and definitely needs to be added to their CV. under the heading of, qualities that demonstrate intelligence. The psychologists argue that driving too fast is compensation for something else, such as having a small penis, (I added that not the psychologists), so could that be the reason?** So, the powers that be decided to re- classify them as **INCIDENTS NOT ACCIDENTS, OR SIMPLY ROAD TRAFFIC COLLISIONS**. Sadly, this is where the euphoria ended because having recognised the facts, decided that deterring future miscreants from such courses of action by imposing the full force of the law, or at least cutting off their private parts so they couldn't wave them at people or produce similar offsprings, was too harsh and contravened **human rights. Instead, let the perpetrators go free, calling it Community Service, to see if they could perfect the art of killing or maiming others in the future.** Preferably, whilst texting on their mobile, drinking a cup of coffee, using their pads, reading a newspaper, listening to their I-pod, playing the radio, whilst trying to look at, and listen to, their sat nav. Not forgetting turning 180 degrees to chastise their offsprings trying to kill each other in the back seats. **"It's really difficult trying to concentrate on my driving M- lud!!"** And TV's answer to assist this increasing crime wave is to put plenty of programmes on TV to show people, 'the tricks of the trade', just in case people were unfamiliar with how to break the law by breaking into a vehicle. **No wonder crime is on the rise because there is simply no deterrent** and nothing gets done because by the time a risk assessment has been made, Health and Safety and infringement of civil liberties has been considered, not forgetting being politically correct, crime figures analysed, the CPS is asked to make a decision on, 'the way forward', the necessary paper work filled out in triplicate and the defence lawyer and do-gooders have made out that the perpetrators of the crime are basically good, decent people, who arrive in court suitably 'suited and booted', the criminals have been given bail and have disappeared up their own backsides, or boarded a plane and were sitting on a beach somewhere in Spain drinking whisky and dry, whilst waving their private parts at the establishment and counting their hard earned proceeds from crime. The film,'7 Pounds', starring Will Smith, was another example of a road traffic incident killing 7 people, and the impact that had on people's lives, caused by a person texting. In the year 2025, there are many who see life in prison as a life choice. **"That wasn't so bad all things considered. She could read, sleep, listen to the radio. She'd be housed, clothed, fed. Better off than 60% of the world's population without access to toilets and clean water."** (Kernick S, 2016. The Witness, PB, 68:395). **As an inmate, sorry inperson, do strikes, energy issues, taxes and inflation etc. affect their stay?** If we once again look at our judicial system it is easy to see why people chose crime over being a law-abiding citizen. When I was teaching and studying law, as part of my on-going professional development, I was informed teachers had approximately 6 organisations they could turn to for help and advice in cases of litigation, whilst the pupils had almost 4 times as many. **"As you are all no doubt aware, suspects in the UK have all kinds of rights. If you're one of the bad guys you'll know them all by heart, and if by some mischance of fate, you're still an amateur and you haven't picked them up yet, don't worry. Your lawyer, who you don't have to pay for, will give you all the info you need."** (Kernick S, 2016. The Witness, PB, 4:36). When I first visited Australia in 1993, as the sole medical person with a schoolboy, U15, Ruby League Tour, I became aware of 'Kangy Bars', on the front of many Australian 4x4's. The bars being related to road kill and absorbing the impact as a kangaroo could suddenly come springing out of the bush, straight in front of the vehicle. Not only was I amazed at the size of the cars, which initially had nothing to do with how many members of the family there were or how many were obese but was about comfort, safety and the duration of even a short journey in Australia. On the tour the Aussies, who are not known for their shy, quiet, reserved personalities often joked that you could actually fit a couple of 'roos' in their cars. I now wonder **who decided and when to introduce these vehicles into the UK? A country 23 times smaller than Australia.** Could the reason be to accommodate the phenomenal rise in overweight, obese people in our country, or to absorb the impact of humans they ploughed into whilst driving too fast? Just a thought as I've yet to see a kangaroo on my travels on the M62 in Lancashire.

The Sporting Theme.

Who decided and when you couldn't play conkers in the school playground, without wearing goggles and protective gloves? When did Wimbledon become the tennis, grunting championships? Who decided, that by grunting when you hit the tennis ball, it ensured a greater technical shot accuracy, or ensured the grunter hit the, 'sweet spot', more frequently, on the racket, than they would do by not grunting? As I see, it only increases the risk of headaches and tonsillitis, or at least a sore throat. If you closed your eyes at times, you might think you were listening to a porn movie with all the oohs and aaahs. Not that I have personal experience of such things, you understand. I cannot recall Rod Laver, Ken Rosewall, Tim Henman, Virginia Wade, Sue Barker, Arthur Ashe or Billie Jean King, or my brother Jack, who was a successful amateur, tennis player, to name but a few, ever grunting at each other on the court. In the days of records being broken by hundredths of a second, with coaching, technological, nutritional, psychological support systems in place to aid the breaking of such, who decided that wearing vast amounts of 'bling', heavy gold chains being one of the favourites, was a great idea to compete in an athletics tournament? In gymnastics there's a dress code, with point deductions if not followed, and in my gym club earrings and such were banned on health and safety grounds. Why historically has there been a dearth of female physiotherapists/sports therapists working at the forefront of the 92 Football League clubs, whilst all other sports that I can think of have a mixed gender backroom staff? Could it be positive discrimination against xx chromosomes or just blatant sexism? Incidentally the x chromosome has been shown to be related to intelligence, so does that mean women have twice as much intelligence than men and if true, you would have thought that the football industry would want that extra intelligence as part of their set-up? I use the term industry, because men's football is now first and foremost a business with commodities, the priority being money, with sport in its purest sense and all that the term implies being very much a secondary consideration. **But unfortunately, as intimated I have struggled, for at least the last 30 years, to associate the word intelligence with many so-called men or women. Is this arrogance or just an informed observation?**

In 2025, with the rise and success of women in sport and the litigation cases in the USA and Europe, especially Great Britain and Spain, hitting the headlines on a regular basis, it puts a huge smile on my face to realise that although it may take a long time, as the wagons are definitely being circled, it's payback time for the racist, sexist, bigoted, misogynistic, male chauvinists I've encountered during my life playing, teaching, coaching, examining and writing about sport. I take up the issues of positive discrimination, misogyny, chauvinism, sexism, racism and masculine toxicity that has, and still pervades, many sports when in Chapter 5, I recount my time spent at Lilleshall National Sports Centre, in Shropshire, studying for my FATOI's diploma.

Brits Abroad.

But even if a person tried to escape the madness of the antics shown by today's generation and seek solace in warmer climates, you still saw these higher forms of intelligence behaving like dogs, urinating on lamp posts and various staging posts to denote territory and warn other animal trespassers away. Couples rutting in the street and discarding their condoms for children, sorry baby goats, to find, just so they could be on a holiday programme about, 'Brits Abroad', or on a reality programme that demonstrated how far society had progressed, or should that be regressed, in its search for fame and fortune? On holiday, the towel on the sun bed farce has nothing to do with nationality, as many would have you believe, but equates to animal behaviour denoting territory and possession and to warn trespassers away. How long will it be before these highest forms of intelligence started urinating on their sun beds? **'Scenting'** as it's called in animal behavioural terms, to warn other potential animals away and how soon, when adopted, would this become normal, acceptable behaviour? I've lost track of the number of times I've been on holiday and seen the mainly, all British holiday makers, who had obviously rushed poolside, in their pajamas, before breakfast, to mark their territory, with not a German in sight, the default mode for many Brits who, as mentioned, find it difficult to accept responsibility for many of their actions. In 2025, the Brits on holiday decided to increase their territorial superiority over the rest of the world by just lying on their towels by the pool if no sun beds were available, just to occupy as much space as possible so these, 'bloody foreigners', couldn't. Does this behaviour happen in Blackpool? **"British forces have deployed a new tactic in the ongoing War of the Sun beds. Every morning troops swarm the area around swimming pools, fighting desperately for the best spot of the day. Men, women and children scatter at the crack of dawn, laying down their weapon of choice – the humble towel. As they join the struggle for freedom from the shade, the bravest of our speedo - clad fighters sacrifice their lie-in, waking at 5 am for the first stage of battle. Early on, you can see some of our fallen heroes, collapsed on their towels, lying semi-conscious in paranoid belief that someone may take their spot."** Metro, 22/7/22. I wonder what the locals thought of these foreigners, who couldn't be bothered learning their language, most Europeans learn English as a second language and many speak it far more eloquently and grammatically correct than their English counterparts, taking their tourism jobs, **expecting** everyone to speak English, probably because many Brits are monoglot, riding slip-shod over their culture and **expecting** full English breakfast, with brown and tomato sauce and expecting mugs of coffee, taking over their country? Not to mention the ex-pats in their Spanish enclaves, who had created, **long before Brexit**, their mini-England. But what do you expect? As mentioned previously history shows that countries such as Australia, Canada and America suffered greatly, due to the influx of mainly white English settlers, in pursuit of wealth and power, showing total disregard for the local, indigenous populations of Maoris and Indian tribes, and riding slipshod over their language, traditional customs and way of life. **And the Brexiteers are bleating on** about immigration. **Is it arrogance, ignorance, dual standards, do as I say not do as I do, hypocrisy, selfishness, or just being in denial? For me it's all of these things and more.** On my world travels I've noticed that it's mainly a British thing, that when travelling on low-cost airlines, the passengers insult the pilot by giving him/her a round of applause after a successful landing. What next, congratulating the bus driver for arriving at the bus stop? That's if they are not on strike. Recently I was on a Ryanair flight to Malta, where because of high cross winds, the pilot made 3 attempts to land, otherwise we were off to Sicilly. **Now I can accept a round of applause for his 3rd and successful attempt.**

Finally, before moving on from travel and Brits abroad, I would like to return to why the rest of the world laughs at us and how I struggle with the claim that we are the highest form of intelligence in the animal kingdom, with specifics on travel. During July 2022, the UK was put on, 'red alert', and given severe weather warnings that a heat-wave was going to occur. Now bear in mind, the Brits spend thousands of pounds every year, Pandemics, air traffic control and rail strikes permitting, on going abroad MAINLY for the hot weather so they can acquire a tan to look like a coloured person. Interesting. Now we had our own hot weather and didn't need to travel but the, 'Winging Poms', went into meltdown and, as previously alluded to when discussing Brexit, the country suggested a whole raft of suggestions to avoid a catastrophe.

To Recap: Where does it all end? What of the future?

"We always seem to be on the eve of destruction, and we always seem to get through it." (Coben, H, 2007, The Woods, 26:282). With Barry McGuire in 1965 singing about such a tragedy. If the reader can't see how much society has degeneratively changed since Marilyn Monroe wrote, 'Wolves I have Known', in the 1950s then some of you are going to get your wish as I'm off to Switzerland to ask them to quietly put me to sleep. I give up. **"Adrian hated the way some people like Ryan seemed to just get away with infecting others, pushing their poison.........Over the years, no matter what had happened, he walked. Either someone else would take the fall for him or witnesses would disappear and every charge resulted in, 'no further action'."** (Diamond K, 2016. The Teacher, PB, 19:183).   All American Murder, by James Patterson, 2018, is another true story of how high-profile figures, with power and money, can virtually get away with murder because they have total disregard for life's rules and regulations. How long will it be before intelligent, compassionate homo sapiens start killing each other because they all don't shop at the same supermarket? Remember with this blogging obsessed society with its hate mentality, anyone is fair game. As an aside, there has always been a snobbery attached to shopping but how long will it be before this becomes overt and an issue for some? **Don't laugh and patronise me by labelling me a sensationalist as many things that I used to laugh about as a youngster growing up, are now reality and part of the reason for writing this book. In 1969 the death penalty was abolished in the UK because it was seen by some as something wicked, cruel and barbaric and left no room for compassion and rehabilitation of the criminals. It is interesting to note we now have the acceptable pastime of trolling, where vitriolic, pure hatred tries to persuade people to kill themselves by harassment and threats. We have white supremists looking for coloured people to attack. We won't watch Strictly Come Dancing, if same sex partnerships are included. We can now trash the White House, if we don't get our own way and send assassins to find people to murder who don't agree with our Modus Operandi.** Back in the day people like Albert Pierrepoint, 'the hang –men', were not only seen as people who punished the guilty but were, more importantly, seen as people who represented justice. **Are trollers, via Tik Tok and anti-social media, now representers of justice or are they just delusional, psychologically disturbed,** biased individuals with an agenda that involves distorting the facts, because they themselves have very little knowledge or qualifications that allows them to interfere in other people's lives and pass judgement? Should trollers instead of being idolised be identified and punished? Sadly, since then criminality, under its many guises, has become more of a way of life for some, for a whole host of reasons. One of the main ones being that there is no ultimate deterrent and so they can literally, 'get away with murder'. Hence the job title, 'Habitual Criminal'. These people seeing repeat offending as free housing, free food, free heating, free education and if so desired free sex, with no responsibility or national insurance stamps and income tax to worry about. All at the expense of law abiding, working class, income tax paying stampers, who question the whole concept of justice and responsibility. In 1987, corporal punishment was banned in State Schools, but it wasn't until 1999 that the independent sector had to follow suit. **36 years on no acceptable, suitable effective deterrent has replaced it, putting teachers at the mercy of young and not so young tyrants.** Without going into too deep a debate about the rights and wrongs of capital and corporal punishment and the abdication of many of societies responsibilities, it's not rocket science to see why society is in the state it's in. With even the police questioning the rationale of so much paper work and protocols at the expense of walking and patrolling the streets, once known as, 'bobbies on the beat'. Could this possibly be one of the reasons why some law enforcement officers, who see the cards heavily stacked against them, adopt the attitude, 'If you can't beat them, join them' and become a, 'bent copper'? Oh, now you are in for a beasting Briggsy. This goes beyond just ic. ists and isms. But take heart from the fact that you can't be hung, although I'm not so sure about drawn and quartered, whatever that meant. **I wonder what the latest job title is for a bent copper?** As mentioned during the 60s and 70s, I taught in some of the most socially deprived areas of Manchester, such as Moss Side, Ardwick, Beswick and Failsworth and in 17 years, only two children ever swore at me and one of those had a prostitute for a mother and a father who spent most of his time at His Majesties' Pleasure. I was told to, wait for it, **'Bugger off'**. I was **never** physically abused or threatened. **I wonder what the statistics would be for psychological and physical abuse of teachers and educators in 2025?** Whilst many teachers such as myself, didn't enjoy 'punishing children', it was, in most cases, an effective deterrent. But if the teacher realised the miscreants were punch drunk from beatings at home, they used their knowledge, skills, experience and expertise to find other solutions that would act as a deterrent. I personally soon realised, not long after entering the teaching profession that, 'a good clip around the ear', was not always the answer to deterring children. When they banned corporal punishment, teachers suddenly became responsible for all of societies' ills and discipline at a time when society was moving in the direction of, 'rights but no responsibilities'. The conveyor belt of ideas and sanctions that many of the politicians, whose own private, elite education included floggings, buggery, humiliation and beastings, came up with **were just not practical, not to mention, fair and just.** Suspending children so they could then roam the streets causing more havoc and mayhem demonstrated just how out of touch politicians were, as to life on the chalk face. **Don't forget that in my career, of all the Education Ministers that teachers were answerable to, only Keith Joseph had actually taught.** When I resigned from full time Primary teaching in 1988, apart from the main reason, I realised that 'my job', if I'd have stayed, was going to be far more psychological, emotional and physically challenging then it had previously been. The relationship between teachers, parents and pupils had changed drastically since I was in teaching, and whilst a collaborative, respectful and civil approach to education would seem to address the issues of authoritarianism, hierarchical teaching styles and disciplines, it has been shown not to work. Accepting that one cap doesn't fit all, what's the answer, never mind the solution? **Going back to my initial** training to become a teacher and to repeat myself, I was told that without discipline, teaching whilst not impossible, was very, very much more difficult and that unless the parents laid the foundation in the first 5 years, the job was one of catch-up. Is this why many of todays' parents gave their children away at the earliest opportunity so someone else can do their job? No further questions Ma Lud, I rest my case, let's move on. The world's most brilliant minds are now designing artificial drones, the first being introduced in 2010, and robots that they think will solve all of life's problems. Today even society is questioning its own intelligence by wanting to devise and create, Artificial Intelligence and Super Intelligence to think for them. But at what cost? Giving such people who think of these things so much power to manipulate, can only lead to doom and gloom because the dangers of modern technology and those who promote and use it are frightening, to say the least. **Revisiting that man Trump again, it has been alleged he suffered from a whole raft of psychological and behavioural problems not least, MUMPSIMUS, (n), is someone who insists they are right despite clear evidence that they are wrong, and IPSEDIXITISM,(n), a dogmatic insistence that something is fact because someone, somewhere says it was, with not a shred of evidence to say it's true to prove it. According to the Washington Post, as of 15/06/20, Trump made over 18,000 false or misleading claims, usually via tweets, since coming into office. Later the January 6th Committee was set up to investigate Trump's involvement in the attack on the White House and his threat to democracy. It showed that tweeting was his main Modus Operandi to try and get his own way. To repeat, 'There is nothing as certain as a closed mind', which is a sign of inflexibility, with Trump being described as, 'a psychological honeypot'. The sad fact is that many less high-profile figures, from all walks of life, suffer from the same conditions.** As previously mentioned, but to reemphasise a point, what I cannot understand is how so-called intelligent humans can believe the lies and bullshit? Or why they vote for such people in the first place. Jon Sopel's book, A Year at The Circus, 2019 was advertised as an insider's guide to the Oval Office and is another reason I question how Homo Sapiens can profess to be intelligent. Just as I can't understand why people just don't switch off their mobiles to stop all the aggravation, now called trolling. Is it because as addicts they couldn't cope without their daily fix? **Or is it because so-called intelligent homo sapiens just love to moan, groan and be abused.** Via the use of algorithms, supposedly innocent pieces of data, create our digital footprint every time modern technology is used, and this in turn can be turned into highly significant factors to alter peoples' mind set, which in the wrong hands can be used to manipulate people. How they think, what they believe and even how they vote can be affected. Psycho Graphics and Twitter played a significant part in Donald Trump's first political campaign to become President and during his first 4 years in office, 220 million Americans were data-mined, to identify groups of people with certain traits and characteristics, that would be sympathetic to, and react positively to, his campaign of, 'building a wall', to keep out the foreigners. Facebook apps ensuring that any disinformation went viral. Once in office, it has been alleged that he targeted such people to incite unrest against people who didn't think he was a wonderful person. But Bill Bryson was not fooled and had Trump's measure, **"-it was the look of someone from outer space, that odd, cunning, malevolent B-movie smile of a face of interplanetary creatures who have taken over a small town in the middle of nowhere as their first step towards becoming .....Earth Masters."** (Bryson B, 1989, The Lost Continent, 16:145). The **'emotional contagion theory'** relates to the idea that the more intense and emotional the content of a message, the more likely it is to go viral. This fact sows distrust and false belief in people, thus changing the democracy of public opinion. **Facebook, which started out as a platform for sharing photographs and chit chat has become a tool that has dramatic implications as to how democracy works. Not forgetting the** fact that it now makes millions of pounds for its founder. "It was easy to manipulate people. Folks had been doing it pretty much forever." (Baldacci D, 2008. The Whole Truth, PB, 8:46). That man Trump again, who by now will be wanting a share of my royalties from this book, gaining a frightening reputation, for challenging and manipulating not only the democratic process, but also the American Presidential landscape, with his volatile rhetoric, via twitter. Taking America back in time to when it was a melting pot of derision between black and white faces. "**The term 'perception management' has firmly entered the public lexicon.....PMs are not spin doctors because they don't spin the facts. They *create* facts and then sell them to the world as the truth........a major untruth can be established so quickly and overwhelmingly across the world, that no digging by anyone after the fact, can make a dent in the public consciousness that it actually isn't true at all. And that is precisely what makes it so dangerous."** (Baldacci D, 2008. The Whole Truth, PB, Authors Note, p547).

"You made up the truth, then you buried the real thing under so much garbage that people grew weary of trying to dig through it and instead just accepted what you offered. It was the easy way out and humans were programmed to always go that way." (Baldacci D, 2008. The Whole Truth, PB, 58:331-2). "**Good information is vital, accidental misinformation regrettable but skilful disinformation is deadly.**" (Forsyth F, 2010. The Cobra, 14:253). **With Presidential, Political and Brexit campaigns having been won and lost on such.**

On 18/11/20, during a TV interview basically to promote his long-awaited autobiography, Barrack Obama , called this manipulation of the facts, **TRUTH DECAY. For Mr Trump in 2024 campaigning for his 2nd spell as President, it was not a question of, 'If at first you don't succeed, try, try again,' but, 'It's worked once let's repeat the process but this time let's see if we can cause more chaos.'** The future appears to be Trump and Musk, hand in hand, striving for world domination. Scary business! In 1995, the film, The Net, starring Sandra Bullock, highlighted the dangers of computer crime and hacking, during which it was stated, "**Our whole world is just sitting there on a computer.....just begging for someone to screw us. They hack into computers and cause chaos.**" So, what do these so-called highest forms of animal intelligence, under the guise of being a human being, do to combat this? They put as much personal information about their lives as is humanly possible, on a daily basis, via facebook etc. to assist the hackers with their crimes. All in pursuit of getting a tap on the LIKE button. Is that sad, scary, pathetic or what? It certainly cannot be classed as exhibiting intelligence. Brexit: The Uncivil War, shown on channel 4 TV, in January 2019. showed how similar tactics as those employed in the first Trump presidential campaign were used to influence the vote. With Cambridge Analytica being employed to identify and target, via people's digital footprint, voters with disinformation tinged with elements of truth, under the slogan, 'Taking Back Control'. But in truth the highest form of intelligence in the animal kingdom was being covertly manipulated, conned and taken for a ride. **Hence the double-decker bus to show how much the UK would benefit from leaving the European Union.** This seems a long way from what Arthur Conan Doyle, the creator of Sherlock Holmes, implied when he said, "*Entia non sunt multiplicanda praetor necessitate.* **When you have eliminated the impossible, whatever remains, however improbable, must be the truth."** This was the basis for what is commonly referred to as Ockham's razor. William of Ockham being a thirteenth century monk who had a profound influence on intellectual thought. In other words, all things being equal, when confronted with choices, the simplest, most obvious answer was usually the right one. Although this argument can be said to be flawed, because it is argued that the impossible cannot be defined, quantified, labelled or listed so how can it be eliminated. Blink: The Power of Thinking Without Thinking, by Malcolm Gladwell, 2006, discusses first impressions, intuition, improvisation, decision making, instinct, adaptive unconsciousness and the power of knowing. With, 'Yea I know' being a yes-but, and a defence mechanism against being challenged. He also talks about 'thin slicing' in relation to positive discrimination. He mentions, 'listening with your eyes', in reference to the words not really being that important as identified in the work of Albert Mehrabian. **"Unfortunately, nothing was ever true for long. In time everything was deconstructed. Black turned out to be white."** (Townsend S, 2012. The Woman Who Went to Bed for a Year, PB, p315). **Also remember proof and truth are two different things, just as deploying words isn't always the same as talking,** and that people make decisions in life based on not only **WHO** we believe, but also **WHAT** we believe. **Social media has lies, deceit and disinformation sitting alongside true stories, making it very difficult for people to differentiate one from the other.** Also, the truth isn't always what you would like it to be. In fact, there's no such thing as truth, just differing points of view depending on the perspective. **That is why the racist, sexist, politically incorrect dispute is flawed.** It can be argued that there are always three viewpoints to any discussion. Yours, the other person's and finally, somewhere in the middle lies the so-called truth. **Finally, from a sociological perspective, when a society loses its agreed values it goes into moral decay, leading to civil disobedience and social unrest and is asking for trouble. The riots of 2011 in the UK and Black Lives Matter in 2020, in the USA are testament to that. This in turn can lead to civil war, which can escalate into global unrest and ultimately global war. Does any of this rhetoric ring alarm bells, or at least raise conscience in 2025, because if it doesn't, can I suggest society takes its head out of the sand, switch off its mobiles, sober up and stop calling itself the highest form of intelligence?**

I was hoping that something as serious as the 2020, Covid-19, virus pandemic may have helped society re-evaluate what was important in life but sadly after an initial scare many reverted to their individualistic or collectivism type, especially once alcohol and eating junk food were introduced back into the equation, and a second lock down had to be introduced. The longer the threat of Covid persisted, there was a definite shift in attitude from initially one of fear to one of complacency, especially if no family member or friends had been affected. We must also not forget those who know the rules, but think that they don't apply to them and who mess it up for the rest of us. They will always be around, as long as there is no deterrent to their selfish behaviour. However, with thousands losing their jobs, and future employment prospects looking bleak, I am not too optimistic that perhaps some may adopt a different attitude towards fellow humans and the value of personal compassion, employment, and who knows work ethic. And whilst this may sound harsh to the thousands who have lost their jobs, something needed to happen because familiarity was definitely breeding contempt and had become enshrined into many people's psyche. **Who knows maybe society may go back to living in the real world, within its means, guided by a moral compass, but I very, very much doubt it.** My last consideration in this section and on the question of Homo Sapiens being the highest form of intelligence in the animal kingdom, is to ask, how the f... Donald Trump became President of the USA **at roughly the same time** as Boris Johnson became Prime Minister of England? Both of whom had a troubled history with a reputation for distorting the truth. And whilst I have suggested how those situations may have come about, how did this highest form of intelligence, under the guise of being the electorate, not see through the bullshit and lies and let it happen? Because I have never voted, I cannot be too critical of the situation or feel smug about any political initiatives or electoral outcomes. Then along came Liz Truss and Rishi Sunak. You've got to laugh, or is that cry?

Food for Thought, (Not Junk Food, Obviously).

Has anyone ever considered what would happen if, as a protest against the sham known as an election, nobody voted? Instead, a committee was set up, consisting of highly qualified, experienced professionals, with no hidden agenda other than to do their job to the best of their ability, once called, 'job satisfaction', representing education, health, sport, commerce, banking, foreign affairs, the farming and food industry etc. and given an attractive salary, and a more than adequate support backup, commensurate with the responsibilities such a job involved. Yes, you could throw in the odd politician to go to Brussels to attend the meetings, and inform the rest of the world what was happening in the UK. I'm convinced some of my ex-colleagues in education, sport and health could do a far better job than the past and present situation, which was and has always been based on jobs for the boys/girls, how much money you had, how you shook hands, which tribe you belonged to or which school or church you had attended. All enveloped in a lack of transparency. In relation to commensurate salary, it should be borne in mind that in the year 2025, a male, professional footballer could earn **in excess of £550,000 PER WEEK,** with perks, for supposedly entertaining the populace, by kicking a football, another player, his partner, a spectator, or maybe the referee, whilst inciting racism, sexism and any other ic.ist or ism you can think of? And today's societal response to my ramblings is to give me an ic, ist or ism label and patronisingly tell me I'm boring, whilst unquestioningly accepting the fact that, 'that's the way it is, James. The world has progressed and this is the way it is now. Get real, stop living in the past'. So, I got real and considered the so-called progress and changes that have been made, in relation to how it used to be when I was, 'naught but a young lad', and very soon realised **WHY I DON'T AND HAVEN'T FOR MANY YEARS EMBRACED THE NOTION THAT PROGRESS AND CHANGE WERE ALWAYS NECESSARY, INEVITABLE AND GOOD.** Ask the hedgehog about the invention of the wheel, the soldiers who sacrificed their limbs, not to mention lives, fighting for their country and Caroline Flack about trolling. And whilst I accept that there is much to be applauded, and there have been some wonderful innovations and discoveries, but are these not partly to blame for the fact that today's world is not a nice place to live in, and is regressing at an alarmingly very, very fast pace? **Have today's 20, 30 and 40 plus year olds lost the Brit sense of humour? They appear incapable of seeing the hilariously funny side of their behaviour and get very aggressive and defensive when such behaviour is highlighted.** They say some people are born old, I wasn't. Neither was I born grumpy, cynical, patronising, angry or depressed. Why did I grow up not wanting to vote, watch the news or read newspapers? Someone or something made it so. Yes, it was the balance of nature and nurture, conditions and circumstance but what and who shaped my being, (the nature), philosophy, (the nurture) and direction, (the conditioning and circumstance)? Which magic moments and pearly words of wisdom. forged my destiny? Foresight is knowing where you are going, hindsight is knowing where you'd been and insight is knowing you'd gone too far.

"Every once in a while, you try to trace your life back to a time when everything was so good. You try to go back and figure out how it started and the path you'd taken and how you ended up here, if there was a moment you could go back to and somehow alter and poof, you wouldn't be here, you'd be someplace else." (Coben H, 2006. Promise Me, p154). **"Memories have the power to shift vast expanses of time into mere instants."** (Grayson AJ, 2017. The Boy in The Park, PB 48:252).

Having hopefully set the scene, I have raised and tried to address many issues and questions relevant to society today. Hopefully I have also started to identify who and when such changes started to occur, and the significant others, events, circumstances and sayings that guided me to my destination. For me, the process being far more important than the end product. The following chapters are about my childhood, upbringing and the rest of my journey through life and my search for more answers. I'm also aware that I could not tell the story the way it happened, but only by the way I remembered it. Verisimilitude and all that. We all glamorise or demonise the past.

So apart from challenging these ideas about progress, change and the supposed fact that Homo Sapiens was the highest form of intelligence in the animal kingdom, who decided and at what point and why did society embrace the changes in the name of progress? "Forgive me. I don't mean to get upset. But you are taking my world away from me, piece by little piece and sometimes it just pisses me off. Sorry." (Bryson B, 1992, The Lost Continent, 22: 202). **How did life and society arrive at such a point becoming more materialistic, addictive, self-centred, two-faced, subservient, corrupt, venal, weak and yet arrogant? Why are youngsters, on one hand, ignored, patronised and sometimes murdered, just because they are trying to draw attention to things that are happening in their lives, whilst on the other, are allowed to overrule weak, misguided adults and cause havoc and chaos? NO is NOT a dirty word so, 'What my children want my children get', can, in my humble opinion, only lead to heartache. Why are the elderly, who have the most experience in the whole of society, ignored and patronised and only seen as cash cows and baby sitters? Why are people driven to suicide because they have been harassed, in all its various forms, by a so called modern, highly intelligent society? Why are people knifed, shot at, beaten, blown up and traumatised just because they belong to a different tribe or have a different coloured skin? Why is the creation of a fairer society that promotes a decent work ethic and values, where the bad guys and gals get punished and the good get rewarded, still considered a pipe dream 75 years after I was born? Oh yes, now I remember, is it because that's what you do? Nearly everyone does it. It's called progress, because we are supposedly the highest form of intelligence on the planet. Or is it just, like sheep, we follow the rest, taking the line of least resistance, with very little thought, other than greed and insecurity, as to the consequences for themselves or society as a whole. Is individualism becoming a thing of the past? What has happened to honesty and a sense of humour? What has happened to MEA CULPA and accepting fault?**

If progress is supposedly a benefit, why is it each successive generation says, 'It wasn't like this when I wer a young un?' And on New Year's Eve the vast majority of the population announce, to anyone that will listen, that they hope the New Year is better than the last because that one was crap? **IN 75 YEARS OF MY LIFE I HAVE VERY RARELY, IF EVER, HEARD ANYONE, APART FROM MYSELF AND A FEW OTHERS, ANNOUNCE ON NEW YEAR'S EVE THAT THEY HAVE HAD A BRILLIANT YEAR AND IF NEXT YEAR WAS HALF AS GOOD, THEY WOULD BE MORE THAN HAPPY.** I'm sure such people exist but they appear to be in a minority and sadly cannot be found in, 'my bubble'. **"If we are so intelligent, why are we so stupid and blind?"** (Donovan, singer/songwriter, Sky Arts, 29th. October, 2021). Or, **"How can we be so rich and so stupid at the same time?"** ...It is the curse of our century - too much money, too little sense." (Bryson B, 1992, Neither Here Nor there, 4:305). In which sector of society are we going to find our next role models and leaders from? Certainly not in the UK, USA or Russia if Johnson, Trump and Putin are the examples. There **must** be some hidden amongst all the dross.

I remember in 1994 walking out of the Roxy Cinema in Hollinwood, Oldham with my friends Wendy and Sian, along with the rest of the audience, in almost total silence, with many in tears after watching the film Schindler's List about the Holocaust and thinking, Why? In 2012, when I started writing this book, and the longer I spent on it I kept asking myself the same question before eventually asking a more pertinent one, What the f... was it all about? Why did our veterans fight in two wars because when they see, or at least those who are still alive, what has become of society with its lies, dishonesty, deceit, greed, materialism, abdication, chauvinistic, racist, sexist, misogynistic, bigotry, surely, they must be asking the same question, Why? In 1988, Henry James wrote, **"Three things in human life are important. The first is to be kind. The second is to be kind. And the third is to be kind."** Which is **totally** at odds with great swathes of today's me, me, me, money, money, money, moan, moan moan, materialistic M Society. But what people forget is that it doesn't matter who you are, there's always a before and after. In 1939, the year England declared war on Germany, Charles Chaplin started to make the film, The Great Dictator, about a tramp, himself and a dictator, Adolf Hitler. Although considered look-alikes the Germans disliked Chaplin labelling him a Jew, which he wasn't. In one of the final scenes, Chaplin orates his first speaking part by addressing the people and aligning himself with the persecuted minority facing extermination, whilst outlining what was wrong with society.

"I'm sorry, but I don't want to be an emperor.
That's not my business.
I don't want to rule or conquer anyone.
I should like to help everyone - if possible - Jew, Gentile - black man - white.
We all want to help one another.
Human beings are like that.
We want to live by each other's happiness - not by each other's misery.
We don't want to hate and despise one another.
In this world there is room for everyone.
And the good earth is rich and can provide for everyone.
The way of life can be free and beautiful, but we have lost the way.
Greed has poisoned men's souls, has barricaded the world with hate, has goose-stepped us into misery and bloodshed.
We have developed speed, but we have shut ourselves in.
Machinery that gives abundance has left us in want.
Our knowledge has made us cynical.
Our cleverness, hard and unkind.
We think too much and feel too little.
More than machinery we need humanity.
More than cleverness we need kindness and gentleness.
Without these qualities, life will be violent and all will be lost.
The aeroplane and the radio have brought us closer together.
The very nature of these inventions cries out for the goodness in men - cries out for universal brotherhood - for the unity of us all.
Even now, my voice is reaching millions throughout the world - millions of despairing men, women, and little children - victims of a system that makes men torture and imprison innocent

people.
To those who can hear me, I say - do not despair.
The misery that is now upon us is but the passing of greed - the bitterness of men who fear the way of human progress.
The hate of men will pass, and dictators die, and the power they took from the people will return to the people.
And so long as men die, liberty will never perish. ...
Soldiers, don't give yourselves to brutes - men who despise you - enslave you - who regiment your lives - tell you what to do - what to think and what to feel!
Who drill you - diet you - treat you like cattle, use you as cannon fodder.
Don't give yourselves to these unnatural men - machine men with machine minds and machine hearts!
You are not machines! You are not cattle! You are men!
You have the love of humanity in your hearts!
You don't hate! Only the unloved hate - the unloved and the unnatural!
Soldiers! Don't fight for slavery! Fight for liberty!
In the 17th Chapter of St Luke it is written: "the Kingdom of God is within man" - not one man nor a group of men, but in all men!
In you!
You, the people have the power - the power to create machines.
The power to create happiness!
You, the people, have the power to make this life free and beautiful, to make this life a wonderful adventure.
Then - in the name of democracy - let us use that power - let us all unite.
Let us fight for a new world - a decent world that will give men a chance to work - that will give youth a future and old age a security.
By the promise of these things, brutes have risen to power.
But they lie!
They do not fulfil that promise.
They never will!
Dictators free themselves but they enslave the people!
Now let us fight to fulfil that promise!
Let us fight to free the world - to do away with national barriers - to do away with greed, with hate and intolerance.
Let us fight for a world of reason, a world where science and progress will lead to all men's happiness. Soldiers!
In the name of democracy, let us all unite!"

    It's ironic that **85 YEARS later** the same speech could apply today with Trump, Putin and others replacing Hitler. In September, 2024, Carol Vorderman's book, What's Gone Wrong with Britain?' became available. On November 16th 2024, in an interview with Mr Holland on, Later With Jools Holland, Joan Armatrading said that society was in a place of all questions with no answers and didn't seem to know to how it had arrived at where it was. Hence the title of her latest CD, 'How Did This Happen and What Does It Mean?'

During my quest to find answers to these and a myriad other questions, I will try to be guided by the words of Sir Michael Caine. **"Never look back in anger, always look forward in hope, and never, never, dream small."** (My Generation, 2017 and shown on BBC2, on the 19/12/2020). In August 2024, I watched a, 'Ben Elton Live', programme where he got a standing ovation for getting laughs by talking about many issues highlighted in this chapter. No comment.

2.
DYSFUNCTIONAL FAMILIES AND CHILDHOOD RECOLLECTIONS: 0-16yrs.

"**Memory is funny – you have these images of a childhood that you constantly re-interpret.**" (Patterson RN, 2011. In The Name of Honour, PB, p204) One such memory is of my brother Jack and mum always whistling. Is this now a dying art form? It is said that by the end, all you are left with are the memories. But the problem with trying to recall the past is that the memories don't come chronologically, the events are random and are triggered at any moment in time. They also appear to be never ending.

Warners:Nidd Hall 2000.

Back Row, L-R:Lilian, James, Marlene, Barry, Stephen Paul. Front, L-R: Jack, mum Lily, Janet.

"**Families guard their secrets – fiercely so, the more dysfunctional they are.**"

(Pattterson R N, 2005, Conviction, PB, p169).

Also, their workings are usually so impenetrable.

"**All families are dysfunctional. It's only a question of degrees.**"(Baldacci D, 2013. King and Maxwell, PB, p32).

"**Family is more than biology.**" (Carver t, Cage of Bones, 2011.83:344).

"**Family is about love and affection, but about friction and separation too. Yet with work and luck, the distances – geographical and emotional – can be shrunk, even made to vanish.**" (Deaver J, 2012. Sealed with a Kiss, Marked with Death, XO, PB, 37:231). "**There's no law that says siblings** have to be close." (Baldacci D, 2011. The Simple Truth, 31:229). And after reading, Too Much and Never Enough by Mary L Trump, 2020, the reader will totally understand why Donald Trump ended up the way he did – one of the world's most dangerous men.

Siblings can have completely different opinions of their childhood. For me childhood was a collection of fragmented episodes, some of which were quite vivid whilst others vague recollections. As for most people, it was also the foundation for future beliefs, morals, thoughts, expectations, aspirations, insecurities, fears and explanations as to why. Upon reflection and introspection, I realised that many things that occurred in my life at a relatively young age, shaped my future thoughts and actions. At what age did I start buying into people's bullshit and conversely, at what age did I start to invent my own? When did I start to become cynical and depressed about society, and when did I decide to isolate myself? Hopefully, as my story unfolds all will be revealed. And whilst I could wax lyrical with many stories related to my parents, brothers and sisters, I feel it's inappropriate to divulge in too much detail what in essence is personal and private. Although at the end of the day, the facts need to be conveyed. Using the expression, 'getting a flavour', is the aim of talking about my family, but as honesty is my default mode, my analysis may be too in-depth for some. **Which I would find strange, as today many are quite happy to tell the whole world what is going on in their lives via, twitter, facebook and snap chat etc. to curry flavour and get a tap on the like button.**

In his autobiography, Trowel and Error, 2002, the gardener and television celebrity, Alan Titchmarsh, a Northerner like myself, waxes lyrical, in much the same way that I have done, by making comparisons between today's society and the one he grew up in. During this chapter his thoughts, along with several other authors, will be referred to. The following is an overview of my life so that comparisons can be made, hypothesis can be postulated, theories can be put forward and questions answered.

My Family: More the Merrier.

Large families in the 50s and 60s were not uncommon. I was born in 1950, just 5 years after the end of the 2nd World War and austerity was the name of the game. As I recall, although I didn't realise it at the time, there was a community spirit and neighbours helped out neighbours in whichever way they could. Be it with leftover food, clothes or looking after little Johnny if mum had a job to do. Even the local shopkeepers knew who you were and where you lived. My parents were named Lily, nee Irish, and my father, James Albert Briggs. Mum was born on 15th January, 1920, dad on the 3rd September, 1918. I believe my father's younger brother was in the navy but sadly died at the age of 21, along with thousands of others at the Dieppe landings in the war, on 19th August, 1942. He was a ship's pilot carrying the troops to the beaches. He had only been married 6 weeks and he was buried in Chadderton Cemetery. My father also had a sister but I knew nothing about her. Mum had one brother, Jimmy, who married Mary and they had two boys Alan and Stephen. Mum was little, being less than 5 foot tall, with red hair, whereas my father was taller at about 5 feet 6 inches, with black hair. I cannot vouch for their genetic make-up or whether their DNA was aligned with Mars but I always found it interesting that their off-springs were all fair haired. At that time, I hadn't studied genetics and wasn't aware of the significance of dominant and recessive genes.

Dad home on leave with mum. In this photo Claire, my niece, has a striking resemblance to my mum.

My parents, Lily and James Albert, at Dee and my wedding, in the grounds of St. Paul's Peel, Little Hulton, 25th August 1975.

Mum's role in life, like most mums in those days, was to provide the ovum, be around at the childbirth, initially look after the house and family, hold down a variety of part-time jobs, whilst whistling, humming or singing. In other words, multi-tasking, long before multi-tasking had entered the public lexicon. Whilst father was handing over his wages, mum was handing over her whistling trait to my eldest brother Jack. When I was a child growing up, whistling was something most people did, or attempted to do. In today's world I hear very few, if any, people whistling as they are going about their daily lives. After returning from the war, dad's role was to provide the sperm, earn the money, tip up his wages every Friday, and administer disciplinary measures as and when appropriate. Handing over the wages was a courtesy afforded to women in those days. Bringing up 7 children on a pittance was, I am led to believe, no mean feat. Before marriage, I know mum worked in the mills as a ring doffer or something like that. However, I only remember her firstly as a cleaner, working either in private houses or in pubs and secondly, as a 'cook and bottle washer', in Chadderton Grammar School kitchen. Being born on a Northern council estate I enjoyed going to private houses with her to help clean, because she was allowed to take a piece of fresh fruit from the fruit bowl as part of her wages and we sometimes shared an apple. In those days, fresh fruit and vegetables for the Briggs family was definitely a luxury. Tinned fruit, not so. In fact, most of our sustenance came out of a tin and was processed. I loved it when she worked in the school kitchens, because some days she would bring home left-overs from the school dinners. I loved the cheese and onion pie, which was like chewing gum. These 'left-overs' were the pre-cursor to my love of school dinners. The antithesis of my dislike of smoking and smokers, which originated from helping mum clean out the ash trays in pubs and clubs she worked in. These experiences and many more provided the blue print for my future attitude towards people's behaviour. To this day I want to slap people who treat waiters, waitresses, cleaners, refuse collectors etc. like a bit of dog shit at the end of their shoe. These people did what can only be referred to as menial jobs, kowtowing to others. When I became a teacher, I'd like to think I always had a healthy respect for the classroom assistants, caretakers, cleaners, and cooks and dinner ladies who cleaned up my mess and fed me. In my teaching career, I came across some teachers who thought they were superior to them, which was pathetic because if some of these classroom assistants, caretakers, cleaners, cooks and dinner ladies had chosen to become fully qualified teachers they would, in my professional opinion, have made far better teachers than these biased, bigoted ones on the staff. Early on in my teaching career at my first school I came across a teacher, who believed only Grammar school educated people should be teachers. Just because certain people, through circumstances beyond their control or just by choice, pursue a particular life style doesn't make them any better or worse than others who have chosen a different path. But as with all things human behaviour isn't that simple because some choose a lifestyle of lies, deceit and crime, usually for material gain and for no other reason than greed. In 2025, such issues are still at the fore, i.e. the 'Black Lives Matter', campaign. Why do some people think they are superior to others just because of money, race, colour or political persuasion? As my knowledge and life education progressed, I started to formulate an idea of what parenting was all about, and where babies came from. During my early childhood, I also thought that all parents and families in the 50s and 60s were like mine. As mentioned, large families were the norm, with 5 and up to 15 children not being uncommon. With single child families being very rare, with not a crèche, childminder or family support officer in sight. How did they cope? Well, they did and sacrificed much along the way. And although my parents had 7 children, the word sex was never mentioned or discussed. I also have zero recollections of them having, 'nookie'. Hence the cry for sex education as part of the school's curriculum. With schools saying it was not their job, and in future how many more responsibilities would parents abdicate? Time has shown that the answer to that question was many. **Many of today's children seem to know very early on in their childhood much about sex and their parents'/partners' mating habits, but this doesn't seem to equate to any sort of family planning later on in life. Some adults find having just one child to look after, just too much as it was, 'doin my head in, I need a drink to cope'. I never once heard mum say she was, 'stressed out and couldn't cope', even when I was a little teenage sh… She just seemed to get on with her lot.**

During the war, my father was billeted at Gosport, Portsmouth, and after the war he became a tin basher/centre lathe turner working in sheet metal after the war. If such jobs still exist, I wonder what fancy title a ring doffer, tin basher and centre lathe turner would be given today? My father was quite liberal with the leather strap that could be found in the top drawer of the wall cupboard in the front room, if any of the family stepped out of line. In today's softly, softly, don't upset anyone, politically correct, pragmatic society, my parents would have been a definite candidate for child abuse, along with the rest of the adult community I grew up in. In those days physical chastisement was the norm and one of several deterrents to keep off-springs on the straight and narrow as lower, working-class people were too busy trying to survive without sitting down to consider the social implications of their actions. **In today's politically correct, hands off, no deterrent world we appear to have far more, maladjusted, psychologically, emotionally and physically damaged individuals than I can ever remember existed when I was a child. Every child seems to have every ailment known to man before reaching adulthood. With many parents happy to announce the fact on national TV or on their smart phones. Add to this the over- zealous 'do-gooders', who provide a cocktail of excuses for people's miscreant behaviour.** My father's drinking, which would eventually lead to his demise, and seeing him yellow, two days before he died, left an indelible mark on me and, once again, subsequently led to my lack of tolerance towards people who became dependent on, and addicted to, alcohol and drugs. Were the culprits in denial as to its possible adverse effects on society and family life? Which I had first- hand experience of, when I entered the teaching profession. My father killed himself doing what he enjoyed, drinking and smoking, and that was his choice. Carrying his coffin with my other brothers at his funeral, I can't recall what I felt. I certainly was not upset as I was at my mother's funeral. I've subsequently felt sad and philosophical, that I never had any attachment to my father in such a way that the following describes. **"My father stayed with me all night in the chair next to my bed. He refilled my water cup and adjusted my blanket. When I cried out in my sleep, he shushed me and stroked my forehead and told me that everything would be OK."** (Coben H, 2009. Long Lost, PB, 23:222).

Born on the 29th March, 1950, I was one of a family of then two brothers, Jack, christened John, 2/9/39, Barry, 12/10/47, and two sisters, Marlene, 27/7/41, and Lillian, 8/5/44. The remaining brother Stephen, 17/9/52, and sister Janet, 15/11/56, had yet to see the light of day. Some people know what time and where they were born, but 75 years on, despite my best endeavours, I've not yet ascertained either. One of my earliest childhood memories of life at 24 Parkway, was wash day and have vague recollections of going to the community washhouse behind Chadderton baths on Middleton Road. At home we had a tub and mangle in which you could boil your clothes, and then manually pass them through two rollers, worked by turning a handle, to squeeze out the water, with no choice of a wash or speed spin cycle. The clothes were then hung on a pulleyed, wooden drying line that was suspended from the kitchen ceiling. But for large amounts of washing, the washhouse was the place to go. The washing was taken in a pram. Here the clothes could be washed, dried and ironed in large washing machines and dryers, whilst the women had a good gossip. The washhouse being the pre-cursor to launderettes. Unfortunately, I ended up having my third birthday in Oldham Royal Infirmary having fractured my right femur, via a slalom, ski-run on a bar of soap that had been left on the kitchen floor, and as a consequence my right leg became half an inch shorter than my left. Perhaps it also stunted the growth of other parts of my anatomy, who knows, but we won't go there. Whether or not this was the reason I had to visit the health clinic as a child to try and correct me being, 'twine toed', I am not sure, but later on in life I found having a right foot that naturally turned in certainly helped with my footballing skills. To this day I am conscious that I turn my right foot in and still try to correct it. My leg length discrepancy has always been a bone of contention for many a girlfriend, who was tasked with turning up my trousers. Being a 27 inch inside leg, in the days when 29 inches was the shortest leg that could be bought off the peg, meant that my trousers were always too long for me unless I could get them shortened, but my leg length discrepancy complicated the task. However, although I was only 'ickle' and had this problem, I grew up to become a very good sprinter but galloped as opposed to running with text book fluidity. You can now buy trousers with 27 inch inside legs. How good is that? That's progress. But wait a minute who decided and when, having vital statistics wasn't important when it came to buying clothes?

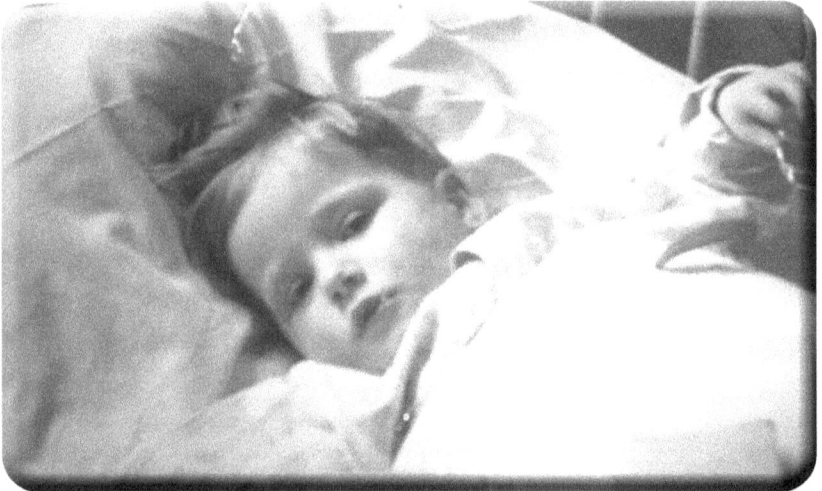

Breaking my right femur and spending my third birthday in Oldham Hospital.

We lived on a council estate in a rented, semi-detached, council, Accrington brick house, at 24, Parkway, Chadderton, Oldham. There was a kitchen, front room, an upstairs toilet, and bathroom, two bedrooms and a box room. My grandma's privy was outside, and toilet paper was courtesy of the local and national newspapers. We had a front, side and back garden. At one point, four boys slept top to toe in one bedroom, my sisters slept in the box room and mum and dad, with baby Janet, in the other bedroom. Such was the closeness of the family community, in more than one sense of the word. I've already referred to the fact that large families were common in the 50s and 60s and some 60 plus years later I can still recall many of the families that lived on Park View, Parkway, Park Gate and Park Field, collectively known as the Park Estate. In those days, if you were lucky, your father might give you a few pence 'pocket money', if you could ambush him before he got to the pub, otherwise you used your initiative, if you had any, to earn a few pence. I would put on 'shows' in the back garden, or have a pavement sale outside our house, and get other children to either come and see the show or to buy your unwanted toys and books. Not that we had very many to start with. Now we have E-Bay and X Factor! Pop from the 'Corona man', and sasparilla, from Johnny Walkers Temperance bar was the nearest thing to alcohol, we youngsters experienced during our pre and early teens. I can recall Monty Python used to enact a 4 Yorkshire Men's sketch, based on poverty and being lucky, with each member trying to out-do the others with their tales of woe. For example, **"You wer lucky, we had to live int shoe box in middle o road." "Luxury, you don't know how well off yer wer. We wer thrashed by ar fathers within an inch of our lives, before we got int shoe box."** You get the idea.

With my 'spends' I sometimes used to buy one green apple, and today I still buy Granny Smith's green apples. I can recall helping my sister Lilian and brother Jack deliver newspapers as it gave me another opportunity to visit private, 'posh houses', not council ones like ours. I eventually delivered papers for Barton's newsagents on Garforth Street, Chadderton, which was miles away, well at least one, near where my grandma Irish lived. My grandma being little and feisty and you definitely didn't mess with my grandma Irish. My granddad Irish being large, portly and definitely Oliver Hardy to my grandma's Stan Laurel in body type. In temperament stakes to me, my Grandma Irish wore the trousers. I walked there and back to Bartons and in between walked my paper round. A distance of at least 5 miles. After a while Barton's let me use a bicycle, which I thought was, 'the bee's knees'. Not that I've ever studied a bee's knees. Not even when I studied Biology at Teacher Training College. Today pedometers are all the rage, so people can tell others how many steps they have walked, whereas in my day walking several miles to and from school, work or just to visit friends was part and parcel of your everyday life. Car, what car? Taxi, what taxi? Bus, OK, but only if you could afford the fare. Fernlea Tennis Club was where I played tennis as a teenager with a girl called Elaine Cash, but more significantly it was where my brother Jack played and where he enjoyed much success with Maurice Mills and Margaret Butterworth, his doubles and mixed doubles partners respectively. The kudos for me playing there was that I was Jack's little brother. Elaine was older than me and because her parents owned the newsagents next to the tennis club, I didn't realise it at the time but I was becoming socially, upwardly mobile. This was long before society understood what becoming socially, upwardly mobile entailed.

But one of my over-riding memories of living on Parkway was of visiting the shops, especially Moore's 'chippy', because I can never recall ever taking money. I was duly despatched by mum with a note to get x portions of chips and after passing me the said goods, Mrs Moore would write on the note a return message to mum, and then make a further note in a book she kept under the counter. Although at the time, I thought this is what everyone did in business, I later realised this was known as **'tick'. A system that was the pre-cursor to the credit card, without the interest.** To this day I never knew who paid off 'the tick', but theoretically it was supposed to be paid off when the main wage earner got paid. In our case James Albert, but as I never saw my father visit any shop, other than the pub, I can only assume all tick was paid off in the local public houses. The chippy also sold tripe, slut and elder, which I was to find out much later in life were the insides of various animals. Whenever I experienced such delicacies, I was told I had to eat it with vinegar, probably to mask the taste. Although as I recall there was very little taste to them. When people recall eating such 'delicacies' they sometimes make gagging sounds, as though they were about to be sick. But to my generation, it was just food, and if that was all there was to eat –you ate it or went hungry. I never recall attending the doctors or hospital with food poisoning. **Today you see parents giving their one, two, three and four year olds a choice of what they would like to eat, and then labelling them fussy eaters.** On the issue of visits to the doctors and hospital in, Chapter 1, Setting the Scene, I looked at the NHS in the year 2024 and tried to find reasons as to why it was on the verge of collapse. Coming to a conclusion that one reason was the interference by people with and in power. But in the 50s, 60s and 70s it was arguably a more simplistic, effective and efficient system. As a child and until I left home at the age of 21, our family doctors were Dr. Lees and Dr.Duthie. The former being male whilst the latter was a female. They had their practice in a large, old house on Middleton Road, Chadderton. If you needed to go to see your doctor, you went to their clinic, sat in the waiting room in the order you arrived. The chairs being arranged in a specific order and when the receptionist arrived, she would go around, starting with the first person to arrive, and write down your details. When the doctor arrived, you would be seen in that order. If 'seriously ill' mum would go to the nearest red, public phone box, and request a home visit. The doctor would come after he/she had finished surgery that very same day. It was so simple and straightforward. No having to book an appointment weeks in advance. No phone calls where you had to press various numbers to get various specialisms, only to then be told that you are number 67 in the Q. No having to wait weeks to get to see ANY doctor, let alone your own, etc. "Good morning, Mr Briggs, how can I help?" "Morning doctor, well actually you can't as I'm feeling as fit as a fiddle." "So why have you come?" "Well 6 weeks ago, when I made the appointment, I was suffering from dehydration, depression, stomach cramps, blurred vision, heartburn, throbbing headaches, and it hurt when I went to try and pee which contained blood."

We NEVER had central heating, double glazing or cavity wall insulation in Parkway, just a coal fire, two gas fires and a paraffin heater. Only experiencing such luxuries after I got married. A hot water bottle to put in bed was something as children we fought over. Getting up in the cold winter mornings to light the coal fire with paper and kindle, was sometimes fraught with danger as the paper that was put across the shovel that had been placed across the fire grate to create a draught, would sometimes catch fire, with the potential to burn everything on the tiled mantelpiece and above. With the least damage being to blacken all in its wake. Putting the trades people on one side, no doubt there will still be some residents that, in true Coronation Street tradition, eat, sleep and exist on the Park Estate today that lived there when I was a child. Have they acquired central heating, cavity wall insulation and double glazing, I hope so. The irony is that some 60 plus years later, I now live in a Residential Park, in Penwortham, Preston, on Park Road with Park Way just around the corner. Is that fate, irony or destiny?

Aunty Lizzie and Uncle Bill, William and Elizabeth McHague to give them their correct titles, were our neighbours but not our real relatives. They just looked after us if mum was not around, and provided us with security, harsh words if we stepped out of line, food, financial help and advice, by giving us a few pence after doing some shopping, and were an integral part of my family's early childhood. Many years later Uncle Bill wrote, in beautiful, cursive handwriting my very first reference for a job at NORWEB in Oldham, when I was 16. Auntie Lizzie suffered from rheumatoid arthritis and was confined to a wheelchair as long as I can remember. Uncle Bill wore a beret, well not all the time, I think he took it off to go to bed, and worked in the offices at Platt's. His beret also made him look slightly French, but the absence of a string of onions around his neck avoided any stereotyping. Not that I knew what stereotyping was at that time. Did he wear his beret in the office? Definitely not.

Today if he did, he would be considered cool and trendy. Platts was a huge firm associated with the textile-cotton industry that was synonymous with Lancashire, and provided livelihoods for many at that time. My brother Barry and my dad also worked there. **Aunty Lizzie and Uncle Bill introduced my brothers and sisters to the concept of saving to buy what you wanted,** by making us save in gold coloured metal, crown, saving jars. The two halves of which were held together with a screw. To further remove the temptation of us trying to remove the crown's contents, by inverting it above your head and using the blade of a knife to slide the coins out, the crowns were kept in a cupboard in Aunty Lizzie's kitchen. At certain times during the year, Whitsuntide, Easter, holiday times and Christmas we would perform the ritual of emptying our crown's contents onto Lizzie and Bill's kitchen table and counting them. This was always an exciting time for me, firstly by seeing how heavy my crown was-the heavier the more money. Secondly, because I felt a sense of achievement, because I had done lots of jobs, made sacrifices, and saved some of my pocket money throughout the year to become 'rich'. At Whitsuntide, you also went around to the neighbours, to show them your new clothes and, if lucky, were given a few pence. The money was spent on birthday or Christmas presents, or was used for spending money if we went on holiday to Mrs Rose's Guest House, on Euston Road, in Morecambe. Spending what seemed half the holiday in Happy Mount Park, as in those days, after breakfast, you had to leave the lodgings and were not allowed to return until tea-time. During retirement, when I started doing casual traffic survey work, I did many surveys in Morecambe and one in particular, outside the York Hotel on Euston Road, prompted a trip to Happy Mount Park but evoked no memories whatsoever. Perhaps my selective memory was kicking in about those days.

Today most of my brothers and sisters are still keen savers, hate debt and **live within their means. A term that is alien to many in today's world. The credit crunch and sub-prime letting scandal would never have happened, if my generation were Chancellor of the Exchequers or ran the country.** We loved going into Lizzie and Bills to play draughts, ludo and such, because **black and white television didn't enter my life until the age of about seven** when Mr and Mrs Brunt, who lived on Park Gate, bought one and I think every child on the estate would go there to watch westerns such as The Lone Ranger and Tonto, Hopalong Cassidy and the Cisco Kid. Uncle Bill also ignited my love of gardening. In retrospect, Aunty Lizzie and Uncle Bill seemed the epitome of a happily married couple. Uncle Bill going to work, coming home and if not spending time with his wife in the house, was in his garden. I can never recall Uncle Bill going to the pub. Aunty Lizzie although crippled with arthritis, looked after the house and made the meals. They never had a car or children and I never asked why. The Briggs's were their adopted family. When Uncle Bill passed away, after going into hospital to have a gangrenous leg removed, which killed him, Auntie Lizzie had to go into various, 'Old Folks Homes', as they were lovingly termed, purely and simply because physically there was no space at 24, Parkway. I remember that she did have a sister, that I once saw but after Uncle Bill's death it was the Briggs's who looked after her. We visited her frequently, and tried to keep her spirits up but she was not a happy bunny. One day when our Jack and I visited her at Hope Cottage in Heywood, she was very depressed and told Jack and I that she just wanted to join Billy. **At that time, I was in my late teens/early twenties, I couldn't understand why someone would want to die. She explained she'd had a good life, loved us all and appreciated us visiting but was ready to go. No amount of Briggs's frivolity could change her mood. Not many weeks later she passed away. For me it was many, many, years later before I fully understood what she meant, and the Euthanasia debate started to germinate in my thought processes and is discussed in later chapters.**

My eldest sister Marlene, who as a child I recall, must have lived next door, with Aunty Lizzie and Uncle Bill, as I never saw much of her at 24 Parkway. Sadly, a trait she carried on when she got married and got older. Her idea of being matriarch of the family appeared to be to distance herself as soon as possible from certain siblings and have very little, if anything, to do with them. Unless of course she wanted something. As I'm aware my sister Marlene has NEVER contacted my younger brother Stephen in 70 plus years to enquire as to his welfare, because she has always viewed him as a loser with nothing to offer her. It seemed we only ever saw her at Christmas, weddings, funerals and Barmitzvas. Made worse by the fact we were not Jewish. I suppose like many children from large families, where personal space was at a premium or non-existent, she probably couldn't wait to escape to a 'better life' or a bigger space. Many years later, not long after Raymond, our Marlene's husband, had passed away with cancer, it was interesting to hear my mum say to me that she recently had never seen so much of her eldest daughter. Was that because our Marlene wanted something, such as sympathy, a hug or a cuddle?

As I grew up, chronologically if not entirely mentally, I realised how living in such an enclosed environment with 8 others would make you want to break free. Cue for a Queen song. I also came to identify individual personality traits in not only myself, but also my family and when I later studied personality at College/University, I was able to classify roughly where each of us approximated in the Briggs/Myer's continuums of introvert-extrovert; stable- unstable, givers-takers, talkers –doers, chiefs-Indians etc. with all the associated sub divisions in between.

I can also recollect a time in my teen years, when the Barlows were considered superior to the Briggs and Dalloways. Our Lilian has admitted that she was just a little envious of her big sister, whose 3 children Craig, Julie and Janine seemed so well behaved, polished and a little superior. Always giving the impression that the Briggs and Dalloways were noisy, crude and lacking in social graces. However, as time progressed and behavioural psychology and the word dysfunctional reared its fascinating, ugly head in my learning curve, I realised the term dysfunctional families could be applied to most families and was only a question of degree. Interestingly our Marlene's three children, Julie, Craig and Janine, like their mother before them, made an early exit from the family home as soon as was humanly possible, never to return, unless serious illness or death entered the equation. Sad, because as children our family's get-togethers at mum's, where the Briggs, Dalloway and Barlow clans collided, always seemed, in my recollections at least, happy, fun affairs. Even into adulthood my rare dealings with Janine, Julie, their partners and offsprings were always more than pleasant, but they always remained on the periphery and appeared aloof. At a distance, they were full of well-meaning platitudes but when they did deign us with their presence, the reality was somewhat different. My last encounter with Janine was at a family do in January, 2023, where Janine's body language informed me that she was unhappy, that I'd chosen to, 'cut out' her mum from my life. Deeming it an inappropriate venue and time to explain my reasons, I invited her and Jonathan to Preston so I could explain. Unfortunately, she craftily asked could she bring her mother to which I replied, no. Although Jonathan took my details and said he would be in touch, I knew it wouldn't happen. Ironic, because Jonathan told me that at that time and for the foreseeable future he was working in Preston. And who says we don't tell lies and are disingenuous? I think it's also pertinent to point out that I felt Janine carried an element of resentment not only towards me, but also her sister, Julie and brother, Craig, for leaving her isolated to care for her aging mother.

Finally, as I entered the world of academia and my knowledge, skills, expertise and not only my qualifications but also life experience increased, our Marlene decided to label me, 'gobby'. But I believe that was only because she didn't appreciate my honesty and playing, 'devil's advocate'. Was she proud of me, I don't know because if she was, I can't recall her telling me. Talking to my sister Marlene was like pulling teeth. You couldn't have a conversation with her because she would only talk about things on a superficial level, and could not be persuaded to change her mind, no matter how powerful a case could be made against her views. **"There is nothing as certain as a closed mind,"** said Dean Spanley. Just as, **"a little knowledge can be a dangerous thing,"** Pope A. **"They say that knowledge is power. But knowledge is power only when it is given away, then it empowers. Knowledge retained is knowledge squandered."**

(Titchmarsh A, 2002. Trowel and Error, PB, 9:58).

My older brother Barry showed certain traits like my sister Marlene in that they both gravitated towards people who they felt would benefit them, for example, my brother Jack, because of what he was supposedly worth or had. When mum died, our Marlene and Barry took on Usain Bolt status by being the first to claim mum's flat screen television. Was this because I am told that my brother Barry, as a youngster, used to follow my sister Marlene around all the time? I gravitated towards my brother Jack not only because of our sporting abilities, but also because of the help and support he gave me, and for the shoulder I knew I could cry on, not because of the material things he possessed. As Barry became older and then met Linda he also, like my sister Marlene, decided to isolate himself from the Briggs family. Another problem with brother Barry, was that he was so hypocritical and always in denial. People who live in glass houses, springs to mind. Perhaps he'd forgotten his drunken exploits as a teenager and relationships with married women as an early adult. He also subscribed to the expression, 'What's mine's mine and what's yours could be mine'. At times, me, myself and I being his three priorities in life. He always had an excuse for not sharing. Again, like my sister Marlene he didn't understand that communication was a two-way process because if he did, he certainly didn't subscribe to it in real life. Once he had met Linda, his wife, he chose to spend most of his time with her family and relatives rather than his own, which upset mum greatly. Linda also came from a large family, I particularly liked her sister Janet, but for some very amusing reason Linda always considered herself superior to the Briggses and by being part of my family she was punching well below her weight. Which at the time, her own could be described as, 'over'. When I first met her, she worked for Hestaire Hope, the educational supplier. She was also a guide mistress, and was well thought of in the work she did for the guides. For me, the issues with my brother Barry and his wife were not a problem. After all, I was best man at their wedding. But in true Barry fashion, he wanted both ends of the stick and the middle by wanting to be kept up to date on the Briggs family news by coining his famous expression, "Nobody tells me anything," whilst spending most of his time with the Peels. But as my brother Jack once pointed out all he had to do was pick up the phone and ask. This involved him being very selective and sparing as to when and with whom he would involve himself in the life of the Briggses. As mum got into her eighties and her quality of life deteriorated, Barry was **shamed** into getting more involved. Just as our Barry would never dream of phoning up his younger brother Stephen to ask about his welfare, because he and my sister Marlene, as previously mentioned, viewed 'our Steve' as a loser. **Social grading at its worst.** Who says blood is thicker than water? Having berated my brother Barry for his one-dimensional approach to life, we were actually quite close in our teenage years and early twenties, so it has been sad but not a hardship for me, to disconnect from him. It helped of course, because I'm not actually sure he was aware we had connected in the first place! He is several years older than me. As teenagers we used to smoke Consulate, menthol cigarettes in a garage on Park Way that we found was not locked when the householders were out at work. How cool was that? There's a pun in there somewhere, menthol-cool!! Never mind. Where we got the cigarettes from, I'm not sure. Our Barry was never short of girlfriends at North Chadderton School, and was one for seeking out adventure, which in the sixties and seventies was the time of drugs, sex and rock and roll. The reader will have gathered by now that referring to family members as our...is a Northern thing. We travelled to many football matches, in my brother Barry's car, supporting our local town team, Oldham AFC. **We went to many concerts together in Manchester, at the Free Trade Hall, never once paying a booking fee, because some materialistic, greedy person in the entertainment business had not yet come up with the idea.** In between girlfriends, our Barry came on holiday with Verna, my girlfriend at the time, and I to Hayle, in Cornwall. I rode on the back of his motorbike to go to the bikers' coffee bars at the other side of Ashton, and he occasionally gave me a lift to football training when I was playing at Oldham Athletic. However, I was so traumatised by the time I arrived at training, it took me a good 15 minutes for my legs to stop shaking. Speed and heights not being my idea of fun. Eventually he moved from two to four wheels, after he built a mini from a basic shell, framework. We frequently visited the Seven Stars in Heywood, to watch Pepper Tree, a pop group he had become involved with. Neil Schofield, 'Scush' as he was nicknamed, also went to North Chadderton, was the 'roadie'. They once played on the radio. Well not actually on top of it. Our Barry was also friends with the Radio 1 and Top of The Pops DJ, Tony Prince. I think he first met him at Baileys' night club in Oldham. I even started up a business with my brother Barry when I was at teacher training college, between 1968 and 1971, selling shirts and ties, hot pants, (then all the rage), nylons, tights etc. I can recall many times I would get on the number 2 or 24 bus at Stevenson Square, Manchester with my briefcase and a dozen boxes of shirt and ties, tied together with string, from the wholesalers in Shudehill, Manchester. Putting them in the luggage space under the stairs of the bus. David Halliwell, a school mate of mine, and my sister Lilian, used to sell a lot of stuff for us. Eventually we had to call a halt to proceedings, as the business was getting too successful and taking up too much of our time, and besides people from our backgrounds didn't go into business. Sir Alan Sugar and 'The Apprentice' had not yet materialised. It's ironic now as I read autobiographies and watch television programmes, about famous and successful people who started from less humble beginnings than myself. Sadly, like my brother Jack and myself, no children materialised from our marriages, although we all wanted children. Eventually we decided that our youngest brother Stephen's contribution to the gene pool would have to do. Although some of his off-springs, especially some of the boys, 'leave plenty to be desired'.

I can't end this section on my brother Barry, without accepting the fact that as he's got older, into his late 60s and 70s, he's slowly made an effort to involve himself more in the family. He now regularly visits Claire, our Stephen's daughter, but I suspect that is only because she can help him with all the modern technology he's acquired. In the past, I offered various olive branches out to him but he declined them. He never attended Heather, my partner's 50th or my 60th birthday celebrations, being the **ONLY ONE** not to RSVP, out of a total of 75 and 68 people respectively. Recently he failed to turn up at my brother Stephen's 70th birthday meal. I didn't ask why as quite simply, I wasn't interested. Dummies, babies and bathwater springs to mind.

My other older sister, Lilian, 'Billie Wizz' or 'Yo Yo', as I affectionately call her, depending on which era of her life you are referring to, or which diet she was on, as she became infamous for losing weight and to celebrate putting it back on by over-eating. Having said that, she has always been the one sister who seems to have been a constancy in my life. As a youngster, she used to take me to the pictures in

Oldham to see films such as, 'The Vikings', with Kirk Douglas. We didn't go with Kirk he just happened to be in the film when we got there. **In those days going to the pictures was a treat, unlike today where for some it's just an excuse to buy an enormous box of popcorn, big enough so that it could be used as roofing insulation for a medium sized house and to help with obesity, and a place to dangle your legs over the seats in front, and use your smart phone, to text and twitter etc. with a blatant disregard for anyone who went to actually watch the films.** Definitely, not cool. She eventually met Jack, of the Dalloway variety. A larger-than-life creation standing six foot five and a half inches against my sister's five feet, or is it foot, and a bit. I suppose, one means you can have five feet as opposed to two and the bit being either a plus or minus half an inch. In 2016, she informed me that she'd 'lost' the bit. 'Jack the Lad', has always been involved in driving for a living, with involved being the operative word, as he always seemed to find a way to play the system to earn a few extra pennies. Something I realised as I got older and entered the workforce, many people were guilty of. As for myself I found school stockrooms a haven of temptation and was sometimes guilty of pilfering the odd piece of chalk. Unfortunately, as society has progressed some, or is that many, people have become more sophisticated, or should I say greedier, in how they play the system and the crime of deception and stealing has become a way of life. This book giving many, many examples of this and so Jack's misdemeanours now seem trivial in comparison. I will never forget being very excited, yet nervous, when I accompanied him on a coach trip to York Races, and I was ushered through the 'free turnstile' reserved for drivers. The look on the security man's face as this teenage runt standing at five foot five was allowed to enter, because, according to Jack, I was his relief driver. My feet didn't even reach the pedals, let alone drive the 52-seater. I could wax lyrical as to my trips and exploits with Jack, but have been sworn to secrecy. As for his relationship with my sister, whilst there have been a few stormy passages, they are still together growing old and grumpy in retirement. Sadly, as aging started to take its toll and the body started to deteriorate and pay you back for all the abuse, cancer and a variety of ailments have taken their toll on both of them. Also, as Jack has gotten older, he's become synonymous with the expression, 'How Much?' and the joke that he'd gone to Poundland to see if there was a sale on. Which for me personally, I found it both sad, yet annoying, that everything, became related to money. It became the yard stick by which life and its occupants were measured. It wasn't that our Lilian and Jack were on the bread line, but they covertly started to resent people, who were enjoying the fruits of their labour, not to mention their financial planning. It wasn't my fault, that she became pregnant in her teenage years and her and Jack didn't adequately, financially plan for their old age and retirement. Life is all about choice. When Jack found out I was having my second book published, he asked how much it had cost me and what royalties I was getting, NOT, well done, Jim. Which brings me nicely onto their two children David, the eldest, and Gary, who both attended St Martin's School, on Fitton Hill, at the same time that I was attending Teacher Training College. Being part of a large family meant, I was never short of individuals to use as actual case studies and I chose David and Gary as part of my child development module. It was obvious early in life, that they were chalk and cheese, which is fairly common when there are only two siblings in a family. The finished written piece, which is now in the hands of Jacqueline, Gary's wife, caused a little upset at the time for my sister, because of its findings but time has shown that much of what I wrote then was fairly accurate. Both ended up as drivers, a common thread in the Dalloway clan, as is money, but that is where the similarities end. I sadly don't see them very often, especially since I moved to Preston, because as we all know, Preston is a very, very long way from Oldham. I seriously cannot recall exactly how many children David is a biological father to, or how many he inherited. I also cannot recall how many partners he has had, but Jack, his dad, seems pleased with his latest, as she has a large, posh house! He had 2 girls, Rachel and Laura with his first wife, Susan. He then met Nicky who had children, before David added to his and her gene pool. When that relationship ended, he moved in with Tracey, who also had several children. Rachael lives with Ryan and they have 3 children Chloe, Casey and Harvey. Whilst Laura is married to Andy and they have 6 children, Harmonie, Livia, Conner, Ava, and the twins, Codie and Logan. With one growing up to look like Ed Sheeran. Gary on the other hand, drives for the NHS but in the past has wanted to do various jobs. He once had private tuition from me to try and pass the police entrance examination and why that ambition never materialised, I'm unsure. He worked for GOTODOC, driving doctors around, who are called out 24/7. He also part owns and coaches at a Martial Arts Centre in Oldham. He has produced two children, Jennifer and Karl. Jennifer, who has a degree in Nursing, is married to Anthony, and they have a little boy, Jack. Whilst Carl, who is excelling in his job in engineering, lives with Helen and they also have a little boy, Lucas. Our Lilian informs me that Helen has been good for keeping Carl on the straight and narrow. Jenny, apart from nursing has a cosmetics business and I am told, she frequently posts pictures of herself on social media, looking like Barbie doll, to promote her business. From conversations I've had with various members of the family, I get the impression she is very materialistic and self-centred. As I have not seen her for many years, I cannot pass personal judgement. Again, as with David, Gary and Jacqueline I have never had any personal issues with her. Her husband Anthony is also not without his critics, looking like a terrorist, Taliban fighter. The last time I saw Carl and Helen was at a family wedding several years ago, when Helen very bluntly told me she didn't approve of, or was it couldn't understand why, I was still seeing my ex-wife for lunch several times a year, especially since Dee had re-married. Why a nicotine junkie, whose present relationship was not without its peaks and troughs, deemed it appropriate to castigate me, I am unsure. Perhaps she wanted to keep me on the straight and narrow. But everyone is entitled to their opinion, and at least she told me to my face. I was not invited to her wedding in October 2023. Dee is my best friend because, as far as I'm aware, she is the only person, including family members, who has never stabbed me in the back. Which is a rarity in a society that struggles with honesty. I am one of many who. in the past, has had issues with our Lilian's view that she couldn't retire to spend more recreational, quality time with Jack because the National Health Service needed her, which is a nonsense because **NO ONE IS INDISPENSABLE.** Eventually coming to the conclusion, that she was either in denial or she needed to go to work because that was her comfort blanket. Staying on at work with all its stresses and strains, especially when you had been diagnosed with cancer at the age of 41, just for the private health insurance seems a perverse, bizarre never-ending spiral, eventually ending in death and then what good is the private insurance? Or perhaps there were other reasons. I re- visit the topic of retirement in Chapter 7. **However, I am more than a little appreciative of both our Lilian and Jack for sharing a part of their lives with me and my partners.** I know Jack had his favourite, Verna. All I've ever wanted out of life, apart from winning the pools and lottery, was acceptance, a smile and a hug. They have given me much more without asking for anything in return. Was this bond because I held our Lilian's hand when she went into labour, in her bedroom in Webster Street, whilst Jack rushed to the nearest public, red, telephone box to phone for an ambulance. **How did we ever cope before all this modern technology? Quite adequately, thank you very much.** Whilst I am proud of my academic achievements **what my sister Lillian and Jack Dalloway gave me in terms of attention, a sanctuary and general life experiences, was priceless and intangible. Thank you, I am indebted to you both.** Unfortunately, as mentioned as they have become older, the expression, 'It's alright for you', has again reared its ugly head, with money and materialism being seen as the passport to health and happiness. Sadly, as my sister's health has deteriorated, I think she is realising that no matter how much money, the number of pension plans you possess, and the possessions you have, it matters not one jot as your body ages and gives you pain. Which brings me onto my eldest brother Jack, christened John but ALWAYS known as Jack, he was and always has been my kindred spirit. My earliest recollections of following in my big brother's, or not that big, footsteps are of watching him play football and cricket for Chadderton Grammar School. The school was then located on Broadway, Chadderton. Today a new Academy has taken its place. **It's an indictment of the divisive nature of political intervention that many Grammar schools were phased out because they were considered elitist but have since been replaced by a system that has Academies. So named because the title conjures up images of high standards and elite education for all, but in essence are just re-labelled Comprehensives. Old wine, new bottles.** I was always known as Jack's little brother and so everyone always appeared huge to me. Our Jack not only played football for his school but played for Chadderton, Lancashire and had trials for England Schoolboys. The first two feats I was to later emulate, although I wasn't aware of at the time, the significance of these achievements. **In today's over inflated world of football, which is riddled with superlatives, our Jack would be worth many, many millions of pounds because he had this rare gift of being able to kick with both feet. Many 'modern day' footballers are so one footed it's embarrassing.** In those days approaches from clubs who had an interest in signing youngsters, on schoolboy forms, made contact through school and home. With usually a personal visit in the case of home and/ or a visit to your school. Financial inducements and such were not allowed, but as with all things in life, there were ways to overcome the restrictions. I remember one club in the Midlands were very keen to sign our Jack and offered him return, train tickets to Birmingham, with tickets to watch that city's team play. Eventually, our Jack ended up at our local club Oldham AFC, which in those days, and unlike today's football teams, had a high percentage of home-grown talent. Being older than me, I never played at Oldham AFC with my brother, but eventually realised my ambition when we both played for a local amateur team George Dews FC. By then, our Jack was carving out a career at the CIS, Cooperative Insurance Society, and studying for various insurance qualifications, and had long ago abandoned the thought of a career in football. He was persuaded to sign for the amateur club, Dews, by his then father-in-law, John Tierney, whose daughter, Christine, my brother Jack had married. Ever since I have known her, she has been a diabetic, which over the years has caused more than a little concern. I believe this was the main reason they never had children because Chris suffered several medical traumas. **A shame, because in my humble opinion, they would have made brilliant parents because they were brought up with the morals and values of a society that accepted its responsibilities. Unlike today's, who are more than happy to abdicate or delegate them.** My brother was a very irritating person to have as your brother because I **NEVER** met anyone who had a bad word to say about him. From work colleagues, neighbours, strangers passing in the street, to sporting mates, they all talked about my brother in glowing terms. No one is that goody, goody. Oh yes, they are. It makes you want to vomit. On his 70th birthday, as a joke, I composed a book to try and dispel the myths, but sadly no one would believe me. In truth he is a very generous person and was always quite happy to throw you the keys of his brand-new Rover or Lexus in case you wanted to have a test drive. We still have disagreements as to who is paying for 'the round' when we meet up for a drink. He used to wind up my brother Barry, when it came to leaving a tip in the restaurant. Our Barry would calculate, to the exact penny, what 10% of the bill was whilst our Jack would just throw a note on the table that was always in excess of this. Seeing our Barry's face at his brother's folly was worth the admission fee alone. He now plays golf and has been known to return home with the odd trophy for his prowess in this domain. If he entered Strictly Come Dancing, he'd probably win the bloody thing!! Sorry for swearing. Incidentally Kelvin Fletcher who won Strictly in 2019 used to live near to and played golf with my brother Jack before he became a farmer. You may have gathered that my rhetoric is not driven by envy or jealousy, but by admiration for someone who never moaned or complained about his lot in life but just got on with it, and reaped the benefits of his hard work and endeavours. However, as he's got older his crown has started to slip, and he is joining the rest of us in being a more opinionated, grumpy, old man, with at least one racist friend whose thoughts on immigrants leave plenty to be desired. My younger brother, Stephen, like us all, has his faults, sadly he is homophobic and a racist, although he would strenuously deny this, because he has a closed mind on many issues related to race, colour and gender identity. Sadly, he is not alone as there are others in the Briggs and Dalloway clans who share his views. He also pontificates about a whole raft of subjects related to life and white supremacy, and whilst everyone is entitled to their opinions, his are based on very scant and at times non-existent, empirical evidence. Having highlighted the negatives, he is a genuine grafter and worker and has feelings and emotions just like anyone else. Unfortunately, he has been stigmatised as being the only one of the children in the family who was just like his biological father. But it's not his fault, that my father chose to share more of his genetic disposition with him than the rest of his boys. There are many stories of our Stephen having to be rescued from himself, but that's what you have brothers and sisters for, isn't it? However, I can't recall spending much time with my brother Stephen, when he was very young. One such rescue was when he went into the army when it was blatantly obvious that he didn't have the skill set, temperament or personality to deal with the psychotic, sergeant majors he would encounter, whose job it was to dehumanise him and condition him to kill. Is it any wonder he ended up in prison. But experience can only be acquired by doing, so undeterred off he trundled to Gamecock Barracks, Leicester, Junior Gunner Briggs, 24138897. Unfortunately, things didn't work out for him and so it was decided to go and see his commanding officer to see if we, my brothers and I, could 'buy him out'. We did get to see him at his passing out parade, but if I recall he got home quicker than we did. It's called going A-wall. Upon his return to civvie street he met and married an Irish, alcohol dependent nurse, who had a strange outlook on life. **Life owes me** seemed to be Anne's mantra. Forming a relationship with someone who drank was not good for a boy, whose father died from sclerosis of the liver. They lived in Ireland for a while, but had to return home because of, amongst other things, the IRA troubles. Their 5 children, the production of which my brother, Stephen Paul, blamed on Guinness, went to Bare Trees school where my friend John Tobin was the head and John used to wax lyrical about Anne's distorted views on education. Anne didn't think children should attend school on their birthdays, and so, she kept them at home. Bugger the lost education. Eventually the relationship with Anne deteriorated to such an extent that a parting of the ways was the only solution. He met Denise after a brief relationship with a lady called Margaret. Initially Denise talked frequently of her ex-husband, Dougie, and over time I found out she had an older sister, Maggie, a brother Dennis, a son in the RAF, Dave and two daughters Vikki and Tina. Denise lost her brother Dennis after a long illness and unfortunately, Denise, like her brother, could never claim to be a fit and healthy individual. Which was surprising as she didn't drink or smoke. Sadly, whilst waiting for a liver transplant and an operation to clear a blockage in her stomach, she passed away on 27th August, 2018 aged 62. Our Stephen still infuriates me, as probably I do him, and at times my patience gets tested, but I still love him. He has been diagnosed with DVT and sleep apnoea, has put on quite a bit of weight after he eventually 'stopped' smoking and 'cut down' on his drinking. He still gets angry when he is accused of being just like my father, but at times seems to have conscientiously or unconscientiously adopted my father's philosophy. If I have to go, I'm going with a smile on my face doing what I want to do. In March 2019, I invited him to accompany me to Nice to celebrate my birthday, and in May 2019, he accompanied me to Rio de Janeiro. Since then, we have re-visited both places and a few others, besides. For both of us it was company, a chance to share and an opportunity for some brotherly bonding, which I had not done with my younger brother for quite some time. I'm pleased to report, a good time was had by all, and whilst I have questioned his views on a whole raft of subjects, and at times he has regurgitated some of the facts I have given him, he is what he is. He also takes the time to come and visit me in Preston, and occasionally buys me 'thank you gifts' which I have always appreciated. He is now in a friendship with a 'young lady' called Irene, who has grown up children of her own. As for his children Mark, Andrew, Jason, Lee and Claire, it's difficult to know where to begin as pre and post hormones, the stories of their exploits came thick and fast. Claire, his daughter, produced a son Noah with David, but sadly, the relationship failed and she now carries the label of single mum. She then had a brief fling with a tattooed footballer, then a relationship with Lee, who had a son and together they have a little girl called Isabelle. In spite of her parent's drinking and self-destructive nature, Claire has always showed loyalty to them and ironically won an Asda competition when she was at primary school, writing an essay about how good her mum was. Unfortunately, she has her parent's temperament and volatility which occasionally rears its ugly head. She has moved on from Lee, and has formed a relationship with Andy. Watch this space. Sadly, I have lost Claire to her smartphone. As for the boys, well boys will be boys. All I will say is that Jason is my godchild, and I failed lamentably in my duty of care as a godparent. They too are all in relationships and have offsprings, therefore increasing the Briggs' gene pool. As I've said my family had to occasionally rescue our Stephen from his impulsive actions and views, but I can never recall anyone having to rescue my youngest sister Janet, other than when she'd been ill. She was born at home, whilst my eldest sister Marlene, who was then 16, and dad sat on the stairs awaiting the arrival of number seven. When my brother Barry came down stairs and saw my newly born sister he asked, "What has mum got a doll for?" Ah bless.

I can't recall much about our Janet's early years, other than she attended Chadderton Hall Primary School and was taught by Eric Harrison, a very good friend of mine. Like our Jack, she attended Chadderton Grammar School on Broadway, and I used to drop her off in my hand painted, battleship grey, Morris Traveller, my first car, on my way to Mather Street School, my first teaching post. How cool was that, Janet? Luckily in those days just having a car was enough to establish, 'street cred'. Other minor details were over looked. The fact that I sometimes had to jump out of the car, lift the bonnet, and hit the petrol pump with a hammer because it had flooded was immaterial. Before meeting Rick, her husband, my sister once went out with a boy from Leeds, called, I think Duncan, who travelled over the Pennines on a motor bike. To this day, she claims her brothers frightened him off as we were protective of our 'younger sis' fraternising with a biker, who drank beer and supported Leeds United FC. I personally cannot recall such behaviour, and put it down to selective memory. She eventually met Rick, who hated to be called Richard, and after a spell living off Westfield Street, Chadderton they moved to Chichester, West Sussex. Before moving South, she worked at Wilson's Brewery, Manchester. I don't specifically know what she did, other than it was in the office, but I definitely know she was not a drayman or should I say person? What are they called today I wonder? I think she met Rick at the dole office in Failsworth, where she worked, and the rest is history so to speak. In Chichester, she worked for the Police and Courts, preparing the paper trail for cases to go to trial. Rick, has a brother Phil, who is married to Carlotta, who also lives down South. Rick, before ill health forced him to take early retirement, worked in the benefits office. He is somewhat of a hypochondriac, computer wizard as well as being a very accomplished photographer. Our Janet is the born carer in the family, and has dedicated her life to ensuring everyone is looked after, including myself, irrespective of the fact that you might not want looking after. She has a steely determination, and at times, you wonder if she is listening. But that is a Briggs trait, we all like to think we are Chiefs not Indians. She just wants everyone to be happy, but sadly, that cannot always be the case which, to be honest, at times has caused family frictions. Unfortunately, as Mark Billingham points out, **"Sometimes people get confused, especially social workers, between caring and meddling."** (Barred 2004, 9:206). **Sadly, just before this book was due for publication, she meddled once too often and asked me, if the family had a right to reply to its contents, without having read one single solitary word of the manuscript.** She doted on my mother, who obviously could do no wrong, and so phoning up the family from hundreds of miles away with instructions on what was needed to be done in Chadderton regarding mum etc. at times, lit the blue touch paper for some, especially our Lilian. Our Janet is still trying to keep us all on the straight and narrow, and I love her for that, but the meddling has become more of an issue. The world needs people who care, and are not guided by selfishness and greed. She told me that I once nearly made her cry, by calling her the carer in the family. But why has she never made me cry by giving me a hug and a cuddle, and telling me she was proud of me and my achievements, irrespective of my faults, other than retrospectively? Our Janet upon retirement from the police and judicial system, had various part time jobs, before securing a position in charge of a Community Hall in the centre of Chichester. In true Janet tradition, embraced her role with gusto. It was her domain, and she treated all jobs from cleaning the toilets to making hire bookings and looking after the visitors with the same care and attention to detail as I have come to expect from her. Her craft hobby of making her own cards and jewellery, also keeps her more than occupied. When I decided to hand over my legacy of organising the annual family, Warner's trip, I had no hesitation in asking my sister Janet. **In today's very volatile and not very nice world, it's nice to know that there are people like my sister Janet and her partner Rick who seem content with their lot in life. They don't drive and don't hanker after an overload of materialistic things.** Don't get me wrong, they would like to win the lottery and wouldn't say no to more money, but as they live within their means they don't appear to wear stress like a badge, as most of the younger generation today do. Sadly, as she has got older, as with the rest of us, her personality traits have become more intense. She watches your lips move, but doesn't fully engage in the listening process, concentrating on trying to instil only her views on how life should be lived. As her experience of life is somewhat limited, this can be galling. As I entered my 70s, I started to wonder why our Janet contacted me, as I'd lost track of the number of times I'd invited her and Rick to Preston only to be predictably presented with yet another excuse. I'd also lost track of the number of times she had travelled North to visit family with no invite for me to join my brothers and sisters. Just like Craig Barlow who never wanted the Briggses and Dalloways to be part of any rare visits to the UK, when he flew in from the Cayman Isles. Obviously, our Janet and Rick had their reasons, but sadly, they have never been honest enough to tell me. **Just like my sister Marlene and brother Barry, her family values had become somewhat distorted.** When studying not only my own but also other families, I've found it fascinating that chromosomes from the same DNA could produce offsprings who could be the antithesis of one another. Finally, it is said that during life everyone has 2 families, the one they are born into and the one they acquire during life's journey. The latter being considered during the remaining pages.

More Childhood Nostalgia.

During the writing of these memoirs, I've alluded to Alan Titchmarsh's autobiography and Our Kid, by Billy Hopkins, published in 1998. The latter being a delightful evocation of a Northern Lancashire boyhood, very similar to my own. Nostalgic, sad and funny, it recalls an upbringing and an environment now almost vanished when mills poured their bile into the rivers, and belched their filth into the skies. Well, perhaps not everything has vanished. Global warming was not an issue. John Osborne's, 'Don't Need The Sunshine', 2013 is another nostalgic look at seaside holidays in the 50s and 60s. 2nd June 1953, was Queen Elizabeth 1 coronation, on the 29th May, 1953, Edmund Hilary conquered Everest and on May 6th 1954, Roger Bannister broke the 4-minute mile record. In 1958, the 'Busby Babes' resided at Old Trafford until the Munich air disaster put an end to many of their careers. In 1963, Kennedy was assassinated and Lee Harvey Oswald became famous. Penny arrow bars, Vimto lollies, jubilees, jammy dodgers, aniseed balls, that when sucked could be used as lipstick, Beech nut chewing gum, gobstoppers, Uncle Joe's mint-balls, Murray mints, 'too good to hurry mints', was the catch phrase for the advert, cap guns, Swan Vesta matches, treacle, sugar, jam, lemon curd, sauce and dripping, (chip fat), butties, sorry sandwiches, dumpling and jam, a rare treat, and Waspi belts abounded. There was and still is Shippam's paste in pots, so small it was difficult to see how anyone could cover anything other than a slice of bread with its contents. There were midget gems that are now going to be re-named by M&S as their name might cause offence, (12/1/22). Oh yes, there was Camp coffee, no comments please, a thick, brown, liquid sludge that you made coffee from. Was this why I was never an avid coffee drinker until I turned 60? When I was about seven, my parents rented a black and white television, in those days renting was the norm. Years later, I can remember that on sunny days, my brother Jack and I balanced the TV on a chair in the front garden, just under the front window, and putting the clothes horse around it, covered in blankets and towels to stop the sun shining on the screen, so we could see the picture whilst sunbathing. The wires and aerial we ran through the window. Obviously, this only worked if the sun was in the right place. Crazy, but true. Did we ever consider what would happen if the television fell off the chair. I don't think so. TV and radio programmes such as Quatermass and The Pit, 1958-59, Hopalong Cassidy and The Cisco Kid, The Lone Ranger and Tonto, famous for Tonto's address to his partner, the Lone Ranger, being, 'Kee Mow Sabbi', Andy Pandy, the Flower Pot Men and Sootie. Who can ever forget Johnny Morris, the 'Hot Chestnut Man', who complemented his story telling by bringing the animal characters in his stories to life, by having a myriad different, individual voices for each one. Each voice giving the animal an individual personality. Brilliant. Did I try to mimic him when, as a teacher, I started reading stories to children, you bet I did? On the cartoon front, courtesy of initially Paramount Studios and then Warner Bros, we had Loony Tunes with Bugs Bunny, Road Runner, Pixie and Dixie, Mr Magoo, Top Cat, and the most violent of them all, Tom and Jerry. Disney also provided us with Popeye, Bluto and Olive Oil which introduced us to spinach in a tin, the green vegetable that supposedly gave you super human powers. Yogi Bear and Boo Boo, The Flintstones and Andy Pandy. Not forgetting Muffin the Mule, and Noggin the Nog, voice over courtesy of Oliver Postgate. All of which in their own ways had subliminal messages in their content about life's ups and downs. Then there was The Beverley Hilbillies, 1962-1971, which was the story of a family of hillbillies, the Clampetts, who struck oil and ended up living in Beverley Hills. Talk about fishes out of water, but a very innocuously funny programme. Although I was only 12 at the time, Ellie May Clampett, the daughter, still made my blood pressure rise. Did I say blood pressure? You get the idea. Finally, its relevance to today is that it provides a stark contrast as to how relatively, 'poor people', who come into money, deal and view their good fortune. Buzz Hawkins, who created the fictitious Bradshaws, a northern family, consisting of Alf, his wife Audrey and son Billy, with his mate 'sken-eyed' Michael, became very popular on both radio and television in the late 60s and 70s because it just oozed nostalgia for people of that generation. Buzz is still doing the rounds and in 2015, with an automated Billy, in the early days he was just a dummy, I went to see him in St Helens and it was instant nostalgia that took me back to a time of austerity, yet simplicity. A time of playground rhymes and games, accompanied by clapping and skipping. Are the last two activities still allowed or are they too dangerous? Rhymes such as, 'Rain, rain go away, Come again another day'. Not knowing that the rain didn't need to be asked to come again, as in Lancashire it never seemed to go away in the first place. Then there was, 'Here comes the bride forty inches wide. Here comes the vicar forty inches thicker. You had to knock the church down to get her bum inside'. Today that would definitely not be allowed with the offending pupils, sorry baby goats, being sent to a penal colony in Tasmania. Conkers was a game where you hung your conker on the end of a piece of string, and then you took turns with your opponent to try and smash to smithereens each other's conker. Obviously, this was a very popular playground game at a time of the year for girls, and boys in autumn when conkers were bountiful. I believe this activity is now banned in schools, unless goggles and gloves are worn, because it contravenes Health and Safety and litigation might become an issue. Obviously, some greedy parent might sue the school because someone had psychologically damaged their sensitive off-spring by beating him/her at conkers. Or perhaps two inanimate, brown objects being swung at one another, was considered racist or too violent. Or perhaps the two combatants gave each other black looks during the game. Sorry off-white looks. **Today we have 'soaps', with Coronation Street being the choice for many Northern families, to help deflect away from their own problems, by seeing how other families deal with the stresses and strains of everyday life.** I recall when it first came onto our black and white television, and I enjoyed watching it, but remember vividly the time when I decided I wasn't going to watch it anymore, and that was when it announced it was starting a ratings war with East Enders. At the time, Coronation Street was an attempt at a fair reflection of life, 'Up North', with funny as well as serious story lines, that was not to be taken too seriously because life, Up North, was grim enough, but didn't involve the whole of it happening on one particular street that provided your every waking need, i.e. food, drink, your next job, sex partner or house. But once it started to compete with East Enders, in my humble opinion, one of the most depressing programmes on TV, the story lines started to border on the ridiculous, with blacks, whites, homophobics, paraplegics, racists, sexists, heterosexual, homosexual, paedophiles, depression, anxiety, many forms of abuse and court cases etc. all squashed into and onto the screens, to not only win the ratings war, but also to avoid any criticism from any bias against any persuasion or denomination. As mentioned, East Enders for me, is one of the most depressing programmes on TV because over the years when I have had the displeasure of watching the odd episode I HAVE NEVER WITNESSED A HAPPY EPISODE. The cast are either crying, screaming at one another, fighting, having sex with anyone within shouting distance, trying to commit suicide, threatening one another with at least death, or taking each other to court, lying, cheating etc. and I often wonder what effect the programme has on lonely, depressed, mentally ill people? East Enders should come with a government health warning for people of a nervous disposition, or those who are having mental health issues. **In retrospect, perhaps all soaps do attempt to represent today's society and in the past, I have not wanted to accept its honesty, because it was just too depressing.** Cardinal red liquid paint and donkey stones were used to clean the front step of your house, with the latter being obtained from the Rag and Bone man in exchange for old clothes. Cardinal red was usually associated with people higher up the social ladder, or those who aspired to do so. The Rag and Bone man travelled around the housing estates on his horse and cart shouting, "Any old rags, any old rags, or, any old iron?" In fact, there was a song by Lonnie Donegan entitled, 'Any old iron?' I suppose this was one of the earliest forms of re-cycling. Everything in those days was re-cycled, long before it became a multi-million-pound industry and charity shops became big business. Hand me downs and left-overs within families, and between families was not uncommon. Donkey stones, the name coming from the logo of the manufacturers found embossed on the stones, were popular in the 50s and 60s and their use died out in the late 1970s. The stones known as scouring stones were composed of powdered stone, bleach and cement. There was also a man who frequented the park at the bottom of our street, who would give you pennies for various bits of scrap metal. **In the year 2025, he would probably be given the label dropout, tramp or even paedophile for hanging around parks, but we just saw him as a scruffy individual who was trying to earn a living.** As many people, certainly those on the council estates, didn't have cars it was quite common in the 50s and 60s for the trades-people to ply their trade, door to door. People then either went out into the street, or went to the door to buy or pay for goods and services. Apart from the rag and bone man there was the rent collector, coal man, insurance salesman, bleach man, Eddie Wilmore, the grocer, the bread man, and the Corona soft drinks man. **Today all the major supermarkets offer home delivery, as though it is something revolutionary and new, and all those trades people would be labelled sexist by referring to themselves as man and not person.** The fact that I never saw a woman enter our cul-de-sac trying to sell, probably because it was their role to stay at home and raise the family, was a sign of those times. In the 70s, there was a popular television comedy called Steptoe and Son, which was about a father and son who were rag and bone men in London. In 2017, Rag and Bone Man topped the charts with a song entitled, "I'm only human after all". I wonder if he got the idea of the name from the TV programme? I can recall collecting tea coupons out of packets of PG tips tea, long before monkeys stole the limelight with their TV adverts. Also, some goods offered picture cards with their products and these you could 'swap' at home and school, to try and get a full set of say birds, animals and trees. The educational value of these sets being, in my opinion, significant. Although at the time, this was not considered. I also recall getting a metal, golliwog badge after collecting tokens from marmalade jars. Today, that would be totally unacceptable. Every family had a Co-op store number, ours was 11540, and periodically the family could collect their 'divi',(dividend). This was years before loyalty cards and bonus points entered the scene. I also recall occasionally going to one of my father's mates' houses, on a Sunday morning to get my hair cut, rather than visit the local barbers on Middleton Road. On a more confessional note, I stole the odd toffee from the Pick and Mix in Woolworths on a Saturday morning, when the assistant turned her back. I also stole apples and gooseberries from gardens in Birch Avenue Chadderton. Both gave me stomach ache as I tried to eat all the evidence as quickly as possible because if I got caught with it and the fruit was covered with my finger prints, that would ensure I got sent to jail for my criminal behaviour. Not forgetting the sadistic past time of putting salt on slugs, and watching them shrivel up and die. Definitely, a hanging offence in today's world. Yes, I know hanging has been abolished. On a lighter note, I helped the milkman on his rounds in exchange for a bottle of orange juice, and delivered leaflets for the local councillor who lived on the Park Estate. This was good practice, as I returned to delivering leaflets, the yellow pages and the phone book, when I retired in my mid-50s. **However, today I want nothing to do with councillors and politicians.** I can recall having an uncle, who was a joiner, and cousins called Peggy and Edith. These memories coincide with the smell of baking fresh bread in mum's kitchen. These relatives used to periodically visit Parkway, and bake with mum, who was not a Sewing

Bee, Masterchef or Bake-Off material. I recall trips with the family to Chew Valley in Grasscroft, Saddleworth, made famous by the Myra Hindley murders, where we had simple picnics, a jam sandwich and drink, and where I stood on a piece of glass and cut my foot. I remember going on my first holiday without my parents, brothers or sisters to Beaumaris on the Isle of Anglesey. It was with Terry Glynn and his parents. My brother, Jack, should have gone but for some reason he didn't and I took his place. We stayed in a cottage at the bottom of a field in which there were cows and many cow-pats. You walked through a huge wrought iron gate to get into this field. Every morning, we went to the farm to get fresh milk. I also remember visiting Beaumaris Castle. As I've said, we had quite a relatively large garden which afforded my brothers, sisters and me, with not only a refuge in which dens and cars could be made with chairs, blankets and clothes horses, but also a place to develop our imagination, interests and talents. I can recall building such dens with a boy called Melvyn Biggs. Melvyn used to live near my Grandma Irish on Garforth Street, Chadderton. Such a garden also provided my brother Jack and me with our own Lord's cricket pitch, albeit dirt, which we used to cover in plastic sheeting, if it rained and our own Wimbledon tennis court. On the side wall of our Accrington brick house, we drew a chalk line, which represented the net. The wall also provided us with a rebound surface from which we could practice not only our hand and eye co-ordination for tennis, but our football skills. The constant rebounding sound against the wall must have been a nightmare to our neighbours Aunty Lizzie and Uncle Bill, but as I recall they never once complained. Well not to me, they didn't. The dustbin, clothes horse, etc. were used as fielders or opposition players. Imagination is a wonderful tool when children, with very few possessions, are left to their own devices. **Sadly, today many are enveloped in so much Health and Safety and materialism, their imagination is directed and stifled.** With regard to play areas, Titchmarsh, in 2002, had this to say. **"They are carefully constructed to remove any danger. Parents feel much more secure as a result. Shame really. We seem to have crafted a childhood influenced more by the threat of litigation, than by the need to grow up and be able to take a few knocks."** (Titchmarsh A, 2002, PB, 4:24). Meanwhile, indoors we developed our speed, hand and eye co-ordination, by trying to catch the mice that regularly visited our kitchen from the field at the back of our house. The park at the bottom of the cul-de-sac, where our house was situated, had a football pitch on which my brother Jack and I and our various friends would spend hours, come snow, wind, rain or shine, playing football and practising our football skills. In my teenage years, footballs were made of leather with a rubber inner. Once blown up, with a bicycle pump and adaptor, the nipple part of the rubber inner was forced inside the leather casing which was then closed and secured with a leather lace. During a game, if you were unfortunate enough to head the ball on this part of the football, you not only had an indentation in your forehead, but you also experienced a sharp stab of pain. **If still in use today, every time a footballer headed the ball, they would have to leave the field for an HIA, head injury assessment.** To prolong the life of your case ball and your boots, and make them waterproof, dubbin could be used. This was a form of grease, similar to Vaseline gel that my father used to put on his hair. Later, when screw in studs entered the sporting arena, my brother Jack and I had to select which set of studs would be suitable for that day's ground conditions. For us this was highly sophisticated stuff just to play football. When not playing football we supported Oldham Athletic FC, who played at Boundary Park, and in the home supporters stand, the Chadderton Road End, we would chant, along with thousands of other fans, zigga-zagga, zigga-zagga, oiy, oiy, oiy. Which as all Northerners know, was a tribal chant to encourage your local team to play well. I now believe, because my friend Ed Whalley is incensed by the fact, that the Chadderton Road end is now the domain of the away supporters. Not forgetting that the club, along with many others, is owned by some foreigner, who it could be argued, knows very little about football, and has taken over the club as a means to use its losses to off-set his tax bill. As previously alluded to, with encouragement from my Uncle Bill, my interest in gardening started to germinate. Sadly, as my hormones started to take control, I can recollect wanting payment for my efforts in our garden, or I would withdraw my labour. Was this my first experience of capitalism? Well, no not really, because as a youngster, I remember being paid one penny for collecting empty mineral bottles. Some of my teenage years proved troublesome to not only my family, but also certain teachers who tried to instil some semblance of education and order into my troubled, rebellious, testosterone driven person. My mother, on more than one occasion, saying that she would, "swing for me one of these days".

Me in our back garden at 24, Parkway.

Please note the absence of Waney Lap or Close Board fencing. Again, at the time, I hadn't a clue what that was.

Which exemplified the anger and frustration she must have felt towards me at that time. And although as I got older, I asked for her forgiveness for those wayward years, I publicly repeated my request during my eulogy at her funeral, and those words still haunt me in my lonely, isolated bubble in Preston. Just off Burnley Lane there was a pond, known as Red Cot, and despite some recent research, still don't know why it was called that. Today it would probably be designated, 'an area of biological or scientific interest'. But for us, it was one of the places we could go and collect frog spawn in a bucket which was brought home so we could watch this semolina like, clear gunge, with black dots in, turn into little tadpoles, then frogs. I can recall spending many hours playing, 'over the lea', which was a piece of land behind Thompson's farm on Burnley Lane, Broadway. It was a valley through which ran the River Irk, and I used to follow vole tracks in the grass, build dens and ambush people who walked past, as I played the part of the local gunslinger in my head. Running with one hand held out front, supposedly holding the horse's reins, whilst the other slapped my buttocks. Or my 'fanny' as the Canadians call the bum. A 'fanny pouch' being a 'bum bag'. All of which was designed to simulate riding a horse, and being the Lone Ranger, Kee Mo Sabby! Oh, the joy of living in your own dream world. **Today most children, along with their parents, live in the manufactured cyber, synth world of their mobiles, where individuality is virtually non –existent because the content is universal.** Later when I attended North Chadderton School, we had to run through the Lea as it was part of the cross-country course. When I took up running, I also used to run through there, before they built the connection to the M62 motorway. As I've previously alluded to pre-M60, Thompsons Farm at the junction of Burnley Lane and Broadway was also there, and where Kathleen Thompson and her sister lived. Both were older than me, and so attended either my elder brothers' or sisters' schools. The Travel Lodge Inn and pub now stand where the farm used to be.

The Hampshire family also lived in the cul-de-sac on Parkway. There was Victor, David, of throwing a slate at my brother Jack's head fame, and 'Birdie' Hampshire, whose boyfriend was called Ralph. I used to go pellet gun shooting with Victor over the cemetery wall, which separated the cemetery from Chadwick's Dye works. To climb and walk along the wall was part of your rite of passage into adulthood, but for me it was another experience that made me realise I had a fear of heights and whilst I would climb and walk along its turrets, I did so, feeling dizzy, nauseous and decidedly not happy. David, who always appeared to be a loner ended up working as a mechanic for Oldham Transport and this was not surprising, as he always seemed to be messing with engine parts etc. Victor ending up as a postman and working with my brother Barry, at the Oldham postal depot, after my brother stopped working at Platt's Textiles. Mrs Hampshire, who lovingly could be described as a battle axe of a lady, not to be messed with, could often be seen berating one or both of her boys for some misdemeanour. **Unlike many today, she certainly did not shirk her duties in accepting responsibilities for her children's wayward behaviour, and she certainly could not be accused of being in denial, as to the true identity of her offsprings. She never blamed others.** Oh, happy days! Another childhood memory that actually is still evident today, is the visit of the travelling fair or circus that usually came several times a year, setting up on the local recreation ground. The former offering rides, whilst the latter offered a show in, 'The Big Top'. The rides comprised of, dodgems, waltzers, and caterpillars, as well as stalls where you threw darts at playing cards, or shot at tins with an air rifle to win either a goldfish in a plastic bag full of water, or a cuddly toy. Or you could try and hook a duck as it floated past in a channel of water. Sometimes, you could throw at a target with a hard ball to win a coconut. Roll a penny was one of my favourites, a variation of which, is now a popular game show on television known as Tipping Point. Sometimes there were freak shows to see people, for a price, with various abnormalities and disabilities. All this enveloped in an atmosphere of flashing lights and loud music. It was an intoxicating place to meet other like-minded souls. Today freak shows are absent, and animal welfare is high on the agenda. **Now that's progress in a positive, caring sense.** We still have Pleasure Beaches and visiting fairs and circuses, the sophisticated version of such is Cirque du Soleil. As a youngster I always enjoyed the lead up to bonfire night. Apart from building dens in your own garden we built community dens, with the wood and skips from the local mills, in the shape of a wigwam, in the field at the back of 24, Parkway. Inside such dens, that afforded some privacy from prying parental eyes, we could get up to all sorts of mischief. Especially, if a young lady could be enticed inside. I recall getting into serious trouble one day, when I was caught red handed with a girl inside our bonfire den. What we were doing was something along the lines of, 'you show me yours if I show you mine'. I also persuaded a girl who was in my class at St Matthews, to also play the game, this time in the fields after school. These episodes being my early experiences of sex in the great outdoors. Night time sorties to other bonfires, to try and steal their wood, were particularly exciting. Bonfire night itself, rockets, Catherine wheels, rip raps, sparklers, bangers and fountains, that you had saved your pocket money to buy, were fascinating and exciting, but they soon disappeared in a whizz, whoosh and flash of colour, in less time than it took to go to the shop to buy them. Today, firework displays are an integral part of the entertainment industry, and are on a much grander scale, usually supporting a classical, music concert in a park, or as part of a pop stars set. The smell of fire that pervaded your whole being for days after the event, was also an olfactory sensation that I can still recall. The blackened potatoes that had been thrown into the glowing embers, and then risking first degree burns to try and rescue your potato before somebody else stole it, were particularly strong memories. The potato's charred exterior transferring itself onto your face, to encircle your mouth like a black and white minstrel. The Black and White Minstrel Show being a very popular television programme that ran from 1958 to 1978, where white showbiz people blackened their faces and whitened their lips and eyes with make-up, and sang popular, creole songs of that era. Today, it would be considered totally unacceptable and very politically incorrect. Just as getting metal gollywog badges to wear from collecting tokens from Robinson's marmalade and jam, would definitely be considered sexist and racist. **But in those days, people just got on with their lives and accepted the entertainment for what it was, a song and dance programme, and not some exercise in microscopic, racist, sexist scrutiny. As I was aware very few people took offence and the BBC switchboard was not overloaded with irate viewers.** I was only aware of Mary Whitehouse and her supporters objecting to such issues as excessive swearing, nudity and sex on the television. I am not trying to justify these issues, and society has been diligent at dealing with many racist, sexist issues but the question I ask myself is, **in 2025 is society any happier, with all this political correctness, or has it become more stressed in having to be mindful of every single thing it says and does?** I think not, as many people now encourage stress, and wear it like a badge, thinking that it portrays them as very important people. Walking, jogging or cycling past Chadderton Park to the canal, besides which stood the vinegar works, at Mills Hill, with its distinctive smell, still evokes an olfactory memory 60 years on. Also, getting to the canal involved going passed the Corona, fizzy drinks factory. **In those days, as far as I was aware, hyperactivity and attention deficit disorder were not the issues as they are today, because society didn't knowingly overdose its children on sugar and perhaps more significantly, children were far, far more naturally active and encouraged to be so. Fizzy drinks for the Briggs family were something of a treat and as mentioned, the Corona man would visit your area periodically to sell such drinks.** Which brings me to a gentleman named Arnold Saville, who lived on Bamford Street, Chadderton, around the corner from Taylor Street, where Hilary Mather, my first, teenage love, lived. Arnold had lodgers, the names I cannot remember but one couple used to make my tea, and pay me a few shillings to take their washing to the launderette on Burnley Lane. I'm unsure what the equivalent would be in today's currency but again any pennies earned in those days were appreciated, and treated as though you had become very wealthy. There was a sense of value in many things related to my childhood. **Unlike today's instant gratification, easily disposable society, where much is expected with very little appreciation, and many people are never content with what they have.** The husband worked at the iron foundry/steel works in Manchester.

His wife was a big lady, both in stature and height. Sometimes, I bought a cream cake, whilst the washing was on its spin cycle and this would take the edge off my appetite, which was criminal on my part, as the meals were delicious and of a much superior standard to the ones prepared at 24 Parkway, sorry mum. Arnold Saville was a bachelor who worked at Park Cake Bakeries, which was one of the main suppliers of cakes and biscuits to Marks and Spencer's. I think he may have been in the navy prior to that. Many years later, I worked at Park Cake Bakeries for a month when I left the teacher training college, just before I took up my first teaching appointment at Mather Street Junior School in 1971. Arnold's house was always full of boys and occasionally girls. In today's world, you could either label him a social worker, or a paedophile. In retrospect, he was both. My brother Barry and I would go and stay for the weekend, with mum's blessing after he'd once visited our house on Parkway and spoken to her. My dad would probably have been at work or in the pub. How and why, he visited 24 Parkway in the first place, I've been unable to find out, and what the conversation was about when he visited, I have no idea, but from then on, visits and holidays were allowed with Arnold Saville. He used to take boys on trips where we stayed in caravans. Incidentally, I can recall trapping my finger in the carriage door of a train at Werneth Station on route to Blackpool with Arnold Saville. I don't recall having stitches, but I do recall having my fingers wrapped in a handkerchief. For years after, I had a scar. Sometimes, you would share Arnold's bed, and be encouraged to show your appreciation for what he was giving you. I, like many of my generation, was full of bravado, but very naive and so at the time it seemed a small price to pay for a holiday away from your parents. He also liked you to say thank you by cuddling up to him on the settee and kissing him. Looking back and writing this, it all sounds very sordid and in hindsight, it was, but at the time, he was a guy that let you stay and use the facilities of his house, and took you away on trips previously not experienced. There was also a chance to meet girls there. From the perspective of a young boy, coming from a large family who had very little material possessions, this situation seemed a good deal. As for the experience, it didn't leave me psychologically scarred for life as I grew up to be a perfectly healthy heterosexual. I can't speak for my brother Barry, as I have never discussed this period of my life with him or anyone else. In fact, it is only since writing this book, that the significance of those times has struck me, and I have never had the desire to want fame and fortune by 'outing' Mr Saville. I have also spent a long time wondering, whether or not I've wanted this part of my childhood to become common knowledge. **It's ironic, now that his surname is synonymous with paedophilia and all things deeply disturbing.** Was he related to Jimmy of DJ fame, I don't know and have no desires to dwell on this part of my childhood, as this is the first time I have ever revealed this part of it to anyone? However, once I understood what, 'catching the other bus', 'batting for the other team', shirt lifter, mincing and being effeminate meant, I realised that there were a few times in my early childhood, when I was in the company of such people but at the time thought it was just part of life's rich tapestry and all youngsters experienced such. Ignorance was not so much bliss, as an opportunity to experience. Later, when talking about football per se, I mention the coach Barry Bennison who is now serving life sentences for sexual misconduct with young footballers. As teenagers on a Sunday afternoon, John Hall, Kenny Dronsfield and I would walk to Johnny Walkers Temperance Bar on Broadway, for a glass of sarsaparilla and two ounces of salted peanuts. Before rushing home to listen to 'Fluff', Alan Freeman, famous for the expression, 'Hi there, pop pickers', going through the top twenty records in the music charts. At the time, this was super cool behaviour and the equivalent of being Clint Eastwood in a Dirty Harry movie, just before he took out his gun and asked the punk to make his day. On the issue of super cool, I possessed a white, PVC, three quarter length coat as a teenager that I wanted to wear come rain or shine. How I acquired it, I have no idea but it was my equivalent of a leather jacket because there was no way in my lifetime, at that time, would I ever be able to afford a real one. I would have loved to have had a photo of me in my jacket, but sadly photography was not part and parcel of everyday life, as it is in today's selfie obsessed society. So having a camera and taking photographs for posterity was a rarity for me as a youngster. I am pleased to say many years later, I owned a black and brown leather jacket. Get you, Briggsy! My earliest recollection of stage fame was, when John Hall, Kenny Dronsfield, myself and several other individuals, who I cannot recall, 'performed' in a school hall, at a scout Jamboree. I curled my lip, perfected my hair quiff, cupped my groin and mimed to Living Doll, by Cliff Richards, whilst the lads imitated the infamous, signature moves of the Shadows behind me. If only Britain's Got Talent and X Factor were around in those days, who knows what would have happened. Yes, I was in St Matthew's scouts for a while, and earned several badges for tying knots, first aid and making a fire! Whilst in the scouts, you could attend the annual Jamboree, a coming together of the different troops. The exciting part being you camped out overnight in Tandlehills Country Park, a few miles from where I lived. Unfortunately, for some reason, probably financial, I was not allowed to stay overnight so I would travel up to Tandlehills, on my bike, and spend the day in camp. As some of the tracks leading to the park were very stony and rutted, falling off your bike and getting punctures was always a possibility. As with most children, finding out how fast your 3 gear Sturmy Archer bike could go, was always exciting, especially if you could emulate some speedway or motor cross hero. Unfortunately, on one particular occasion, as I hit a large stone I went straight over my handlebars and virtually somersaulted to the ground. Spectacular, but painful. Did I cry, was I bruised and battered, was I bleeding? Yes, and more. Did I survive, well obviously, but I did have to push my bike all the way home, as my front wheel was buckled? I now watch the Tour de France on television and wince when there is a crash, recalling my own personal mishaps in that department. Bradley Wiggins and Geraint Thomas eat your heart out.

People who are born during a certain time in history, say that was how it was and it is no different for me. For all generations it's a case of dealing with the day-to-day circumstances that presented themselves, and how you overcame them, believing that all families dealt with life just like yours did. I distinctly remember ironing my clothes on Sunday night in preparation for school the next day and putting a crease in my shorts. Why, I hadn't a clue I just did. Didn't everyone have a crease in their shorts? On many an occasion, I was left to my own devices, which meant I either copied or made it up as I went along. If what I did, didn't get me into trouble I carried on doing it. Of course, like most children, I got away with things that I thought or knew were wrong but at some stage I had to pay the price for my indiscretions, as there were suitable deterrents., such as a, 'clip 'round the ear'. Sadly lacking in today's world. Also, I don't remember there being a naughty step as I was growing up.

What has happened to family values?

Sadly, very few, if any, of the values that mum and her generation brought her children up to respect, don't exist anymore and if they do, they are certainly not extolled as the way forward. As well as the word children, the word respect seemed to have been devalued and under used. Today's society is big on rights but not so hot on responsibilities. Mum had 7 children, not 2.5 as sometimes quoted as the national average and exercised her responsibilities, to bring them up without a crèche, childminder or support service within a million miles of 24, Parkway. I've often wondered how can you have 0.5 of a child? Parkway was no easy street, but a place where we never went hungry (well most of the time we didn't) and we always had clothes on our backs, even if the hand-knitted, swimming trunks ended up below your testicles as soon as you entered the water. We never wondered where mum was, or when she was coming home, or what, or who she was coming home with. She just seemed to be there. Her mum and dad were around, but in those days a grandparent's role in simplicity, was to pass on society's agreed values, help and advise their children in the vagarities of childrearing, and periodically spoil their grandchildren at their convenience. **The problem today is that we as a society can't agree on anything, and the grandchildren are usually spoiled, being over burdened with materialistic garbage, before the grandparents can exert any influence. To repeat, "What my children want my children get," is not a good philosophy if related to materialism.** Mum's philosophy was the same as it was for all women of her generation. I have chosen to bring them into the world so it's **MY** responsibility to love, care, educate, chastise and develop them to the best of my ability. **Not some stranger, sporting a posh title.** She also exercised her responsibilities to live within her means, without the aid of a bank account, loan, mortgage, credit card or parents, that she could turn to for a financial handout, or free babysitting duties. In fact, my mum thought that the credit crunch was a form of breakfast cereal, and would probably have thought the same of Brexit. In mum's day there were shopping catalogues such as Kays or Littlewoods, from which purchases could be made and then paid for, at so much a week. She must have been under considerable daily strain to make ends meet, but never once threw a sickie or screamed, **"You're doin my hed in."** In fact, she hadn't a clue what a sickie was, as they hadn't yet crept into the public's lexicon. On the 14th August, 2010, at 0220 hrs when she passed away at the age of ninety, she didn't have one, single solitary penny of debt; didn't own a credit card or a bank account, and left several thousand pounds to pay for her funeral. She didn't possess a mobile phone, and never once had she abandoned her children to go away on holiday. She hadn't a clue where the nearest nursery, childminder or crèche resided. What a claim to fame in today's abdicating, troubled, debt ridden, greedy, jealous, two-faced, envious world. I miss her for many reasons, and on many levels, but expressions such as, "He's a bad bugger, I've had seven but none are as bad as him/her," which she would utter, whenever she came across a newspaper, radio or TV item depicting a local or national miscreant, are etched in my memory bank. She was also famous for her expression, "I've always wanted one of those," and in her later years when such requests were denied, she would sulk. The fact she already had at least more than one of those items was immaterial. **"All of us do it to some extent, embellishing our recollections to conform to one agenda or another, whatever it may be."** (Case J, 2001. Trance State, PB, p252). Academics refer to the 'half-life of facts' because over time what we know now, will become obsolete/untrue. New research, better technology and a greater understanding, will always question what was believed in the past. Also, whilst trying to recall my earliest recollections, it's very easy to slip into the time honoured tradition of saying, **'It wasn't like it woz when I wer a lad'**, no matter how true. To be honest, despite all the changes and progress, some of which has been necessary and at times beneficial, **I have NEVER MET anyone in my life** that has said, **'Today's world is a much happier and safer place to live in than when I was young.'** Without getting into too deep a sociological debate my childhood, whilst appearing very carefree, was in actual fact very structured because there were agreed values in society and boundaries, so you knew what you could and could not do, and where you could and could not do it. It was also an age of relative innocence as you groped around in the dark looking for answers. You got to understand that your actions had consequences and there were also deterrents, if you transgressed. At times, like all children, I transgressed, just to see what would happen and eventually realised it wasn't worth the effort. Today with the breakdown of agreed values in society, where there appears to be no boundaries, resulting in moral decay and social unrest, there are very little, if any, effective deterrents. Lots of empty threats and political posturing, but no meaningful deterrents. Over the years I've been bored stupid, hearing yet another parent say, "If you do that again", with no resultant follow up. Probably because they couldn't spend the time away from pecking, tapping, swiping, scrolling and trolling. What has happened to the rule of 3 when, after the perpetrator has transgressed twice, a suitable deterrent was implemented? My generation had very little early on in their lives, but appreciated what they had. Today, so much is taken for granted and not appreciated, leading to greed, selfishness, and dishonesty. In fact, for many these traits are seen as a genuine way of life. The more they have the more they desire –there never seems to be a saturation point of having too much. In my opinion, the politicians and do-gooders with their political correctness and desire to curry favour, whilst trying to please everyone, which is never going to happen, have helped destroy the fabric of society. Television programmers haven't helped by making so called reality programmes showing the least desirable aspects of human behaviour, under the guise of catering for all ages, genres, tastes and predilections. I suppose their argument being is that you don't have to watch them, but if the name of the game is viewing figures, then I can't quite see the logic in alienating vast swathes of the aging population. Or is that just another example of discrimination against the elderly? Psychiatrists always try to blame and relate childhood experiences on most things that are negative in people's lives, but if a comparison can be made with my physical, sensory and emotional childhood experiences with today's children, which for many consists of staring at screens, tapping keys and swiping battery operated gadgets, whilst being driven here, there and everywhere, at the same time as being overdosed on sugar and junk food, it's not rocket science to see where the problems lie. Especially in relation to the multitude of labels regarding their health issues. With many parents only too pleased to announce to the world, via any form of media available to them, how many labels their child had been given, to justify their behaviour. Finally, because of postcode gangs, knife crime and abusive parents, today it is a far more dangerous world for children to live in than it was when I was a schoolboy. In 2004, the Children's Act, first implemented in 1989, was updated to make it easier for local authorities to step in, when they knew a child was at risk. In February 2021, the total of children murdered by abusive parents was, yet again, on the increase, the total at that time being 69. (Geraldine McKelvie, Investigation Editor for the Mail, 20/02/21). What's happened to the expression, 'When you are young the world's your oyster?' Now the world is anti-social technology.

Early Childhood Educational and Religious Influences.

My total memories of all my time at Primary School are episodic and sketchy, which is usually a sign of not enjoying something, but for me that was not the case. I may be corrected by my elder brothers and sisters, but I have no recollection of being dragged screaming, shouting and crying, to be deposited at the main gates of St Matthew's Primary School, on Burnley Lane, Chadderton. I generally enjoyed most of my schooldays up until I left Secondary education at the age of 16years, in spite of minor blips and hiccups. I probably saw my first school as an adventure because in those days and at the age of five any journey over half a mile from home was exciting. As the school was C of E it was right next to the church and therefore religious festivals usually involved a trip by the whole school, to the church. Why a church school, as I cannot ever remember religion being an integral part of my childhood? However, when I eventually qualified to become a certified teacher at the age of 21, I understood all about catchment areas, denominational and non-denominational schools and the issues surrounding entrance into these establishments. In the 1950s these issues were not as fiercely contested as they are today in 2025. Although during my educational journey, in spite of what many researchers and in fact, parents claim, my experience showed that up until the advent of multiple car families, parental choice was usually based solely on location. I also remember as a teenager attending Garforth Street Methodist Church with a lad called John Hall, whose father was a Methodist minister. At that time, I hadn't formulated any definitive views on religion, other than to associate going to church with meeting girls and an annual trip to the seaside. When it came to that time of year, when the annual church trip to the seaside for the children of church goers was imminent, it appeared as if the whole world had suddenly been converted, seen the error of their ways and had all seen the light! **This early cynicism towards religion, and all things related to brain washing stayed with me the rest of my life.** Whenever I've watched 'Songs of Praise' on television, with churches filled to the rafters with a congregation singing its heart and soul out, with the odd individual acknowledging the camera as it panned around, the word hypocrisy sprung to mind. Because whenever I'd attended churches, when the television cameras were not present, I could count the numbers in the congregation on one hand, with the Catholics having more cars in the car park on a Sunday, than other religious groups, whether the television cameras were there or not. But I suspected that was more to do with the fear of retribution, hell and damnation, instilled by the Pope and his mafia, than trips to the seaside. These political manoeuvrings to get your child on the annual seaside trip, was of absolutely no consequence to me. I also thought that Catholics had more money than non-Catholics because they could afford cars.   At St. Matthew's Primary I once carried the cross in church, probably because it was my turn, or was it because I was told it was an honour? For me it was just because I enjoyed singing? Later in a school report I was described as an enthusiastic member of the choir.

Early Sporting Prowess and the Therapy of Exercise.

As a child, like most other children of my generation, my brothers and sisters walked to school. And once in school, we would go on Nature walks with the teacher. Since those early days, I've continued walking for pleasure. As transport was mainly buses, with very few cars around, I'd run to catch the bus, or run to and from the shops. To be frank, even when given bus fare, which was rare, I would run from stop to stop, trying to beat the bus before it arrived, and pocket the money to buy sweets, a cake, or a piece of fruit. To be fair, the amount of traffic on the roads during the 50s and 60s was minimal compared to today. I cannot recall very many obese children attending my Primary or Secondary School. Overweight occasionally, obese not so sure. **Who decided and when, that children had to be chauffeured everywhere, whilst staring at a computer, swiping a mobile, whilst eating junk food, by shovelling spoonfuls of sugar down their throats, constituted a healthy life style? Oh yes, it's because of the nasty people that exist today, as though such people have suddenly appeared on the scene. It's not as though today's society is unaware of the dangers of such a lifestyle.**

Over the years, no matter where I was in the world, walking was, and still is, an essential part of my holiday. The jogging started as competitive running, as early on in my time at St. Matthew's Primary School, I remember being successful on sports days, despite being one of the smallest in class, whether or not it was in a sack, skipping with a rope, or carrying an egg and spoon. Unfortunately, as soon as I realised the eggs for the egg and spoon race were not real, I dismissed the idea of trying to steal them, to take home for mum to add to the weekly shop. However, I have no recollections of being tied at the ankles with another pupil, to participate in the, 'three-legged race'.

Is such a practice still allowed in Primary schools in 2025 or would it be considered a paedophilic, S and M practice with the teachers involved being brought to boot for their actions? My footballing skills were discovered and developed at St Matthew's where every playtime, Briggsy could be seen dribbling a tennis ball around the school yard, pursued by a posse of boys and some girls, trying to avoid collisions with others playing skipping, hop scotch or just wanting to do less physical activities such as coloured stone crushing. Which involved grinding down small coloured stones, with a larger one, to create a kind of coloured salt and pepper. The fact that even junior sized footballs were nowhere to be seen, was more to do with the reality that no one could afford them, rather than they were banned. I loved games periods when the teacher would bring out wire baskets which contained 'real' footballs. The fact that they would come up to my knees, and if asked to trap and control one I could easily be knocked off my feet, was only a slight problem to be overcome. I have a vivid recollection of playing football in the fog against St Marks School. Mrs Patterson, the Headmistress, **walked us there,** a distance of at least a few miles. We never had a PE teacher, let alone a male presence in my Primary School, and so I think the boys in the juniors picked the team themselves, based on their playground prowess. Obviously, the boy that provided the tennis ball at playtime was in the team. By the time I became a PE teacher in Primary schools, men had infiltrated this mainly female domain and specialist teachers could be found dotted about the Primary Schools in Oldham LEA. Up until then, I think the male species felt that teaching any child younger than 12 was a slight on their manhood. On the issue of playing football in the playground with the girls as a child, was simply something that occurred but because society at that time was conditioned into the 3-tier class system and gender roles were clearly defined, the boys just laughed at the girls in their attempts to kick a ball. Throw and catch yes, but kick, no. Little knowing what an issue, women in sport was later to become and what that threat to male chauvinism invited. In the past, several people have commented that I had a complex about my size. I could at this point go into an aside that size matters and little gems are priceless, but I won't. Today it would appear that all playground games to develop physical prowess, not least hand and eye co-ordination, are banned unless the pupils, wear suits of armour. **But don't forget, even if you wrap children in cotton wool, you run the risk of suffocating them.**

Some of my teachers at St Matthew's, who ensured you learned your tables by sometimes poking you in the small of your back if you faltered, and made a mistake, would be guilty of a whole raft of criminal offences today, but whilst I don't condone violence per se **it didn't** leave me psychologically scarred for life, and I did learn my tables. Today adult, 'celebrity contestants', are asked on the television programme, Weakest Link, December 2021, what is 6x7 and struggle to give an answer. One female contestant was asked, "How many beds would you find in a twin room?" To which she replied, after some thought, one. And she wasn't playing for laughs, but to raise money for charity. Talking to many of my Catholic friends who were taught by nuns, violence towards pupils was an integral part of their education. **In the history of education, the three Rs were an integral part of schooling, the irony being that two of the three, arithmetic and writing, didn't begin with the letter R.** In my class were the Barrat sisters, I think they were twins, with round, smiley faces and red, chubby cheeks who lived on a farm. **Today, they would be a brilliant advert for an alternative healthy lifestyle spent outdoors, as opposed to one spent indoors glued to a TV, computer, game boy or smart phone screen. Also in those days, prison was a massive deterrent to erring off the straight and narrow, even for children and not seen as free board and lodgings and a free Master's Degree as it is today. All in the name of rehabilitation. In 2025, if a comparison is made with what law abiding, elderly**

people are entitled to from the state and what they have to pay for, after a lifetime's contributions paying tax and National Insurance contributions, and what prisoners got, all paid for by the tax payer, just for being a criminal, there would be a strong case in itself for a crime against humanity. If state entitlements could be reversed with prisoners paying from the proceeds of their activities and the elderly getting most, if not all, of what criminals got for free, what a much fairer society we would live in. It's not rocket science to see why certain elements in society are labelled habitual criminals and certain elements in society make crime a career choice. St Matthew's was where I was first made aware of the term suicide, after a boy in our class didn't turn up for school for a few days and the rumour going around school was that he had committed suicide, whatever that was. St Matthew's was also where I experienced my first kiss, from someone who was not a member of my family. I say from but that is an exaggeration because one day, whilst waiting outside the classroom, I ran up to a girl in the queue, named Wendy Robinson, and tried to plant a kiss on her cheek. Well, some people do say that the sooner you start to perfect your life skills the better you become, but at that time in my life becoming a gigolo was not on my radar? I never did find out why Peter took his own life, unlike Brian, our neighbour, who ran straight under a car whilst playing, 'Knock a door run away'. Brian is back left on this infant school photograph and looking at my old school photographs it surprises me how many names I recall. Looking directly at the photograph, and starting back row left, my classmates were; Brian Duffy, Graham Wolstenholme, Janet Wroe, Jennifer Jackson, I can't recall the next girl's name, Graham Walker and Graham Hilton. Next row down starting from the left as you look, the wonderful Wendy Robinson, aka 'stolen kiss', Graham Cordingley, I can't recall the name of the next pupil, my good self, John Boardman, the next three boys I can't recall and finally Dorothy Dodds. The next row, as you look, right to left, the first two girls I can't recall, Audrey Hilton, I can't recall the next, Sylvia Yates and finally, the Barrat twins. On the front row, left to right, I don't recall the first boy, but the other two were Kenny Bridges and Charlie Allen. It's interesting looking at a much later photograph of my school friends at St Matthew's, not only from the point of view of physical development but also any additions and omissions. I appeared to have lost the Barrat twins and acquired a certain Vincent Eyes.

What's App Ened? Or What The F... Was All That About?

Again, starting back left: Brian Kay, whose parents owned the ironmonger's, Graham Hilton, Vincent Eyes, Graham Walker, my artistic saviour in Paul Hesketh's art class at North Chadderton Secondary Modern School, Paul Hegginbotham, whose parents owned the butcher's, Graham Wolstenholme and John Boardman. John becoming one of my best friends at North Chadderton. On the next row was Kenny Hughes, who I now suspect, suffered from dwarfism but at the time I just considered him as being little, which, next to Master Butterworth, who as you can see enjoyed his food, the difference in size being exaggerated. Next was yours truly, Master Briggs, who loved wearing a tie, even if a suitable shirt was not available, and having a 'quiff' as part of his hairstyle. Then there's Jennifer Jackson, who together with Dorothy Dodds, sat in front of her, were two of the tallest in the class. Next came Graham Cordingley, David Halliwell and I'm sorry, but I can't recall the last pupil. David Halliwell lived across the back field from my family. Upon leaving school, he secured a job as a drayman, with Lees Brewery, and to this day, still works there. On the front row, were Audrey Hilton, who became a nurse, Sylvia Yates, Janet Wroe, who became a district nurse, Dorothy Dodds, Miss Goodyear, Wendy Robinson, aka 'stolen kiss' and Gillian Griffiths. You will notice that Wendy had taken on a more European, Spanish look as she got older. It's interesting to note several things in relation to the photographs. Both of which were significant issues when I myself became a teacher. **Firstly, the difference between chronological age, related to your birthday and physical age, the age related to your physical development at that time.** Whilst it was a fact that our birthdays were all within a certain chronological age, we differed greatly in size and stature. **Research shows at 10/11 years there can be as much as 5 years difference between the two.** The other significant age is developmental age, which related to sociological and psychological parameters. Secondly, the class sizes on the photographs are interesting because in education this was always an issue.

Research in the 70s and 80s had shown that an optimum size in primary school, that was beneficial to both pupil and teacher, was 25-30. Class sizes in excess of that, meant that the social implications of teaching became more of an issue than the educational ones. And that the larger the number of pupils in the class, over 30, the more the teacher was just babysitting, and trying to be a social worker instead of being an educator. Teachers are not trained to be social workers or expert behavioural psychologists, but today in 2025 that is primarily their role, dealing with many issues related to a dysfunctional society.

Early on in my career when I taught, 'problem children', i.e. slow learners, educationally subnormal or special educational needs, depending on what label the powers that be at the time deemed appropriate to give them, the class sizes were kept relatively small because discipline, classroom control and individual attention were more of an issue than in the 'normal classes'. However, the issue of labelling pupils, which I experienced in all my 35 years of working in education, was more a political initiative than an educational one. On the 20/5/21, the BBC aired a documentary, Educationally Subnormal: A British Scandal, which was about categorising, stigmatising and labelling certain pupils as educationally subnormal in the 1960's and 70s. With almost twice as many coloured immigrants as their white counterparts being given such a label, with very little, if any, objective criteria to justify such. The ramifications of such are still being felt today, as the never-ending debate on racism and discrimination continues. The 1981 Education Act abolished the category, to later replace it with the term Special Educational Needs, (SENS). In my experience categorising children, who possibly needed 'extra help', was a double-edged sword. On one hand it could be seen as educationally good, by identifying children in need requiring specialist help, but on the other hand, bad, as some parents didn't like their offsprings to be separated from their peers and labelled, 'not as clever as the rest'. Their words not mine. As for class sizes in my primary school teaching career, class numbers between 25-30 were rare, with my last classes, before I resigned in 1987, being in excess of 40 pupils. **When I later worked as a lecturer in Higher Education the same issues arose where, 'bums on seats', each bum being worth money, became more important than the quality of education.**

The room at the top of the stairs at St Matthew's was an early recollection for me of my fear of heights. The room being where we had story time, but sometimes, we had to wait half way up the stairs for another class to exit. To me that was the equivalent of looking down from Blackpool Tower, not that I've ever done so.

Who can forget the visit of the 'nit nurse' who visited schools to rummage through each child's hair looking for head lice? If detected, the chosen one would be sent home with a tube of shampoo/head lice cream to destroy the little buggers. Once home, my mother, or one of my sisters, would frequently run a comb through my hair, and if any nits were found they would be crushed between their thumb nails. **Although phased out in the late 1980s and 90s, can you imagine if this infringement of civil liberties occurred in 2025? Front page headlines, six o'clock news, a storyline plot in the soaps, and a guaranteed slot on Loose Women. Greenpeace would be fighting for the rights of the head lice, Social Services would be investigating child abuse, and the nurses involved would at least be looking at a custodial sentence or being stoned to death.**

In the 1950s, urban sprawl was not an issue as Chadderton was quite rural, certainly not inner city. In summer, I frequently took a shortcut home from St Matthew's across the farmer's field. In the summer and autumnal months, we would play for hours hiding and 'tracking' in these fields of corn. Sting, the musician, later sang about such fields, but not particularly the ones in Chadderton. One of my final recollections of St Matthew's, is of waiting at the school gates for others to arrive in the morning to see who had passed their eleven plus exam, and were going to Grammar School. I was not going because it was rumoured, I had failed my entrance exam on purpose, but recall not being too disappointed, as my parents, as far as I was aware, didn't put my brothers and sisters under any pressures to succeed. Today in the year 2025, with reference to parental expectations, the expression, 'trying to make a silk purse out of a sow's ear', springs to mind. As the psychologists point out, success and failure in people's lives can usually be attributed to early influences, but as I've mentioned, my brothers and sisters' subsequent successes and failures were based purely on individual and personal endeavour, rather than excessive, early parental pressure, guidance and ambition. In retrospect, we were never burdened with the fear of failure, with the only pressures coming from a society that was geared to the three-class system of upper, middle and lower. You may have noticed there is no mention of my sibling's attendance at St Matthew's, and that's because I have no recollection of seeing any of my brothers or sisters there. Perhaps they skipped Primary school and went straight to Secondary, which are now known as Academies. Yet another label to give the impression that implies, pathway to excellence. What was wrong with Grammar, Modern and Technical that categorised children based on their academic and technical/practical potential to succeed? As the next chapter on my educational journey will show, my Secondary Modern education certainly did not hinder me in reaching my potential.

I can't end this section without further reference to a book that I've read more than once, 'Our Kid, A Lancashire Childhood', by Billy Hopkins, 1998. **"OUR KID is a delightful evocation of a Northern boyhood. Nostalgic, sad and funny, it recalls an upbringing and an environment now** vanished." Starting in 1928, 22 years before I was born, the story was based around Manchester, especially Bolton, and for me upon first reading evoked so many memories of my childhood, that it inspired me to read the follow up books, and planted the seed of me wanting to not only read more about other peoples' lives, but also write my own story. Another, Nab End and Beyond, 2006, by William Woodruff, which even pre dates Our Kid and starts in 1916, 2 years before my father and 4 years before mum was born. Born in Blackburn, during the depths of the economic depression and detailing what it was like as a child living during the war years, Woodruff brutally depicts the reality of being poor, hungry and desperate. It also details the rise and fall, of the textile industry in the North West. After reading it, I had a greater insight in perhaps why my father behaved the way he did. Finally, Take It Like a Man, by George Alan Dowd, (Boy George), written when he was only 33, was another piece of work about a person's upbringing, **that epitomised the term, Dysfunctional Families.** It also made me realise, that it was not only, 'Grim Up North', in the 1950s but could be just as grim, if not worse, down South in the 1960s when Boy George was conceived. In fact, there were times when I winced when reading its brutally honest, graphic details. Giving me further insights into human behaviour, cloaked under the guise of the highest form of intelligence in the animal kingdom. I would like to end this section by using some of Mr Woodruff's recollections, **"I was proud to be a Lancastrian. Lancashire had given me the freedom to run as wild as I wanted. I had always had the freedom to run from dark streets and alleyway into the open rolling countryside. My heritage was joyful as well as bleak. I knew not only the squalor of a factory town, but also the unforgettable beauty of the surrounding fields, moors, hills and rugged fells. As a boy running wild, I had never known boredom."** (The Road to Nab End. 13:406-407). **My own childhood recollections are of OUTDOOR PLAY, ANTICIPATION, DISCOVERY AND DISAPPOINTMENT. I WAS VERY RARELY BORED. Sadly, a great many of today's children are immersed in THUMB AND FINGER PLAY, MATERIALISM, EXPECTATION AND PLASTIC LOVE, WITH FREQUENT MUTTERINGS OF, "I'M BORED."** It is also interesting to note that the TV programme, 'Call The Midwife', is annually the winner of many TV awards. Is that because, for many viewers it depicts a time long before progress reared its materialistic, abdicating, greedy head?

North Chadderton Secondary Modern School: Hormones, Rejection My First Love and Leaving Home.

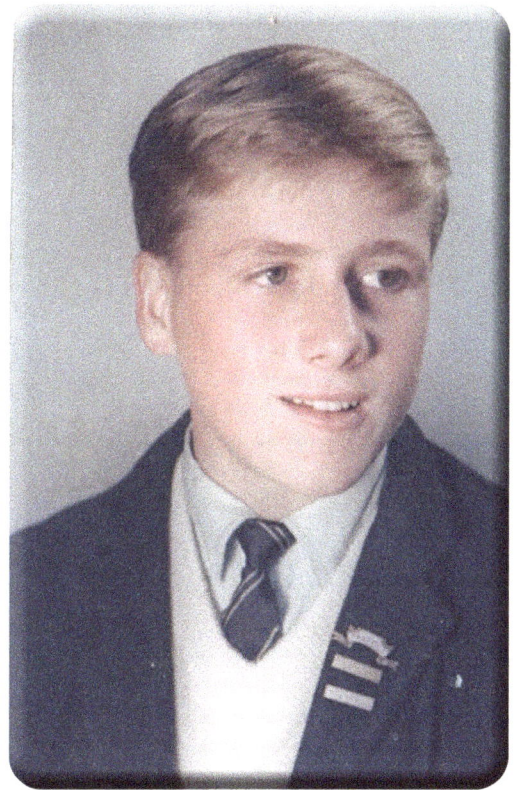

The boy who failed his 11 and 12 plus.

Adolescence is a war, filled with pressures both imagined and real. It is a bitch and is on the cusp between childhood and adult, when the body and hormones are just starting to come to a boil. Peer pressure is intense and affects the way you look, act and who you have as your friends. It is a time when the child becomes a frustrated lawyer, questioning, finding loopholes and demanding impossible levels of proof whilst attacking the most minute of minutia. (Coben H). Stephen Fry in his book, The Liar, 1991, 1:12, refers to adolescence as, **"Six hundred suits of skin oozing with postules, six hundred scalps weeping oil, twelve hundred armpits shooting out hair, twelve hundred inner thighs exploding with fungus and six hundred minds filling themselves with suicidal drivel."**

North Chadderton First X1 Football Team.

I enjoyed playing on the first team with lads such as Les Thewlis, Jimmy Brown, Colin Brooks, Roy Dickenson, Kevin Hilton, and Stewart Meredith. Colin being back left next to me on the photograph, 3rd along, back row left, Les Thewlis, then Jimmy Brown, Colin Brooks and then my good self. Front row 3rd along from the left, Roy Dickinson, then Kevin Hilton and finally, Stuart Meredith. Apologies to the other lads, whose names I cannot recall. In later years, I would re-unite with several of the lads, who ended up playing for local amateur teams.

During my first year at North Chadderton Secondary, I was top, or near the top of the class, with good reports, so where the rumour I had purposely failed both my 11 and 12 plus to gain entry into Grammar School came from, I am not sure as I always tried to give my best, knowing in reality there must have been times when I momentarily took my foot off the gas.

In those days, the tri-partite system was in existence, Grammar, Technical and Secondary Modern. Secondary Modern suited me as I was not an academic, and although history shows I later became relatively, academically successful, I really did have to work hard and apply my limited personal resources to the maximum. A photographic memory I had not. Secondary Moderns were perceived as places of containment, rather than education, before you were sent out into the big, bad world of industry and commerce, landing a job in either an office, or in the local factory. If lucky, you could be offered an apprenticeship. Higher education and degrees being the domain of only the privately educated and elite, Grammar school pupils. **What has annoyed me over the years is, how many pupils failed to take advantage of the opportunities that were afforded to them, that didn't exist when I was a schoolboy. Carrying this annoyance into when I crossed over to the other side, when I trained, and then became a teacher.** Having said that, my passage through secondary education was not all sweetness and light, in spite of all my academic and sporting successes. Unfortunately, once North Chadderton Girls amalgamated with the boys, in 1962, large doses of the male hormone testosterone took over, and I displayed all the hallmarks of an adolescent teenager; alienation, rejection, moody, distrustful, randomly alternating between resentful silence and confrontational malice. My first term's report in class 2A speaks for itself. I wanted to keep up my grades, play football and seek attention from the opposite sex, but my hormones wouldn't allow that to happen. A big part of the problem was, that I had a violent temper and if the red mist descended, as it frequently did, then fists, arms and legs would fly. But for me, my temper was a bonus as it meant that if distracted from my goal, (no pun intended), of getting my class and homework done so I could concentrate on my sport, with needless macho posturing, I could quickly dispense my opponent to somewhere that dealt with cuts, bruises, broken bones etc. Becoming form captain at the end of my second year, and then shortly afterwards being threatened, that I would lose my form captain's badge and would not be considered for selection on any of the sports teams, unless my behaviour improved, must have had some positive effect on me and seemed to settle me down. Before that, I would occasionally take the odd day off school. I nearly lost my Head Prefect's badge at school, as a result of going to Glasgow with brother-in-law Jack, because I wanted to see what it was like, instead of attending classes at North Chadderton. Scotland being on the other side of the world at that time, because I had not yet taken my Geography O' Level. When asked the following day by the head, Jack Graham, being an honest soul, after all I was Head Prefect, I proudly told him that as I had no exams that day, so I took the opportunity to go to Glasgow with my brother-in-law. Needless to say, this response was not greeted with, "Well done Briggs, you've shown tremendous insight and initiative into improving your life experiences, and your trip will look good on your CV and subsequent job applications." It was more akin to, "Look Briggs if I, the Head and my staff, have to drag ourselves here to try and impart some knowledge into little pricks like you, the least you can do is turn up, you little gob shite," or something similar. How did he know I had a small penis? I digress. During my third year, I was back enjoying the academic side of schooling and continued representing the first eleven at football. During my final year, I was suddenly given the label of, 'cock of school', which when hormones are raging, seemed an inappropriate title as it had nothing to do with sex. Although little in stature, you didn't mess with Briggsy. Not that I was always the victor, as I once went to play for Chadderton schoolboys nursing a beautiful black eye and swollen lip. When I moved to North Chadderton Secondary, my sporting prowess continued to flourish, with the PE department probably being my main inspiration for a career in sport. Colin Cunningham, who also taught me Biology in my final year, was certainly more supportive of my sporting prowess, than Neil Whitmarsh, head of PE, whom I found aloof. Jack Sutcliffe, who was a maths teacher who occasionally taught games, always found time to give me words of encouragement. The Head, Jack Graham, was always there and, as I was later to find out, a staunch supporter of Jimmy Briggs. The most negative influence came from a person named Clifford Taylor, whom as I recall once slapped me, after a games period, probably for answering back. As a representative of the school for both Chadderton and Lancashire schoolboys at football, top of my class, form prefect and Head Prefect for the school, allied to my philosophy of work hard, play hard and fight hard seemed to strike a chord with certain, if not all of my teachers. Later, once I'd entered the teaching profession, Taylor, who had sought sanctuary in the Primary sector, seeing it as a better prospect for promotion, even though he had very little experience other than teaching practice and a short time at Chadderton Hall Primary, was to later suffer from amnesia and deny any knowledge of such behaviour. Which was typical of the man who spent much of his teaching career in denial or back in the Victorian times.

Chadderton and Lancashire Schoolboys.

I played for Chadderton schoolboys over a two-year period, alongside my mate, Colin Brookes, and I still have some of the press cuttings from the Oldham Evening Chronicle, 1964.   With regard to Lancashire Schoolboys, I was selected to play for them 6 times although I only played 5 times because of a lack of communication, to get me to a game on Boxing Day. Don't forget, in those days there were no mobile phones or e-mail and we certainly didn't possess a land line at 24 Parkway, the nearest red, phone box being at the corner of Beech Avenue and Burnley Lane. Therefore, communication was by Royal Mail or word of mouth. Usually, North Chadderton School was contacted, and I was summoned by Jack Graham, the Head, to be given my instructions. Having a car was somewhat of a luxury, and catching local transport to games was not uncommon. But I do recall one of the teachers would become involved, and drive me to the meeting place to pick up the coach, not literally you understand. I was primarily right footed, although I spent many hours practising kicking with my left foot. Spending equally many hours practising scoring a goal, in exactly the area of the goal I wanted to put it in such as trying to score from the corner flag by, 'bending the ball', using first the outside and then the inside of the foot. **Sorry folks, but Mr Beckham, not that I had anything against David, did not invent making the ball curve by striking it with different parts of your foot. Today we are subjected by pundits, to a diatribe of information, a posh way of saying bullshit, designed to sell the game of football, and extol the skill of the players who ply their trade. It makes people of mine and previous generations laugh with, 'the spin'. It also amazes me with the lack of accuracy, so-called world class strikers lack with, 'shots on goal'. So much so, they actually use it as a statistic and quote it to quantify and qualify why player x is worth only £24 billion pounds and player Z is only worth £100.**

Playing for Lancashire was very different in many respects than playing for Chadderton, not least of all having to adjust to all the regional accents and senses of humour. I found it fascinating, that although we were all Lancastrians, the difference between the Wigan accent and the Liverpudlian took some getting used to. Together with local colloquialisms, it was at times quite challenging. Put into the mix, the opposition accents, which in my first game was mainly 'geordie' and my second 'brummie', I didn't realise that playing football was much more than just kicking a football. These issues not only whetting my appetite to discover more about people and their individuality but also provided me with first-hand experience of these differences. Later on, in my career I realised there was no such thing as a North East accent or a Lancastrian accent, as just travelling 10 miles down the road, the accent could noticeably change. Also initially playing for Lancashire, I knew no one on the team and I had to travel a fair distance just to meet the coach. Whereas, I knew many of the lads on the Chadderton team, and we usually travelled alone to the various venues, which, on the whole, were not a million miles away. Sometimes playing for Lancashire, pre-motorway days, whilst exciting, could be pretty tiring. Playing under floodlights for the first time in a night match at Deepdale, Preston North Ends' ground, was exciting and after the game, several scouts came into the changing rooms, to see if I had signed schoolboy forms for anyone. What's that saying, what goes around comes around? As I write this memoir Deepdale, Preston is only a few miles down the road from where I now live.

I loved my sport and whilst representing Chadderton and Lancashire Schoolboys at football, I had a plethora of scouts visiting not only me but also my brother Jack, who was a better all-round sportsman than me. He was also my role model, whenever I went to watch him play cricket or football for school, town or county. In those days professional clubs could only sign you on schoolboy forms until you were 16, and would try and woo you with free tickets to games etc. Now the vast sums of money and inducements that are wafted in front of parents' noses, to entice them to let their child sign for their club, not long after their child has come out of nappies, raise many moral and ethical arguments. It takes a very strong will for an adult to ignore the promise of a relatively lot of money, especially if you are deemed as coming from a socially deprived area. I will revisit this and other issues when we look at sporting academies and child abuse in sport in later chapters.

I remember WBA offering to pay for our Jack to travel to West Bromwich to watch a game. Where was West Bromwich we wondered and how many buses would we need to catch to get there? Jimmy Adamson, the ex-Irish international, who was the boss at Burnley, came to our house, one night at tea time, to discuss with my parents about the possibility of me going to Burnley to train. In those days, Burnley was at least two bus rides away and motorways were few and far between, with only the M6 around Preston being under construction. Don't forget, my father needed to be on the 6.30 bus to get to the pub and Mr Adamson called after 6. Yes, you've guessed, James Albert departed at 6.20 leaving Mr Adamson and me, I'm not sure but mum must have been around, to finalise me travelling over to Burnley, to have a look around. I've no recollection of ever going to Turf Moor. **So much for parental guidance from my father**. To be fair to my dad, he did travel with me when I spent a day at Bury FC training, which, if my memory serves me correctly, was on Gigg Lane car park at the side of the ground. Sadly, as I write this episode in my life, Bury AFC has fallen on hard times. My father also organised several pub trips to go and watch my brother play, with Crewe and Nelson springing to mind. After one Lancashire game, Manchester United's head scout approached Jack Graham at school about the possibility of me travelling to Old Trafford for training. Manchester United, are you kidding? Yes please, sir.

Manchester United FC and Oldham Athletic FC.

After signing schoolboy forms for Manchester United at the age of 15, and taking two buses to get to Old Trafford in Stretford, I ran up and down the steps of the Stretford End, and spent much time doing laps around the pitch. However, I eventually made the decision that it was costing me too much in terms of time, effort and finance, travelling to Old Trafford. Eventually I wrote a letter to United asking them to release me from my schoolboy contract. Remember I was making these decisions, which involved my whole career, myself, with the only help and guidance coming from the football clubs involved, school and my brother Jack, which in hindsight was pretty scary. I resigned from Manchester United in August 1965 and signed for Oldham Athletic FC in September, 1965, purely and simply on the strength that it was considerably nearer to 24, Parkway, Chadderton. Did my father know where I was during this period in my development, because if he did, he was noticeable by his absence? **Note the letter is addressed to me not my parents. Interesting.**

Manchester United Football Club Ltd.

M. BUSBY, C.B.E., Manager   L. OLIVE, Secretary

TELEGRAPHIC ADDRESS:
STADIUM, MANCHESTER
TELEPHONE TRAFFORD PARK
1661 & 1662

Old Trafford,
Manchester, 16.

LO/AG

2nd August, 1965.

Mr. J. Briggs,
24, Parkway,
CHADDERTON,
Nr. Oldham.

Dear James,

    As requested, we have today written to The Football League asking them to cancel your Associated Schoolboy registration with our Club.

    Mr. Busby wishes me to thank you for your interest and assistance during the time you have been with us, and we all send our very best wishes to you for the future.

Yours sincerely,

L. Olive

Secretary.

At Oldham Athletic, I played on their A, Youth and Reserve teams. I was a happy bunny there, and **I was the very first youngster to be offered one of their six apprentice professional places.** At that time, this was a big deal as only a few clubs in the North West offered such contracts, Burnley being the first, whilst Huddersfield, Burnley and Bury also wanted me to join them. These apprentice professional places were in no small way due to the influx of money injected into the club by a millionaire called Ken Bates who became the Chairman. Now he would have to be a Chairperson. It was also whilst playing at Oldham, that I was associated with a football scandal at the club that went under investigation for, 'Financial Irregularities'. As we got expenses, playing on the A team you got 15 shillings and, on the reserves, you got 30 shillings, to cover travel and kit expenses. I worried that I might become embroiled in the scandal, not realising that paedophiles masquerading as sports coaches were a far greater threat. I'm sorry, but I cannot do the maths conversion to say how much those expenses would be in today's money. In the 60s playing in the first team at Oldham, as a professional, you got considerably less than £100 in old money/pre-decimalisation. Since the days of Mr Bates at Oldham, who incidentally was at Chelsea FC before coming to Oldham, there has been a catalogue of scandals associated with not only millionaires taking over football and other sports clubs, but also a conveyor belt of issues such as paedophilia, bribery, corruption, chauvinism, drug abuse, sexism and racism affecting many sports. At that time, screw in studs had become the latest sporting must have and I had two sets, with accompanying spanner of course, one long set and another short, as well as my rubber moulded boots. This meant I could theoretically play on all kinds of surfaces, without slipping. I paid for the studs out of my own pocket money, as asking my parents for money was hit and miss, if not futile. To be fair, there just was no spare cash available. At that time, Oldham were in Division 4, with Manchester and Liverpool being in Division 1, for me things didn't get much better than this. I loved my time at Oldham as there was camaraderie, because most of the lads I played with, were mainly locals. My brother Jack also ended up at Oldham. From where we lived on the Park Estate, we only had to walk across Clayton playing fields and we were at the ground. Unfortunately, because he was older than me, my brother and I never played on the same team together at Oldham. He frequently played on the reserves, whereas I only played a few times on the reserves. My sporting career was relatively injury free, and when I did get an injury, it usually didn't keep me out of action too long. It is worth mentioning that during my time at Oldham, Jim Kelly, was the 'physio', but little did I realise that many years later, I would be looking after sports people myself as a sports therapist. In those days, 'the physio', was not as high a profile figure and an integral part of the medical back-up team, as it is today. But more the 'kit, bucket and sponge, man'. He was usually an ex-pro who was given the role as reward for loyalty to the club or his sport. Nowadays the 'physio' has to have a minimum qualification of the FA Diploma in the Treatment and Management of Injuries and more, before being offered a position at a club. Also, in those days there was no minimum wage, as Jimmy Hill and the Players Union had not yet won the battle, to have it as part of a player's contract. Players didn't have agents and usually negotiated their own contracts. **Today many professional sports people are seen as commodities, not people.** The contracts being fairly basic and wages, as I've intimated, were peanuts compared to today's over-inflated, ridiculous sums. And so, at the end of their careers and sometimes during, many players had to seek alternative employment, usually in sales, using their name and reputation, hoping someone would buy the latest vacuum cleaner from them. Going to 'the physio' in those days was optional, you just turned up at the ground on Sunday morning. I recall picking up a muscle strain, and was told to report to the ground first thing Sunday morning. This may sound perverse, but I was very excited as I had never been to see a physiotherapist before. It was just my luck that I was the first to arrive that day, going straight after my paper round, and was the only one in the treatment room at the time. Sometimes there could be many. Later in my career, footballers were banned from treatment areas unless receiving actual treatment, as it was found that for some it was an opportunity to, 'have a laugh', at their mates' expense, by adjusting the controls on treatment machines behind the physios' back. When I entered the sports therapy world, and worked for a short while in football, I talked to many professionals about their career and exploits finding out that some, even at international level, had personality clashes with other professionals, and did not want to share a room with them when playing away, because they couldn't stand their loutish, childish behaviour. Nothing has changed there then! One very famous international player was known to urinate out of the hotel window, rather than go to the bathroom after he'd had a few celebratory drinks after the game. Why, because he could. After all, who was going to stop him? Sid Jolley, who played on the opposite wing to me on Oldham Athletic's Youth team, ended up signing as an amateur for George Dews in the Manchester Industrial Premier League, who my brother Jack and I had signed for. Sid, like me, had opted for a career in teaching, with our Jack becoming a boss at CIS insurance. Sid spent many years at Dews with my brother and me, but sadly died of cancer in his fifties, leaving his wife Kath to mourn with his children. Before his death, our Jack and I went around to visit him at his house in Spring Gardens, Hollinwood and shared a few beers with him, reminisced and watched a game involving Manchester United on television. It was very sad to see him, and made you realise how life could be so cruel. I cannot recall the exact moment that I stopped playing for Oldham, but I do recall getting very frustrated that Jimmy McIlroy kept bringing many Irish lads over for trials, at the expense of local talent and talent from other parts of Lancashire. **52 years later, the FA and Brexit reflected a similar theme that foreigners were depriving local talent of jobs.** I think Mr M was searching for another George Best, but as far as I was aware never found one. Sadly, Jimmy Mac died on 20th August, 2018. **As for football, nothing much has changed as, 'jobs for the boys', with the emphasis on boys, has always been rife in football. It is and always will be a very select, private club that fastidiously looks after its male members, irrespective of what skulduggery they get up to. Later when I became a Sports Therapist and gained my FA Diploma in the Treatment and Rehabilitation of Injuries and then working for the FA, I had first-hand experience and insight into what goes on behind closed doors in football.** Eventually I just stopped going to Oldham, as I'd become a little disillusioned with football and for a while didn't play at all, before eventually signing for George Dews in the Manchester Amateur Industrial League. During my 'wilderness years' Terry Casey one of the PE staff at Mather Teaching College, tried to persuade me to play for Nantwich Town in the Cheshire league and Dave Roberts, an insurance guy, wanted me to go to Ashton United but I declined both. Who knows what would have happened, if I'd have stayed at Manchester United or signed for Oldham, Nantwich or Ashton? Many, many, years later watching programmes on television on peoples' sporting lives, they recalled how their families and especially their fathers, played a significant role in their development and ultimate success, i.e. Tiger Woods, golf, Brian Lara, cricket. Brian Lara stating that, up until his father's demise, his father had not missed one single game of cricket his son played. Where was my father during all these wonderful times? In the pub I suspect. I cannot recall one single, solitary game of football my father watched me play in 30 plus years, and only several involving my brother Jack, which were organised pub outings. I know he used to shout out in the pub, that his lads had just arrived, whenever our Jack and I turned up with our girlfriends, to meet mum for a drink. I think he was proud of me but if he was, he never told me or never showed me, as I never received a hug or a cuddle. So very, very sad. Finally, my brother decided to shun the footballing pathway in preference to carving out a career at the Co-operative Insurance Society, whilst playing sport as an amateur. As far as I was aware he had no help or guidance from any significant other. So, what should I do, sign professional forms, when I was old enough, or should I do something else? My brother Jack pointing out that if I broke my leg, my career would be over before it had started. Now I know why my brother Jack passed his 11 plus and I failed mine.

At the age of 14/15, whilst practising for an inter-school athletics competition, I was 'spiked' by another member of the relay squad during a baton change-over on Westwood running track, in preparation for the local inter-schools' athletic meeting. This resulted in me having to attend Oldham Royal Infirmary to have stitches and a tetanus injection. I was given half the booster dose, to see if I was allergic to the tetanus jab. Three hours later, and two anaphylactic fits, the answer was yes, I was. Sometimes, allergic reactions can be fatal. In respect of this episode, the reader must appreciate that wearing a pair of running spikes and having different 'screw-in studs' for your football boots, as I had at Oldham AFC, was a big deal.

> **OLDHAM ATHLETIC ASSOCIATION FOOTBALL CLUB LTD**
>
> Chairman: K. W. BATES
> Secretary:
> Team Manager: J. McILROY
> Telephone and Telegrams: MAin (Oldham) 4972
>
> Registered Office and Ground:
> **BOUNDARY PARK - OLDHAM**
>
> 7 July 66.
>
> Dear Jimmy,
>
> Thank you for your letter asking for your release. Mr. McIlroy is on holiday at present, so I can't give you a definite answer.
>
> I can tell you this however, I personally feel that there is a future for you here, & shall do all I can to persuade the club to retain you. The fact that a lot of new faces will be here will not in any way jeopardise your chances.
>
> Should you still not be happy with my reply, I suggest that you ring or write to the manager after 21st July.
>
> Yours faithfully,

In terms of exercise and sport, I realised whilst attending North Chadderton and after, when I left, that I was reasonably successful at most sports, apart from swimming and high jump. But to this day, I have never found it necessary to, go to the gym and take steroids, to bulk up or acquire an image. Being an outdoor type, meant spending time indoors never appealed, unless it was a means to an end. Also, my work and life style meant I was always active, in one guise or another, and so didn't need to sign up at the gym to pose on the running machine. Going out for a walk, or a jog, with my partner, family, friends and neighbours was as much a social as a physical event. Especially, if it meant raising money for charity, or a local cause that was close to my heart. I loved playing squash, either socially with my teaching colleagues, once a week, or more competitively, at weekends, at Maple Squash Club on Broadway. I never, however, wanted to play on any of the teams. Strange though it may seem I was never ultra-competitive. I liked to win but not at all costs, and as long as I did my best and, more importantly, enjoyed myself, I was happy. People who don't exercise don't appreciate the 'high' that is experienced from exercise, which releases the bodies' own endorphins and encephalin. **Who needs nicotine, steroids, alcohol, crack, cocaine or heroin?** I walk and jog, because it enhances the quality of my life, not because I think it will make me live longer. Also, I have **NEVER** come across walkers or joggers arguing or fighting. Stress kills and today certain people argue it's an unavoidable fact of life. Well, I suppose it is if you go looking for it and wear it like a badge of honour. Don't forget life is about choices. Although I didn't fully appreciate it at the time, but during my teenage years, especially at North Chadderton, rejection was not something I dealt with very easily as my girlfriend at the time, Hilary, can attest to. **This difficulty of dealing with rejection became a blue print for the rest of my**

life. After Hilary had 'chucked me' for an older person of the male species, just prior to taking my GCE O' levels, I left home for a while to visit Cornwall, via Cheltenham bus station and the rugby ground. Drawing all my savings out of my Post Office savings account, which couldn't have amounted to much, I caught the number 6 bus into Oldham and boarded a Yellowway coach to Cheltenham. Spending one night in a B&B, courtesy of a total stranger, and the other in the groundsman's shed at the rugby ground. Arriving in Hayle, with nowhere to stay, and having spent several hours sitting on a bench outside a school, I decided that I had better return home to do my O'Levels. As I write this account, I have no recollection of where I slept after Cheltenham, how I got to Hayle, or how I returned home. I do, however, recall going straight to Hilary's house when I returned to Chadderton and being very tearful in their kitchen. Hilary was not impressed with my cry for help. Her mum Hilda was brilliant, but her father Jack thought, and quite rightly so, that we were far too young to take our relationship that seriously. But don't all teenagers finding themselves in similar situations, feel their world has come to an end? After the police arrived, I was taken home and remember talking to my brother Jack in the bedroom about my exploits. In hindsight, I just considered it an adventure and was totally unaware of the distress it had caused to others. Was this my first inkling of wanting to be a traveller? In those days, as it is today, leaving home was a serious business but in my teenage years I wasn't aware of this. But, as mentioned, teenagers threaten and commit all kinds of acts in failing relationships – it's a sign of emotional immaturity and a possible way to attract attention to your plight. Many an author, e.g. Linwood Barclay, has earned a living by writing about teenage angst, leaving home, abduction, self-abuse etc., all under the guise of ignorant youth and emotional immaturity. It was surprising, where one could get to in the 60s on a few pounds saved in a Post Office account. However, after this initial setback during my teenage, hormonal years, I was lucky to have many experiences with women. After all, what are hormones for? My biggest problem was that, whilst I pretended I knew, I hadn't a clue what to do during these experiences beyond a kiss and a cuddle. Also, in my search for, 'the love of my life', although at the time I wasn't aware that I was looking, and coming across males whose attitude towards women left plenty to be desired, coupled with my lack of respect for my father, eventually led to me to becoming very anti male chauvinist. Although, I was later to discover female chauvinists could be just as bad. Sorry ladies, but not all men are bastards. My experience with Hilary, although quite early in my life as mentioned, set the precedent for how I dealt with future rejection, by possibly running away and isolating myself. Later, realising confronting and as they now say, 'owning it' was the answer. **Like many teenagers, I was melodramatic and needed acceptance, love, a hug and a cuddle and Hilary highlighted that personality trait in me. Subsequent episodes and relationships in my life, also highlighted that fact.** Such a personality characteristic was probably the reason for my positive decision making, when I felt I was not wanted in a particular situation. Having realised I didn't handle rejection, in its many guises, very well, I reacted by either running away or resigning from the position I had found myself in. The reader will recognise these responses to many episodes that occurred in my life, as my story unfolds. As I matured and developed, I recognised my positive decision making as a plus rather than a minus. And whilst some, quite rightly, would argue I could be a little irrational and melodramatic at times, I certainly was comfortable with this facet of my personality. My management style was certainly not laissez faire. Also, as I grew up, I chose not to run away from the issues instead chose to confront them, no matter how upsetting, at times with little diplomacy. Anyhow back to being a teenager scholar and sportsperson. My hormones were raging and I was desperately trying to find some stability and meaning to life. I wanted a stable, loving, caring environment. Yes, I know it's a cliché, but I somehow felt cheated that I had somehow missed out. Others talked about mum this and mum that, dad this and dad that. I felt my parents only entered my realm when I had been or was in trouble. How the rest of my brothers and sisters felt, I wasn't sure because it was not something we sat around the table at meal times to discuss. The nearest I got to counselling was from my brother Jack talking to me when I returned home from my sojourn to Cornwall. I smile now as upon my return, I expected hugs, kisses and forgiveness not all the negative attention. I was distraught. Hilary's father, didn't know what all the fuss was about. Hilary called me melodramatic, which I later found out was not a compliment. The Police gave me a rollicking for taking up so much of their valuable time and my return to school was akin to a wake. No banners or trumpets. Years later when in our 60s Colin Brooks and I met quite by chance, and over a few drinks he told me he never forgave me for the police interrogation he had to endure as a teenager, when I suddenly disappeared. At that time the police believed he knew where I had gone, when in actual fact I had only briefly mentioned it to a few of my other mates. After all that time he said he secretly still lusted after Ann Lidle, Hilary's friend, who incidentally had nothing to do with establishing the chain of German food stores throughout the UK, but with a wife and several children in tow, I put it down to an old man reminiscing! In 2012, at the age of 62 reading the book, "The Summer that never was", by Peter Robinson, I relived all those 50s and 60s memories as the plot centred around a boy called Graham Marshall that had supposedly run away, and his mate Alan Banks was interviewed by the police as to his whereabouts. Years later, when Alan Banks became a policeman, he reminisced about not enjoying the experience of being interviewed as a teenager. So once again Colin, sorry, not only for my leaving home but also how our friendship ended all those years previously. Unfortunately, I am not proud to say, that it ended after I lost my temper during a disagreement and the red mist descended. I think the disagreement being over Ann Lidle. Years later, I invited Colin to my 60th birthday celebration, but he politely declined by choosing instead to attend a wedding. Perhaps he still never forgave me for the interview and spat on Broadway over Ann. Very sad. Unfortunately, my latter days at North Chadderton Secondary School was not about all my academic and sporting achievements, but was synonymous with my relationship with Hilary and my 'running away'. **Leaving home was front page news. Being Head Prefect at the time was also a bit of a slight on the teaching staff in their selection procedure for head boy.** Personality profiling being in its infancy at the time. The last I heard Hilary was homeless, in the sense that she was spending half the time living with her daughter, the very bubbly Nicola, and the rest with her son, the very serious Robert, whom I never met. Her father, Jack, succumbed to the drink and died in his 60s whilst Hilda remained fiercely independent, living in Shaw but sadly, the last time I visited her was showing signs of dementia. I then lost touch but recently found she was living in Chadderton Health Care, where my own mother spent the final months of her life. I've visited her on several occasions and found it very distressing for obvious reasons, but at the same time I'm pleased to have made the effort. Finally, returning to the theme of a teacher's influence I always hoped that any teacher I knew, who didn't find it easy to impart knowledge to my good self, take credit that JB ended up an acting headmaster, with a degree, a published author, external examiner, senior lecturer and Fellow of the Higher Education Academy. Thank you. As for those who influenced my decision to become a teacher there was Mr Worth, my English teacher, Robert Hadfield, my woodwork teacher; Miss Jo Hill, the PE mistress and for a while my form mistress, who later became Mrs Jo Hadfield. I was later to become friends with Jo and Robert when I entered the teaching profession. Vernon Oldland was my geography teacher and whilst later not enjoying the same friendship as I had with Robert and Jo, I did cross paths with Vernon's wife Cath, who was a headmistress in Primary/Infant Education. Jo Hadfield also ending up with her own Primary/Infant school to manage. Sadly, Robert died of cancer but I still managed to keep in touch with Jo, who moved to Durham to be nearer her daughter. There was Mr. 'Doggy' Dawson, who taught maths. Not my strongest suit although I did try hard, or was it I was very trying? Adrian Reid was the music teacher, but was more known for doing cross country. There was also Harvey Wright, my technical drawing teacher, who played cricket for Milnrow, and was a leading spin bowler in the CLL league. I remember one year playing on the staff versus boys' cricket match and Harvey bowling me around my legs with a ball I'm certain turned 90 degrees-Honest! Wendy Wadsworth, was one of my form mistresses, who tried to teach me French at a time when I was going through my most rebellious phase. I am still trying to master the French language on my travels. I also remember Miss Sumitri, who was a young, probationary teacher and became my form teacher in my second year at North Chadderton. As mentioned, the boys' and girls' school had recently amalgamated and before then, although on the same site, the boys' and girls' school were run as two separate entities. N'er the twain shall meet-upon pain of death. Well, behind the cemetery wall maybe. You can imagine the potential mayhem that was to ensue when all those hormones were allowed to mix. Even at a time when discipline in schools was not the issue that it is today, because the do –gooders and politicians had not yet worked out a way to mess it up. So therefore, I was more interested in showing off to the girls than showing respect to Miss Sumitri. Sorry, Miss Sumitri. Years later, when I started going on teaching practice, as part of my teacher education, I hoped, beyond all hope, that I didn't get a Jimmy Briggs in my class. On the whole, my time at North Chadderton was full of happy memories, and it goes without saying that was where my talent was recognised, encouraged and rewarded. Also, although I didn't realise it at the time, it was to lay the foundation for my eventual journey, thanks to Verna Dale Howarth and Frank Gorner, into the honourable, teaching profession. I left with 4 GCE O' levels and a few CSEs, failing my English Language but passing my re-sit. As I was only allowed to take a maximum of 5 GCEs I was pleased I eventually passed them all.

3.
CONNECTING WITH THE ADULT WORLD: 16-21years.

Norweb.

Upon leaving school at 16, I was, in hindsight, rudder less. My mother was still trying to juggle and keep the balls in the air with 7 children, many of whom now had jobs and if not already done so were considering, 'leaving the nest'. Whereas, my father was still trying to identify which political party he belonged to, by becoming a member of the Conservative and Labour clubs at the same time. Patronising both with a frequency that was directly correlated to the price of the beer the affiliated clubs pumped out into his glass. If still alive today, the Lib Dems, BNP, Loony Party, Green and Pink Parties would probably get the same consideration. Therefore, as previously alluded to, I have no recollection of any parental help, support and advice, apart from chasing my father down the street to ask for some pocket money, and could pretty much do as I pleased. I suspect the rest of my brothers and sisters were in the same boat. Realising, with the help of my eldest brother Jack, that football was too risky, even if the few pounds win bonus was highly attractive, I applied for a job at NORWEB, The North Western Electricity Board, or as it was known, 'The Board', on Union Street in Oldham, where I worked for several months in the accounts department. Admittedly, school leavers in my day did have a plethora of choices as to what to do upon leaving secondary school, but it was in essence very stereotyped by class and education. Certainly, unless Grammar school material, a professional route was not on the radar. Even my eldest brother Jack and my youngest sister Janet didn't consider University an option. If they did, they certainly didn't tell me. My choice to go for a job at 'The Board', was based purely and simply on the £4 plus a week, wage. At this juncture I can tell you that **my dream as a 16-year-old, in the year England won the football world cup in 1966, was to earn £1,000 pa, own a car and a flat. If by some miracle I managed to achieve these things before I died, I would have considered myself a very successful bunny indeed.** My boss at the Board was a guy named Frank Airey who was responsible for disconnecting people who didn't pay their electricity bills. The emphasis being on responsible. This was a time when, 'passing the buck', had not yet become a workplace pastime and society knew who was responsible for what. The switchboard, which was adequately manned/womaned, would put the caller straight through to the appropriate department and/or person. **Today as a result of sophisticated, technological progress, after a 10/15 minute phone call, most of which is spent pressing buttons, 1 for a person with a soft voice, 2 for a grumpy person with a loud voice, and so on, or by providing information to save time when you theoretically get through to the correct department or person, only to be greeted by, "Oh, we don't deal with that, I'll put you back on hold," for another 10 minutes so you can listen to some music and consider if it is worth staying on the line, as it is probably quicker to walk the 100 miles to visit the office personally. Such music being interrupted with a message pointing out that the company value your custom and thank you for not giving up on life. If by some miracle, you actually do get through to speak to someone, and can remember why you needed to make the phone call in the first place, they will then have to take you through a privacy screening by asking all the questions you have previously**

provided the answers to, whilst being put on hold. Seriously, this is progress?

Frank was not the most popular person in the local community and working for him was my first introduction to people management, diplomacy and personal survival. People who came to see Frank were not bearing gold, frankincense or myrrh. This was in an era when you lived within your means or you suffered the consequences. In this particular case no heating or lights. No credit cards. Plenty of 'tick' and under the counter credit with weekly pay back, but no living beyond your means. More like living to survive. Oh, there were terms such as social class and social deprivation floating around but in hindsight, most of the people I grew up with could fall into the latter and social class, although I didn't know it at the time, was the thing that glued and cemented society together because people just accepted who they were and tried to make the best of the cards they had been dealt. The TV programme, 'That was the Week that Was', the title track being sung by Millicent Martin, was fronted by David Frost and created the now famous, **Social Class Sketch**, with the two Ronnies, Barker and Corbett, and John Cleese. For those who were not around to watch this master piece it was visually and verbally a reflection of the class system that pervaded society at the time. Ronnie Corbett, the little one, representing the downtrodden, lower class and Cleese, the tallest, representing the privileged, upper class. Ronnie Barker, 'knew his place', as the middle-class person who looked up to Cleese and down upon Corbett. Upon entering higher education and academia, this very subject was the topic for a study I was to become involved in, looking at what effect the class system had on not only education and educability, but also job and career opportunities. Margaret Thatcher tried to challenge the class system by telling everyone, together with Norman Tebbit, to get on their bikes and 'go for it', irrespective of a person's background. Whilst I definitely benefitted from Maggie's mantra, I was old enough to appreciate that the class system, whilst being considered derisive and divisive by the scholars and academics, nevertheless gave people a sense of belonging. To quote Ronnie Corbett, "I know my place." Josephine Klein, in her researches in the 60s and 70s talked about social ascenders and social descenders. I subsequently became a social ascender, thanks to Verna Dale Howarth and Frank Gorner, whom I met when I worked at Manchester University. Josephine Klein's work considered how early life experiences could lay the foundation for future growth, development and personality. It clarified for me my station in life as a social ascender. Looking at the class system and the question of nature and nurture, genotypes and phenotypes, Klein identified people in life that moved either upwards, later to be known as upwardly mobile, or downwards, from one stratum, or class in society, to another. The reasons given for this mobility being the individual's own efforts, positively or negatively, and not because of societal position, which school one went to, or how much money a person possessed. A significant other in my life at that time, was Joan O'Hara, who befriended, mothered, helped and guided me. Joan was a class act and my first introduction to the difference between a lady of class, and a female pretending to be classy. She exuded dignity. No swear words, tattoos, pints and dressing like a hooker for Joan. **"There's no future in disconnecting people from the National Electricity grid, James, so if you aren't going to play football what do you want to do with your life?"** said Joan. She was a very articulate and soft-spoken lady, with husky, smouldering, sexy intonation and diction. Seven months later, I found myself working in the Department of Education, at Manchester University.

My time at Norweb, was fittingly curtailed by Joan O'Hara, who having taken me under her wing and nurtured me, pointed me in the direction of Manchester University. Not to study I might add, that was to come later, but to work. So, after 6 months at NORWEB I applied for a job in Computer and Statistics in the Dept. Of Education at Manchester University, which involved two bus rides from home in Chadderton. In the 1980s Norman Tebbitt urged the nation to, 'get on its' bike', to find employment, but thanks to Joan, I was getting on my bike at the age of 17 to become a social ascender. Not knowing at the time that I was starting on such a journey, and that my bike was in fact several double decker buses and a Fiat 500 motor car. Also, in looking for answers I've realised that as a 17-year-old setting out on my career, although at that age, work just meant earning money, and even though career officers existed I cannot recall ever speaking to one, the term, **'job satisfaction',** was in daily use. As I got older, and I did have a definite career path, albeit a path that occasionally changed direction, this expression was seen as a definite no, no, and that going to work was not meant to be satisfying but just a means to an end. Today in 2025, I very rarely, if ever, hear the term. As time went on, and society began to change, I realised by steadfastly refusing to join the, 'Bah, Bah, Instant Gratification, Easily Disposable Society', people were isolating themselves. In 2025, for some, 'getting on your bike', as Norman Tebbit wanted us to do in the 80s would be considered just too much exercise, but jumping in the car to go and buy a newspaper from the local Spar or newsagents, that was 200 metres away, was a much more preferred option. **Self-induced illness rules, OK!**

The Education Department and School of Education, Manchester University:

Meeting Atlas and Anita.

If pre 16 years was the time in my life when the foundation was laid, post 16 was the period when building blocks were added and my life started to change significantly. My time at the Department of Education, at the ripe old age of 17, proved to be very, if not the most, significant of my life. Not least because it was where I first met Verna Dale Howarth, in the School of Education. She was single and 6 years older than me, and was being pursued by a certain Peter Woolsey, who drove an AC Bristol sports car and fancied himself as a lady's man. He also had money. In hindsight, he reminded me of a Jeeves and Wooster character. Verna's 'side kick' was Coreen Collinson, a darker version of Kylie Minogue, 5 foot tall, very attractive, with high, high heels and married to Fred, who worked for British Rail. Privatisation had not yet entered the scene for many utility services. Coreen, apart from working in the same department as Verna, was also given a lift home by her. Verna was the personal secretary to Frank Gorner, whose correct departmental title I cannot remember, but he was very well connected to many educational establishments. Coreen on the other hand, worked for Vera Southgate Booth, who pioneered the Initial Teaching Alphabet system of reading. The ITA system was considered a revolutionary way of teaching children to read, based on phonetic and letter blends but after being trialed by many local education authorities, and in many schools, it died a death never to be seen or heard of again. Both the Dept of Education and School of Education were housed in the Humanities Building, next to the University theatre, and Joint Matriculation Examination Board, (JMB), building from where GCE O'level results were collated and distributed. During summer, the octagonal building was filled to capacity with mainly young females that would, during their break times, spill out onto the grass lawns to enjoy the sunshine. Yes, Manchester sunshine, would you believe? In fact, my time at the Dept of Ed. seemed to be blessed with good weather. I likened this event to releasing prisoners out of their cells for exercise, and something of a phenomenon that David Attenborough would include in one of his whispering, highly acclaimed documentaries. You had to see it to believe it, and we alpha males certainly did as the room I worked in with Jim Morris, a computer programmer, and Peter Cole, a fanatical Manchester United supporter, overlooked the JMB. Needless to say, there were times when a direct, significant correlation could be made between negative, work output in the office and JMB break times. I must emphasise that this was the period of hot pants, mini-skirts, drugs, sex, and rock and roll. I had never in my 17 years seen so much of the opposite sex in such a concentrated space, and to be honest I just wanted to run amok amongst them all asking for a hug, or cuddle but obviously not sex. Because although it was a period of drugs, sex and rock and roll, I had not yet drugged, sexed or rock and rolled and was still a virgin. Yes, in those days most girls had self-respect, and so first base was all one could hope for. Now the term is synonymous with a gentleman named Richard Branson. Perhaps Joan at Norweb knew that this was the place for Briggsy to lose his virginity, as well as enhancing his career prospects, and that is why she encouraged me to apply for the job of Computer and Statistics Analyst. Looking back, I cannot for the life of me remember going for an interview or how I got the job, especially when maths was definitely not my strong point. But I did, and here I was staring out of the window at all that oestrogen on legs. I am sad to report that I never got to date, never mind impregnate, by having rampant, no holds barred sex with any one of them, and only ever visited the JMB building on the odd occasion to deliver some package or other. Oh well, such was life. My boss in the office on the second floor was an Irish guy called Tom Fitzpatrick, known as Fitz, who was in charge of several research projects. The Dept of Education housed several large research projects at the time, all with varying degrees of pressure related to deadlines and financial restraints, not to mention obtaining results that justified the time, effort and financial sacrifice which would hopefully ensure further time, effort and more funding. Which meant Fitz could be an unpredictable, volatile boss to say the least. Higher education in simplicity consisted of teaching, research and publications. All lecturers being encouraged to participate in research in the hope of going to publication, as there was, and still is, a certain kudos to having an impressive research portfolio and being a published author. As well as these areas, lecturers were expected to fulfil their teaching commitment. Needless to say, there are many who prefer one more than the other, which can lead to problems as both require commitment and a delicate balancing act. Tom Fitz preferred the research side and had obviously secured a position that required most of his efforts in this direction. To counter Fitz's irascible nature was Professor Warburton, the kindest, gentlest man you could ever wish to meet, but who was the epitome of the absent-minded Professor. His secretary, Rosamund, Roz, was from Knutsford, very posh, and as expected, super-efficient. She had to be as Prof, as he was known, was prone to doing all kinds of hilarious things which could send his students into varying states of apoplexy. Talk about the mad Professor. but in this case Prof Warby, as he was known, was far from mad, just very forgetful. He once left the only copy of a mature student's final dissertation, the result of many years' work, on a train from Bowden/Altrincham. **In those days, work was either hand written or typed, not word processed and stored on a desk computer, memory stick or laptop. Many copies being carbon copies not photo copies.** But when Prof would later recall his version of events, he would relate it in such a way that he thought everyone did these things and it was no big deal. Needless to say, I loved the man, not literally but you know what I mean, because he made me think as to what actually was important in your life. **So many people get hung up and stressed, 'you're doing my head in', being a popular modernism, on so much materialistic trivia, it's quite pathetic in the grand scheme of things.** Later in my career, as I entered the world of Higher Education and academia, I came across many like Prof Warburton and understood that these people, whilst being experts in their particular fields of study, found daily, mundane tasks, that we all have to do in our lives, not that important and tended to disregard their significance and/or impact on others. It was not a deliberate disregard or a slight on their mental health, but just their hierarchical importance as to coin a phrase, 'what floated their boat'. This is why some academics can be very, very, boring and tiresome in social situations, because all they want to talk about is some obscure piece of research, that many people don't even understand the title of, let alone understand its content or relevance. In my career, I've met some of these people, who could be quite rude and dismissive of your presence, if they realised you lived in a different mind-set. So, I had to learn how to be diplomatic when trying to communicate with them. At first, I found this very difficult as my philosophy in life was, 'give someone a smile, they may not have one of their own', and be honest. **Little knowing many people didn't do honesty, preferring instead, two-faced backstabbing.** This was of course, after I had found out what philosophy was. I also realised that some people don't want a free smile, even when given with good intention, and interpret your intentions as flippant behaviour. It's not about learning diplomacy, although that may apply in some cases, but more about accepting the simple fact that, **you are never going to please all of the people all of the time, so don't even try.** People are very quick to compartmentalise you within a few minutes of the initial meeting, and can take an awful lot of persuading that they have got it wrong and, in some cases, totally wrong. **This was no more so than when it comes to accents.** Back in the department there was another typist who worked within the same office as Roz, who lived in Knutsford but whose name unfortunately escapes me. I wonder why? My first impressions of her was, that she was very snooty, and **related strong Lancashire dialect to a lack of intelligence** and so therefore, she tried to belittle me because of the way I spoke. This must have been some form of political incorrectness and an 'ic, ist or an 'ism, but being as political correctness had not yet reared its ugly head, she felt perfectly safe in adopting such tactics. I very quickly realised that everyone in the department commuted in from South Manchester, the Bowdens, Knutsfords, Stockports and Hales of this world, whilst I was the only one from North Manchester. I said things like, "fur hur and buzzes", in rather a broad, Lancashire accent, whilst others would say, "fair, hair and buses" in a slightly more refined tone. Many years later, when watching on television Michael Palin's, Ripping Yarns, I laughed at his portrayal of characters such as Eric Olthwaite and Gordon Ottershaw, who spoke with very broad Yorkshire accents, and wondered how some of the staff in the School of Education back in 1967, would have coped with such. To be honest, during my life and even now, I need interpretation as to what someone is saying, because they are speaking in a very broad regional dialect. Again, although I didn't know it at the time, this was another aspect of human behaviour, which led me into wanting to investigate the subject of communication, eventually lecturing on the subject. Three to four years later, my mother told me I had become posh because I didn't say 'fur hur' any more but fair hair. **This was testament to my training at Mather College. Not that they tried to change your accent, but the tutors just pointed out that every single thing you said and did as a teacher, including what you wore and the way you spoke, influenced young, impressionable minds.** And so, wanting to be good at my job I took this fact to heart and whenever I stood in front of an audience, be they 4- or 40-year-olds, I was aware I was a role model. I was also told at college, that children do not come out of the womb, 'efffing and jeffing', but that someone had influenced such language. For every foul-mouthed slob of a son or daughter, there probably was a foul mouthed, slob of an adult close by, who had influenced them. Everyone else in the department was fine about the way I spoke, and so I decided to use it to my advantage. I'd realised I could make people laugh, because I had a flair for mimicry, impersonations and accents. Not to Jon Culshaw, Jan Ravens, Alistair McGowan or Rory Bremner standards, but finding this gained me attention, a possible hug, and certainly a laugh or two, I decided to work on the act. Also realising, I had the ability to make people laugh was a wonderful asset. This was in no way meant to be disrespectful but anything that gave me the attention I so craved, I went for it. Obviously, Roz's secretarial, snooty colleague, whom I decided to totally ignore unless she spoke to me was now in my sights for some serious, fun and games. Every time she said anything, I would repeat it but with differing emphasis and tonation on the phonetical pronunciation in the form of a question. In simplicity, do you say the name of a letter or do you say its sound? I remember, she once remarked about going to listen to a famous PIANIST at the Free Trade Hall in Manchester but I ignorantly enquired in my broadest Lancashire dialect, 'How dust tha spell pianist love, PENIS'? When I later started teaching children with learning difficulties, I found many spelt words phonetically. Over time my laughs were superseding her bigotry, and when she realised that I could mimic her so called posh accent with ease she started to try and mimic my broad one. RESULT. So, whenever I went to the many parties the department were invited to, my strategy was to bring my soul LPs for dancing, and hold court by trying to make people laugh. I was also realising I could attempt different regional accents. Without being arrogant, I found I just saw the funny side of certain situations and could turn it into a little amusing sketch. Together with taking off various people at work, the sincerest form of flattery, I started to enjoy my time amongst all these 'posh folk'. Especially, when one of the programmers stated that she would only go to a party if Bloggsy was going. Bloggsy being my adopted nickname. Whilst Ivy teased me about my accent, it was done in fun and Ivy and I shared many happy frivolous moments. I was now getting the attention for positive reasons and loved it. I also gained a reputation for having a vinyl, record collection that people said, "If it's got a black face on the sleeve, Bloggsy will have it." I was very much into the American, imported R&B, Soul, Otis Redding, Aretha Franklin, Stax and Wilson Pickett sound. Was this my first appreciation of colour, little knowing that racism, together with religion, was and still is, a toxic subject that is sometimes the reason for deeply ingrained hatred that can lead to war? **MURDER BY COLOUR** as I call it. I will return to the topic of prejudice and racism later. At the University, computer programmers were treated with a lot of respect by the researchers because they were the ones who would write programmes to try and convert all the data that was being collected and collated, and transform it into information, with statistical relevance, that could later be published as significant knowledge to be added to the existing knowledge on a particular subject. These programmes were written to order and so were untested, which put a great deal of pressure on Jim and Ivy. Myself, along with others, were tasked with putting numerical data onto machines that produced either card or paper full of holes, which related to binary notation. Each hole relating to a one or a nought, which in turn had a pattern that related to a number. This was known as the Hollerith – based punched card system. Bill Gates and Microsoft had not yet entered the scene. **Manchester University had one of the first IBM computers in the country, called Atlas, which was housed on a whole floor in the Reynold Building.** Yes, a whole floor, it was enormous, with not a desk top in sight. Upon entering the Atlas domain, it reminded me of entering a quiet, cotton mill. A contradiction in terms, if ever there was one, because there was this constant humming and buzzing, with the occasional mechanical click. You left your labelled tray-box, full of paper or card, in the appropriate place and the staff would load the data, when a department's time became available on the computer. Time allocation was noted and once a department's time was all used up, no further access was allowed until the following day, or week. After dropping off the data, you went to the other end of the floor to collect the data that had been analysed. This was highly significant, because if the printout showed no results or limited results, it meant there was a mistake in the data or programme, and it all had to be checked, probably re-written and re-entered into the computer, using up more of the department's allotted time. Time on the computer was precious. This meant there was a great deal of overt and covert wheeling and dealing to get your data onto the computer, to be statistically analysed. **Apart from Atlas the University**

also had one of the earliest desk calculators called Anita. In its time, it was an all singing and dancing machine and much prized. Between Atlas and Anita, we had at our disposal the very first pieces of kit that was to herald the dawn of the IT revolution. Little did I know at that time, what my future would have been if I'd stayed working in the Department of Education. And although I was attending St John's College in Manchester, to study A Level Pure Maths and Statistics, the fact of the matter was I never really saw myself working in mathematics or computers. I did, however, enjoy the statistics side, until I had to revisit the subject later whilst working in Higher Education. I then realised I had made the correct choice all those years ago, in not pursuing a career in computers. The class system at the time did not accept that people from my lower, working-class background should not have (or should have?) aspirations above their station in life. Opponents of the 1870, William Foster Education Act, 'Education For All', saying, **"that to educate the masses would make them discontent with their station in life."** Because our department had programmers, data collators, typists, statisticians, who could interpret the data, with access to Atlas the computer and Anita the calculator, I soon realised why we got invited to so many parties and why, at certain times, a box of chocolates or cakes would find its way into the office. Getting your research analysed on a computer saved the student literally hours and hours of time, working out statistical calculations by hand. The programmers could write specific programmes to do this for them, and then all they had to do was interpret the results, so the girls could then 'write up' the results.

Again, in hindsight I now realise that **by the age of 17or18, opportunities for careers in both football and information technology had presented themselves,** but at the time it was not apparent to me as I was just aimlessly taking each day at a time. Enter Verna Howarth and Coreen, two very attractive ladies, way out of my league, but nevertheless they became part of my dream world. If Joan O'Hara, at Norweb, had started the process of my re-education and socialisation, Verna and Coreen continued it.

I cannot recall the precise moment, when Verna and I ended up going out together but I do remember our first meeting. It was a seminal moment in my life that just happened, and materialised out of circumstance. For many of my generation, many things and everyday occurrences that would now be considered boring, were exciting and adventurous. For me catching two buses, one into Manchester, Stevenson Square and another from Piccadilly, out to Old Trafford or Manchester University, was in itself an adventure. Going to all night parties with people who talked posh, and not only read books, but also wrote them, was a heady cocktail for me to swallow. At times, I felt out of my depth but as long as I could keep them laughing and listening to my records, I would carry on until they found me out, and asked me to leave the party. Back to Verna in the School of Education. One day I found myself having to visit the School of Education, which was in the same building as the Department of Education, but on the Oxford Road side, not the JMB side. I was asked to deliver a package to a Mr Frank Gorner, and ended up going into the front office of the school during a coffee break time, when unbeknown to me all the girls in the school were assembled doing what all people do, 'chinwagging', whilst drinking tea and coffee. After a polite knock, that got no response, I banged on the door louder and heard many female voices shout, "Come in." For some reason, flashbacks to entering the Norweb's typing pool entered my thoughts.

Upon entering, I was confronted with several stunningly attractive, female forms sat atop various desks and swivel chairs displaying sufficient stockinged leg, to instantly trigger my testosterone levels to rise as well as causing idiopathic, craniofacial erythema, blushing to you and me. Now up until that moment in time I was not aware that Jim Briggs blushed easily, but being as my entrance was also accompanied by "Hiya Bloggsy," my instant recognition was too much to deal with. The fact that the words were uttered by a darker version of Kylie Minogue, in a short skirt as opposed to hot pants, was just all too much for the cocky, little bastard from Chadderton. How did they know who I was, I had never seen any of them in my life, and even had to ask directions as to how to find them? Luckily, an elderly lady, called Sylvia, rescued me before I was eaten alive by these female Praying Mantises. "Can I help you?" she enquired. No impersonations this time, in fact, I opened my mouth but very little came out, causing another bout of idiopathic, craniofacial erythema. I was actually in seventh heaven but because I had no experience of first, let alone seventh, I was truly not sure where this was going. I just know I loved the attention. "Leave him alone," said another girl, "it's not often we get male species in this part of the world, unless it's in the form of a student who has lost his way." At this juncture, I must point out that I have always turned up for work dressed for the part, and would never ever attend anything public looking scruffy. I would never go to work in jeans, let alone ones that were torn, ripped and distressed! Also, whilst I cannot swear to it, I will have been in a collar, tie and trousers. The last item being compulsory in those days. Looking at my class photographs at Primary school, show that even at an early age I wore a tie if I could find one. I must also point out that my recollection of this moment in my life whilst vivid as to the visual, the verbal aspect is very sketchy and so I have had to use authors' licence. Also, in those days I was very blonde. In fact, an Australian lady who worked in the department, once asked me had I ever visited Down Under, and I thought she was talking either about oral sex or cleaning under the bed. Either way I replied in the negative. I have since visited Australia on several occasions and understood why she asked. Eventually I managed to utter the reason for me being there, and Kylie slithered off her perch like Kaa out of Jungle book, a snake ensnaring its prey and said, "Come with me, Bloggsy." Could this get any better? To be honest, if she had taken me to the nearest stockroom and told me to have my wicked way with her I would probably have fainted. This woman oozed sex appeal and class and furthermore she knew it. No disrespect to the girls at NORWEB, but these girls were in another league. At the end of the corridor Kylie, soon to become Coreen, knocked on a door and without waiting to be summoned inside, opened it, walked in and said, "Verna there's a little, blonde bombshell to see you." By this stage, my blushing was reaching boiling point as Coreen, nee Kylie, turned, smiled and said, "Bye." I can't remember but I must have replied with a, "Thank you," because I had been brought up to be polite. "That's Coreen," said Verna, "take no notice, she's only teasing." Take no notice, you would have to be totally devoid of all your senses to take no notice of Coreen. It's ironic that I was later to become a massive fan of Miss Minogue, and have seen her several times live in concert. I still can't look at Kylie without thinking of Coreen. Anyhow back to Verna, I was now taking notice of an entirely different animal. Long, dark mousy hair, slim, very attractive, a genuine smile, that showed off her immaculate incisors and taller than Coreen. I'm sorry but my recollections from now on are to say the least, non-existent but we must have chatted because I ended up, a short while after this first encounter, being offered a lift home on the days I was not working late. This was not all the way home, but to Moston Baths on Broadway, which meant I only had to catch one bus to Chadderon. What was also good about the lift, apart from saving me money, Verna refusing to accept any petrol money, was that by the time the 2 and 24 buses from Manchester arrived at Moston, they had started to become less congested and so, I nearly always not only got on the bus but also actually got a seat, which was not always the case when getting on at Stevenson Square, Manchester.

Verna and I became close friends and our relationship lasted 3 years. She introduced me to the theatre, bridge, cashew nuts and we played tennis with her parents, Frank and Nora. Frank was a boss at British Aerospace and Nora was a teacher in Further Education. Frank was a lovely man and never once patronised me, but must have thought I was not the right material for his only daughter. Nora was dipsy and dotty, full of airs and graces but again always treated me fairly.

When I first met Verna, as I've said, she was being pursued by a guy called Peter Woolsey, who was of a similar age to her and he lived in Knightsbridge, London. At the time having never visited the capital, I was unaware of the significance of this area of London. I'm not sure when or how he had entered her life, but Verna informed me that she was not interested but he kept cropping up like a bad penny! I do recall that when a party invite in Kilburn was extended to the School and Department of Education, Verna arranged for us to stay at Mr Woolsey's place in Knightsbridge. I also recall that Verna had told Peter that if she was going to stay at his place, I was part of the package and begrudgingly, he agreed. I travelled down to London in his AC Bristol sports car whilst Verna followed in her mini. Well, not literally, because the journey was my first experience of travelling at speed. At times on the M1, we reached 100 mph. I didn't get the buzz that some people get from travelling at speed, but arrived in London unscathed, with underpants unsoiled. His flat was massive, but then again for a runt from Lancashire, who had shared a council house with 8 other people, I must have easily been impressed. The reader might think this episode in my life strange, but in hindsight I realised that my relationship with Verna was more symbiotic than sexual. We got on well together, liked the same things, I made her laugh and being an only child, my brothers and sisters provided her with something she missed in her life, other siblings to love and fall out with. Unfortunately, because of our age difference Verna was always trying to encourage me to find a more suitable partner. It's not that she didn't care, in fact it was the opposite. Being many years older than me, she said she wasn't interested in marriage or having children and thought I was wasting time being with her, when I should be looking for a more suitable girlfriend. She never actually qualified what constituted, 'more suitable', other than someone of my own age. As I became more worldly wise, I later realised age differences were subjective and personally speaking, you were as old as who you felt. From my point of view, I was very happy, thank you very much, enjoying the moment, being chauffeured around by an intelligent, attractive, classy, young lady. To be honest, I think she liked my company because I appreciated her for who she was, and not some kind of prized possession I could link arms with. The only negative for Verna was that she smoked, and history will show that she was the only woman I ever dated that was a nicotine junkie. To be fair to Verna, she never smoked in my presence and sucked polo mints. No comment. We spent a lot of time with my sister Lilian and Jack Dalloway, who had moved from Webster Street to Fitton Hill, Oldham and with my brother Jack and Chris at Marlborough Road, Royton. She frequently visited Parkway.

Jack Dalloway, my sister Lilian, myself and Verna, in the Sun Inn Middleton Rd. Chadderton. Note the cravat, very posh.

In those days going to the pub was a, **'night out'**, for **ADULTS**, with not a child in sight, unless they were waiting for an adult to come out. The night consisted of face-to-face chatter, a few drinks and the odd bag of crisps, and in larger establishments, an entertainer. The men drank mild, bitter, mixed or a bottle of stout, and the ladies drank Babycham, Cherry Bs or cider. All from a glass and definitely **NOT STRAIGHT FROM THE BOTTLE**. Incidentally, my father referred to Cherry Bs as, 'leg openers'. I'll say no more, but again, in those days the object of the exercise for both sexes, was enjoyment. **Unlike today, where there are more children than adults in the pub, and the enjoyment factor appears to be a competition of who can get sclerosis of the liver the fastest.**

As our relationship developed, Verna soon picked up on the fact that I was rudderless, and so she was always asking me what I wanted to do as a career, now that I had decided against one in football. Having 5, GCE O' levels and a few CSEs and studying for an A Level at John Dalton College in Manchester, she once asked me had I considered going to university, and a career in teaching? To which I replied, "Are you serious? People from my background don't think such things."

"A mental abyss separated the likes of us from Universities." (Woodruff W, 2006, Beyond Nab End, 4:479).

"Why not, I think you'd make a great PE teacher." She eventually persuaded me to talk to her boss Frank Gorner, whose wife was a lecturer at Mather Teacher Training College Manchester. He informed me that I had the qualifications to secure a place in a Teacher Training College, and that he would ask Miss Jean Murray, the Principal of Mather TT College, Whitworth Street, Manchester, a friend of his, to invite me for an interview. He would also act as my sponsor, and give me a reference. I was choked, because apart from my brother Jack, I had never had any kind of help, support or guidance as to what to do with my life.

Arriving home that night, after talking to Frank, I spoke to mum about the possibility of going to Teacher Training College. I cannot recollect the conversation, but the issue that would have been paramount was leaving my paid employment at the University to become an unpaid student, albeit hopefully with a grant. This meant I wouldn't be able to continue making a contribution, like my brothers and sisters were doing, to the Parkway budget, and as grants were means tested, based on your parents' income, may have involved them in contributing to my grant. Mum must have said something like she would manage, but I now had the problem of firstly talking to dad and explaining to him that in order for me to get a grant he, as the main wage earner, would have to fill in some pink forms disclosing his earnings. Memory recall is a fascinating thing as great chunks of history can be forgotten, whilst the colour of some forms, that were filled in years previously, can be recalled in an instant. Several days later, I remember sitting on the settee in the front room, asking him to fill in various sections of these pink, salmon-coloured forms that referred to his gross income. I, together with mum, had filled in the rest of the grant application, and must have succeeded in achieving my goal as I was given a grant of £246 pa, plus a parental contribution of approximately £40 pa. The £246 was to be given in 3 lumps, as semester cheques. The reason I cannot recall the exact amount of the parental contribution was, because it had to be given directly to me by my dad, and I decided I had no intentions of chasing my father 3 times a year along Parkway. He struggled giving us pocket money, so the thought of intercepting him for larger sums for my college education didn't appeal. I would get part time jobs between semesters, as many students did, to supplement my grant. After a successful interview with Jean Murray, I was offered a place at Mather and with a successful grant application, everything was in place to start the next journey in my life. The rest is history so to speak, and why Verna has always had a special place in my heart. I can never thank her and Frank enough, for pointing me in the right direction.

"Learning aroused my curiosity and imagination. There was wonder and adventure – an entirely new way of looking at life had opened up." (Woodruff W, 2006, Beyond Nab End, 4:478).

When I became a published author, in 2001, I dedicated my book to the pair of them. Sadly, during my second year at Mather College, Verna accepted a position in a 5-star hotel in Bermuda, I didn't even know where Bermuda was. It was as though she wanted to ensure I was OK and that I didn't need her help and guidance anymore, before she considered her own career, but that was Verna. I cannot recall how long her contract was for, but I do remember her returning to the UK to visit her parents during my final year's teaching at Mather Street School. In making the decision to leave the School of Education and accept a contract in Bermuda, she was putting herself out of arm's length. Although our relationship had never been intense and in retrospect was fairly fluid, to say the least, she always felt I should find someone younger and, in the end, she probably felt that by accepting the position in Bermuda, I would have a better opportunity with her out of the way. To say I was once again gutted was an understatement. I definitely was realising that I somehow did not have the skill set to deal with rejection, especially as I felt I had done nothing wrong to warrant being told the party was over. I will always remember our last time together as she drove away from 24 Park Way in her white mini. I was, to say the least, a very unhappy bunny. Rejected again.

It's ironic that Verna eventually ended up marrying a much younger guy than herself, called Rob Fraser. They had two children, Samantha and Victoria and she returned to this country to live permanently in Scotland with Rob. When her father became ill, she returned to live back in Moston, next door to her parents. Over the years birthday and Christmas cards were exchanged between her and some of my family. My brother, Jack and his wife, Christine actually visited the Frasers in Scotland. As both Verna and I were married, it didn't seem appropriate that we should communicate, but we did eventually re-unite, if that's the correct term, when she and Rob attended my brother Jack's family do at the Maple Squash Club on Broadway, Royton. From then on, our paths crossed at various times in my life and we will re-visit Verna and the Frasers later.

Verna and I on holiday in Cornwall, 1968.

TV, Radio, Music, DJ's, Films, Musicals and the Theatre.

As my life experiences increased, in many cases due to the people I was meeting, it became apparent that, even as a late teenager, music, reading, writing, the theatre and exercise were becoming my daily drugs, and without them I became restless and unhappy. Each day gave me numerous escapism opportunities, via my 'fixes'. I could go back to a time when the world was a far different place; solve a murder mystery or crime, via my latest read or, like Alan Bennett the Northern Playwright, be in the here and now. As my music collection grew, it was also defining specific times in my life. **"When I write a book I find there are songs that, 'keep me company', at various points."** (Bruce A, 2011, The Siren P293). In Alan Bennett's case his choice of music was classical whereas, apart from folk, I tried to embrace all types. In fact, I could have written this autobiography and defined my life via my list of favourite music tracks, and later via my choice of authors. The latter beginning at Mather TT College, when I realised reading could be the portal to other worlds and therefore could broaden my horizons, whilst making me realise that a library was not just a building, but somewhere you could visit for a reason. I was 14 when I bought my first vinyl LP, Vanilla Fudge, featuring a drummer named Carmine Appice, who later went on to work with Rod Stewart. Before the age of 14, my influences in entertainment can be attributed to radio DJs, especially pirate radio such as Luxemburg and Caroline. I still listen to Tony Blackburn on, 'Sounds of the 60s', on Radio 2 Saturday mornings. When TV did enter the music scene, The Six Five Special, with Pete Murray, Ready Steady Go, with Cathy McGowan, who married Michael Ball, Juke Box Jury with David Jacobs and his female co-presenter who would, 'Give it five', in her strong Brummie accent, all became firm favourites with me. Not forgetting Top of the Pops, The Old Grey Whistle Test, with DJ whispering Bob Harris, and The Tube with Jools Holland. At the age of 74, I can say that I have never bought a singles record in my life, only ever purchasing LPs, cassettes and CDs. In my early teenage days, my record collection related to black soul and American R&B music. Am I allowed to say black soul? Too late, I've said it. I then moved onto heavy rock, classical and engaged with the disco era. **During which time I enjoyed asking a lady, "Please would you like a dance or, could I have this dance?" Very rarely were you refused because in those days Neolithic grunting, rapping man and 'Big Brother, Love Island girl', both with a high dependency on alcohol, six packs and Botox, had not yet materialised, and self-respect, courtesy and manners existed.** If, by chance, you managed to stay on the dance floor for more than one dance, your adrenaline started to pump as there was a slight possibility that the young lady liked you. The decision being arrived at with, 'a clear head', not a drug induced haze. **Today in the year 2025, the world is a different place and men don't ask, they just pose at the bar, or dance alone, or with their mates, spinning on their heads, mincing and body waving across the floor.** Do the ladies still form a circle around their handbags? Because if they do, the bags most probably have been replaced by alcohol. Shots being more important than shuffles. Or the handbags now belong to a male, rather than a female. Is this called gender bending? **How do you bend a gender and is it the same thing as a 'bent copper'?** Which, we now know, has a monetary value. I know all this homophobic, rhetoric will incur the wrath of some microbiotic, seaweed eater, but being an honest biologist, I'm just reporting what I see or know, and have no particular gripe how people live their lives or how they want to be perceived. **But I am adamant that I am not going to be conned or hoodwinked into thinking that these people are behaving this way, because that is genuinely who they are.** In my day, the tribes were mods and rockers, denoted by dress and music preference. **Today, it appears these tribes are very transient and the lines are blurred, depending on what is the latest get rich quick gimmick/trend to become famous with. To me, I find it disingenuous.** Disco has become hip-hop, house, garage and we now have aficionados of music and a multitude of variations on a theme. Debbie Harry of Blondie fame was one of the first artists to rap on Rapture in 1980, and you could tell what she was saying. In 2025, so called artists can now talk gibberish to music, with the obligatory eff and geff words, probably because the artist has a limited vocabulary, and their singing is questionable, and call it rap. Or as James Patterson in his 2005 novel, Honeymoon, calls it, **'Rap Crap'.** The lyrics consisting of a few monosyllabic lines that are constantly repeated, whilst holding their crotch, very much like Homo Erectus Slack Arse, and there you have it, Social Conscience. Even Tini Tempa, when talking to Lenny Henry in his documentary, 2023, admitted that rap was for people who can't sing. **"I'd rather listen to a strangled cat cough up phlegm, says Pops, than listen to rap."** (Coben H, 2011. Caught, 13:126). With the development of technology and the demise of the mafia like industry moguls, with artists having a much greater input as to their contracts and careers, the music industry has changed and in terms of the actual music, I'm pleased to say, on the whole, for the better. But it's not all wine and roses. In the 60s, 70s and 80s it was all about exploiting individual musical talent, with dodgy contracts, whereas, today musical talent is being exploited and promoted in other ways. In the 1960s and 70s backing singers and dancers, appropriately suited and booted, had wonderful, if somewhat robotic routines, that provided hours of amusement for people of my generation to copy. Of course, you will always get the alternative to the rule, but this was mainly as a gimmick to stand out from the crowd. **So, who decided and when did the lead, background singers and dancers have to wear as few clothes as possible, ensuring the music industry became an off shoot of the soft and in some cases, not so soft porn industry?** It has been suggested the advent of the MTV music videos, when bands who could sing, play and write their own songs were in decline, to be replaced by soft porn videos to promote artists. What is the next stage in this so-called progress, total nudity? **Playing my music instantly projects me back in time, with various recording artists and tracks from their albums reminding me of personal relationships, good and some of the bad times, that are still too raw in my psyche to listen to, physically reducing me to tears with their evocative memories. Whilst others can immediately make me want to head bang, air guitar and hold concerts in my lounge, in front of thousands of screaming, adoring fans, with or without the aid of a hair brush or tennis racket as my prop.** Not forgetting being a DJ and helping thousands to party in Ibiza. My musical educational foundation in 60s, 70s and 80s was about the lyrics, and knowing the story behind the words. The autobiography of Ronnie Woods of Faces and Rolling Stones fame, in 2007, is testimony to the diversity of music on offer in the 50s, 60s and 70s and afforded me a wonderful trip down memory lane. **My generation can still sing most of the Lennon and McCartney, Beatle's songs. In 30 plus years I wonder if the music populace will be able to repeat the lyrics to the rap of 2025?** When I was growing up, and going out 'clubbing' most artists and groups were distinctive, different and individual. **Today, many are manufactured and cloned and like many male footballers, who are hyperbolized into stratospheric, delusional superstars. What musical, lyrical legacy will today's soft porn, rap artist leave? Watch Ben Elton's last Live Stand-Up DVDs for the answer.** As an aside my Wharfedale Litton speakers are at least 50 years old, and have NEVER needed repairing. In 2024, you can't buy anything without being offered an extended warranty because after 12 months it could break down.

During the late 70s and early 80s Dee, my wife and I had season tickets to go and listen to the Halle orchestra in Manchester and most Sundays, during the season, we would travel to the Free Trade Hall to listen to Stravinsky, Rachmaninov, Beethoven, Dvorak and Shostakovich, to name but a few. We loved attending, even though we did find some people a little pretentious, to say the least. I, especially, loved watching the old dears going to sleep during the quiet second movement of a piece and listening to their own personal movements before the comfort break.

Over the years I have seen many music artists and groups live and as time went on, I came to realise the difference between 2 hours plus, non-stop, musical extravaganza such as those given by the likes of Madonna, Phil Collins and Kyli Minogue, as opposed to going to see a group play live which consisted of instrumentals and songs, interspersed with chat. I was present at Kylie Minogue's comeback, Showgirls tour, in Manchester, in 2006, after she had recovered from cancer. She had a 5-minute, standing ovation when she first came on stage, before she had sung a note. It was very emotional. It is interesting to note that in 1967 you could see 4 groups, including the 'supergroup' Cream, live at the Manchester University Rag Ball, for £2 for a double ticket, or in 1970, The Who, for 15 shillings at the same venue. By 1980, it cost £1.50 to see Human League. **THERE WERE NO BOOKING FEES INVOLVED so who decided and when did booking fees become standard practice?** In 2023, the booking fee costs considerably more than it costs to see all the groups live in my student days? **How are booking fees justified? Who benefits from these extra fees? Have the promoters not already factored in all the costs, which include venue hire, before deciding the ticket cost?** The answer to the last question being **yes**. How do I know, because many years ago a football mate of mine went out with a female music promoter, and she would inform us what the job involved and how the promoter arrived at a ticket price. **But as the highest form of intelligence in the animal kingdom, vast swathes of today's society appear happy to pay the booking fee and be 'ripped-off'.** My love of all things related to being entertained, started long before I worked at Marianne Jepson's Dance and Drama College as a forty-two-year-old, and started meeting people from the entertainment world. Remember

I was not born with a TV, transistor radio or Hi-Fi system providing background noise, but with the sounds of my mum and brother Jack, whistling, humming or singing a tune. We had a radio which provided a diet of plays, sing along shows, serious discussion or programmes that could be put under the umbrella of family entertainment, but the radio was not a constancy in the Briggs' household, as choice of stations was limited. The radio was only put on at certain times. Shows such as Workers Playtime, Two Way Family Favourites, Quatermass and the Pit, that used to scare the listener, Al Read and that all time Sunday favourite – Sing Something Simple with Cliff Adams and The Adams Singers. As I generally hated Sundays, this programme, which if I remember was on just after teatime, 6 o'clock, was my first encounter, as a teenager, with the idea of committing suicide. Only joking, not. It was just there every week and it wouldn't go away. Later in my childhood, Alan Freeman, "Hi there, pop pickers," used to give us a rundown of the pop charts. This was brilliant as TV's, Top of the Pops and Radio One had not yet entered the scene. Pirate radio was in its infancy, and trying to locate such stations as Radio Caroline and Luxemburg on our, 'tube radio', that took a few minutes to warm up, was a real challenge. My earliest recollections of self entertainment were of some of my brothers and sisters singing around a black, upright piano. Did we have a piano and if so, how could we afford one? Who played it? I don't know. Nevertheless, that was what I recall. I can also remember a portable record player suddenly arriving in our front room one Sunday, after my father had 'gone out', with half a dozen single records which were neatly stacked, and secured on a central arm and then dropped one at a time to be played. Cliff Richards and The Shadows, springs to mind. Obviously as my sister Lilian has been in love with Cliff Richards since she was born, it stands to reason he had to be on the play list. Records were just played and repeated continually, and so learning the tunes and all the lyrics was the done thing. **Today advertising, brain washing and soft pornography tend to sell many records.** I think our next-door neighbours, Duffy's, provided the record player. No relation to the singer. And yes, Brian was the boy that ran in front of a car and was killed. **In those days there was a community spirit of sharing, from food left-overs to the latest invention by those who could afford such things. Now we have programmes on television entitled, 'Neighbours from Hell' and How to steal a car/ bicycle.**

Our nearest picture houses were The Casino and Lyric, off Middleton Road. The latter affectionately known as the 'Bug House', but then didn't all towns have picture houses referred to as such? On Saturdays, we sometimes went to the matinees to watch Superman and his arch rival Ming. Paying 6d, (pence) to sit at the front and, when the lights were dimmed, crawling under all the seats to the 1 shilling and three pence, or was it nine pence, at the back, was a favourite pastime for many children? Unfortunately, the usherettes were trained in Rottweiler control and so with their high-powered torches nothing got past them or for that matter under them. As I got older, and earned my own, 'pocket money', I would sometimes go out on a Friday night alone, or with mates to watch a film. Afterwards frequenting Dorges chip shop for sausage, chips, with gravy, in a tray. Luxury. Today a two-ton box of popcorn, with a gallon of coke appears to be the norm. What interpretation the reader wants to put on the word coke, I will leave up to them. There were other picture houses, apart from the Lyric and theatres in Oldham. Picture houses on Union Street, such as the Odeon, with another one near Featherstall Road as well as the Coliseum Theatre. Baileys Night Club, at the Star Inn traffic lights, was originally an ABC cinema, where, if I'm not mistaken, my brother went to see the Beatles. In those days, these places were old time, entertainment theatres before becoming cinemas. The Coliseum is where, when I was old enough to appreciate live theatre, I spent many, many hours watching plays and productions. As a repertory theatre company many 'soap stars' learned their stage craft at the Coliseum. Actors such as Sarah Lancashire, Siobhan Finneran, Barbara Knox, Anna Friel, Roy Barraclough, Michael Lavelle, Judith Barker and Kenneth Alan Taylor, to name but a few. My early cinema exploits, apart from the Lyric, were courtesy of my sister Lilian who took me to see such classics as Oklahoma, West Side Story, 7 Brides for 7 Brothers, and South Pacific. The ratings for some of these meant you had to have, 'a responsible adult' to accompany you. Sometimes, you would go up and down the queue outside, and ask if some adult would take you in. **Today, some adults can't even look after themselves never mind anyone else. Also, today's society would have a hissy fit at this practice but in those days, community spirit was very much in evidence. Also, many people today prefer Netflix rather than going out to the cinema, probably because it doesn't involve too much strenuous activity, only pressing buttons.**

I was 8, when I saw one of my first films in a 'picture house' when I got in to watch Kirk Douglas in The Vikings. I'll never forget the dimple on Kirk's chin. 9 years later I watched Julie Andrews in Sound of Music, with Verna at Manchester Playhouse. And in my 20s, whilst on holiday with my future wife Dee, in Torquay I saw Saturday Night Fever, starring John Travolta, at a late night screening at the picture house in Paignton. Films such as Dr. Zhivago, ET, Close Encounters of a Third Kind, Schindler's List, 7 Pounds, Pretty Woman, Love Story, Railway Children, Great Expectations and Saving Mr Banks, starring Emma Thompson and Tom Hanks, in 2013, not forgetting Educating Rita, are just a few of my favourites. Being a massive Monty Python fan, their films, In Search of the Holy Grail and Life of Brian would have to be high up on my list of favourites. I love anything that makes me laugh uncontrollably. Comedy films with Tina Fey, Steve Carelli and Mila Kunis in, such as Bad Mums 1 and 2, I can watch over and over again. Bill Cranson in, Why Him? Then there was Toy Story, Happy Feet, Shrek, Cars, Ratatouille, Flushed Away and Ants. In fact, most animated children's films that educate and entertain. However, once I'd experienced my first live theatre and musicals, such as Barnum with Michael Crawford and Billie Liar, with Tom Courtney in Manchester, with Verna, I was hooked. Enter Cameron Mackintosh, Andrew Lloyd Webber and Tim Rice – Jesus Christ Superstar, Evita, Phantom of the Opera, Cats, Chess, Starlight Express, Les Miserables, Chicago, Cabaret, 42nd Street, (I love tap), Grease, Billie Elliot, Sweeney Todd, The Demon Barber of Fleet St, Stephen Sondheim. Blood Brothers and Boys from the Black Stuff by Alan Bleasdale and Oliver by Lionel Bart. Not forgetting the films Burlesque and Moulin Rouge, starring Nicole Kidman and Ewan Mc Gregor. When Denis Potter entered my world, I loved his plays as they not only appealed to my extrovert personality, but also to my anti- establishment, non-conformist, rebellious streak. Finally, Michael Flatley's Riverdance, which I saw live in Manchester, with Margaret Bradbury, her children, Jenny, Jo and Ruth, is entertainment at its best. My favourite actors include Jodie Foster, Julia Roberts, Sandra Bullock, Sarah Lancashire, Suranne Jones, Nicola Walker, Sheridan Smith, Julie Walters, Meryl Streep, Harrison Ford, Tom Hanks, Stephen Tomkinson, James Morrison, Martin Clunes, John Sims, Stephen Graham, Jody Comer and David Tennant to name but a few. It goes without saying that I have just scratched the surface of my favourites in each of the above categories, but because entertainment has been such an integral part of my life, I felt I had to devote some of my autobiography to it. As for the music and songs, TV dramas, comedies in the guise of Kenny Everet, Monty Python, Hi Di Hi and Hello, Hello, entertainment and documentaries etc. these have been integral reference points during the writing of this book.

Extract from Soul Manchester Magazine, P24.

Crossing Over to the Other side:

Mather Teacher Training College, Manchester University, 18-21yrs.

"That's the thing about teaching – no matter how organised you are, how many systems you put in place, you can't plan for people. They interrupt, they're early, they're late. They can't get it together." (Jordon T, 2008. Addition, p57).

My ID photo for college.

I remember my first day at Mather, being a very excited bunny. As alluded to before, with the class system firmly entrenched into the fabric of life, people from my background didn't go to university or attend Teacher Training College. But here I was in the entrance hall to Mather Teacher Training College, Whitworth Street, Manchester, which was part of the Manchester University campus. As the entrance hall became more and more congested, I remember ending up being corralled into a corner with two other lads, George Bradbury and Eddie Whalley, who subsequently became two of my best mates during and after college, as they both came from the Oldham area. George from Diggle, in Saddleworth and Ed from Werneth, Oldham. I honestly have no recollection of what happened next, but we all must have been shepherded up to the main hall to be addressed by the Principal, Jean Murray. A slight framed lady, with greying hair who had interviewed me not too long ago, as my application to attend the course was, as I'd mentioned, on the last minute to say the least. My interview with the principal having been arranged by Verna and her boss Frank Gorner, who acted as my referees. Frank's wife also worked at Mather as a French tutor, and so, to say I had some help getting in was not an over exaggeration. **For this reason, I attended Mather not wanting to let anyone down,** and add this to the fact that I felt I didn't really belong in such an establishment meant my work ethic, although I say so myself, was excellent. I secretly dreaded being asked to leave because I wasn't good enough. Long before I knew what Imposter Syndrome was. **Very sadly, my later experiences in Higher Education have found some students arrive because they think it is their right, with an attitude and work ethic that centres around the belief that they are doing the lecturers a favour, turning up for lectures, workshops and tutorials.** As I will address later, **universities themselves, once fees started to become an issue, considered prospective candidates as cash cows rather than potential academics.** Anyhow back to my interview with Miss Murray. The only question I remember from the interview was, "Why do you want to be a teacher, James?" and being told by my mentors Verna and Frank **not to reply,** "Because of the money and holidays." The stock answer being, because you loved children, or something equally cheesy and insipid. I could have given her the old standard joke, 'I love children but can't manage a full one', but I suspect she would have heard it on more than one occasion and was getting just a tad bored with it. During the ensuing week I was introduced to my biology tutors, Keith Weston and Roy Amos, who used to teach biology at Chadderton Grammar School where my youngest sister and eldest brother attended. The biology group consisted of 14 girls and 2 lads. Yes, 14 girls and 2 lads. My recollections of my biology course with its field trips to The Lake District, North Yorkshire and days out to Derbyshire, to study the local flora and fauna, was one of enjoyment and happiness. As I recall there was no bitchiness amongst the girls, Roger and I didn't vie for the Alpha male slot, the tutors were approachable and tried to make the lectures and workshops interesting and the group, as a whole, got on really well. My PE Tutors were Terry Casey, Bill Craven and Shirley Munday, the boss. Terry was an alpha male, who also, part-time, managed Nantwich Town FC in the Cheshire League. Terry tried to get me to play for Nantwich Town, but the fact was I had lost a little of my earlier enthusiasm for the national game, and was channelling all my efforts into becoming a teacher and had abandoned thoughts of playing professional football. Although playing for Nantwich Town would have been semi-professional, it seemed an awfully long way to go on a bus to play a game of football. In those days, the M6 only went as far as the Penkridge and Gailey roundabout in Staffordshire. Added to the fact, I couldn't drive and didn't own a car, made my decision to decline Terry's offer easy. But I was none the less flattered.

In those drugs, sex and rock and roll days, just like today, there were many distractions to actual studying, and stable relationships could be put under a great deal of strain. There were so many new temptations and distractions to experience. People arriving at College/University, with a school-day relationship in tow, were suddenly confronted with peer group pressure on a higher plane. **This, 'group tribal behaviour', was quite simply where people become desperate, 'to belong', for fear of becoming a, 'Billy No Mates'.** So, if as a student decided to display a body language which said, 'hands off, I'm spoken for', they were in actual fact excluding themselves from many social situations at university. For me, this time of being away from home was a massive social learning curve that I feel everyone, who has the opportunity, should embrace. **This 'belonging' and 'group tribal behaviour', akin to peer group pressure as a teenager, manifests itself in many guises such as football hooliganism, sexism, chauvinism, bigotry, racism, and a whole variety of ics, ists and isms in social situations.** Brexit was partially driven by such behaviour. In the 70s and 80s people were either a mod or rocker, into the Beatles, the Rolling Stones, Ska or Reggae music. Later on in my teaching career, from 2003-6, when I was lecturing at Teesside University, tribal groups was one of the subjects I chose, whilst studying for my PgCTLHE and then becoming a Fellow of the Higher Education

Academy, which in itself could be considered an academic tribal group, based on belonging to a group who shared a specific knowledge, in a certain sphere of education. As mentioned at the onset of writing this book I have purposely avoided writing about personal stuff unless it was relevant to highlighting a point, and more pertinently to not embarrass the people involved unless, in my humble opinion, the criticism was justified. But needless to say, if only I'd have known then what I know now, a career in script writing, or comedy, was beckoning. After I retired, I went to watch Gervais Finn, at Bolton Town Hall. Gervais was a retired teacher and HMI, (Her Majesties' Inspectorate), who had found a niche entertaining and writing about his exploits in teaching. The place was packed, and he was very funny. During the interval, my then partner, Heather, remarked, "You could do that." Thanks, Heather. If only. Which leads me onto someone who did choose to trip the lights and walk the boards instead of becoming a teacher, Mike Harding. Mr Harding was a year above me at Mather, and successfully ran the folk club and did the odd gig in and around the folk clubs in Manchester. As is now history, Mr Harding became famous as, the Rochdale Cowboy, and penned northern comedy plays such as, 'Fur Coat and No Knickers'. Teaching was a tremendous source of observational, as well as other forms of comedy. In the early days, much of Mr Harding's material was taken from his classroom and school experiences, but occasionally, he was guilty of plagiarism as some of his stories were not his own. There was a student John C who, after one teaching practice, had us in stitches because some of the children had set fire to one of the desks. I can still see him now waxing lyrical about the little bastards, who had given him nothing but grief. Later Mr Harding was to experience such laughter when he related this story as his own. Was Mr Harding confused or in denial? On the 29/9/2022, Mr Harding could be seen in an episode of, All Creatures Great and Small, as a cantankerous old farmer. In the late 60s and early 70s Manchester conurbation consisted of Ardwick, Moss Side, Failsworth, Newton Heath, Levenshulme, Failsworth etc. These places were full of life's rich tapestry, long before social commentators came up with terms such as social deprivation, disadvantaged, no-go areas, etc. They were to me the foundation of my early teaching experiences, and a rich source of material to pass on to future teaching generations. Apart from the obvious student haunts of the student union and college bar, we sometimes could be found in the Rembrandt pub behind Chorlton Street bus station, Piccadilly. It was situated next to the canal, on Canal Street, which was and, as far as I'm still aware, the place for the prostitutes and rent boys to hang out. My PE course more than adequately prepared me for what lay ahead, as all three tutors, in their own inimitable ways, contributed to my development. Sadly, I heard not long into my teaching career, that Trevor Duerden, one of the lads on the PE course, who was in a relationship at the time with a Swedish bombshell, suddenly died of a heart attack, aetiology unknown! He was in his twenties. The one person with whom I became most associated with at college, was a guy 6 years my senior, who was studying Art and Design, called Peter Holland. Peter could sell sand to the Arabs and was a 'Jack, the lad'. Pete had roguish good looks and the fact he drove a Triumph Spitfire did no harm to his 'street cred', when it came to, 'pulling the birds'. Apart from studying art, Peter used to work for an old police mate of his dad, who was a private detective. So, serving summons, following people, doing what is termed, leg and grunt work, were things Pete got involved with, and paid for when not studying to become an art teacher. He also used to buy and sell stuff by visiting wholesalers in Shude Hill, Manchester. Not long after becoming mates with Pete, he helped my brother Barry and me to set up a little business venture, that provided us with a little extra spending money. At college, Pete and I embraced the social aspects of college to the full, but we both applied ourselves to work, as and when it was required, and were both quite disciplined when it came time to, 'knuckling-down', to our studies. My philosophy to studying being much the same as it was at secondary school, work hard, play hard, in that order. I frequently travelled to ollege on the 2 or 24 bus to Manchester, alighting at Stevenson's Square and passing several reputable barbers' shops, whose main source of income seemed to be derived from selling, 'packets of three', as opposed to giving someone a short back and sides. **Now they use all kinds of number codes to basically shave your head, but in those days, hair was a valued commodity and not something most people, especially the guys, were in any rush to lose.** I had several brief relationships whilst at Mather, but with no disrespect to the women involved, nothing serious, or which could have been called serious, until I met Dee. And even though, Verna had left for pastures new, I always felt she was always there for me, perched on my shoulder, guiding and advising. **Pete, being Pete, always had a project on the go, other than his academic studies and making money, which usually included the female variety, and it was on one of Pete's escapades that I first met Alma Johnson, Dee, who was to become my wife.** The venue was the University of Manchester Institute of Science and Technology, UMIST, on a Wednesday evening, during my third year at Mather. For people who are not aware, traditionally, Wednesday afternoon in Higher Education is given over to the pastoral, social and the sports side of education, when teams vent their spleens against one another, whilst others look for drugs, sex and rock and roll. A few students actually go to the library to work on their latest assignments, which, being a goody –two-shoes, sometimes included me. The Students' Union was also active in organising various events and pastimes which, in the evenings, meant that the latest, musical phenomena would hit town, and for the equivalent of 50p, plus your Student Union card, you got to see groups such as Free, a heavy rock band, Barclay James Harvest, 'a prog rock group', coming from the Saddleworth area, and Osibissa, a multi –cultural group of happy chappies, full of rhythm and happiness, were just a few of the ones I saw. The University circuit then being, as it still is today, part and parcel of the live music, comedy and entertainment circuit. On this particular Wednesday night, I had been out during the day with Peter, in his red sports car, following a garage salesman, who was suspected of being up to no good with his employer's motor vehicles, by selling them to friends and family, by 'cooking the books'. We had arranged to meet the rest of the lads in either the student bar at Mather or at UMIST, the distance between the two venues being less than a mile. What made this particular night special, apart from meeting my future wife, was my friend Pete. In his own inimitable way, he had arranged to meet not one, but also two other female students at UMIST. Unfortunately, during the day he'd found out that his girlfriend Janet was also planning on arriving as a surprise, OOOPS!!! As mobile phones had yet to enter the scene, I am not sure how he came by such information. Anyhow, I was tasked with Plan A as to how we, that is his mates, were going to help him out of his predicament. As the reader is probably wanting to read all the juicy details, I am sadly going to disappoint to avoid embarrassment to those concerned. Only to say that no one got their nose bloodied or ended up being murdered! Enter the Didsbury girls, Barbara Hinchliffe, Alma Johnson and Janet Higginbottom, who later became Hutchinson, after marrying Alan. Didsbury Teacher Training College was a far more established TT college than Mather, and we were perceived as the somewhat poorer relations. However, UMIST was the place to be, and so as long as you had your student union card anyone was welcome. To cut a long story short, as opposed to my hair, my mates and I ended up chatting with these girls and I decided I would like to see if I could get a date with Alma. How I ended up seeing Alma, later re-named Dee, again I am not really sure but my mate Eddy's lack of social skills may have helped. She was a year younger than me, and therefore a year below me at Didsbury College, where she was studying music. I think I may have bribed her to go out with me, on the promise of helping her with her assignments and teaching practice. I do however, remember one of our first dates when I travelled to Heaton Moor to see her and after going to the local pub for a drink, being the gentleman that I was, walked her back to the flat she shared with the other three girls. In my mind's eye I can see us now hurrying down Heaton Moor Road near to the railway station. "Hurry up or it will be closed," she said, as I increased my pace. To be honest I had no idea where we were rushing to, but got the impression that for Dee it was important. Eventually we arrived at the local chip shop where she immediately ordered chips in a tray, with gravy. A very well known, local, Northern delicacy. Walking along a road sharing chips and gravy, with plastic forks, with a member of the opposite sex, is what cements a relationship, don't you think? Why is it food, in this case chips, tends to taste better in the fresh air? Anyhow more about Alma Johnson, or Dee as she later became known, and our married life, in the following chapters but for now here is a photo of her during her student days.

Dee: rolled neck sweaters were all the fashion rage in the late 60s early 70s.

As mentioned before, it was only at the age of 18, when I attended Mather Teacher Training College/University Manchester for 3 years and studied PE, Biology, Child Development, Psychology, Sociology and every other 'ology' you could think of, did I realise the significance of my pre 18-year-old memories. Helped tremendously by the fact you were encouraged to relate your studies to your own particular upbringing and circumstances. Up until then, I thought all children, apart from the rich and posh folk, had roughly the same upbringing, with the emphasis being on rough. My almost total ignorance of nature, nurture, genotypes and phenotypes was soon exposed. **Today with 12-month PGCEs the emphasis is not so much on the social aspects of teaching and the massive implications this has on the job, but on the pedagogical skills of lesson preparation, time management and targets, to satisfy political initiatives, from a National Curriculum. My generation, on the other hand, had it drilled into us as student teachers that the first 5 years of a child's life were vital** and the template for future development. In other words, a foundation on which to build, and without such future attempts at socialisation, and education would prove at best, difficult and at least, almost impossible. The message and research evidence was: Compensatory education could never replace what has been missed early on in life. To re-emphasise, the first five years being the time when adults could provide a loving, caring, secure, stimulating, environment in which the child could start to grow and develop linguistically, emotionally, spiritually, physically, and intellectually into an independent, responsible adult. The irony of this being that if the adults, especially the parents, were successful in building such a foundation, they may have built a rod for their own back when their children became headstrong, independent, rebellious souls. Our standard text at college was Lovell's, 'The First Five Years', or something similar, which was a must read if you were to pass your theory exams. I gained a commendation in my finals, so I must have read it cover to cover. The never-ending 'Nature versus Nurture' debate rumbled on. Biologists and geneticists related everything to X and Y chromosomes, spirals and helix. The sociologists related such to environmental factors, one parent families, etc. Whilst psychologists emphasised conditioning, id versus ego and quality parenting. A. M. Foucault, 1973, summed it all up by saying, **'the diagnosis depended on the gaze'.** This was actually in relation to musculoskeletal, differential diagnosis, as opposed to child development, but personally speaking and using author's licence, I felt it was just as relevant in an educational context. **So, when parents started to give their children away not long after they were born, I couldn't understand what was happening and have since written extensively about what I think of the practice and the consequences of such.**

At college, I was introduced to a plethora of 'buzz words' such as 'slow learners', statemented, special educational needs, educationally sub-normal, disadvantaged, retarded, intellectually disabled, dysfunctional, blah, blah, blah. Some of which have stood the test of time, whilst others have been replaced with more politically correct, user-friendly terms so as not to offend a one-legged frog, who has aspirations to win X factor by croaking to victory, because it had had a troubled life in the swamp and deserved a break, living in an off-white pool. That seaside town in Lancashire, famous for illuminations.

College was also the awakening of my interest and love of reading which, whilst providing me with not only the facts and figures to not only extend my knowledge via non-fictional books, but also provided me with an escape into the world of fiction. Both arming me with a plethora of topics which enabled me to enter the social strata of dinner parties, with all its airs and social graces. **Sadly, now even the dinner party has been debased and bastardised on TV with a bunch of 'guests' being invited for a meal at each other's house with the prime purpose of being insincere and 'slagging off', the host/hostess, off camera off course, and then giving them a mark for all their efforts. This was after they had perfected the art of being totally two faced in front of the guests. Don't forget this is all in the name of progress and reality.**

When I was growing up we never had many books at Parkway, apart from the odd romantic novel, usually Mills and Boon, that could be found at the side of my parents' bed, a set of second-hand encyclopaedias, that for me was my only source of information, if I had to find out about anything, and copies of the News of the World, Oldham Evening Chronicle and Green Final newspapers. Hard copy, as opposed to kindle and google, was the name of the game. Occasionally, we would get a book in our Christmas pillow case which you would consider a real treat. I remember, as a child under 10, once getting a hard backed book about the life of a salmon and being fascinated with its journey from sea to river, so much so that I started looking for salmon in the River Irk. As the Irk was so polluted, from the factories and mills nearby, it was unlikely anything lived in it, never mind a salmon looking to lay eggs. But my serious love of reading didn't really begin until I started teacher training college at the age of 18, and I've been making up for lost time ever since. But hard copy reading was not for everyone.

> "...books were over-rated and very unhygienic. You never knew who had been messing with the pages."

(Townsend S, 2012. The Woman Who Went to Bed For a Year, p42).

Obviously with the advent of computers, kindles and tablets etc. this observation may need qualifying. My brother Jack, who although going to Grammar school, has only recently become a reader. The massive plus for me on the advantage of having an interest in reading, was that, although the characters at times were fictional, it gave me an opportunity to escape into and become immersed into another life, character, or world. I started to associate and relate with the plots and characters within the books. At times, and for a time, they became part of my own persona. Like the actor I could play another role, and, if I so wished, temporarily forget about the reality of my own situation. Over the years I've wished that Jack Reacher, one of the central characters in Lee Child's novels, could just suddenly materialise, and eliminate all that was bad in the world. **Unfortunately, when several of Child's books were made into films one of the biggest miscastings in the history of film making saw the 5 feet 7-inch Tom Cruise being cast as Reacher.** Now for those of you not familiar with the character of Jack Reacher, he is a 6 feet 5 plus inches, ex-military investigator and has been likened to the Incredible Hulk, in both size and stature. A man mountain of a person. So, for Tom Cruise to be given the role was, to put it mildly, ludicrous and meant I couldn't bring myself to go and watch the films. Whilst appreciating that characters in the books were fictional, but could be based on a certain, real-life character I could empathise and appreciate that person's journey was similar to my own, albeit via a different route, arriving at their destination and to conclude, that to all intents and purposes, our lives were not that dissimilar. Reading can give a person a wider perspective of the content of life and clarifies and intensifies their views, vagaries, similarities, complexities and anomalies. Although I'm aware, that fiction is not always a helpful guide on how to live. Allay this to personal experience, and you have a powerful tool with which to view a subject. People who don't read and seek new experiences, ideas, views and perspectives could arrive at Dean Spamley's, **"There is nothing as certain as a closed mind."**

Reading autobiographies helped me to put my own life into perspective, confirming or denying my own doubts, suspicions and perspectives. Knowing there were and are people with the same fears, aspirations, upsets, highs and lows, as myself, somehow made me feel that I was not ploughing a lone furrow. I was not alone, which for me was a massive plus, to be able to escape into the book and not feel so isolated when the Black Dog was on my back.

Like music, writing and exercise, reading for me was a form of therapy and I'm convinced I would not have survived the dark days and loneliness without literature. Unlike alcohol and drugs, there were no known side effects in that after reading, I didn't start effing and jeffing or physically beating my partner. There was no unwanted pregnancy to deal with. I didn't jump into my car so I could knowingly kill another, who chose not to drink and drive, whilst making or taking a phone call. I could wake up the following day without a hangover, with no thought of 'throwing yet another sickie'. The only known side effect for me was that I became even more of a dreamer, than Stuart Ford thought I was when I was in my 30s. Whilst the worst that could happen was that both during and after reading a book, I could be an emotional wreck with tears rolling down my cheeks. Whilst writing this piece of work and proof reading it, I have been able to live in three different worlds. The here and now, be the character in a book in a specific era, and go back in time and re-live my past. Not only have I physically travelled the world but also, via the books I've read, mentally travelled the world and been a part of many of its character's lives.

During my time as an educationalist, I have had to read many factual books and over time it not only made me a more professional student, in that my interests and search for the truth ensured I never stopped searching, but also made me aware of how little I knew. I used to have a file on the subject of knowledge, which of course related to all the categories and sub divisions of the term, depending on which definition you wanted to use. My search for the answers started in childhood with why, why, why and will end with my last breath. Now aged 75, isolated, alone and at times feeling sorry for myself, reading is still one of the pastimes that helps me through the day.

My headteacher friend, Stuart Ford, once told me that education never changed because the questions were always the same, it was just the answers that they kept swapping about, depending on a changing perspective. They being the politicians who always felt the need, upon coming to power, to reform the educational and NHS services. Irrespective of whether or not they needed reforming, and in many cases all they needed was more resources in specific areas. **Very galling for those involved in such reforms when the appointed Education and Health Ministers had usually never taught or even acquired an up to date First Aid qualification. Their only qualifications for the jobs being that they once went to school and had once visited a doctor or hospital. Both of which were usually from the private sector.** If I recall in my first 17 years in education, Keith Joseph was the only Education Minister who had any background in the subject, he was a minister in. Margaret Thatcher's 1979 Government deciding that Comprehensive Education was the way forward, which in essence meant bringing every student **down** to the same level, had a cabinet which comprised of above 90% privately, educated politicians. What politicians **HAVE NEVER** seemed to realise is that what they were actually doing, was creating more mayhem than the previous incumbents.

There was an excellent e-book published in 2007, entitled, 'Stitches', by Dr Nick Edwards, which basically was a day-to-day account of life on an Accident and Emergency Unit. The author having had 8 years' experience in A&E. Upon reading it, not only did I soon realise that Nick and I, (no I've never met the man but feel I'd known him all my life), shared not only the same sense of humour, but also scepticism for everything political. His views on the continual political interference into the NHS, were very much simpatico with mine on their pathetic attempts at so called educational and health reform. His book should be a must read for all student nurses and doctors and should be placed on the Essential and Recommended reading lists of all teaching, political and medical establishments. There are now several TV programmes, Hospital and 24 Hours in Accident and Emergency being just two, which are just as revealing as to the state of the NHS, after constant interference from the politicians, and the impact this has on hard, working, dedicated staff, even before the Covid Pandemic entered the scene, who keep the system going **INSPITE OF POLITICAL INTERFERENCE. It's alright saying we need more medical staff and teachers as there is a drastic shortage, but who would want to be a doctor, nurse or teacher in the year 2025? How can you be expected to do a job, whilst being blindfolded, with your hands and feet tied together, without sufficient, appropriate resources, whilst constantly being told by a suit, you need to be more efficient, 24 hours before you have your first nervous breakdown?** America is constantly being referred to as one of our closest allies and sadly, what happens in America tends to also happen in the UK and vice versa, and what I've just discussed is relevant to this observation. As this book is all about human behaviour, I would like to mention the Mueller Report, a 400-page document that saw the light of day in March 2019, and was all about the alleged Russian involvement in Trump's Election Campaign and Trump's alleged obstruction of Justice related to the enquiry. After the report became public, research was conducted by ABC and the Washington Post, which revealed that **58% of Americans polled were absolutely clear he had lied, while only a third thought he had told the truth.** But, wait for it, 'his supporters' said, **"We know he's a liar but let's do nothing about it."** (Jon Sopel, 2019, A Year at The Circus, 10:338). This is an American President we are talking about, who, at the time of writing, may get another term in office. I couldn't make this stuff, if I sat at my computer for weeks at a time. And we profess to be intelligent.

Christmas Post, Butlins, Park Cake Bakery, The Unions and Strike Action.

My grant at Mather Teacher Training College was means tested, based on my father's income, and although my father was also supposed to make a contribution, I never asked him for it. Trying to get him to help me fill out the grant application forms was like asking MI5 to divulge its innermost secrets. So, having achieved such I decided to trouble him no further by asking him to share his beer money with his son who had miraculously been accepted into Teacher Training college, with all the prestige and pride that supposedly went with the invitation. So therefore, during my time at Mather, I did what many students did and supplemented my grant by working during the inter semester breaks. In those days, finding work was not the issue it later became as the local employment office, or 'the dole', as it was then known, always had seasonal or temporary vacancies to offer for those willing to work. **I emphasise the phrase willing to work, because in the late 60s and early 70s working was not a dirty word and 'the sickie' had not yet entered the scene.** There was something pleasing about earning your own money, via sweat and graft, no matter how insignificant the amount. **There are many in today's world that are ensconced in a philosophy of the world owes me a living, with a work ethic of a sloth and viewing significant others as a soft touch or a cash cow.**

I remember working at the Oldham sorting office, on Hamilton Street, on Christmas post, during my first year at college and enjoying delivering mail in Oldham Town Centre. Originally, I went out with the guy whose round I was helping on. After an early start sorting out the mail, which was almost done by the time I arrived at around 7a.m., we left the sorting office with two bags, one of which was left in the entrance to Barclay Bank Chambers, next to Oldham church, to be collected after emptying the first bag. This reminded me of when I used to deliver Sunday papers, leaving a bag in one of the doorways of a house on Moira Avenue, Chadderton. In the late 60s there were no postcodes, and mail sorting was mainly done by hand, throwing the post into the relevant pigeon hole. If it didn't fit it was considered a parcel/package and was thrown into a wire cage. Once sorted, the post person set off to deliver the first post. In those days, there were two deliveries a day. However, I was informed that getting back to the depot too early pleased the management, but was frowned upon by the Unions, because although time and motion studies were still in their infancy, they, the unions, liked everyone to 'toe the line' with policy. This involved, as I could ascertain, not breaking into too much of a sweat to do the job. My early insight into unions and management was the intransigence that seemed to exist between the two with NO MIDDLE GROUND. The unions wanting its members to do one hour's work for six hours' pay, whilst management wanted six hours' work for one hour's pay. This is a slight exaggeration but hopefully the reader gets the idea. I also soon realised that the unions were powerful entities, with many of its leaders bordering on Bolshevik, communist, mafia types who were so far removed from the 'coal face' and could only reminisce about what doing a full day's work entailed, that any negotiations were doomed to fail before they had even begun. History has subsequently shown the power of the unions, which ensured management found it extremely difficult to manage, whilst at times, the arrogance of management beggared belief, before Margaret Thatcher entered the foray and decided to, 'take on the unions'. The rest is history, so to speak. Many years later my brother Barry became a postal union rep. Perhaps that was when he learned to swear so eloquently. I enjoyed working on the post and signed up again the following year. Being a good boy, I toed the union line so as not to upset the apple cart. Unfortunately, my last casual job at Park Cake Bakeries, in Hathershaw, Oldham, before joining the teaching force, proved a little more confrontational. But before visiting the bakery let's toddle off to Billy Butlin's Holiday Camp.

I think Eddie and I decided to go to work for Billy Butlin, at Pwllheli, North Wales after seeing an advertisement for staff in the job centre, at the end of our second year at Mather College. Up until then I had only been to Rhyl, Beaumaris in Anglesey and Cornwall with Verna. At that time holiday camp holidays, such as Pontins and Butlins, were all the rage for Northern working-class families. The TV comedy hit, Hi Di Hi and the fictitious Maplins, had not yet hit the TV screens, but being a Butlin's Red Coat, at one of the many camps that adorned the country, was the breeding ground for aspiring artists and history has shown that many television celebrities started their careers as a holiday camp entertainer. I had no such aspirations or pretentions of fame and fortune in the entertainment world, and accepted a job in the kitchens, basically washing plates, pots, pans, knives and forks. Then mopping the floor and wiping down surfaces before being allowed to sign off. Although you were issued with thick rubber gloves and the dirty cutlery, pots pans and plates were put in large dishwashers, the gloves soon became ripped and torn, and so, after a very short time, several days to be precise, your hands became cut, blistered and bruised. The TV advert, 'Now hands that do dishes can feel soft as your face with mild, green, Fairy liquid', springs to mind.

The contract, was for six weeks. If you honoured the six weeks, you got a monetary bonus, which was an incentive as the pay was not very good. Minimum wages not being part of employment law in 1970. Upon arrival, you would be paid out of pocket travel expenses, whilst work clothes, board and lodgings were provided. Overtime could be earned by working double shifts or working in the bars at night. Sounds good to me, thought Ed and I, as we boarded the train to North Wales. Unfortunately, we should have realised as soon as we arrived at the camp to, 'sign in', that this trip was not going to be as exciting and lucrative as we had envisaged. My younger brother Stephen has been in the army, so you will have to ask him for a comparison but as soon as we arrived, we were treated as morons, by people who were perhaps considered not psychotic and sado-masochistic enough to be training, army sergeant majors, but who thought Butlins was the next best thing. In actual fact, many of these people were basically arse lickers who had worked at Butlins previously. We were shepherded from hut A to B to C and so on, first to collect your 'kit', which was given out with no consideration to waist size, chest measurement, leg length or shoe size. This was flippantly dismissed with the excuse that they had run out of your particular size. Being 'ickle' everything was far too big for me and when I complained, they told me I could always go back home but would not be given any financial assistance to help pay for the trip. The fact that I hadn't received any financial assistance to date for my travel expenses so far, made this threat a little strange. Next was a trip to personnel to check you were, 'fit for duty', and finally to the administration block, to sign your life away and advise them of your next of kin, in case you contracted malaria from the sheep in deepest, darkest Wales. Or you lost your bearings, one night, on the way home from the kitchens, and never saw your family and friends again. Our accommodation was in staff chalets, which from the outside looked like any other offered to, 'the campers', but inside lacked anything other than the basics of a sink, bed, and a set of drawers. We started work early in the morning, in our case we were woken up, after the cooks, at 5 o'clock by security tapping on your door three times with a baton. Sorry did I say tapping, I meant banging. Our shift in the kitchen should have ended at 2 p.m., after lunch, but as they were short staffed, they asked us to work a double shift until after the evening meal, which could be any time up until 9 p.m. Obviously, we would be paid for the extra shift. Or at least that is what they told us. During your lunch break you could go over to staff HQ and sign up to work in the bars at night as a glass collector, shelf stacker, waiter etc. If you waited-on, you had an opportunity to earn tips and an opportunity to, 'pull the birds', sorry meet young ladies, but obviously these jobs were the first to go. I rarely got a job as a waiter in the time I was there, so could only gaze at the, 'holiday totty', as I lay on the pavement outside the kitchen, falling asleep with my co-inmates during my breaks. Yes, I know that to refer to the females, in 2025, as, 'totty' is an ic, ist or an ism, but that was acceptable expression at the time. In fact, some females liked the idea of being, 'totty', as it conjured up images of being desirable. When I did get to work in the bars, some being quieter than others, I did earn a few tips. I distinctly remember one girl asking me for my chalet key, because she thought I was a RED COAT, but fraternisation with the campers was frowned upon, which could lead to instant dismissal. Not that this stopped anyone, as testosterone and oestrogen was far more powerful than common sense. Well, that's a general overview of life at Billy Butlin's Holiday Camp but after a week, we soon realised the reality, and experience was probably designed to encourage you to leave, so that they didn't have to pay you a bonus. Butlins was a non-Union environment and working conditions and things being, 'fit for purpose', and employees' rights were not high priority for management. Happy paying campers were. Every day some member of staff, who had had enough, went, 'a-wall'. **Any complaint was always met with, "Well, if you're not happy you know what you can do."** And being as we were still waiting for payment of our initial travel expenses, or any payment for that matter, our options were limited. If only BBC Watchdog and the team were screened in those days, they would have had a field day. The TV adverts doing the rounds at the time might have encouraged people to book their holidays at Butlins, but the grim realities, behind the scenes, painted a totally different picture. **It is true to say that some 51 years later, the front of house image of many jobs and careers still disguise the actual reality.** Especially where jobs in the Leisure and Tourism industry are concerned, where working long hours, for poor wages, can still be the norm. In the cruise industry, passengers are asked to pay on average £10 pppd in 'tips', or is it gratuities, to top up the workers' wages because they are paid a pittance? The same can be said for drivers and Tour Guides working in the travel industry, who rely on the passengers for tips, or as my brother–in-law Jack used to say, 'whippy', which I think stems from the expression, to whip round with the hat, to earn a decent wage. What are airline stewardesses but glorified 'trolly dollies'?

At Butlins where we had to work a week in hand and were told any extra shifts would only be paid the following week. Was this designed to confuse the less mathematical of us and a ruse to delay paying you as long as possible? We also realised that many of the supervisors were people, who had previously survived the regime and so could pre-empt problems and trouble. **In essence, the place was a melting pot for anarchy.** Any opportunity to get back at Billy Butlin and his merry men, was grasped with both hands. At times the place was scary, especially in the staff bar on Thursday night when some people who had been paid, and had sampled too much of the local fire water went looking for someone, or something, to vent their pent-up emotions on. The main focus of physical assault was sometimes directed at the foreign student workers, who were protected by some employment regulation which said they could not be sacked, unless they tried to blow up the place, or raped and buggered Billy Butlin's wife and family. This crazy ruling meant that many foreigners, but not all, didn't pull their weight on the job. Unfortunately, they all got tarred with the same brush and were frequently assaulted, especially if they banged on your door at 4.30 in the morning. My first night, I worked a double shift in the kitchen, 0700 till 2100, and had signed up to work in the bars until 2 p.m. the following day, ensured more sleeping on the pavement during the day. On one occasion, I had just finished mopping the floor in the kitchen and asked one of my fellow workers, who had been left in charge but was not a regular supervisor, what to do with the dirty, disinfected water, bucket and mop. He promptly took it out of my hand and poured it in the huge vat of tomato soup, that was being served the following day. After giving it a stir with a huge wooden ladle he said, "That should clean their insides and stuff their bellies." When I looked at him in amazement he said, "I thought you wanted to get off to work in the bars?" I nodded. "Well, fuck off then," he said. Another time I was stacking shelves from behind the bar with bottles of various drinks, and then collecting empties from the tables. These were then placed in large trolleys that were wheeled back behind the bars, down a ramp into the cellars, to be put back into larger crates. Re-cycling was not the hot topic it was later to become. Even if it was, it certainly was not high priority at Butlins. I do, however, remember, as a child, being paid one penny for collecting empty mineral bottles. Working in twos, my fellow worker took the empties' trolley to the top of the ramp leading to the cellars, and when he saw no one was looking gave it a shove with his foot, down the ramp, where at the bottom the trolley tipped and disgorged many glass bottles out onto the concrete floor to a cacophony of sound. When the bar manager asked him what had happened, he said he was sorry but the trolley slipped out of his hand. The sound of breaking glass and porcelain was a common occurrence at Butlins and was usually the trigger for anyone in the local vicinity carrying anything, to immediately drop it, saying sorry when glared at by the boss. The mentality being that they might fire one person on the spot, but not the whole kitchen or bar staff, so unity was the name of the game. Not joining in was frowned upon by your fellow workers, resulting in you being, 'sent to Coventry', or Istanbul, or Morecambe – you get my drift. All this tension and tiredness meant I was occasionally visited by the black dog and just wanted a kiss, cuddle or a hug. I missed Verna's guiding hand. I admired my mate Ed who fulfilled his contract, because after a month I had had enough of having my intelligence insulted. In fact, every fibre of my body had been insulted, apart from my...... I left with the princely sum of £60, which to be honest, in those days, was not to be sniffed at. Ed decided that Butlins was still a better proposition than going back home to mummy and daddy. My experiences at Butlins certainly left an indelible impression on me. Times were not all bad but I had never experienced falling asleep on the pavement before, through sheer exhaustion, with people walking past. Many's the time I have seen beggars asleep in the street, and my mind has returned to Butlins. If only I had taken a dog and blanket with me, I might have made a few bob in my breaks. Happy days. Anyhow enough of these carefree, unionless, working environments, let's get back to what happened next.   I remember Eddie and I, fresh from saying our good byes to Mather College and securing probationary, teaching positions for Lancashire Education Authority, Ed in Ashton and me in Failsworth, meeting in Oldham to find a job for the summer, before starting full time as teachers in September 1971. Within hours of walking into the job centre in Oldham, we found ourselves on the number 9 bus to Ashton, getting off in Hathershaw, to have an informal interview with the personnel manager at the Park Cake Bakery, on Honeywell Lane. We were offered jobs on the condition we both had a haircut, and that we agreed to wear hair nets. A white tunic would be provided that would actually fit. After Butlin's this was a definite move in the right direction. The pay was also considerably better. Another massive contrast from Butlin's was that Park Cake Bakeries was very union orientated, as it provided cakes for Marks and Spencer's, and had very strict Health and Safety rules. Long before Health and Safety became the force it is today. I promptly visited the barbers to have a haircut, but Eddie was allowed to tie his hair up. In those days long hair was fashionable and short hair, number one cuts and wearing head apparel inside buildings, were only for those with head lice and nits. Or for those recovering from brain surgery or chemotherapy, after cancer treatment. **It's fascinating how historically these so-called highest forms of intelligence in the animal kingdom, can, at times, be so gullible in accepting and embracing the latest fad and fashion, in case it loses them, 'street cred', without question, rhyme or reason, as to its possible detriment to the individuals involved, or society as a whole. Refusing to join the flock mentality, and being an individual has somehow always been viewed with suspicion, labelling such people odd, weird or rebellious.** Park Cake consisted of five bakeries, each responsible for producing different cakes. I worked in Honeywell Lane Bakery and Ed in Dowry. I was assigned to work in the mixing room preparing the cake mixes for the mainly female staff, who prepared them for putting them in the ovens to bake. On the spot, no warning inspections, were not uncommon and so everything had to be kept spotlessly clean. I also had to clean the mixing machines bowls at the end of my shift. There was one particular machine known as, 'the Jap Machine', a stainless-steel machine designed by, yes, you've guessed, the Japanese to assist in the making of Eccles cakes. Now this machine had to be stripped down, cleaned and reassembled after each shift. I worked with a guy called Frank Fullalove, what a fabulous surname, who showed me the ropes, how to mix, and the general rules and regulations of life in Honeywell Lane Bakery. He was affectionately known as FS Fullalove, although his stature was nothing like a battleship. He was the only mixing operative, in Honeywell Bakery, who could strip, clean, re-assemble and work the Jap machine. In relation to the name Frank, there were more Franks in Honeywell bakery than you could shake a stick at. The bakery boss who was also called Frank, but whom you only ever called Mr., Big Frank, the works Convenor, and Little Frank, the union guy, who kept calling me brother. The fact that I had 3 biological brothers before I arrived at the bakery didn't seem to faze him, as he ignored my pleas to be referred to as Jim or James. I started work at 5 o'clock or was it 7, I'm not sure, but had to get a mix ready for when the girls arrived. The mixes ranged from Eccles cakes, bread, certain buns and Christmas cake. **I couldn't believe, I was being paid for putting 3,000 buns in the oven a day**. A mix would take me thirty minutes maximum to prepare, and I must not keep the girls waiting. The mixes had to prepared to order and so you couldn't make them up, until told to do so by Frank F. I finished work at 4 p.m. A 9 hour plus shift with breaks in the morning, afternoon and at lunch. One of the things Frank had warned me against was getting into the lift alone, with the girls, to visit the cafeteria during my breaks. Come on Frank, I'm a young, virile 21-year-old, PE teacher, full of testosterone, who the girls find irresistible-give me a break. "That may be as such, Briggsy, but a lot of these girls are nymphomaniacs and are always on the lookout for, "young bits of fresh meat," said Frank. Now I had never been referred to in this way before and took it as a complement. The reader needs to realise that when I was 21 years of age, although flower power was in California, in Oldham, virgins abounded, you treated girls with respect and many dates ensued long before first base was reached. First base being a feel through the clothes of a pert, firm young breast. I know that's unacceptable language in 2025, but what the hell. **For their part, girls didn't get blindingly drunk on shots, wine and pints, before even leaving the house, offer full sex, oral and anal, all on the first date, swear, wear clothes that left nothing to the imagination, and danced as**

though in a porn movie. So, you can imagine I'd thought I'd landed in some kind of hedonistic Eutopia. To be honest, whilst I was full of bluster and blow, I found girls hunting in packs quite daunting. Also, as I've alluded to, my sexual experience up until this time had been limited, to say the least. It would also be remiss of me to mention that because of the hot environment, many of the girls wore little or nothing under their white, bakery overalls. Why I didn't walk around the bakery with a permanent erection, I will never know. Sorry, mum, for that indiscretion. One particular day, Ed was sharing my break in Honeywell Bakery and as we approached the lift, Ed's bakery didn't have a lift, armed with cake, I noticed there were no other males in sight and as the lift doors opened, it was full of girls. "Wait," I said to Ed, although the girls had kept the door open beckoning us into their harem. Suddenly hearing Frank F's words in my ears, and suffering a sudden panic attack I said, "Thanks girls, but no thanks." Unfortunately, Ed had not had the benefit of Frank's pearly words of wisdom and virtually ran to get in the lift. Leaving me shaking my head shouting, "Don't do it, you're too young to die." As I watched the numbers on the lift move to denote its passage to the next level, and then seconds later, its descent back to me, I thought perhaps Frank was wrong and my fears had been unwarranted. At that moment, the lift doors opened and there was Ed curled up in the corner of the lift, stripped-bollock-naked, trying to hide his manhood. His clothes had mysteriously disappeared, including his elastic band and hairnet to keep his hair tidy. Thinking of taking off my white tunic, so as to save my mate's blushes and offer a sympathetic hand, I realised I had failed miserably at both, as I was in fits of laughter, along with a sizeable crowd that had witnessed the de-frocking of one of my mates. Go, Girls, Go!

As you can imagine life was never dull in the bakery and, for most of the time, I loved working there. Incidentally, any cakes that didn't reach the exacting standards of the clients were sold off, discounted to the workforce, in the on-site shop. Yes, every Friday, Briggs could be seen walking out of the factory gates with two large, brown, paper bags in tow, full of misshapen cake. Another time when I was loading the ovens, I was approached by what can only be described as a deputation of three girls, informing me that I had to be in the Honeywell Arms pub, after work, on Friday and not to be late. After which, I was summarily dismissed. Frank upon seeing this, asked what had been said. It transpired that one of the young girls, who worked in the packaging and despatch area, was something of 'a looker', am I allowed to say that or is it too sexist, with many of the guys in our bakery, single and otherwise, asking her out for a date, only to be politely turned down. For some reason she had sent her mates to inform me, that I had just won the pools, there was no lottery in those days, and admiring me from afar had decided I was the chosen one for drinks and a possible trip to first base. Apart from Frank taking the Michael, as to what the hell she saw in me, I firstly, had no recollection of ever seeing her and secondly, had never been asked out on a blind date in Mafia style before. Frank assured me I would not be disappointed. How did he know? However, to cut to the chase, I was dating my future wife, Dee, although I think at the time we were enjoying some me time apart, and so I never turned up at the pub. I had also recently bought my first car, and so didn't need to queue at the bus stop, which was next to the pub. My first car cost me £40 and was a hand painted, battleship grey, Morris Traveller. I later sold it to Eddie Whalley, so he could learn to drive. To this day, why I never went I can't give a reason, but worried that I might end up in a ditch, down near the canal, with both my legs broken. I possibly also thought that I was being set up again, as I was slowly getting to know about life in the workplace. Everyone being able to tell their tale of being sent for a jar of elbow grease, on their first day at work. On Monday, I soon realised it was not a set up as word spread like wild fire, of my decision not to go to the pub. Trying to save face, I cockily informed one and all that she mustn't think much of me, if she had to send her mates to ask me out. Although getting your mates to do your dirty work, because you hadn't the balls, was not an uncommon practice, especially in secondary school. I honestly cannot even remember her name. Frank F thought I was queer for not turning up or was it stupid. I can't remember? Anyhow enough of the girls, and my non-existent sex life and back to upsetting big and little Frank, of union fame. Now as you know, I had been brought up a proud Lancastrian, who cleaned up his own mess, put in a decent day's work, for a decent day's wage and respected the ladies and my elders. Working 8 hours a day and taking 30 minutes to do a mix and being told not to do more than five mixes a day was, to put it bluntly, not stretching my resources to the full. I was told by my boss Frank F, so I didn't upset the Unions, that in between mixes, I was to look busy without actually doing any work. We don't want to let management see that you could, without breaking sweat, improve productivity. Back to the buns, or in this case, Eccles cake mixes. Frank used to tell me to grab a paper, and disappear to the loo for half an hour, but after several days of this ducking and diving, all I had to show for it was a sore arse. One day I spilt some flour and after finishing the mix and taking it to the girls, immediately grabbed a brush to clean up my work area. **WRONG.** Within minutes of finishing my clean up, realised that I was alone in the mixing room. After checking personal hygiene, especially under my arms for body odour, I decided to see where everyone had gone. Although the mixing room never had the same level of activity as the main rooms, where the ovens blazed, I was immediately met by Frank F who told to stay by my mixer, as either big Frank or little Frank would shortly be summoning me to account for my actions. Evidently there was a meeting going on with unions and shop floor, because someone had done a job that was not theirs, yours truly, and this constituted doing someone out of a job. If management could be shown **that a mixer could mix and clean up his own shit,** then the sweeper-upper could be out of a job. I was struggling to come to terms with this nonsense and was not taking it too seriously. **WRONG.** For the union guys, this was equivalent to the British and Americans invading Iraq to depose Sadam Hussain. Frank told me to eat humble pie and apologise, which I did purely out of respect for Frank F. In hindsight, I think because I was a student, who as yet didn't pay tax, I was placed under constant surveillance from day one by the unions, who saw me as some kind of subversive, who wanted to do a decent day's work for a decent day's pay, and that would never be allowed. It could just have been pure jealousy, because an attractive young lady had asked me out for a drink, and not them and to add insult to injury, the cocky little shit, yours truly, had stood her up.

Another example of the stupidity and intransigence of the unions in the 70s was when the big boss Frank, asked Frank Fullalove, to show me the ropes regarding stripping down, cleaning and re-assembling the Jap machine. This made sense to one and all because if Frank was ever ill or off work, which as far as I was aware he never was, I would be able to cover for him. Why they hadn't thought of this eventuality before I arrived on the scene, I'm not sure, but don't forget Homo Sapiens are the highest form of intelligence on the planet! To be fair, this was pre-sickie days, when people rarely had days off work, and so the thought of Frank F being off work perhaps, had never crossed management's mind. In view of what had gone on before with the unions, I asked Frank if this had been cleared by them, as I felt a full-time worker, rather than a casual student who could and would be leaving at any time, would be more suitable to train up. They assured me my fears were ungrounded and I think they thought, as a smart-arse student, I could speak many languages, including Japanese, and must have the mental capacity of Einstein. In retrospect, whilst working, stripping, cleaning and re-assembling the Jap machine was not rocket science, I think some of the union guys might have struggled. The following Friday HMS, as I was now allowed to call him, told me that Frank, the 'big boss', wanted to see me in his office. Fearing that my time at the bakery was due to be terminated, due to the fact I was a womanising, communist, terrorist, agitator who incidentally didn't pay tax, I was pleasantly surprised to be told that management was pleased with my work ethic, and as I was now virtually doing the same job as Frank Fullalove, without the responsibility, I was to be put on a mixing rate, which in essence was a pay rise from the casual rate I'd originally been put on. Brilliant, more money for putting more buns in the oven, with a nymphomaniac, work force. Could this get any better? I had risen from £4 plus a week working at the Electricity Board in Oldham at 16, to earning £35 plus a week, with overtime, and all the cake in the world I could eat free, at the age of 21. By contrast, when I started teaching, my first pay slip, when I was put on emergency tax, was something like £50 for a month. Who said getting an education would set you up for life? Granted, I liked working overtime because the bakery offered all kinds of bonuses, if you worked more than your normal shift, and there were many glassy eyed, zombies walking around the place who virtually lived at the bakery. Yes, you've gathered, my euphoria was soon to incur the wrath of the unions, yet again. Frank F decided to have a Saturday off to attend a wedding, which was virtually unheard of before my arrival, and asked the boss if I could cover for him. It involved working not only with the Jap machine, but also with the girls who only came in on certain nights and Saturday mornings. I was approached by big boss Frank and re-assured I was taking no one's over time off them, and to be honest there was no one else who could cover for HMS. As Saturday work was double time, I agreed. **WRONG.** World war three broke out this time and the work force 'downed tools and hairnets' for an hour, until the dispute was resolved. The simple fact of the matter was I was not used to working Saturday, and didn't have a wife and family depending on me, so it was no skin off my nose if someone else took Frank F's place. The fact that there was no one who could replace Frank, on this particular occasion, seemed to be overlooked and was not an issue for discussion by the unions! Talk about, **'there is nothing as certain as the closed mind'.** However, unless the Eccles cake machine was operative on the Saturday morning, a dozen ladies missed getting their Saturday pay and it was my fault. When I found out why I had been sent to Coventry by, 'my brothers', I immediately went to see the boss and declined the offer of working Saturday. I was told it was too late to change as there was not enough time to inform the Saturday staff that they could not work Saturday, crazy. Don't forget mobiles, e-mails etc. had not yet entered the scene. There was an impasse whilst management and unions 'worked out a deal', because management had not consulted the unions on how they should manage, again, crazy. My last memory of the bakery was taking a few hours off to go and take my driving test in Failsworth, which I am pleased to say I passed first time. Is there no end to this boy's talent?

These early sorties into the work place and the power of the unions, coupled with my scepticism of politicians, were the basis for me never voting in a General Election and not wanting to join a union, unless forced to do so. To me, both politicians and union leaders, had agendas that had nothing to do with the working-class person, with openness, fairness and equality on the agenda. But had more to do with covert, two faced backstabbing and what's in it for me and what can I get out of this before the bubble bursts, or I get found out? To repeat, I have never voted in a General Election and have no obvious political persuasion, one way or another, as they are all tarred with the same brush. Having said that, people have told me over the years that I am a staunch Conservative because I was a teacher and all teachers are Conservatives. Not forgetting the person who said I obviously, was a Conservative because I always wore blue. What do these

people do for kicks? Have they ever tried sex? So, when Margaret Thatcher decided to take on the unions she had my support, irrespective of what I thought of her or her politics. Looking at the topics I've considered so far, it could be argued that not a lot has changed with covert greed, apathy and selfishness ruling the roost. But as this work is about trying to identify the significant changes in my life, I'll end this chapter by saying that whilst it's true some things would appear never to change, it's the perception that we need to look at. Today ME, MYSELF, I and SICKIES are many peoples' priorities but what has happened to a positive work ethic, honesty, compassion, sympathy, common sense and decency? I am aware that many of these values still exist, especially in people of my generation and their offsprings but sadly, they seem to be enveloped more and more, with the passage of time, in their misguided ways of dealing with life's challenges by choosing to live in the, 'synthetic world', via their smartphones.

4.
THE PRIMARY TEACHING YEARS, 1971 to 1987: 21-37 years,

Mather Street Infant and Junior School, 1971-76.
"**Learning is of less importance than what you do with it.**" (Woodruff WW, 2006. Beyond Nab End, PB, 6:518).

Armed with my newly acquired Teachers' Certificate in Education, I remember arriving for my first visit to Mather Street Junior School, Failsworth, to meet the head Mr Plimmer, who because of a typing error, 'typo', in my letter from Lancashire Education department, offering me the position, I thought was called Plummer and envisaged someone out of the Christopher, film star mode. Although only a preliminary visit, before the real action started, my probationary teaching year, I experienced a gamut of emotions from excited to apprehensive but most of all raring to get started in my first teaching post. I didn't want to let Verna or Frank down. I also thought that it was irony, fate, or was it just coincidence, that my first love at Secondary School was Hilary Mather, my 3-year teacher training, was at Mather Colllege, Manchester and my first teaching post, was at Mather Street, Failsworth?

The Accrington brick building itself was typical of many schools at that time, old, possibly Victorian and t-shaped. There was no signage to warn visitors, staff or pupils as to trip hazards, or the potential threat to life if one felt the desire to throw themselves, head first, off the top step of the entrance to the building. **In today's Health and Safety, politically correct, crazy world, the entrances would immediately be condemned as lethal and the worst entrances ever built. With the legal profession rubbing their hands to the possibility of massive litigation claims against Lancashire Education and County Council.** As a young 21-year-old, in 1971, these thought processes were not even in my memory bank. Failsworth, was what one could call a socially deprived area, which again was typical of many parts of North Manchester and the type of area to which I was sent, on many of my teaching practices, whilst at Teacher Training College. Much of the housing was back-to-back terraced properties, with an early Coronation Street community spirit. But Failsworth did have its respectable areas, or 'posh parts', as we say, 'up North'.

As I entered the building, I had no sooner started wiping my feet on the large core fibre, rubber mat strategically placed in the well that was designed for such, and before I had barely time to appreciate the smell of the cloakroom and toilets facing me, a loud voice from up the corridor on my right called out, "Mr Briggs, I presume." Was this a statement of fact or a question, I'm not sure? Upon turning to my right, I saw this slightly built, elderly gentleman, atop a pair of stepladders, painting one of many friezes that could be found on either side of the corridor. **Had he been trained to use those and had he filled in the necessary Health and Safety documentation in triplicate,** I didn't ask, but you get my drift? Mr Plimmer was sporting an overall over his suit, collar and tie. Coming down off the steps he seemed genuinely pleased to see me, which immediately put me at ease. Many, many years later, when I started lecturing on communication, I used this occasion as one example of, **'you don't get a second chance to make a first impression'.** And was just one of the many lessons I was fortunate to experience on people management. As for Mr Plummer, sorry Plimmer, having your name bastardised was part and parcel of schooling, education and being a teacher. At school I was Briggsy, pigs' ears, and having been Bloggsy at the School of Education years previously, I had to be careful to refer to my boss with his correct title. Having said that, I have nothing but fond memories of my time spent under his headship. For me, he was old school. He preferred being out and about with staff and pupils, rather than stuck in the office moving paper around, especially addendums to a memorandum. **In December 2024, I attended St John's Infant- Junior School to watch their Nativity, where the headteacher was conspicuous by her absence. When I enquired where she was, I was informed in her office where she spends most of her time. How the hell did she get the job when she treats the parents, staff, children and ancillary staff, the most vital components of running a school, as not worthy of her presence?** Mr Plimmer genuinely preferred teaching to managing, which didn't go down well with certain members of staff, but as he was my first boss in education, I learned much from his style of leadership. Using some of his traits and qualities, as I subsequently developed my own teaching and leadership style. **In retrospect, he wouldn't have survived long in today's harsh environment of OFSTED, targets and mis-placed quality control,** but as I now picture him in my mind's eye, conducting the school choir in the Christmas Carol Concert, he would knock spots off some so-called modern heads, who have been moved upstairs, away from the chalkface, because their teaching skills had become embarrassing, and the powers that be didn't quite know what to do with them. Let alone admit they had made a mistake in appointing them to such a privileged position. Or to be blunt, because they belonged to a certain tribe.

There was also a newly appointed head of the infants, Miss Moir, which meant the staff had to adjust to an influx of not only new, but also, male blood into the building. As alluded to previously, in those days, men in infant-junior schools were rare because it was considered that as the children were young, they needed a more maternal, feminine type of teaching, whatever that meant? Is that statement now an ic, ist or an ism? It was also thought a man could possibly frighten the little darlings. Which was utter balderdash, when you considered how many female teachers roamed the corridors in those days, putting the fear of whatever into the children. More 'ics 'isms and 'ists to be guilty of. There was also the male chauvinist point of view, that teaching young children was a little demeaning for the male species. Initially I was asked to teach a mixed, junior one and two class, of 7- to 9-year-olds, who were classed as, 'slow learners'. It was usually the norm for Probationary Teachers to be given the more difficult classes to teach, the thought being that if you could teach those you had earned the right to teach brighter, more responsive children later in your career. Whatever slow learners, brighter, more responsive meant. During my 35 years in education children, pupils, scholars and students were given more labels than days in the year. The number in the class was about 18, which in terms of logistics was easily manageable, but if I didn't already know from my training, I soon realised teaching was not only about class size, but also about educability and the potent mix of factors that are included in such. Many of these little darlings coming from poor socio-economic backgrounds, and for many the home environment was not conducive to complementing the educational process offered by schools. **In hindsight, I can honestly say, without any shadow of a doubt, that those first few years at Mather Street, together with my training at Mather TT College, provided me with a foundation that was not only to be the basis for my future success as a teacher, but also a thorough grounding in the vagaries of human behaviour. I realised that teaching itself, or should I say the transference of knowledge, was relatively straight forward, but appreciating and overcoming the factors that hindered such transference was extremely challenging.** Throwing myself into my role with positivity and enthusiasm, I found my organisational skills a definite bonus for the day-to-day pedagogy of classroom teaching. **Without organisation and discipline, teaching becomes very difficult, as you spend most of the day just child minding. The Deputy Head, Betty Needham, also taught me that respect had to be earned with dedication and hard work, not by waving certificates, degrees and qualifications at people, or trying to impress them by hinting at who you knew.** She always mentioned that she had a glass of sherry after school, with her husband and for a while I thought that was the norm for all teachers as they became more senior, and denoted their success in the profession. Ah bless! Of course, there were teachers who were the antithesis to Mrs Needham and, in my humble opinion, were not very good teachers. Often wondering, why they had entered the honourable profession in the first place. As I grew older and my life experience increased, I realised that in all jobs there was an element of people whose motivation for the job was almost zero, and their only reason for going to work was to do as little as possible and take the money. There was such a teacher at Mather Street who used to spend her time in the staff room causing trouble with her two-faced backstabbing of people who were not present. She lacked any kind of empathy with the children in her care, and saw them as the enemy. She also knew exactly how long it was to the next holiday, as soon as she'd just come back from her summer break. She thought the boss was a fool and that no one should be a teacher unless they had previously attended Grammar school. As several of the young staff, including myself, had attended Secondary Modern, it was difficult working with such a biased, bigoted individual. She could be a nasty piece of work, loved confrontation and I wondered why she was teaching. So, once I had settled into a routine, under the tutelage of Betty and Frank, I decided to completely ignore her, for fear that one day my temper would erupt and I would, as my hero Clint Eastwood had once done in a film, hit her in the face with a frying pan. Failing your probationary year was rare, but could happen and so I decided not to take a frying pan to school. In hindsight, a stronger head would have 'sorted her out' and when, years later, I started to study management issues, I used this teacher and Clifford Taylor, at Blackshaw Lane Primary School, as, in my opinion, as two of my worst examples of personnel in the teaching profession. But again, I suppose teaching was and is no different to many jobs, in that there's a mix of individuals, with different personalities, knowledge, skills, expertise and agendas, all masquerading under the same umbrella. It's what makes the world go around. Which brings me to another individual whom I met at Mather Street. And whilst I had no axe to grind with her in terms of her attitude to the job, one day, on one of the rare occasions I was in the staff room, she totally out of the blue announced that if it was a choice between her dog and her husband, the latter would have to go. I couldn't believe my ears and thought it was said tongue in cheek. When challenged by another member of staff, she affirmed where her loyalties lay. How could someone say such a thing? But during my life's subsequent journey and many years later, when I discovered the, 'dog mafia', I understood a little more of the significance of pets and the transference of love between different members of the animal species. After teaching for several years at Mather Street, I did start to formulate in my mind not only issues that I would address if ever I was to become a headteacher, but also a growing awareness of the sociological issues that pervaded society and ultimately education. Although I didn't know at the time, it could be argued I was becoming a political animal, not in the sense of voting, but in the sense that I needed to be aware of the massive negative impact that politics, the unions and religion could have on education. I also started to keep an anecdotal file of instances, incidents and happenings that occurred, making me, at the very least, smile but at times, cry with laughter. I did, as the years went by, think these episodes would make a good read, until I realised others in the profession had beaten me to the punch. Gervais Finn, a retired teacher and HMI Inspector, whom I saw at Bolton Town Hall many years later, shortly after I'd retired as a teacher, sold many books and played to packed houses, at venues all around the country, eulogising about his time in education. Drat and double drat, he'd beaten me to it. However, here are a few examples of what life in the fast lane as a teacher at Mather Street was all about.

In the 70s teachers were respected, appreciated and on the whole, left to get on with their jobs. Words such as children and respect abounded, with not a baby goat in sight. There was always and always will be the exception to the rule because you are never going to please everyone all of the time, so don't even try. Parents showed their appreciation, by showering you with gifts several times a year, cajoled by their off-springs. Now there were a couple of brothers in the juniors who were scruffy, little urchins but lovable rogues. Unlike another pupil who, even as a 9-year-old, was not a pleasant individual and eventually ended up in prison. **In today's blame culture that would be the teacher's fault, Germans, or the fault of the immigrants.** In the case of all three children their home environments left a lot to be desired, and were classic examples of the influence of the home environment on a growing child and educability. The troublesome pupil had a father who was in prison and, it was alleged, a mother who, 'entertained'. As for the brothers both would frequently arrive at school in the same state they had left the previous day. Probably as a result of having slept on the couch overnight in their school clothes, with a bag of crisps and a bottle of pop, with very little consideration of personal hygiene. Their mum enjoyed a drink, and their father enjoyed using his fists and I am led to believe had also served time at her Majesty's pleasure. It was difficult to see how the pair of them could stay on the straight and narrow. As a young, naive, caring teacher, it was easy to get upset as to the plight of these little darlings until it was pointed out, although the theory would have been pointed out and would have been a part of teacher training, that, at times, teaching was more to do with social work than education. Something teachers are not trained in, teachers are primarily educators, and must not get emotionally attached to pupils. Personally, I found this aspect of the job, trying to dissociate one from the other, very difficult, but nevertheless you had to try. At Christmas, I always gathered my class around my desk to make a fuss of opening the presents they had bought me and trying to give each gift 100% approval, and that it was the best gift I had ever received. When it came to one of the brothers, which was wrapped in newspaper, I carefully smelt it and touched it, trying to guess what it was, before un-wrapping it. The children were not allowed to shout out if they knew but could have a guess, along with Mr Briggs. Da Dah- **it was half a bottle of after shave, with SAMPLE, PROPERTY OF BOOTS, written across it.** Later I found out his brother in another class had bought Jean Tate, a female member of staff, half a bottle of perfume, 'bought' for with exactly the same writing on. Priceless, in every sense of the word. Incidentally the Tate family lived on the same council estate I was brought up on.

On another occasion I had given a very simple descriptive passage to the children, that we would read aloud together, followed by a few questions to see if they understood. This was a comprehension exercise found in First Aid in English. The passage was about a buccaneer, who was dressed accordingly, with a hat from which hung a cock feather, boots, sword etc. When one question asked, how could you tell the man was a fierce sailor? The reply from one child was, "Because he had a big cock hanging down in front of him." Oh! the age of innocence. Honestly, you can't make these things up. What is the name of a person who plays the piano? A PENIS. Obvious, isn't it? Does a contortionist have a twisted sense of humour? Actually, that's one I have just made up. These are not so much amusing anecdotes, but examples of how teaching becomes an all-encompassing part of your life and once invited to the party, it can be very difficult to leave. I suppose that is why some teachers can acquire a reputation for being boring bastards, because it is very difficult to switch off. Not that the humour always stemmed from others. As a young twenty odd year old I and other members of staff would sometimes have, 'a night out', and after one such night out, when I arrived at school the next morning, or should I say later that morning, the boss asked me to take morning assembly. This was rare, but he had to attend a meeting and the deputy Mrs Needham, had to see a parent deputation. I had never arrived at school still slightly hung over before, as I took my professional responsibilities very seriously, but decided in the comfort of my own classroom, with black coffee and polo mints, (remember the mint with a hole?), I could blag my way through the morning, until I sobered up. The request to take assembly, whilst invaluable experience for me, completely threw me because I would be in the hall with all the pupils, staff, support staff and a few parents gazing upon my being. The head cook was sure to make an appearance as the word on the grapevine was she fancied Mr B. Managing to get through the, good mornings and first hymn, I was convinced nobody had sussed I was half pissed. The problem arose when it came to prayers. Putting my palms together and closing my eyes, so we could think about what we were saying, and asking the children to do likewise, I realised that the little tots on the front row of the infants would copy **exactly** what Mr B did. If he left his eyes open, so would they. Shit, what could I do? Every time I closed my eyes, I felt nauseous and suffered a massive vertigo attack. It would not go down too well with the powers that be, who decided on my promotion prospects, not to mention the parents, if during the morning act of worship I fell on and vomited over a dozen infant children sitting cross legged in front of me. I remember Peter, the guy I had been out with, standing at the back of the hall wondering if he should go for a bucket and mop, just in case. How I survived I don't know, but **I NEVER, EVER** did anything remotely like that again. As I've said, I started to keep a book of these episodes with a view to publication but as of yet I've not got around to it. Whilst I taught at Mather Street and the other schools and educational establishments I worked at during my career, I formed lots of friendships with not only members of staff, some of whom I socialised with, but also parents, who would help me by providing lifts for the children, to various sporting events. The dinner ladies who looked after me and the caretakers and cleaners who cleaned up my mess. Whilst I went on to become Acting Head of Blackshaw Lane Primary School, Royton, Peter went on to become a head teacher of Lydgate School, Grasscroft, Saddleworth. There must be a moral in there somewhere.

At the age of 64, I suffered a serious vertigo attack caused by a virus, which, apart from frightening me, brought back memories of my morning assembly at Mather Street, 42 years previously.

Not long after starting at Mather Street I attended a meeting of the Chadderton and District School's Sports Association, which had been formed by the teachers in Lancashire Division 23, who were interested in organising inter school sporting leagues, events and tournaments, such as swimming galas, bridge tournaments, five and eleven a side football, cricket and netball etc. In those days, Lancashire was educationally split into divisions. Division 23 included Failsworth, Chadderton, Royton, Crompton and Shaw. It was through the association that I met many of my teaching friends and colleagues, who became an integral part of not only my teaching sojourn, but also my social life. People such as Neil Sinker, who later was to become my best man, Stuart Firth and Stuart Ford, Brian Chicot, Eric Harrison and their partners, Marilyn, Alison, Tina and Hilary, all became friends outside school. Eric Harrison taught my youngest sister, Janet, when he taught at Chadderton Hall. Dave Farrington, John Higham, Rick Gibbon, Don Smith, John Tobin, Peter Grundy, young Cliff Taylor and several others, whose names I cannot instantly recall became an integral part of my life. When I became the organiser for the Chadderton and Failsworth Swimming gala, I was indebted to the twenty or so staff, who annually helped me make it a successful event. None of them receiving a penny in overtime, although I did take them all to the pub afterwards for a drink, but not before checking if I was taking morning assembly the following day. **These were some of the most rewarding times in my life, being surrounded by these dedicated people who weren't materialistic or driven by financial gain, but who gave freely of their time so that little Johnny or Usrah could pit their sporting potential against others.** Whilst on the question of a teacher's dedication, commitment and motivation, during one holiday period I received a phone call from Mr Plimmer asking me if I could come into school to help the caretaker and cleaners clear up, as a burst pipe had flooded the school. Arriving at school, I was greeted by several inches of sludge covering the corridors and classrooms. It was heartbreaking to see the mess and found that all the staff, who were not away on holiday, had come in **voluntarily** to help clean up. I felt quite proud to be part of a profession that acted in such a way. Unfortunately, this episode was marred when I overheard one of the temporary cleaners remark, that the teachers had only come in because they got, 'double time'. **That has always been the problem with education, everyone is an expert because they have all been to school but in reality, have no idea what the job involves.** In my day, if teachers had been paid overtime, I would have been able to financially retire at 46 not 56. Later on in my career, when I taught at Blackshaw Lane, teachers were asked to work to rule by the unions because teachers' contracts had been suggested. They wanted to show the difficulties of implementing a job description and job specification that could be applied to **ALL** teachers, as well as remind people of what hours teachers were actually, legally obliged to teach. As part of the exercise, teachers were also asked to log how many hours they actually worked. Never being asked to do this before, I was intrigued as to what my results would show. At the time, teachers were legally obliged to be on the premises 15 minutes before the start of school, and 15 minutes after. In total, they had to work 38.5 hrs a week. Remember a 40-hour week was the norm for many jobs. I discovered I was working 66 hours a week on school related business and this was just slightly higher than the norm, but by no means was the highest. As I was aware, most teachers were intrigued as to how their contracts when implemented, would reflect the actual hours many teachers worked without **A MASSIVE PAY INCREASE**, which was never going to happen. In the end, contracts were handed out and teachers got an ex-gratia payment, if they did dinner duty as well as a free lunch. During my career of 35 years in education, I personally never met any teacher that was in it for the money. In relation to finance, the only conversation related was about how long it would take the finance department to give us our pay rise and back pay.

During my early career when I felt a need to justify my vocation, I frequently said to people who were critical of teachers, if it is so well paid, with fabulous holidays why don't you come and join us. One such person, who will remain nameless, took up my offer but had a nervous breakdown after a few years of trying to motivate hormonal teenagers. He was found locked in a toilet crying his eyes out chanting, like a mantra, 'I can't do this anymore'. Whilst writing this book, I often wonder how many teachers today, feel the same way?

Independence: Carnarvon Castle, Meals on Wheels, Les Dawson and George Dews FC.

Not long after starting teaching at Mather Street, I decided it was time to find a place of my own and leave Parkway. I felt a little guilty because my financial contribution to Parkway up to this point had been minimal, but like many, who initially had to share council house space with 8 other bodies and a bedroom with three other boys, the prospect of having my own space, especially my own bedroom, was very appealing. A flat at 33, Carnarvon Street, Hollinwood, Oldham, later to be fondly referred to as, 'The Castle', proved to be my first sortie into the world of independence. In actual fact, it was the top floor of an old property, owned by an elderly couple Jack and Janet Edwards. Carnarvon Street was tree lined, and was only a short bus ride to Mather Street. In Jack and Janet's eyes, being a teacher was more than acceptable and added to the fact that I was not one for making lots of noise, they were more than happy to share their house and lives with me. I sometimes attended bingo in Harpurhey with them, and this was my first introduction to the passion of gaming, slot machines and gambling as experienced by the elderly. Here handbags, pens and anything that could be used as projectile missiles was hurled when someone called **HOUSE**. This word was always greeted with a unanimous groan from the assembled throng, and abuse was hurled at the caller, who always seemed to be the most despised person in the room. No one had a nice word to say about a winner, apart from the winner and his/her friends, and the bingo caller was always accused of not shaking up the numbers, as the same people always seemed to win. Or at least that's what the assembled crowd seemed convinced of. In reality, this was not the case but was the result of pent-up emotion and frustration by the many folks, who would flock to the Bingo Hall several times a week. Here they would buy several 'books' and pour the rest of their hard-earned cash, or pensions, into the one-armed bandits, in the hope that they would return home to their terraced fortress with the jackpot. I was fascinated by the passion and adroitness of these people, who could sit and chat, whilst they checked off their numbers on not one, or two, but up to six cards at a time. Whilst I, the so-called educated teacher, struggled to concentrate on two. Upon hearing the word **HOUSE**, the talking stopped and these people morphed into aliens bent on revenge. It was fascinating, and another reason for me wanting to study more about human behaviour. Having sold my first car to my mate Eddie Whalley, who had a garage in which to put it, I bought another white Morris traveller, but that needed a new engine and I sold it at a loss, on the advice of my brother Barry. So, I arrived at Carnarvon Street, without any mode of transport. However, I was offered the use of a bike, so I could cycle to school, by a friend Jenny Lavin, who lived in a block of flats behind Carnarvon Street. One lunch time, as I was cycling back to school down Mather Street, I was attacked by an Alsatian dog, who I subsequently learned was not only owned by John O'Hara's parents, a pupil at the school, but had also attacked others before. I was taken to Oldham hospital to have the gash in my ankle stitched and upon returning to school, later that afternoon, I was met by the caretaker, Joe Austerbury, who after enquiring as to my health remarked, **"Obviously, the dog thought you were, Meals on Wheels, Mr Briggs."** Hilarious, Mr Austerbury, I like your sense of humour. The dog was eventually put down, but not before a policeman and I visited the O'Hara's house, so that I could identify the culprit. Imagine the scene of me being led into their back garden, to see this beast enclosed in a wire cage jumping, barking and snarling, and being asked if that was the dog that took a chunk out of your ankle? I don't know who was more nervous, me or the policeman, but I won the race to exit the garden. Obviously Failsworth was becoming the spawning ground for future stand-up comedians and Olympic sprinters. Whilst living at the castle I bought my third car from Jack, a silver and red, Humber Sceptre. This was a beast of a car where the handbrake and lever to alter the position of the back of the driver's seat, were on opposite sides of what I was used to. This meant that sometimes upon stopping at traffic lights, I would suddenly disappear from view much to the shock of the cars next to me. Also, my memory escapes me as to the actual chain of events but there was a time, whilst living at Carnarvon Street, when Dee and I had temporarily fallen out, and it was during such a time that I enjoyed my time at 'the Castle' because considering myself as a, 'free agent' I could do what I wanted, when I wanted and with whom I wanted, within reason. I say within reason, because Jack and Janet frowned upon late night parties and too many visitors. Janet, in particular, liked to know who was under the same roof as her and quite rightly so. As we both used the same entrance hall, it was difficult trying to enter without being heard or seen. I did occasionally sneak the odd female into the house, and was fortunate enough never to be caught in flagrante delicto. It's not that Jack and Janet were prudes, it was just that as an elderly couple, with failing health, I didn't want to upset them unnecessarily. There was only one occasion when I incurred Janet's wrath and that was when I met up with my mate from college, Pete Holland with whom I was still in touch. Pete had started teaching art at Burnage High School and was, at the time, dating a dancer, who also lived in South Manchester. I cannot recall the dancer's name or, more significantly, what had happened to Janet, his long-suffering girlfriend. Peter, as long as I had known him, always appeared to have more than one lady friend at a time. A lovable rogue, springs to mind. One day Pete contacted me asking if I wanted to attend an after-show party. Apparently, Les Dawson, the comedian, was appearing in Pantomime, at Leeds Playhouse Theatre, and Pete's young lady was one of the show's dancers. She also confessed to knowing Les Dawson, because she had previously worked with him. Mr Dawson, well he was just as you saw him on TV. He was the star of the show and as a friend of Pete's girlfriend, I was introduced to him and shared a couch with him. Fame at last, not that I was looking for it, but who knows I might have landed a part in a Pantomime. However, Les didn't appear to appreciate the fact I could raise a laugh or two, and could do a few impersonations, as I was genuinely surprised that he should feel threatened or intimidated by a schoolteacher from Chadderton. Perhaps I was picking up the wrong signals, and the honest truth was he probably just didn't like me. Years later, I was to find out that many 'entertainment, show biz', people are very insecure, escaping into a role, or persona, that has been created. This is not to decry the fact that they are, to all intents and purposes, decent people, but the business in which they work is very cut throat and at times, cruel. I'd said Pete could stay at my place, with his woman, but had not told Jack and Janet and so, lots of shushing and tip toeing was called for, as we didn't arrive back until the early hours of the morning. Unfortunately, Peter and his young lady were quite vocal during the night, I think she was rehearsing her dance moves, so much so, that even I had trouble sleeping. In the morning, the atmosphere was a little frosty with Jack and Janet, when I waved off Peter and friend later that day. Years later, I had another dalliance into the world of show business when I caught up with an ex North Chadderton pupil, Shiela Carter and ending up working in Marianne Jepson's dance, drama college in Oldham. Also, whilst living there, I started to play amateur football for George Dews, in the Manchester Industrial League. Mainly because my brother, Jack, was playing for them. The team was managed by John Tierney, my brother's father-in law, and a guy called Kenny Hughes. Ken had a reputation for driving the team bus like a formula one racing driver, which meant we frequently arrived at the opponent's ground, just glad to be alive. We never suffered pre-match nerves worrying about the opposition. In fact, many's the time we were pleased to see them. Ken was a brilliant club man as he would do anything for the players, but his knowledge of football left plenty to be desired. And so, it came as not only a shock to me, but also very sad, when many years later, as Ken grew older, he was found guilty of paedophilia, and appeared on the front page of the Oldham Evening Chronicle. Ken lived at home with his mum, and never seemed to have a social life, and his world revolved around George Dews. Writing this now, I smile at the time I had at Dews, but I still feel shocked about Ken. My brother Jack had been persuaded to play for them by John, and I thought it would be great to play on the same team as my brother. Something I had so far never managed to achieve, although we both played at Oldham Athletic. I loved playing for Dews, as they were some of the happiest times in my early teaching days. Some players are known as medal hunters, because they only want to play for teams who had a chance of winning something. For me that was never the case, and Dews was the only amateur team I ever played for, and the fact we consistently had a good squad of players was the icing on the cake. We had a big enough squad to play two teams, with many on the second team graduating to the first. We were a close-knit bunch and enjoyed each other's sense of humour and company. **Nowadays many youngsters will only agree to play for teams, if they are chauffeured to the ground.** Our rivalry with other local, amateur teams, such as Chamber FC, was well known, especially as I used to train the lads from Chamber, at Fitton Hill night school. One time I was training both Dews and Chamber, but my loyalty was always with Dews. Dews was also the team where I was re-united with some of the players I played with at Oldham Athletic. Players such as Kevyn Gibbons and Sid Jolley. As mentioned previously, Sid played for Oldham Athletic on their youth team, and it was great to renew our footballing partnership many years later, at Dews. Before Sid's death, at the age of 57, with cancer, our Jack and I went around to visit him at his house in Spring Gardens, Hollinwood. We shared a few beers, reminisced and watched a game involving Manchester United on television. It was very sad to see him, and made me realise how life could be so cruel. His best mate at Dews was Joe Gibson, known as chopper, don't ask. Up until the age of 66, my brother and I still attended re-unions, organised by Joe Gibson, involving lads from Dews. Sadly, at each re-union the numbers declined, as other players, besides Sid Jolley passed away. After Len Charnock, who occasionally used to bring his two small children to home matches, passed away, one of his sons attended one of our re-unions. Unfortunately, in the summer of 2016, Joey himself passed away. His funeral at Hollinwood Crematorium was very emotional for me, for many reasons as the Black Dog was also on my back. The funeral was well attended as Joe had not only many children, I think five, but also many friends. He was a well-known taxi driver in Oldham. It was also whilst playing football for Dews, I suffered a hairline fracture of the skull, just over my right ear, and ending up having an apoplectic fit and severely lacerating my tongue. Many people arguing that I never fully recovered from the brain shaking, and it was a shame that my tongue healed, allowing me to be able to speak properly again. Jealousy is a terrible thing. Finally, it was also whilst living at Carnarvon Street and playing for Dews, that I got sent off for breaking a player's jaw and was banned for 6 weeks. The red mist descended and I was not proud of my actions. During my time at Dews, I also played alongside my brother Jack for their Sunday team in the Blackley Amateur League, and was selected to play for their league team, earning myself a league badge.

George Dews FC. As you look at the photograph, on the left in the leather jacket is John Tierney and next to him is Len Charnock. Ken Hughes is on the right with my brother Jack, two along from Ken, on the back row. Can you spot me on the front row with the bulky shin pads?

Our First Home, Financial and Family Planning and Living within Your Means.

After I got married on Monday, the 25th August. 1975, it was an August Bank holiday, Dee and I spent the first few months living at 33, Carnarvon Street, Hollinwood. Jim Widd, a financial representative for the National Association of Schoolmasters, NAS, came to see Dee and myself, at Carnarvon Street, regarding getting a mortgage. I had a few endowment policies that I'd started from the age of 16, and so was looking for an endowment mortgage. Both Dee and I were now teaching full time and so getting a mortgage was not an issue. It was just a question of what kind of a mortgage and how much could we borrow. We had decided that all the finances for the mortgage would be based solely on my salary, and so if Dee became pregnant and stopped work, money would not become an issue. We had also been saving for the deposit, and all the other expenses that go with buying a house. We eventually bought a town house in Mendip Close, Royton for £7,200. It was in a block of six and ours was next to the end were Ray and Audrey Poxon lived with their children Andrew, Stephen, affectionately known as Pocco and Michelle, the eldest. Our other neighbours were Brian and Alice Shaw. At the time we bought the house, unbeknown to us, Brian, a self-employed kitchen installer, was a good friend of my mums. They had one daughter, Tracey, a good-looking girl, who attended St Paul's in Royton, where my friends Stewart and Marilyn Firth worked. Two of the three Poxon children, Michelle, the eldest and Stephen, also attended St. Paul's. Michelle was an early developer and, like Tracey, an attractive young girl, so both attracted a lot of attention from the boys. Audrey and Ray's other son, Andrew was educationally sub-normal and attended Ferneyfield, on Broadway, a school that dealt with children with various learning difficulties. Andrew needed a lot of care and attention, but all the children were well behaved and we never had any issues with any of them, in all the time we lived in Mendip. Andrew would frequently be waiting for me to come home from school, sitting on our top step. He was fascinated by sounds, and would follow bumble bees around the garden, mimicking the buzz sound. He also used to ask me to sound out various words such as equals, with emphasis on the ee. He also loved going through my vinyl record collection to find various symbols and loved the Warner Brothers' symbol. Unfortunately, you could always tell when he had done so because my records were strewn all over the lounge floor. Ray and Audrey would always tell Dee and me to send him home, when we had had enough but he was such an affectionate child we never once sent him home, even though sometimes we were both shattered from a day on the chalk face. **Like most newlyweds, in those days, we were just happy spending time decorating, doing DIY and looking at items of furniture we'd love to buy, once we had saved up enough money to buy them. If you couldn't afford it, you didn't buy it, until you had at least, saved up the deposit.** Until such time, all donations were gratefully received. Hilary Sinker's parents gave us a wardrobe, which we thought was brilliant. Sitting on a pair of deck chairs in the lounge, which someone had kindly given us, listening to my records, was for Dee and me, pretty cool! **As intimated in, Setting the Scene, many newlyweds today want to move into a brand new fully furnished, detached, with all singing, all dancing fixtures and fittings to impress their fickle, materialistic, so-called friends. Moving into a terraced house, for many, or accepting some one's second hand, cast offs is somehow frowned upon and, if possible, avoided. It would also appear that financial and family planning, and living within one's means are not items on the agenda.**

Now before the reader snaps this book closed, and puts the it on the rubbish tip, thinking that I don't know what I talking about, I have in the introduction to this book and periodically throughout its pages, pointed out that there will always be exceptions to the rule, but as I am searching for answers to many questions, the exceptions to the rule today, were mainly the norm in my day. I can only write what I have seen, experienced and have knowledge of, with reference to other people's opinions, published studies and research to emphasise a point. For my generation, 'doing up your first property', and spending time in, 'your own place', was part of the process of developing and building the foundation for a life of living together as a couple. It was something that cemented your relationship. **Nowadays many, but not all, after spending a small fortune, usually from their parent's retirement fund, on the wedding and securing their first home, the first thing the couple appear to want to do is exit stage left, only returning to go to bed. No wonder, the relationships only last a few years. Apart from sex there's no foundation holding the relationship together, and in some cases, there isn't even that. And as all people in long term relationships will tell you, the sex doesn't last forever. Whilst the words, 'love you', are bandied about as often as the meaningless expression, 'see you later'. As for family planning, I re-visit the subject in Chapter 6, Personal Stuff.**

Our local pub was The Greyhound, in Elly Clough, a five-minute walk from Mendip. The Greyhound at that time was the equivalent to a modern-day Spar as every conceivable household necessity could be purloined from its sanctuary. Bacon, televisions, books, firelighters, cooked meats, top soil etc. could all be bought and acquired from someone who passed through its portals. No questions asked, just pay the man and take your goods. This meant there was no shortage of, 'Jack the Lads', that frequented the pub. What today's non-political equivalent of this expression would be, I'm not sure. Answers on a postcard, please. **I am also unsure if this practice exists today, as visits to the pub just seem to be with a sole purpose to drink as much as possible. With the community spirit being related to drinking as much of the spirit as possible.** Mendip Close, or should I say in the tap room of the Greyhound, was where I also increased my knowledge and experience of human behaviour, when I was re-introduced to the fervour I'd come across in the bingo hall, in Newton Heath years earlier, with Jack and Janet. In simplicity, I foolishly won a game of cards, I think it was 9 card don, or something to do with the Italian mafia, in the company of some serious, hardened, professional card players, who were convinced I was a ringer or plant. One Sunday night, shortly after we had moved into Mendip, I was invited by my neighbours, Brian and Ray, to attend the Greyhound for, 'a swift one and a game of cards'. I knew I was a swift runner, but I was neither a drinker nor a card player, other than snap at Christmas, but I agreed and found myself being cajoled into playing cards. Now this invite was not only a friendly gesture to make the new kid on the block feel welcome, but also, I suspected, a chance for the boys in the tap room to impress me with their expertise in the art of card playing. Unfortunately, no one had told me the script and the friendliness turned to mild hostility, as I started to win a few hands. This was purely and simply based on luck and statistical probability, and had nothing to do with skill and expertise. But try telling that to a guy called Steve, who was close to tears and convinced I was, 'taking the proverbial piss'. Oh no, not again, was I going to end up pressed against a wall? Even when I said, "Thank you but no, thank you," to another game, they, the local card mafia, insisted I continue playing. No pressure there then, Mr Briggs. In the end Brian and Ray rescued me by pleading insanity, and convinced the boys I was, no disrespect to Andrew Poxon, mentally retarded and couldn't be held responsible for my actions. To this day, I have never played cards in the tap room of any pub. It's called being a coward. Another fond memory of our time living at Mendip, was when Dee and I bought a sliver, Renault 5TL, motor car, with a dash board gear stick. Which Dee loved, because she could hook her handbag on it. Now for those of you that are not familiar this make and model of car, the gear stick stuck out of the dash at 90 degrees, with a handle at the end and changing gears consisted of pulling out, or pushing in, the stick with various turns to the left or right depending on which gear was to be selected. It was simplicity personified, and I loved it. Eventually we part exchanged it for a Datsun Cherry, which was to be the first in a long line of cars from Datsun, later to be re-branded Nissan, when a new car plant was opened in Washington, in the North East.

It was also, whilst living at Mendip that Dee started teaching keep fit classes in Manchester and I joined Parkfield Country Club, Moorside. Every Tuesday Neil Sinker, Stuart Ford, Stuart Firth and Eric Harrison would visit Parkfield, for a boy's night out, playing squash, having a swim/sauna, playing dominoes or darts and a few beers and taking turns to drive. Notice, no mention of playing cards. When Maple squash Club opened on Broadway we moved our allegiance there. My final memory of living in Mendip was when Dee and Janet H's relationship took a turn for the worse when she and her husband Alan came up from the Midlands, to visit for the weekend, with their two children. Remember Dee had shared a flat with Janet and two other girls, Barbra and Marilyn during her time at Didsbury Teacher Training College. As is the case with many families where there are two children, they were chalk and cheese. The girl was lovely, whilst the boy was horrendously, badly behaved and it was when he decided to wipe his chocolate covered hands on our new red, velvet curtains, whilst his loving mother gazed on without saying a word, that enough was enough. So, Dee and I decided to take the law into our own hands. After all it was our house, not to mention curtains, and decided to chastise him for his errant ways. This was not a problem for Alan his dad, who was just about to separate his son's breath from his body, but for Janet it was all too much for her fabulous, beautiful, intelligent, sensitive off-spring, who was copiously weeping, as he was not used to such barbaric behaviour from Northern adults. This obviously put a tremendous strain on the rest of the weekend, and, to cut a long story short, to this day we never saw Janet and Alan again. This for me was sad, because Alan was a great guy but he married someone who, in my honest Northern opinion, was a spoilt brat, who although trained as an infant teacher, thought loving your children was to spoil them to the extent that first degree murder was acceptable behaviour by them, and was to be rewarded with a chocolate bar. During the weekend the atmosphere was tense, to say the least, as Janet and Alan battled for supremacy as to what was the best way to parent their children. Alan, going for the deterrent method, and Janet, the rewards one, and whilst both have their merits, Janet failed to embrace the fact that, 'one cap doesn't fit all', and was steadfastly opposed to Alan's methods. At the time, Dee and I were under tremendous societal pressures to have children. "After all what was the point in getting married," said Stuart Ford, "if you weren't going to have children?" And so, for Dee and me, weekends such as these made us both realise the enormity of the task of bringing children into the world. Eric Harrison, threw his hat into the ring by reminding us that if we thought about children too long, we'd never have them, or we would be too old to appreciate them. Having pontificated earlier about, Family Planning, Children and Parenting, I suppose this recollection was the first signpost to when the then acceptable, historical practices on the subject of parenting started to be challenged, and the 'old order' was starting to be replaced. This episode also brings me nicely around to perhaps the unhappiest time in my early teaching career when, after four plus wonderful years at Mather Street School, I applied for and was offered a Scale two post at Whitegate End Primary School, on Broadway, Chadderton. Before moving on, I recall the special assembly that was arranged for my leaving Mather Street. It was an emotional occasion not only for me, but for other people whom I didn't expect to feel that strongly about my departure. Were they tears of joy or sadness I thought, could they be both? Prior to the assembly, Mr Plimmer had been to see me, telling me that they had raised a certain amount of money for a leaving gift, and whilst some of my colleagues had several ideas, such as a new whistle for my PE lessons, he wanted to know if there was anything in particular, I would like within a certain budget. I obviously wanted something that I could treasure, and remind me of my first teaching post. I chose two porcelain figures from 'a posh' furniture shop in Oldham, called Squire Bancofts, where Dee and I had bought, after saving up to buy it of course, our first dining table and chairs. I can visualise the scene now, as I was made the centre of attention and presented with my gifts. The hall was packed with not only the children, staff and parents from the Primary School, but also staff from the Infants and Nursery. I felt quite choked that I had made such an impact, and quietly thought of Verna and Frank knowing I hadn't let them down. Although I hadn't yet been introduced to one of my favourite verses, in retrospect Mather Street was the first time it took on a collective, practical significance. I make no apologies for repeating;

'Some people come into our lives and quickly go

Some people move our soles to dance.

They awaken us to new understanding with the passing whispers of their wisdom.

Some people make the sky more beautiful to gaze upon.

They stay in our lives for a while, leave footprints in our hearts and we are never, ever the same.'

The porcelain figures still have pride of place in my home, and I still have the whistle. I haven't kept count of how many times I've used it, but it's a lot!

More of this in Chapter 6 when I discuss friends and acquaintances.

Whitegate End Primary School, 1976-1979.

My first visit to Whitegate End Primary School on Butterworth Lane, Chadderton, was when I was invited by the head, Mr Tom Goring, to attend their sports day, in the summer prior to starting teaching there in September. This was an opportunity to meet the staff, children and parents, and get an initial impression of what my new teaching environment was going to be like. Leaving Mather Street was the right thing to do for my career, but it was difficult leaving somewhere that had become my comfort zone. At Mather Street, I had earned the respect of the children, my peers, parents and support staff and in return I had been given the help and support that all teachers need during their early teaching years. Mather Street was an old Victorian school, run along traditional lines, with a democratic, bordering on laissez faire head, who believed in corporal punishment as one deterrent to maintain discipline. Whitegate End was a modern building, on a split site and split level, that was run by a very autocratic head, who didn't subscribe to, 'a clout around the ear', to erring miscreants. Not that in my 35 years in education, I ever saw a teacher give a pupil a, 'clout around the ear'. Flying board dusters and chalk yes, but clouts around the head, no, even in my Secondary school days when physical chastisement of one kind or another was not uncommon. Mr Goring had asked me, how I felt about this when I attended an interview, and I honestly said I would look upon it as a challenge as I strongly felt that without discipline, teaching was virtually impossible and teachers should use their discretion as to the appropriate method of deterrent. We disagreed, as he told me corporal punishment was off the menu at his school. Furthermore, Tommy Goring was head, not only of Whitegate End but also the NAHT, The National Association of Head Teachers. In other words, he made a powerful enemy. In spite of this difference of opinion, he still invited me to join his staff. The word on the street was that he was not a well-liked Head and was difficult to work for, but for me, because the school was so different to what I had experienced during my first 4-5 years, I looked upon the move as part of my personal development as a teacher. I needed to not only acquire more of the theoretical underpinning, but also the pedagogical skills allied to my profession. Following the advice that you stay in a situation long enough to take and learn from it, whilst long enough to give what you can to it, I felt I had achieved what I could in a small school such as Mather Street, with 168 pupils and was looking forward, with slight trepidation, to the challenge Whitegate End would present with its 250 plus pupils.

As highlighted the modern site was not only split level, three to be exact, but also in two parts, with the infant block adjacent, but separate from the Juniors. The school was also next to South Chadderton Secondary School, with whom it shared the playing fields. Although, sharing was not strictly true as both schools had their own allocated spaces. The deputy Head, Christine Cooke, was located in the infant block, along with Gillian Lloyd and one other member of staff. In the juniors were Valerie Beresford, Don Colley, Francis Norris, Chris Anderson and myself. I was assigned to a Junior two class of 8–9-year-olds. Personally, for me the physicality of the site presented problems when it came to continuity of education, as you were always going up and down stairs or going from one building to the other. I personally felt isolated as my classroom, whilst much more modern, light and airy than I had been used to at Mather Street, was on the lowest level, two down from the main entrance. However, the fact that the school was modern and was surrounded by extensive playing fields, meant there were plenty of pluses for me as a PE specialist. One of the reasons I had secured the job was that although, Whitegate End had several members of staff, such as Val Beresford, Chris Anderson and Don Colley, all involved in running various teams, there wasn't an actual PE specialist in the school. In fact, when I first entered the teaching profession PE specialists were a rarity in Primary Education, as they tended to gravitate towards the secondary sector, for reasons I've already alluded to. Unfortunately, because of the way Mr Goring allocated scale posts for certain responsibilities, it soon became apparent that using my knowledge, skill and expertise in PE to benefit the school, was not going to be easy as most staff seemed to have a scale post equivalent to mine. It wasn't that I wanted to be the big honcho, but at Mather Street Mr Plimmer left me to develop the PE side of the curriculum with very little interference, but plenty of support, whereas at Whitegate, I was conscious of not wanting to tread on people's toes. Also, as Mr Colley ran the school football eleven, my role was one of support rather than direction and leadership. Whilst Don was a good guy, he was not the strongest personality I had come across in teaching, and he wasn't a person immersed in exercise and sport. He did, however, have a life outside teaching, whilst on the other hand Valerie Beresford ate, slept and drank teaching and didn't appear to have much, if any, of a social life. I liked Val, and got on really well with her and although, I had only been in the profession for less than half a dozen years, I had come to realise that it was **vital that teachers had to be able to 'switch off', unless of course you wanted a nervous breakdown. Sadly, Valerie passed away in her early 60s and, as far as I know, never married. I have often remarked, with tongue in cheek, that you needed to be schizophrenic, or have a split personality, to be a successful teacher, as it can be all consuming. Also, unless people had actually taught, as opposed to being an expert because they'd just been to school, it was difficult for them to appreciate the pressures that teaching presented. I also appreciated that just because you had trained to be a teacher and possessed a certificate, diploma or degree, it didn't necessarily mean you would be good at it. This truism can be applied to many jobs.** As my knowledge, skill and expertise developed, and I started to become interested in human behaviour and teacher education, by attending courses and becoming involved in research, I realised that it took a certain type of personality to be a successful teacher. I also realised that many parents and classroom support staff, who hadn't chosen teaching as a career, would make far better teachers than some of my colleagues. Having experienced first-hand the Mrs Hallets of this world at Mather Steet, and later to come face to face with my old PE teacher from North Chadderton, Clifford Taylor, now trying to help his promotion prospects by working in Primary education, I realised what a negative impact these individuals can have on a child's education and the morale of staff, who have to try and work with these people. This ultimately leading to my resignation from the honourable profession on more than one occasion.

Anyhow, back to Whitegate End. I respected many of the staff at Whitegate, and set about trying to earn their respect. However, it soon became apparent all was not well, as Mr Goring was frequently away from school on union business and the fact the school had a non-corporal punishment policy, it always felt to me as if it was permanently simmering on the verge of anarchy. Regarding discipline, I was told that you should only tell a child twice before stronger measures are required to dissuade him/her from continuing their errant ways. After the first time you can presume, they were watching your lips move but not listening. The second time they either listened, but ignored you, or they had an auditory or other problem that needed further investigation. If, in your professional opinion, this was not the case then the third time they were waiting to see what would happen if they transgressed again. Don't forget children learn to lie to avoid getting into trouble as early as 4 years of age, (Serota K, Levine Timothy R, Boster Franklin J, 2010. Human Communication Research), and Whitegate End seemed to have a lot of children immune to verbal chastisement. How many times do you say, no, if you do that again I'll..? Add that to the fact that because the social demographic of the area meant parental pressure was far greater than at Mather Street, the pressures came from not only the children. Basically, little

Johnny was the greatest and cleverest thing since sliced bread, and could do no wrong. If he, or she, was not top of the class, or near to it, then it **MUST BE** the teacher's fault. At Mather Street parents left you to get on with trying to do your best and, on the whole, appreciated your efforts, whereas at Whitegate End I always felt I was under the microscope. Not that I had anything to hide, it's just that the parental microscope at Whitegate End needed cleaning. This ultimately led to my first major setback in teaching and a blot on my, so far, unblemished reputation.

Having started an after school gymnastics' club, with Chris Anderson, I found myself one night being pushed to the limit of my patience by one of the pupils. Now this child, who shall remain nameless, had developed a reputation, long before my arrival, as one of the naughtier children in school, but more significantly his mother had locked horns with Mr Goring on more than one occasion. The psychologists and sociologists, if asked, would come up with a raft of labels, when in simplicity, he was a hyperactive, spoilt, little brat. To cut to the chase, gymnastics was steeped in health and safety, long before health and safety became steeped. So, after this child had repeatedly disobeyed my requests to stop trying to cause an accident in the session, with a defiant look of, what are you going to do about it if I don't? I reacted instinctively, with no malice aforethought, and paddled his backside with the palm of my hand. This did the trick, and I thought nothing about it, until the following morning, when I was summoned to the boss's room during Christine Cook's assembly. Evidently his mother had stormed into school to see Mr Goring, because Mr Briggs had physically assaulted her son and had my finger print marks on his backside to prove it. Shit!!! I'd intended to inform Mr Goring at the earliest opportunity but hadn't. I could use the excuse that it was a long walk from my classroom to his office, but I didn't. Now Tommy Goring may have had his faults, but he was loyal to his staff, as long as he knew what he was defending them for. The fact that he was dealing with this problem in the dark, didn't make him a happy bunny. The outcome of the incident was that he had placated the mother on the understanding that the matter would be dealt with internally, with a letter of apology from Mr B. The word overzealous with my discipline springing to mind. What upset Mr Goring was, he was unaware of what I'd done, until it was too late, and for that I got a bollocking. The incident was one of the blackest in my career, but definitely cemented my thoughts on discipline within schools. **When the politicians eventually did away with corporal punishment as a deterrent in schools, NEVER TO THIS DAY TO BE REPLACED BY ANY OTHER EQUALLY EFFECTIVE METHOD, I realised that was the time when education became the survival of the fittest, as it is today.**

"Running a school, working in a school, it's not like it used to be, you know? I mean, you always had tough kids but it's worse now. They're armed. Their parents don't give a shit." (Barclay L, 2017. No Time For Goodbye, PB, 18:160). Today I tell youngsters wanting to become teachers, "Have you thought of becoming a Prison Officer instead, at least you can lock up the little buggers?" **Poor teaching is now blamed for all the ills in society, but what many people fail to realise is that teachers are trained to educate, they are not social workers. Although a percentage of teaching involves having to deal with the problems in society. Discipline starts in the home. Remember the first five years of a child's life are vital. To repeat, teachers are not social workers, prison officers or policemen.** Don't get me wrong, not all children are socially inept and many want to learn, and I've always argued, why should those who want to learn have to put up with those who don't, won't or can't? A topic I was to study in greater depth, years later, when I re-entered full time education as a lecturer in Higher Education. Another, but entirely different example of the distorted view that some parents had of seeing education as a two-way process, between parent and school, where both are singing from the same hymn sheet, was a child called Martin. He lived in a large detached house near school, and his parents gave the impression that they were not short of money. Martin, their youngest son, could frequently be seen driving his go cart around the back garden after school. The parents were well meaning, middle-class, well-spoken people, who loved their children and only wanted the best for them. **Sadly, as many parents today do, they interpreted love as a materialistic thing and so the children were smothered in money, materialism and possessions.** Martin was also dressed very smartly, and added to the fact that, as he got older, he was destined to break many a young lady's heart, meant he could charm the socks off many unsuspecting adults. In actual fact he was a lazy sod, and was punching way below his weight in an educational context, especially with his reading. When I diplomatically, pointed this out to mum and dad, who had earmarked Martin for great things, they laughed and thanked me for my honesty. "Is there anything we can do to help Mr Briggs?" Well, in my humble opinion, humility can help in situations like this, I said that he was quite capable of being further on in the reading scheme and developing his higher order skills of reading, than he was at present. This meant reading so that he comprehends, can skim and scan, can predict, anticipate and analyse and is not just reading parrot fashion to finish the book. These being known, along with others, as the higher order skills of reading. After explaining how we could achieve this, they promised their whole hearted support. Unfortunately, several weeks later I overheard Martin telling his classmates that his parents had just bought him a brand-new TV for his bedroom, because he'd finished his reading book. A dog is for life not just for Christmas, springs to mind. I don't think he ever completed the reading scheme. To be honest why should he, life was hunky dory without all these higher order skills of reading.

I would have liked to have waxed lyrical about my time at Tommy Goring's school, but I didn't enjoy the experience and decided that two years was an acceptable time to serve, before I started looking for pastures new. As for the experience, I was pleased I had made the decision to go there. Tom Goring taught me much, and I was appreciative of that. Apart from watching him wheel and deal, under the guise of school management, he would sometimes give me a lift home and impart pearly words of wisdom. He was always asking me to justify myself, which was something I was not used to with Mr Plimmer, but I soon realised he was grooming me for greater things. Thanks, Mr Goring. On our journeys home, he would say such things as, "Jim, you are never going to please everybody all of the time, so don't even try or you'll have a nervous breakdown." Or, "Democracy is all well and good in theory, but as the boss you are paid to kick arse, so don't shirk it." Rich coming from a man, who was against corporal punishment. Also, "Asking your staff what they think, is all well and good, but at the end of the day it's what's best for the children's education, not Mrs/Mr X's personal wish list. Children and their parents, in that order, are your priority when it comes to making decisions, because without them you have an empty school." One of the most interesting things I learned from Mr Goring, was his style of leadership. Yes, it was definitely autocratic, but he openly admitted to me that he wasn't interested in being friends with his staff and knew what they thought of him. Knowing they would nearly always vote against him in staff meetings, which he saw as a plus that made decision making easy. Different factions in the staff meant, people were either for or against you, so no matter what you did, someone was going to be unhappy. But as he believed all his staff were against him, it was easy to make decisions. He either pleased or upset them all en bloc. This was not strictly true, as not everyone disliked him, both Christine Cooke and I, both respected him, and although I didn't subscribe to his style of management, I nevertheless saw merits in it. Later in my career, when I became a head of department, deputy and acting head, I integrated some of his philosophies into my leadership style. Sadly, Tom passed away not long after he retired, along with Valerie Beresford, but not before I'd thanked him, for helping me with my career, especially after I'd moved to Blackshaw Lane. After several years at Whitegate End, an opportunity arose to apply for a Scale 3 post at Blackshaw Lane. Tommy Goring, whilst supporting my application, didn't think it was a good career move for me at that time. In his position, as head of NAHT, he must have known something, but because I'd decided I wanted away from Whitegate End, I was not clever enough to read the hidden message Tom was giving me. His caution at going to work with Mr CJ Taylor was justified as I eventually resigned from teaching, after fighting for many years to have Mr Taylor removed from his position of earning a lot of money, under false pretences. Even the masons, whom it was said had more than a hand in securing his appointment, were acutely embarrassed, as it became blatantly obvious that he should never have been put in such a position.

Blackshaw Lane Infant and Junior School, 1979-1987,

- Venture Week.

If Whitegate End was one of my unhappiest and frustrating times in my teaching career, Blackshaw Lane was certainly the most professionally and personally challenging. As I've mentioned previously, it was at a time when there was a definite policy to not only encourage more men into Primary Education, but also it was a time when some secondary male teachers saw such a move as advantageous for promotion. For some the thinking being that if you could teach older, secondary pupils, then teaching younger, primary children, would present no problems. How wrong could they be? Where this hierarchical misconception came from that the older the age group you taught, by inference, the more intelligent, and pedagogically skilful you had to be, and the more difficult it was, I am not sure. But for me that was the biggest load of bollocks I'd ever heard, and I frequently challenged my secondary colleagues, who genuinely believed that all you did in junior schools was play in the sand and water, to do a job swap, but no one ever accepted my invitation. For me, I felt teaching infant/junior children should be a compulsory part of **all** teacher training as I have nothing but the utmost respect for most infant teachers. I say most because as in all jobs there are always the weak links. **In the 70s and 80s, infant junior teachers taught and educated, secondary teachers instructed and directed. Nowadays, both just try to survive.** It was also a time of massive upheaval in Secondary Education, after Margaret Thatcher's elitist government, 90% plus coming from a private/boarding school background, had steamrollered **Comprehensive Education** into the educational mix, seeing it as a massive vote getter. One of the government arguments was that it would do away with stereotyping children, having all abilities under one roof. This was against the advice of the teaching unions, who opposed it on the grounds that it would bring every pupil **down** to the same level. The emphasis being on **down** and that teachers teaching in such, especially the ones that had been used to teaching the academically brightest and cleverest ones in the Grammar schools, would have to be retrained to deal with the vast variances in ability and, most importantly, behaviour. **The research evidence also said that it would only work, if such schools were kept to a maximum of 450 pupils,** as having numbers greater than that would not allow such ranges of ability to be taught effectively. What actually happened when integration took place was that very few Comprehensives, if indeed any, had 450, or less, pupils, many exceeding that by hundreds. Also, many of the old, Grammar school teachers were given the senior positions, over their secondary modern counterparts, with no further training. This not only alienated half the secondary teaching population, but also it became more and more acutely obvious that the grammar school orientated teachers were struggling to cope with some of the anti-school, anti-social pupil element found in the old secondary modern schools. Anarchy was rearing its ugly head, both in and out of the classroom. To deal with this, the new comprehensives started streaming children according to their ability. Was this not what the Tri –Partite system of Grammar, Secondary Modern and Technical Schools had done before they abandoned/disbanded it? Of course, it was **but what did the Education Minister of the time know about teaching as he/she had never taught or been trained to teach?** The government was also coming under increasing pressure, from various bodies, to do away with corporal punishment, but hadn't a clue what to put in its place to act as a deterrent and keep law and order against the anti-social behaviour. **Without discipline or an effective deterrent structure in place, teaching becomes ineffective, ineffectual and a waste of time, space and effort, because teachers just become child minders, quasi-social workers/ prison officers.** I was personally aware of several teachers, one a head of maths in the old grammar system, who had nervous breakdowns, trying to teach in a comprehensive. I say personally, because before Mrs Thatcher's vote enticing, 'bright' ideas to con the public into thinking the government was on the side of the 'common man', these people were decent human beings, trying to just do their jobs as best they could. So, this was the background for many secondary teachers, both male and female, to look to the Primary, Further and Higher Education sectors for sanctuary. I can recall four such teachers in Oldham Education Authority, two male and two female, who entered Primary Education via the Secondary Education route. Furthermore, these people were given fairly senior management positions, which personally I had no problems with, if they possessed the necessary knowledge, skill set and expertise. Clifford Taylor, **who openly admitted in the local pubs, that going to church and joining the masons was one way to enhance a person's career prospects,** was **NOT ONE** such person. **Diplomacy being absent in Taylor's skill set which, at times, caused embarrassment to his fellow masons and teachers.** Before being appointed Head at Blackshaw Lane Infant Junior School, Taylor had earned himself a reputation, not only teaching PE at my old Secondary school, but also at Chadderton Hall Primary, for being an, 'odd bod'. It soon became obvious to me that Taylor's overall grasp of what his role entailed, was not ground in modern day pedagogy and research thinking, but a Victorian model involving mincing around in gowns and mortar boards. What made the situation more bizarre was that as he didn't have a degree, he borrowed a gown from one of the parents. He had some very strange Victorian ideals, which were at odds and the antithesis of Primary thinking at the time. How much experience of team teaching, with a thematic approach, in an open plan environment, was open to conjecture, but I suspect he had none. But upon becoming a member of staff at Blackshaw Lane, it became obvious that Taylor favoured the more traditional approach of seating children in rows of desks, where they all did an exercise from a text book, whilst the teacher sat at the front, overseeing proceedings. I was informed by others, 'in the know', that he had applied unsuccessfully for many Primary headships, but was told he needed more practical experience in this field of expertise. So, it came as a bit of a shock, to say the least, to not only myself but others, who had only ever worked in Primary Education, when he was appointed head at Blackshaw Lane, one of the largest in the borough. There were rumours and it was alleged that Taylor had been given the job because he was a mason and a church man. Or was the authority trying to send a message to other ex- Secondary teachers that joining the junior ranks, from secondary, was not demotion but a possible promotion? Was Tommy Goring trying to tell me something, when I told him I wanted to apply for a job at Blackshaw Lane? To recap, Taylor became Headmaster at Blackshaw Lane Primary School, via being a PE teacher at North Chadderton, where I first met him as a pupil, then Deputy Head at Chadderton Hall Primary, my youngest sister Janet's old school, under Stephen Perfect, the head. Years later, when the problems at Blackshaw Lane became more than just rumour and the authority was trying to silence me by suggesting I apply for a transfer, Mr Perfect and several other heads said they would be more than happy to have me as their deputy. At that time, as I was virtually ploughing a lone furrow, by wanting Taylor removed from office, by asking the authority to admit they had made a mistake and rectify the situation as diplomatically as possible. Unfortunately, **whilst many may not agree with what they see as injustice or a mistake, at the end of the day they have bills to pay and families to feed and so clear consciences, morals, ethics and rectifying such mistakes become just words.** Not long after arriving at Blackshaw Lane, as Head of Juniors, on a Scale 3 post, the then deputy, Mavis Butterworth, who was responsible for the infants, was seconded for 12 months, never to return. She made no bones of the fact that although Taylor had only been in situ for a very short while, she had seen enough and wanted to put as much distance between herself and Clifford Taylor as possible. Talk about you don't get a second chance to make a first impression. Anyone with

Primary school management experience soon realised that Taylor, whilst talking the talk, was out of his depth trying to lead, inspire, motivate and innovate in respect of infants and juniors. In the short time I worked with Mavis, our relationship was 'edgy', to say the least, as she saw me as a mate of Taylor, and I'd only been given the job on the back of being, 'one of the boys'. Her departure also meant that I immediately became acting deputy. I also soon realised that Blackshaw Lane, under Taylor, was in serious need of radical surgery, and it was going to take more than one operation, to get both the infants and junior departments talking from the same hymn sheet. To be fair, there were probably issues that needed addressing at the school before Taylor arrived, but the fact that he couldn't see much wrong, and if he did, he either didn't know how to put it right or couldn't be bothered. For me it was a combination of both, and so was just another indication of how tough my job was going to be. It was not in my psyche to ignore its failings and just take the money, my responsibility was to the pupils. **Without pupils, teachers don't have jobs.** Unfortunately, Taylor, whilst totally agreeing with me and anyone else who cared to listen, and whose responsibility it ultimately was, appeared clueless as to how to instigate change, never mind innovative change. He hated any kind of discussions with me on the subject because it was blatantly obvious, he had very little to contribute, other than to blame members of staff who saw him for what he was and refused to make his life any easier. **Power you can take, respect you have to earn.** To start with, there were 23 different reading schemes on offer, scattered throughout the infant and junior departments. There were no generic schemes of work that the staff could refer to, and staff development was virtually non-existent. There were no clear communication channels and chains of command. There were two members of staff with special responsibility for music, neither of whom knew definitively what musical equipment was available in school. Whilst certain members of staff viewed PE lessons as something to deprive naughty children of, if they stepped out of line. This was a red rag to a bull for an enthusiastic PE teacher such as myself, who saw PE as the third most important subject on the curriculum, after literacy and numeracy. Rising to the challenge I adopted the attitude that I had made my bed and therefore must lie in it, and any efforts to stabilise the ship and move it forward had to be done, **in spite of the head, Taylor,** who basically was in denial as to his failings and was only interested in spreading the gospel according to the free masons, and **flouncing around in his borrowed University gown. He hadn't a degree but persuaded one of the parents to lend him a gown to wear in school.** Look at me, I'm a headteacher. Curriculum Development, innovation, self-analysis and introspection were not something Taylor was familiar with and even if he was, was not prepared to share his thoughts with, 'us rabble', as he sometimes referred to certain members of staff. If he had been honest and quietly admitted he was out of his depth, I could have respected him, but to try and bullshit his way through the job, at the expense of children's education was, to say the least, arrogant, disrespectful and undermined the profession I represented. Add that to the fact that he was being paid a lot of money for shopping in Asda, and looking at cars in exchange and Mart, during school time, made his status even more ludicrous. Years later, when I was preparing my case against him and the Chief Primary Officer, Chris Pickup, was asking him what curriculum development had he been involved in whilst at Blackshaw Lane, the honest answer being very little, he claimed he had updated the maths curriculum to gain an ACP, (Associate of the College of Preceptors). **What he had actually done was submit a copy of Mavis Butterworth's work, the then Deputy Head, that she had submitted as part of her secondment, claiming it as his own. As these things were not physically checked as accurate, but only underwent academic rigour, he was awarded the diploma. Unbeknown to Taylor I had found a copy of such hidden away in his office. In Higher Education this is known as plagiarism and is a serious offence. Punishable by students being** thrown off the course. But if you're a Headmaster, with connections, the crime is overlooked or **ignored.** Added to this lack of leadership, there were also difficult members of staff, steeped in union tradition, who could be frequently seen around the pot, creating their next brew, and plotting their next dastardly deed, and Taylor had no idea how to deal with them. Unfortunately, for me they wanted to make life as difficult for anyone wanting to improve Blackshaw Lane, which may have involved taking them out of their comfort zones. If the school acquired a poor reputation, then maybe Taylor would be held accountable and so they certainly didn't want anyone improving things, which Taylor would undoubtedly take credit for. And there lay the problem because whilst I sympathised with them, having inherited Taylor for a boss, as deputy I was expected to support him. What I was also aware of was, that teachers like them needed watching or they could destabilize any institution. As they saw me as a mate of Clifford, I was doomed from the start and even though I was prepared to earn respect from the staff, I soon realised some were not prepared to give it to me. Nevertheless, I decided to accept the challenge, knuckle down and try to achieve my aims. I also realised it was going to take time. To be honest, I embraced the role because I could get on with it, and if other members of staff wanted to also become involved, they could, otherwise I'd plough a lone furrow. I kept them aware of what I was doing and virtually paid lip service to Taylor's lack of leadership. Many times, I held staff meetings in Taylor's absence. Oh, he was aware of them, because I always sought his permission regarding curriculum development, but because he didn't think there was any need for change, he felt he had better things to do like looking at cars, that his car dealer mate was selling, or going to Asda, because it was quiet when all the children were in school! **I often thought that it would have made a fabulous reality TV programme, that would top Biker Groves and Waterloo Rd. in the ratings.** One must also remember that at the time National Curriculums and OFSTED had not yet been fully created and released into the educational domain. It must also be realised that the Authority, as time went on, was becoming more aware of the situation, once the facts emerged, via the educational gossip, hot line. Also, when I was approached on the quiet to present a case for his dismissal, I labelled it, Spycatcher II, after the recent political scandal that had been in the news. This was not appreciated by the powers that be, as they didn't share my sense of humour. When the shit did eventually hit the proverbial fan and Taylor was brought to task, in his defence, he couldn't even differentiate between abdicate and delegate responsibility. Once immersed in the task I started to enjoy myself, treating the exercise as excellent training, and on the chalk face experience for when I eventually got my own headship. I also realised that my time with Tom Goring had been invaluable and frequently heard his pearly words of wisdom ringing in my ears. Even though, I had a class of 38 plus junior fours to teach, I set out my long-term strategy and plan, devoting many hours after school to the task.

Two people became very significant, not only in my attempt to make my time at Blackshaw Lane an important step in my quest to become a head, but also in my private and personal life, Barbara B and Lynne D. Add to these Eileen T, another member of staff that initially I clashed with, but eventually came to respect me, and who eventually joined my inner sanctum.

My first Junior 4 class at Blackshaw Lane.

Barbara Lynch, nee Bolwell, nee Cooper, entered my life when she walked into Blackshaw Lane Primary school in 1980, a few days before term started. It was her first teaching appointment, since leaving teacher training college, and was soon informed that she had only just returned from a trip to India with her boyfriend. It was also ironic that she had attended Chadderton Grammar School, and was in the same class as my youngest sister Janet. Barbara proved to be one of those members of staff, that you want on your team. She was conscientious, reliable and appreciated **teaching was a job, that was very difficult to put into a contract with a job description and role specification. It was a job where the rewards equated to your attitude, work ethic and input and although, the financial rewards didn't equate to such, job satisfaction was key.** Barbara would ask, if she was unsure or was not happy, unlike a lot of teachers who felt that a few years of training equipped them for a lifetime on the chalk face. **On-going professional development,** at the time, was only seen as something you did if you wanted to get more money and promotion and so therefore, was never an issue for the less ambitious teachers. Oh, they wanted more money but didn't want to justify it with increased knowledge, skill and expertise. It was pleasing, to say the least, to see Barbara become more and more confident in the classroom, and take on more and more responsibility. I, more than anyone, appreciated the value of having a mentor when you first started teaching, and so when I became management, I took it upon myself to help probationary teachers all I could. In my humble opinion teaching in primary education had always been more about the sociological and environmental, rather than the educational aspects. **You don't find people in books.** I also wanted to protect her from Taylor, who had even less idea of how to communicate with female members of staff, than he did of male ones. But I need not have worried, as it didn't take her long, even with her very limited experience, to 'suss' him out. Once she was aware of Venture Week and what it entailed, she enquired if she could be considered as the female member of staff to accompany me. This was one of the first responsibilities, apart from after school sports clubs, that I took on not soon after arriving, at the school. To be honest Jack Verity, my predecessor, had started the idea and I was excited to develop it and make it an integral part of the children's final year, before going to, 'the big school'.

Butlins Venture Weeks, like PGL and other such organisations, was where children could be taken away from their home and school environment, and be involved in a variety of educational and physical activities, ranging from basket making, abseiling, roller skating, First Aid, gymnastics, to performing on stage in the end of week show. Off site visits to wild life parks, show caves, steam engine grave yards, not to mention 8-mile walks and pony trekking. This was possible as Butlins Holiday Camps made its facilities available, before they opened their doors for the holiday season. Seeing it as not only a good advertisement and PR exercise, but also an opportunity for them to train staff and get the camps up and running before the paying customers arrived. Not that Venture week was free to schools, but the charges were basically just to cover their overheads. A good PR exercise. Schools travelled from all over the country and so, apart from the many obvious health benefits such weeks provided, it had massive sociological benefit for the children to integrate with other children from differing race, colour and social backgrounds. Watching Northern children listening to a conversation between a cockney, brummie, Welsh person and a scouser, and the reverse was something to behold. On my first Venture week, I took 30 children from mainly Junior 4 and a few from Junior 3, to Barry Island, South Wales. Made famous by the television programme Gavin and Stacey. **This was no picnic as Loco Parentis, in place of the parent, was very much to the fore and accepting responsibility for 30, 9- to 11-year-old children, 24/7 was a massive task.** Especially, as 12 of them had never done anything at all away from mum and dad. It was scheduled during school time, before Easter, and I obviously needed a female member of staff to not only accompany me, but also to look after the girls. Also, permission had to be sought from the LEA and school governors, and took many months to plan and organise, with supply staff having to be found, to cover our classes, whilst we were away. If I could do nothing else, organisation was my forte and so I relished dotting the i's and crossing the t's. This particular year, my first, Eileen Turner and Barbara Cooper, had shown an interest in coming. I had no preferences, but it was decided by the Head, Clifford Taylor and the governors, that as the children were upper juniors, Barbara would be the least disruptive choice, as she was teaching Junior 3. Eileen at the time was teaching lower juniors. It would also be invaluable experience not only for me, but also Miss Cooper to see how other teachers and schools behaved away from the classroom. In 1980, the educational environment was one of respecting a teacher's organisational skills to arrange these out of school trips, and as long as the parents appreciated its relevance and the necessary paper work was completed, the local LEA would approve it and provide the necessary supply staff in a teacher's absence. I loved every second of my Venture Weeks.

Venture Week, Barry Island, 1980, Miss Cooper with the children.

As I got to know Barbara better, rightly or wrongly, I started to take an interest in her personal as well as her professional development. Occasionally we went out for a drink, when I sometimes made my views on her relationship, with her boyfriend John, known to Barbara. I suppose I was stepping out of my role as mentor, but what harm were we doing? Little did I know. When Barbara suddenly announced, that she and John had set a date to marry, more as a statement of fact than as a subject for discussion, and then surprisingly, actually got married to John, I realised my views had fallen on deaf ears. If that was what she wanted, I was happy for her, and our relationship as work colleagues and friends continued. I valued her friendship and was absolutely shocked, surprised and saddened when one evening, after we had been out with some of the staff, after some after school do, she told me she only married John because I was unavailable, and she hoped that when she announced she was getting married, I would leave Dee and set up home with her. With no disrespect to Barb, she had misinterpreted my help and advice, or had I planted a seed of doubt/hope? Again, I am unsure as to how it happened, but not long after she married, it was obvious she was unhappy and sought solace in my company. When I eventually left Blackshaw Lane, to set up my clinic, at the same time that Dee and I had agreed to separate and she'd left, to initially go and live with her sister Brenda, Barbara was very upset, and as a true friend continued to be supportive. I, on the other hand, felt very, very guilty I had messed up my marriage, and didn't want to cause further distress to anyone else, least of all Barbara, and so withdrew into myself. As the loneliness and black dog took hold, Barbara continued to want to share with me. Ego is a powerful thing, for both men and women, and takes very strong will power to oppose the consequences, when some woman is stroking it. I was single again, so what was wrong with encouraging attention from the opposite sex? Things were not helped, when Barbara told me John was having an affair, with a girl in Sheffield, and announced he was going to live with her. Barbara left Blackshaw Lane, shortly after I resigned and left. But the following year she contacted me, as she was very upset, when her school had OFSTED, which had not been very kind to her with its findings. On both occasions, I felt I needed to be there to support her, although I was heavily into a relationship with a lady called Deborah at the time. Unfortunately, I didn't inform Debs, that Barbara and I had history, and when she confronted me, she decided to call a halt to things, eventually going to live in Sunshine Bay on the West coast of Canada with her boss, Derek Alltree. There they set up their own jewellery business. With Barbara things finally came to a head, after she further informed me that she only married John to spite me, and at one time she would have done anything for me. In return all I had done was taken her for granted, and used her when it was convenient. Not long afterwards, she exited my life and I have never seen her since. **I am not proud of what I did to her, and that moment is one that I will take with me to my grave.** Most men would consider themselves fortunate to have the love of one woman in their lives, I had had two, and had seriously hurt and upset both. I heard that Barbara eventually remarried, and was called Lynch. Over the years, whilst I have managed to make my peace with Dee, I have never managed to find Barbara and do the same, especially since she has remarried. Whilst writing this, I feel nothing but sadness and a deep loathing of myself for the way I behaved. I hope Barbara is a happy bunny, and has produced some wonderful children. I've often thought of trying to contact her, to look her in the eyes and to say sorry, but wondered what it would achieve 30 plus years after the fact. I am still wanting to find her and apologise. Lynne Doherty arrived at Blackshaw Lane, after asking for a transfer from Byron Street infants, Royton. After visiting to have a look around, and deciding on the move, subject to both Heads agreeing, she was offered the job. I'm not sure why she wanted to come to Blackshaw Lane, perhaps as an Infant Junior School, she saw more prospects, I don't know. Also, perhaps Clifford Taylor's reputation had not permeated through to Byron Street at that time. She arrived as Head of Infants and as I was Head of Juniors, and we both worked in the same building, it was obvious to both of us that a good working relationship was necessary. I could learn from Lynn and vice versa. I liked working with Lynn and helped her deal with difficult staff. Unfortunately, Lynne had not been afforded such luxuries of working with Tom Goring and, at times, found the personnel management side of the job difficult. Sometimes she just needed a shoulder to cry on, and the shoulder sometimes involved a drink after work. Yes, lightning struck twice. What led to the demise of our friendship was twofold. Lynn became pregnant, not by me I hasten to add, with Helen her second child, and secondly, I **resigned** from Blackshaw Lane.

Resigning from teaching was, and still is, a big deal. The issues with Taylor, my friendships with Barbara and Lynne just proved too much. When I eventually left Blackshaw Lane, after fighting for almost three years to get Taylor removed, it coincided with the final breakup of my marriage, and the last time I saw Lynne was, when she came to see me, at Alandale Drive, to bring me some leaving presents. I was not in work the last few days at Blackshaw Lane, the stress of trying to oust Taylor had eventually taken its toll. It was a tearful affair. Again, I hope Lynn is happy and that her children have made her proud. I often think of her. It may appear that I was having a whale of a time at Blackshaw Lane, having the attention of not one but two ladies, and whilst I cannot deny that I was enjoying the attention these females gave me, it became obvious that what I really was enjoying, in a strange kind of way, was the freedom Taylor's abdication of his responsibilities and lack of involvement in Blackshaw Lane, gave me. The more immersed I became in life at Blackshaw Lane developing the curriculum, mentoring, liaising, after school activities such as football, cricket, gymnastics, not to mention helping to establish parent teacher relationships etc, the more I thrived. I could say Taylor was not daft, knowing that in his absence I could steer the ship. But that is being too kind to him, because I don't think he had a pilot's licence and so, was unaware of what steering the ship involved. In fact, during his first 6 months in charge he was rushed into hospital, with seriously high blood pressure, just weeks after I arrived, leaving me to now become acting head. Was my arrival and Mavis's departure the trigger, or was he finding it just too stressful going to Asda, during school time, without being seen? Or perhaps he was bored, sitting in his office, not knowing what to do, other than pester Mrs Buckley the school secretary with tittle tattle and gossip. As for me, my fast-track promotion was really getting too silly, but I was not complaining.

Acting Headmaster.

Classroom assistant, Eileen Turner, Paul Firth, Mary Riley, Lyn Doherty. Peripatetic Teacher, Christine Ashworth, Mr B, Barbara Cooper, Mrs Buckley, School secretary.

But not everything was doom and gloom, as Venture week went from strength to strength and became extremely popular, with not only the children, but also parents. From Christmas onwards, the fourth-year curriculum was geared towards a multi-disciplinary approach, which involved a parents' before and after film evening, incorporating a photograph competition. A Fuji camera being donated by one of the parents as first prize. Other schools, also wanting to set up Venture Week in their school timetables, were ringing me up for help and advice. I was slowly implementing some of the curriculum and staff changes I felt necessary. Some staff were enjoying having the opportunity to have a say in what they would like in their classrooms, if money was available. Taylor's philosophy on school requisition was that **he** would decide what to order, and considered asking staff, apart from those he liked, as the equivalent to giving them money to buy themselves a present. The first year he had just ordered what had been previously ordered, with no consultation with the staff, and irrespective of what was actually required. Resulting in the school running out of some essential supplies just after Christmas. But hey, his son Matthew, who had recently joined the school, had a computer at home he could use. It was rumoured, courtesy of Blackshaw Lane, on loan. Taylor's significant role in daily management, which included teaching, curriculum development, requisitioning, planning and suggesting ongoing professional staff development as well as organising schedules and meetings, was to go shopping to Hestaire Hope, the educational suppliers, in Royton, and weekly trips to buy biscuits, from the Cash and Carry. Meanwhile, I was also working on curriculum schemes of work for both the infant and juniors, that again staff were encouraged to have an input, if they wished. This was a subject I chose to study doing my B.Ed Honours degree. It came as no surprise, that Taylor didn't feel he had the necessary experience to help, and so was happy for me to forge ahead, so he could leave the building at 4 o'clock and not have to stay after school. Also, Christine Ashworth adopted the attitude that, why should she help to do my job for me, when I was getting much more money than she was. A perfectly valid argument against the people who pontificate about being part of a team, and all being in it together. Let's all go on a jolly bonding day. Bollocks. Briggsy, you get paid the big bucks, and so you make the decisions, so we can then criticise you, if they don't work out. Enter Tommy Goring's words ringing in my ears, **'You're never going to please all of the people all of the time, Jim, so don't even try.'** Meanwhile, under my tutelage, we also, for the first time as far as I was aware, in the school's history, won the final of the Oldham Schools' Home Safety competition, held at Royton Assembly Hall.

In the meantime, Taylor, probably feeling isolated and bored just visiting Asda, looking in car mart and pestering the school secretary, decided to surround himself with yes people. Enter Hilary Sinker, my best man Neil's wife. Neil was one of the lads, together with Eric Harrison, Stuart Firth and Stuart Ford, who I've said, I met up with, when I was introduced to the Sports Association. Neil and Hilary, together with Stuart and Marilyn Firth, became Dee's and my best friends and whilst socially I was happy with Hilary, I soon decided she was not someone I would choose to have on my team for many reasons. The main one being she was very unprofessional, and loved to gossip out of school and not someone Blackshaw Lane needed at that time, or any time for that matter. Hilary also saw teaching as just a position that paid very well, especially when she became a supply teacher, and so therefore, because she basically was a lazy teacher, she knew with Taylor she could get away with minimum, whist trying to impress the staff with stories of Mr B and Mr T. That was more fuel to the fire for my detractors. On the other hand, Marilyn Firth was more my cup of tea in terms of attitude, work ethic and professionalism. The Firths lived not far from Blackshaw Lane, and I taught both James and Ian Firth whilst they lived there. Hilary and Marilyn returned to teaching, via the supply route, after maternity leave. Previously, Hilary had taught at Greenfield Lane, with Stuart Ford, and Marilyn, at St. Paul's, with Stephen Perfect. Eventually, both Hilary and Marilyn ended up at Blackshaw Lane on supply, Taylor seeing them as someone he could go and talk to, to fill his lonely days. Also, because he had very little personnel management skills, he was very quick to pigeon-hole people, and saw Hilary and Marilyn as allies. Whereas, I avoided working with family and friends, especially when you are paid to, 'kick arse'. It always ended in tears. At least, Marilyn appreciated my situation and respected my professional distance, and just kept her head down and tried not to get involved by taking sides. As for me, I immersed myself more and more into all things educational. Needless to say, these appointments, although initially only temporary, not only added to the tensions and problems within the school, but also put a strain on our friendships. If that was not enough, Taylor, decided to enrol his son Matthew into the infant department, which gave him another ideal excuse to leave Blackshaw Lane shortly after 03.15p.m., when the infants finished. The junior department finishing 30 minutes later. Taylor didn't see anything wrong with leaving, 'his school', to go home for tea, whilst half the children and staff, were still on the premises. I repeat, you can't make this stuff up to read any sillier.

Home Safety Quiz Winners: Kam Hung, Michelle, Heather McBride, Carl and John Holden. Apologies for not remembering all the names.

Putting all the problems aside I was inspired by what I was achieving, and I approached the authority, and asked, if they would pay for me to do The College of Preceptors, Diploma in Management of Schools, with the emphasis on legalities in the Primary School. I had recently attended a day's seminar at Manchester University, where Nick Adams, an educational legal bod, was speaking, and I was enthused and fascinated by what he had to say. This was the start of another of my interests, the legalities of not only education, but also health care. Unfortunately, the authority refused my application, but instead, as I had left teacher training college with, **ONLY a three-year teaching certificate,** they would consider an application from me to do a three-year Bachelor of Education Honours degree. **The move at the time was to make teaching an all-graduate profession, based on the mis-guided assumption that if you stood in front of several hundred pupils, some of whom didn't actually want to be there, and waved a piece of paper at them, that somewhere on it said degree, they would all start to behave responsibly and do as they were told.** As for the management and legal stuff, the authority said they already had a management course in place at Padgate College, Warrington, and were in negotiations with the Open University, to make available Management courses for all its heads and deputies. If I was to study for a B. Ed., they told me they would look favourably on sending me to Padgate, or putting me on an OU course. After discussing it with Dee, I applied and was accepted on a B.Ed. Honours degree course, starting at De La Salle College for one year and then two years at Charlotte Mason College, Manchester. Both under the umbrella of the University of Manchester. To say I was excited, was an understatement, and immediately tried to contact Verna to tell her my good news. Whilst finding both the degree and OU Management courses hard work, yes, the authority did keep their word, they provided me with a wealth of theoretical underpinning to support my pedagogical classroom skills. **Unfortunately, the down side to all this extra knowledge and experience, was that the more I mixed with other heads and deputies, and studied the research, the angrier I became at the**

Clifford Taylor situation. Things came to a head when I was asked to go on a week's course, under the guise of appraising a new management course, at Florence Boot Hall, Nottingham University, so that the advisory staff of Mrs Evans, John Ap-Thomas and Chris Pickup could spend a week in Blackshaw Lane, in my absence, to see Mr Taylor in action for themselves. I'm sorry, did I say action? Sorry, slip of the tongue. This course proved to be the best I'd ever been on, not least for dressing up as Dame Edna and camping it up with David Johnson, the then Head of Primary Education in Manchester.

For me having to relate the theory to my own personal situation, which of course meant Blackshaw Lane and Taylor, the more embarrassed and depressed I became. **I will never forget reading, that a school that was run under a passive, tinged with Bourbon Head, (Jennifer Nias, 1979), with ritual traditional authority, (Ronald King, using Weber, 1973), who displays characteristics of aloofness, prefers to disintegrate rather than delegate, (J Watts,1980), and exists in a closed climate, (Halpin, 1966), will eventually be in need of radical surgery, (Halpin, 1966). This was the opening paragraph when I was asked to put in writing my grievances against Clifford Taylor.** Not long after finishing all my educational, on-going professional development courses, I was so downhearted, that it was obvious that there was no way the educational establishment was going to admit it had made a monumental, cock-up, or that the system would allow a deputy to do a hatchet job on his boss, that I started to consider what I could do, if I resigned.

Dressing up as Dame Edna and camping it up with David Johnson, the then Head of Primary Education in Manchester.

In 1987, in a blaze of pure, unadulterated anger, sadness and depression, I handed in my resignation. As my whole world collapsed around my ears, with my errant ways also leading to the break-up of my marriage, I found that I was unable to motivate myself into performing even the simplest of personal tasks, such as cleaning my teeth, and escaped into a relaxed, slightly euphoric state of lassitude, that the mood altering, relaxing drug Mogadon offered, courtesy of my doctor. I blamed my conceited arrogance for my personal situation, but wanted to shout from the roof tops, that the situation regarding Taylor, at Blackshaw Lane, had not been satisfactorily resolved after I'd been assured it would be. Despite parent protests, and the outcry of some high-profile educational figures, not least Derek Smallwood, my PE advisor, Taylor still remained in situ. I was totally and utterly demoralised, when I was flippantly informed that there were other teachers out there like CJ Taylor. Years later, I met Mr Pickup, the senior Primary Advisor, on the island of Crete. He was sunbathing and admiring the view when Heather, my partner at the time, and I disturbed his reverie. To say the meeting was terse would be understating it as Heather, who had never met the man, wondered why I gave the impression, I wanted to cause serious physical damage to a man twice my size.

My B.Ed. Honours Degree.

It's strange but I have very few recollections of doing my degree, and then my graduation, other than to say it was hard graft having to study after a day's teaching at Blackshaw Lane with all its problems. It could be argued it provided a break from the day-to-day stress, but in actual fact the more I studied, the more it highlighted the problematic issues I encountered, associated with teaching, on a daily basis. This was even more an issue, when attending management courses. My first year I attended De La Salle College, Middleton, North Manchester, to do the access modules before transferring to Charlotte Mason College, South Manchester, both colleges being affiliated to Manchester University. I was resentful of having to go to De La Salle just to re-hash most of the stuff I'd done at Mather College, whilst acquiring my 3-year Teacher's Certificate, namely Philosophy, Psychology and Sociology, but now 12 years into my teaching career, and now wearing a different hat I could see the relevance, or otherwise, of how the theory could be applied to the practice. This situation led to some interesting discussions during seminars and lectures. For me Philosophy was a subject I titled, 'What do I mean by what do I mean?' Because, once it appeared that a consensus of opinion had been agreed upon in the discussion, it was summarily dismissed and questioned by what ifs, buts or howevers. I remember one evening during a philosophy seminar, Brother Bernard getting very heated, to say the least, because we kept dismissing his thoughts and pontifications just to try and keep ourselves awake. To put things into context, that whilst Oldham Education was funding our studies, because money was available to try and make teaching an all-graduate profession, teachers were doing the course in their own time, after a hard day on the chalk-face. Secondment only being granted rarely and to a few. This sometimes meant, that by 8 o'clock in the evening, no matter how interesting the subject matter or dynamic the lecturer, we were suffering from, 'brain fag'. In my career, I had come across many in the teaching profession, who churned out the same old stuff year after year. When I later became a lecturer, I tried to keep my lectures as up to date as possible, and deliver them as interestingly as possible. But soon realised, that even Cochran research could be as much as five years out of date. Now Roy Beardsworth, who was the course leader at Charlotte Mason, laid his cards on the table, by telling us we were the up-to-date, chalk- face troops, which he respected and hoped the course would give us food for thought, to question and challenge our views. Roy, unlike others I came across, practised what he preached, and was quite happy to engage in healthy debate, as to the relevance of the theory. By this stage in my career, I was of the opinion that **sound theory underpinned good practice,** and so was always looking to better my pedagogical skills, via theoretical models. It was also the time when I seriously got into human behaviour and teacher development, and so seriously questioned some of the stuff I'd just soaked up at Mather Teacher Training College, as an 18- to 21-year-old. Now at the age of 75, I'm still questioning, and fascinated with human behaviour. I also realised back then, that very little changed in education, the answers nearly always being the same, with just slight adjustments to give the impression of progressive thought, and it was just the questions that kept getting swopped around. By choosing History of Education, Curriculum Development and Primary Education, I had a good overview to realise that progress, for the academics, meant a new posh title, but the underlying problems were still the same. Class sizes, role definition, lack of funding, discipline, etc.

Eventually I graduated with a 2:2 degree which, to be honest, was not going to put me in the top percentiles of academia, but considering I did it virtually alone, without a computer, google, spell check, or search engines, and the numerous aids that today's students have at their disposal, I was thrilled to bits just to get any kind of degree. All my assignments were hand written, including my dissertation, with Alison Ford typing it up for me, in exchange for a blue, suede jacket because, as a friend, she didn't want payment. My literature search consisted of going to the library and reading books and taking notes, long hand. But that's what everyone did, so at the end of the day, it was just a question of getting on with it.

My graduation, at Manchester University, on November 7th, 1985, was attended by Dee and mum. I also had a family celebration at the White Hart Public House on Oldham Edge. Yes, I may have failed my 11 and 12 plus, but here I was a Deputy Head of a large Primary School in Oldham, and a graduate of Manchester University.

Thank you, Verna, thank you, Frank and last but not least, thank you, Dee for your loyalty, belief and support.

Dee, myself, and mum, at my Manchester University graduation, November 1985.

Alandale Drive, Jim's Gym Club and It's a Knockout.

Eighteen months after I arrived at Blackshaw Lane, 1981 to be precise, Eric Harrison and I were persuaded by Derek Smallwood, the PE Advisor for Oldham, to do a BAGA, (British Amateur Gymnastic Association), Club Coach, Level 4, award. As there were no facilities in Oldham at the time, although a new Sports Stadium, next to the Church in the centre of Oldham, was in the pipeline, at weekends we had to travel to the Thomson Leisure Centre in Burnley and then North Manchester Gymnastic Centre, in Gorton, to attend the nearest course. The head coach, at North Manchester Gym Club, was a guy called Colin Lee, who looked like Mike Harding, the Rochdale Cowboy. Colin ran the BAGA course. He was one of the early club coaches that developed, and raised the profile of men's gymnastics in this country. Later on in my career, I was fortunate enough to work with Colin Still, an England Gymnastics coach. His wife, Christine Still, was a commentator on TV, at major gymnastic competitions. The sport has progressed a long way since the late 80s, and in 2016, Team GB had World Gold medal champions. Derek Smallwood also wanted a vehicle to raise his profile, since securing his position, and saw gymnastics, in a new Oldham Sports Stadium, as the way forward. Prior to his appointment, he was a lecturer at Oldham College, but his all-round teaching experience in Primary was lacking. He was therefore trying to recruit teachers, especially from the Primary sector, but not exclusively, who could and would help him achieve his goal. He set up satellite gymnastic clubs, in various areas of Oldham, that would not only provide specialist gymnastic sessions, but also identify young talent that could be fed into Oldham Metro Gym Club, to enter competitions at local, county and national levels. He decided to enter competitions in the emerging Sports Acrobatics category, which would give Oldham Metro more chances of success, than in the conventional, established 4-piece floor, bars, rings and vault competitions. Under the guise of Educational Sports Acrobatics, the philosophy was one of participation and enjoyment, rather than must win at all costs. For some 'pushy' parents, this was a difficult concept to encompass. In simplicity, children were invited to join Oldham Metro firstly, because of their potential and ability, but secondly, because they wanted to, and not because their parents wanted to relive their own childhood failings, but this time, hopefully, with more favourable outcomes. Initially, Diane Trees was asked to establish Saddleworth Gym club, who, along with Alan Davey, were Heads of PE at Saddleworth School. But after a whiplash injury she was forced to, 'give up', the Saturday morning gym club. I was approached by Derek Smallwood, to see if I would be interested in taking over. After being told that I would be paid, something teachers were not used to for taking sports teams, after school and on Saturday mornings, I accepted. After receiving my first payment for my coaching I recalled the school cleaner at Mather Street in 1973, who thought all teachers were paid over-time, with Saturday mornings being double pay.

The feeder intake for the gym club was from the local, Saddleworth Primary Schools. However, I soon realised that some parents saw the gym club as a place to dump their children, whilst they went shopping. So, I started having a waiting list, so if children were brought into the sports hall, crying, kicking and screaming, and it was obvious they didn't want to be dumped at the Gym club, it allowed a cooling off period, before being invited to join. Whilst well intentioned and on the whole conscientious, parents in Saddleworth were not used to being refused, and so my arrival was met initially, in some quarters, with mild hostility. So, I prepared my battle plan on the grounds of health and safety, my enjoyment and voluntary participation philosophy, and the fact that children crying in the sessions would be unsettling to the other children. Having achieved my first goal, it was not long before I had a waiting list for my first beginners' group. My second group was made up of older children, who had attained a certain level of competency. BAGA had an awards structure, based on the difficulty of ten moves starting at level four, with the basics of handstands, rolls and balances, and descending to level one, which involved more complex movement and combined routines. To pass, the gymnast had to satisfy the examiner that they could do 6 out of the ten, and, if successful, were awarded a badge and certificate. I never put a child in for their award, until I was happy, they could do all 10. This was not to flout the system, but ensure the gymnasts didn't pass awards four and three, and then progress no further, because the more difficult moves had not been achieved. There being an obvious increase in difficulty from three to two, and certainly two to one. Whilst the awards acted as an incentive and motivation, I didn't see them as a tool to boost my credibility or ego. **Smiling faces and children trying their best to do a 'roly poly', gave me immense satisfaction. In hindsight, that's the reason I never fully 'fitted in' with certain sports, especially men's football, as I never saw sport as the be all and end all in life.** Obviously, certain parents saw them as trophies to be gained, in the shortest time possible. But as age has many facets and can relate to chronological, physical and developmental stages, pushing children too early, before their bodies and minds had reached a certain level of maturity, can be detrimental to their well-being. **"What is the point of having a mantelpiece full of cups and medals if your child is in a wheel chair at 21?"** (Peterson L and Renstrom P, 2001, Sports Injuries, The Prevention and Treatment). **In Chapter 5, when discussing football, I continue to discuss the subject of child abuse in sport, something I have written and spoken about on more than one occasion in my career. But as I am talking about my gym club, I wish to highlight the ITV programme, Gymnastics: A Culture of Abuse, shown in February, 2024. It talked about Stan Wild, ex Olympian turned coach and torch bearer in York for the 2020 Olympics, who 'CONNED A WHOLE CITY' before EVENTUALLY being banned from the sport. Stewart Wood, who was promoted to the higher echelons of coaching by the BAGA, but who was EVENTUALLY jailed for 11 years for sex offences against children. And finally, David Schadek, who was EVENTUALLY jailed for 4.5 years for sex offences. Eventually is highlighted because all three had been brought to the attention of the BAGA, by, amongst others, Darren Norman, a coach and judge up to 20 YEARS previously. The story centred around Nikki O'Donnel, an ex-gymnast, who was suing the BAGA for its part in the perpetrated crimes, and basically ruining her life. The other 'culprits' in the scandal being the CPS who, for reasons only known to themselves, always seemed to find a reason for not prosecuting. It wasn't until the Ann White Report in 2020, written over 2 years, and which considered over 400 submissions and, 'shook the sport to its core', were 64 coaches banned. For someone who has been involved in sport from an early age as a participant, PE coach, therapist, observer and writer, it makes me physically sick, angry and depressed hearing about such crimes, in not only football and gymnastics, but also many other sports.**

Back to my gym club. I also decided to take certain children who showed potential from my gymnastics' club at Blackshaw Lane to Saddleworth to get more practice, with the possibility of introducing them to the main Oldham Metro gymnastic squad, based at Oldham Sports Centre. Sian Davies and Jill Talbot being two such girls I took to my Saddleworth Gym Club, after going to visit both sets of parents, to get their permission. Mrs Davies, Wendy, was initially a little reticent to send her daughter off with me, from 8'o'clock Saturday morning, until 1 o'clock in the afternoon. I understood her concerns but as Sian, a 100% bundle of sheer, delightful energy, and not to say talent, was keen to give it a go, she agreed. This was the start of a long and fruitful relationship, both professionally and personally, with Sian and Wendy. Sian later joined Oldham Metro Gym Club, and her mum joined the coaching staff. Sian became part of the Sports Acro team that travelled the country entering competitions, with Mr B as her coach and chauffeur. Wendy didn't have transport. By this time, both Sian and I had left Blackshaw Lane, she going to Royton and Crompton Secondary, and I to set up my Osteopathy and Sports Therapy Clinic in Chadderton. She was also part of my support team at Saddleworth, helping with my first group of beginners, along with children from Saddleworth Secondary, Lucy Wright, Catherine Hearns, Maxinne and Helen Lowe. These girls grew up and became successful teachers, solicitors and physiotherapists. Not to mention, wives and parents in their own right. Sian also became a physiotherapist, wife and mother. Now, whenever I travel to Saddleworth to see my friends George and Margaret, whose three girls, Jenny, Jo and Ruth all attended my gym club, I'm always brought up to date with what is happening to the gymnasts I coached. The latest being, in 2016 when I attended Jo Bradbury's wedding and caught up with several of the girls, one of whom, Jayne Harthan, was living in Kathmandu, being involved in treks, cycling and religious experiences.

Because I was seeing Sian and her mum frequently, Wendy and I became friends to the extent we invited each other to one another's house for meals, and also attended certain social events. I was living on my own at the time, as Dee and I had separated. I was also invited firstly to Sian's brother, Gareth's wedding, and then to Sian's own wedding to Daren or Daz, as he was known. I taught Sian to drive, and after she had passed her test, would lend her my car some weekends. They acquired a King Charles spaniel, that Sian named Dillon, I think after the children's TV programme, Magic Roundabout. I recall looking after Dillon, for several weeks, whilst they went on holiday. Who says I was not a pet lover long before the dog mafia became a talking point? To put it quite simply, if I'd have had children, I would have been more than happy, for one of them to have been Sian, which was a testament to Wendy's parenting, her father leaving them when Sian was very young and was rarely, if ever, mentioned. Although, I did meet him at the weddings. My relationship with Wendy was always purely platonic. After marriage, Sian and Daz bought a house in Royton, and gave birth to two children. But sadly, once I had met Heather and we moved to Preston, the Davieses and I drifted apart. I invited them to Preston, on more than one occasion, but visits, for one excuse or another, never materialised. It still saddens me, because at the time Sian became very special to me and whilst I was a realist and knew you couldn't just borrow other people's children to suit your own purposes, Sian and I did much together. Wendy used to say, "Our Sian tells you things she wouldn't tell me." Anyhow back to my gym club, now nicknamed Jim's Club because one of the children, upon finding out my Christian name, thought it was named after me. I loved every minute of my time at Saddleworth. The parents respected what I was trying to do, and frequently thanked me for all my efforts, even if little Johnny or Sally didn't make it to the Olympics. Some parents even offering their services to help run the club, but diplomacy is sometimes needed at times like that when you suspect such parents may have ulterior motives for offering to help. I also had a child in the club who secured the lead role in Orphan Annie at the Palace Theatre, on Oxford Road, in Manchester and went to see her perform. Unfortunately, not long after she had set off on her journey to fame and fortune, she was involved in a road traffic accident in Saddleworth, which put paid to any aspirations she had of becoming a gymnast or stage performer. Life can be so cruel at times.

At one time I was attending my gym club on Saturday morning, and then driving over to Blackpool to teach at the NIM, Northern Institute of Massage in the afternoon. How lucky was I, doing things I loved doing? But as usual the politics and religion kicked in, and the Education Authority wanted to start charging children to attend the gym sessions, and moving them from Saturday to mid-week.

Needless to say, I was not happy and objected to these initiatives. Eventually, the gym was forced to close. My leaving day was again very emotional with very little gymnastics being performed, but with plenty of present opening, hugs and thank yous. I even had a personal message box in the local newspaper, that some parents had put in thanking me for all my efforts. Meanwhile, Derek Smallwood had entered a team from Oldham, made up of mainly secondary PE teachers, to compete in the highly successful television BBC game show, 'It's a Knockout', fronted by Stuart Hall and Eddie Waring. Originating in Europe, as Jeux Sans Frontieres, Games Without Frontiers, or something like that, it featured teams from different European Countries, dressed in outrageous costumes, competing to earn points, in equally bizarre, but hugely funny games. The show was a massive hit on TV in the late 70s early 80s. Sid Jolley and Eric Fitzsimmons, with whom I played football at Dews, were part of the Oldham squad that, as I recall, reached the quarter final stage. 'Fitz', later becoming boss at Oldham RLFC, when I was working as a sports therapist at Batley RLFC. As mentioned, Sid passed away at the age of 57. As for Derek Smallwood he became one of my strongest allies, when I resigned from Blackshaw Lane. Not long after I left, he announced, to Wendy Davies and myself, before a gym session at Oldham Stadium, that he was taking early retirement, as he no longer knew who he was, or what he was supposed to do, as the political powers that be, kept changing his job title. He moved to Porter Soller, on the island of Majorca, where he had an apartment, with his partner Diane Cook, another ex-PE teacher. Whilst resigning from Blackshaw Lane had been a traumatic time for me, both professionally and personally, Derek, and to a lesser extent, Diane, had tried to soften the blow by offering me part time work gym coaching, whilst I recovered and established my new career in osteopathy and sports therapy.

As I have said on more than one occasion, you need people who believe in you and appreciate the fact you are just doing your best to participate in this game, called life. Thank you, Derek and Diane. The last time I heard about Derek was, that he was suffering poor health and had sadly, passed away.

> **PERSONAL**
>
> **"GYM" BRIGGS**
>
> **THANK YOU**
> for giving a flying start to our little gymnasts at
>
> **SADDLEWORTH GYM CLUB**
>
> from their Parents

Alandale Drive, our second home, was a very significant period in my life and can be easily split into two distinct parts: married and working in Primary Education, pre-1987, and separated, working for myself in healthcare and education, post 1987. Tuesdays, Thursdays, Saturday and Sundays, Haydn, Tom, Brian, John and I would go out jogging and would occasionally do charity runs. They were fun, happy times and a nice break from the pressures of work. I also used to play squash, twice a week, at both Maple Squash Club on Broadway and The Squash, Country Club at Moorside. During the week, it was with Neil Sinker, my best man, Stuart Firth and Ford and Eric Harrison. At weekends, there were several opponents, Maurice Mills, our Jack's tennis mate, and Andrew Needham, son of Betty, who I worked with at Mather Street. There were also various others, who would ring up to see if I was available. It was also whilst living on Alandale Drive, that I resumed attending Sportsman's Dinners, something that I was first introduced to, when I started teaching. I suppose now they would have to be called Sportsperson's Dinners, but as yet I haven't heard of any sportswomen on the after dinner speaking circuit. Is that another, 'ism or 'ic remark? Do you know what? I don't care. Royton Cricket, Tennis and Bowling Club held an annual Sportsman's Dinner, that was always very well attended. Over the years, I've listened to Peter Parfitt, the cricketer, and footballers Duncan McKenzie, Jackie Charlton, Steve Kinder and George Best. Yes, George was slightly inebriated and was not very good, but the best speaker for me, by far, was not a sportsperson but an ex, air-traffic controller, called Gunnerson. Apart from being an interesting and eloquent narrator he didn't need to try and impress the audience by using foul language every other word.

As the reader has been made aware, I enjoyed being in the spotlight with an audience, loved, 'holding court', and entertaining, but found difficulty dealing with rejection. I always took it very personally. In hindsight, this flaw in my character was something I was not particularly proud of, and now, in retrospect, I am greatly saddened by the upset it caused. The factors leading up to the break-up of my marriage were decided in isolation, but were inexorably linked; meeting Neil and Hilary Sinker, my time spent at and eventually resigning from Blackshaw Lane.

At the time I was not aware of anyone that voluntarily resigned from teaching, many preferring instead to suffer in silence, have a possible nervous breakdown, and take the money and run. Not forgetting the 6% that you paid into the teacher's superannuation scheme. So, this was a very big deal especially, as I didn't want to betray Verna and Frank, and all those people who had nurtured my career in teaching. However, such was my personality, that once the seed was planted, I knew it would not be long, before I acted. But if I did take the step of throwing away my career in Primary Education, I needed to consider my options and becoming a 'physio', and working in sport was something that certainly appealed. Apart from my teaching certificate and B. Ed. Honours degree, I had various coaching qualifications and many years' experience of participating in, teaching and coaching in sport.

Gaining further qualifications at weekends, or in the evenings, appeared to be the answer. In much the same way I'd studied whilst teaching full time, but this time with no financial assistance from my employers. Dee was supportive of my plan of action, and said that financially we would be OK. My savings hopefully, seeing me through the first year until I became established in my new career. Although not for the first time in my life the greedy bankers, decided to relieve Dee and me of our savings, when Black Friday reared its ugly head in October, 1987, causing a catastrophic Stock Market collapse, resulting in us losing almost £10,000 of our investments. Finding myself with very little savings and no regular income, although to be fair to Dee, she was still contributing to the upkeep of Alandale, I decided to go self-employed, and applied to set up my business with an Enterprise Allowance. In reality, this amounted to the princely sum of £20 a week. Derek Smallwood was also keen for me to carry on coaching and found some extra hours and money for me, by juggling his PE budget around. Cheers, Derek. I attended several free business courses and seeing an advertisement, in a local newspaper, to study remedial massage, at Alan Mooney's Private Clinic, in Ashton, I decided to apply with the relevant fee before the bankers stole that too. After which I continued to re-train by enrolling at the NIM, the Northern Institute of Massage, in Blackpool. Whilst training at the Northern, I also enrolled for the two-year, FA's Treatment of Injuries Course, at Lilleshall, Shropshire.

I don't want to move onto the next chapter in my life without further reference to the parents, children, certain members of staff and support staff, and dinner ladies who made my final years in Primary teaching a time I will remember with great love and affection. Although, at times, it was stressful and challenging these people were always in my thoughts as to the reason I went into teaching. Thank you all.

The wonderful kitchen staff.

5.
A Change of Direction: 1988 onwards.

Ashton Private Clinic.

Ashton Private Clinic was run by an ex Northern Institute of Massage student Alan Mooney, who, like many before and certainly many after, felt there was money to be made from teaching massage, and all related complementary therapies. The course was run at weekends, and consisted of theory in the mornings, and practical in the afternoons. As I recall there were only 6 to 8 people enrolled, with the theory being delivered by a nurse, and the practical by Alan Mooney. Although Alan proved to be very similar to his nemesis at the NIM, Ken Woodward, in that he considered pounds before people. I personally had no axe to grind with the course, and found both aspects gave me a good grounding in massage. The first lady I ever massaged was Loraine Dinely. Her partner was Brian, and I subsequently became good friends with the pair of them. Not long after Dee and I split, I spent a New Year with them in a remote cottage, near Bala Lake, Wales, chopping wood and pumping water by hand. Brian, amongst other things, was a Buddhist, and I found him a very calming influence. He had this wonderful way, during conversation, of getting you to discuss your inner most secrets, whilst betraying none of his own. Unfortunately, Loraine and Brian were to split up.

The Northern Institute of Massage, (NIM), and the Northern School of Osteopathy, (NSO).

Training at the Northern Institute of Massage, NIM, in Blackpool, 1987-1990, and subsequently lecturing and tutoring was a significant time in my life, as it saw the severing of connections from full time teaching in Primary Education, with all that that involved, and the starting of a whole new lifestyle of friends, colleagues and acquaintances. During my association with the Northern, from its base in Blackpool to its moving, and in my opinion, subsequent loss of identity, to Bury, my life took on a whole new perspective. I set new goals, and recaptured some of my enthusiasm, dreams, hopes and aspirations. As it turned out, my teaching qualifications would prove to be invaluable, as virtually within two years of leaving full time education, I was earning almost as much as I was when I left full time education, and paying less tax!!! How good was that? Unfortunately, deep down inside I was very lonely, periodically fighting off the 'Black Dog' and true to form, sought solace in more relationships. Always in the hope that I would find someone who would accept me for what I was, and not whom they wanted me to be. That is not a slight on the women who shared my PJs, and I accept I am not the easiest person in the world to please or put up with, but just the fact that most people have a hidden agenda when it comes to relationships. Sometimes, that was overtly displayed but many's the time it was covertly hidden.

When I first started, the staff at the Northern consisted of Ken Woodward, the boss, an ex-newspaper man from Bradford and his wife, Audrey, a beautician. Unfortunately, Ken being a Yorkshire man was blunt and related life to, "How much?" Not that all Yorkshire people were like that, but putting pennies before people, was, personally speaking, not a good trait in an industry where physical contact, communication, compassion and empathy were vital. Starting off with good intentions and surrounded by a few friends, he helped build the reputation of the Northern, but later failed to adapt, and innovate to a changing educational and sociological scene. This was purely and simply down to the fact that although he appeared to appreciate adaptation and change were sometimes a necessary evil, he seemed incapable of actually implementing it. Losing control and an old dog learning new tricks, spring to mind. Towards the end of my training and after I qualified, gaining a diploma and higher diploma in remedial massage and manipulation, Ed Caldwell and I were asked to join the teaching staff. Both with not only the pedagogical skills, but the knowledge, skills and expertise to develop the courses. But having secured the services of people who could initiate such change, and bring the Northern into the twenty first century, Ken saw such people as wanting to steal his baby. This led to, 'trouble in't camp', on more than one occasion, as such people realised that although Ken could talk the talk, he was all bluster and blow and couldn't let go. Ken had no social life to speak of, and struggled to accept that others had a life away from their work and careers. In Ken's case the Northern and the money it generated, was Ken's reason for getting out of bed every day. Many years later, when he eventually did capitulate and hand over the reins to Ed Caldwell, the opportunity for me and several others had passed. Not just because I had moved onto pastures new, but because the personnel was not available, and the climate had changed. Ed moving the Northern to unsuitable premises in Bury and turning it into a family business, and although I renewed my connection with Ed, by delivering a Sports Therapy Diploma course and a link with the Society of Sports Therapists, things didn't work out and, for the second time, I severed my connections with the Northern.

Whilst under Ken's control, the rest of the teaching staff, only a few of whom had teaching qualifications that I was aware of, were Beryl Harper from Rawtenstall, Mel Tozer from the South West, Stan Duscombe, Coventry, Keith Brimelow, Oban, Russel Dick, Blackpool and Harry Hawes, the North East. Each bringing their own brand of knowledge, skill, expertise and experience to the course, as well as their strengths and weaknesses, or should I say, areas for development. Not forgetting the backroom staff such as dear old Mona, the tea lady, who was not to be crossed when it came to comfort breaks, and Shiela Hardy who worked in the office, and who supplied the staff with sandwiches and tea at appropriate times. Although, like Ken, some were just one trick ponies, albeit good at the tricks, but not for innovation and change. Beryl Harper, who did have teaching qualification possessed the qualities that many teachers I had met and worked with, didn't possess. What's the point of having a degree if you have very little common sense, compassion, empathy and a poor work ethic? If I owed my teaching career to Verna Dale Howarth I owed, in part, my therapy career to Beryl Bessie Harper. Not only did she teach me massage, but became a teaching colleague when I joined the staff, a friend and my therapist when I became old, and past my sell by date. I still visit her practice as and when, and Beryl is the only person in my life that without fail, gives me a proper, heart to heart hug.

There were also many visiting lecturers and speakers drafted in for certain courses, and for the LCSP Conference, which was held once a year at the Savoy Hotel, North Shore, Blackpool. Sometimes these guest speakers and practitioners would travel from as far afield as Canada. The London and Counties Society of Physiologists register was the umbrella organisation that students joined, to provide not only insurance cover but also help and support to its members. When I was associated with the LCSP, its numbers ran into several thousand. In 2019, the LCSP achieved 100 years of continuous service, but because of various reasons its days were numbered. The structure of the course was that once you had sent off your application, and money with a direct debit for monthly instalments to be debited as you progressed, you received your theory lessons for home study, and then you would arrange to attend for practicals at the Northern, at the appropriate level you were at. Students such as Maggie Brookes, Tom Macmullen, Clive and Cilla Warden, Dave Mason and later on, Penny Walker and Jeanette Stokes, to name but a few, became friends. When I started teaching at the Northern, John Waller also entered my life. I also became friends with some of the proprietors and guest house owners such as Val and Bob, who were from the North East and Geoff and Maureen, who originated from Yorkshire, in so much as after a while, for me their lodgings became a second home and helped stave off my feelings of loneliness and isolation. You may find that strange that being surrounded by many people one could feel lonely and isolated, but loneliness wraps around you like a blanket but doesn't give you any warmth and comfort whatsoever. During my training to become a masseur with Alan Mooney, and then at The Northern I was told that after a while they, the patient, just became another body. In much the same way, as the medical profession have to personally try to detach themselves from death and their patients' problems. One misdemeanour meant a career in tatters, and so I did not have difficulty in treating patients as, 'just another body', and whilst my mates would salivate when seeing attractive ladies enter my practice, and later try to get me to divulge information with a glint in their eyes, I always remained focussed, much to the annoyance of my mates. One of my best mates at the time, Tim, thought I had the best job in the world.

As a teacher I was trained to always be professional, and so adopting the same mind set as a physical therapist and not give the slightest suggestion that masseurs and masseuses were anything but professionally trained, physical therapists offering treatment, was not a problem. Distancing ourselves from the personal column of the local newspaper advertisements where, 'massage with extras' was offered. Incidentally the Society of Chartered Physiotherapist started out as an organisation of trained masseurs and masseuses, but after they gained a Charter the physicality of hands-on slowly became replaced with exercise prescription, and the use of electrotherapy. I always embraced the philosophy of physical therapy, in that it treated an individual person with a problem, not just the problem because everyone was different and you didn't find real people in books. If we did, then we were instant millionaires. That's what I loved about therapy, you had an individual with a problem and you had to decide, after the consultation and examination, whether your therapy would help. If not, then you could refer them to someone who may be able to. To re-visit **Foucault, 1973, 'the diagnosis depended on the gaze'.** Sometimes, the therapy was to show compassion, empathise or to care. How could you quantify these in a world of financial constraints, targets, time-management and bonuses?

I joined the teaching staff at NIM after I had finished my basic training, and was on their advanced programme. I was approached by Eddie Caldwell, who was also on the advanced programme and who had only recently joined the teaching staff, to consider asking Ken Woodward, 'Woody', if he wanted any more tutors. Ed, an ex-PE teacher like myself, and very much involved in sport, a pro wrestler being part of his CV, was teaching the sports element of the advanced programme. I had been to Lilleshall and completed the FA Diploma in the Treatment of Injuries, and Ed thought we would make a good team to develop the sports side of the programme. Ken Woodward was delighted to have two fully qualified teachers as members of his team, and I subsequently joined the staff. To an educationalist this may have appeared to have been a step in the right direction, to appease the claims that the NIM lacked tutors with actual teaching qualifications and experience, and whilst existing tutors, Beryl Harper in particular, endorsed this move and welcomed both Ed and me, others doubted Ken would embrace change and criticism, no matter how constructive. Also, one of the subjects I studied to gain my B. Ed. Honours degree was Curriculum Development. Ken's background was in the newspaper business before buying the Northern, and I don't actually think Ken knew what Curriculum Development was. He was a business man not an educationalist. I was asked by Ken to have a look at the possibility of updating the basic course, but when finished I was reticent to give Ken my finished product. This subsequently proved to be a wise move as Ken had no intentions of introducing my work. Later, after I had left the Northern, and Graham Smith asked me to join his teaching team, which delivered courses on not only his Sports Rehab and Education courses, but also on behalf of the Society of Sports Therapists, all my hard work at the Northern was rewarded. I modified my efforts designed for the Northern, and the course work became the very first module to be offered on the Sports Therapy degree course, at the University of North London some years later. In 1994 or 1995 I decided to do Harry Hawes's Osteopathy course at Usher Hall, County Durham. Harry, following others such as Alan Mooney and Mel Tozer, who had fallen out with Ken Woodward, for one reason or another, and left the Northern. These ex NIM tutors had decided to set up courses themselves, sometimes, in direct competition to the NIM. Mel being based near Bristol, teaching massage with another ex NIM lady, whose name escapes me, with Harry teaching Osteopathy at Usher Hall, near Durham. In my opinion, both were excellent practitioners but, as far as I was aware, had no qualifications or experience of teaching, other than what they did at the Northern. When I went to join Mel, Harry and Russel Dick at Usher Hall, I was re-united with several students I had previously taught at NIM. Russel was also an ex NIM student/tutor. To be a little arrogant, Harry felt having me on board, would give some credence to the course and that I may want, at some stage, to teach on it. Thank you, Harry.

I met Penny Walker and Jeanette Stokes, 'Netty', whilst training at the Northern Institute of Massage between 1987 and 1990. I cannot recall the exact moment, but Penny came first and Netty, one of Penny's friends at the time, came second. Both came from Yorkshire, Penny from Mirfield, and Netty from near Leeds. Jeanette having gone to Leeds University many years earlier, as a student. Again, I cannot recall how Penny and I went from sitting in class together to visiting each other's house but that's what happened. Penny's family was steeped in rugby league as her father, 'Tug Walker', as he was affectionately known in rugby league circles, held the distinction at that time of being the top try scorer for a hooker at Batley Rugby club. Penny had worked with Maurice Bamford, the ex-Great Britain coach, at Dewsbury and Wakefield, and was at the time we became friends working as, 'the physio', at Bramley RFC.

Penny and I celebrating my 47th birthday.

Apart from watching sport Penny and I enjoyed each other's company and socialised as and when, with either her coming over to Royton/Chadderton or me going to Mirfield. Sometimes we would meet up with Netty, but a lot of the time it was just Penny and myself. Our friendship never developed from being purely platonic, although, on more than one occasion it did cross my mind to chance my luck, but never did. I suppose I didn't want to have to deal with the possibility of rejection, that would mar our friendship. Apart from training at the NIM and socialising, I ended up working at Bramley RLFC with Penny. At the time, I was doing my FA Diploma Treatment and Management of Injuries course at Lilleshall, and wanted to get more experience at club level, running on pitches and treating players in the club environment. I was looking after the gymnasts, cricketers and dancers in the Oldham area, but attaching myself to a club would increase my practical experience. Penny had a word with the head coach, Maurice Bamford, and he agreed I could attend on match days, but the club couldn't pay me. That was fine by me as it was experience, I was after not remuneration. Also, because games were mostly on a Sunday, or mid-week in the evening, it didn't clash with any of my other commitments. In those days, and it's not much different today, apart from a few clubs with millionaire backers, rugby league at grassroots level was constantly striving to financially make ends meet. One time after a home game, Maurice came to pay Penny with a cash bag that was obviously the takings from one of the turnstiles, as it was full of coins. Before retiring to the players' lounge, we sat in the changing rooms counting it to see if there was enough to pay Penny her 'wages'. **In my youth, I could have pursued a career in football, but as I became older my love of men's football diminished, and my love of rugby and many other sports, especially women's, increased, and this was mainly due to the honesty of the players. The way they respected the referee and opposition players, didn't feign injury, didn't blame everyone for their own shortcomings are all synonymous with rugby league, and alien to football to the extent that I never wanted to work full time in football, but loved working in rugby. I was approached to work at a high-profile football club, but declined.** One of my fondest memories of my time at Bramley was, when we played Oldham RLFC at Watersheddings, in a mid-week cup game under floodlights. A ground I had spent many an hour cheering on the, 'Roughyheads', as they were known. At the time Eric Fitzsimmons, an old football friend of our Jack and mine, was the boss at Oldham, having also swopped his allegiance from football to rugby. Eric was also an ex-PE teacher, and represented Oldham on the very popular TV programme, 'It's a Knockout'. Usually Penny and I would share, 'running on the pitch duties', as in rugby the action doesn't stop just because a player has 'gone down', and so you were constantly on the alert. But on this occasion, Penny asked if I wanted to do all the on the pitch stuff as it was my home town, and she would deal with any dressing room problems. Sitting pitchside in the dug-out you are totally focussed on the game in terms of incidents and injury, and shut out much of the banter from the terraces, and sometimes you are even unaware of the score. But on this particular evening, I couldn't help but smile at the comments coming my way, the first time I ran on to attend one of the Bramley players. Obviously, word had gone out to the terraces, especially where I used to stand with my mates, that Briggsy was in town looking after the opposition. Being only 5 Feet 5 inches, I must have looked 'ickle' running onto the pitch to attend to 6 feet plus, rugby lads, and the terraces were quick to point it out. It was also apparent from their comments, that they preferred looking at the backside of 'the blonde lass' sitting next to me, running onto the pitch rather than mine, I wonder why? Not long after Penny and I had attended a Sports Therapy Conference in Warwickshire, she told me she was pregnant by an Aussie rugby league player, and informed me she was not intending to get married, but intended having the baby. When it was born, she called it Harvey Jack, and asked if I would be a godparent, along with her sister Caroline. I agreed and Harvey Jack was christened in a lovely little church on the outskirts of Dewsbury, with the reception at a working men's club in the town. I recall that it was not the friendliest occasion I had ever attended, and the fact that I was a Lancastrian in Yorkshire, to boot, didn't help, but I survived the ordeal. I continued to visit Penny and Harvey whenever I could, and opened up a savings account for Harvey, but slowly, probably because Penny was now in a relationship, we drifted apart and the last I heard of Penny was that she had gone to live in Australia. As for Netty, we also saw less of one another as our lives went in different directions but I caught up with her, when years later, Heather and I moved to Preston, and I became a Countryside Ranger. One Sunday on visiting a Ranger friend, John Dimsdale's house, in Chorley, and chatting with his wife, she mentioned that a masseuse, named Jeanette, lived in the same close, and her partner was a gentleman with two girls. After knocking on the door, I was thrilled to see it was Netty. Sadly, I felt that the bond we'd once shared, was no longer apparent, and when I mentioned Penny, it was obvious that something had happened between her and

Penny, that had caused a bitter rift. The nearest I got to finding out was that it involved an Australian male. The last I heard of Netty was, that she was still in Chorley, but after pushing a note through her front door, and not receiving a reply, I decided to accept that yet another friendship had sadly run its course. In 1994 or 1995, I decided to do Harry Hawes's Osteopathy course, which was held at Usher Hall, County Durham. Towards the end of the course, a young lady named Irene Baker and I got together, by arranging to visit each other alternatively to prepare for our final exams. Practising physical therapy, involving manipulations and mobilisations was extremely difficult on your own. Irene was an ex-NIM student. I would drive over to Driffield, East Yorkshire, and she would either drive or catch the train to visit me in Royton. As this involved a journey of several hours, it was agreed that 'sleep overs' were permitted. Obviously, Irene had to, 'sort out', Darren, her disabled son, before anything could be finalised. To cut to the chase, on our first study weekend, which involved Irene coming to Royton, the physical therapy we practised was more than remedial massage, manipulations and mobilisations. Although, some would argue that our hand and body positions were just variations on a theme. We kept the relationship fairly quiet, because that was what it was, mainly because of the distance between us. Also, Irene had Darren to consider. We helped each other pass our final exams, interspersed with trips to Bridlington, local walks with Darren, drives out and social dos to conferences and birthday parties. Things continued to just roll along, but I personally found it difficult when we attended study days or conferences to keep my distance from Irene. We hadn't actually agreed to keep our fling a secret, and as far as I was aware we both liked each other. But eventually as Irene only considered our relationship as a bit of fun, it petered out. Many years later, when I was asked to give a talk at an LCSP Conference, in Scarborough, Irene was in the audience. Travelling up from London on the Saturday, where I'd attended a conference, I wondered if she would attend and if so, what would the re-union be like. All my fears were allayed, as after my talk we smiled, hugged and then chatted briefly. After thanking her for attending, she informed me that once she had seen the list of speakers for the conference, she had to come to see, how her old study partner was getting on. She emphasised the word old. She still had that cheeky twinkle in her eyes, and I would have loved to have spent more time with her, but it was not to be. Although only, 'a bit of fun', I often think of her and Darren, hoping they are both happy bunnies. As for me, **I continued my search for emotional stability, a hug and a cuddle. All you can do in life is go forward, you can't undo, you can't change the past, all you can do is deal with the here and now.** As I've mentioned, I was prone to the odd panic attack which I started having after Dee and I split. They were frightening, because I was suddenly seized with the feeling of not wanting to go on, because I couldn't rationalize the futility of doing so. I was also starting to consider how much time I had spent alone since my childhood, when I used to sit on my own at the top of the slide on the park on Parkway waiting for Uncle Bill to come home from work.

PS. The NIM ceased trading in 2018/19 with the retirement of Ed and Marie Caldwell.

Sheila Carter, Alan Ayckbourn, Sir Andrew Lloyd Webber, John Denver and Marianne Jepson's School of Dance and Drama.

I first started working at Marianne Jepson's School of Dance and Drama in 1992, after an ex- North Chadderton school pupil, Sheila Carter, had recommended me to Marianne. Incidentally, Jennifer Dalloway, my great niece, attended Jepson's, on a Saturday morning. Sheila was married to Mark Stratton, an actor from Thirsk, who had worked in TV on Heartbeat, The Bill and Emmerdale, as well as treading the boards and plying his trade as a jobbing actor in the theatre. Sheila, like many in the entertainment business, had kept her maiden name for professional reasons. Marianne was married to Jack Doughty, a boxing promoter, and she also was known by her maiden name, and like Sheila was addressed as Miss. Sheila had trained at Marianne's college, and since passing her dance exams, had kept ties with Marianne. Marianne was quite an influential person in the dance circles, and was, together with Sheila, an examiner for the Imperial Society of Teachers of Dancing. This meant travelling extensively around the UK, as well as occasional trips abroad. There were several different dance organisations, that dancers could become affiliated to. Sheila ran her dance classes from rooms in Chadderton Library, and she contacted me one day to not only catch up on gossip, as I had not seen her from North Chadderton School days, but also to ask me if I could give her private tuition in Anatomy, Physiology and Injury Prevention, as part of her On Going Professional Development. For me, the opportunity to work in the dance arena with teachers and dancers would also develop my knowledge, skills and expertise by understanding not only the mechanics of dance but also the aetiology of dance injuries. As a Sports Therapist, I advised, treated and helped rehabilitate any person with an exercise related injury, irrespective of which pastime or profession they belonged to, sport they played, or at what level the participant performed at. The more sports I was familiar with, the more I could empathise and treat with confidence. As with many exercise related activities that people turn to professionally, initially there are choices as to whether or not they wish to be solely a performer or go down other routes, i.e., the teaching route. Usually, the shelf life of professional sport is limited in the performance stakes, because of the stresses and strains that the body is subjected to, and then alternative avenues **have** to be explored. In acting, decisions are made because of type casting, roles offered etc. Sheila was doing very well for herself not only teaching and examining, but also choreographing certain shows around the country. Later when she moved to Glaisdale, near Whitby, North Yorkshire, she started working for the famous playwright, Alan Ayckbourn, at the Keith Joseph Theatre in Scarborough. Alan, subsequently introduced her to Sir Andrew Lloyd Webber, and Sheila choreographed one of his shows, travelling to Boston for the opening night. During the time I tutored her, we occasionally got together socially, and Sheila made me more aware of the insecure, 'luvvy world' of the theatre. As mentioned before, many in the entertainment business hide behind a persona, or role, and can be very insecure if not surrounded by like-minded souls, or they have to play themselves. Also, they are all looking for not only fame and fortune, but love and acceptance. I could relate to that. That's why long-term relationships could be difficult to sustain, as people in the entertainment business have to travel where the work is, and can sometimes be away from home, as well as out of work, for long periods of time, which can put a tremendous strain on any relationship. As well as the insecurity, it could also be a lonely life. Also, many 'batted for the other team', or 'got on the other bus', or even tried both buses. I personally found these social classes to be very mischievous, funny but ruthlessly hard edged, if you decided to try and ridicule them, as I can attest to on more than one occasion. Their ripostes could be, let's say a little crude, if not downright defamatory. The entertainment world was also no different to lots of other professions, in that there was an element of who you knew, or in some cases, whom you'd slept with. Nepotism was also not uncommon.

During my career it always fascinated and intrigued me how certain jobs, careers and professions attracted certain social types and personalities. As a generalisation, I found cooks and music teachers could be highly volatile. With Gordon Ramsey later earning a fortune for being a foul-mouthed bully, in Hell's Kitchen. **Today in the crazy world of homophobia, bigotry and political correctness, honesty and stating the facts is frowned upon, if it is perceived as possibly upsetting a particular group in society. Playing the, 'race card', or blaming the immigrants is always a good excuse to ignore the facts.** I was once accused of being racist, because I failed several Greek students in an exam. There were no complaints from the other students, and the fact that the Greeks had not prepared well enough for such an exam, seemed to be completely ignored by the purse holders. Personally, it never bothered me to be in the company of lesbians, homosexuals and bisexuals, during my career because that was the case on more than one occasion, either because of work or a particular social occasion. Whilst at Mather College, I had long blonde hair, and wore a gold ring on my little finger, long before I knew the significance of this, and was 'hit upon' on several occasions in the Rembrandt pub, near Canal Street, next to the Bridgewater Canal, Manchester. At the time, the Rembrandt was not only the College's local, apart from the Students Union, but also one of the gay bars in Manchester. Canal Street being a local favourite pick up place for homosexuals, rent-boys, lesbians and prostitutes. The fact that our college was right next door, was pure coincidence. This usually freaked out my mate Ed, as he was, mainly because of his parents, sadly lacking in social awareness, and so attending Teacher Training College was a whole new learning curve for him. I used to love having entertainment friends around for a meal, or attending functions where they were in the majority, as they related many a story of goings on back stage, and the highs and lows of treading the boards, or bouncing the bed springs. Stories of actors, 'falling in love', with fellow actors and showing undying love for them, by waving their private parts at their victims, for want of a better term, from the wings, whilst those on stage were trying to deliver their lines, was hilarious. This being done discreetly of course, out of sight of the director. Although, some directors themselves had reputations for not only having favourites, but also could insist that providing personal favours was part of the contract, for landing a particular role. Of recent times, an American very high-profile film director, named Harvey, has been outed and put on trial for such behaviour. Max Clifford, the 'PR guru', was another high-profile personality, who believed he could do what he wanted, because he had the power and the money. I could also relate to why actors put up with long periods of inactivity, as the roles dried up because of the adrenaline buzz from the applause of an audience. I related it to waiting for your next fix. Not that I had first-hand experience of taking drugs, although there were many opportunities. For me fresh air, exercise and adrenaline were enough. However, I did understand and appreciate that standing in front of an audience, whether acting or teaching, was all about playing a role, with an expected response from them, be they young or old. The fact that Mark and Sheila had stayed together so long, as far as I know they still are, was a true testimony of their relationship. Apart from what you hear in the press about, 'celebs', I am personally aware of several couples, who I've shared an evening with, having succumbed to the pressures of the entertainment world. Don't get me wrong, the entertainment industry, in my limited experience, wasn't one big sex romp, but I certainly understood the temptations and pressures of being involved in it. Also, at that time in my life I was living on my own, and was fair game for any actor/actress or dancer that came my way. There was more than one occasion that my resolve, or should I say my professionalism, was put to the test. Sheila also introduced me to Kenneth Alan Taylor, infamous for his 'Dame' roles in pantomime, and his wife Judith Barker, famous for many a TV role, the latest being, Last Tango in Halifax with Derek Jacobi. Kenneth and Judith who still live in Oldham, were also instrumental in establishing Oldham Theatre Workshop, to develop the young talent in and around the Oldham area. My apologies for any other actor who I have slighted, by not including them at this time. My mother always claimed she knew Judith from school days. Kenneth at the time was Artistic Director of Oldham Coliseum, a place I had patronised with not only family, especially mum, but also with several girlfriends, since being old enough to appreciate the theatre. Formerly known as Oldham Repertory, Rep, as it was known in those days, spawned many a famous actor and actress, i.e. Roy Barraclough, who worked with Les Dawson; Sarah Lancashire and Siobhan Finneran to name but a few. The popularity of rep. in those days meant that, actors attached to a company got the opportunity, and gained invaluable experience of playing many different roles, and so didn't become type cast as they can do today. So not only were Sheila and Mark fighting my corner, visiting my clinic for treatment and recommending me to others, but now I also had Kenneth and Judith doing the same. The reader must also realise that then, as is now perhaps still the case in certain quarters, massage meant different things to different people. As alluded to previously, I was trained to always be professional and not give the slightest suggestion that masseurs and masseuses were anything but professionally trained, physical therapists, offering treatment and advice, as did the Chartered Physiotherapists, and we distanced ourselves from the personal columns of the local newspaper advertisements, offering other services. I can recall quite vividly, or more than one occasion, not only because of the hilarity of the situation, but also because they were stark reminders of the importance of communication, and dealing with people from all walks of life, having my professionalism put to the test. Communication and control being a subject, I later lectured on and wrote about when working in colleges and universities. Sheila, if working locally, would sometimes refer an actor to me for treatment, and inform me to take no nonsense from him/her. To protect identity and libel laws, I do not feel it appropriate to relate such stories in detail, no matter how amusing, in this book. However, having dangled the carrot, I am more than happy to give the reader a flavour of some of the expressions, comments, rants, tirades and situations, that I was subjected to. On one occasion, after making eye contact, I entered his personal space, in a non-threatening way, by proffering my hand and said in a warm, welcoming way, "Hello……., pleased to meet you, I'm James Briggs, do please take a seat." Without letting go of my hand, and looking me straight in the eyes, and showing no signs of discomfort from his injury he replied, "Fuckin' hell, that bitch Carter didn't tell me you were this fuckin' gorgeous." The secret of success in many jobs is to remain calm under pressure, although, to be honest all I really wanted to do on this particular occasion was, to burst out laughing. During the consultation, the patient continued to berate Miss Carter in choice language for his present predicament, saying that if she hadn't asked him to do a ball, step, shuffle tap, followed by an arabesque, his fuckin' neck wouldn't have gone into spasm. After all it was only panto' at Oldham Rep. and not fuckin' RADA, with Sir John Gielgud. Please appreciate, I have used author's licence as to the exact dance moves, he was asked to do and his choice of language. When I asked him not to use such choice language, and to stop slandering Miss Carter, he profusely apologised, became very contrite, and apart from asking me not to tell her, looked me straight in the eyes, and asked if there was anything he could do, to make it up to me. Talk about an Oscar winning RADA performance. Moments such as these were fascinating challenges, me the teacher playing a role and he/she, the actor, reciprocating, but with no script. In the words of Craig Revell-Halwood, of Strictly Come Dancing fame, 'FAB-U-LOUS, DARLING'. In clinic gaining informed consent is vital by explaining to the patient, what it is you would like to do, so after the consultation, I would inform them that I would like to examine them, and if they would mind removing certain items of clothing. Normally, for this I would provide the patient with a large bath towel with which to cover themselves, after disrobing, and direct them to the sectioned off changing area. On this particular occasion, I'd no sooner got my informed consent, and requested that they just remove only certain items of clothing, than the patient had virtually stripped down to his underwear, and stood there with a glint in their eye and said, "Where do you want me?" Now I do not want to give the impression that everyone in the entertainment world is promiscuous, because that was definitely not the case, in fact my elderly patients, who had done it all, seen it all and wore the tee-shirt, could be innocently just as bad. Taking off their clothes, without going into the changing area, and informing me that they had nothing to hide. **I used to say to students, "You can't buy this stuff, fast track it, go to University and get a degree in it – it's gold dust, and it's called life experience."**

Now for anyone that has not had a massage, administered by someone professionally trained, they will be unaware that, in my humble opinion, it is the best thing since sliced bread. A northern expression meaning very, very good. I've never understood the relationship between all things very good with sliced bread, but there you are. For the therapist relaxing a patient, who is in pain, during massage is one of the aims. With total relaxation of sleep being the ultimate compliment. But verbal announcements from the patient of being in love with you, whilst you were working, I was unaware of. Still, you never stop learning. Later when I spoke to Sheila, sorry Miss Carter, some hours later, she asked me tongue in cheek, although I couldn't actually see if this was so, how I'd coped? Thanking me for all my efforts, she then proceeded to inform me that since the actor had returned to the theatre, he was telling every man and his dog to go and see me, aches or not, as I was the best physio' they had ever been to see. Word of mouth when you are self-employed, is the best advertising you can have. Needless to say, his return visit was a little more subdued, which for him was still OTT, sorry, over the top. You see once you mix with the stars, you can become affected, or is it effected, and you start to use the language? In those days, jobbing actors got set rates of payment set by the professional body, irrespective of a show's popularity at the box office, which was not as much as many people thought. Also, on tour they had out of pocket expenses, staying at various lodgings which 'took in' people from the entertainment world, knowing that their job was not 9 to 5. This particular actor didn't return to clinic, because the theatre wouldn't pay as he had fully recovered, but in all the weeks he was at the Coliseum, doing Pantomime, he continued to spread the gospel according to James Briggs. The last time I saw him was at Churchill's Restaurant in Oldham at the last night after show party, which is traditional in the theatre. According to Sheila, he had reserved a seat next to him, and told the other members of that cast that he would scratch their fuckin eyes out, if any one tried to hit on me during the evening. Apart from the odd stray hand on my knee, during dessert, I had a great night.

Some years later I received a phone call from the Apollo Theatre in Manchester from John Denver's PA asking if I could, 'attend to John', whilst he was in Manchester. He was scheduled to do several concerts and I had been recommended by a fellow practitioner who had 'looked after him' when he appeared in Nottingham, a few days previously. They would pay my fee and cover all my expenses. At that time John Denver was big box office in the world of country music with top 20 hits. However, the fact that he was not on my list of favourite artistes was ignored but unfortunately, I couldn't oblige at such short notice, as I had my own clinic and a gymnastics club to attend. Such is life but for a while I did consider having a tee-shirt printed saying, **I NEARLY MASSAGED JOHN DENVER**. When

Sheila moved from Chadderton to Glaisdale, she sold her Dance Studio to one of her students, Julie Milnes, and kept strong ties with Chadderton, mainly because her mum lived near to Boundary Park, Oldham Athletics' football ground. Sheila had a son from her first marriage, Paul, who went into journalism. For a time, he worked at the Advertiser in Oldham and interviewed me for an article he was writing on my forthcoming trip with NW Counties Under 15's Rugby Tour to Australia, New Zealand and Fiji in 1993. I was travelling as their Sports Therapist. The last I heard from Sheila was that her husband Mark had started up the Esk Valley Summer Theatre, and was writing plays as well as doing his day job travelling the country treading the boards. After receiving some literature, I always intended to travel to Whitby to see one of his productions, but unfortunately the dates always clashed with my teaching schedule and therapy commitments. When working at Teesside I tried on several occasions to arrange a meeting with Sheila but in true thespian tradition, people in the entertainment world can, at times, be notoriously unreliable, there was always some reason why it wasn't possible. In September 2016, I saw Mark on TV in an advert for cancer, and shortly afterwards found out that he had in fact, suffered from cancer himself.

As for Julie Milnes, I first met her when Sheila brought her to my clinic with a recurring problem she wanted me to look at. Over the years, Julie continued to patronise my clinic, and at one stage, I had treated most of her family and relatives. I always attended both Sheila's and then Julie's annual dance shows, as well as Pat Dysons and Marianne Jepsons, which was usually performed at Oldham Coliseum, or Ashton Hippodrome, as it was then known. Back to Jeppy's, as she was fondly known, not to her face, you understand. Her dance studio was on Back Street, near to King Street traffic lights in Oldham, which was a nightmare to park outside, and so I frequently used Sainsbury's car park nearby. Sainsbury's has now moved, and given way to the new Metro Link to Oldham from Manchester. Every time I visit Oldham something has either closed down or disappeared. The historic Oldham landmark known as Mumps Bridge is no longer there, and so when I reminisce about when I was a teacher training student being given assignments to do about my local community, and what made it special, has led me to the conclusion that **I definitely don't agree that progress is always for the best, when beautiful historical structures are replaced with yet another B&Q or Superstore.**

Teaching at Marianne Jepson's was to put it bluntly, 'back to basics' but in a masochistic way I enjoyed it, mainly because of the students. I was always happiest when left alone with students, whether they be 5 or 55 years of age, to do the job I loved, passing on my knowledge, skill and expertise. The rooms were cold, there were very few desks or chairs, and if there were there were never enough, and many times the students had to sit on a hard floor taking notes. Sometimes, I had a heater in the room, but that barely raised the temperature. The students themselves were a mixed bunch of females with the odd male, no pun intended, but I tried to cram as much relevant knowledge into their brains, so that with enough revision they could pass their Royal Society of Arts Anatomy exams. A further qualification was related to, Applied Anatomy and Injury Prevention. My mantra to them being, **'By failing to prepare you are preparing to fail', (Abraham Lincoln).** Because the practical aspects of the course were considered more important, I wasn't given as much time as I would have liked with the students, but Marianne wanted the kudos of having these extra qualifications as part of her curriculum. There were some clever bunnies in the group, as well as some who were less academic, and so trying to pitch my content at a level that would hopefully retain all their attentions was a challenge. Also, the students were challenged by having to not only learn all the terminology related to their dance moves, but also, they had to learn a whole new set of terms related to Anatomy, Physiology and Pathology. The students had to travel to Leeds to sit their exams with other dance students from other colleges, and I used to travel over the Pennines with them for moral support. The first cohort of successes were Collette Wood, Victoria Walker, Rachel Durass and Pauline Gee, which warranted a bit of publicity in the Oldham Evening Chronicle. Other students whom I remember were Roberta Knox, Joanne Scaddon, Emma Williams, Lyndsey Phillips, Amanda Polwin and Rebecca Southern. Several of the teaching staff also attended my sessions, including Mrs Ashworth, who was, 'in charge', whenever Marianne was away. Because I love live theatre, and I love to be entertained I have many fond memories of the time involved with the dancers. To me it was a reciprocal relationship, I passed on my knowledge, skill and expertise related to Anatomy, Physiology and Pathology, and they in return taught me how this related to dance and drama movement. I was always the first to attend the shows, and loved seeing the little dots stop dancing, to wave to their parents in the audience, whilst the teachers were going ballistic, screaming at them, with a smile on their faces of course, to carry on dancing because they were all dominoing into one another. Seeing the older girls perform, was also a treat, knowing that several of them would end up in shows/musicals, on cruise ships or with their own dance schools. Since retirement, I have been on two cruises, and always paid particular attention to the dancers on the entertainment team. To know you have a played a miniscule part in someone's career, for me, was very, very rewarding. Why I stopped working at Jepsons I'm not quite sure, other than a combination of circumstances. Someone moved the goalpost, I became involved in the next phase of my career, or Marianne decided not to re-employ me after a few students failed their Anatomy exams. I honestly can't remember but Marianne always used to send me a Christmas card every year, long after I finished working for her. Sadly, Marianne passed away in January 2008 and Pat Dyson in September, 2010.

During one visit to Oldham in November, 2013, I noticed that there was a Pauline G Dance School in Lees. St John's the Baptist, Stamford Road, OL4 3LH to be precise, and decided perhaps I'd pop in one day to say hello. Well in September 2019, I spent a lovely 60 minutes with her in a cafe in Uppermill, Saddleworth. She informed me she had two grown up sons, and her dance school was doing very well. She also seemed genuinely pleased, that I'd made the effort to contact her. At the time, she was unaware that I was suffering from loneliness and depression, and therefore was and still is unaware, unless she reads this, of the effect the kind words she said about me had. I think the best description would be tears of joy, hidden behind my sunglasses, as I walked down Uppermill High Street, back to my car.

When I lived at Eaves Lane, in Chadderton, I used to treat a local Chadderton singer, Janice Yorke, who, together with her group, was the warm up act for comedian Bernard Manning, whose club was not far away in North Manchester. Bernard was an extremely popular, but controversial Northern comedian who divided audiences because of his extreme material, and his style of entertainment. Roy Chubby Brown was another such comedian, who hailed from the North East. Even at the time in the 70s and 80s, Bernard was considered a racist, sexist bigot. When I eventually got to see him, I found him extremely funny, and as Bernard used to say in interviews, "If you don't find my act funny, you don't have to attend." Years later, when I was involved in going on a rugby tour to Australia, we held a fund-raising evening at Bernard Manning's club. As for Janice, I still have a cassette tape of Janice, that she very kindly gave me after I got her to do a gig at Royton Cricket club. As for Bernard, Janice says he was a very generous person, and did lots of charity work, but turned down many contracts, worth thousands of pounds, to appear in the States and Australia, because he didn't want to travel that far to work, or because he didn't want to compromise his act. Obviously, TV executives weren't keen to sign him up, which Janice says didn't bother him. Today nothing has changed in that, the entertainment world still has its controversial characters and as the saying goes, 'you make your choice and pay your money', or something like that. Curtains, 1997, by Katy Hayes, is a lovely read about theatre life.

Finally, before moving on, as the title of this chapter is, A Change of Direction, I feel here is an appropriate place to include the Fletcher family of Kelvin, Liz, Marnie, Myler, Mateusz and Maximus, whose life changes are documented on the television programme, Fletcher's Farm. Just as my career changed direction, there are lots of connections with the Fletchers related to this book. As mentioned, Kelvin used to live near my brother Jack and occasionally, he played golf with my brother and another neighbour Frank. In one episode, Kelvin was actually helping his son to putt. Some of Kelvin's family still live in the area. Incidentally, Frank, like Kelvin and Liz, is also in the entertainment industry. Although I have never personally met Kelvin or Liz, I only discovered he was my brother's neighbour, when he won Strictly Come Dancing. A programme I have avidly watched over the years, because I've always loved to be entertained or to entertain. Or is that annoying? Also, I have friends who are actors or dancers/choreographers, and for several years worked in a Dance Drama College, and had associations with Oldham Coliseum Theatre. I also used to lecture on face-to-face communication. As this book decries many changes that have taken place, that are relevant to my upbringing and career development, some of these are also relevant to the Fletchers such as parenting, child development and communication etc. When I watch the television programme, it always fills me with joy and happiness knowing, if you'll excuse the pun, Liz and Kelvin have decided not to join the bah, bah, instant gratification society. I've no doubt Kelvin and Liz have embraced modern technology, but during the programmes there are no smartphones, game boys or computers to be seen, other than the odd photo to celebrate success at the Cheshire Show. Neither is the programme interrupted with, **"Excuse me, whilst I just take this call."** Conversations amongst the adults and children are in well spoken English, with no effing and jeffing, like ye know babes. I've yet to see a temper tantrum. Although I've no doubt they occur. There are lots of hugs, cuddles, patient encouragement, play, time spent, effort, energy, adventure, participation, sharing, laughter and tears with no abdication of responsibilities. Treats involve ice creams and the odd glass of alcohol, not materialistic crap. Unless you include a tractor as, 'a must have accessory'. For me, the Fletchers are a shining example of what parenting is all about. Thank you, Liz and Kelvin, for showing me that there are still adults out there, that take their responsibilities seriously.

Writing and becoming a published author.

> "Writing is talking to oneself. You don't put yourself into what you write, you find yourself there." Alan Bennett, playwright.

Writing for me was a therapy. I loved putting order to my thoughts on paper. I was and always have been an organised, lists man, but one that never owned a filo-fax, and so when I was approached by a representative from Corpus and Human Kinetics Publishing, whilst tutoring at the NIM in Blackpool, and asked if I would be interested in writing a book, I jumped at the opportunity. At the time there were many books on massage therapy, but very few on Sports Therapy, and so I decided I would try and write a book, that clearly outlined what sports therapy was and how it differed from physiotherapy, and others working in the sports field. I acknowledged in the book, that some of the material was from Graham Smith's diploma course material, but at the time thought that this was relevant to raise the profile of sports therapy in the world of sport. Taking me twelve months to write, and four months to proof and fine tune, in October 2001 the finished product appeared on the book shelf. Having recently accepted a lecturing post at the University of North London, on the very first Sports Therapy degree course, and having written the massage therapy module to start the first year, I was in a wonderful bubble of professional contentment. Having tutored and examined all over the country, for Graham Smith on his Sports Therapy diploma course, and then to be offered a lecturing post, teaching my own module, whilst becoming an author, with my own ISBN number, was for me, just reward for all the hard work and dedication I had put into re-building my career since leaving Blackshaw Lane Primary. I had come a long way, from sitting in my bedroom as a teenager at 24, Parkway, writing poetry and coming up with lines such as, 'dripping in awesome majesty', to describe a man sat on a bar stool. For those of you wondering, an ISBN number **is only** assigned to published books and although I had written many assignments, articles, publications and modules, during my career for various qualifications and courses, this was my first ISBN. Unfortunately, years later, when I wanted to write the follow up to the book in collaboration with John Macreadie and Stephen Smelt, colleagues of mine at Teesside University, with input from Natalie Hardaker and Colin Jackson, Graham Smith was not best pleased, because I had not consulted him beforehand. Sorry, but I was not aware that I needed his permission to pursue various avenues in my life. In a letter that he sent, he not very subtly reminded me that I had used some of his material previously, and would not be allowed to do so again. He also patronisingly proffered advice on what I needed to do with the book, to give it more gravitas. What Graham failed to realise was, that I had been doing a lot of the background research for this second book for at least 12 months, and knew exactly what I wanted to include. Hence, the collaboration with other colleagues. Baby and bath water springs to mind, and let's have a pissing competition. I suspected Graham was pissed off, I hadn't asked him to be part of the process. The book entitled, Sports Therapy 2, Evidence Informed Practice, was a far more detailed and in-depth work and was planned and meticulously researched but never written up, because I resigned from UCLAN not long after moving there. By now, the reader may have realised that there was a pattern emerging, of Mr B resigning from high profile positions, if he felt injustices were being carried out. All the information for the book is still sitting in a box in my spare bedroom at 4 Park Rd., many years later. During my short time at UCLAN, Professor Jim Richards said that it would have been a wonderful addition to the Sports Therapy degree course. But I resigned from teaching, for much the same reasons I had many years previously, politics, hypocrisy, and disillusionment with the falling standards, and the professional jealousy that pervaded the job. **Also, as with most things today, education is all about finance but I repeat, bums on seats do not and never will equate to quality**

education. It was also sad to see a side to Graham Smith that I suspected existed, namely bullying and intimidation, but never personally experienced, resulting in his displaying the, 'pouting bottom lip'. I'd regarded Graham as not only a true friend, but also as someone who had helped and encouraged me to get where I was, after leaving Primary Education. I have not spoken to Graham Smith, since leaving UCLAN in 2006, although he has asked me, via a third party, to give him a ring, my conscience has always been clear. No, Mr Smith, you ring me, you are not that important in the grand scheme of things. Ask the undertaker.

This latest piece of writing will be my biggest to date, but I am equally proud of all my previous attempts at putting my thoughts and knowledge onto paper.

November, 2001 – Improving Safety and Effectiveness Course.

August, 2001 – Sports Therapy Tutor and Examiners Course material.

May, 2001 – Sports Therapy: Theoretical and Practical Thoughts and Considerations. Corpus Publications. ISBN 1 903333 040 0.

February, 1999 – Ways to Improve R.O.M. and E.O.M. Course.

November, 1999 – Sports Therapy Course. Updated 2003.

June, 1997 – Introduction to Sports Massage Course.

September, 1996/97 – Degree Module for University of North London, Soft Tissue Manipulation.

April, 1996 – Diploma in Soft Tissue Manipulation – Remedial Massage and Mobilisation.

October, 1994 – Sports Care Journal, 'Children in Sport'.

1993 – Society of Sports Therapy Journal, "Down Under with the Boys".

July, 1991 – Society Sports Therapy Journal, 'Are Sports People Getting the Massage?'

Whilst writing this autobiographical piece of work it has made me realise that I could quite easily have become, with a little encouragement, a script writer, possibly in the comedy genre, as various people over the years have asked me, "Do you do stand up?" or, "Are you a script writer?" There is nothing as funny as the reality of life. Look at Peter Kay who used to deliver leaflets, just like me, before perfecting the art of writing about people's idiosyncrasies. Whether or not the scripts would have been accepted, is another matter but to coin a phrase, you have to be in it to win it.

Ed Caldwell and I posing for a photo shoot at the NIM.

National Coaching Foundation/Sports Coach UK, 1991 to 2003.

I started to tutor for the National Coaching Foundation, NCF, after I had attended several of their courses, which led me to apply for one of their tutorial positions. The head of the organisation was Sue Campbell, who later became a Baroness, was on the Olympic committee, and became a leading light in women's football during Sarina Wiegman's reign as England's manager. First and foremost, you had to have coaching qualifications, and qualifications both theoretical and practical in your chosen field of expertise. With coaching qualifications in football, handball, gymnastics and athletics, I applied to tutor on the Coaching Children and Injury Prevention, and The Treatment of Injuries Courses. There were several levels of qualification for each subject, and the courses lasted from several hours to several days. These were offered all over the country. Tutors were offered courses nearest to where they lived, although, occasionally you were asked to travel a little further afield, if there was a tutor shortage in a particular subject. There was a tutorial package with each course, that was primarily delivered via lectures and workshops. Each package consisted of the course handbook, which was sent to each participant or given out at the beginning of the course, a set of overhead acetates and evaluation sheets, to be completed at the end of the course. The delivery of the material was left to the discretion of the tutor, but in order to ensure the key points and specific areas were definitely covered by different tutors offering the same course, tutorial days were arranged, so that all tutors could get together, and make sure we were all talking from the same page. These days were not only useful in that you could put names to faces, but also because teaching pedagogy could be exchanged between fellow tutors. Denis Wright and Lyn Booth were other tutors working on my courses. Both were Chartered Physiotherapists and worked together in the NHS in Rochdale. Denis worked for a time at Wigan Rugby League, whilst Lyn was involved in women's hockey. Although I met him and attended some of his talks, I never worked with Denis but respected his help and advice, but the more I worked with Lyn, the more respect we developed, coming from different backgrounds. During such training days there was also a generic session, led by senior tutors, which would be useful adjuncts to your teaching tool-kit, no matter what courses you tutored. I particularly enjoyed the ice-breaker sessions, which primarily were different ways to get a group of total strangers to interact at the beginning of a session in a workshop setting. The aim of the NCF, which was later re-named Sports Coach UK, was to complement courses offered by the major sports organisations, many integrating them into their main coaching qualifications, and to generally improve the level of coaching in the UK. Just because an athlete had been successful in their own careers, it didn't necessarily follow that they would be successful coaches, or for that matter managers. 'What makes a successful coach?' was one such course offered by the NCF/Sports Coach UK. The courses were also designed to, 'raise consciousness', as to some of the bad practices, mind sets and intransigence to change, **that pervaded and still pervades certain sports. Issues such as sexism, male chauvinism, racism, illegal payments, bribery, alcohol abuse, sexual and drug abuse, child grooming and paedophilia, whilst perpetuating a culture of fear and bullying. All being allowed to germinate, because of a lack of transparency.** Although, during my time whilst working for the NCF, many of these serious issues were still being swept under the carpet and so, not raised. **There is nothing as certain as the closed mind, and teaching old dogs new tricks, are expressions that immediately spring to mind.** Also, as with all aspects of life the political arena was never very far away, and Head Office was always sending some, 'big wig', to pontificate as to the way forward. Many of them never to be seen again, as the political climate changed. After a while I started to feel sorry for them, as Sue Campbell introduced them to the team and the team immediately adopted a, 'It must be election time again', demeanour. **It is very difficult to have respect for someone who pontificates about a subject in which they have very little, if any, knowledge, skill, expertise or experience.** During my tenure as a tutor, there were many innovations as Nutrition, Sports Psychology, Sports Mechanics, Sports Sciences, Communication skills and financial acumen etc. that became significant in the sporting arena. An understanding of Anatomy, Physiology and Pathology, equipment and environmental factors came under scrutiny, and subsequently became vital elements to help 'athletes' reach peak performance. Gone were the days of, let's do a few warm up laps, a couple of stretches, plenty of sit ups and press ups, here is your bucket and sponge, off you go. With some sports more receptive to change, than others. The quantity- quality debate was never far away, until research and science showed that training to the max every day, was not always the best way forward and rest days were not just for, 'softies'. **Paid and lottery funded athletes were encouraged to become more professional, as they became commodities and income generators for sports clubs, and therefore their physical and psychological wellbeing needed to be looked after, and their shelf- life needed to be extended.** An athlete's public persona also became a massive issue. Enter the sports agents to negotiate the contracts, some of whom it has been shown, had agendas not in the best interests of the athlete. Athletes were also made more aware of what higher profile meant, as they were going to be scrutinised more, and finding the 'cheats', became an item on the agenda. Enter the legal profession who also became an integral part of the mix, and the PR gurus with their spin. All this leading to the advent of teams of people, supposedly respecting each other's expertise, and working towards a common goal. Unfortunately, sometimes the common goal was not in the best interest of the athlete's health and welfare, with systemic abuse and sexual misconduct not uncommon. Something I personally found out about, when working in full time education, health and sport. Egos and insecurities usually getting in the way, not ignoring the power and greed factor, and as mentioned, you can't escape the fact that as soon as you put a group of people together, you are going to get personality clashes. I thoroughly enjoyed my time as a tutor, and not only learned much from my fellow tutors, but also developed a greater understanding of **sporting mentality, which for me was the key to survival in sport, and the reason I never wanted to work full time in certain sporting environments. Spitting, swearing, physical, sexual and psychological abuse, macho posturing, pissing competitions, chauvinism, and working with paedophiles and psychotic tossers, was not for me.** Oh dear, now you're in trouble, Jim. I've told you before, that honesty is never well received. However, it was great to see how certain sports developed, and became successful by adopting the multi-disciplinary approach to sporting success, and employing specialist expertise as and when required. Track cycling immediately springs to mind, but even that has been shown to have its hidden agendas. Unfortunately, others still adopted a closed shop mentality of, 'jobs for the boys' and 'that's the way we've always done it.' In 1994, I had an article published in the Sports Care Journal, Vol. 1, No 5, entitled, Children in Sport, emphasising the fact that children should not be treated as mini adults. It referred to not only a child's physical development, but also their mental, psychological, emotional adjustment and behaviour. How much has changed since then, is open to debate but **as soon as money enters the arena greed, bribery and corruption become issues, and over the years, evidence of this at the highest levels of sport has been discovered. But even at an amateur level, these abuses continue to be reported. The Yates Report in 2022, related to National Women's Football in the USA being the latest scandal. Sadly, for me this will always remain a major issue, until the deterrent becomes greater than the incentive and many of the issues are reported as crimes, and not just sporting issues. Pathetic short-term bans and temporary suspensions, bearing** absolutely no relevance to the crimes committed. **With sports coaches being allowed to virtually get away with sexually abusing 16 plus athletes, purely and simply, because he or she was over 16 years of age. One year younger and that becomes criminal behaviour, but was not reported as such. Athletics, cycling, swimming, gymnastics, rowing, bobsleigh, cricket, archery and canoeing to name but a few of the culprits.** (Fletcher P, 27/11/20. Cycling News: Burst bubbles and blurred lines). The Lance Armstrong scandal being one such scandal, that was highlighted in the article. In September 2020, an investigation into Yorkshire Cricket Club found it guilty of breaching, 'anti-racism rules'. In February, 2021, 37 former gymnasts, including 3 Olympians, were taking legal action against British Gymnastics over its alleged abuse of those, to whom it had a duty of care. These 37 representing, 'the tip of the iceberg', with over 100 clubs and 100 coaches being identified. During the 2020/21 Olympics, Simone Biles, the American gymnast, who was tipped to win gold medals, suddenly withdrew from part of the competition, citing excessive stress and pressure that affected her ability to perform. In April 2021, prior to the boat race, there was a sexual assault, misconduct allegation, pertaining to a rape case on one of the girls on the Oxford crew that was, **'dismissed'**, by Oxford University, and was deemed **not worthy of investigation.** It is interesting to note that during my time at Sports Coach UK, some 25 years ago, the initiative to tackle the thorny issue of drugs in sport, became a priority and at that time, Michelle Veronique was tasked with the job. Sports Coach UK asked the coaches if they were interested in getting involved, but at the time I was happy enough doing what I was doing. Many years later, Michelle resigned because **it was alleged, she felt not all governing bodies in sport were totally committed to the deterrents, especially if it impacted on revenue or national pride.** She has subsequently been proven right, as many sports have hit the headlines for all the wrong reasons. We still see athletes at the highest level plying their trade after being 'banned' for substance abuse, with many athletic coaches still grooming and sexually abusing young athletes, to whom they have a duty of care. On the 20/9/21 The BBC screened a programme, Nowhere to Run: Abused by our Coach, which was about manipulative coaches who preyed on vulnerable young athletes, as young as 12 years of age, who just wanted to be successful at any cost. The central characters were Charlie Webster, an athlete and journalist from Sheffield, and her athletics coach, Paul North, who sexually abused Charlie, and some of her running mates some 20 plus years earlier. What made me angry was, that the abuse started with massage, my profession. As if massage has not had to suffer enough from its nudge, nudge, wink, wink stigma. Massage in football was considered something for 'puffs' until Arsene Wenger appeared on the scene at Arsenal, with his multi-disciplinary back-up team. Sadly, one of North's victims took her own life, by overdosing, at the age of 18, as she never got over the trauma. **The coach North was eventually jailed for 10 years, after which time he would be free to repeat offend.** The programme ended with the mention of HYDRANT, a police task force, that had been set up to look into reported criminality, including child abuse in athletics. To date, they have 11,000 victims and 9,000 suspects on their data base. In 2016, there was an initial move to ban the WHOLE Russian athletics team. **But as in life, bad practice will never be totally eradicated, because those with power and an invested interest in, 'perpetuating the myth', will do anything to ensure it continues. Muirfield Golf Club only allowed women to join in 2017. Why is Russia still being allowed to participate in any sports competitions, with its track record of substance abuse and cheating?** Chris Boardman, the Olympic cyclist, remarked in commentary during the 2021 Road Cycling World Championships, that sport was a play without a script and that is why we love it. But even when there is a script relating to children's welfare, certain people still chose to ignore it.

Simply the Best: NW Counties, Junior Rugby League U15s, Tour to Fiji, New Zealand and Australia, 1993.

Now I don't know if the reader believes in fate or destiny, no, not Destiny's Child, the other one, but on this particular day in 1992, I'd decided to have an early night and scan through some travel brochures I had collected the previous few weeks on Australia and New Zealand. Going there was one of my to dos on my bucket list, and that particular night I decided that as I was now working for myself, and free of the constraints that being in full time employment had on you, in the not-too-distant future I would take time out and travel Down Under.

The following day I was in my office, the small back bedroom at Alandale Drive, when the phone rang. It was Steve Bitthell, known as 'Bith', a friend of my neighbour Hadyn. Many of Haydn's mates, whilst being good eggs, were nevertheless 'Jack the Lads' and could always be relied upon to make your time spent with them interesting and entertaining. Now I had met Steve on several occasions when out with Haydn, and knew he was one of his mates that went to the sauna every Friday, and the pub most Friday evenings to watch rugby on Sky Sports. Whilst I never went to the sauna, because of my teaching commitment at Marianne Jepsons and my clinic, I sometimes went to the pub. The following telephone conversation is roughly how I recall it.

"Hi Jim, Steve Bith, how's it going?"

"Oh, Hi, Steve, I'm well thank you and your good self?"

"Jim, I don't know if you are aware but I'm involved in this North West Counties Rugby League Under 15s tour to Australia, New Zealand and Fiji. As the league executive representative, I will be travelling as Team Manager. Haydn Walker, the head Coach, who has previously toured Down Under is looking for a male physiotherapist, because last time they took a female physio but with all that testosterone around, it didn't work out, and so this time they are looking, if possible, to take a male and I've thrown your name into the hat. Do you fancy taking 6 weeks out of your schedule next year, June or July to be precise, to join the squad? It's an unpaid position but the prestige and experience could prove invaluable. We are fund raising at present, and we need to raise £92,000. Each person has to raise approximately £2,000 each. There are 8 officials and 36 players, chosen from all NW amateur clubs."

Now thinking back to what I was doing in bed only hours previously, no, not that, I'm thinking this is either a wind up or very, very spooky. Also, I was not aware that Steve was involved in such a venture.

"Steve are you serious or are you just bored and want a laugh?"

"No, Jim, I'm deadly serious. You don't have to give an answer right now but at a meeting in Warrington last night I told the committee, I would give you a call to see if you were firstly, available and secondly, would you be interested. At present we don't have a Tour Manager or a physio, and we need to fill those positions as soon as possible. I thought even if you can't go, you might know someone who would be interested in either or both of the positions."

"Well thanks for the vote of confidence, Steve but I would obviously need to know much more before committing one way or another. My next patient is due soon, and so if I can get back to you later today for more details would that be OK?"

"No probs, Jim, thanks for your time."

Now Steve was a sales rep, and had a reputation for being able to sell sand to the Arabs and was well known for, 'doing a deal', and so as soon as I put the phone down, I wondered was this deal for real? How could it be that less than twenty-four hours after deciding I was going to go to Australia and New Zealand, sooner rather than later, I would receive a phone call offering me such an opportunity? Financially, I had some savings for a rainy day. Was this opportunity such a rainy day? Could I take time out from clinic, and my teaching commitments for 6 weeks? All of these questions started whizzing through my mind, but first of all I had several more patients to see that day who needed my undivided attention.

Needless to say, the rest of the day was taken up with organising my thoughts. To be honest how could I say no, what a tremendous opportunity to put my knowledge, skills, expertise and experience to the test at the other side of the world? After further conversations with Steve, I was invited to Birchwood, Warrington to meet the players and officials. It was at this stage that I suggested my friend and recently retired headteacher, Don Smith, as a possible Tour Manager. Like myself, Don was an avid Oldham rugby league supporter, and added to the fact that he had quite recently been to Australia and enjoyed his sport both as a youngster, playing football, and now as a spectator, watching Oldham Rugby League, I certainly felt he was worth approaching. As Tour Manager he would be a figure head, meeting dignitaries, making speeches, and generally giving the tour an air of respectability and professionalism. A role I had no doubt Don would be good at, but would Alice, his wife, give him her blessing to return to Australia, but this time for 6 weeks with a group of rough, tough, testosterone fuelled rugby players and coaches? Alice gave her blessing and the rest is history, so to speak. The following months were taken up with attending training sessions, meetings, fund raising events and planning the logistics of travelling to the other side of the world, with the responsibility of caring for 44 people. No pressure there, then Mr B. Steve, Don and I organised a Sportsman's dinner in Royton to raise funds, and my family and friends, especially brother Jack, did their bit to help and support my efforts. Dee was always there in the background lending her support.

For me, the tour itself was a mixture of highs and lows, and so was not just, Simply the Best, by Tina Turner, which was played in the dressing room before every game. To reiterate, whenever you put people together in a group, for a period of time, you will more often than not, get personality clashes, that's human nature. When you put 44 sports people together, each one an individual in their own right, each with their own sporting, competitive mentality, and where 36 of them are flooded with teenage hormones, there are inevitably going to be flash points. How such flare-ups are managed, is dependent on the personalities tasked with dealing with such. Role definition is vital in such circumstances. Some sports tours abroad have both medical and non-medical back up, but I had sole responsibility for all things related to health, and so my focus was ensuring I brought back to Blighty, 44 people in roughly the same healthy condition as they were before they left. Yes, battered, bruised and mentally scarred, after a little, 'Pommy Bashing', but nevertheless in roughly the same shape. To this end, the tour was a success for me. Other people's definition of success was dependent on their role in the squad, and that in itself created tensions. Also, for me the tour re-enforced my view, shaped whilst working with the National Coaching Foundation, later to be re-branded Sports Coach UK, that working in sport full time was not for me. Years later, I was thrilled to find out that some of the boys had made full time, professional rugby players, Kevin Mannion, Lee Briers, Alan Cross, Neil Baynes and Andrew Coley. Kevin Mannion actually signed for Oldham, and we had a mini re-union on the pitch at Spotland, Rochdale after one local derby match. Lee Briers became a Welsh international, and a key player and the coach for many years at Warrington. As far as I'm aware, he is still working at Warrington. Obviously, the tour looked good on my CV, and resulted in several published articles. In October 1993, I had an article published in the Society of Sports Therapist's magazine, entitled, 'Down under with the Boys', outlining my experiences related to the tour. Not least my cultural experience, when I realised Australians always asked a question, and then gave you the answer in the same sentence. What's your favourite colour, blue? What's your name, Sheila? But I digress.

Kevin Mannion, Jonathan Gwilliam, Lee Briers, Mr B, and Alan Cross enjoying Coolangata.

L-R: Rob Davidson, Jim Briggs, Keith Babcock, Steven Wilson, Keiron Royales, Chris Wheelan, Wes Roberts, Steve Bitthell, Don Smith.

Sport, the FA, FATOI's, Positive Discrimination, Disillusionment, Bullshit and Balderdash.

Whilst at the NIM Tommy McMullen, who at the time was working for the Scottish RFU, mentioned this new course covering the treatment of injuries that was being run by the Football Association at Lilleshall, the National Sports Centre, Shropshire. At that time, the late 1980s, many professional sports were not very professional, in the way they looked after their most valuable assets, the players and competitors. Also, traditionally football professionals who were coming to the end of their careers, and who wanted to continue doing something in the sport, other than manage or coach, were given a bucket and sponge, and started running on to the pitch whenever there was an injury. This together with putting out kit on match days, and doing various other tasks constituted their role as 'physio'. Apart from having played the game, very few of these people had much knowledge, skill or expertise and very little, if any, qualifications in treating sports people and just basically mimicked what they had experienced as players. Many didn't even have a First Aid certificate. Serious situations were dealt with by paramedics, a trained physiotherapist or a doctor with an interest in sport. However, on February 9th, 1979 when Trevor Francis became the first million-pound footballer, the FA felt a more professional approach was needed in their welfare. So, it was decided that anyone wanting to work in football, on the medical side, would need to have a minimum qualification and decided to set up a course themselves, the Football Association Treatment and Management of Injuries Diploma, attendees being lovingly referred to as FATOIs.

It was also apparent that there was a dearth of trained first aiders working in football, especially at amateur level, and that was not only unacceptable for our national game, but had implications for insurance and litigation. As for those who did have a First Aid qualification, it wasn't actually relevant to sport, but was more suited to either the work place or road traffic injury management. How many road traffic incidents have to be dealt with on a football field? Another fact being, that of the 30,000 plus trained Chartered Physiotherapists, only a few thousand actually worked in sports and that was after they had undergone post graduate training. The Course Director appointed by the FA was Graham Smith, a Chartered Physiotherapist, who had worked in professional football and had gained a reputation, whilst at Lilleshall, for sending players back to their clubs after attending Lilleshall for rehabilitation, not only fully recovered from injury, but much fitter than before they attended. Lilleshall being somewhere that players with long standing injuries, or injuries the club physiotherapist couldn't 'fix' were sent. The staff at these Centres of Excellence supposedly having specific knowledge, skill and expertise above and beyond traditional physiotherapy.

Tom mentioned that I might be interested in doing the course, but as for himself was a little put off by the cost and the fact that he had a successful cleaning business, was working in rugby and needed to consider his family. The course was over a two-year period, Year 1, Lower Body and Year 2, Upper Body, with 12 days being spent in residence each year at Lilleshall itself. The intervening time being spent on revision, and gaining practical experience. A First Aid certificate was the pre-requisite for attendance. I was now running a clinic, doing further courses at the Northern, coaching and travelling with Oldham Metro Gymnastic, as well as running my gymnastic club, but decided working with experienced people from within football, especially on the rehabilitation side, would be invaluable and well worth the financial outlay. I had always had a current First Aid qualification, ever since I started training to be a PE teacher in 1968, and the theoretical aspects of the course, after all the training I had undergone as a physical therapist, seemed well within my grasp. I applied and was accepted. To be honest, I'm still not sure what the entry criteria was, apart from the First Aid Certificate, other than, can you pay?

On my first day at Lilleshall, I found out I was sharing accommodation with a guy called Paul Miller, a fireman, who was also working for a part time club in Hinckley Town. Arriving in the dormitory room after registration, I noticed Mr Miller, or 'Mills' as he was later to be known, had already settled in, as there was a box of skeletal bones on his bed and several text books. My immediate thoughts were, that I was sharing with either a swot or a guy with an intimidatory sense of humour. When I eventually caught up with Paul, as he returned whilst I was unpacking, we got on like a house on fire, if you will excuse the fireman pun, from the moment we exchanged initial pleasantries. He was a tall, self-deprecating guy, and towered over me by many inches. Little and large was an understatement. Our senses of humour just intertwined, and our times at Lilleshall were nothing, if not filled with joyous hilarity. There was a mixed bunch of people on the course, mainly male, many attached to football clubs in the Football Leagues, but there were **only two girls.** One, was called Shona, who together with her friend, if I remember correctly worked at Hitchen Town. Now I was used to being in the company of and working with females, as either my equal or my superiors, but it soon became obvious that some of the guys, who were entrenched in football mentality, viewed these two lasses with not only interest, but also scepticism. Women in football was definitely not on the agenda, as football traditionally was and still, despite the rhetoric and the advancement of the women's game, hides pockets of male chauvinism. Why I chose the word pockets, will soon be revealed. **Toxic masculinity** as it has sometimes been referred to. In fact at the time, I was only aware of one female 'physio' in football, Caroline B, who had worked at Wimbledon. At that time, Wimbledon was infamous for having Vinnie Jones as one of its star players. I was also aware that the first woman to work as a 'physio' with an English league club, was Judith Lo, who worked part-time at Tranmere Rovers, between 1982 and1985.

The cohort of students at Lilleshall, June, 1989, with Graham Smith on the left as you look at the photo, Miller, back row, second from the left and myself squatting front centre.

This issue of the dearth of women physios working in men's football, has been one that has consistently been in my thought processes, since I became aware of its significance when I first attended Lilleshall in 1989. In 2011, Sir Alex Ferguson was involved in a sexism in football row, when a rejection letter he wrote in 1994 was leaked to the Mail on Sunday newspaper. The letter was his reply to a 20-year-old girl's request to be considered for a physiotherapist work placement at Manchester United, leaving the girl hurt and insulted, not to mention quite shocked by the tone of the letter. How many women physiotherapists work in men's football at the highest level in 2025, I'm unsure but it's a few more than when I attended Lilleshall in the late 1980s and early 90s. It's certainly not very many, relative to men. How has football been able to get away with this restriction of practice and discrimination against women over the years? The words culture, racism and sexism spring to mind. With the rise and success of women's sports in general, it has become more difficult for this blatant discrimination to be overlooked, with a greater scrutiny of the historical treatment of not only women, but also coloured people in sport, with its homophobic view of life. Referred to online as football's racist underbelly. Although, men's football is certainly not alone with such tunnel vision. Before moving on, we now have, **Gender neutrality and abrusexual, to name but two of the expressions that have suddenly appeared on the scene. But since studying for my biology O' level at 16, I have been trained, taught and educated into the fact THAT MEN AND WOMEN ARE DIFFERENT. Over the years, I have answered several examination questions, explaining why this is so to gain my qualifications. I'm confused. Introduced in 1976, by Michael Foucault as a term to erode the cultural, biological, psychological and social role of gender within society, has the term now been re-introduced, 48 years later, to address the issue of gender discrimination? I am also informed that the term, non-Binary, relates to being neither male nor female. More confusion.** In a Chartered Society of Physiotherapist's article in 2005, Vol 11, Issue 10, 'Soccer Women Physios Push Forward', it was stated that in the season, 2004-2005, only two women worked with first team squads amongst the 92 English professional clubs. But in the same article, Alan Hodson said that with the rise of the football academies, he **estimated** 30-35% of the total physios working in them were now women. However, in 2020, the WiF, **"aims to improve women's representation at all levels of the game by challenging discrimination and lobbying for change."** The 2014, 2016 and most recent 2020 WiF Surveys highlighted that **there is much work still to do in key areas such as widening the talent pool of diverse women across the game, achieving gender balance on boards and committees, and instilling confidence in reporting discriminatory behaviour and abuse. With 66% of women working in the industry having witnessed sexism in the workplace.** Karen Dobres, 'Pitch Invasion', 2025, is about a feminist and the abuse she received as a Board member of a football club. Over the years even if a woman did secure a position, it appeared that her role was not as extensive as her male counterpart, and she was probably paid less than her male counterpart for doing the same job. With the girls now entering the punditry/commentary realm, it has been interesting to watch the dynamics of the mixed gender teams. Many years ago, I was informed by one such woman that she was asked **NOT** to sit in the dugout, because of the bad language during the match. Perhaps women working in other sports, for example rugby, are not subjected to swearing and bad language and so are allowed access to the dugout. In recent times, a certain Chelsea manager hit the headlines with his abusive treatment of the female club doctor. You would have thought these male chauvinistic, stone-age attitudes towards women would have changed, considering the history of women in football. In July 2017, the BBC screened, 'When Football Banned Women', which charted the rise of women's football, during and after the first world war. Dick Kerr's Ladies played to crowds in excess of 50,000 and support for the ladies' game was huge. Incidentally, there is a wall plaque dedicated to Dick Kerr's ladies' football, not more than a mile away from where I live in Preston. But on the 5th December 1921, the FA banned women from playing football in their grounds, citing spurious complaints, but saying the game was quite unsuitable for women. This was after the women had worked tirelessly in the munitions factories, assisting the war effort. Tara Lynne O'Neil's debut play, Rough Girls, in 2012, was all about the growth of women's football in Northern Ireland, and the first NI Women's football team. In 2022, NI women qualified for the first time in their history for the European Championships, with basically a non-professional squad, and they then qualified for the Women's World cup in 2023. In July 2025, BBC television screened, Euro 2025: Together Stronger, after the Welsh women's football team made history, by qualifying for the Euros. It charted how this was achieved, against the male opposition to their very existence. What right, other than sexist arrogance, has one gender got to tell another it cannot kick a football? It wasn't until 1971, that the FA's ban on women's football was lifted. Words used on the 2017 programme were **SCANDALOUS AND DIGRACEFUL,** but could easily be ascribed to the 2025 one. I'm also aware that initially only men got the England women's football's manager's job but as they fell by the wayside, **'for various reasons',** it was only when Sarina Wiegman took over, in September, 2021, that serious progress was made. Surely it should be the best person for the job irrespective of culture, gender, race, creed, special handshakes or political persuasion. I would love to still be alive to witness the first woman manager to take over a high-profile men's football league club, with perhaps Karen Brady as the chairperson. Many years ago, when I was working at the University of North London, on the very first Sports Therapy Degree course, a student of ours, who desperately wanted to work in football, sent a letter to Alan Hodson at the FA, asking why was there a dearth of women physios working in football? I am unaware of the contents of the reply, but would be interested to know what reasons were given at that time. But all is not doom and gloom, because as a season ticket holder for Blackburn Rover's Ladies, **I DO WATCH women's football for all of the 90 plus minutes,** purely and simply, because they play the game like my brother Jack and I used to play, with positivism, enjoyment, by respecting the referee's decisions with very little, if any, dissent, and not wanting to spend as much of the game as possible rolling around, as though being pole axed after a challenge, whilst seeing every opportunity, upon entering, 'the box', as another chance to practice their acting skills to, secure a penalty. Need I go on? **How long this will last, I'm not sure as more money creeps into the women's game. Whilst very happy with the growth of women in sport, with the Independent, 27/9/24, reporting a 4-year, record growth in women's and girl's football, I fear the male influence will start to affect attitudes and behaviour. And whilst I would like to see the men taking a lead from the women's game, I don't think that will happen and why should they, as long as someone continues to pay them £550,000 plus a week for kicking a football, or anything else that moves within their personal space?** On this issue, during the Women's World Cup, in France, in June 2019, the USA national football team's record-breaking win, 13-0 against Thailand, sparked a heated discussion about gender pay inequality in football. Not least with social media. The win was the biggest winning margin in World Cup history, across both the men and women's tournaments. The achievement prompting the statisticians to point out that in spite of the women's team achievements over the years, they were still paid considerably less than their male counterparts, who incidentally had not even qualified for their World Cup. It was pointed out that they had won 3 Women's World Cup titles, 4 Olympic gold medals and had scored more goals than the men during the past 3 World Cups. In 2016, five members of the USA women's national football team filed a lawsuit against the US Soccer federation, with regard to wage discrimination. Pointing out the women had generated $20M, (£15.71M), more revenue in 2015 than the men's team, but the women only earned a quarter of what the men were paid. In March 2019, 28 members of the USA women's team filed a gender discrimination lawsuit with the US Soccer Federation, stating, **"Despite the fact that these female and male players are called upon to perform the same job responsibilities on their teams, and participate in international competitions for their single common employer, the USSF, the female players have consistently been paid less than their male counterparts. ….Even though their performance has been superior to that of the male players- with female players, in contrast to male players, becoming world champions."** A follow up to this was the Yates Report in 2022. In 2022, the England Lionesses football team reached and won the final of the European Cup at Wembley. The tournament attracted record crowds, with 87,192 spectators attending the game, and gave much joy and inspiration to a nation suffering from a pandemic and Brexit. Incidentally in 2022, the women's game generated the largest crowds in football, 91,553, Barcelona versus Real Madrid in March, and 91,648, Barcelona versus Wolfsburg, in April. Also, in June 2022 Alex Scott an ex-England player and commentator was involved in making another documentary, Women in Football, but this time charting the rise of the women's game, shown before and during the European cup. After England won, she condemned the attitude of the men's FA towards hosting the Euros with only a handful of clubs wanting to be involved, and said that was now their misfortune as, 'The train had left the station.' In 2025, the Lionesses repeated their success by winning the European Cup for the second time. But why are people surprised, as after all, it is men's football we are talking about, where very little, if anything, apart from the financial side of the game, unless shamed or forced to do so, changes. As mentioned, changing culture takes more than just kneeling down before a game, and in the case of certain sports, a long, long time. I suppose it's fitting that the final words go to Alex Scott, now a television commentator, who said that she no longer needed to go cap in hand to the boys, to ask for their support or permission. On the 7th October, 2022 in front of **a FULL HOUSE,** England Lionesses, the European Champions, played the USA, the World Champions, need I say anymore? **Personally, I would be interested to see the statistics making a comparison between men and women's football, on how much time is spent actually making contact with the ball and playing the game in 90plus minutes as opposed to arguing, fighting, wasting time, diving, play acting, feigning death and trying to con the referee. And even arguing that VAR had got it wrong.** There's a theory that the more time that the male players spend during the game not actually playing football, the less time the spectators have to assess the players' skill levels. Whereas, in the women's game it is there for all to see. The gender debate, not only in football but many other sports, will no doubt rumble on but before returning to Lilleshall and the people on the course, I need to update the reader to the fact that I no longer go to watch Blackburn Rovers Ladies after Blackburn Rovers, seeing the rise in women's football decided in 2024, as a cost cutting exercise to return the girls to being a part time outfit, whilst appointing a man to look after them after Gemma had left. To repeat again, culture takes time to change and sometimes may never be achievable whilst HOMO SAPIENS roam the planet. Back to Lilleshall. To say I was a little disappointed with the level of anatomical, physiological and pathological knowledge some of them possessed, considering they were attached to professional clubs, would be understating things. **Sound theory underpins all good practice, and by doing the course, I hoped to add to not only my theoretical knowledge but also my practical skills.** Unfortunately, several viewed my attendance with suspicion, because I wasn't attached to a football club. It was as though they couldn't allow a spy in the camp. The fact that my qualifications were at least equivalent to many already working on the 'medical side' of the sport, counted for nothing. Whilst some of the course participants could probably handle physical intimidation, they found academic intimidation took them out of their comfort zone and was a tad difficult. It was also obvious to the people on the course, not actually attached to a football club, that some of the tutors, despite their protestations, had their favourites, especially if they were high profile ex-pros. It was also becoming obvious that I, along with several others, were not finding the theoretical aspects too daunting, whilst others, who desperately needed the qualification to stay working in football, were finding it, to say the least, very stressful. Sometimes this stress manifested itself in verbal confrontation. As I personally was not attached to any football club, it meant that at times there was a little antagonism towards myself, and the non-football fraternity from the football people, who couldn't understand how anybody was not in love with men's football. I remember one day after we had just been given the results of an on-course assessment, and I was one of the top three, one of the guys, asked me what the heck I was doing on the course, if I knew everything and didn't intend working full time in football? Another then waded in with, "What the fuck did you get wrong Briggsy, your bleedin name?" Hey Ho, such was the banter. In spite of this, I got on with most of the participants as they realised rather than shower me with abuse, I could be useful when it came to revision. Miller telling everyone he spoke to, that I had been a great help, 'sorting out his bones'. He loved to ask me to test him on various aspects of the course, and would come out with a variety of expletives, if he got things wrong. Also, when they found out I did have a background in football, as a player and coach, and was also a qualified PE teacher and had qualifications in physical therapy, many would come to our room for extra tuition. I was happy to oblige, as it was also good revision for me. As my friendship with Paul blossomed, together with several others, Pete Brown at Northampton Town FC being another, my time at Lilleshall became less confrontational and more enjoyable. Lilleshall was, at the time, one of the Centres of Excellence for gymnastics and I would go, time permitting, to watch the British gymnasts attending training camps. Don't forget, I was a gymnastic coach and had run my own gymnastic club. During my second year at Lilleshall, I met a female gym coach who, as part of her degree course at Newcastle University, had been seconded to Lilleshall for work experience. A J was a gymnast herself, of some repute, unlike my good self who considered myself a better coach, than I was a gymnast. She became a slight distraction for a while, until either I returned home, or she had to return to her digs in Jesmond, Newcastle, or home in Wellingborough, Northampton. Mills loved to involve himself in pranks, whenever I returned to our room. I always had to be prepared for the fact, that he had usually done something to my bed. His favourite was putting all his bones under my covers so that when I got into bed, I stubbed my toes. Another was, filling my bed with cutlery he had borrowed from the canteen, so that I nearly lacerated all my private parts. Sometimes, he would find a skeleton from the anatomy room, and put it in my bed as a bed partner. He also took great delight in tying the sheets together, so I couldn't get into bed, or completely stripping the bed and hiding the covers. As it could sometimes be the early hours of the morning when I returned to our room, I stumbled about in the dark trying to get undressed, before being confronted with these assault course traps he had set for me. Cursing, swearing, but laughing at the same time, I could hear giggles coming from Miller's bed and, "You dirty little bastard, that'll teach you to go with nubile gymnasts, when you should be here with me helping with my bones. During my first-year final exams, Gary Lewin, who at the time was the Arsenal and England Physiotherapist, was my examiner and I must have done everything asked of me, as I passed. This meant I could return the following year and take Part 2. But after the first year, we found out that Graham Smith had left, 'under a cloud', and that Alan Hodson was to take over and further develop the course. **Upon completing my FA Treatment of Injury course, if I wasn't fully aware during the course I certainly realised after, of the insular behaviour that existed in football.** Once it was known that I was not going to attach myself to a football club, instead continue running a private clinic, my membership to the boys' club was certainly going to be curtailed, if not rescinded. Upon qualifying, Alan Hodson, The Head of Medical Training, told me to, "Go and fill your boots, Briggsy," with work on the First Aid and Diploma course the FA had started to roll out. "Just contact Alan Leeming, at the FA Headquarters in Preston, and he will give you as much work as you want." As I sit here, writing these memoirs 16 plus years after retirement, Mr Leeming, if he is still in situ, has never offered me one single teaching position. My involvement with the FA being restricted to teaching First Aid on the Coaching Courses, run by a young lad who lived in Milnrow, who phoned me personally and asked if I would cover the First Aid for him. It was ironic that I was later to move to Preston, and only live a few miles from the FA headquarters, in Leyland, where Blackburn Rovers Ladies sometimes play.

As previously mentioned, in today's over inflated world of men's football, mediocrity appears to be rewarded, and the game itself is riddled with superlatives. Some footballers today appear to be so one footed, it's embarrassing. In my career I came across many footballers, coaches and 'physios', attached to football, who were incapable of talking without an f, t or c word, f..ing and jeffing this, that and the other in virtually every sentence. And, as is known, swearing demonstrates a lack of vocabulary. Their mentality being that to be a man, you had to be able to do sit-ups, press ups, spit, swear, and abuse authority, not to mention your partner, be they male or female. Oh yes, and firmly believing a woman's role in life was in bed, with a chain around her neck long enough to reach the oven. Their words not mine. I'm pleased to say there were some, who didn't have this mentality but, in my experience, they appeared to be in the minority. Or was it like homosexuality, many kept quiet for fear of being stigmatised? And so, having hyped these footballers into super star status, who is going to admit that they are not, but are really just the survivors of, at times, a male chauvinistic, closed shop system, that has been shown on more than one occasion to abuse young talent, relies on blind patronage and rewards, if you'll pardon my English, arse licking. Many managers surrounding themselves with sycophants and mates. A system that certainly closes ranks at the merest sniff of abuse, corruption and denial. With the rise of women's football, these and other issues have become more evident.

Football, like many institutions, has always looked after its own, and personally speaking, there is nothing wrong with that, as long as the word transparency enters the domain. As has been previously intimated, over the years football has not been alone in being guilty of perpetuating a culture of fear, bullying, illegal payments, racism, alcohol addiction, child grooming, body shaming, sexual and drug abuse, paedophilia, male chauvinism and bribery. All being allowed to germinate, because of a lack of transparency when issues of sponsorship, funding, national pride, and vast sums of money are involved. Sports such as cycling, (Lance Armstrong), gymnastics, (Simone Byles), tennis, (Arthur Ashe), and rugby, (the Welsh national team), to name but a few, have been found guilty of misdemeanours in the past and present. Not forgetting the alleged abuse taking place in several top ballet schools, whilst Charles and Camilla were Patrons. During the 70s Arthur Ashe and Billie Jean King were trying to overcome the racism and sexism that pervaded tennis, whilst Basil D'Olivera was being subjected to racism on the cricket field in the 60s. On the 18/7/ 2023, Channel 4 asked the question, Is Cricket Racist? The programme centred on Yorkshire cricket, where up until 1992, only people born in Yorkshire could play for the county. A bit like certain Scottish golf clubs where up until quite recently, women were not allowed to enter certain areas of the club house. As Monty Python, in Life of Brian, chanted, "Unclean, unclean bring out your dead." Without going into the many issues that the programme

covered, it found that related to Women's cricket, there was widespread misogyny, racism, sexism and chauvinism. In terms of racism generally, it found, since the Salman Rushdie Affair and 9/11, the racism was related to hate and abuse, and in particular, Islamophobia. Just before the 2023, Six Nations Rugby Championships, yet another damning documentary shown on Welsh television, highlighted the culture of bullying, racism, sexism etc. in Welsh rugby. In February 2024, an ITV documentary, Gymnastics: A Culture of Abuse? was shown. On 19/5/2025, The Dark Side of Swimming Clubs, was shown on Panorama, covering the issues of body/fat shaming, verbal and sexual abuse, inappropriate discipline, bullying, grooming, manipulation and young, female swimmers being made to train, whilst injured and ill, with lung infections. High-profile coaches such as John Rudd, David Painter and Anthony James were cited as being just some of the guilty parties. Of course, denials and mission statements by the individuals and SWIM ENGLAND abounded. Rudd being found guilty, after 17 witnesses testified against him. He was supposedly suspended for 4 months, but this never happened. Instead, his career blossomed and he moved to SWIM IRELAND and then to Canada. But James was eventually jailed for 21 years for, amongst other things, rape. As for Painter, he continued to claim the accusations against him were untrue and defamatory. Recent investigations going back over 20 years involving over 15,000 cases, looked at this TOXIC CULTURE in swimming where performance was more important than children's welfare. When does it all end?

Returning to men's football, but this time to the issue of sports agents, who it has been shown, have repeatedly broken the law by offering financial and other inducement to families of pre-adolescent children to sign for certain clubs, with the aim of cashing in on potential, young, footballing talent. And in some cases, the clubs involved being complicit in the practice. This practice being highlighted in a BBC, Panorama programme, Football's Broken Dreams, shown on 20/9/2021. It highlighted the practice of agents targeting single parent, lower social class families, who perhaps would be more vulnerable, or is that amenable, to such approaches? It also showed how scant regard was given to the youngster's mental health and physical wellbeing as they were under tremendous pressure to succeed. The factory farm mentality of the academies to find the next superstar, being the breeding ground for such activities, where the hope of making it in the cruel world of sport could be shattered at the drop of a hat or a young person's underpants. In March 2021 a 3-part, TV documentary, Football's Darkest Secrets, Abuse of Power, highlighted how teenage boys were physically, psychologically and emotionally traumatised, as a result of sexual abuse by youth team coaches, between the mid-1970s and mid-1990, and who for years were too frightened to speak out, for fear of being stigmatised. It was only when a tearful Andy Woodward appeared on a television interview, that others plucked up the courage to come forward. Between November 2016 and March 2018, 849 survivors came forward to the police in relation to historical sexual abuse in football. Most being ex professionals and even England internationals, with wives and families. Over 300 alleged suspects were identified, and 332 clubs were named. Because in the 1960s I was playing youth team football at Oldham FC, and wanting to become a professional footballer myself, the programme reduced me to tears, seeing these grown men crying on television because some power crazed, paedophile coach had ruined their lives. On March 17th 2021, 4 years after it launched the independent review into child sexual abuse in football, published its findings. **"We must do everything we can to ensure that we learn the lessons, and never see a repeat of this again."** I'm sorry to be cynical again, but have we not heard this rhetoric before, in not only football but in other sports and other walks of life?

THE ONLY THING INTELLIGENT HOMO SAPIENS HAVE LEARNT FROM HISTORY IS, THAT WE NEVER LEARN FROM HISTORY.

In August /September 2022, Channel 4 screened 6 programmes, Football Dreams: The Academy, but after 3 programmes, I stopped watching. To be honest, on the surface much appears to have changed in sport and in particular football, with many checks, or should that be cheques, and measures are now in place to try and avoid another Barry Bennison scandal. But has it? On the 15th August 2025, William Woods, a football coach, in the Crewe area was jailed for 31 years, for subjecting minors to a torrent of sexual and physical abuse. I do not doubt that in the year 2025, many personnel involved in the football academies, with specialist knowledge, skills, expertise and experience, who are trying to prepare these youngsters for the harsh realities of a possible life in football, have the best of intentions, but I ask at what price? We see how even if, these youngsters are not offered contracts at one club they move onto, or is it passed onto, another? But how many never make it, and again I ask, at what cost to these young impressionable minds? The programme was quite honest, as to the brutality of the success rate stating that, **"In the Academies, the pressure to perform never stops."** (Episode 3, 26/8/22). How many end up like some of the fathers shown on the programme trying to re-live their failures, through their own children? The programme highlighted several parents guilty of such practice using the excuse, 'I want what's best for my child,' or, 'It's what my child wants.' But wait a minute, have I not already discussed this subject during Chapter 1, Setting the Scene, Financial Planning, Self-respect, Children and Family Planning? Yes, but let's add more fuel to the fire. These children are barely out of nappies, and virtually have no experience of life itself, and need a moral compass, help and guidance, which is not based purely on materialistic criteria, but on emotional, psychological and physical wellbeing. For many viewers to hear some of these children, as young as 8, talking to camera as to what and who they would spend their money on, if they became professional footballers they would probably say, 'Ah, Bless', but for me it made me both sad and angry. To return to the topic of parenting and child rearing, where a loving caring, stimulating environment is essential, is a daily routine of testing, football drills and practices the answer? But no matter how well intentioned these adults involved in the process are, I suspect they themselves have been conditioned, if that's the correct word, and only see the world through blinkered eyes. **'There is nothing as certain as a closed mind,'** said Dean Spamley. Also, one must bear in mind that being filmed for a TV documentary, all the participants will want to show, 'Good Practice and Due Diligence', but the reality is often what goes on, when the camera stops rolling. Not that I'm suggesting malpractice, but just to say that it's human nature to put on your best face for the photo shoot. As for myself, being trained as a PE Primary School teacher, my training and experiences have been one of developing children, based on how they grow and develop at various stages in their lives **NOT** how much could they be worth in the future? **As far back as the 1980s research informed us, that sporting specialisation before and during puberty could lead to problems as the child grows and develops.** During the programme, they actually admitted that very few of the youngsters achieved their goal. My article, Children in Sport, written in the Sports Care Journal, in 1994, and my book, Sports Therapy, Theoretical and Practical Thoughts and Considerations, published in 2001, discussed such issues. It emphasised that, **CHILDREN ARE NOT MINI ADULTS physically, socially, psychologically or skilfully, but are growing organisms in the process of physical, and psychological adaptation, adjustment and development. (P103)**. Pointing out that, **"Prescription coaching, doesn't allow for individuality." (P99)**. And, **"Intensified training (for children) has no physiological or educational justification."** (Sports Health, 1991).

Whilst stating, **"Abuse can be verbal, emotional, physical, psychological and sexual, and many children are crucified physiologically, psychologically and as Peterson and Renstrom, 1986, put it, 'orthopaedically', long before they reach maturity."** (Briggs J, 2001, Sports Therapy, Theoretical and Practical Thoughts and Considerations, 2001. 1: part 6:99).

"The game is not the thing, the child is." (Margaret Talbot, PEA Fellows Lecture, 1987).

So again, I raise the question, as so-called intelligent beings, **what have we learned from history, what has changed, and will kneeling down before a game alter historical fact, culture and precedent? Answers on a postcard, please.** In 2016 Sam Allardyce, 'Big Sam', was sacked as England manager, after only being in situ for several months, for I believe, some indiscretion. In 2017, the manager of the Women's England's World Cup squad actually got his marching orders, after alleged racist behaviour towards one of the coloured players. In October, 2011, there was the Anton Ferdinand and John Terry racist language incident. A TV follow up programme, BBC TV, November 2020, 'Football Racism and Me', showed that 9 years later, such issues were still on the agenda. With Dee Albert, Psychotherapist, stating that, **"The initial reaction to racism is silence."** Was this directed at John Terry who, years after the event, it was alleged, had still not apologised to Anton? But personally speaking, racism has been endemic in society since I was born, in the 1950s. Just ask John Barnes the ex-England footballer. In 2020, the, Black Lives Matter, was the latest chapter in this on-going saga and I ask again, **will kneeling down before a game change the mind set of some of these power crazed, sexist, racist individuals?** Which other institution sacks its manager because he has supposedly failed by not gaining the club instant promotion, or he has committed some indiscretion or another, is then offered another job, with another club, probably on more money than he was on before? This said person then returning to his previous club, to buy some of the players who got him the sack in the first place. Interesting. **At times, the rhetoric used in football, now known as punditry and sometimes referred to as, 'clumsy phrasing', (Susanne Wrack, 30/12/20), is so inane, as to be farcical and with the rise of the women's game and its resultant increased media exposure, this is sadly not just restricted to the men's game.** Let's get the ball rolling, if you'll excuse the pun, with, **'That was a goal and a half.'** How can you score half a goal? **"He's got quick feet."** Does this mean the other players have slow feet? Referring to Helen Greenwood during the England v Japan game, 5th March, 2019, **"She's got a sweet left foot."** Obviously, her right foot being sour. This obsession with highlighting the players' feet should not cause concern as it is after all football, but at times the analysis is questionable. Lucy Ward, one of my favourite commentators/pundits, as she always makes me smile and shake my head, **likes to highlight feet as being cultured** during a Manchester derby, 13/2/22. Sometimes the commentators ask the question, **"How good is he with his feet?"** Are they seriously expecting some deep analytical, comparative reply by pointing out that some players can do more than just walk and run? **"Bonmati's feet are unreal,"** declares Rachel Finnis-Brown, during the Women's World cup final in August 2023. Does this imply that some players' feet are fake? **"Harder has the ability to glide with the ball at her feet."** (Lucy Ward, Chelsea v Man City, 9/2/22). Perhaps Harder should consider entering the Winter Olympics. But sometimes this issue of a player's feet, and where they are located can be a cause for concern as Lucy Ward informs us that in the same match, **"Chelsea are just finding their feet towards the end of this first half."** Excuse me, but are your feet not at the distal end of the tibia and fibula, before encountering the tarsals, metatarsals and phalanges? Siobhan Chamberlain during the Aston Villa v Manchester United women's game, 1/10/23, was quite impressed with Rachel Corse's defending, because to do so, she had to stand on her feet. Thanks for that, Siobhan. Referring back to my earlier references of, 'bending the ball like Beckham', we are told, during a women's football game between Manchester United and Chelsea, that, **"she opens up her hips and bends it in."** The mind boggles. The 'she' referring to Lauren J of Manchester United and that, **"the goal had woken Chelsea up, because during this second half they have been asleep."** Could that be classed as being over confident and disrespectful to the opposition? Should we ask the commentators on the game, Adam Somerton and Karen Carney? Sometimes total dismay enters the commentary when it is declared that, **"He's unplayable."** Referring to JJ after 55 minutes of the Liverpool versus Watford match, 16/10/21. What this observation suggests I am not quite sure. Perhaps if he's unplayable, the opposition should stop playing and just observe the 'Master Class'. During the Women's European Cup final, 31/7/22, Rachel Finnis Brown, got in on the act again by saying, after England scored the goal, **"England were unplayable, just as Germany have been unstoppable." This is the lady who considers time wasting as one of the roles of a goalkeeper, to help out her team mates,** (September 2022). Unfortunately, RFB, if I could be so bold as to use the title, used to, 'keep goal', but now as a pundit she has become like many others, 'thrown in at the deep end', an expert on every position on the pitch, including coaching and refereeing. Rachel, I am not questioning your goalkeeping skills, but please don't pontificate just to impress.

Again, but not surprising, another fixation appears to be related to the actual football. We are told, **"Not to put the ball at risk,"** (Cameroon versus Netherlands, 15/6/2019). However, Lucy Ward, Chelsea v Man City, 9/2/22, informs us, **"At some point, and quite early in this second half, City will have to put the ball at risk a little bit more in the final third."** This mantra being repeated in the Germany versus Spain and Germany versus France, July 2022, European Cup. Or, we need to, "Respect the ball more." How can you respect or put at risk an inanimate object? A living being yes, but a football that has not one shred of life in its entirety, I think not. You would have thought that kicking it for 90 plus minutes was enough abuse, but what do I know? Perhaps, if the male players respected the referee and their fellow/female competitors more, the game would be a far more entertaining, genuine and honest spectacle. Even managers such as Mark Skinner inform us that, **"We need to be more aggressive with the ball."** (Manchester derby, 27/2/2021). **"The ball was given away too cheaply,"** is another favourite comment. I'm thinking for how much and with so many foreign players, in which currency are they selling footballs? Are they using E Bay? Is Amazon involved? Is cashback involved? Will Brexit affect the price? From what I've heard of some of the demands made by player's agents before the player will sign a contract, I wouldn't be surprised if perhaps it's part of their contract, that they are allowed to sell so many footballs, buy so many free kicks and penalties, per season. On the question of retail therapy, we are also informed, (England versus the Czechs, 17/11/19), that football players can also now buy free kicks as it was clever play by Beth Mead, because after being fouled she was, **"Buying a free kick to get England on the front foot."** Oh no, now it would appear we have front and back feet as well as left and right, cultured, real and unreal, and not forgetting sweet and sour. Is the last phrase to cater for the Chinese players in the game? **Is that an ic, ist or an ism?** Also does it cost more to buy a penalty, as opposed to a free-kick? **We are also being educated, and I use that term loosely, via punditry, that footballers are also artists. No snide comments please, because they can now draw a foul.** What one looks like on paper or canvas I'm not sure, but there you go. What do I know? Jill Scott, herself now a pundit, has appeared as a model on Portrait Artist of The Year, November 2024, and so perhaps she could enlighten me. As a young child we played a game called, 'I draw a snake upon your back', which was done with your finger, and the person being abused, as would be the case in 2025, had to guess who was doing the drawing. I wonder if the game could now be called, 'I draw a foul'? **I've often wondered, why we now have professional fouls but not amateur ones?** Also, I was not aware, until educated by Siobhan Chamberlain, that Georgia Stanway, **"knows when to do a tactical foul."** (England v Brazil, 1/7/23). So now we can have tactical fouls.

Sometimes there is so much concern for the ball that we are told, **"They need to get hold of the ball and keep it for 5 minutes."** To be fair we all need a bit of tender loving care, a hug and a cuddle occasionally, but sometimes the rhetoric causes confusion. **"Perhaps France put the ball at risk too much in the first half,"** (France v Norway, 1st June, 2019). But a week later Japan, playing against Argentina, were criticised because, **"they don't put the ball at risk in the final third."** Whilst other teams, **"Need a bit more quality in the final third."** (Siobhan Chamberlain, Philippines v Switzerland, 20/7/21). Obviously, the final third of a football pitch could be too risky to take the ball into, but if the team has a bit more quality, these obstacles could be overcome. Sometimes, this quality issue can refer to the whole team as, **"England need to have more quality going forward,"** (England versus USA 2/7/19). However, all is not lost as no mention was made of going backwards. **Also, can someone please define the word quality for me in relation to football?** Of recent times I have been told, well not personally, that a foreign manager who had just taken over at a certain club, it was obviously his turn in the revolving door, had made a massive difference on the pitch and to team morale because, **"He had taught the team how to hold onto the ball better, and made them better at knowing when to pass."** Especially, as we are informed the said manager, **"Was a genius at manufacturing players."** I'm wondering what else he manufactures, whilst the players are busy buying free kicks and selling their footballs? I particularly liked Sarina Weigman's comment before the opening match World Cup game, England v Haiti, 22/7/23, when she said, **"If we're on the ball, they can't use it."** She unfortunately, didn't say whether or not the ball could be sold, which would obviously not please the agents. We are even informed that, **"today's players are getting better at knowing when to close the ball down."** What does that mean? Are there opening and closing times for footballs? Do footballs need a hug and a cuddle, because all the players do is abuse them? These are male Premier League, stratospheric, dominantly, one footed, superstar footballers on £550,000 plus a week, not Junior School children. Sometimes, it all becomes just too much with Jo Montemurro, before he left for pastures new, admitting, **"We couldn't find any solutions with the ball,"** and added, **"They also played,"** (Manchester versus Arsenal, November, 2020). What did he expect the opposition to do, have a picnic or like Chelsea, have a nap? Was this the reason he eventually left the club? During an Australia v Norway last 16 game, one team was, **"Asking a different question."** I thought this was football, not a police interrogation or oral examination. **"The boys got vision,"** I hear another analyst remark. Well, if he hadn't, he'd be blind and with no disrespect to the 2024 winner, perhaps he could appear on Strictly Come Dancing. Paul Merson decided to have a go. Does this also imply, that his team mates don't have any vision? In the FA ladies cup final, Chelsea versus Manchester City, 2018 to be precise, we were informed that for one player, **"Her vision had improved since moving to Barcelona."** Perhaps the opticians are more efficient in Spain, and maybe one of the reasons Keira Walsh decided on a move to Barcelona in 2022. Megan Rapinoe, one of the American players in the Women's World Cup final, in 2019, was singled out for special praise because, **"She's got quality vision."** Perhaps the rest of her team mates need to visit the opticians, to see if they can get their vision up to her standard. But perhaps, having good vision is not all that important, because after Sam Kerr scored the first goal in the league cup final on the 5th May, 2022, we were informed by the commentator, **"She didn't even need to look as she knew where** the goal was." As a sportsperson, I suppose it does help to have such insight. Another one of my favourite pieces of, **'clumsy phrasing'**, was given by Farah Williams, when she was 'punditing' on the Liverpool versus Arsenal women's game 23/10/22, when she remarked that, **"You can just see, when you take your eye off the ball."** With Seb Hutchinson, during the 2023, Women's World Cup, Brazil v Panama, 24/7/23, saying, **"Many teams would have difficulty seeing past Brazil and Panama,"** and then went on to become worried about, **"How much Panama will see of the ball."** Perhaps, he had forgotten that Barcelona was the place to go, to improve one's vision. Many years ago, long before 'punditry' superseded commentating, on the eve of a Liverpool versus Manchester United game, Gordon Strachan informed the listeners on the radio that the reason United were better than many of their opponents was, **"because they can trap, and pass a ball better."** I used to cover those basic skills when I taught in junior school, and you would have thought that being professionals, being paid a lot of money to ply their trade, they would have more sophisticated, physical skills. Evidently, trapping and passing well are not a 'gimme' for all teams. Years later, Robert de Pauw, during the Liverpool v Aston Villa match said of Missy B, **"She is good at passing and also knows where to find the goal."** Yes, it does help to have these skills as a footballer. Lucy Ward during the Italy v Argentine World Cup game informed us, that Italy were not making best use of the ball and although they, **"Were good in terms of passing, and one or two touch, but doing it in the wrong areas of the pitch."** Obviously, since I used to play football, the coaching manuals insist that you can only pass, and play two touch football in certain parts of the pitch. Does this take into consideration the fact, that some players might have stretched it and altered the dimensions? During a game on the 27th February 2019, England versus Brazil, in Philadelphia, after I was informed, not personally I might add, of the existence of, **'a clinical pass'**, I wondered if it could be related to, **'a clinical finish'**? If so, were they connected to the National Health Service, or would we need to go private, because during my training and pursuit of knowledge, anything clinical was related to healthcare? Let us move on, did you know some players in the modern game have, **"The ability to break between lines."** What, wind? Sometimes, **"She finds little pockets of space in between the units."** (Sue Smith, Manchester City versus Everton, Women's Cup Final, 2/11/20). Are we on a football pitch or an Industrial Estate? Whilst, **"Press started the move, dropping into a pocket to receive the ball."** (Manchester United v Tottenham, 24/4/21, commentators Vick Sparks and another). But they are not the only players who are, **"good at picking up pockets."** Ella Toon and Lauren James, according to Siobhan Chamberlain, (England v Brazil, 1/7/23), could just as easily join Fagin's crew of pick pockets. **Seriously, are we talking football here or crime, snooker and billiards?** Even cricket pundits have now been given 'the script' by introducing pockets into their analysis of the bat and ball game. **"He uses the space well."** Sometimes the whole team can influence the space. **"We stepped up and squeezed the space."** (Carla Ward, 15/1/21, Aston Villa v Man City). With Helen White, during the Chelsea v Aston Villa women's game, Sept. 2024, being impressed because a certain Vivianne Miedema was, **"Really smart at holding the space."** I believe these days players are allocated spaces and pockets, that they can fill, use, hold and squeeze, but must not wander out, for fear of getting lost, perhaps they needed a sat nav. or more significantly, substituted because they weren't doing what they were f...ing told. Don't forget the 'Modern Game' is all about processes, analysis, laptops and touchline conference debates. Accompanied by the obligatory arm waving and gestures. Not content with referring to units, spaces, lines and pockets, teams can now influence the dimensions of the pitch. **"That's when England have been at their most dangerous today, when they have stretched the pitch."** (Steph Hawkins and Siobhan Chamberlain commentating on the England Lionesses game against Austria, 27/11/21). On the 10th November 2024, Chelsea were better at opening up the pitch than Liverpool. Is that why they won, and not because they scored more goals than the opposition? However, during a Netherlands v Portugal game, 23/7/23, Robin Cowen and Anita Asanti were worried because, **"Nobody was stretching the back line."** But that girl Harder of Chelsea is singled out again, but this time for her immense strength. **"Harder's causing a lot of problems, where she's picking up areas she's causing a problem for City."** (Lucy Ward, 6/2/22). Obviously, all that weight training was starting to pay dividends for Miss Harder. But what about if a player comes across, 'an intelligent space'? No worries, as Anita Asanti, during a France v Morrocco game, 8/8/23, tells us that the French player Dall, **"picks up intelligent spaces."** I'm wondering, if football players can influence spaces and areas, can they alter the dimensions of the property they live in? **"They are playing a flat back four,"** is another piece of information to help the viewer appreciate the finer technical details of the beloved game. However, I've been informed that in certain American states, 'flat backers', is a slang term for prostitutes. Is this then the reason the men take off their clothes, when they score a goal and dive on the floor, so their mates can then lie on top of them? Perhaps the dancing around the corner flag prior to this, is a foreplay ritual, who knows? Perhaps, it's part of their contract, that sex can follow after scoring a goal. Don't ask, you certainly won't get an honest answer, and are more likely to receive a Glasgow kiss free of charge. Also, the players always seem to lie face down, and not on their backs and so perhaps they are suffering an identity crisis, allowing their mates to dive on them from behind. No comment. Whilst on the subject of sex, during the European Championships in June 2021, in an analysis session involving Gabby Logan and another pundit, sorry but the name escapes me, the viewers were informed that, **"we need to see more of him opening his legs." No comment.** And did you know that, according to Sue Smith, Kim Weir, **"can open up a side."** Which, left, right, in or outside? Are we talking football here or a can of beans? Sometimes from the amateur touch line we hear, **"Stand him up, stand him up,"** accompanied by the odd eff and geff. I wonder, from whom they got that gem of coaching advice, Lilleshall, Bisham Abbey or wherever they run the courses these days.? In my day when you scored you got a handshake, with most sports now having progressed to, 'high fives', or a, 'fist bump', but in men's football you now run the risk of getting covered in love bites or being buggered. Sometimes the punditry advice of, 'Stand him up', is given directly to six-foot five-inch goalkeepers, when an opposing player is coming towards them at speed, **"You must make yourself big,"** is the advice. How big I ask myself? Perhaps RF Brown can educate me, but I warn you Rachel I'm only five, four. If the player concerned was any taller, he/she wouldn't fit under the crossbar. Could this piece of advice be related to the now common piece of punditry of teams, **"growing into the game."** (Siobhan Chamberlain, Australia v New Zealand, 20/7/23?). I'm aware of child development growth spurts but I'm a little confused as to what this has to do with adult football. In the 2020 Olympics, during the GB v Chile game, Sue Smith was at it again, stating that she was worried about Chile as **"it was a team that was growing."** Despite the fact that many of the Chile players were over 30 years of age, or perhaps Chileans have very, very, late growth spurts. During a Chelsea game during the 2023 season, we were informed that, **"Lily Bright grew into the first half."** Whilst Georgia Stanway, **"has grown into her position."** (Siobhan Chamberlain, England v Brazil, 1/7/23). Mark Chapman commenting on the Match of the Day, Tottenham v Chelsea game, informed us that one player, **"made himself smaller instead of bigger."** Moving from growing to jumping, during an England v South Africa final, we are informed that a certain player when jumping for a high ball when moving, **"owns the air."** Obviously, football is moving into the airline industry. Matt Bee, the assistant coach at Blackburn Rovers women, during the 2/10/22 season, sent a message onto the field to tell a player, that when she jumped for the ball to head it she had to jump higher. I was standing only metres away from him. More on Mr Bee shortly.

I repeat once again, where does it all end?

Footballers are already buying and selling free kicks, penalties and footballs; manufacturing players; filling, using, holding and squeezing lines, pockets and spaces; not forgetting the ability to open their legs, stretch a pitch and pick up areas of such, but now they want to own the air. Not forgetting that football is now a game, that during the match, players and teams can, if they so wish, irrespective of growth spurts and such like, grow into games, or particular positions. None of which was available to my brother and me, when we played football for Chadderton Lancashire and Oldham Athletic football club. Are we jealous? Are we envious? **NO. On the 26/12/2023 Sam Allison was the first black referee in 15 years, to referee a Premiership game, whilst Rebecca Welch, a female, refereed the Fulham v Burnley men's football match.** Well, it's a start – 'small steps' springs to mind. During a Blackburn Rovers women's game, 2/10/22, at which I was in attendance, I am after all a season ticket holder, I heard and noted the following instructions from the touchline, from Mr M. Bee, the then assistant coach at Blackburn Rovers, who always appeared to be on the verge, or is that the touchline, of a nervous breakdown? Starting 15 minutes after the kick off, these were his pearly words of coaching wisdom, **'Tuck her in', 'Pin her in', 'lock her in', 'Hook in', 'Squeeze her in', second by second, 'Open up and delay'.** As mentioned, this was the guy who in a previous match had sent a message onto the field, to tell a player that when she jumped for the ball to head it she had to jump higher. No wonder some of the girls look disillusioned, with all these instructions being thrown at them every few minutes. I also heard the Leicester boss shouting to his girls to, **"Get 'em off"**. No comment. Here are a few questions for Mr Bee. Mr Bee, are you aware that these girls are part-timers? How many instructions can a teenage /early twenties female absorb, assimilate and put into practice in the space of 10 minutes? Mr Bee, have you EVER attended a course on Motivation? Mr Bee, has it ever crossed your mind that the girls are trying their best. Giving them a hug, (oh dear!) and high fives, during warm up and as they leave the pitch, is not fooling anyone. **POWER YOU CAN TAKE, BUT RESPECT YOU HAVE TO EARN.** When Gemma Donelly left the club at the end of the 2022- 2023 season, she was replaced by Simon Parker who brought in his 'own team', of, as far as I can tell from the stand, **ALL MEN**. The only coaching staff to remain was Mr Bee. I've also noted that on match days, most of the touchline shouting and aggressive behaviour is coming from the men, not the women. As for my fellow spectators standing next to me, I hear comments such as, **'What the fuck have they got a man and a woman as linesmen for, surely it should be two men?'** But abuse in all its many guises, both on and off the pitch, at all levels of men's football is nothing new. During a Manchester United v Millwall game, 18th March, 2023, 2 players and a manager were red carded, with many neutral commentators concerned about this violence setting a terrible example to youngsters watching the game. Personally speaking, I would also be concerned if it was during my playing days, but today many youngsters are subjected to so much violence by what they are allowed to see on television and their games' consoles, that I think they have become immune to its significance. **Since watching Blackburn Rovers Ladies live, home games, I have never heard any female manager or coach from either team come out constantly with foul language.** From some players yes, but not the boss. I'm not daft, women swear but they don't see it as something they need to demonstrate to identify their gender superiority. **"Twenty–four-year-old girl, forty –three –year-old man. Pretty much parity in terms of emotional development, I'd say."** (Elton B, 2003, High Society, PB, P145).

As mentioned, I've had my share of verbal and physical abuse in the past, when I've deemed to offer an opinion, or a tongue in cheek observation, on the game of football. I was once pinned up against a wall at Lilleshall, and asked if I was taking the f...ing piss, when I informed my male attacker that football was a simple game, in that the team that scored the most goals was the winner. How did he know I had an irritable bladder, and was on medication for my condition of frequent toilet visits? But I accept the game has, 'moved on', and scoring goals would appear **NOT** to be the primary object of the exercise anymore. It is now a game that from the kick off, the ball **MUST** travel backwards toward your own goalkeeper, or is it now a minder so he/she can get an early feel of the ball? Ah, bless. The game plan being to, 'play out from the back', by seeing how many passes can be made sideways and backwards. Meanwhile, whilst this is happening, the opposition can pop off to the touch line for light refreshments, only needing to return to the gladiatorial arena, when the ball enters their half of the field, which could take ages, or they've been told to implement**, a press.** And even if the ball does arrive in and around the opposition goal area, the same plan is adopted. How many passes can we make, before the team is left with very little option but to shoot at goal. No wonder, shots on goal are now an integral part of the statistics for the game, because they are a rarity. Also, if a player just out of instinct takes a shot at goal from outside the box and scores, they are immediately hailed as, 'something special'. When my brother and I played we, like all soccer mad youngsters, practised for hours trying to improve our skills. Drills such as 'keepy uppy' and trying to score a goal from the corner flags by swerving the ball, using both the outside and inside of our feet. Now known as, 'bending the ball like Beckham'. We also practised relentlessly, taking penalty kicks so the ball went into the top and bottom corners of the goal. Whilst training at Manchester United and Oldham, I spent many hours aiming to land my crosses, from all areas of the field, but mainly the dead ball line, onto the penalty spot where I expected my centre forward to be. If during a game we didn't have at least a 90% success rate of shots on goal, we thought we'd had a poor game. This was long before coaches attended places such Bisham Abbey, Lilleshall and such like to get their coaching awards and badges, so they could come up with such mind-blowing tactics of playing one person, 'up front', so they can pontificate about why their team wasn't scoring many goals. **"The teams lost its shape."** Does this mean their arms have fallen off? But fear not, according to Lucy Ward, 9/2/22, **"Chelsea's shape out of position is very good."** Staying with Lucy Ward and why not, during a ladies Manchester derby match, 13/2/22, referring to Hayley Ladd of Manchester United, she informed the viewers, **"You only realise how good a player she is, when she is not playing." I think at this moment in time this is one of my all-time pieces of, 'clumsy phrasing', with the expression, 'Engage your brain before opening your mouth', springing to mind.** Things are getting so ridiculous that Gilly Flaherty suggests **"Asseyi, needs to stay more in the box and be alive."** WHU v Arsenal 4/2 24. Well yes, it does help if you've not already passed away, Gilly. This style of commentary, **NOT** evident when Kenneth Wolstenholme commentated on the Football World Cup in 1966, or Bill McClaren on the rugby, has slowly crept in since television coverage of the beloved game now ensures there are more pundits in the studio and pitch side, than there are actual players on the pitch, including the officials, ball boys and substitutes, all with varying degrees of communication skills. Or should I say lack of? When I was much younger Joan Bakewell took elocution lessons, before being offered a job at the BBC. Today street slang and bastardised English seems totally acceptable**, Ye no wot, like I'm finkin bruvah. What has happened to commentating with clarity, professionalism and common sense be men or women?** Television coverage also now ensures that at least half a dozen replays, at varying speeds, can be seen to definitively prove that a player actually slid into the tackle with ALL studs showing, with the intention of permanent damage to the opponent. Just so the said player could tell his boss that he, 'took him out of the game', as requested. But even then, the pundits won't come to a unanimous decision, about whether or not the player should have been sent off or not. Let alone be banned indefinitely, which will then lead on to another studio debate as to the integrity and qualifications of the match officials. Meanwhile, the pundits have missed another 10 minutes of the game because they are too busy arguing. Bottom lip pouting, baby and bath water are expressions that immediately spring to mind. Grow up why don't you, or should I say, make yourself tall? Sadly, football is not alone in slow motion, video analysis debates that at times, can take up almost half of the programme's allotted time slot. To re-iterate, I find it amusing that as a sportsperson's career is coming to an end, they are invited to become a pundit, and suddenly become an expert on every position and every aspect in their chosen sport. **So, I ask again are we meant to take their observations and analysis seriously? I often wonder, when people are asked to be a pundit/commentator, if their communication skills are taken into consideration, or are they just given a script of ludicrous, meaningless and inane expressions, that must be included in their commentary or analysis?** And dare I suggest, they also should be encouraged to at least try and speak grammatically correct English and common sense, irrespective of their regional accents. After all, is that not what they are paid for, to commentate, NOT to initiate the viewer into slang, bastardised, English, text speak terminology? The inability of certain commentators /pundits to pronounce basic letters, blends, phonemes etc., is shocking. **A TH blend is NOT an F,** which is what I used to teach in Primary schools, is alarming, to say the least. One of my many roles was to help children, pupils, students, develop their language skills. I then moved on to lecturing on Communication in Universities. But it would appear that with the advent of smart phones and modern technological gadgetry it doesn't really matter, or should I say ma er, what comes out of your mouth. I accept that for some, English is not their first language, and have taken into consideration regional accents etc. Now you've done it, Briggsy, you can't say that. You can't be HONEST. More ics, ists and isms, social media and the 'boys club' will definitely target you and want you electrocuted at least. That's if they can get a grant to pay for the increased cost of electricity, post Brexit. Burn him at the stake, crucify him, remove his testicles? Obviously, it's the teachers' fault they don't speak as one would expect? **Does it matter? Well yes, it does, otherwise why historically, have teachers bothered teaching children to read and speak correctly? Why offer degrees in English language? Why is English language considered a subject in its own right?** Who decided and when that correct pronunciation was to become a thing of the past, superseded by rap slang all in the name of progress, or were they just being lazy because they couldn't be bothered to put their tongue between their teeth to pronounce TH?

I also, cannot leave the subject of pundits, commentators and interviews, without considering what qualifications do interviewers need, to be given such a role on television, and I'm not just referring to sport? **As I've mentioned, certainly for some not a command of the English Language.** I've lost count of the times I have heard an announcer use bastardised English by pronouncing TH as F, such as, "Next is a friller that's deeper than you fink," BBC Sunday night, 6/2/22. Or by lazily not bothering to pronounce the letters at the ends of words so that running becomes runnin and riding becomes ridin. When did the letter T become obsolete or a double e or an i so that party became pa ee or pa i? My tutors at teacher training college must be holding their heads in disbelief, that's if they could perform such a feat? I have also lost track of the number of times an interviewer has asked the most inane, stupid question? Just like some of the pundits, are these supposedly intelligent life forms given a script, or are they just not aware of the ridiculousness of the questions they ask, and are television bosses not bothered about using Queen's English? Sorry, should that now be King's English? Or are these questions asked to create, good television because the viewer wants to know? Deeply, analytical probing questions, which must include phrases such as, well, going forward and what would winning mean to you? Questions such as: **How important is it to keep up the intensity? OR, to go through the structures and processes?** During the European Indoor Athletics championships, 3/3/2023, Janette Kwakye asked Daryl Nita, **"What would winning a gold medal mean to you?"** What would happen if Daryl replied, "Fuck all?" Let's consider more questions and possible replies. **"Do you think winning the competition/a gold medal will change your life?"** Reply, "Not one jot." "How significant was that last minute, winning goal that stopped the club being relegated?" Reply: "Actually now I come to think of it, it wasn't in the slightest bit significant." "I can see you are upset, but can you tell us how you are feeling?" (Winter Olympics, 2022). If I was that person, I would have head butted the interviewer and replied, "Does that answer your stupid question?" In the 2021 Tokyo Olympics, Matthew Pinsent, when interviewing Imogen Grant, rower, after she failed to achieve her goal by one hundredths of a second, asked, "How does that leave you feeling?" Why she didn't poke him in the eye with a paddle/oar or knee him in the groin, I have no idea. During the European Championships in 2022, Non Stanford won gold in her last triathlon before retirement. Mr. Pinsent asked her, "What will be the emotion, when you finally take off that tri-suit and pack up that GB kit for the last time?" Reply: "I won't feel a thing, Matthew, other than to think what to cook for tea." During an interview with Hannah Blundell by Jane Mc Dougal, Hannah was asked, "How much would it mean to the club to win a trophy?" Followed by, "How much will being in front of home fans, be an advantage?" "In answer to your first question, Jane, "Jack shit," and to the second, "No advantage what so ever, happy?" Whilst in other sports a driver is asked, "Do you think getting a puncture during the final lap cost you the race?" Reply: "No, I wouldn't have won anyway, because I intended to crash on the last lap anyhow." Another one of my favourite comments regarding sport occurred, when Ash Goulding of Huddersfield Giants rugby league club was asked for his opinion of James Roby, during a Salford v St Helens rugby game, 13/5/23. Roby was a player who had made 574 appearances, a career and club record for St Helens. "You cannot put into one word, what he's achieved, it's immortal," he replied. Finally, how does one create, 'Good television coverage'? Is it part of an interviewer's role, to cause people in tears greater distress? During the 2024 Paris Olympics, a female diver, whose father was a famous French celebrity, was distraught for many reasons, informing the interviewer that 12 months ago, she had contemplated suicide. So did the interviewer show her compassion, console her, give her a hug or a cuddle? No, instead he wanted the gritty details, just to increase her depression, sadness and upset. This was a world-wide sporting event, not a documentary on euthanasia and suicide. And please don't tell me he would have got into trouble by showing empathy and compassion, because that would further demonstrate how bad things have become. In fact, if further evidence is needed, during an Invincibles v Trent Rocket's cricket match, 14.8.24, Finn commented that one of the players, Zampa, **"Had a lovely earring."** In true Briggs tradition, I could go on and on, and on, because I cannot un-know what I know, and will **NEVER** apologise for my knowledge, skills, expertise, qualifications and experience, but I won't. Hopefully, the reader gets the idea, and I've no hesitation or doubt in saying the reader will also have many examples themselves, that could be included here. **But beware, social media will hunt you down, troll you, create vindictive hatred and force you into considering suicide, if you dare to be honest and embarrass someone with the truth.**

Referring to personal experiences, when my brother and I played football by the time we ran onto the pitch, we knew what our role was and what to do to deal with the 'What if, scenarios', called, 'on the field decision making'. But in today's technological world, before a substitute goes onto the field for the last 60 seconds of the game, so they have time to make an impact, they need to have an updated, laptop lecture/tutorial/lesson of what is expected of them. It's called PROGRESS. Or is it just another excuse to tap, scroll and swipe to satisfy the daily fix? At this point, I would like to refer to an interview Emma Hayes, the then Chelsea Ladies manager, gave with Tom Garry in January 2024, in relation to Eni Aluko, Lucy Ward and Joey Barton's attacks on female pundits. Whilst mine are just examples of 'clumsy phrasing', his was personal. But then with his track record, whilst being a professional player what did you expect? Emma saying misogynistic comments about female pundits are symptomatic of a "sexist society" within English football. In 2024, she was to have an altercation with the Arsenal manager because of his aggressive behaviour during the game. She also said that the issue was "more prevalent here", compared to the USA. An interesting observation, considering she had just accepted the job as head of the USA national ladies' squad, and was leaving Chelsea at the end of the season. Her opinions also highlighted many of the topics I've discussed, whilst writing this book. She said, **"If you think about lots of things in the last 10 years in this country, from Brexit, to our populism, to our division in politics, for me, this is just another moment that's escalated because sadly, a little bit of social media can create such a divide, in such a vitriolic way, instead of us having 'sensible conversations'. Unfortunately, you can't do that at this moment in time."**

Although I could continue with my observations, it's not rocket science to see why since 1966 the men's England national team has not led the world in football. If you flood the English leagues with many foreign imports, in both management and playing staff, the opportunity for home grown talent to develop is restricted, and the English manager has a relatively small pool of players with the necessary skill set and experience to choose from. All sports in England are now searching for any talented individual, who has the merest tenuous link to being a UK citizen, to poach them from another country. Or perhaps the pool of young talent is small, because of the various forms of abuse they have been subjected to, during their early development. Kevin Keegan in his autobiography, My Life in Football, 2018, was refreshingly candid about this reluctance of the big clubs to give male English talent a chance, despite nurturing it in the academies, and the exultation of foreign managers who park their bus and are called defensive maestros. **Don't forget one of the main reasons for Brexit was, the claim that 'foreigners' were taking up jobs that were meant for the UK residents, and these 'foreigners' should be sent back to where they came from. Interesting. Many ardent supporters still love football but HATE the industry. It's been very sad for me that over the years, since considering football as a career in the 1960s, and watching my local team Oldham Athletic, play in front of 12,000 plus spectators and win the FORD SPORTING LEAGUE, to have become totally and utterly bored and disillusioned with the men's game I used to love.** At times, it just appears to be paid, macho thuggery, and not a competition of skill versus skill. **As our national sport, it sets a terrible example to young impressionable minds.** Why don't they just do away with the referee, not literally, and after entering the gladiatorial arena, pair off and have 11 fights, with or without boxing gloves, accompanied by the compulsory swearing and spitting, and the team with the most bouts won and most mucus/phlegm expelled, being declared the winner, with the resultant bragging rights until the next 'match'? Or perhaps they could just stay in the changing rooms, and have a pissing competition to see which players could urinate the highest up the wall. I know of one ex England player who had not only a drink problem, but also a reputation for urinating anywhere and everywhere. What about a penis measuring contest?

Year after year, the public have been subjected to the rhetoric and hype, waiting for yet another scandal, knowing full well that nothing would change. Money, greed, power, a closed shop toxic mentality and jobs for the boys, easily springs to mind. Like politics and religion, the questions are always the same it's just the answers that keep getting swapped around. What has happened to the Busby and Shankly mantra of, football should be a team game played to entertain the working man? Now working man needs to earn a small fortune, or to have won the lottery or pools, just to afford to buy a ticket to go and watch their local team spitting, swearing, posturing, play acting, dancing, diving, inciting the crowd with histrionics, and pleading absolution for their crimes, after abusing or trying to con the referee. During the spring/summer of 2023, whilst on holiday in Europe, I watched a few minutes of the Manchester City v Inter Milan cup game, before becoming bored and deciding to go for a walk instead. The amount of negativity, hatred and abuse, both on and off the pitch was farcical, yet frightening. I was thinking, why do they bother trying to pretend this is a skilful sporting competition between two teams? **To repeat, will kneeling down on one knee change a systemic, endemic mind set, and much of the bad practice that has been entrenched in men's football, since I was a teenager seeking fame and fortune as a Lancashire schoolboy in the 1960s?** Personally speaking, I think not. Would Mr Busby still be proud of Mr Giggs who, between August 2017 and November 2020, it was alleged assaulted Emma and Kate Grenville, both describing him as scheming, manipulative and devious? Are we meant to still appreciate Mr Rooney, who admitted in a Channel 4, documentary, 'Rooney',20.11.23, that he frequently went out with his mates looking for a fight and sometimes wore longer studs because he wanted to, 'hurt somebody', during a Manchester United v Chelsea game. But I suppose, if you are hailed as one of the finest, by scarring opposition players, who probably had partners and children, so they ended up on crutches, was acceptable just so Mr Rooney could prove to the onlookers what a pathetic, childish, brat could do, if he didn't get his own way. Many arguing, 'Winning at all cost', is the name of the game, whilst football's toxic mentality once again reared its ugly head. I found it interesting that during the programme, whilst many admitted he was, 'a hot head', no mention was made of anyone wanting to pour ice cubes over his skull or help him, by offering Anger Management help and advice. Sometimes referred to as, 'Toxic Time Outs', to curb aggression and temper tantrums. No wonder, Colleen escaped into the jungle. Instead, football decided to offer him various football management posts, before realising he wasn't very good at that, and politely suggested he consider alternative employment.

Having said all that, I recall my time at Lilleshall with a smile on my face. I learned plenty, especially on the rehabilitation side of things, and thank goodness not all the lads and lasses ate, slept and drank men's football. After meeting up with Paul Miller, on several occasions after Lilleshall, me travelling south and he north, I introduced him to the game of rugby league. He asked me the same question, that has been asked time and time again by many observers, **"Why doesn't football adopt the same refereeing standards as rugby, with the players giving the referee the same respect?"** I recall many years ago an ex professional player and high-profile manager, who I will diplomatically not name for fear of retribution, physical harm or being trolled, being asked the same question. His reply, as I can remember, was along the lines of that there wouldn't be many players left on the park at the end of the game. Whether this was said with tongue in cheek or to dismiss the question as trivial, I'm not sure. Years later, during two rugby league, televised games, in June 2023, two players were first yellow carded and then red carded, for verbally abusing the referee during the first 15 minutes of the game. The decisions were accepted by all, on and off the pitch and the match continued. One team actually winning the game, after playing the remainder of the game with only 12 players. If that had been men's football, the heated discussion would still be raging with heart attacks pending, and retribution would be in the advanced planning stage. Finally, so as not to incur the total wrath of most of the male population, I did watch most of England v Malta's televised game, 17/11/23, where the commentary team of Steve Bower and Dion Dublin, did just that, commentate on the game. Thank you, gentlemen. Unfortunately, the 3 half time 'pundits' were not as obliging with their bastardised, English rhetoric and bullshit. So, Briggsy, what is your solution? Well, I now regularly turn off the sound on the television and play a CD whilst watching the action. I've also stopped supporting Blackburn Rovers Ladies, since the club decided to relegate them to part timers on minimal wages, whilst still retaining its mainly all male coaching staff. In other words, I've tried to eliminate the stressors. 'Silly but it's true what loneliness can do', sang Susan Maughan in the 60s.

The Society of Sports Therapists.

As mentioned, I met Graham Smith as one of my tutors at Lilleshall, but after my first year, I heard he had left Lilleshall, under somewhat of a cloud to go back into football with Glasgow Rangers. I think one of the issues Graham had, was the development of the course, to include all sports in the injury and rehabilitation course, and not restrict it to just football. Obviously, being run by such a closed shop as the FA, this was, personally speaking, never going to happen. Enter Keith Waldron, or Waldo as he was known to his friends, who like Graham Smith was a Chartered Physiotherapist, who worked in football with people such as Terry Venables and, if my memory serves me correctly, had been assistant manager at Portsmouth FC. Keith was the one to see, if you needed an entry into the world of the FA. Graham was running his own sports rehabilitation courses, Sports Rehab and Education, from an office in Glasgow, and Keith was building up a business of private sports injury clinics mainly down south. It was Keith Waldron along with Graham Smith, who first mooted the idea of a Society of Sports Therapists, which would be an umbrella **organisation, that would include all sports and therapies.** This would not be as direct competition to the FA course, but as an alternative for people not necessarily wanting to work in football. Unfortunately, the politics kicked in and this organisation, if established, would be seen to challenge the idea that only Chartered Physiotherapists were suitably trained and qualified to treat musculo-skeletal problems and 'sports injuries'. An argument that I and my fellow colleagues in the massage world had been fighting against, since I first entered the world of physical therapy. Graham and Keith, although Chartered, appreciated the fact that there were suitably trained and qualified people out in the real world, working in Complementary Medicine, that were also working in, or attached to, sports clubs that were not Chartered Physiotherapists. Citing me and some of the people trained at the NIM, as examples. In fact, of the 33,000 Chartered Physiotherapists working at that time, only a few thousand actually worked in sport, and that was only after they had attended a post graduate course in sports injury management. Also, many of these were not actually sport participants themselves, but just liked the idea of working in sport. The goal for the SST was, to train individuals who had a background in sport, either as a participant, coach, teacher etc. with, from day one, sport as its main emphasis. Chartered physiotherapists, with all due respect, are trained primarily to work in the National Health, where the bulk of the work was with the elderly, stroke and heart attack patients. Obviously, anatomy, physiology and pathology are generic to both camps, but sporting mentality is what separates them. Unless you understand the psychology of sports people, you are never successfully going to treat them. As for the term sports injury, a sprained ankle is a sprained ankle, no matter what the aetiology and should be treated accordingly. However, the person whose ankle has been injured, can seriously affect its recovery. In simplicity, it was a case of horses for courses. After Graham left the FA in 1989, he contacted many of the students he had met whilst working at Lilleshall, outlining his and Waldo's ideas and that is when I became involved. I joined the Society in 1990, and became member 49. I started working for Graham on his Sports and Rehab courses, mainly at Keele University, after a chance meeting at a Stratford hotel that was the venue for his annual Sports Conference. I had taken Penny Walker with me, as Professor Craig Sharp was one of the speakers, a physiologist who worked with many top athletes, including Steve Redgrave the 5 times Olympic gold medallist in rowing. Knowing I played sport, taught it, was a coach in several disciplines, and that I was teaching massage at the NIM, Graham must have seen me as an ideal person to bring on board, not only to be a tutor on his own courses, but also to possibly assist in the development of the SST aims. **The ultimate aim was to have a pool of tutors, preferably with teaching qualifications, as well as** backgrounds in sport, who could not only deliver the course, but develop it into a multi-sport organisation. In other words, walk the walk and talk the talk. During the time I worked for Graham, I found him to be a good employer, and enjoyed working with people such as Reg Brassington, Mark Eales, Paul Darby, Sandra Airey, and Debbie Annett, who treated jockeys. Although, Graham and I may have disagreed on certain aspects of the teaching of massage, we became good friends and I got to know his wife Alison, a wee Scottish lass, who had nursed Graham back to good health, after a serious road traffic accident in South Africa had almost ended his life. Recently I watched a Runrig concert on TV, which was to be their farewell concert and I recall Graham and Alison taking me to a Runrig concert, complete with tartan scarf, in Glasgow, many years previously. Graham introduced me to Marianne Tidswell, who was course director for the Chartered Physiotherapy course at Keele University, and at the time was looking for someone to teach the massage aspects of the Chartered Physiotherapy course. But upon learning it was **only 12 hours in total,** I declined. No wonder, Graham and I disagreed, but he must have appreciated my expertise to recommend me. Or was it because Reg Brassington had **actually** seen me teach before 'singing my praises' to Mr Smith? Thank you, Reg. Unfortunately, the more I got to know Graham, I realised that he was somewhat of an insecure, dare I say, control freak, and it was alleged, used and associated only with people who would benefit his cause? He sometimes expected the red-carpet treatment wherever he went, and gained a reputation for throwing a hissy fit, if he didn't get his own way. For some, this could be intimidating. For me, it was more experience in my human behaviour journey. Certain aspects of the sports world, as seen through the eyes of Graham, were certainly not open for discussion, and there was a succession of people who suddenly disappeared from the scene. Well, not literally, as I was aware he didn't have links to professional assassins. Joke. Once someone had upset him for whatever reason, Graham would usually jettison them from his thought processes. Also, as he sometimes was a key witness in physiotherapy trial cases, he was not a person that others wanted to upset. He was definitely not happy, when on one occasion I reminded him that I had trained initially for three years specifically to be a PE teacher, and then attended many courses related to teaching after that, and was not, like many, someone who had just stuck a one year post graduate teaching certificate on the end of a degree. Many years later, when he got his professorship, he started to expect the red-carpet treatment more often. Don't get me wrong, I never doubted Graham's knowledge, skill and expertise on the rehabilitation side of sport, and he taught me so much, but he could be a little dismissive of anyone proffering an alternative, as to how he perceived all things sporty, and at times lacked a little humility. I also knew that, because initially I had chosen to work in Primary Schools, Graham always viewed me as a, 'light weight', because I enjoyed laying the foundations and working with pupils/students at the beginning of their studies. Whereas, I think Graham Neil Smith preferred them when they had been sanitized, and did not ask too many questions or create too many problems. To me, lecturing was relatively easy after trying to teach 35, 4 and 5 year old children to read on a daily basis, but I'm not sure if Graham realised, that to teach youngsters you had to have many strings to your bow and many tools in your tool box, not least of all the ability to consider other alternatives to the script. If he did, he certainly didn't demonstrate such pedagogical skills in my presence. Whilst I respect the efforts of all who work in education, for me, different age groups need different skill sets. For me, lecturing was all about putting acetates on an overhead projector, or power points to show on a screen, whilst delivering the script and exiting stage left. Teaching involves having 35 plus pupils, from 0900 to 1600, with very little respite, at least 5 days a week. During my training, I was once asked, 'How do you know for certain that the message you think you are giving to your pupils/students, is the same message they are receiving?' **In my humble opinion, teaching and**

lecturing are not the same. I think most teachers I have worked with could lecture, but I doubt if many lecturers could teach effectively. I was grateful to Graham for the opportunities he gave me, the doors he opened and his initial friendship, but I wasn't daft and knew at some time my turn would come to exit the revolving door. Since resigning from UCLAN some 17 years ago, I've never spoken to Graham. He once told Steve Smelt to ask me to phone him, but why couldn't he phone me himself? Despite his protestations, he was a football man with a football mentality, which eventually led to me leaving the Society. Sadly, football was never very far away from steering the society ship, in spite of what some would have you believe. When I first signed up to the cause it was meant to be a multi-disciplinary, sports organisation, not a stopping off post for the football fraternity, until another job became available back in football. Having said all that, I always enjoyed working with students who had not only paid to be on the courses, but were there because they wanted to be and not because they had to be. It makes teaching so much easier, as all your preparation and efforts are appreciated. I loved working on the GPs in Sport weekends, the only downside being they were sponsored by pharmaceutical companies such as Lederle. On them we lectured and ran workshops for GPs, to make them more aware of what was available for referral in not only complementary, but also allopathic medicine. Again, this gave me an opportunity to not only work alongside the medical profession, but also with people such as Colin Still, a GB gymnastics coach. There was usually a doctor from Northern Ireland, whose name for the life of me I cannot recall, who became a regular fixture as part of Graham's 'team', that I particularly liked spending time with.

Finally, how the Society decided to offer degree programmes, and how I was persuaded to return to full time education to teach on the very first programme, albeit for a short while, will be explained later.

My First Clinic: Eaves Lane and the Crown Prosecution Service.

Initially, I set up a treatment room in the front bedroom at Alandale, mainly to practice in and decided to take each day as it came. Sadly, Dee had gone to live with her sister Brenda, in Eccles, whilst I continued living in Alandale Drive, Royton trying to sort out my future and where to live. Sooner, rather than later, we would have to sell Alandale, and I would have to find suitable premises to use as a clinic to start up my business as a physical therapist. Having a background in sport, especially football and gymnastics, and being a PE teacher and coach, helped me to spread the word that I was setting up practice as a physical therapist, and slowly but surely, I managed to attract patients, not least from the local Royton Cricket and Tennis Club. I also managed to get onto the local speakers' circuit, giving talks to local groups, Townswomen's Guilds and Lions in exchange for publicity and free food for my efforts. Eventually, we decided to sell Alandale, and Dee bought a house on Hollins Lane, Bury, whilst I found a house on Eaves Lane that would suit my purposes very nicely.

26, Eaves Lane was chosen as my first clinic, because it was an end terrace, provided parking spaces and was on a bus route, but its main selling point for me was, that it was opposite the South Chadderton Health Centre, a definite plus in terms of projecting a more professional image. Eaves Lane was a seminal time for me professionally, and to a lesser degree personally, in that it signified a definite break with my past married life, as a full-time teacher in education, to an uncertain future as a single person, as a sole trader, in a new profession. Obviously, one can never escape the past, and the break was never absolute. I never got divorced until many years later, once I'd moved to Preston, but Eaves Lane was my place and the success or failure of my clinic and future exploits, was down to me and me alone, with the emphasis on **alone**. Sadly, the emphasis on alone was to come back and haunt me many years later, when I realised all my life's efforts had counted for virtually nothing. And so, I concentrated on building up my practice, whilst considering work opportunities as and when they presented themselves. However, as one door closed another seemed to open, and in retrospect there were more doors opening than closing. My number of patients was steadily increasing, because of my local connections and the fact that many people knew me, from my footballing and full-time teaching days. This, together with me being introduced to Kenneth Alan Taylor and Judith Barker by Sheila Carter, thus giving me a link to Oldham Repertory Theatre, meant even more doors started to open. Also, my work at Marianne Jepson's Dance College was not going unrecognised, and links to other dance schools, such as Pat Dyson's was helping to enhance my reputation. I was still tutoring occasionally for Sports Coach UK, and initially my tutoring at the NIM meant I could pay the bills, whilst doing something I truly enjoyed. Being self-employed also meant, I only did things on my terms, without interference from the politics. I was also becoming more involved on the educational side with the Society of Sports Therapists, and Graham Smith's Sports Therapy Diploma course, not only as a tutor but also an examiner. When Graham asked to meet me at The Thistle hotel, Haydock, to discuss joining the team to teach on the very first Sports Therapy degree course to be offered at The University of North London, on Holloway Road, I knew that things were in the ascendancy. I took along the work I had done, to update the courses at the NIM Blackpool and my ideas for its development, incorporating Sports Therapy, as up until then my efforts were just sitting in my office looking for a new home. Enter the degree course. Both Keith Waldron and Graham had put a lot of effort into establishing the need for a degree course, to raise the profile of Sports Therapy, 18 months to be precise, and negotiations at the University of North London were at the advanced stage, and Graham and Keith were trying to put together the teaching team. I was flattered that they saw me as a possible candidate to get the first module, involving physical therapy, up and running. To write and teach my own module, was an exciting prospect but there were several problems. Firstly, I had no desires to go back into full time education, and give up my clinic and freedom. Secondly, I wasn't trained to teach in Higher Education, but was not daunted by the idea of teaching older students. However, after Graham had pointed out that for the first year I could just travel down to London and deliver my module over several days, and as long as I attended any academic meetings related to the course, that would cover any contractual obligations I would have. In actual fact, I never signed a contract, but was just paid a fee for my services. What should I do as I was adamant I didn't want to return to the politics and hassle of full-time education? However, Graham's faith in me and the fact that for three months' work I was to be paid a very generous sum of money, persuaded me that I should give it my best shot. Adopting the strategy of being organised, preparing properly, sticking to the script, not bullshitting and accepting that someone in my audience may know more than I did, I prepared to set out on the next part of my teaching journey. What would Verna and Frank think?

But before all that materialised, I concentrated all my efforts on my patients, who had become an integral part of my life, as each not only brought me physical problems to solve, but also their own personal stories and tragedies. After a while, I realised that unless one could empathise with these people, whilst remaining detached from their everyday troubles, one could never become a successful therapist. It also taught me that all problems in life are relative. I'll never forget one lady, who had made a full recovery from her injury, bursting into tears when I told her I didn't want to see her again. Little did I realise how lonely she was, and how much her visits meant to her. Again, another insight into the world of loneliness that would come back to haunt me, many years later. For her coming to Mr Briggs was equivalent to a day out, the therapy being almost secondary. Then there was a very elderly patient who quite bluntly said, "I am just waiting to die, Mr Briggs, have you any suggestions?" He assertively told me not to pity him, but he felt living as long as he had was too long and he was frustrated and annoyed that God had kept him going, and his doctor wanted to keep giving him tablets to keep him alive. Whilst working at Eaves Lane, I encountered many patients who brought more than just a physical problem to the clinic. I had always embraced the philosophy that in physical therapy you treated an individual person with a problem, not just the problem, because everyone was different, and you didn't find real people in books. If we did, then I would have become an instant millionaire. That's what I loved about therapy, you had an individual with a problem and you had to decide, after the consultation and examination, whether your therapy would be appropriate, and help. If not, then you could refer them to someone who may be able to do so. To re-visit Foucault, 1973, **'the diagnosis depended on the gaze'. Sometimes, the therapy was to show compassion, empathise or to just care. In today's world, how can you quantify and qualify these, in a world of targets, statistics, effectiveness, efficiency, time-management and bonuses?**

Now it has been clearly emphasised in this book, that I have never been and was not a religious person, and struggled with expressions such as, 'It's God's will', or 'It is the work of Allah', but running my clinic on Eaves Lane, was my first serious introduction to the debate on old age, loneliness and euthanasia. It also threw into the melting pot, my first moral and ethical questions pertaining to patient confidentiality. Had I a moral, ethical obligation to report what some patients told me in confidence? Yes, of course, I did but when it involved life threatening issues, these became serious matters of principle. My experiences certainly helped, when I later found myself lecturing on professionalism, ethics and morals at various universities. Meanwhile, although my professional life flourished, my personal life was in tatters. I can remember the first Friday night I moved into Eaves Lane, sitting in the upstairs lounge on the floor with my back against the wall, in darkness, **feeling so alone.** And whilst Ed W was good for escaping the realities of my situation, because he himself was so needy, my only go-to was Tim, one of my best mates. Tim, who had banking running through his soul, was instrumental in arranging my financial move to Eaves Lane, as well as being the only person who actually understood me. And so, it was very sad when years later, we parted company because of his errant behaviour. Both of them provided social support when I needed to get out there and meet people, but to be honest, we never went out with the sole purpose of finding Jim, 'a new woman'. My school friends were also around in the background, and Alison Ford, known as the social secretary, was always asking me to join Stuart Firth, Stuart Ford, Neil and Eric and their wives to various social events, but I couldn't be arsed with the pettiness of it all. A single person entering the scene sometimes, can unsettle the social equilibrium. Jealous husbands and unhappy wives, to name but two of life's obstacles. But eventually I succumbed and eventually accepted one of Alison's invitations to a dinner party at their friend Lesley and Kevin's house.

Anne, Hannah and Christopher.

I can't say it was love at first sight, as I sat next to this lady called Anne Macmillan, but during the evening we shared a laugh and joke. Her baggage was two young children, Christopher and Hannah, and a truck load of angst over her divorce from an accountant who had, according to Anne, stopped her having a promising career in the Crown Prosecution Services, because she had to take time out to bring up her children. Was I missing something here? Had she been forced by her husband Charlie into starting a family? During the evening, I tried to keep personal stuff to a minimum, but after the evening, which I enjoyed, I decided that rather than sit at home feeling sorry for myself and playing at Shirley Valentine, talking to the wall, I should at least see if she wanted to have a date with me. Something inside told me, I owed it to Alison to at least give it a whirl. So, the following week I phoned Alison, and asked her for Anne's phone number. Anne agreed to meet me to go to the cinema one night, and the relationship grew from there. It wasn't a match made in heaven, and the baggage kept getting in the way. Nothing new there then. Taking on board other people's children was not going to be easy, and during my teaching career I had seen the damage parents' separation could cause to children's lives. Whatever I did, I knew I was always going to be piggy in the middle. Anne was always asking me why I wasn't divorced, and couldn't understand why I wouldn't, 'slag off', Dee. She also asked if I intended to be involved in the children's upbringing, which seemed a little strange. Did she think I was just going to ignore their existence? The relationship lasted for two and a half years, before she decided I wasn't committed and she couldn't trust me, because I was still married and was frequently surrounded by all these young female students. **If people don't trust, then what chance have you got?** And because I wouldn't put a piece of metal around her finger, this proved conclusively I wasn't committed enough. I was summarily dismissed, and my services were no longer required. At this juncture, I could present my case for proving that I was committed to the cause, but as I've said if it's not relevant to the aim of this book, I will not go into too much detail. I will, however, say that Hannah and I became very close, and that Christopher sadly grew up to become a thief by stealing from his mother and 'doing drugs'. As for Hannah, the last I heard, from Anne's brother Tony, was that she was in Australia with a young man, doing what youngsters do. As for Anne's family, I always got on well with mum and dad, her two brothers and their partners, even though they were big Burnley football supporters. In fact, after we split up, Tony and Margaret contacted me to say I was sadly missed, which meant a lot to someone who was starting to think that he was destined to spend the rest of his life alone. I often think of Hannah, because, to say the least, at the time I was very upset as I've said I became very attached to her, and watched her blossom into a lovely teenager. Not two words that you instantly put together. Not forgetting I didn't deal with rejection easily. But as time went by, I realised Anne did me a massive favour. Her spitefulness upon finding out that after dispensing with my services, a certain Heather Thorpe had decided to take up the mantle of accepting James Briggs into her life was eye opening. She immediately stopped me seeing the children, even though Hannah asked specifically, that although mum had fallen out with Jim, could she still visit me occasionally. For a while, I would pick the children up, and take them to Manchester to watch ice hockey. Anne was happy for me to let that happen, because it gave her more free time to socialise and play bridge. It was also interesting that whilst my family and friends accepted my relationships with an open mind, and asked about them even after I had announced another one had, 'kicked me in touch', to this day, no one has ever enquired about Anne's welfare. Did they know something I didn't?

Moira Bailey, Accountant.

I cannot move on without mention of my accountant, Moira Bailey, whom I met whilst living at Eaves Lane. She had taken over from my previous accountant, who had premises on Middleton Rd. Chadderton. Over time we became good friends. Like me, she enjoyed dining and walking and whilst we enjoyed several meals at the Hoghton Arms in Chadderton, we never spent a day tramping the countryside, although it had been suggested on more than one occasion. Moira was an only child, and when I first met her, she was looking after her father, who had been diagnosed with Dementia. So initially, when we first met, her life mainly consisted of looking after her dad, her dog and being an accountant. As it was obvious this was very stressful, I always tried to bring a little sunshine into her life, and she always said she was pleased to see me as I made her smile. I even invited her and her friend Dorothy to my 60th birthday party.

Thanks, Moira for sharing, and your friendship and whilst I liked the honesty of your friend Dorothy, I didn't enjoy meeting your patronising Masonic neighbour. I wonder why?

Finally, how ironic is it that my great niece, Jennifer Dalloway, and her husband, Anthony Jones, bought Eaves Lane many, many years later?

University of North London-BSc Sports Science and Sports Therapy, 1996-1997.

As previously outlined, the opportunity to return to mainstream education, this time in Higher rather than Primary Education, arose during my time at Eaves Lane, and my focus once I'd accepted the challenge was, from day one, to give it my best shot and see what happened. Early meetings with Graham at the Thistle Hotel, Haydock, to consider being part of a degree course to which I would write the very first module and then with Dr Mike Roberts, my liaison at the University, were the first major steps to get the degree up and running. It began with me arriving with a list of questions and to-dos, which I was informed Mike had not been used to. Being a scientist, he was tasked with heading up the course whilst working in close liaison with Graham Smith and his team, which at that time was Keith Waldron, Graham and myself. Mike was usually the one doing the asking and telling. However, as massage was not his field of expertise, and this was going to be the very first module on the very first degree course of its kind in the country, and all concerned wanted it to be a success, he graciously allowed me to take centre stage, whilst advising me of the politics, ways and customs of working in Higher Education. I liked Mike, and over the time I knew him, found him to be a genuinely good guy. His academic knowledge was obviously beyond reproach, and I learned much from him. **He was not, as some I found, insecure and up his own backside.**

The University was 4 stops from Euston, on the Northern Line, and the building on Holloway Road, which acted as the base for the course, was facing, 'The Tower Block', which was the main building. Our block was just across the road from the underground station entrance, and so once I'd arrived at Euston train station in London, I became a mole only surfacing to cross Holloway Road. I say this because, apart from the underground, the building itself was a maze of different levels and stairways, and if a wrong turn was initiated you could quite easily, end up in the wrong place. Our first intake was 24 plus, and it was my responsibility to teach them the art and science of remedial massage, whilst creating a good first impression, and laying a foundation for future Sports Therapy courses. I loved the responsibility and became more and more excited as equipment arrived, and my little domain took shape. Fitting 15 massage plinths so that students could work on them, without causing major trauma to each other, into an old science laboratory, was no mean feat. I had my own key and code to open the door. Eventually, the time arrived when Graham and I would meet the students, but not before Mike had given me a sheet containing the names and passport photos of the students. I noticed there was a Storm Nuttall, whose mother I found out was called Gail and I often wondered, but never asked, if her father was the infamous snooker player, Alex 'Hurricane' Higgins. Memories of Quentin Cumber came flooding back from my Primary school teaching days. Not forgetting Sarah Blizzard, the weather reporter and Mrs Fiddler, the Brittania Building Society manageress. Iris Ferguson's brother was the Scottish international footballer, Duncan. One of the students, Howard Piccaver, eventually took over my module, after both Steve Smelt and myself had left North London, for pastures new. Howard, later successfully ran a clinic in Peterborough, after also leaving North London. Another student, Carolina Mischiati, eventually secured a lecturing position at the University of Chichester, on their recently started Sports Therapy degree. Whilst Kate Cady ended up on the Society of Sports Therapy committee. Not bad for a new intake. I was not sure where the other students ended up, but have no doubt most of them found some position or another in sport, as they were a hard-working, conscientious group. As many of them were mature students, they were bringing life skills and a different attitude to study than the usual 18-year-olds. This was no slight on the 18-year-old, but you can't buy life experience, and all they had usually experienced was academia.

Being a new course, the University was unsure as to the number of students it would attract but at our first meeting with the potential first year intake, there appeared to be far more than two dozen. I hoped that the University had not enrolled them purely and simply as a numbers exercise. We wanted students who were attracted to what the Sports Therapy degree was offering, and was what they wanted to do from the outset, we hoped this would negate the need to 'jump ship', later. Known as a retention strategy Universities didn't want to lose students, who for a variety of reasons wanted to leave. As it turned out, only one student, left the course during the first year. As previously mentioned, apart from the odd hiccough, the students were dedicated, applied themselves and flew the flag for our profession which, at that time, was being very closely scrutinised by others, not only in the sports world but also the therapy world. Our aim was to get all the students a good class of Honours degree, from hard work, dedication and application. Little did I know, that several years later this application and dedication was to be the corner stone on which I based my decision to resign from university lecturing and leave the Society of Sports Therapy.

Once students had got used to my Lancastrian accent and ways of teaching, things went from good to better than good. Spending time with students who for some of that time, are in various stages of undress and working in pairs, **where respect for your partner is paramount,** brings a certain bonding and rapport within a group. As the professional relationship between the students and myself developed, some started to mimic my Lancashire accent. **Would that be allowed today or would it be a breach of some etiquette, code, an ic, ist, or an ism?** I had also told the students just to be honest, if for whatever reason, they were going to be late or absent. As a result of this, one week I was just about to start a practical session when there was a knock on the door, and an out of breath voice was heard to say,

"Please can I come in, Mr Briggs, I'm sorry for being late, but last night I had too much to drink, I overslept and missed my train."

To which I replied, tongue in cheek, "Come in, but because you are late, you can take the class."

"I'd love to, Mr B, but I can't do a Lancashire accent."

For me, this was heart-warming to hear, as it was all part and parcel of what is known as, 'the hidden curriculum'. The students having taken on board that in life, especially when working with other people, in high pressure situations, a sense of humour was vital. This was why I loved my job. Obviously, during my time, there were the odd personality clashes as some academics didn't know how to take me. Lacking my sense of humour, and me being a Northerner, I think some secretly thought I was a bit of a dickhead, but a dickhead the students and fellow lecturers seemed to like. As the university's agreement with the Society was one where the Society initially chose the teaching staff to deliver the course, these people were reluctantly stuck with me. I loved saying things to gauge their reaction. As I had decided, I was only going to work at the university to get the degree course up and running, and was not interested in staying full time as it gained momentum, I was certainly not going to, 'lick arse'. I think this was very unsettling for some. All I wanted was, to be left alone to do the job I knew I was good at, and as long as Graham, Mike and the students were happy then so was I. I certainly had no time to kowtow to insecure people who wanted me to doff my cap when in their presence. Don't get me wrong, I respected their positions and understood procedures and protocols, but at the end of the day these people only had, if they were lucky, two arms, two legs and a bit in the middle, like the rest of us. As mentioned many times before, I found myself in places in which I never in a million years expected to be, but once there I was determined to not let people down who had shown faith in me. I was once asked to 'look after' Mr Angus Wallace, Professor of Orthopaedic and Accident Surgeons Medicine. This was a person who had performed an operative procedure, with a coat hanger on a BA flight from Hong Kong to London. As time went on, I realised that there were many people who, not only did not possess my knowledge, skill, expertise and experience, but were in positions, I felt they should have not been put in. This obviously had a massive impact on the way I perceived people in positions of so-called responsibility and power. **I was once again reminded that power you could take, but respect you had to earn.**

The 1997 SST Conference held at High Wycombe FC that many of the University of North London students attended. Graham Smith is on the left with Vania Barbera linking him. Kate Cady is back row 2nd from the left, with David Jones, Wycombe Wanderers, on her right and Joel Harris on her left. Keith Waldron on the far right, with Dr Mike Roberts in the glasses on the back row, directly behind Mr B. To his left is Howard Piccaver.

I had let it be known from the onset I did not want a full-time position at the university, and so I was paid a fee for my services per semester, and had suggested when I decided to leave, for course continuity, I would be prepared to team teach and let someone shadow me for 12 weeks, so they could eventually take over the teaching of my module. Technically, the course belonged to the University, as part of one of their courses, but as I was the one that wrote and taught it, and had the most experience in hands-on therapy, it seemed only fair for people teaching on it to at least shadow me for a while, to see how it was delivered. This avoided student confusion, a common problem in education, who, as the course numbers increased, were taught by different teachers and lecturers. This to me was obviously the way forward, and how I envisaged my gradual withdrawal from the course. **But sadly, the university**

was opposed to the idea on financial grounds! Not educational grounds I might add. Not unduly upset but a little miffed at their intransigence, I returned North, with my head held high, knowing I had achieved my goal but unaware that Graham was already in the process of approaching one of his football cronies, to see if they were interested in a full-time appointment at the university. Not long after my return to Eaves Lane, I received a phone call from a Steve Smelt, the newly appointed full-time lecturer at the university, who had fallen out of love with his beloved football, for reasons I do not feel are appropriate for me to put in print. His background was initially similar to mine, in that he started his working life as a PE teacher but in secondary education, before joining the football ranks. As a teacher and England Youth team coach, with experience of working in the real world, he seemed an ideal candidate to compliment the team. He was offered the position of full-time lecturer at the university as my replacement. Unbeknown to Steve, he was to be put in the position of delivering a physical therapy module with very little, if any, experience of teaching remedial massage. Without going into details of copyright etc. and who owns what, the author or the institution it was written for, he was faced with the prospect of having to deliver a course he was unfamiliar with, and with very little time in which to prepare for it. To be blunt, it would appear he had moved from one pile of shit to another. The gist of his phone call was, that he basically wanted to know if I was happy for him to use, if not all, then some of my course material next semester. This request was accompanied by suitable grovelling words, as to how brilliant he thought my course was. Whilst I appreciated the fact that he had phoned me up personally, at first, I told him that as the university had declined my offer of sticking around to help a smooth transition with whoever was to take over, I was not inclined to help them out of their present situation. I pointed out that it was nothing personal against Steve Smelt. However, eventually after several phone calls where Steve said he appreciated my position and didn't blame me for my stance, I decided I would consent to him using all my course material. From that moment on, Steve and I became good mates, to the extent that we eventually ended up teaching at Teesside University together, where I enjoyed some of the happiest times of my higher education career. But that was not before I once again returned to the University of North London to, 'dig them out of another hole', but this time as a favour to Keith Waldron, after the University appointed Howard Piccaver, an ex-student on the first cohort, onto the teaching side, after Steve Smelt had left to take up a post at Teesside University. Again, whilst I had no axe to grind with Howard, he had no experience of how to teach the massage module, other than having been a student on my course. To go from being a student on a course, to then becoming a lecturer on that course, with no actual experience of putting that knowledge, skill and expertise to the test in the real world was, personally speaking, a giant leap of faith and quite frankly, not fair on Howard. Of course, the newly qualified students want employment, but they initially need an experienced hand to guide them. This was always going to be an issue for the Sports Therapy degree course as it grew and developed, staff recruitment and quality control. Not to mention jobs for the graduate students. Having secured degree status, the Society was trying to get state registration and recognition, and it was having to jump through all kinds of hoops, to be considered for such. There were many hurdles to overcome, and many other organisations on the list for the Health Professions Council to consider. One of the dilemmas the Society had, was numbers of members. Having Degree status had opened the door for students to consider a career working in sport, with an alternative route other than via Chartered Physiotherapy. As far as the Society was concerned, the more Universities that came on board, the more their numbers would increase. **Whilst the number of Universities wanting to join the party, as they immediately saw this as a massive income generator, was steadily growing, the quality control and staff recruitment issues kept raising their ugly heads. Over the**

ensuing years, these issues became more and more of a problem, and eventually became another of the reasons I finally resigned from UCLAN. I felt the quality control was not there, and the courses, like all courses, had become a bums on seats, number crunching, financial exercise and not a quality control, educational excellence issue. Also, it was becoming noticeable that whenever a vacancy occurred, Graham would turn to football to try and fill the void. Usually with personnel who had fallen out or had been released by their clubs, and so Graham, 'threw them a lifeline', irrespective of whether they had a teaching qualification or not. **As the initial aim had been to develop Sports Therapy in its broadest sense, incorporating ALL sports, now that things were expanding, student numbers wise, it seemed to be contracting teaching personnel wise. I was becoming surrounded by either people who had been attached to a football club in one capacity or another, or those who had football as their number one sport.**

The first graduation ceremony for the University of North London was held at the Barbican in London, and it is difficult to describe how I felt, watching the first cohort of students going up on stage to receive their degrees. The boy from Chadderton, who don't forget, had supposedly purposely failed his 11 and 12 plus, had done well. Sitting next to Keith Waldron watching some of the students look up in our direction and smile and wave, was a picture that sadly is not on a file on my computer but is nevertheless in my memory bank, and will stay with me until the end. During my time at North London, both as lecturer and later a visiting examiner, I met many people who for a short time I viewed as friends as well as colleagues. These people were to set the ball rolling, making the SST stronger with a higher profile. These people had set the benchmark. To Mike Roberts, Vania Souto, nee Barbera and Carolina Mischiati, David Jones, Howard Piccaver, Colin Jackson, Victoria Davis, nee Cummings and Joel Harris can I say, thank you for your involvement, enthusiasm, tolerance when I went into performance mode, laughing at my jokes and sharing. Sadly, one of the themes constantly repeated throughout this autobiography, is that once I retired, I was no longer on their radar and we have lost touch. On several occasions, even if I did make the effort and managed to trace their whereabouts and make contact, I felt that my efforts were not going to be reciprocated. So sad. But as I will mention in the next chapter of my journey, this lack of appreciation, that communication is a two-way process, is not uncommon.

Keith and myself at the graduation ceremony at the Barbican, 1999.

Arnside Close, Hoghton, Preston, Sunseekers and Asking Prices.

I met Heather Thorpe on holiday, 2001, in the Comics British pub in Alcudia, Majorca. I was on holiday with my brother Stephen and his daughter Claire, who was 17 at the time and Heather was on holiday alone. She was getting over two failed marriages, and had plucked up the courage to go on an all-inclusive holiday by herself. She informed me that her 3 children, Mark, Paul and Melanie, were grown up and were now big enough to look after themselves, and her middle son, Paul, who was still living with her, would have to find a place of his own, if she decided to move house. She wanted some me time. For a short while we courted, if that's the right word. Heather had decided that if Anne Macmillan didn't want Mr B. for whatever reasons, she was quite happy to take on the mantle of being his partner. And so, after she had joined me at Eaves Lane, storing a lot of her stuff in the double garage, we decided that we both wanted to make a clean break from the past and find a place together. York, Chester or somewhere between Lancashire and the Midlands were all considered, but after visiting Chadderton virtually every other week, with me travelling, work permitting, to Hinkley in between, Heather decided that Lancashire was big enough, and friendly enough to put roots down there. For me, this was music to my ears as Lancashire was in my blood and where my roots were. Was her decision swayed because she knew this, and just wanted to please me or did she genuinely like what she had seen and experienced since visiting Eaves Lane? I genuinely felt it was both, but knowing Heather, knew she wouldn't have moved to Lancashire purely and simply just to please me. **"It's time the children stood**

on their own two feet, it's now my time," she informed me. Little did she know that although, her children gave her their blessing with, **"As long as mum's happy, that's all that matters,"** what they forgot to add was, **"But if she isn't living just around the corner from us, that could potentially be an issue."** As for her parents, Betty and Reg Bird, who lived in Rugby, I'm not sure what they felt, but as Heather was very close to both of them, especially her dad, I was very conscious that the move was not taken lightly by Heather. What I did know was that at first, they both thought I was a little gregarious. Also, as Heather's previous two marriages had failed, for various reasons, all her family was hoping she was not being a little hasty in moving away.

Before she moved, 'up North', I was tasked with finding a place for us to live. Whenever she came up for the weekend, we spent at least one day house hunting, and the rest of the time I travelled about looking for suitable houses. At that time the house market was crazy, with many properties being sold either before they went on the market or very shortly afterwards. Heather sold her house within weeks, which prompted her move to Eaves Lane. We'd decided that selling one house at a time was the more sensible, practical thing to do. In the meantime, I was travelling over to Preston, from Chadderton, every week viewing houses. I viewed Arnside Close, Hoghton, one late Thursday night, not ever having heard of Hoghton, or knowing it existed, until I consulted a map and the internet. I immediately fell in love with the size of the place, that was owned by a policeman George, his teacher wife and his children. There was a lot of interest in the 4 bedroomed, semi-detached house and I was informed there were many viewings arranged for the following few days. To cut the long story short by 7.25 p.m. the following day, we had offered the full asking price and shaken hands with George and his wife to buy their house. We loved the property moving in via the Acme Removal Company, namely Melanie, Heather's daughter, Jason, her boyfriend, who incidentally hailed from Darwen, brother Jack, Tim, my mate, as well as Heather and myself. Melanie was not convinced mum was doing the right thing moving up North, as she herself had moved up years before to be with Jay, not long after they had met, and had not enjoyed the experience. As a result, they both moved back to Hinkley, near to her mum. Jay found work soon after, and they were happily ensconced in their little house just around the corner from Heather in Hinkley. The bond between Heather and Melanie was very strong. Therefore, mum moving 2 hours plus up the M6 was not something Mel was happy about, but to her credit she was helping her mum make the transition. Which is more than can be said for eldest son Mark, who couldn't find Hoghton because it was too far from his local pub, with its 24/7 football screen, to visit. Alcohol dependency played a significant part in Mark's existence. Also, his wife Charlotte was not a happy bunny because, "We've lost a baby sitter," she was heard to utter. It soon became apparent that whilst the children were happy for us to travel South down the M6 every month, apart from Mel and Jay, reciprocal gestures were few and far between. All Heather's friends from Hinkley were also conspicuous by their absence. This was very frustrating, because one of the main reasons we had bought Arnside Close was its size and we had plenty of bedrooms, so people could visit and stay. During the time there, we had 2 extensions built giving us extra toilets and bathrooms. Meanwhile, Heather had secured a sales job at MASTA, Medical Advisory Services for Travellers Abroad, selling travel vaccines, whose head office was near to Leeds and Bradford airport. She loved it, and became top sales executive for several years. She was making new friends both at work and home, and to broaden her circle of friends decided to do Art and Craft courses at Runshaw College, Euxton. I had secured premises in Leyland at Sunseekers, a tanning salon, not ideal, but having visited the place on several occasions and talking to the owners and manager, decided it would suit my purposes. All I now needed to do was build up my clientele. I was still working at the NIM, which had now moved to Bury with Ed Caldwell, delivering my sports therapy diploma course, as well as still tutoring for Sports Coach UK. I was also travelling to London and Glasgow, working for the Society of Sports Therapists.

All in all, life was good as we settled into living in Hoghton, inviting James and Diane, friends of Heather from work, Alan Walker, a local builder, and his wife, who built our second extension, neighbours George and Alice, Michael and Pauline, round for meals. Heather also became friends with the local hairdresser, Helen, who not long after meeting Heather, started visiting my clinic for treatment. Oh yes, and there was Roy, who ran the local Texaco petrol station and all the staff at the Royal Oak Pub. These things, as well as working on the house and garden as and when, enabled our new life and dream home to take shape. As my clinic was taking time to become a going concern, I decided to apply for a position as a Sports Therapy lecturer at Teesside University and after discussing the implications of leaving Heather alone in Hoghton, whilst I worked in Middlesborough 4 days a week, and being offered the job, I accepted. To be honest, Heather being an independent bunny seemed quite excited at the prospect of having the remote controls to the TV and Freeview box all to herself, 4 evenings a week. My time at Teesside turning out to become some of the happiest, if challenging, in my teaching career. Added to the fact I loved driving home on Thursday to see Heather. We loved Hoghton and jogged, walked and visited many local restaurants and pubs. Located between Blackburn and Preston, and only 5 minutes from the M65 motorway made it an ideal place to travel from and to. To add to our experiences there, we had a mini tornado pass over Hoghton that hit the local and national news, May 3rd, 2005. We also became, 'Friends of the Charter Theatre', and frequented both the Guild Hall and Charter Theatre, as well as patronising the local, amateur dramatic scene, such as Hoghton Players, whenever they put on a production. We also travelled as often as possible, both in the UK and abroad. Towards the end of our time in Hoghton, I made the agonizing decision to leave Teesside and apply for a post at UCLAN, which as the reader will shortly find out proved to be a mistake. Resigning from my position, after only a few months in situ, and because I'd become disillusioned with teaching, for the second time in my career, decided to semi-retire, certainly from full time education and eventually, therapy. Also, because it had become apparent that Hoghton was just not somewhere friends and family wanted to visit, especially for Heather's connections, we decided to sell up and down size, releasing capital to help the finances, and so I could attack my bucket list. As mentioned, whilst Heather's friends and family were quite happy for us to travel to Warwickshire once a month, the gesture was rarely, if ever, reciprocated. This issue was always a contentious one. I had started delivering leaflets, Yellow Pages and the Phone Book, and enjoyed it by looking upon it as being paid for going for a walk!

I understood from previous sales, a house was only worth what someone would pay for it, but the whole business of employing estate agents just seemed to me to be a paper exercise. Whatever figure they came up with, after all their measuring, calculations and research, people never accepted their, 'professional judgement', and made up their own mind as to what to offer. Even the term, 'guide price' seemed to be ignored by some potential buyers. Eventually we agreed to sell to a lady called Cath and her two daughters, and so on August 10th 2004, we moved from Hoghton to Claughton Avenue, Leyland.

Claughton Avenue,
Leyland, Preston.

Having left UCLAN for the first time and being semi-retired, Heather and I decided to downsize and move to smaller premises. This would not only release capital, until my pensions and investments matured at 60, but also give us more money to travel. On August 10th 2004 we moved from Hoghton to Claughton.

We quickly made friends with the neighbours Cameron and Teryl, on our left and Matthew, the accountant, on our right. Cameron was in IT and Teryl was a bank nurse, who worked nights. They had this arrangement so that their young son, Josh, would have a parental upbringing and would not be, 'farmed out', to the local childminder. You can imagine how this arrangement was music to my ears, and immediately endeared them to me. Cameron had a teenage girl, called Jade, from a previous relationship, who also lived with them, visiting her mum in Colne at weekend. Shirley was directly opposite us, and initially we just used to wave to her when she was getting into her car on the way to the gym. She was in her mid-seventies but looked and was extremely well preserved for her age. Later we became good friends with Shirley as Heather used to see her at the local gym, and I did jobs for her in the garden. She was also invited to our house for a meal on more than one occasion. As for Matthew, he very much kept to himself, but was always polite and would exchange a few words as and when the occasion arose. Occasionally, a female was seen visiting Matthew's premises. Sometimes his mates would arrive on their mountain bikes, and off they would ride into the sunset, returning several hours later caked in mud and water. One Sunday I was on the drive between our two properties, and I could hear heavy breathing and grunting coming from Matthew's garage. As Heather was in the kitchen baking, I asked her to step outside to share the moment. Yes, sure enough, we both agreed that on this particular day, Matthew was not getting his exercise by going out on his bike with his mates, but had probably got a female visitor. Unless his mates were in the garage as observers. Heather returned to her baking, and after about ten minutes the noises emanating from his garage stopped, and as Matthew's garage door opened, he had an electrically controlled one, he emerged in his shorts and tee shirt, sweating profusely.

"Morning, Matthew, had a good work out?" says I, tongue in cheek.

"Hi, Jim, yes I've just smashed the f... out of Laura."

"Oh," says I, not quite sure what to say next, until I saw his punch bag, that hung from inside his garage roof, still swinging.

"Oh, I've not introduced you, have I? Jim, this is Laura," he said pointing to the punch bag, "Laura, this is Jim."

I love a sense of humour, don't you? It's not until you physically move house, do you realise the advantages and disadvantages of such major decisions. As well as the financial gain, which was one of the major reasons for moving, the advantages certainly outweighed the disadvantages. It was nearer to the M6, M65 and M61 for both our commuting. Leyland Railway station provided easier access to Preston. The local petrol station was one of the cheapest in Preston. Having Cuerden Country Park on our doorstep was brilliant for walking, jogging and cycling. The Hayrick pub, our local, served cheap and cheerful fare, and had entertainment on most Saturday Nights. Whilst the local butcher, next to the chippy, gave 10% discount if you spent over a certain amount. What more could we ask for? All that was left to do was enjoy, and travel around the world. As for Heather's family, well Mark and Paul, her sons, graced us with their presence to attend their mother's 50th birthday party at 'The Pines', and my 60th at the Ley Inn, both in Whittle-le-Woods but only visited one other time to view the property. After that, they left the task of visiting mum to Mel and Jay, as travelling the M6 was just too much trouble. After Heather's dad passed away Betty, her mum, was reluctant to travel, but she did come up on the train to view the property. I vividly recall meeting her at Preston Railway station and entertaining her, until Heather returned from work. As for Heather's brother David and his partner Sue, well they just didn't bother. This apathy towards visiting Heather in Preston being one of the major issues in our eventual break-up.

Teesside University.

Having been very pleased that I had been instrumental in helping to set up and establish the first Sports Therapy degree course in the country, I was merrily going about my business at Eaves Lane, getting on with life as you do, or don't, as the case may be. I, along with others, were being tasked to address the quality control issue by externally examining on the Society's courses and being involved in interviews to recruit new staff. Andrew Cunningham, whom I had met when examining on Graham Smith's Advanced Diploma course at Keele University, had been appointed to set up and develop the latest degree course at Teesside University, and I was asked if I would travel to Teesside, to examine the massage module. This for me was going to be interesting, as I was curious as to how my module had been taught away from the University of North London. Meeting Andy in the hotel where I was staying, he presented me with a timetable of examination times and students that quite frankly, was unacceptable to me because it involved examining blocks of students, that didn't allow time to see if the students were **safe and effective. A student could be safe and not effective and vice versa. For the Society they had to be both.** After a little negotiation, we reached a compromise. I was also aware, that I had never actually seen Andy teach physical therapy/massage. On the day of the examinations, the biggest issue I encountered was not the physicality of the hands on, but in establishing if the students understood the significance of what and why they were doing it. This involved asking pertinent questions whenever they came up with very superficial answers or, as is the case in physical therapy, why they performed a particular technique. This applied to all examinations, irrespective of the course. Not only does it give the examiner a better chance to give students a better grade by extracting relevant information, but it also sorts out students who have not done the required amount of study and revision and would have to re-sit. **For students for whom English was not their first language, this proved very difficult as for some their command of English was only rudimentary, which meant at times, they didn't even fully understand the questions being asked. Now this was and still is a very sensitive issue in a politically correct climate, leading to claims of victimisation, sexism, racism and a whole raft of...ists, isms and ics. The plain truth of the matter was that if a student's command of the language was only basic, then when academic rigour was applied the student was always going to be found wanting. Which ultimately could lead to failing the module. But to the University, more students meant more money. More foreign students meant even more money.** As long as they'd the requisite number of points for entry, they were usually accepted. But this brought into question the validity of qualifications, not only between different academic organisations in the same country, but between different countries. There was also the issue of foreign students with wealthy parents arriving in this country, with possibly bogus qualifications thought to have been acquired dubiously. This put considerable strain on the admissions department tasked with checking out not the validity of such qualifications, but also if such qualifications were of a comparable standard. As more universities entered the scene, the more universities fought for the numbers. To re-iterate, **BUMS ON SEATS DO NOT EQUATE TO EDUCATIONAL QUALITY CONTROL.** The issue of quality and academic standards was down to the lecturers. Losing students because they didn't meet academic rigour, and exacting standards meant loss of revenue to the University. So, everything was done to help students to pass their re-sits, which sometimes was more than just once. Unfortunately, it's not rocket science to see how this placed lecturers in an invidious position. On this particular occasion, **I FAILED SEVERAL GREEK STUDENTS** who quite frankly, should not have been put in that position. **Obviously, leaving myself open to claims of racism, sexism, favouritism and victimisation. Which seems to be a favourite default mode for some students, when they are given a few home truths.** Also, if these students couldn't pass muster in their first year, what chance would they have in their third year? Once again, politics reared its ugly head but I won't bore the reader with what transpired next, other than to use a Margaret Thatcher euphemism, Jim Briggs was, 'not for turning'. This was the first of several visits to Teesside to examine students and with each subsequent visit, I became very impressed with how the standards of the students had risen since my first forays to the North East. I will always remember one student called Natalie who impressed me with her demeanour, attitude, knowledge and skill, and was not surprised that she eventually got a first-class honours. The reason I have singled out Natalie Hardaker is, that upon graduating she was offered a job as a research assistant at UCLAN in Preston, where I eventually ended up several years later, sharing an office with her. Andy Cunningham having just moved there from Teesside to set up their new Sports Therapy Course, after Teesside refused to give him a Principal Lecturer's position. By now new universities were coming on board at the rate of at least two a year, and staff recruitment was starting to become an issue. As newly qualified students, with PGCE qualifications, became available, they became an option to fill certain positions, but the dearth of experienced lecturers to fill senior positions, was becoming the main issue. I had played, coached, taught, written about and treated all things related to sport in the real world, even at the other side of the world, but whilst there was no shortage of teachers to teach topics such as Anatomy, Physiology, Pathophysiology and Psychology etc. very few of these had experienced working or even being involved in a sporting environment. After examining and before setting off on the journey home along the A66 over the moors, a beautiful journey by the way, I had been informed that there was a vacancy coming up at Teesside and Steve Smelt, who had recently moved there from the University of North London, had casually inquired if I was interested. Steve being, 'a smoggy', from Middleborough jumped at the chance, when a post at Teesside came up. He tried to massage my ego, excuse the pun, by saying with me on board with Andy, it would make a brilliant team. As I just looked at him, he took it as a, thank you but no, thank you. However, the more I thought about it, the more the idea appealed. So much so, that by the time I'd arrived home to Hoghton, I wanted to discuss the possibility with Heather. The reader may think that by now Sports Therapy was becoming a bit of a merry go round and not unlike football, jobs for the boys. Something I was very keen to avoid and if I had any influence at all, I frequently let my views on the subject be known to Graham Smith and Keith Waldron. **I wanted a teaching pool of lecturers, male and female, from as many different sports as possible. After all, when Graham Smith fell out with the FA and set up the Society, I believed this is what he envisaged.** Considering going back into full time teaching was not something I had envisaged when I moved to Preston, but as long as Heather was happy, I had this gut feeling all would be well. Also, since moving to Preston, I knew it would take time to establish my practice at Sunseekers, in Leyland, purely and simply because no one knew me or my background and apart from trying out, 'the new kid on the block' I was virtually starting from scratch. Therefore, I relied on other sources of revenue such as teaching, tutoring and examining to pay the bills. Add this to the fact that I was not getting any younger and getting a contract in HE would certainly help me achieve my financial goal of retiring mid-50s.

On the day of the interview, I found out that a guy called Mark Leather, a Chartered physiotherapist **who worked in football but had recently fallen out with his club, was one of my main rivals. Is the reader picking up on a recurring theme here?** To cut to the quick I was offered the post. Well done, Briggsy. Apart from Heather, I wanted to contact Verna to tell her the news. From then on things seemed to move very quickly. The issues of commuting to Middlesbrough from Preston, on a weekly basis, and where to stay whilst there, had to be sorted. I shared a downstairs office with Dominic White, 'Dom', the lab technician. I got on well with Dom and he was very helpful during my first few weeks, until I became familiar with procedures and protocols. It was also decided that although I had a B. Ed. Honours degree and a 3-year teaching certificate, I had no specific qualification for teaching in Higher Education, and I would be enrolled on a 2-year PgCLTHE. As it turned out, although it involved one afternoon a week attending lectures etc and weekly assignments, I thoroughly enjoyed it and , learned a great deal and was chuffed when I was invited to be a Fellow of the Higher Education Academy after successfully passing. Slowly, I found my feet and was never happier than when teaching. Teesside had three cohorts of students who, on the whole where a conscientious bunch, and I enjoyed working with Pat Turner, our departmental leader, a South African physiotherapist, Andy, the course leader and Steve, who as I've said, had arrived from the University of North London. Initially Jim Golby, a research guy that came from Leeds University, was 'the boss' but it became obvious that Jim was old school and wasn't 100% happy with flying the Sports Therapy flag. The course was also run in conjunction with the Sports Science department with Jocelyn T, our liaison, to cover the anatomical, physiological, nutritional and psychological aspects of the curriculum. People such as Ian Speers, who later became Dr Ian Speers, and Lyndsey Bainbridge being part of the team. Lyndsey was a Sports Psychologist, and we got on really well together. The office personnel, which consisted of two ladies and a gentleman, were good at dealing with admissions etc. and understood what type of students we were looking to attract. Unfortunately, because of this liaison with the Sports Scientists, we had to teach certain aspects of the Sports Science courses. For me, I found this challenging because some of the students didn't have the same drive and commitment as the Sports Therapy ones. We also had to work and liaise with lecturers and teachers from local colleges, some of whom had, 'bees in their bonnets', at not being perceived as carrying the same kudos or status as university lecturers, and who were not paid the same. Where this insecurity came from, I am not sure because as I'm aware my colleagues and I just viewed these people as part of a team. At one point, I was afraid that the politics was going to spoil my party, and that my decision to return to full time education was not a good one. However, as time went on, and the course and its reputation steadily grew, these issues became minor in the grand scheme of things. I took over the responsibility for the running of an in-house clinic, which was established to give the second and third year students, the experience of dealing with real life injuries and problems under supervision. With thousands of personnel on campus there was no shortage of patients. I also, was responsible for taking second and third year students to 'The Great North Run' to work in the tented Village, providing post event massage to runners representing various charities. This initiative was initially started by Andy, before he left for pastures new in Preston. Each year we would offer the students' services free to two charities, i.e., Childline, Epilepsy in Action etc. to do post event massage. For the students, it provided them with experience of working at a top sporting event, which in September 2019, had 57,000 runners. John Macreadie, **another football casualty,** joined us from Glasgow. John was not a trained or natural teacher, and was immediately put on in-house courses to develop his weaknesses, sorry 'areas for development', and once he'd found his feet, proved to be a valuable asset on the team. I continued to develop the massage course in year one, by incorporating a massage monitor, which became part of a student's assessment. This proved very successful as first year students were peer assessed by providing massage to two other students, one a third year, and the other a second year.

An early morning start for the students to get to the Great North Run and ready for action, in the 'Tented Village'. September, 2004.

Unfortunately, as with all things in life, the good times only seem to have a limited shelf life as Andy applied for the vacant post to set up the Sports Therapy course at UCLAN after Teesside had refused to offer him a Principal Lecturer's post. There was also an ongoing clash of personalities between certain members of senior staff. This came at a time when the number of applicants was steadily rising, as the reputation of the Sports Therapy course grew, and so we were always looking to strengthen the team by bringing in more personnel, with backgrounds in a variety of sports. We were now without a course leader and the three of us, Steve, John and myself closed ranks and pulled together to just get on with it. Steve immediately threw my name into the hat to take over, which was very nice, but I definitely wasn't interested. In the end, Steve himself decided to take up the mantle whilst we kept trying to consider others, who could strengthen the team. I was very keen to strengthen and balance the team with women from non-football backgrounds, and had at least two women that I wanted to sound out, as to the possibility of joining the team. One such person was Roz Nottingham, who I tutored on my Sports Therapy diploma course at the NIM, and then joined me to team-teach after she had qualified. I was also her external tutor on the Teaching course she did at De Montford, Leicester. Roz had experience of working with Rugby Union players, as her partner played for the local club in Grantham. We were also considering others who had crossed our paths, and had previously kindly commented that Teesside had a strong team and they would love to work with the team there. Dispelling the myth of, jobs for the boys, was easy because the people I wanted to sound out were women, who had no affiliation with football. Also, it was not a question of just offering these people jobs, as they had to go through university job protocols, but if we could attract people who fitted the Sports Therapy job descriptions and job specifications, then selection would be so much easier. Unfortunately, such people were a rarity and even if certain people could be identified, for one reason or another, they were not available. One such reason was the commute to Middlesborough. Also, other universities were on the lookout for suitable personnel. Ian Littlejohn, **who had a footballing background,** had just been offered a job at Chichester, and was also looking for staff.

At Teesside, we had Dr Jane Dunbar as our external examiner, who most definitely understood what we were trying to achieve and brought, with no disrespect to Pat Turner, a refreshing external feminine presence to all this testosterone. Also, there was a rumour going around that I was going to join Andy at UCLAN as I lived in Preston, and the university was just on my doorstep. To be honest, it never crossed my mind as I was more than happy at Teesside and had planned to stay at least three years, to see at least one cohort through from first year to graduation. At times, it was presented to me as though my move was signed, sealed and delivered. That sounds like a cue for a song from Mr Wonder. Another Steve, this of the Smelt variety, appreciated my honesty and loyalty for not applying for the subsequent posts that became available at UCLAN. Unfortunately, as time went on, little cracks started to appear in the smooth running of the course as Steve tried to be all things to all people, whilst Pat Turner, our course leader was busy involving us all in a course re-write. Up until this point, I was the happiest I had been in a long time. My working relationship with the students and staff was good. During my time at Teesside, I had increased the number of students choosing to study massage related topics for their final year dissertations, from the odd one to over a dozen. Prior to that they had virtually been dissuaded, because of the challenges it presented. From my perspective more research was needed to prove the efficacy of the therapy, not less, and challenged students to at least try and overcome the obstacles by making their studies repeatable and comparable. In simplicity, **LIFE WAS GOOD FOR MR B.** So why did I choose to leave and apply for a post at UCLAN? Apart from the obvious financial gains and the fact that I could live at home, as mentioned, little issues had started to rear their ugly head and I feared that the Sports Therapy course was not receiving the help and support it deserved. Also, there was the growing, 'bee in my bonnet', that whenever a position became vacant, either full or part time, a name was reeled out that had a footballing or associated footballing background. I remember one very heated discussion, involving Graham Smith and the boys, where I was told to shut up as I pointed out that with so many ex-football people in the building, we were fast becoming a watered-down version of the FATOIS course run by the FA. This was like a red rag to a bull to Mr Smith who reverted to default mode of bullying and intimidation. As pointed out, Graham was famous for throwing a wobbly if he didn't get his own way, or if the red carpet was not rolled out for him. In the meantime, Mark Leather, who I'd initially met during my interview, was brought onto the team part time, to help on my 2nd Year, Examination and Assessment module. **Yes, you've guessed, Mark's background was football.** He was also a Chartered Physiotherapist and whilst I didn't have a problem with this and respected Mark's knowledge, skill and expertise he was not, in my humble opinion, a team player. As soon as he came on board, I specifically pointed out that we taught things differently to the Physiotherapy department and we all needed to talk from the same page. Unfortunately, once in situ I found he was, 'doing his own thing', and deviated from the script. Preferring instead to put forward alternatives, which obviously was going to confuse the students. Not that these variations on a theme were not credible but for me remained in the domain of, On Going Professional Development, **AFTER** the student had qualified. For the first time since arriving at Teesside, students started to get confused because what Mark was teaching was different from what Mr B was teaching, and the other members of the team. He was also constantly challenging why we taught this and not that. I was not in the least concerned with justifying our methods, and on several occasions had words with Mark and whilst smiling nicely and accepting my arguments he still continued to, 'do his own thing'. **I felt Mark was**

not happy having a non-Chartered physio, non-FA bod, such as myself, telling him what to do. He was also tasked with developing the Master's Course which was seen as a massive plus as it would be the very first of its kind in the country, and of course would generate more income. This obviously meant for some Mark's teaching indiscretions, were not an issue. I also feared that the Master's Programme would become a variation on the Physiotherapists Master's Degree. The fact of the matter was that whenever the Sports Therapists came into contact with the 'physios' our students were always amazed as to how little time the 'physios' had spent studying certain things compared to them. For example, their whole physical therapy programme consisted of 12 hours of massage, whilst ours consisted of three times that amount over three years. Whilst I not only expressed my concerns to Mark about the disruption to the E&A module, I also expressed them to Steve and John. Sadly, they didn't see this as an issue, and the football mentality kicked in of circling the wagons and closing ranks. I also got the impression that Mark was just passing time and as soon as another position in football presented itself, he would seriously consider it. We had also just undergone a massive re-write of the whole course as the University changed from 12-week semesters to 10-week ones to bring it in line with other Universities. Pat was brilliant at pulling all our efforts together, as we were all tasked with dealing with different aspects of the course depending on our knowledge, skill, expertise and experience. Unfortunately, just prior to this Pat had recruited another physiotherapist, Penny Minnoch, from the physio department, to help me with the physical therapy side of things and again whilst I respected Penny's knowledge, skill and expertise she was trained as a Chartered Physiotherapist, and I suspected wanted to join the team because of its growing reputation not because of a burning desire to promote Sports Therapy. Eventually after finding out that a position was to come up at UCLAN, and after that they would have their full complement of staff for the foreseeable future, I considered applying for it. Deep down inside, I wanted to stay at Teesside but felt I was banging my head against a brick wall as the numbers game was once again taking precedent over the quality of the course. **Bums on seats with a lecturer in front of them to deliver the power point, irrespective of who that person was, seemed to be becoming more and more a reality.** Another reality that had to be addressed was, as the number of graduates grew where would these people find work? In theory, it would appear that in sport per se, with all its dangers and pitfalls, there would be ample employment opportunities for people who wanted to look after their welfare. However, the reality was that there were still many issues to be resolved regarding insurance, historical precedent, social grading, racial profiling etc and the fact that the term sports therapist was not yet State Registered meant, there were still many barriers to break down. The SST was pro-active in addressing such issues but it started to become a question of prioritising. The society needed more members to justify State Registration, but as the number of universities offering the course increased, so did the number of graduates needing employment. **I loved the students with their enthusiasm and commitment, but felt they were getting a raw deal because statistics, tables, targets and egos, not to mention money, seemed more important than trying to ensure there were ample opportunities for paid employment for these graduates. On 12/03/2018, whilst researching this question of employment, I came across a first class honours graduate student, Pok Wong, who was suing Anglia Ruskin University Business School for more than £60,000, after claiming her two years of study had not helped her career, despite claims by the university to, provide a quality of education and prospects of employment after graduation. If successful, it would definitely set a precedent that would make all universities re-think its marketing strategy. I REPEAT BUMS ON SEATS DO NOT EQUATE TO QUALITY OF EDUCATION OR GUARANTEED EMPLOYMENT.**

Back to the chalk face, I certainly felt standards were slipping and whilst we as a Society had come a long way from the first module on Holloway Road, North London, the foundation that had been laid in those early days was beginning to become frayed, if not crumbled. So, with a heavy heart I reluctantly applied for the post at UCLAN hoping that if I got the job, I could get back to winning ways with Andy at UCLAN. How wrong could I have been, and moving there proved to be the straw that broke the camel's back. Well, if not the camels, certainly mine. As can be seen from the good luck cards and e-mails I received, I was not the only one to think I was making a mistake. These e-mails have been included straight from the computer as they were sent.

Hi there, Jim! Just Wanted to wish you well in your new venture, it's been a real pleasure learning from you, I've learned so much in the past fourteen weeks that I've been here and I'm sorry to see you leave , but I'll always remember your quote 'ENJOY' So I'll say to you ENJOY your time as you will be sorely missed.

ALLMOST FORGOT PLEASE THANK YOUR 'MOTHER' , (THE MOST IMPORTANT LADY), FOR IF IT WASN'T FOR HER, WE WOULDN'T HAVE THE KNOWLEDGE OF WHAT WE KNOW NOW, AND THE WEALTH OF YOUR EXPERIENCE THANKS, JIM FOR ALL YOU HAVE DONE FOR US AS A CLASS HAS BEEN TRULY APPRECIATED!! KM, 25th January 2006 1535.

Mr Briggs, what's this nonsense I've been hearing that you are leaving us for happier times in central Lancashire? Do you not love your second years anymore? Who on earth is going to make me laugh now? I really don't think you have thought this through properly! Well, if this is true I suppose I should wish you well ! Miss B. 25th November 2005 11:14.

Hi, Jim I've just heard the news about your departure to Central Lancashire. I'm very sorry to hear you're going and I'm sure you will be missed as a valuable member of staff. Do you remember a conversation I had with you about 2 years ago when Andy announced his departure?? I expressed concern at Mr Cunningham poaching Teesside staff and you laughed at my "conspiracy theory"!!! Good luck, anyway, I'm sure it won't take you long to miss us all(not!) Helen. H O 24th November2005 1537.

11 years later, Helen was for a few years a lecturer at Teesside University before moving, having secured a position at Leeds University.

But I didn't leave Teesside before having a wonderful send off from the students, with lots of e-mails and cards, not forgetting several leaving parties. I will never forget driving home along the A66 after my last day, very upset. Soft sod, pull yourself together man. I still find it difficult to read the cards and e-mails and even worse looking at the pictorial memories.

On 6th July, 2016 I received a phone call from Steve Smelt, informing me he had just retired. Whilst it was great to hear from him, it was sad that he informed me that the course at Teesside had changed because management was interfering too much, and so his decision wasn't too difficult to make. His final words being, **"It wasn't like it was in our day, Briggsy."** So sad.

University of Central Lancashire: Final Straws and Camel's Backs.

Following Andy Cunningham to UCLAN in 2006, was a big decision for me but in the end the financial benefits, reduction in travel-time and being able to spend more time with Heather won the day. Finding Colin Jackson, who I had taught at North London, was also going to be joining me, after he was one of my rivals at the interview stage, and that Natalie Hardaker, a top-class student I had examined at Teesside, was also there as a research assistant, were massive bonuses. Andy was trying to build a staff of Sports Therapists to produce Sports Therapists, 'fit for purpose'. Or at least that's what I thought. There was only Colin Hayes, a Chartered physiotherapist, on the staff whom I didn't know. That was not an issue for me, as long as it didn't create another Mark Leather scenario. My initial dealings with Colin were that he talked the talk, and appreciated where we were trying to take Sports Therapy as a profession, but I had reservations until I'd actually worked with him. I was also a little concerned, that Andy was excited that he had quite a few students on the course that had been unsuccessful in getting on the physiotherapist course and saw Sports Therapy as second choice. Well, I've already made my views perfectly known on that topic and if I'd have known that before accepting the post, I may have reconsidered. During the first few weeks, I was informed that James Self would contact me, once I had settled in, regarding the publication of another book, which would have been my second, considering, Evidence Informed Practice, as opposed to Evidence Based Medicine. Again, I was excited with the prospect of writing the book in collaboration with John McCreadie and Steve Smelt at Teesside. Add this to the fact, that I found that Dr Jim Richards, who was part of the faculty, was also keen to get involved, and that I could approach Colin Jackson and Natalie Hardaker for input, I was really buzzing to get stated. My initial impressions were that UCLAN would be far more supportive of getting my second book to publication, than Teesside would have been. James was one of the guys tasked with ensuring that all the lecturers developed their research portfolios. With a name like James, I felt we were going to get on well! Meanwhile, Graham Smith was singing Andy's praises, and was excited that Andy was taking the course into the 21st century with his ideas for development and, on paper, these seemed to be steps in the right direction. Knowing Graham as I knew him, I was wondering at what point, no disrespect to Andy, had Mr Smith become part of the Andy Cunningham mutual admiration society, because when he was at Teesside this overt enthusiasm had not been apparent. Certainly not to me, it hadn't. On the curriculum development front, don't forget that this subject had been one of my options whilst studying for my B. Ed. Honours degree, I personally felt that things that had proven successful at Teesside could be fine-tuned and be just as successful at UCLAN. My initial thoughts were, that Andy would use my knowledge, skills, expertise and experience to take over the physical therapy modules, and develop the clinical side of things. Unfortunately, once I was in situ Andy saw it differently and now that he had a full team, appeared to want to fit square pegs into round holes. He asked me to take over Research and Development, to put it mildly, not my strongest suit, whilst helping Natalie, who was a keen researcher with very little appetite for teaching, with some of the teaching of the Anatomy, Examination and Assessment modules. He wanted Colin Jackson, who was, in my humble opinion, good on the research and development side, to take over the massage modules, with Colin Hayes, a physiotherapist, developing the in-house clinic. This together with his excitement of having students who saw Sports Therapy as second best, was like a red rag to a bull to me, but Andy saw it as a feather in his cap. I was also made aware, that Andy had bought a sports shop in Lytham, with Cath, his wife, being front of house, with Andy steering the ship from UCLAN. I was a little confused as to what Andy's motivations were since leaving Teesside, as he certainly didn't appear to be the same guy I had worked with at Teesside. I went to see Andy to air my views, and he in turn explained his reasoning, which I respected but didn't agree with. Why was he not using my strengths instead of throwing me in at the deep end with Research and Development, with both Natalie and Colin J being far more suited to the subject than myself? He didn't see it that way, arguing that as a published author I should be au fait with R&D, and so we begged to differ. The issue being the degree or what definition was being used for the term, au fait.

Unfortunately, I never really settled as one thing after another kept annoying me, everything seemed so disjointed. I understood it would take time as it was a relatively new course with lots of new staff, but the Sports Therapy family that I'd gotten used to at the University of North London and Teesside, just wasn't there at UCLAN, as everyone seemed to be doing their own thing, instead of complementing one another. I channelled my energies into mentoring and helping Natalie with her teaching, as we team taught some of the sessions. It appeared she had also been thrown in at the deep end, having been under the impression she was only going to do research. Again, square pegs in round holes sprung to mind. No disrespect to Nats, as she liked to be called, but as mentioned many times before, you need to shadow experience for a while, before being thrown to the lions. For me, the main thing was the attitude of certain students. I had left cohorts of committed students at North London and Teesside, to teach students who appeared to lack identity, and who also appeared to be just going through the motions, and doing favours to lecturers by turning up. Was I being impatient, no, I was the 49th member of the Society of Sports Therapists, and my worst fears were becoming a reality.

As mentioned previously, in its desire to get State Registration, and to get more Universities signed up, the quality of not only the course but the input of students was, in my opinion, suffering. You can't just conjure up experienced sports people, that can not only walk the walk but also can talk the talk. Sticking raw recruits, such as newly qualified students, into the fray without any shadowing and expect miracles, or to paper over the cracks, is not a sound teaching strategy. There needs to be periods of analysis, evaluation and consolidation. But what the hell do I know, I was, in certain people's eyes, 'just a little old, Primary school teacher'. Had such a scenario not been discussed with Graham Smith and Keith Waldron, when we started the very first, degree course at the University of North London? Yes. Also, it was during my first few weeks at UCLAN that I had contacted Graham, outlining my ideas for my second book, and as I've mentioned, was shocked, but realistically, not surprised, with his reply. Professor Graham Smith was not the Graham Smith I had started the journey with. To give him a hug now would probably mean I needed an appointment. I will always appreciate what Graham did for me, but he asked me to join him on the journey, not the other way around, but now he appeared to have pigeon holed me as second division. He may have initially invited me to the party, but Mr B was seriously considering leaving it. I had left behind at Teesside a group of students who, on the whole had a work ethic and attitude that personally I felt would guarantee success in wanting to become Sports Therapists. Yes, it had taken time to get some of them to adopt such an approach, the rest arriving on the course with a positivity that needed no guidance or steering, and here I was having to deal with some students that wanted to contribute very little to promote the Sports Therapy brand. Suddenly, my doubts and concerns about leaving the Teesside students for a post nearer home, and the financial package that went with the move, raised its head again.

What price happiness and job satisfaction?

Universities adopted a theoretical, two-way, verbal contract of respect, agreed with students at the beginning of the course. Unfortunately, some students, especially the, should I say, less mature ones, adopted the attitude that as lecturers were paid vast sums of money to do their jobs, why should they be afforded such courtesies? **This attitude of displaying a lack of social maturity would hopefully disappear, as students gained more life experiences of living in the real, as opposed to the virtual reality world of computers, mobiles, tablets wi-fis etc. "Time to move on, Jim, you don't need this crap, you're not a social worker."**

I decided my letter of resignation would be handed in to Andy Cunningham, as soon as he arrived at work the following day. My retirement would begin, just as soon as I could serve out my notice and clear my desk. I would inform Heather and sleep on my decision, even though I would write out my resignation that night. As usual once an idea had germinated and it had, after only a few weeks of arriving at UCLAN, that I had made a big mistake moving from Teesside, it festered until I acted upon it. As this autobiography has shown, I was never one to shirk a responsibility just for an easy life. Andrew Cunningham's response to my letter was, to suggest that if I was finding it difficult teaching certain students, he would move them into another group. He mistook my anger and perhaps depressed demeanour as, "he's having a break down and can't cope." Which I suppose if you've not got your eye on the ball, and are more concerned with how your new sports shop is doing, then that would appear to be a good excuse to report back to the superiors, when questions are asked. **What a bloody insult.** He did ask me to dub down my letter of resignation, which was not complimentary to his leadership, which I did out of respect to our relationship of previous times.

To be honest I was not at UCLAN long enough to have any strong feelings about the place one way or another, but I was in no doubt that I had lost my motivation to continue working in that environment. My biggest regret was not finishing my second book, which is still in a box in my back bedroom. I would have liked to have got it published with John, Steve, Natalie and Colin and other personnel involved. Would Graham have been happy, I think not, as he had not been asked to be up front and centre stage from the onset?

Upon retirement I chose to write this book rather than return to my thoughts on Evidence Informed Practice in the world of Sports Therapy.

As this was my last teaching appointment, I was very sad it was so short lived, and left me with a bad taste in my mouth. In much the same way, as when I had left Blackshaw Lane and Primary Education in 1987. Yes, I left with a tear in my eye but that was out of frustration, unlike Teesside which was because of what I was leaving behind. As Heather and I socialised with both Colin Jackson and Natalie Hardaker away from the University, they were shocked with my resignation, but within the following 18 months both Natalie and Colin had left UCLAN for pastures new. Colin back to Scotland, and Natalie to join her brother James in New Zealand. Both had their own personnel reasons for leaving, and as they were considerably younger than I and unlike me, a long way from retirement, they would have been diplomatic as to why they were leaving, but I was aware some of those reasons were not dissimilar to Mr B's. As for Natalie, she became one of the top triathletes in New Zealand in her age range, whilst studying for a PhD and has secured a position as Senior Injury Prevention Specialist for Community and Sport ACC, in Wellington, New Zealand. Periodically, we exchange an e-mail and I recently caught up with her when she visited her parents Barry and Prudence, as her father was recovering from a recent operation. I occasionally meet up with her parents for a catch-up, and to go walking. It's ironic that Natalie and I used to joke about writing a book together, on what was happening in society as we used to, 'put the world to rights', when she sometimes stayed with Heather and me, when she worked at UCLAN. As for Colin Jackson and John McCreadie, I have not heard from them since I retired. Recently, in summer 2019, I saw Andrew Cunningham in Preston, but he pathetically pretended he hadn't seen me. I just smiled. And people wonder, why you become cynical. In July 2015, there were 21 universities and 26 accredited programmes associated with SST. Was that a success story? Well, numerically yes, but at what cost to quality? What those figures are in 2025, I am not sure and has the Society secured State Registration yet? Is Mr Smith still expecting the red carpet? Sadly, I can't be bothered to find out.

Natalie and I at the Thyme Restaurant in Hoghton, February, 2008.

UCLAN, Voluntarily Revisited: The School of Medicine.

In January, 2019, 13 years after I had left, I returned to UCLAN but this time as a Volunteer Patient, connected to the School of Medicine, in the Allen building. Right next to the Harrington building, where I'd spent my final months in full time education. I had a few reservations about returning to UCLAN, but once in situ, I quickly realised that being back in a room full of enthusiastic students was a happy place for me. Although there were tutors, lecturers, doctors and other health care workers in the same room, who were responsible for the teaching and examining, my role as a volunteer was one of just being a member of the public, to create a realistic scenario in which the students could acquire the necessary knowledge, skills and expertise to become doctors, nurses and other allied health professionals. Role play was minimal, as they brought in actors when such occasions required this. Some tutors, who became aware of my background, appreciated any feedback and help, when asked, I could give to the students. **I was, however, fully aware that my role was purely and simply one of being, 'a body'.** The volunteer programme was run by Joanna Clarkson, who herself had a background in health care. I liked Joanna, but also appreciated that, at times, she had to be more than a little diplomatic. She was, as one would expect, very appreciative, as were the students and staff, of the role the volunteers played. Unfortunately, after a honeymoon period during which I applauded the significance of students training to be doctors and nurses having to communicate with Joe Public from day one, and really enjoying being part of that process, **I started to realise that old issues such as not all staff talking from the same page, both in practice sessions and assessments, bums on seats versus quality of education and pissing competitions between so called adults, started to raise their ugly heads. And sadly, just as I was really enjoying my time back in an educational environment, I was accused of being, 'not very helpful to the students', and was asked to explain my version of events.** Whilst I don't think it's pertinent to highlight in detail such issues in this book, I nevertheless feel obliged to point out the facts as I saw them, especially as I felt my character was being questioned. I loathe to use the word defamed. The gist of my e-mail to UCLAN was,

"Thank you for my feedback from yesterday, and perhaps the issues raised are clarified. I am very conscious of the fact, that I do not offer my services as a volunteer wearing my external examiner's hat, my senior lecturer's or my author's hat and I'm just Joe Public being asked to do whatever. But I, like the students, get confused and find it difficult to ignore what I see and experience. The problem I have is, that not all the staff appear to be talking from the same hymn sheet, not only in practice sessions but during assessments. I'm aware that when issues are raised in any situation, there is a temptation to circle the wagons and look after one another. I repeat, I was not volunteering to assess and critique, but I do not subscribe to the fact that ignorance is bliss and having a high pass rate looks good for all concerned. I think the issues raised against me are from the junior members of staff, who perhaps didn't appreciate my honest reply to their question, and haven't the experience of examining and were perhaps not as diligent as the more experienced. You have to start somewhere, and I appreciate that, but if the criteria for pass and fail are questionable then that is not my fault. Also, if you don't get the reply you want from someone you barely know, don't ask the question. How a student can pass an assessment, which involves looking at spinal curvatures and feeling for skin temperature changes, without asking the 'model' to remove their tops, or standing in the correct place to observe and without appropriately touching them, is not something I understand. But hey folks, we've a high pass rate, whoopie!! Finally, if my presence as a volunteer is viewed with suspicion, and not appreciated then the solution is very simple. For me, the students are paying a lot of money to be on the course and deserve, 'a fair crack of the whip'. I'm sorry, Joanna, but quite frankly, I am saddened that certain members of the staff see me as some smart arse, but if my comments in this e-mail are not seen as constructive criticism, then a quote readily springs to mind, 'There is nothing as certain as a closed mind.' (Dean Spamley). Will I see you next week? I think for all concerned, I think not. James."

A week later, I received a diplomatic reply from the Course Leader, John, addressing my concerns and agreed that my withdrawal as a volunteer was perhaps, the best course of action. For whom I wondered.

I am aware that during my career, I have never been afraid to confront issues that I feel need addressing but during my journey, I have realised that many would prefer such issues to be swept under the carpet. I make no apologies for my passionate behaviour, and I am proud of standing

up for what I believe in, even when at times, I've asked myself, why was I even bothering? The answer to my doubts is that I prefer being like a dog with a bone, and not like a sheep that just follows. Who said I was not a dog lover?

On the 19th December, 2019, a Channel 4 programme titled, The Cure, about the high mortality rate at a Staffordshire hospital, where financial stringency was prioritised over patent wellbeing and safety, showed the lengths to which the 'powers that be' will go to hide unacceptable practice. The person who started the campaign to get something done about the management, was subjected to all kinds of abuse for daring to take on the establishment. Does that sound familiar? But someone has to stand up to the power crazed bullies. As I watched the programme, guess whose side I was cheering on?

6.
PERSONAL STUFF.

Marriage and Children.

"Once you've been married to someone, they're always part of your life, good or bad." (Gerritsen T, 2004. Body Double, PB, p126).

25/8/'85 Dee and I at our wedding reception at Swinton Civic Hall.

I cannot actually remember getting down on one knee with the ring in my hand, and asking Dee to marry me. As I recall, we had been seeing each other for some time, after the initial night at the university and then the chips in a tray with gravy, night out. Yes, we had one or two fall outs, probably because I was being a dick head, but I do recall being at Dee's parents, walking along Longshaw Drive, Little Hulton, when it somehow just cropped up in the conversation, and the rest is history so to speak. Not very romantic, you may say but that is how I recall it. Perhaps Dee has a different recollection, we'd have to ask her. Sometimes, there's an intensity that people talk about in relationships, but that was not the case for Dee and me. Sometimes, people say it's good to have a row every so often, so you can then, 'make up', but I cannot recall ever having a severe row with Dee. My marriage to Dee was never volatile. For some, such volatility is part of the territory, but as Dee preferred the waters to be calm and smooth, she never sought confrontation, or stressful situations. She was like her father Les. Les was a lovely man, but I used to get frustrated with him as he was the chief cook and bottle washer in the house, whilst Olive, his wife, used to spend most of her time reading Mills and Boon novels. This sounds like the beginning of a long tirade against the mother-in-law. Remember, I had met Les Dawson who was famous for his jokes about mothers –in-law, such as, **What is the difference** between in-laws and outlaws? Outlaws are wanted. But that was never the case for me, as I got on very well with Dee's parents and they were very good to me. I know, they were hurt when Dee and I split. Les once told me, that he behaved the way he did, because it made for an easier life. With Dee informing me, that her mum used to be a very industrious mum and wife, but had somehow lost her 'mojo'. Oh, don't get me wrong, she would cook and do her bit, but Les was **ALWAYS** on the go. The favourite request being, 'Les, put on the kettle.' As I got into my sixties, I understood how the elderly can suddenly become less active and it's not always to do with the aging process. Dee had a younger sister, Brenda, who started going out with Paul, a music teacher, and Ian, a younger brother, whom we used to pick up from the local Primary School. Dee, who was christened Alma, got her nickname after we had been to see, Walt Disney's, The Aristocrats, at a cinema in Bolton. One of the cats, Duchess, had beautiful eyes, like Alma, and as I was not particularly fond of the name Alma, I gave her the name Dee, for Duchess. Everyone in my family knew her as Dee, and only a few people, her mum and dad of course, called her Alma. Her sister referred to her as Al. After courting for 5 years, with one break apart, whilst I sorted myself out, and Dee had a brief relationship with another young man, we both decided that that there was more than enough compatibility between us, and so chose to get married on Bank Holiday Monday, 25th August, 1975, at St Paul's Peel, Little Hutton. Like many couples who are seeing someone over a period of time, courting as it was known, we were subjected to the societal pressures of constantly being asked, by family and friends, when we were going to tie the knot. **Do couples still court or do they skip that phase and just go for the posh wedding?** Having committed, we saved to pay for our wedding and honeymoon, as we didn't expect parents on either side to have the resources to pay. My parents certainly didn't have any savings, that I was aware of. Having said that, both parents, in their own ways, wanted to contribute as best they could. My father citing himself at the bar during the reception, to buy everyone a drink. The word pride springs to mind. **According to the website, Hitched, a survey carried out in 2016, said the average cost of a UK wedding, including the honeymoon was £25,090, with much of this expense coming courtesy of mummy and daddy.** It would also appear that, today some couples just want the wedding but not the marriage. Being the centre of attention for a day, with all its trimmings, and inviting as many people as possible to share their special day. Many of whom the bride and groom will probably never see again, appears to be the norm. However, working at the marriage was not something it would appear, they had given much thought to. This attitude certainly fits with the instant gratification, easily disposable tag, I've given to many in today's society.

"They say a woman marries a man with the belief she can change him, and she can't. A man marries a woman with the belief that she won't change, and she does."(Grisham J, 2015, Grey Mountain, PB, 17:227). Also, saving up for a deposit for a modest property, such as a terraced house, and beg, steal and borrow to furnish it, somehow seems beneath some couples. Opting instead for a brand new semi-detached, with all the mod cons. No wonder they can't get on the property ladder, with such high expectations. If, however, they do manage to secure a property via a mortgage, as opposed to renting, staying at home to paint, wallpaper, clean, dust, cut the grass, dig the soil, plant etc. appears too much of a lifestyle change out of the limelight. No wonder they get bored, and utter such endearing terms as, "You're doin my hed in." Hand in hand with this attitude is, what would appear to be a total lack of suitable criteria to help find a partner with whom they wished to happily spend the rest of their lives. In other words, the glue to bind the relationship, or put another way, what baggage are you bringing to the party? **This compatibility to include such criteria as friendship, significant** others, shared interests, individual interests, chemistry, personality, hopes, disposition, dreams and ambitions to name but a few, now seems to have been condensed down to sex, tattoos, the ability to drink copious amounts of alcohol, and very little eye to eye conversation, because spending as much time on anti-social media appears to be the priority. In many instances, both parties don't appear to even like each other, and could certainly not be classed as friends. Dee is still my friend after 55 years. In fact, **she is my best friend.** Again, this instant gratification aspect of today's generation rears its ugly head, with the easily disposable aspect following on, when 6 months down the line, rumours start to emerge as to the stability of the marriage. As said, they appear to be excited at the prospect of an expensive wedding and honeymoon, but are not too keen on what follows. **Also, today optional wedding presents have been superseded by subtle requests for contributions to a Caribbean Cruise as part of their honeymoon. Cheeky bastards. Could this be one reason, why several years later they are both, 'lawyered up', going through an acrimonious divorce, contesting who gets what? Sadly, in 2022, getting divorced is like puberty, a stage most people go through. With the actor, Robson Green once stating that if we invest in people emotionally, not financially, the rewards will come.** Dee and I never got engaged, because as I recall, like marriage, the topic never seriously entered the conversation. We were too busy trying to enjoy life, by sharing and caring, and starting our teaching careers, myself at Mather Street, Failsworth, and Dee at Holy Trinity, Manchester. We were not religious people, but never considered anything other than a church, white wedding. St Paul's, where we got married, was 'high-church' but the Registry Office alternative was not even considered. In hindsight, I was hypocritical, because I subsequently became firmly convinced that politics and religion were the root of all evil. At the time, I was living in Carnarvon Street, Hollinwood, and so my wedding banns were read out at St Margaret's Church, Hollinwood. On the day Neil Sinker, my best man, picked me up from Carnarvon Street, and drove me to Little Hutton. The standing joke for Neil Sinker was that he became the swimming secretary for Chadderton and District School's Sports Association. That Bank Holiday Monday was a gorgeously, sunny day and, as I recall, all went well but for both Dee and myself. Our strongest recollection of the ceremony was a spider crawling up Mr Watt's, the vicar's cassock, as we were taking our vows. The reception was held at Swinton Civic Halls, and in the evening Dee and I stayed at the Wendover hotel, in Eccles, before returning to Carnarvon Street. I recall emptying the car the day after the wedding, when we'd returned to Carnarvon Street, feeling emotionally very low. **Today's society probably has a label for my then emotional state, possibly Post Traumatic Wedding Syndrome, which could be used against their partner in any subsequent divorce proceedings.** But for me, with all the planning, organisation and hype that had gone into the wedding, it was not surprising we would suffer some reaction. So here we were, just the two of us, isolated and alone. It wasn't that nobody cared, it was just not the done thing, in the 1970s, to contact people, immediately after their wedding. Time had to be given for the couple to consummate the marriage as virgins still roamed the planet. **I wonder how many texts, emojis and photos are exchanged during wedding nights in 2025? Also, today the word virgin is associated with banking, air and rail travel, and could now possibly be the title of a game, 'Find the Altar Virgin'.** According to research by Professor Wolfinger, who looked at the US Surveys of Family Growth 2002, 2006-2010 and 2011-2013, virgins were a fast shrinking population, with over half the brides in the 1980s being virgins, whereas by 2010, this was only true of just 28%. I can't see the figures for the UK being significantly different to these. However, for me this isolation was another reminder of how I hated saying goodbyes and rejection. Silly really, as it was not as though I would never see my family and friends again, or that I'd been rejected by anyone, but I felt very emotional. Because of this, I said to Dee that once we'd unpacked the presents, we would re-pack and go away for a few days. We hadn't planned a honeymoon, but I certainly didn't want to stay at, 'The Castle', and make Dee miserable. We honeymooned in Grasmere, in the Lake District, at a lovely hotel with a stream running through the grounds. No Caribbean cruises for our generation, as they would only come after years of grafting and saving. Perhaps we should have asked for cheques, cash and pin numbers, as many do today, to fund one. And I know what the response would have been from most of our family and friends, if I'd have asked for such. One member of my extended family for his SECOND marriage asked for money, but as far as I know didn't even bother with the honeymoon, and just pocketed the cash. They have since split up. Was I shocked, angry, saddened or upset. Not really. **After all, Jim, that's the way it is today, get real, IT'S CALLED PROGRESS. Followed by a patronising pat on the leg. Which will probably be the only exercise they do that day, apart from tapping, pecking, scrolling and swiping. You can lie, cheat, disrespect, patronise, abdicate your responsibilities, steal, (Swiping in my day meant stealing), claim as many benefits as you can lay your hands on, get drunk on a regular basis, hoping to get sclerosis of the liver, eat junk food, hoping beyond all hope that you'll get obesity and type 2 diabetes, smoke and do drugs, in the hope that you'll at the least get lung cancer, dress your children up to look like hookers, hoping they will get pregnant, long before they know what a tampon is, (Not forgetting that what my children want, my children get!) etc. etc. etc. but no one bats an eyelid, (heavily laden down with false eyelashes, of course), except for my generation, but what do we know? Not forgetting, we are supposedly the highest form of intelligence.**

During the writing of this book, there are many references to Dee, along with Verna and later Heather, because they, along with certain family members, just accepted me for what I was, warts and all. I still feel guilty about my marriage break up, and subsequent divorce. That's why I never asked for a second chance. I know Dee forgave me but **I NEVER forgave myself.** I felt I needed to pay a price for what I did to her. After all, according to Stephen Fry, **"Love is supposed to be creative, not destructive."** (The Liar, 1991, PB, 4:156). **"Falling in love really amounted to, your brain on drugs. Adrenaline and dopamine, oxytocin and serotonin. Chemical insanity, celebrated by poets."** (Gerritsen T, 2012, 9:108). As I've got older and travel became a big part of my life, with no disrespect to my other partners at the time, I did so miss taking the rest of my life's journey with her. Dee and I are still friends, in fact, **she is my best friend**. She is married to John. We exchange birthday and Christmas cards, and occasionally meet up for lunch, to catch up on the news and gossip. **Today in the world of acrimonious divorces, there are many who consider this more than a little strange, but that is their problem not ours.** I met John, before they decided to get married, and I'm not sure what he thinks of his wife meeting up with her ex., but Dee tells me he's a fairly laid-back guy and just accepts it. Thank you, John. Perhaps, he thinks that if we are having sex in the Travelodge in Preston, Jim can't be any good at it because she still comes home to him. In today's instant gratification, easily disposable society, how long is it from celebrating an engagement to celebrating the divorce, weeks, months?

Children.

In previous chapters, the topic of children and parenting, and its relevance to child development has been considered on more than one occasion. **I've even tried to find out when a child became a baby goat and a commodity, instead of someone you love, entertain, guide and educate,** even referring to the television programme, Call The Midwife, as an example of life during my childhood. **Caregivers** and shapers affect how children see the world. Do today's children actually see themselves as baby goats or just as items who are participants in a game of, 'pass the parcel'?

"If we are lucky, we have, as infants and toddlers, at least one emotionally available parent who consistently fills our needs, and responds to our needs and responds to our desires for attention. Being held and comforted, having our feelings acknowledged. and our upsets soothed are all critical for the healthy development of children. This kind of attention creates a sense of safety and security, that ultimately allows us to explore the world around us without excessive fear and unmanageable anxiety, because we know we can count on the bedrock support of at least one caregiver. Mirroring, the process through which an attuned parent reflects, processes, and then gives back to the baby the baby's own feelings, is another crucial part of a young child's development. Without mirroring, children are denied crucial information about how their minds work and how to understand the world. Just as a secure attachment to a primary care giver can lead to higher levels of emotional intelligence, mirroring is the root of empathy." (Trump ML, 2020, Too Much and Never Enough, 1:23).

Unfortunately, many parents today misinterpret the expression, 'What my children want, my children get', smothering and enveloping them in materialism and sugar. And the reason I've included this quote by a member of the Trump family, is to demonstrate what happens when this happens. The title, Too Much and Never Enough, is a brilliant description of Donald Trump. Moving on, I want to make the topic more personal to myself and Dee, and relate it to our experiences both in and out of the classroom. This will mean I may go over certain issues raised previously. **"Do you know what's ahead? Months of sleepless nights. And for some of you, the end of your life as you know it. All the sacrifices you'll both make over the years to come? Will you produce geniuses who'll change the world for the better, or ungrateful little bastards who'll turn you into an anxious mess? The gamble of life. A good kid or a waste of space? Nature, nurture; good parents, crap parents. You need a licence to keep certain animals, but any irresponsible idiot can have kids."** (James P, 2020. I Follow You, PB, 1:11). **"because let's face it –who'd want to bring children into this world?** (Hunter A, 2023, The Serial Killer's Sister, PB, 48:386). Look out, James, the troll merchants will be after you. Don't forget, many of today's generation find it difficult to accept any responsibility for many of their actions. When my wife and I taught in nursery, infant and junior schools, parents were usually the first to accept that their child was naughty, or lazy and needed strong discipline etc. Whatever that means, and also whether this was the case in school or not. However, discussing with parents that their child may be, say dyslexic, was sometimes difficult as they didn't want their child stigmatised with a label, and the thought of special educational measures, that in theory was beneficial, was strangely something they were keen to avoid. Nowadays, with drastic changes in society we return to the issue of why and who is responsible? Advances in teacher training has meant it has become easier to identify children with, 'problems', that may need specialist help. Unfortunately, as I see it, it would appear some parents are only too quick and pleased to attach a label to their offspring, and there are many to choose from, and that announcing to whoever might want to hear, that their child had Attention Deficit Disorder, ADD, was a good way to distract attention away from the fact, that their parenting skills left a lot to be desired. Long before this plethora of terms entered the scene, children were seen as little darlings or as lazy, disruptive, un co-operative little so and sos? Also, when I taught in primary education, children had very few, if any, technological gadgets to occupy their time, but today maybe the child has been allowed to stay up late, sometimes all night, playing on a games console or computer, or smartphone and so by the time it came to concentrating for more than several minutes on school work, they were found wanting. There's research evidence and several television documentaries highlighting the facts. In my personal experiences, reading a book under the covers was as bad as it got. Now before I am given another ic, ist or ism and society is going to pass judgment on me, **I AM NOT SAYING THAT MANY CHILDREN HAVEN'T GOT EDUCATIONAL ISSUES THAT PREVIOUSLY WERE NOT IDENTIFIED. ALL I AM SAYING IS THAT THESE LABELS HAVE GIVEN CERTAIN PARENTS A READY-MADE EXCUSE FOR THEIR PARENTING NEGLECT. DON'T FORGET, THAT IN AN EDUCATIONAL CONTEXT THE FIRST FIVE YEARS OF A CHILDS' LIFE ARE VITAL. HOW MANY OF TODAY'S PARENTS EVEN CONSIDER SPENDING ONE YEAR, LET ALONE FIVE ON THE TASK?**

"**I don't have children……Perhaps, that's because I don't want all that pain.**" French N, 2012, Blue Monday, PB, p308. "**Ruddy kids. They take up the best years of your lives and then they bugger off. I'd tell them they were ungrateful if they stuck around long enough to listen.**" Titchmarsh A, 2002. Trowel and Error, PB 28:217. "**…it was Rousseau who began in Western culture the worship of the child, innocent and perfect in nature. Anyone who has raised a human from scratch knows this is a lie. Children are savages-egocentric little brutes who by the age of three master every form of human misconduct, including violence, fraud and bribery, in order to get what they want.**" Turow S, 1993, Pleading Guilty, HB, p86. "**-the early moments of parenthood when you try to figure out how to survive nature's slyest tricks, using love to produce someone to come between you. There is no divorcing your children.**"

Turow S, 2007. Limitations, 16:150. "**When your children are young, they tread on your feet. When they get older, they tread on your heart.**"

Cole M, 1992. Dangerous Lady, PB, 6:103.

To this we could easily add, **and on your wallet.**

"**What is the first thing they'll tell you? That their children come out a certain way. Hardwired. Nature over nurture. Parents can steer them and try to keep them on the right road, but in the end, they are little more than caregivers. Some children will end up sweet, no matter what. Others will end up psychotic. You know friends who have raised their kids identically. One kid is outgoing, one is quiet, one is miserable, one is generous. Parents quickly learn that their influence is limited.**" (Coben H, 2010. Long Lost, PB, p365).

As previously alluded to, is the fact that many can't be bothered to try. It's also interesting to note how, in the last reference, the words kid and children are used and referred to as though they are the same thing. Some authors and researchers seem unclear as to the difference, which I find staggering, when such people use words as their main communication tool. WC Fields was attributed with the tag line, "**A man that hates women, cats and dogs can't be all that bad.**" And when asked specifically how he liked children he replied, "**Fried.**" When I was at Teacher Training College, as part of the Child Development course, we had a lecture that highlighted the many reasons why people had children, ranging from to continue the species to having someone to look after you in old age. The latter being the least desirable as it was grounded in selfishness. Also having children to save a relationship, and to divert attention away from the real issues as to why a relationship was failing, was considered disastrous.

"**I want to have kids, Dick.**"

"You think it would be OK to introduce a kid into this mess?"

"Don't call it a mess."

"But that's what it is. You can hardly be civil to me, and I can't stand the sight of you."

"That's not true. We just say those things, but they're not true."

"They're true." (Hayes K, 1997. Curtains, PB, p225).

Remember my teacher training was at the end of the sixties and early seventies when ethics and morals were more clearly defined by society, crèches and child minders were in a minority, if not totally absent, grandparents were respected and appreciated, not abused and seen as babysitters and cash cows, and virgins roamed the planet. Parenting was seen as a skill learned through experience, not by abdication of responsibilities by giving your children away for somebody else to look after. Household roles were defined with the man being the bread winner, and the woman the housekeeper. Today, with all the changes that have taken place in society a whole raft of issues have come to light, some of which already existed but were never talked about or tackled. Issues such as the 'dead-beat' dads who didn't, or couldn't contribute to raising their children; the parents who abuse their off-springs, not forgetting that abuse can take many forms; the middle-class parents who never leave work early to spend time with their children, and spend forty grand on a new car but find spending forty minutes with their children just downright inconvenient. Men who still believe that sharing their sperm with a woman is their ONLY role in the parenting stakes, as it's solely the role of the woman to look after the children, whilst they watch football and pop off to the pub, again. Articles such as, The Myths and Reality of Deadbeat Dads, (Andrew Yarrow, 6/9/2019) and Kids Turn Central, 15/2/21, have shown that these dead-beat dads are usually responsible for the dead-beat teenagers who create many problems, and have no respect for women because they've never seen a woman being respected. As a biologist, I understand men are the tups of the human species, but why do they not have their chests painted with a bright colour, so people could see how many women they had impregnated, as is the case in the farming community? At the other end of the scale, some would argue that feminism has created a sub-culture of women who had no idea how to put a meal on the table, and couldn't be bothered to learn. Also, spending time with their children was proving difficult as it clashed with bonding with their girl-friends and raising their fists to girl power. When I was born in the 1950s, many children were considered under nourished, now they quite easily fall into the category of over nourished, with sugar and fat, falling into the obese category. Or they are deprived of, 'essential amino acids', because mummy and daddy are vegetarians or vegans.

As mentioned, at college we were given the latest research as to why people didn't have children, which ranged from couples wanting to concentrate on their careers, which initially included Dee and myself, to couples accepting that children were selfish, money sapping and difficult and would eventually move away, if not geographically then psychologically, and so they didn't feel they had the necessary skill set to be able to cope. Which at the time left me a little confused, because I never asked the question, "Who was the most selfish, the parents or the children?" However, as my knowledge of human behaviour grew, both from an experiential as well as a theoretical perspective, **I soon realised that you didn't find people in books, and some aspects of life just couldn't be theorised, hypothesised, postulated or rationalised.** Which returned me to the childhood loop of asking why, why, why? Dee and I both wanted children, but being teachers had a checklist of parenting dos and don'ts. As time went on, and I saw our friends getting married and having children and becoming a family, not only did societal pressures to have a child increase, but I also realised that, 'making a baby', and rearing them wasn't as simple as just exchanging sperm, as some would have you believe. Eventually, I settled for the blue print of if we are absolutely certain we both wanted them and we did, then, after conception, we had to **lay the foundation, in the first few years,** by providing a loving, caring, secure, stimulating environment, in which the child could develop physically, emotionally etc. But in the final analysis, it was quite simply about laying the foundation and then crossing your fingers and hoping they would be fine. I have purposely avoided listing all the criteria to define fine, or indeed stimulating, as it can mean different things to different people.

"Active parenting, the enlightened and child focused philosophies, that usually end up with the child being a spoilt brat, because they hadn't been subjected to, or had to compete with other children, who would put them in their place." (Tsiolkas C, 2008. The Slap, PB p394). I also realised that no matter how hard you tried to protect them from the world, the world would eventually claim them. In the meantime, as our careers flourished and things started to be taken for granted in the relationship, we slowly started to 'drift apart' and having children was not the main topic of conversation. Dee, although an excellent teacher, yes, I am biased but honest, was not sure whether she wanted extra responsibilities and promotion at school, whilst I was driven by not wanting to let anyone down, especially Verna and Frank, and to do the best that I could in my career. Obviously, the longer this situation continued, the greater the societal pressures became, as society needed to have us labelled and, in a box and didn't look kindly upon people who didn't play the game.

As a biologist, I understand that unless people have children the species become extinct, and so in that respect my existence has been a failure, but the barrage of abuse that people who chose to make life choices that are different to others, is crazy. Enter the now acceptable world of blogging, cyber bullying and trolling. Sometimes, it may be that these people just do not want to be sheep. I remember Stuart Ford, who had two boys, Jonathan and Christopher, saying to me, **"Jim, if you didn't intend to have children, why did you marry Dee?"** Whilst vividly remembering the question, I can honestly say I cannot remember my reply other than to question his assumption, that because at that time we didn't have any children, we didn't want any. Married couples who didn't have children are considered to have, 'something wrong with them', irrespective of the real reasons. He must be impotent, he can't get wood, she's a lesbian, he's a puff, she's frigid etc. Even today, women who choose not to have children are heavily stigmatised, with the misguided assumption that women who do, are good parents and those who don't are not, and should not have an opinion at all on the subject. **Remember, that sound theory underpins good practice**. Just as people who have sex, usually as a result of too much alcohol resulting in pregnancy, think they are the experts on all things related to the topic. **"It is possible the world is divided into three genders – there are men, there are women, and then there are women who choose to have nothing to do with children. How about men without children ...aren't they different from fathers? No, all men are the same."** (Tsiolkas C, 2008. The Slap, PB p397). How this quote is viewed in 2025 I'll let the reader decide.

Over the years, as I became more and more stigmatised for not having children, and my patience became tested, my standard reply became, **"We decided not to have children, because we realised, we would make crap parents and didn't want to subject society to our little brats, what's your excuse for having them?"**

One of the big issues at the time for us, and which subsequently provided the basis of why I am so critical of today's society on the issue of parenting, was that although we both wanted children, the overriding concern was, who was going to stop work and stay at home to provide this loving, caring, stable environment? **In those days, family planning was a very simplistic, but relevant topic, and issues such as crèches, child minding, designer babies, cloning, house husbands and contractual agreements allowing parents to be paid to have so much time off, with full pay and then half pay, were either in their infancy or non-existent.**

QUITE SIMPLY THE CHILDREN WERE YOUR RESPONSIBILITY AND IF YOU DIDN'T WANT TO ACCEPT THAT, THEN YOU SHOULDN'T HAVE THEM. YOU WERE EXPECTED TO LOOK AFTER THEM - NO ONE ELSE. Sadly, many of today's generation are shocked to find out that after having had unprotected sex, they didn't win a brand new 42" colour TV, or a holiday to the Bahamas, but instead were burdened with a tiny, living being. In disgust, many can't wait to get rid of their offspring to anyone who will accept responsibility for them. **For my generation asking our elderly parents just to babysit for one evening was a last resort, whilst looking after them 5 days a week, so we could return to the task of generating money and material possessions, before the placenta had been cut, was not even considered.**

I remember that I seriously considered giving up my career, for at least the first few years, to be at home with any children we had, but Dee did not think that was fair but she herself wasn't 100% certain she wanted to be at home all day either. As the issue never materialised, it was never resolved as we continued to absorb ourselves into our work. **BUT WHAT WE BOTH AGREED UPON WAS THAT ONE OF US WAS STAYING AT HOME FOR AT LEAST A FEW YEARS.** For me, teaching was not a good career to have when considering children, as you were constantly bombarded with the everyday realities of parenting and child rearing in your classroom. We were informed that child rearing and parenting were not the same thing, and were not exact sciences but as sound theory underpinned good practice, we had to absorb facts, figures, research and the arguments for and against, relating to all things to do with child development. Which meant that, in the end you were either totally confused, as to the best thing to do, or you had a checklist of things you would never do, if you started a family. Only death and change being absolutes in life. In simplicity, the strategy was to do your best, then keep your fingers crossed. Or should that be, in the case of the ladies, your legs? Another ic, ist and ism label. You also saw first-hand the devastation caused by misguided parenting, divorce and a lack of family planning. The result being that in my experience, teachers didn't necessarily make the best parents. **Today's generation being so confused that it has either turned itself into servants and secretaries of their offsprings or decided that a hands-off, abdication approach was less demanding, whereas others accept their responsibilities. Some extremists suggest that parents should be licensed.** As an aside I found the book, Perfect People, by James Patterson, 2011, a very enlightening read regarding designer babies. I always wanted children, preferably two, and especially a daughter, and hopefully they wouldn't get spoiled, whatever that means. Strangely enough, I never hankered after boys, who I could play football with, and during my life have always gravitated towards the girls as opposed to the boys. I wanted to call my daughter Victoria Charlotte, but friends said that sounded like a cake. That was another thing about teaching in primary schools, names not only reminded you of things, but also mainly, they reminded you of pupils, or things, which could instantly dissuade you from adopting a particular name. Also, the playground is a harsh, cruel environment and most names get bastardised. My best man Neil, who had two girls, said that if he had a boy, he would call him Phillip, Ian, Stuart, until it was pointed out to him that with a surname such as Sinker, his son would soon become PISS. I once became aware of a pupil who had a surname Cumber, and his parents called him Quentin. Work it out, the playground soon did, resulting in lots of tears, and parents arriving at school complaining of bullying. Did they not realise from their own school days, that we all acquire nick-names at school? **I've already alluded to the fact that my generation was never cyber bullied or trolled. Bullied yes, but not cyber bullied or trolled, which to me is a self-perpetuated situation.** On the issue of names, I've always been interested, well since I started teaching in primary education, how people got their names. In previous chapters, this issue has been raised when discussing family and friends. I've already mentioned Neil Sinker, swimming secretary, but what about my old Britannia Building Society boss, Mrs Fidler? Then there's the stunt arranger on the TV named Stuart Fell. The weather forecaster, Sarah Blizzard. Not forgetting, when I worked at the University of North London, I taught a student called Storm, whose mother was Gail. Was her father Alex 'Hurricane' Higgins? Then we have the actress, sorry, actor, Tuppence Middleton. Finally, my mate Ed, when working in the tax office had to deal with a Peter Niss, who always referred to himself as P Niss.

After Dee and I separated, when I was 38, I soon realised that finding another partner, not that I was seriously looking, was going to involve some serious baggage, i.e. children, ex-husbands, acrimonious divorces etc. As for me, I was childless and so a biological failure. My baggage was me, my family and friends. The journey was at times difficult, and sometimes heartbreaking. The issue of the degree to which you commit to sharing the parenting, doesn't alter the fact that you are not their biological father but 'the boyfriend', partner, or substitute, male guardian. **Seeing some of these little darlings being used as materialistic pawns in the judicial game of chess during divorce settlements, has caused me untold sadness and anger.** Watching them having to spend a weekend here with mum and a weekend there with dad, or another, and the rest of the time with grandma and granddad, or the childminder, was difficult. Seeing your children for a few hours on Christmas Day, and a few hours on their birthday must be, for many parents, gut wrenching. The argument that having, 'significant others', in a child's life is a perfectly valid argument, and can be advantageous for a growing child but as mentioned before it's a question of, **do you delegate responsibilities or abdicate your responsibilities?** Also, I had my own agenda of what I felt my role was, but sometimes this was at odds with the biological mummy and daddy. After all what did I know? Not having children myself, perhaps, exposed an emotional deficiency that meant, for one reason or another, my relationships with women, who had children, eventually ended. Each of my forays into playing happy families, added to my life's experience and CV. And even in my sixties when I met Denise, who had no children because at the age of fourteen she had informed her mum she never wanted them, and had stuck to the plan, things didn't work out. With no disrespect to all the other children who entered my life, via the non-educational route, Sian D and Hannah M were the nearest I got to finding that daughter I never had. **To this day, I am still very sad as to why the adults no longer wanted my friendship and as if to punish me, I was denied any further access to their children.** The last time I heard, Sian had two children but I never was invited to view, never mind hold. As for Hannah, the last I heard she was in Australia with her boyfriend. I hope both Sian and Hannah are fit, well, healthy but more importantly, happy and their children are likewise. I often think of them and smile or shed a tear.

Children, do I regret not having them? Yes, but when I see what has happened to society in my lifetime I'm relieved I didn't. **On 21st July, 2025, ITV screened, Breaking The Silence: Katie's Story. It encapsulated many of the issues raised in this book.** It was about a Conservative, Cabinet Minister,

Andrew Griffiths who repeatedly abused his wife, even raping her, and the documentary was about how his wife, Katie and many other women, including a female doctor and police woman, fought for many years to get justice. Katie herself becoming a government minister to stand up against her husband. No pun intended. The programme documented how these women whilst not only being abused by their partners, were also being abused by the Family Court System. A system where hearings were held behind closed doors, where those involved couldn't talk about the discussions and decisions taking place, for fear of being incarcerated for several years. Thus, ensuring the court's dirty linen was not aired in public. A system that developed **a culture of consistently NOT BELIEVING THE VICTIMS, that forced many to sort it out themselves.** A system where Parental Alienation was used by the abuser, to get custody of the children. A system where the court ordered and forced children to be with their abusive fathers. A system where, by March 2024, 262 children had died as a result of its decisions. Let's also briefly return to the topic of life, which I started this book with, to consider another reason why perhaps, I'm relieved.

"Parents are always surprised by what their kids will do. They raise them from the time they are babies, spend each and every day with them, think they are these goddamn fucking angels, and then one day the cops come to the door and say hey, guess what, parents? Your kids just bashed some other kid's head in with a baseball bat. Or you're the kid and you think things are pretty fucking OK, and then one day this person who's supposed to be your dad, says so long, have a nice life. And you think, what the fuck is this? So, years later, your mum ends up living with another guy, and he seems OK, but you think, when's it coming? That's what life is. Life is always asking yourself, when's it coming? Because if it hasn't come for a long, long time, you know you're fucking due." Barclay L, 2007, No Time For Goodbye. PB, 18:164.

Finally, to end on a positive note, 'The Fletcher Family Farm', shown on ITV from 2021 to the present, as well as making me laugh, smile and cry all at the same time, made me realise that there are still some wonderful, well-adjusted families out there. It was also testament to the fact that if adults put in the time and effort to bring up their offsprings, the results can be so rewarding. The reader must also appreciate and realise that although Kelvin was born in Oldham and for a time lived near my brother Jack, with whom he played golf, was also a successful actor who won Strictly Come Dancing, had nothing to do with influencing my decision to include him in my book. And who says we don't tell lies? Thank you, Kelvin and Liz –Stay safe.

Friends, Acquaintances, Colleagues and Significant Others.

There's a strong social urge in humans to be needed.

"We all of us – the fools, the geniuses, the beggars, the A listers – we all need to be loved and we all need love." (Townsend S, 2012. The Woman Who Went to Bed for a Year, PB, p399). **"You need friends, Pat. Everybody does."** (Quick, M, 2008.The Silver Linings Playbook, p288).Sadly, it's difficult to ignore the tissue paper reality of friendships, where if you spit on them, they dissolve. For someone, who needed attention, a cuddle and a hug from an early age, those around me played a dominant role and so friends, acquaintances, colleagues and the significance of others was extremely important. But as I got older, and not only realised the differences between these people in my life but also, I found it strange that someone that you'd had a very close relationship with, could suddenly fade and virtually disappear from your radar, as if the connection, similar to pressing the delete button on the computer, was something best expunged.

"It was difficult to grasp. The people who had been around, furnished your life, could simply evaporate and you never saw them again. Except in dreams." (Nesbo J. 2015. The Son, PB. 36:521). As Carol King would sing, 'When you're down and troubled and need a helping hand, you've got a friend.' Or had you? Differentiating between these significant others, whilst appearing obvious, was something I used to get confused about. For me, loss of contact with significant others coincided with some of my saddest moments in life. It also took me a long time to accept and understand, **the tissue paper reality of friendship,** not realising it until I became much older and then very starkly, when I retired at the age of 56. **"You must have friends, I did, at least I thought I did, but everything changed."** (Gerritsen T, 1993. Presumed Guilty, p111).

"Friendships are fickle, bloody things. You think you have lifelong mates, joined by some sort of superglue and then one thing changes. What happens to the friendships? What fucking friendships? I might well have died for all my friends' care. Where are you? Have you changed your lives? Do you come to visit? The answer is of course not." (Fox K, 2007. Skin and Bone, PB, p217-218). On the issue of staying in touch,

"We'll have to keep in touch." "We both knew it was bullshit." " it took an hour to get 17 years of catching up out of the way..... I find that depressing." (Richards J, 2003. Winters End, 4:73). Are these observations fact or fiction? Could they be due to the fact, as mentioned on several occasions in this book, that people are very quick to judge and pigeon hole within the first few minutes of meeting someone, but in reality, these first few contacts could be the bases for future relationships, which unfortunately can sometimes be based on very fickle criteria? These criteria being an extension of the demographic classification tool used since the 1960s known as, **'Social Grading'.** To that we can add, **'Racial Profiling'.** The former being a powerful social discriminator based on occupation and a household's Chief Income Earner. Social grading being very much in evidence in any social gathering, be it at work or at play, because certain facts need to be established, after the initial handshake and eye contact, if a friendship or relationship is to be cultivated. Social grading becomes number one priority. What is the person's income bracket or profession? Are they in a relationship? What kind of a relationship? Have they got children? Where do they reside? In the work scenario, this can be, to put it bluntly, somewhat of a 'pissing competition', as insecurity of some, especially if one is in a more senior position, can create tension. The replies to these casual enquires, answered accurately, or with just a little author's licence, will determine if that person can be a candidate for a friendship or, as Gary Glitter sang, 'Do you want to be in my gang, my gang, my gang?' And we all know what kind of friendships Mr, Gadd and Mr. Saville liked. As for, 'Racial Profiling', this was very much in evidence during Brexit, when people's quick acceptance and perceptions of not only the disinformation being touted by the politicians, but also the misguided, misinformed, white supremacist bigots and racists in society, who caused subsequent mayhem during its implementation. During these initial encounters, there can also be what the psychotherapists call, Negative Transference, which is an instinctive hostile reaction to someone you've just met, that you cannot explain, even if they seem a perfectly decent person. **In my experience, the vast majority of people need to have others pigeon holed and slotted into a box as soon as possible.** It is said that true friendships take time to cultivate, but unfortunately, **society is very quick to judge, and so the instant gratification label can be applied.** It can also be argued that in much the same way as many social addictions, friendships and subsequent relationships are also about dependency. As the Travelling Wilburys sang, 'Everybody needs somebody to lean on.' Friendships are also about usage and being fit for purpose. What can these people bring to my party? In other words, friendships or relationships can be a convenience based on shifting self-interest. Joseph Parry reminding us that you can make new friends, but you can't make old ones.

"It was so hard to keep up with old friends, when they weren't immediately useful." (Hayes K, Curtains, 1997, PB, p87).

Which in essence is a very shallow basis for a long-term relationship because once that person's situation changes, i.e. becomes divorced, retires or decides to out themselves etc., then the question is raised, what good are they to us now? Also, as we get older, friendships become harder to cultivate, WHY?

As we get older, we have more experience, becoming more discriminatory and less forgiving.

Perhaps by middle age, most people have enough friends, and don't feel the need to acquire more.

Perhaps every individual has a quota and when it's filled, they have to wait for someone to die or retire to get on the list.

Perhaps slowly you, 'give up the ghost', as the ones you have, call less often, send fewer letters, e-mails or just don't accept that communication is a two-way process between the giver and receiver. The stark realisation being, that those you thought of as true friends were just happy to receive, but not give. In life, there are givers and takers, with far more takers than givers.

In today's fickle, disingenuous society, friendships appear to be determined by how many times the thumbs up, like button is tapped on the latest technology.

Ricky Gervais reminded us in the television programme Derek, 2012, that,

"You make a living from what you get. You make a life from what you give."

Some would argue it's not what you have in your life, but who you've got in your life. But is this just a blurring of the perceived reality against the fact. Humans are quite capable of deceit, and it is argued that people who won't look you in the eye, are not telling the truth! This issue of eye contact has always been an interesting topic for me once I started to travel, especially south of Watford. There was definitely a North-South divide, with many a patronising, disingenuous, southerner actually believing in their superiority over their northern counterparts, but wouldn't or couldn't look them in the eye to tell them that is what they thought. Ah, bless!

"In your life there are a lot of foxes in the hen house." (Evans C, 2010. 'It's Not What You Think,' p10). **"Adults use you and lose you."** (Timmy Mallet, DJ, Radio and TV presenter).

"There was always a small secretive corner of someone's life that was unknown even to the people closest to them." (Booth s, 2018. Fall Down Dead, PB, 11:121).

The book, Behind Closed Doors, by BA Paris 2016, is an excellent read on such a subject. Linwood Barclay, an American author, says that people are very seldom who we think they are. **"Sometimes we think we know other people, especially those we supposedly are close to, but if we really knew them, why are we so often surprised by the shit they do?** (Barclay L, 2007. No Time for Goodbye, PB, 18:163-4).

My friend of twenty plus years, Tim Kinder, was a prime example of that. As a former bank manager for HSBC, he was found guilty of theft, deception and fraud, related to not only his professional life but also his personal life. These accusations primarily centred upon his son's rugby club, Waterhead RFC, Oldham, where he was treasurer, and the fact that he used his partner's credit card to buy presents for one of his, 'other women in his life at that time'. I have not made any contact with him since he was given a 9 months', suspended prison sentence and ordered to do 300 hours of unpaid work in the community. I could end this by saying that he is still laughing all the way to the bank with his sentence, but that would be to trivialise his actions. I do, however, miss seeing his 3 children, Bethan, Angharad and Luc who are now adults themselves with children of their own.

Finally, another reason why some people do not want to commit to friendship is perhaps they do not want to be entangled into another's sticky web of need and become embroiled in the condition known as, 'Compassion Fatigue'.

"He reckoned that basically there was always a good reason why people lost touch with one another. Sometimes it was an effort to keep a friendship going; when geography was against you or whatever. If the friendship was really worth it, though, you made the effort. Simple as that. If not, let it go, and like as not the other person was thinking the same as you, and letting it go at exactly the same time........If an effort was made later to get back in touch, there was a good chance that the party making the effort wanted something.....But, a decade or more down the road, you want different things, don't you? (Billingham M, 2004, Lifeless, 2005, p186).

At the end of the day, we all have very few friends but many acquaintances. In fact, the enemy of my enemy is my friend. Or so said the Arabs, or was it the Chinese?

"People came and went, lived and died, loved and hated. But at the end of the day, they were always alone. Life was just a relentless flow of strangers passing through the same space. Seconds, minutes, hours, days. Years apart....On and on.....over and over....Never really connecting." (Heller M, 2005. The Charmer, PB p79).

Which is a shame because,

'Some people come into our lives and quickly go,

Some people move our soles to dance.

They awaken us to new understanding with the passing whispers of their wisdom.

Some people make the sky more beautiful to gaze upon. They stay in our lives for a while, leave footprints in our hearts and we are never, ever the same.' Flavia Weedn.

I will always be indebted to Barbara Lynch, nee Bolwell, nee Cooper, for introducing me to this gem of a verse in my 40s that has stayed with me ever since. Barbara was a significant other in my life and feel happiness tinged with great sadness when recalling our times together, and the last time I saw her. I still have two books she bought me, The Wisdom of the Millennium and Seize the Day! Enjoy the Moment. Some of the verses still reduce me to tears because they are so poignant and nostalgic. As Dr. Edmond Locard, French medic, quoting his Exchange Principle, **"Every contact leaves a trace,"** and **"All of our lives have someone's finger prints on them."** (Patterson RN, 2007, Exile, 22:327).

At this juncture I would like to mention several young ladies, Zoe and Khushi. Heather and I met Zoe early in 2003, when she worked in Wilko. We were both impressed with her effectiveness and efficiency when dealing with our requests. She then moved to The Range, where she still works. I occasionally pop in to see how she and her family are and I'm always greeted with a smile and a wave. And this is one of the many reasons I've wanted to include her in my story. She has always treated me with respect, and always given me the impression she was pleased to see me. Recently she lost her father and she was grieving, but still managed to put on a brave face. She is just a lovely, honest, genuine individual and if there were more like her in life it would be a much better place to be part of. Thank you, Zoe. As for Khushi, I think that's how you spell her name, she used to stroll, and I do mean stroll, through the Residential Park delivering newspapers for her parents, who owned a shop on Leyland Lane. Khushi has a wickedly, infectious laugh and over the time I've known her, we've shared many a joyous moment just chatting. Whenever I asked her what she had been up to she always replied, "Nothing really." She teased me that she hadn't any friends, male or female, didn't go out much, didn't drink or smoke or misbehave and was a good Muslim girl. I once bumped into her, well not literally, on the bridge over the River Ribble and she was dressed in this wonderful, colourful attire. When I said, "Hi Khushi, got a date or are you out clubbing with the girls?" she just giggled and said, I always made her laugh. Again, she is one of those youngsters I feel sorry for surrounded by all the Neolithic, grunting dross that roam the planet in 2025.

Whilst reading this autobiography, it should become apparent that I have been fortunate, which is an understatement, of meeting many people who not only, 'left footprints in my heart', but also played a significant role in my personal life and career. They have appeared and hopefully will continue to do so, as this writing unfolds. Likewise, I have felt great sadness and let down by people, including family, who I thought would support and appreciate me, and friends that left footprints, but for the wrong reasons and when my usefulness, or is that uselessness, was past its sell by date, left? **What would be the point of naming and shaming? I know who my true friends are because I have told them so, and they have reciprocated.** Also, I'd always thought I am what Sigmund Freud called, **MENSCHENKENNER,** which loosely translated means, **'a good judge of character'.** After I retired in 2006, I seriously questioned my MENSCHENKENNER, realising that I was no different to the rest of society in that, at times, I had made a grave error of judgement, or was it a giant leap of faith, in believing certain people were not only my colleagues, but also my friends. When in actual fact, many were merely ships passing in the night and very, very few were actually true friends once I had outlived my usefulness, or left, 'the bubble'. A term that was to become a term everyone became familiar with in 2020, because of the Covid pandemic. In retrospect, several only wanted to use me for my contacts to widen their horizons, after which my usefulness became diminished. Was that a compliment to my status at the time, or an inevitable part of career advancement? Had I also been guilty of such? Of course I had, but whilst I still wanted to retain some kind of contact with such people it became obvious, they, for whatever reason, didn't wish to reciprocate. **"In the end the only friend you've got is yourself, 'cos all the others they'll let you down in the end. We all stand alone in the end."** (Connolly J, 1999. Every Dead Thing. PB, 40:342). These so-called friends know who they are, and probably have not even considered the significance of their actions, probably citing me as the guilty party, because I'd decided to move house, get promotion or retire earlier than I should have done, and in doing so, moved out of their bubble. Not an easy pill to swallow for someone who spent a great deal of his working life, fascinated by and studying human behaviour. **How could I have been so wrong?** Not that I ever considered myself too important, to forget my roots. After all I am a very proud Lancastrian and was guided in my career by the following verse:

> **The Indispensable Man.**
>
> **Sometime when you are feeling important**
>
> **Sometime when your ego's in bloom,**
>
> **Sometime when you take it for granted,**
>
> **You're the best qualified man in the room.**
>
> **Some time when you feel that your going**
>
> **Would leave an unfillable hole.**
>
> **Just follow these simple instructions**
>
> **And, see how they humble your soul.**
>
> **Take a bucket and fill it with water**
>
> **Put your hands in it up to your wrists**
>
> **Pull them out and the hole that remains**
>
> **Is the measure of how much you will be missed.**
>
> **You may splash all you please when you enter,**
>
> **You may stir up the waters galore**
>
> **But stop! And you'll find in a minute**
>
> **That it looks just the same as before.**
>
> **The moral of this quaint example**
>
> **Is do just the best that you can.**
>
> **Be proud of yourself, but remember**
>
> **There is no indispensable man**. Saxon White Kessinger.

I suppose, in today's politically incorrect world and to appease the insecure, this verse should be updated replacing the word man with person. Where Non-Binary, Gender Neutrals fit I'm not sure. As mentioned earlier, many authors including Linwood Barclay, centred their story lines around supposedly everyday people, supposedly doing everyday things, in supposedly acceptable ways, but nearly always revealed that people who thought they knew people actually ended up not knowing anybody at all. This going way beyond the simple Lancashire expression, 'there's nowt funnier than folk.' To repeat myself, who would have thought, least of all me, that my ex-Grammar school, bank manager friend, Timothy

Kinder, would have behaved in the way he did? Was it purely all about greed and sex? Or was it about the insecurity or selfishness of being an only child? Let the psychologists debate that one.

Personality Inventory Tests and various authorities have, over the years, placed people into myriad classifications. To me, the reality of dealing with life's curve balls is to know where you fit and being adaptable enough, to change to suit the circumstance. Since my thirties, I have been aware of peoples' need to socially grade and racially profile, either consciously or unconsciously, and because of this, I have sometimes decided not to play the game with the result being that, at times, I've been guilty of not being serious enough or honest. Edward Hall an anthropologist talks about relationships in terms of social space, and the distance people keep between themselves. Are you a DIGGER, a person who can't hear enough, or a DODGER, one who prefers to hear nothing at all? Frequently referred to as, 'nosey buggers' and 'apathetic sods'. As alluded to previously, in life there are more talkers than doers. I am proud of the fact that whilst I am a definite talker, I'm also a definite doer. Unfortunately, sometimes doing is not the wisest course of action. POSITIVE PLACEBOS are generally happy people, but are viewed with suspicion, whilst NEGATIVE NOCEBOS are generally wingers and moaners, wallowing in the self-indulgent expression, "It's alright for you." **Reality being, that they need to blame someone, in fact anyone, for their inability to make decent judgments and decisions. These people usually find solace in social as well as medical hypochondria. I could quite easily continue this fascinating topic, but feel I have adequately conveyed my message.**

Relationships and their Baggage – Struggling with Rejection.

"**A relationship is like a fire. You got a few months of flame, a year of ember, then the rest is smoke.**" (Deaver J, 1992, Shallow Graves, 17:229).

Whilst writing this book I made a conscious decision, not to go into intimate details about my personal relationships, other than to highlight how they materialised and eventually ended. Also, out of respect to the people involved, I can't on one hand complain about people who pour out their bile on anti-social media, telling their life stories on facebook, twitter etc, hoping to get trolled, and then become guilty myself by telling all in my autobiography. Obviously, pertinent details are included to illustrate certain issues, and the idiosyncrasies of human behaviour. In relationships, everyone in life comes to the party with baggage and expectations. I was no exception as I was looking for love, hugs, cuddles and someone to share my life with. As for myself, I look back with a smile on my face, on the times I've shared with others. I am also proud of the fact that although, for one reason or another, I haven't seen them for many years we remain friends to this day. But why, oh why, is it that when some single people meet a new partner, they consciously or unconsciously decide to jettison their existing friends? Again, I could go into a discussion about why this occurs, such as not knowing the new partner is a jealous, possessive, control freak and covertly tries to isolate them, etc., but feel as I have raised the issue, I will let the reader arrive at their own conclusions. Why, oh why, is history so intimidating to people's future? In my experience, these discarded friends are usually the first port of call, when the relationship goes wrong and a shoulder to cry on is required.

"**A true relationship is two imperfect people, refusing to give up on each other in spite of their obvious differences.**" (Mary Wright, 'The Power of Silence').

Returning to the considerations given to me as a young lad to help choose a suitable partner: you have to be friends; have shared interests as well as individual interests; there has to be sexual chemistry and finally, an acceptance that change is going to happen the longer the relationship continues, is at least a helpful guide, but not an absolute to ensure a successful outcome. Mainly, because of the fact that people do change. Also, over the years what I and many others have found fascinating, not forgetting we are supposedly the highest form of intelligence in the animal kingdom, is the obligatory aspect of staying in a toxic, abusive relationship. Can't these people differentiate between caring and sharing, and controlling and abusing? Over the years, I've been made aware of the fear factor, but many relationships, for one reason or another die, usually because sex can only keep it glued together for so long, because there are only so many variations on a theme. But to stay because their partner cries and SAYS sorry, and they do love them after using them as a punch-bag is beyond my comprehension. OK, perhaps rough sex comes into the equation, and I know the answer isn't, in some cases, a simple one, but one of the aims of writing this book is to try and disprove that we are the highest form of intelligence in the animal kingdom. How am I doing? I could move onto today's societal pursuit of infamy and fame, and entering into a relationship because one or the other is famous, but I won't other than to recall a television interview many years ago, before political correctness raised its silly head, conducted by Mrs Merton, aka Caroline Aherne, when she asked Debbie Magee, **"Other than his money, why did you marry Paul Daniels?"** or words to that effect. The reality of friendships and relationships and their associated baggage is a minefield. The significance for me was that I realised after, **'my heart had been slammed up against a wall,'** (Bonnie Rait), by Hilary Mather, at the tender age of 16, **I subsequently struggled at dealing with rejection.** As I started to learn more and more about myself, via self-analysis, introspection and life experiences, I became more comfortable in my own skin. As a result, I realised that apart from not wanting to let anyone down, especially those who had faith in me, I also wanted acceptance and by projecting myself forward and into the limelight, which during my teacher training I was encouraged to do, I sometimes became the fall guy, entertainer and life and soul of the party. Whether this was genuine acceptance or a false assumption, I wasn't sure, I just realised I didn't want to be a shrinking violet. As previously mentioned, during my late teens I would get invited to parties, because I had a lot of Stax and Soul LPs. American Soul music being all the rage during the 60s and 70s and was happy to oblige by turning up with my vinyl LPs in tow. I was also happy to entertain the troops for a few minutes with a few jokes, witticisms and tall stories, as well as throw a few moves on the dance floor. Like many, I thought I was a mean dancer, and this was long before I'd been introduced to the world of entertainment at Marianne Jepson's Dance and Drama College and later, Strictly Come Dancing. Make 'em laugh in my experience was not a bad philosophy, to endear you to the populace, especially the female kind. Subsequently, entertaining, attending and organising dinner parties and quizzes became something I enjoyed immensely, as it put me in the spotlight. Could I be labelled an attention seeker? Of course, by some, but I never considered myself as such. After all, if that was the case it could be argued that all who stood in front of an audience, for whatever reason, could also be given the same label. To be able to make people smile was, and is, a wonderful gift. To be able to make people laugh with you and not at you, is a talent. But this was my dichotomy: **I LOVED THE ACCEPTANCE AND ATTENTION, BUT FOUND IT DIFFICULT DEALING WITH THE REJECTION, THAT FOR WHATEVER REASON INEVITABLY COULD FOLLOW, ESPECIALLY ONCE A RELATIONSHIP HAD RUN ITS COURSE. I HAVE ALSO HATED GOODBYES.** I've spent a lot of my later years, from 40 onwards, in buses, railway stations and airports, and whilst they can be exciting and vibrant places, they can also be sad, lonely places. I took rejection personally and as a slight on my personality, when the reality was that, in many instances, it was just a natural progression to finding a suitable partner, or a realisation that one or the other in the relationship wanted out. As for goodbyes, I realised that I just found railway stations, bus depots and airports, sad places, even though once I got the travel bug I purposely spent a great deal of time in them. So, finding myself 'single' again at the age of 38, after the breakdown of my marriage, was difficult to deal with. Apart from the obvious heartache, I found myself alone with no audience. Of course, the expression there are plenty more fish in the sea, sprung to mind. But were there? Numerically yes, but suitability wise, perhaps not. Having spent 5 years courting, to establish if Alma Johnson was the one, before deciding to get married and then after 12 years of living together to find that the marriage had 'failed', after investing 17 years of time and energy, didn't fill me with confidence in finding another with whom to share my life. Especially, when I now know, I didn't make a mistake in choosing Dee in the first place. Not that I was looking for another matrimonial partner, not then or at any other time in the future. This as it turned out was both a blessing and a problem for future relationships. It also took me a long time to stop looking for Dee number 2, by making comparisons. For me, there was only one Verna and one Dee and I realised I was delusional in thinking I could find another. It is said that you come to a new relationship shedding the skin of the old ones, but there is always a lasting imprint that can tarnish the future. When young, both men and women, look for their ideal partners on a, 'level playing field', but if they enter the playing field in their late 30s, in my case 38 plus, there is the question of how much baggage are both parties bringing onto the pitch? As mentioned for me, the issue was usually children not the women themselves. Taking on-board someone else's off-springs is fraught with problems, ranging from issues such as not being their biological father, ex partners, teenage hormones, motives and differing perspectives on parenting. As I've had relationships involving very young children, teenagers and adult children I can say, without fear of contradiction, that I've experienced the full gamut of issues. Which at times, made me seriously question was it worth all the hassle just to say you had a partner? As I got older and arguably wiser, it didn't make sense to waste energy on relationships that would only pull me under some emotional waterfall, from which I'd never catch my breath. As I sit here at the age of 75, tapping the keys my views of women have not changed, since I discovered testosterone as a teenager. I love them dearly, prefer their company to talking football, tits and booze with the boys, will always have them on my team but **will never, never, understand them. "Any man says he can understand how a woman thinks is living in a fool's paradise."** (Barclay L, 2016. The Twenty Three, PB 20:176). Was it important to do so? For me yes, if I was going to establish any kind of relationship with them beyond sex. Which in itself, could be an issue. "All you want me for is sex," said a few whilst others said sex wasn't everything. I am looking for a man, that wants me for who I am, warts and all. Whilst others tried to convince me that sex was the foundation of all long-term relationships, but ignored the reality that there were only so many ways that you could skin a cat. Like everything else in life, familiarity breeds contempt, and after a while many start to think the grass was greener somewhere else? Do you succumb to the temptation, or drift into acceptance that birthdays and Christmas are going to be your only sexual highlights? Are these good analogies, perhaps not, but you know what I mean. For me, the basis of any relationship was friendship and trust, other facets added to its rich tapestry, but that takes time, and time is not what some ladies are prepared to give you, because unless you play all your cards early, YOU'RE NOT COMMITTED, or you are hiding something. If you're honest, some ladies don't like the answers to their questions. So why ask them, unless they needed an answer? The time-honoured question of, "Does my bum look big in this dress?" springs to mind. Relationships can't be based on walking on egg shells. Don't get me wrong, sex is the best thing since sliced bread, Warburtons of course, and when you find a partner whose chemistry mixes and explodes with yours, oh, such joy. But is that enough to sustain a long-term relationship? Conversely whilst the woman may be fabulously attractive, intelligent, witty, charming, etc. etc. if there is nothing happening in the basement, no matter how hard you try, another pun, she is not meant for you sexually. Unfortunately, ladies can take it very personally and label you queer, or ask if you catch the other bus, whilst reminding you that all men are bastards, and are only after one thing. Don't forget, that people need you in a box. All of the ladies mentioned in this autobiography, like myself at the time we met, were not necessarily looking for a serious relationship or marriage, but someone to just share their lives with, or a shoulder to cry on, because most had suffered some kind of relationship breakdown and wanted to rebuild self-esteem, enjoy the moment and move on. Also, I am not proud of the fact that some relationships were on-going at the same time, as a new one was in its infancy. I have no intention of disclosing the intimate details of my sexual relationship with them, because that was personal between ourselves. Also, the fact remains that they and their children were a part of my life, and added to its colour. Some colours were brighter than others, but I still regard these people with fondness and as my friends, even though I may not have seen or spoken to them for a long time. Apart from those already mentioned there were,

Deborah and Ross.

It was whilst I was re-training to become a physical therapist that I met Deborah Warburton, her son Ross and subsequently her family, Bette and Bill, her parents, her sister Jane, Jane's husband, David and their two children, Jo, (Joanna Whalley look alike), and Martin. During our initial meeting, in a cafe in Ashton, Deborah informed me she was a single mum and had a son, Ross, named after Poldark, of TV fame. As I recall he was 4 years of age. After this initial contact, I kept recalling this chatty, bubbly person I had met at lunch time, whilst trying to concentrate on acquiring the skills of massage. In a short space of time we started to, 'see each other'. Again, out of respect to Debs, her family and friends, I don't think it's pertinent to go into intimate detail about our time spent together. But what I will say is, that my time with Ross and Deborah was special, but initially I was not in a good place professionally, because I had recently resigned from a job I loved, and emotionally, as my marriage was under pressure and Dee and I were to eventually separate. To this day, I've always felt that if I had met Debs 12 plus months later than I did, we would possibly still be together. Whether or not DW would agree with that, I have never asked. Sometime after our relationship ended, I found out that Deborah had started a relationship with her boss, Derek Alltree, a respected jeweller and designer, and they both emigrated to Canada, in 2008. This was somewhere her parents always used to talk about, because they had friends there and visited them as often as possible. It was also somewhere Deborah's best friend had moved, many years previous. In 2009, Derek and Debs opened, 'Coast Jewellery', at Lee Bay, on the Sunshine Coast, North West of Vancouver, BC. In true Briggs tradition, I remained friends with her family for many years after that, but lost contact. Finally, Deb's father, before his demise, was one of my staunchest supporters. Thank you, Bill, or should I say Mr Booth? As I've said my contact with the family had all but ended, but I did receive an e-mail from Debs when I discovered an e-mail address on some publicity, whilst researching a trip to Canada in 2014. She said she was disappointed I didn't visit her on my trip, but as I was in a relationship with a lady called Denise Walsh at the time, I didn't think it appropriate. Why, I haven't a clue, as Denise and I split up not long after. In November 2020, I received a Christmas card from Jane Carter, Debs's sister and after a follow up reply by myself, I received a 5 page, double sided, hand written letter. How good was that? Who in the year 2020, sends hand written letters? Well Jane Carter does. She has also proof read this book. Thanks, Jane. I have also received several e-mails from Debs as a result of Jane's communications. In one such e-mail Debs thanked me for the time that I spent with Ross, during our relationship, and who was now an adult, and she informed me that he still remembers me. I often think of her and Ross.

Audrey, Anne-Marie and Stuart.

Audrey proved to be another brief flirtation in my quest to find a hug, cuddle and possible happiness by sharing my life. Still living in Royton after Dee and I had split, I was keeping myself occupied and busy trying to start getting clients to massage, gymnastic coaching and accepting the odd teaching assignment offers. I met Audrey in Monty's nightclub, Oldham. Monty's has long since gone, coinciding with the arrival of the Metro in Oldham, along with Mumps Bridge, which was very much a landmark in the annals of historical Oldham. The evening ended with an exchange of phone numbers. The following night, Saturday, the phone rang and a very croaky voice asked me why I had not rung. At first, I couldn't recognise the voice but was not opposed to a female, croaky voice, giving me a heavy breathing, dirty phone call. It was Audrey, full of a cold, obviously not man flu, otherwise she would not have had the strength to talk, asking me how I was and did I fancy getting together. Now as you know I am into equality, and was not opposed to women taking the initiative, but I thought that she was being a little too keen and pushy. But then again, I had given her my number so what did I expect and why was I surprised? To be honest, I could only recall one other member of the opposite sex having phoned me up before, asking for a date, and that was when I first started teaching at Mather Street. Was I flattered, was my ego massaged-it must have been? That was the start of it all. But I recall not expecting too much and certainly not so soon, after Debs and I had gone our separate ways. Did I want another relationship? After all being on my own, I could do what I wanted, when I wanted, where I wanted, with whom I wanted and as long as I didn't hurt my family or friends, it was OK, or so I convinced myself. All I remember is that emotionally my head was still all over the place and survival was the name of the game, and so logical reasoning, on a personal level, was a little off centre.

Audrey was separated from her husband but had custody of their two small children, Stuart and Ann-Marie. Stuart was a cheeky, chappie and a handful, whilst Ann-Marie was a girlie, girl. Is that another ic, ist or ism? Do you know what, I don't care. Their father was Duncan D, who I soon found out worked with my brother Barry on the post. So, I was getting two versions of why the Dickies had split up, Audrey's and my brother's. The latter being incidentally given in a casual conversation one day with my brother. I am not sure to this day, if my brother Barry ever knew I was seeing Duncan's wife, but it soon became apparent where my brother's loyalties lay, and it was not with Mrs Audrey Dickie. Obviously, my brother would not have approved but then again, I was not in the habit of running to family and friends as soon as a new female arrived on the block. I was also intrigued as to whether Duncan ever knew I was Barry's brother, because the children must have mentioned me when he saw them. I never lost sleep over the situation, but in hindsight it was an interesting situation. Not gritty enough for a Martina Cole novel, but a good story line for writers of family intrigue. Audrey lived in a council flat in the Clarksfield area and thought my semi-detached, in Royton, very posh. She worked as an insurance clerk in Hollinwood, and I was once invited to lunch with some of her workmates. As I recall, Duncan saw the children most weekends and although I never met the guy, he was a good guy, according to my brother, who was better off without the bitch, or something equally complimentary. I saw the children whenever we had a day out, or I visited the flat. As I recall, the children never came to Alandale Drive, why I'm not sure. I never slept over, when the children were there. As a teacher I was familiar with many stories from the children in my care, of 'Uncle Johnny' staying the night, and the effect broken relationships had on the children, and I always tried not to be part of it. Yes, I did have some morals and I felt very strongly, about what effect my relationships had on the children involved, although reading these memoirs, you may doubt the sincerity of such. As far as I was concerned, we were not an item and so I avoided going to dos where family or friends might be in attendance. As for Audrey, she just accepted things and was not possessive in any way. As for me, I tried to share my social life with her and helped in domestic issues when I could. I never felt the relationship was going anywhere, and called it a day after I had arranged to take Audrey and her children to the Isle of White on holiday, but then had second thoughts. The last time I saw Audrey was at the Colosseum Theatre in Oldham. I was with my then girlfriend, Anne Macmillan, who thought Audrey and I were a little too familiar, for such a brief encounter. But then again Anne, who you will later find out, never fully trusted me, so there was no surprise there. Do you blame her? Audrey looked good, and we both wished each other well. I believe she eventually went to the Isle of White with another James, but this one lived in the flat above her. As I have not shared intimacies with my brother for years, I never knew what happened to Audrey, Duncan, Stuart or Ann-Marie.

Gillian and Emma Smith.

As mentioned, whilst living on Alandale Drive, I frequently visited the local Royton Cricket and Tennis Club, to watch both sports and attend many of their social functions. It was also a place I knew I could frequent, as I had treated many of the players, and was friends with many of the club members. Joan, my neighbour had also been treasurer for the cricket section and with her husband, Haydn, had, before children had arrived at the Mason household, provided accommodation, on several occasions, for the visiting cricket professional. Joan and Haydn had all the inside information and gossip associated with the club. One weekend, after Dee had gone to live with her sister, I found myself squashed, along with many other sweaty bodies, including Haydn, against the bar in the club house. There was a young lady there, with what can only be described as bleached and spiky hair. She was a little taller than I was, and could be described as slight in stature. I was informed that she had had a relationship with the last professional cricketer to be hired. She had also been in a long-term relationship with a guy named Bo, the result of which was a young child, named Emma. I subsequently found out she did office work in Manchester and was a part-time barmaid at the Greyhound pub, in Elly Clough, my old local. She liked tennis, and played on one of the club's teams, coaching the younger members. Enter my world, Miss Gillian Smith. The year was June 1989, give or take twelve months. It is difficult to describe my relationship with Gill over the following months, without appearing to be over critical, but the facts are the reason the relationship never gathered any momentum and eventually, 'fizzled out'. We do, however, as is the case with many of my partners, remain friends to this day, although after she met Brian, communication was less frequent to say the least. I have always considered Gill a friend, irrespective of whom she or I were sharing a bed with. In fact, Gill has met several of my lady friends. Before meeting Brian, Gill invited me to Emma's birthday bash, and then her father's funeral. I also met her and mum at the Royal Toby Restaurant, just before her mum passed away. Her parents Margaret and Ken were both patients of mine. The problem was her daughter who, at that time, wanted Gill all to herself, and saw me as someone who would not allow that to happen. The relationship with her brother David, and his partner and her parents, Margaret and Kenneth, was fraught and soap orientated. There was always some crises or fallout. Gill was also hyper and a worrier, constantly finding things to stress about. The relationship with her ex, Bo, was always an issue. I personally felt Gill found parenting, at times a little inconvenient. She felt she was missing out by having to deal with Emma. Whilst we saw each other and I, to a point, sympathised, all of these issues bubbled beneath the surface, or periodically erupted. As for me, I got on well with her parents and brother. In fact, as I've said, her parents attended my clinic. I dealt with Emma as I found her, and many years later at a family get together, to celebrate Emma's birthday, Emma and I, with captive audience, talked about me helping her with her gymnastics when she was a little girl in a leotard. Emma grew up having two children of her own, Jamie, a girl and Thomas. Eventually, the relationship moved to being one of boyfriend-girlfriend to just friends. I can't recall any particular time or instance when it happened. There was no argument or fallout. Many years later, when I lived in Preston with Heather, and Emma was married and working at BAE at Salmesbury, whilst living in Blackburn, Gill was tasked with looking after her grandchildren. Occasionally, she'd bring them to Preston and we'd take them to Witton Park to burn off their energy. Unfortunately, once Gill met Brian, and although she and Emma attended my 60th birthday celebration at the Ley Inn, our contact was now restricted to the odd Christmas card and e-mail. However, I was invited to her 60th birthday, at one of the hospitality suites at Oldham AFC. It felt strange re-visiting the ground I'd once played football on, some 50 years previously. Unfortunately, my evening was spoilt by being introduced to her brother David's latest partner, who within minutes of meeting me, decided to, 'put me in my place'. Why, I hadn't a clue but decided I couldn't be bothered to find out, and left quite soon afterwards. Sadly, Brian passed away in 2018 and so, I presume as I have heard very little from her, she is back living on her own.

Lyn, Lisa and Jonathan.

The second Lyn, sorry it's shocking but I can't recall her surname, entered the scene when I answered an advertisement in the Oldham Evening Chronicle. At that time internet dating was in its infancy but personal ads, in local newspapers were becoming an acceptable way of finding someone to share with. I think Lynn was initially attracted to the fact that I used to play for Oldham Athletic AFC, as she and her two children Lisa and Jonathan were avid fans. Lisa, the elder, was courting Tony and Jonathan, who also had a girlfriend, was still at secondary school. Lynn worked for the Police as a civilian, organising policing for sporting events, one of which was at Boundary Park, where Oldham AFC played. Lynne's ex, was known to my neighbour Haydn Mason, as he used to drink in the local pubs around Chadderton and Royton. She lived on Birch Avenue, on the corner with Beech Avenue. A garden I used to pinch gooseberries from, as a child. Years later my accountant Moira Bailey set up her practice several doors down from where Lyn lived. The first time we dated we went for a drink. But the first time I visited her house and I met Lisa, I distinctly remember wearing my red, 'Benny hat'. For those of you not old enough to remember, Benny was a not very clever character, in a TV programme called Crossroads, who always wore a bob hat, **long before it was cool and trendy to wear headwear twenty-four seven.** In those days the hat denoted being a simpleton. I could say, so nothing has changed then, but I won't. We would visit each other's house and I spent Christmas with her and the children. At that time there was a possibility, that I and several other people were going to take over the Northern Institute of Massage, in Blackpool, as Ken Woodward, the principal, was thinking of handing over the reins. The sceptics said it would never happen, and it was to be many years later before Ed Caldwell eventually took over. Anyhow, at that time I was trying to find suitable premises to start up my business, commuting to Blackpool to teach, and trying to stabilise my personal life. In hindsight, whilst Lynn was an attractive proposition, the chemistry wasn't there, and I always felt I was treading water. In spite of going on holiday together to Turkey, she eventually wrote to me telling me that it was over. In true Briggs tradition, I took the rejection badly and despite buckets of tears and asking for another stab to make it work, I knew deep down that she was doing me a favour. Not long after we split, I gave her friend, who was a market trader, a lift home and she asked me, if I was gay. Why, I hadn't a clue? I was now not only a reject but also a homosexual reject. It's a cruel, funny old world, isn't it? Tony and Lisa ended up buying a house near to me when I moved and set up my clinic on Eaves Lane, Chadderton.

Glynis Rafferty, nee Cottam, Ryan and Leah.

Glynis entered the scene one Friday evening, when Ed Whalley and I were having a beer, or two, in the Junction pub in Royton. She was with her mate Sharon and how we got talking I can't recall, but we ended up going into the Tram tracks nightclub, across the road from the pub, with them. Ed was seeing a lady called Jackie at the time and was reluctant to be led astray by Sharon, whilst I was more than happy for Glynis to lead me astray. Not that Glynis was a one-night stand but she invited me back for coffee, whilst Ed returned home to 241, Turf Lane, Royton, and Sharon returned to her place, just around the corner from where Glynis lived, in a semi, on Thorp Farm, just at the back of Alandale. We arranged to meet up, after I had been to rugby the following day. That was the start of a friendship that has lasted up until now, although I only occasionally exchange the odd e-mail. Glynis was separated from Kevin, a good-looking guy if I might add, and had two children, Leah and Ryan. Was she named after the Star Wars heroine, I'm not sure? She was a lovely child, whilst Ryan was a teenage handful. Glynis was an edgy, nervy person and added to the fact that she also had a few medical issues, she was not someone who was ever far from stress. She was a practice nurse. Don't get me wrong,

Glynis could party with the best of them but her personal situation always hung over her like a cloud. I on the other hand, was trying to rebuild after separation and was throwing all my energies into trying to move forward. Glynis always seemed to be stuck in the groove. I never asked what her expectations were. For one reason or another, our relationship never strayed beyond platonic, which didn't seem to bother her. As for me, I was happy to share. I'm not sure how long we saw each other, but it was never considered serious. It was just one of those friendships, that we both accepted for what it was. We never went away on holiday together, or anything like that. We just seemed to fit each other, into what was happening in our lives at the time. Glynis came to my 60th birthday bash at the Ley Inn, in Leyland, and it was good to see her. Although, to be honest, we didn't get much chance to catch-up. On several occasions, I have tried to call to see her, when visiting family in Chadderton, but she has never been at home when I called. Perhaps she was hiding behind the settee. Although, I did manage to catch her and Leah at home, just after Leah had bought a house. I remember giving Leah some stuff, to help set up home. The last I heard was that she was in a relationship, and had found happiness and contentment in her life. As for myself, I look back with fondness of the brief time we shared together. Thanks, Glynis.

As for my struggles with rejection I still, on a regular basis, ask myself what it is that I have done terribly wrong for some people, including family, to consider me as just a gobby little shit? Perhaps, I was looked upon in much the same way as the white people of Alabama used to look upon the blacks, as people who shouldn't be allowed to breathe. Answers on a postcard please.

Glynis, unfortunately, I have no photo of her with her children.

It's alright for you, you've not got children!

Christopher and Hannah.

Debs and Ross.

Gill and Emma.

Personality Studies Re-visited: The Link, Lancashire Dining Club and the Last Chance Saloon.

Schadenfreude: German from Schaden, meaning harm and Freude, meaning joy.

Collins English Dictionary, delight in another's misfortune, when something bad happens to someone. Satisfaction or pleasure felt at someone's misfortune.

I joined the Lancashire Dining Club, (LDC), attending my first evening on Saturday, 12th April, 2014. This was a, 'Hollywood meets the Brits', evening and was held at The Royal Toby in Castleton, Rochdale. Paul Nugent and I were invited to join by a Scottish gentleman named Duncan M Lees, whom I'd nicknamed, 'the silver fox', and had met at a Link social event at the Hoghton Arms near Riley Green, Preston. That's also how I met Paul.

The LDC was, "for single people with exceedingly good taste". Although, theoretically there were no age restrictions, it catered primarily for the over 50s. The LDC first dined together in 2000 and its aim was to increase the social circle of both sexes with both good food and good company. The dining venues were mainly in and around the Bury, Bolton and Rochdale areas. During 2014, there were 8 dinners planned and each evening was themed. It was run and organised by a lady named Yvonne Wright, nicknamed, 'the Dinner Lady', who was a councillor. The format of the evening was pre-meal drinks, a 3-course meal with wine and coffee, followed by a disco. During the course of the evening, there were various quizzes and interactive activities designed to increase the communication between diners. For example, between each course the gentlemen, who were fewer in number than the ladies, had to move around the table clockwise and change places. All newcomers had a little flag as part of their place-setting to indicate that it was their first time and needed looking after. There were approximately 70 to 80 diners, sitting in tables of 8. I was placedt next to a lady on my left, who it just so happened was also attending for the first time, and a lady on my right called Lynn. These place settings proved to be significant in more ways than one. Firstly, the lady sitting on my right was a former North Chadderton school pupil, and knew more about me and my life, since leaving North Chadderton School, than I did. She said she was around during my younger brother Stephen's time. Paul and I thoroughly enjoyed our first outing, and I was very impressed with the organisation of the evening. So much so that at the end of the evening, on impulse, I ended up asking the lady who initially was sat on my left, for her phone number. Since Heather and I parted, over 18 months previously, this was the first lady I had summoned up the energy, enthusiasm and courage to want to meet again.

"When this stuff comes back so late in life, completely unexpected, completely unwanted, it comes back with such force and there's nothing you can do about it, there's nothing to dilute it........Doing something that makes no sense at all and potentially disastrous for all concerned."
Anthony Hopkins in the film, Human Stain, 2003.

Quite simply, I'd resigned myself to the fact that at the age of 64, I had neither the motivation nor inclination to try and become involved with another female, even if I was fortunate enough to find someone who would have me and my baggage. As for taking on board someone else's baggage, well I definitely could not be arsed.

What made this lady different, was the fact that initially and for a time, she restored my mojo, gave me back my dignity, my pride, my ability to make people laugh and most importantly, a purpose to the remaining time I had left in life. For that I was more than grateful. Add this to the fact, that she was

13 years my junior, was single, didn't have any children, didn't smoke or drink and was quite happy to drive, when alcohol was going to be consumed, made her a very suitable prospect indeed. Doing some research, I came across this lovely quote regarding sex and age differences in a relationship, especially when the man is considerably older than the woman.

"You want the soap at the end of your rope to be fresh."

(Slaughter K, 2017. The Good Daughter, PB, 17:423).

But as with most things in life there's a price to pay and it wasn't long before alarm bells started to ring and the situation could prove, 'potentially disastrous for all concerned'. Going somewhat against my aim, of not divulging too much personal stuff regarding my relationships, I've decided to make an exception in this case, as the relationship proved to be a fascinating human behavioural study. If you can call, being verbally and psychologically abused, fascinating. Unfortunately, after our first few dates, it was apparent we had very little in common. The fact that her girlfriends called her, 'Bolshy…….,' should have been enough of a clue. She informed me that she had recently moved back up North to Wigan from Reading, after her marriage failed. She had this confidence about her philosophy and take on life that, whilst to be admired, bordered on arrogance and most certainly could be interpreted as female chauvinistic. However, upon closer inspection and with several sessions of introspection and self-analysis, it was apparent that her views were mainly subjective and lacked academic rigour. Not that this put her off. It was apparent that, just like her father, she was not used to having her very forthright views challenged, and became very defensive when I played devil's advocate. She had this habit of asking why, about generally accepted human, behavioural traits, in much the same way as a child, but for her it appeared to be, so she could provoke a response. For example, she hadn't any children and told me she never wanted any, and whilst I respected this, she couldn't understand why other couples wanted them. Pointing out that biologically it was the role of men and women to continue the species, and by abstaining, maybe, that would be the end of civilisation as we know it. But she didn't appear to accept that fact. When asked why she had not taken her husband's surname and become a Mrs when she married, she dismissed the question with, "Why should I?" I had no wish to change her, heaven forbid she was not a person who saw any reason to change, at times she begrudgingly would compromise, albeit temporarily, which was why I stayed along for the ride. But **in hindsight, I was delusional in thinking the relationship would last.** Unfortunately, old habits die hard and her intransigent, confrontational personality kept rearing its ugly head, which put considerable strain on not only me, but also our relationship. She appeared for one reason or another to enjoy confrontation. I'm sure that she had issues with me and she did, but when asked why she stayed with me, she never proffered an answer one way or another. There were several times when I was ready to walk away, because I thought our relationship wasn't working. Surely, she must have felt the same way. I wanted companionship and to share, but she only appeared to want part time sharing. She didn't appear to want what I was offering. I was aware that people have differing personalities and priorities in life, but the whole scenario just frustrated me. You could say we were **partners of convenience,** but I frequently wondered what she was getting out of it. **To be blunt I had never met anyone like her before.** I never knew where I stood, as she had this Jekyll and Hyde disposition and within a very short space of time, could swing from one to the other. **People with potential 'Borderline Personality Disorder' are characterised by an inability to introspect or self-analyse. Their dissociative identity disorder involves the existence of two or more personality states within one person. Could Mr Trump also have such a condition, along with the others I've already identified? Because if so, it may be something one should**

consider, as it could get you the Presidency of the USA, not once but twice. Which personality would turn up on our next date was always on my mind? Did others see this almost bi-polar disposition in her personality? I suspected people who had known her many years did as I was sometimes asked, with a hidden agenda look in their eyes, "How are things with you and ......?" In spite of this, there were times when I would look at her and see this childlike vulnerability, and just wanted to give her a hug and a cuddle. But in all honesty, for me the reason I stayed was I dreaded returning to a life of loneliness and so bit my tongue on many occasions, when a younger Jim Briggs would have said, "Bugger this for a game of soldiers," and would have called time, I didn't. I sometimes decided it must be me, but when I received a card or e-mail thanking me for my help in the garden, or for making her smile, or cheering her up, it appeared that this was not the case. I just wanted to share my life, and was always suggesting trips out, holidays etc. but as mentioned, she only wanted to do limited share. It was a shame because without her bolshy, belligerent, attitude, she could be a kind, generous and lovely person but I always felt when she was with me, she wanted to prove a point to the world. In fact, such was her personality she wanted to prove several. Once I got to meet and to know her parents and find out about her three brothers, only ever meeting one of them, the middle son, everything became much clearer. Chapter two of this autobiography is all about my family and dysfunctional families and all that they entail, and so hers was no different to others, and like others they had their own idiosyncrasies, which seemed to be an on-going topic of conversation. Having said all that, as usual I always got on really well with her mum and dad and they always treated me with respect. After all, her mum wasn't that much older than me. Did they know what was going on in our relationship? After helping them to move house, her mum said that I was now part of the family as I had done more for them, in the short time I had been around, than her sons had done for her in years. Thanks, mum. Now no one likes to have their family criticised and she was no different, but she would frequently say to me, "James, you can say what you like, you won't offend me." Whilst I had better things to occupy my time than denigrate other families, preferring instead to, 'stay out of it', these facts are relevant to understanding our relationship and why it wasn't sustainable. My first serious attempt to end the relationship resulted in me just walking out the door, Monday, 16th March, 2015, and then sending her an e-mail explaining my actions. But after a short time apart, we drifted back together and carried on with the pretence. In an academic sense, she was a fascinating study for the behavioural psychologist, but the reality and re-occurring theme for me was, that whilst I was trying to fulfil my desire to tick off as many things on my bucket list as possible, before old age and senility seriously kicked in, I constantly wondered, why did she keep agreeing to join me? She didn't enjoy the sunshine and avoided it like the plague. She never liked getting out of bed early, whether we were on holiday or not, and we frequently disagreed as to what constituted a good day. Bed time and sleep were always contentious issues. As far as I'm aware, everyone snores to varying degrees and we both were no different to others. Unfortunately, whilst I accepted this and explained my conditions making suggestions, such as I'd sleep in the other room, she appeared to want me to sleep with her, probably to belittle me if I suddenly awoke, gasping for air. At the age of 38, I discovered I suffered from **sleep apnoea**, which for those who have shared my bed can be scary. I can wake up suddenly, gasping for breath. The significance of this condition is, that during sleep the person stops breathing, therefore depriving the brain of oxygen, hypoxia. And as all first aiders will tell you, that can lead to brain damage-No comment! I am also a male over 50 and so frequent trips to the toilet, during the night, is not uncommon. Are these facts too much of an overshare for an autobiography, perhaps, but I like to dot the i's and cross the t's? Matters were not helped, because she appeared to be in denial as to how badly she snored, and there were many, many occasions when I would leave the bed at 2 or

3, in the early hours of the morning, because she was snoring so loudly, go into the lounge, read for maybe an hour, watch a little TV, fall asleep on the settee, before returning to the bed several hours later, absolutely knackered. Upon waking up a short while later, I would be met with an abusive, verbal assault, accusing me of keeping her awake all night because of **my snoring, gasps for air and visits to the loo.** I'd like to say,

"The extraordinary sensations of sleeping with someone after a lifetime alone, made the night one long embrace."

Turow S, 2006. Limitations, HB, p117.

but unfortunately, it was more like trying to sleep on egg shells without breaking any. Our differences and approach to not only holidays, but day to day life itself always seemed to be at odds. In the end, I stopped staying at her place because she was a different person than when she visited me in Penwortham. Early on in our friendship, she'd had asked me did I like dogs? Cynophobia is the fear of dogs and recalling my episode with O'Hara's Alsatian, whilst teaching at Mather Street, I diplomatically shrugged my shoulders. She informed me she had always had a dog, but upon returning home from Reading, decided they were too constraining but occasionally looked after a friend's dog, a German Shepherd dog called Fritz. This friend ran a very successful business, and had a partner that didn't like big dogs and so it was somewhat neglected. In stepped her good self. She also informed me that Fritz could tell, if people were nervous in its company. No pressure there then, James. As it turned out, I got on really well with the mutt, but she NEVER believed or accepted that I'd never owned a dog and wasn't particularly fond of pets. **I suppose you could say I'd finally joined the dog mafia.** Unfortunately, as big dogs were not allowed on the Penwortham Residential Park, he never visited 4 Park Road. Why did we put up with each other's company for so long? I cannot speak for her, just for me. **I JUST DREADED BEING BACK ON MY OWN AGAIN, LONELY, DEPRESSED AND, if you'll excuse the pun, WITH THE BLACK DOG ON MY BACK.** To many she was this lovely, polite, funny, bubbly person but like Jekyll and Hyde, could morph into this very aggressive, argumentative, opinionated, provocative, annoying, frustrating individual. I often wondered, if she would agree to taking a Myers-Briggs Type Indicator, or a Princeton Personality Indicator, which are particularly useful in diagnosing personality disorders, especially with people who appear to be someone they are not.

History has shown that many individuals have spent time in jail, because they had been fooled by a member of the opposite sex. I wasn't fooled by her, or beguiled, I was just fascinated, or was I just stupid?

I stayed with her because I desperately wanted the relationship to work, as returning to solitude didn't bear thinking about. But in the end, at 6.30 a.m., 1st January, 2016, to be precise, after agreeing to spend New Year with her, something I hadn't done for months, after one final verbal assault, where I was blamed for yet another night of keeping her awake, I quietly packed my bag, didn't say good bye, only saying it to Fritz, got in my car and drove home to Penwortham. Whereas, Heather had rescued me, she had just extended my existence and allowed me more time to achieve my goals, and for that, I thank her. Although, when she found out I was writing my autobiography, she was adamant that I should not include her in it. I wonder why? I didn't bear her any ill will and hoped, corny as it always sounds, we could remain friends, as I'd been with most of my ex-girlfriends. But knowing how stability was a rare commodity with her, and her family, as there was always some crisis or another, I doubted that would be possible. In the end I had to admit defeat.

"9 M people from all walks of life in Britain are affected by loneliness."

MSM, 14/06/2018.

How many more people stay in abusive relationships to avoid adding to this statistic, is uncertain. My sister Lilian still believes I stayed with her, because she was an interesting case study. In most of my relationships with members of the opposite gender our times together, no matter how long or brief, were an integral part of my search for a hug and a cuddle and the fact that they offered more, and in some cases much more, is something that I and only I can appreciate. The chronology of when such ladies entered my life is not exact, but the fact that they did at various times and left, 'footprints on my heart', is something that cannot be taken away from me. Unfortunately, the fact that either their baggage or mine, and in some cases both, prevented our lives travelling further along the same paths, is a sad reflection of the complexity of relationships, especially when you genuinely wanted things to 'work out' but the people involved were intelligent enough to realise they couldn't continue. Yes, there are still some intelligent life forms out there immersed in all the dross. One of these ladies, who shall also remain nameless, but who was called Diane – yes, you see I can also tell lies - had had over 200 dates, via dating agencies, before finding 'Mr Right', after her first marriage failed. But because I have not seen or heard from her in years, I cannot comment on whether or not they are still together. No, I was not part of the dating agencies she had subscribed to, as our paths had crossed via another route but we frequently met up and over a meal and glass of wine to overview, if that's the right word, her latest computer match. Our own attempts to form a serious relationship had long ago fizzled out, when we both realised, we couldn't offer what each was looking for. She wanting materialism and marriage, and I acceptance, a hug, a cuddle and someone to share with. After Dee, I never felt the desire to go down the matrimonial path again, or should I say the aisle? But we remained good friends, and both wanted the best for each other. I'd like to end this section by concluding that in spite of all the research and theorising the Northern expression, **'There's nowt funnier than folk,'** will do very nicely, thank you.

At the age of 65, I came across the author Matt Dunn who wrote some hilarious books on relationships. Best Man, Ex Girlfriend United, Ex Boyfriend Handbook and The Good Bride Guide, to name but a few. At this juncture can I suggest, 'From Here to Paternity', for an amusing fictional read into choosing a, 'suitable partner'. Perhaps if he'd started writing earlier, I may have used the books as a tongue in cheek guide to help me deal with the opposite sex and their baggage.

If it's the innocence of childhood and the arrogance of youth, what is it for adulthood, stupidity and frustration?

As for Lancashire Diners I did attend one other dinner after our relationship ended, and I had parted company and as a result, spent an enjoyable half day walking along the sea front at Lytham and St Anne's with a lady called Sharon, but no further meetings materialised. I think she had spoken to Denise for a character reference. So sad.

Warners For Adults.

Another thing that I am immensely proud of and view as part of my legacy, is, in 1999, getting the family to agree to go away for a few days, once a year, as a family. I was first made aware of Warners For Adults, when it was part of a Judith Chalmer's holiday programme on TV, when I lived on Alandale Drive. After moving from Alandale Drive to Eaves Lane, and not long after meeting Anne Macmillan whom I took to Nidd Hall, for 2 days as a birthday treat, that the idea of taking mum to Warners, Nidd Hall, for her 80th birthday came to me. In fact, as I was 50 in the same year and it was my sister Lilian's wedding anniversary, I thought it would be a great idea to see if the rest of my brothers and sisters would be interested. As many of us were still working, it would have to be a Friday and Saturday night stay, travelling home Sunday. Visiting each member of the family, including my mum's cousin Amy and her husband Bill, I canvassed my views. Surprisingly, and much to the rest of my family's surprise, my sister Marlene didn't take much persuading. Only my brother Barry was reticent, as he didn't want to bring in a locum to run his newspaper business for a few days. I think, he feared they might find out how much money he had and would return at some time in the future to relieve him of all his hard-earned cash. He also panicked at the thought of having to drive his own car, or even worse give someone a lift to Yorkshire. There was also the realisation that he would have to spend several days with his mum, brothers and sisters. In the end, he came up with a compromise, that he would leave Linda in the shop to guard the safe and he would come as long as someone gave him a lift. Making the excuse, that he had to leave Linda the car. However, this was a risky strategy for Barry because although, Linda had passed her test, being a woman, he was unsure how she would cope driving on her own, because up until that moment in time HE HAD ALWAYS DRIVEN. Even taking and going to pick her up from guides every week. Well, she couldn't take her guides class **and** drive all in the same evening, could she? Tim, my mate, was also invited. The rest is history, so to speak, and the start of a family tradition that lasted 18 years. Since the first Warner's weekend, many people have been part of the annual get together, George and Margaret Bradbury, Amy and Bill, Barbara Bollwell and Gordon and Jean Masters. Sadly, over the years we lost several members of the Warner's brigade, not least of all mum, Raymond, Bill and Gordon, but the party still went on even though, being at a Briggs family get together could be somewhat of an auditory and sensory barrage, as we are all chiefs wanting to be heard with no Indians to listen. This was never more evident than at the hilarious, annual bowling challenge where various members of the family would proffer advice on how to become an expert, and then being told where they could put their advice.

As the years rolled by, it was always my idea to get the younger members of the extended family to join and on more than one occasion invited our Marlene and Lilian's children to join us. Gary and Jacqueline, our Lilian's son and his wife, accepted the invitation and became a permanent fixture. Claire, our Stephen's daughter, also became another regular, until children and financial constraints ended her tenancy. Unfortunately, our Marlene's offsprings, Julie and Janine, have only attended once, and that was on their mother's 70th birthday. After a while, I withdrew their invitation because of, 'The Boy Who Cried Wolf', but in this case it was a girl, and 'Matilda, Told Such Dreadful Lies', kept springing to mind. Why can't people just be honest and say they don't want to attend, but thank you for the invite. I was particularly chuffed when we went to Bembridge on the Isle of Wight in 2013, when Jennifer and Anthony, Helen and Karl joined the regulars. Jennifer and Karl being our Gary's two children.

On a personal note, over the years I have attended with various partners, with and without my family, and my family have always made them welcome. When I see how other families are so dysfunctional, as to not even function, I am proud to be a Briggs.

The Warner's Diary.

Each of these visits evokes wonderful memories for me:

1999, 2000, 2001 and 2005, 2014 Nidd Hall, Harrogate, West Yorkshire.

2002 and 2016, Bodelwyddan Castle, North Wales.

2003, 2004, 2005 and 2006, 2012, 2014 and 2018, Thoresby Hall, Nottingham.

2007, 2015, 2017, Alveston Hall, Nantwich, Cheshire.

1999, 2010, Sinah Warren and 2015, Lakeside Coastal Village, Hayling Island.

2008, Littlecote House, Newbury.

2009, 2011, Holme Lacy, Hereford. Marlene's 70th.

2013, Bembridge, and Norton Grange, Isle of Wight.

I became a Concierge member in 2015, and a Silver Club member in 2018. I can't leave the Warner's story without saying a special thank you to my sister Janet and her husband Rick for pictorially documenting the journey every year, and then in 2012 taking over the mantle of organising the annual get together when I felt it was time to, 'let go'. **But after Warners, I often wondered, 'What's Happened' from the start of Warners to its demise, for some of my family to start stabbing me in the back, which of course they will vehemently deny?**

Holme Lacy 2009, the aging process was catching up.

Starting back left: Jack B, Rick and Jack D.
Middle left: Lilian, Janet, Marlene and Amy.
Front left: mum and Chris. Is our Stephen taking the photo?

7.
RETIREMENT, VOLUNTARY WORK AND BUCKET LISTS: 56+years.

No work, no worries, no problems, however,

"Having work is so important. You are defined by it. So, I suppose when you decide to resign yourself from your work you are losing your definition and identity and becoming invisible." (Eamon Holmes, TV Presenter, Daily Mail, 'Weekend', 2012).

But all is not doom and gloom, because when you are in full time employment, paying a Class 1 stamp, you get x number of days off per annum which you cherish, appreciate, cosset, protect and treasure and try not to waste, but when you are in retirement you don't need anyone's signature or approval to take a break. I was fairly clear in my mind, how I was going to deal with my retirement, but what I was not prepared for was, how invisible I would actually become. As mentioned in Chapter 1, when considering Aging and the Elderly, it's as though when you retire, others still working adopt the attitude that you have prematurely expired. Also, as I've stated leaving UCLAN was a very upsetting experience for me, not because of the actual physicality of leaving but because of the frustration the short experience engendered. It also took me about 18 months to come to terms with the reality of retirement from full time work. Nixon said a month after resigning from the White House, **"The unhappiest people in the whole world are retired – they have no purpose."** Probably, because they missed what they used to be, and what they used to do. For me It was not that I had no purpose, and I certainly was not unhappy. I had plenty of plans but it was accepting the reality and wondering what I had done wrong to so many so-called friends, acquaintances and colleagues, many of whom I had known for a long time, that made them treat me as though I'd acquired some contagious disease. During your life, you are surrounded by people who you like/dislike, please /annoy, fascinate/bore, leave footprints in your heart/a bad taste in your mouth, but then you decide to retire and whoosh, most of them disappear. Excommunicated.

"Enjoy whilst you are hot because once you are cold no one wants to know."

(Evans C, 2015, Call the Midlife).

"Retirement? These days you're useless long before you get to sixty-five."

(Booth S, 2003, Blood on The Tongue, 9:149).

As far as I was concerned, I'd resigned from a post I had barely started and decided that it was also a good a time as any to realise my retirement ambitions, which were mainly walking, reading, writing, gardening, voluntary work and travelling. Heather was also a little taken aback as to why the telephone stopped ringing for me once the surprise, or was it novelty, of my resignation had worn off? The answer was fairly simple, and highlighted the fickle nature of human beings, I had moved out of the work bubble, and into another, ensuring that I was severing my connections with my past and, apart from historical rhetoric, had very little in common with the people I had left behind and, in their eyes, was of no further use. Or as Jennifer Saunders put it in her autobiography, **"You are loved as long as you are useful."** Saunders J, 2013, Bonkers: My Life in Laughs. People who I had known for years didn't return my calls or e-mails, and if they did, it was with insincere platitudes and excuses. How could I have been so wrong about friendship and its frailty and significance? To repeat myself, here I was at 56, feeling the full force of leaving the socially acceptable bubble of the workplace, rushing around all day with a supposed purpose, all for the sake of a pay cheque, to the unacceptable bubble of retirement. No mortgage, no managers, no morons, no health and safety; no addendums to a memorandum; no griping, whinging, whining, moaning work force; no targets and no full-time work. Unfortunately, I couldn't say no politics and religion, they are enshrined in society and would always be. So, nursing my shattered pride there was nothing left for me, but to get on with my life and together with Heather's support, put my future plans into fruition whilst accepting,

"Everything I've done, everything I've worked for, gone in a moment as soon as I walk out of that door, just to be another old man on a park bench. You've earned that space on that bench, embrace it." (White N, 2017, From The Shadows). And,

"That swagger tends to go when you retire." (Jensen M, 2019. What was, What is and What might have been. 20:249).

My thoughts on retirement were fairly simple. You spend a third of your life growing, developing and learning, a third continuing your education and accumulating, via work, and the last third, retirement, enjoying, spending and sharing. That's if there's anyone around, to share with. Learning and experiencing a continuous thread running through all phases. **Once the deed was done, I turned to my bucket list of things I wanted to do. The alternative being a useless list of things you have no intentions of doing.** Financially I would be OK, but just needed a meeting with Derek Winsland, my financial advisor, as to how to maximise my savings and investments to give me a monthly income, off which I could live and afford several trips abroad every year. By the time I received my OAP, in March 2015, some 9 years later, my pension pot was only £2,000 less than the starting pay for a trolley dolly, working for Virgin Atlantic. I'm not sure what the significance of that was but, as those who know me will tell you, I hate wasting useless pieces of information.

My first priority was planning and organising a trip around the world for Heather and myself. This was well documented with a daily diary, e-mails home to our families and photos. All of which can be found in a cardboard storage box, in my spare bedroom at Park Road. Another book waiting to be written. Next, I decided that if I could find myself a part time job, not in health care or education, it would serve the dual purpose of providing me with not only extra finances to fund more travel, but also keep me socially active and in touch with the reality of, 'the modern world'. Although, to be honest, I'm not quite sure what that expression actually infers as I was struggling reconciling myself with much that was going on around me, and becoming more and more detached from the modern world. Coupled with the fact that stress kills you, and so avoiding the stressors was beneficial. So, I decided to try and find jobs where I was doing things I thought I would enjoy, whilst at the same time giving me a fair degree of autonomy. I thought doing voluntary work and giving something back to a life that up until then had, on the whole, been relatively kind to me, was one option. Volunteering for St Catherine's Hospice and joining the Countryside Ranger Service, whilst working for CTS Traffic and Transport, provided the solutions. Also, becoming a house husband, although we were not married, and supporting Heather with her work and chosen pastimes was never an issue, but a done deal. So that was the plan, all I had to do was put it into fruition and try to enjoy every moment. **"The problem and** the pleasure of retirement was this: so much time to fill, but so much enjoyment in trying to fill it." (White N, 2011. Cold Kill. PB, p166).

My Travel Log and Bucket List: Being chased by 4 ton of rhino on Safari.

According to Simon Calder, The Independent, 6/9/24, **"Large airports are on a par with prisons and hospitals-no one wants to be there and everyone wants to get out as soon as possible."**

Upon retirement when my travelling to foreign shores and cultures increased, I was frequently asked, why I travelled so much, my answer being three-fold: Keep moving so the tax man doesn't know where you are. Keep moving because it's more difficult for people to stab you in the back. Keep moving because it helps with depression by avoiding the stressors in your life. As should now be obvious many of the stressors in my life came from, 'the Whinging Poms'. I suppose one could say that later on in my life, when financially I could afford to take more trips I became a bird of flight, fleeing from society, hurt, rejection and a desire to hear the English language spoken correctly.

"Explore, Dream, Discover." Mark Twain.

"It is better to see something once, than to hear about it a thousand times." Asian Proverb.

"The world is a book, and those who do not travel read only a page." St Augustine.

"There is something about the momentum of travelling, that makes you want to just keep moving, to never stop." (Bryson B, 1992. Neither Here Nor There, 22: 498).

My earliest travel recollections as a youngster were of day trips to Fleetwood and Knott End, courtesy of Chadderton Congregational Church, the local Conservative and Labour clubs. There was my trip to Beaumaris, on the Isle of Anglesey, with Terry Glynn and his parents, when my brother, Jack, couldn't go because of illness, and I was drafted in as a last-minute replacement. But when I visited Beaumaris, some 50 plus years later in 2015, with Denise Walsh and walked around the town one Sunday morning in the cold and rain, other than the castle, nothing else registered. Then there were the family holidays to Mrs Rose's Guest House in Euston Road, Morecambe with visits to Happy Mount Park, of which I have absolutely no memories, other than its name. Not forgetting good old Blackpool, with its illuminations, with or without Arnold Saville, 'the kiddy fiddler'. Apart from this, my first holiday as a teenager without my family, was with Colin Brooks to Blackpool, where Colin was, 'set upon', by some lads when he ventured out one night on his own. Where I was at the time, I have no idea. Not that me being with him, would have avoided the altercation. In those days, during the fifties and sixties, these places were teeming with holiday makers as the factories closed for the local, 'Wakes Weeks'. Then there was the camping trip to Paignton and Torquay, Devon, with my teenage mates, Pete Fletcher, Jimmy Hughes and Kenny Clough.

For the first forty years of my life, I had been happy to explore my native shores, even though Freddie Laker was trying to tempt us to fly abroad, with his early 'package holidays'. During my courtship and subsequent marriage to Dee, I acquired a liking for Cornwall, Devon and the Channel Islands and in particular Jersey. One of our first holidays together was on the train to Torquay, and after arriving quite late in the day, visited the Tourist Information office to see if they could find us somewhere to stay. "Yes, no problem," said the lady, but as internet and e-mails were not the sophisticated tools that they are today, the arrangements were made over the telephone. Yes, landline, no mobiles. How did we ever cope? The hotel even said they would pay for a taxi to collect us. At that time in my life, travelling in a taxi was considered, 'posh'. No sooner said than done, a taxi arrived and took us to this hotel where the proprietor met us at the door, and paid for the taxi. What a nice man! During the booking in process, he explained that he couldn't accommodate us in the same room all our stay, but if it was acceptable, he would find us a more permanent room in a few days. Being tired and just happy to have found somewhere to sleep, we had no problems with that. Finally, on the booking form we had left the occupation space blank. Don't forget, this was long before demographic, data collection and mining were an integral part of life. Asking us politely, if we could please fill that in, he joked that we really could put anything in the space as long as it didn't say, 'Working for the Inland Revenue'. Was he joking? Later, I realised that by fitting us in at the last moment, and moving rooms, he probably was not going to process us through the books. But hey, what did we care, as we had a dirty weekend planned in Torquay. It has often amused me, how we use certain expressions which if taken literally, are very amusing. What is a dirty weekend? One where you roll around in the mud? I digress. Well, it was more than a weekend. It's interesting that the holiday was not immaculately organised, but once I'd got the travel bug, many of my subsequent holidays were. As I got older, the planning and organising of such, became an endless source of enjoyment, especially during the times I found myself alone. The process being just as enjoyable as the holiday itself. Also, don't forget, in those days information technology was not the addiction it was later to become, and so travel agents and tourist information centres ruled the roost. Years later, I returned to Torquay to holiday with Deborah Warburton and her son Ross, and in May 2017, I travelled alone to Torquay for a 4-day nostalgia break. Staying at a guest house advertising itself as a modern, Fawlty Towers, which the owners thought was a good advertising ploy, but I don't think they realised it could have put many people off staying there. Having said that, it was an excellent place to stay and wouldn't hesitate to stay there again.

As for Dee and our love affair with Jersey, visiting three times, we seriously considered living there so we could change from being a grockle to a resident. In Jersey, holiday makers were known as grockles. However, in the 70s if you wanted to live in Jersey, you couldn't just pack your bags and arrive uninvited at the docks or airport. Although, initially we always travelled on the overnight ferry from Weymouth or Portsmouth, as cheap flights were few and far between. In order to be allowed to stay, other than as a tourist, you had to have secured a job, which was of some value to the community, have enough money to live on, until you started earning, or money you intended to invest into the island's economy. If my memory serves me correctly, the money to stay in Jersey at that time, without a job, was in excess of £100,000. In today's terms a month's bonus for someone working in the city, or a day's wages for a Premier League footballer. Whatever is meant by an average footballer I will let the reader define. In 2019, I would imagine the lump sum might be considerably more than £100,000. Unlike in England where, in spite of all the rhetoric by the politicians, we appear to have a virtual open-door policy to immigration that causes resentment, unrest, bigotry, anarchy and chaos. Enter Brexit, or should that be exit Europe? It's been interesting travelling the globe, to find out what the rest of the world thought of the UK and its citizens. Without going into depth and to put it in simple terms the nickname, pre-Brexit, was 'Spongers Paradise', and that applied to not only immigrants, but also certain UK residents, with the attitude of, 'the world owes me'. I also have friends who, over the years, have abandoned the UK and have taken up residence in other countries, and all have said they were given nothing to reside in New Zealand, Spain and France, apart from a job, but would never return to the UK. That's not to say countries with a specialised labour shortage, i.e. teachers, engineers etc. don't offer incentives to recruit people but the question of residence has become more sophisticated and somewhat of a political hot potato, and a long way from the £10 voyages, in the 50s, to attract people from the UK to Australia. As both Dee and I were teachers, it was just a question of scouring the Times Educational Supplement for jobs in the Channel Islands, and then trying to secure a couple of teaching posts on the island. Easier said than done, as competition was fierce because not only was the lifestyle less frenetic and stressful than on the mainland, but it was also a tax haven. After work many islanders going to the beach for a swim, before their evening meal. During the day, the beaches were full of not only grockles but also mums spending the day with their little off-springs, with not a crèche, child minder, babysitter or grandmother in sight. The only downside to what appeared to be this idyllic lifestyle was, the fact you had to live on the island for 10 years, before you could own property. Unless of course, you were called Alan Wicker or Jim Bergerac, (John Nettles), both high profile celebrities on TV at that time. This meant 10 years in rented, B&B accommodation. This was to ensure that people genuinely wanted to become an islander, and not just someone who wanted to take advantage of the tax laws and benefits of being a Channel Islander. Our first holiday to Jersey happened quite by accident. At the time, we lived on Alandale Drive, Royton, which was only a fifteen-minute walk from the town centre. On this particular Friday morning, at the start of our school summer break, I had left Dee ironing, whilst I went into Royton to visit the bank and do a little shopping. Oh bugger, could that be construed as sexist? Probably, but as it's a fact, am not bothered. A few hours later, I returned with very little shopping, but had booked our car, Dee and myself on the midnight ferry to Jersey from Portsmouth, or was it Weymouth, the following day, I can't remember? As I walked through the front door, Dee asked why it had taken me so long, who had I been talking to and where was the bread and cheese? Teachers didn't eat very well in those days. I explained that after visiting the bank, I just popped into the travel agents to pick up a few brochures, and the only thing I remember after that was paying for the tickets. The sales girl must have had big, blue eyes, dark hair and a decent cleavage. Now that's definitely sexist, guilty as charged, your honour. Although being very organised, I loved spontaneity and impulse. "The deal was too good to miss, Dee," I said, as she looked at me as if to say, OK, I had better start putting this ironing into a suitcase and start packing. "It also means we will be on the island at the time of, The Battle of the Flowers, which Dee had once mentioned she would like to see. To those who are unfamiliar with Channel Island folklore, the Battle of the Flowers was equivalent to France on Bastille Day, or during the Tour de France cycle race. It was a massive event and Jersey would be full of tourists. Leaving very early the following morning, which was a Saturday, we had several stops on the way down to the South coast, one being before lunch to phone the tourist information in St Helier to secure some accommodation, as the deal I had secured with the travel agent was only for the ferry crossing. As we had booked accommodation via the tourist information before, we were not too worried about getting somewhere to stay. This was done from a red, public phone box at the service station and not via Trivago. This was the era of red, public, phone boxes, putting money into the box, when you heard the beeps and pressing button A, to connect, or B, to get your money back. So, a lengthy phone call had to be planned with military precision, unless you wanted to be cut off just as you were getting to the important part of the call. Not to forget the line of people outside the box, also waiting to use the phone, looking at you with angry eyes. Cue for another song. Also, in my excitement to book and get home to tell Dee about this great deal I had just secured, I had not taken into consideration the fact that securing accommodation in Jersey during the Battle of the Flowers week was like finding a needle in a haystack. Not that I've ever had to look, but I've been led to believe was an appropriate expression to use. Upon getting through to the nice lady in tourist information in St Helier, Jersey, and telling her what we wanted, I was greeted with a stony silence and then, "I'm sorry, sir, the island is fully booked up." No, you're jesting, you're having a giraffe, I thought to myself. How can an island the size of Jersey with all its hotels, B&Bs and guest houses be fully booked up? After all, had we not brought with us several travel brochures from the travel agent, that were full of places to stay? "The only thing I can suggest, sir, is when you arrive, come straight to us when we open at 0900 and we'll see if we've had any late cancellations, or acquired any late bed availability, but at the moment there is nothing." Putting down the phone, I looked at Dee and smiling, said, "Well that's that, love, tomorrow we are sleeping under the stars, or under the pier as a grockle." I didn't even know if Jersey had a pier, but as I'd been to Blackpool, which had three piers, I thought all seaside resorts had them. As we journeyed further South, Dee had managed to scour the brochures for accommodation agencies that might, for a fee, have somewhere to stay. Stopping again near Newbury and finding a phone box, off the A34, we tried several of these places, and managed to book a few nights in a private house, but only if we paid cash upon arrival to the agent, who would take their fee before paying the proprietors. As we were given details over the phone, we didn't stop to think too much of, 'the cash in hand', implications, as long as we initially had somewhere to stay and would worry about having to move after a few days, once we had arrived on the island. After all, we were used to living on the edge after our experiences during our trip to Torquay. As it turned out the accommodation was very good, and right near the route of the Battle of Flowers parade. The owners only took in guests on a casual basis and then via recommendation, or people who had stayed with them before, but once they realised, we were a young professional teaching couple, they allowed us to stay with them for the duration of our time in Jersey. Little did they know we could have been tax officers from Torquay. Needless to say, we fell in love with the Channel Islands for many reasons, but for me the main one was they didn't suffer fools gladly and took a dim view of grockles, who just wanted to come to their islands and disrespect and abuse it with drunken, loutish behaviour, or by throwing stones through the local jeweller's window, just for a laugh. **Today in 2025, this kind of behaviour is a good reason to make a TV programme.** One of the islands' attractions for holiday makers was its drinking laws which allowed pubs to be open all day, well from 10 am, which for us was something we were unfamiliar with, and somewhat of a novelty. **It was only when the UK joined the European Union, that pub hours were brought in line with the rest of Europe. The thinking behind longer drinking hours being that it would reduce the prevalence of drunkenness, as people could drink more leisurely and didn't have to buy doubles for, 'last orders'. Unfortunately, this was not proven to be the case, because it didn't consider the UK's obsession and dependency with and on alcohol. For me, this extending of drinking hours could have been the precursor to what was to follow with regard to alcohol abuse and addiction.** At that time in Jersey, holiday makers guilty of misdemeanours, no matter how petty, would be brought before the island's judiciary as soon as possible, given a hefty fine and or a possible prison sentence, if they transgressed again. But to avoid such an eventuality, they were put on the first ferry back to the UK mainland. The first ferry being the 0630 from St Helier and was known by the locals as the, 'undesirable's ferry'. Every morning just before it was due to set sail, a police transit van would pull up at the dockside and escort said miscreants onto the ship. I say escort, it was more like throw. **We loved it and was a million miles away from the liberal, British penal system, with all the kowtowing that goes on today with criminals and people who flout the law, with no deterrent whatsoever.** For several years after that, older and wiser after our first visit, we holidayed on the island during our 6-week summer break, by renting a house, in St Lawrence, from a young couple called John and Carol. John was a Yorkshireman who had holidayed in Jersey, met Carol, fell in love and got married to the local girl. Her parents were not short of a few bob, and owned quite a large house in St Lawrence and a holiday home in the South of France. As such, the residency laws didn't apply to John after marriage, and so John and Carol had recently moved into their own home, which was, 'just around the corner', from her parents' place. Seeing our advertisement in the local paper, and resigned to the fact they probably wouldn't be able to afford a holiday that year, because they lived within their means. So, they hit upon the idea of renting out their semi-detached, so they could holiday in her parents' villa, in the South of France. Again, another sign of the times were parents, even if they had the cash, didn't just hand it over to their offsprings, to make life easier. As for me, ever since I had entered the teaching profession and started to consider myself as an upwardly mobile, social ascender, (Josephine Klein), I had thought it would be great to go away for more than the normal week, ten days or fortnight. And so, after our first holiday there, and knowing some locals did rent out their homes we put an advert in the Jersey Post along the lines of: **Professional teaching couple, with no children, seek holiday home to rent for minimum of four weeks between July and September**. We provided contact details, and received three replies. In those days, contact was either by telephone or letter, now known as ,'snail mail'. To cut a long story short, we ended up arranging to meet John and his wife as we drove off the midnight ferry in St Helier, Jersey at 0630, to be escorted up to their property in the centre of the island, at St Lawrence. As they had never done anything like that before, they were very nervous about letting their property to someone they didn't know for 3-4 weeks. The plan was for them to spend a day with us, showing us around their place and introducing us to the neighbours, and then the following day they would depart for the South of France with her mum and dad. All our fears were allayed, as we got on really well, loved their house, and were introduced to not only the neighbours, but also the local publican. Being aware of local customs is no bad thing, as there was a protocol for getting served in the bar, that for those who were not aware could prove to be frustrating. Dee and I spent many a night sitting and watching the mainly English grockles clicking their fingers, expecting the locals to jump to attention and being completely ignored. The more they clicked, the more they were ignored. If only they knew, that if they exercised good manners and didn't treat the locals as lackeys , they would be served in due course. Whilst grockles, did bolster the economy and were good for business, the locals didn't enjoy being patronised by them. Was this arrogance or ignorance? In fact, the locals provided most businesses with a decent living, so they certainly were not going to kowtow to these people from the mainland. **Some 40 to 50 years later, a vast majority of Brits travelling abroad still expect other nationalities to provide a little England for them, where everyone should speak English and provide full English breakfast, with brown or tomato sauce, with absolutely no attempt to speak the language of the country they are visiting or respect their customs and values.** Yet the Brits slander immigrants and visitors to this country, for doing the same. Why? I have wondered post Brexit, 2016, when we said to the rest of Europe, we don't need you, we are going to go it alone. Europe then says, fine, English people who travel to other countries on holiday or chose to live abroad, will be ostracised if they don't make an effort to speak the language, and respect local customs and cultures. Interesting! No wonder we are perceived as arrogant, alcohol obsessed, foul mouthed, white supremacist bigots. Back to Jersey, as we had been introduced as friends of John and Carol, we soon lost our grockle label and quickly learned the local traditions and folklore. We soon learned that people in Jersey saw Guernsey as a place to go if you wanted to die, and people in Guernsey saw a trip to Jersey as somewhere to go, if you wanted to catch a sexually transmitted disease, or die of a drug overdose. In simplicity, Jersey was seen as a vibrant, happening place to live, with Guernsey having a much more laid-back approach to life, and somewhere you might want to retire for a peaceful existence. As I have never visited Sark or Alderney I can't comment on them.

During that first day, we were invited to enough barbeques to last us a month, and when I told John and Carol that we enjoyed gardening, and could we spend time cutting the grass etc. our relationship blossomed further, as John hated gardening. It was strange on that first night in St Lawrence, after they had taken us to the local pub, to introduce us to several of their neighbours, and from there inviting them into **their house** for coffee. Weird! Needless to say, we had a fabulous time, and not only kept their garden in trim, but also tidied out the garage so we could fit our car in, and bought them a wall clock as they didn't have one anywhere in the house. All of this of course, under the watchful gaze of the neighbours, who had obviously promised to, 'keep an eye on us', in case we trashed the place. As if, had we not on our first visit to the island, proved to be model, law-abiding citizens? It was after this second holiday, that we seriously considered living in the Channel Islands, returning to the house on one other occasion, after John and Carol had had their first child. Sadly, after our third visit to the island, both theirs and our relationships took a turn for the worse, and the Channel Islands became a distant memory. They split up and sadly, so did Dee and myself. In June 2017, I flew to Jersey alone on another nostalgic, return trip and within 24 hours of arriving back on the island, realised why Dee and I had wanted to live there many years previously. Yes, it had changed but not for the worse. Was I sad, what do you think? I didn't fly until I was 40, but within a few years I had travelled around the world on a rugby tour in 1993, visiting Los Angeles, Fiji, New Zealand and Australia. The next time I was to circumnavigate the globe was with Heather, 27-09-2008 to 29-12-2008, to be precise. During our sojourn we visited Boston, New England, and from there went on a 9-day, coach tour titled, New England in the Fall. It's interesting to note that whilst the Brits go to New England in autumn to see the spectacular leaf colours, the Americans visit the UK to visit the New Forest to see our leaves change colour. In America, they call it, leaf peeping, which I think is a lovely term. We then spent a month touring the North and South Island, New Zealand in a camper van. In Australia, we travelled from Cairns to Sydney, via plane and train, including stops in Brisbane and Coolangata, on the Sunshine Coast. From Melbourne to Adelaide, we hired a car and travelled along the Great Ocean Road, and from Adelaide flew to Perth. In South Africa, after visiting Johannesburg and Soweto, we then hired another car and travelled along, 'The Garden Route', from Port Elizabeth to Cape Town, via Kariega Wildlife Safari Park, with stops in Knysna and Plettenberg Bay. On our Around the World Trip Heather and I kept a diary, together with photographs, charting our time away, which we later turned into specific folders, and which is another record of a time in my life, which could provide material for yet another book. In the meantime, here is an extract from our diary from our time in South Africa, spent at Kariega Wildlife Safari Park, 141kms from Port Elizabeth. Tuesday, 16th September, 2008.

"On the afternoon game drive, we set off to look for the lioness and her 3 cubs, and after 20 minutes, we were going up a one-way track, with no exit routes, when we came upon two very grumpy male rhinos. The rule is we give way to them not the other way around. Temba, (our guide), put the 4x4 in reverse and started to back down the track. Suddenly, the rhinos started to run towards us and at this point, we could smell something and Jim started to tell Heather he loved her, and where he had hidden his will. Temba was brilliant as he reversed at speed until he eventually, found a small turn off before the rhinos passed us at speed seconds later. What an adrenaline rush. Temba asked if we were OK and said they were very naughty boys for doing that to us."

Being chased by 4 ton of rhino on Safari. 'Naughty Boys.'

Several years later, 2010, we re-visited California and Nevada, on a coach tour which included stops in Los Angeles, Palm Springs, Las Vegas, Yosemite NP, and finally San Francisco before leaving the tour to fly to Hawaii for my birthday. The final leg being my birthday present from Heather. On our return journey back to the UK, we had an unscheduled stopover in San Francisco because of the Icelandic ash cloud, arising from the volcano Eyjafjallajokull, which ground all flights in the Northern Hemisphere for several days. In the intervening 15 years between the rugby tour and travelling around the world with Heather, I travelled to many European destinations. My first plane journey abroad, was to the Nestor hotel in Ayia Napa, Cyprus, the first of many journeys I undertook alone. My brother Jack took me to the airport and as he waved me goodbye, and as I headed for the security check, I had this overwhelming feeling of loneliness. A recurring feeling that was to become an integral part of my later life and which led to many periods of depression. Whilst not ideal going on holiday alone, I argued that it was better than talking to the wall, auditioning for Shirley Valentine, and staying at home. Although separated the following year, I returned to the same hotel but this time with Dee as we had kept in touch and both felt guilty about our, 'failed marriage'. Would we get back together? I suppose this question was asked regularly, until Dee eventually married John B many, many years later.

"I always think it is better to travel alone, isn't it? Stops you being a tourist and really helps you get into the local culture." (Macdonald H, 2000. The Mind Game).

Whilst I don't totally agree with this sentiment, I understand what the advantages of travelling alone can be. In the 80s and early 90s holidays for singles were in their infancy and the most one could hope for was, no single supplements. Long before political correctness became a pain in the arse, there were serious cases of positive discrimination against people who, through no fault of their own, found themselves single. I remember walking into a Travel Agents in Oldham, on one wet Tuesday afternoon, when there was no one in the shop apart from two young girls selling holidays. I suppose I should call them Travel Consultants as they probably had done a B. Tech. at Oldham College, in Tourism and Leisure. What they are called in 2024, I wouldn't know? "Can I help you sir?" said one. "Yes, you can," came my reply as I took a seat to get their undivided attention. "I'm looking for a holiday to Cyprus, Spain or Greece, but I have several allergies that you need to know about." Now I really did have their undivided attention, because there was only the three of us in the shop. Or to be more accurate, I could only see two girls besides myself. "You see every time I see supplements added, when I want to fly from my local airport, Manchester, I come out in a rash. Also, every time I am asked to pay £100 supplement because I am classed as, 'Billy No Mates', I start frothing at the mouth and could have an epileptic fit. So, if you could find me a holiday that addresses these issues I would appreciate it." Silence. After about 10 seconds, which was a long time for me to keep quiet, one of the girls started to smile and asked if I was being serious. "Deadly," I replied. "I refuse to be victimised and discriminated against just because I am a sad, lonely person, with no one to travel with, and I have decided not to have children." "Well, let's see what we can do for you, sir," said the boss, who had just appeared on the scene after obviously responding to the alarm/panic button that one of the girls must have pressed under her desk, when they realised a potential trouble causer had come into the shop. About an hour later I left, after several biscuits and a cup of tea, but not before booking a holiday to Aghios Nicolas, in Crete. "Thank you for your custom, Mr Briggs, and for brightening up our afternoon with your funny wit and repartee." I think that's what they said, or was it, "Pillock?" Don't forget my mantra: **Give someone a smile, as they might not have one of their own. As intimated in Chapter 1, Setting the Scene, over the years I've been sorely tempted to walk into a travel agent, followed by the press and a television crew, with 2 baby goats on leads, and request 2 free kids' holidays.**

My first flying travel companion, apart from Dee, was a young lady called Lynn with whom I travelled to Marmaris in Turkey, summer 1991. Apart from the fact that Lynn and I had a good holiday, I remember it for one character whom we met who was staying in our hotel. He was a West Country gentleman with quite a strong, west country, Bristol accent, who used to work for British Rail, as a train driver, but had just retired. Virgin Trains, franchises and competitive tendering had not yet taken a stranglehold on the economy. If my memory serves me correctly this was in 1997. Upon retirement he had been presented with a camcorder, which in those days was the something, 'every home should have'. He could be seen wandering around the hotel filming everybody and everything, none of this invasion of privacy business. He seemed particularly fascinated with towels on sunbeds, that were not being used by anyone at the time of filming. One day he was swimming off the private jetty, that was part of the hotel grounds, when he made a bee-line for Lynn and myself as we rested, dangling our feet in the water, having just had a little dip in the sea ourselves. It was pretty obvious, and early into our conversation, that he was anti Royal family and anti-German. "What do you think of old jug ears then?" he enquired after the initial introductory salvo. "Jug ears?" I enquired. "Prince, bloody Charles and that gorgeous Diana. What the fuck, sorry luv, is she doing with that wanker? Hopefully, she'll get shut once she realises what she's done." Now as everyone knows I'm a chatter box but being bombarded with so much information to which I was expected to reply, was, even for me, a little daunting. Especially as it was obvious he wouldn't listen to any counter arguments to his point of view. Don't forget, 'there is nothing as certain as the closed mind.' So, of course I did what most people do in such a situation, I just smiled and hoped Lynn would distract him in her slinky bikini. No such luck and barely giving us much time to reply, even if we wanted to, he went off on a tirade about the Germans. "I'm sick of 'em," he said, "they wanted all the bloody sand in Africa during the war and Monty wouldn't let them have it, and now they want fucking world domination of sunbeds. Sorry luv. Well, I'm not having it." And with that he jumped up, went over to all the sunbeds that had towels on with no occupants, and proceeded to throw them, the towels not the sunbeds, into the hotel swimming pool. He then stood there defying anybody to challenge his actions. He was not a skinny chap and I would describe his demeanour as intimidating. Lynn burst out laughing, quietly of course, and I loved it, because our bed was not one he had targeted for his mini tirade. A moment in time that could have been a classic for actual, 'Reality Television'. To be honest, the gentleman and his wife were a nice couple, as we spent several occasions socialising with them during our fortnight's holiday. It's ironic, if that's the right word, that later on in my life towels on sunbeds and Prince Charles, now King Charles, became issues for me so much so that I had to include them in my autobiography.

Now I used to get up early in a morning, if I intended to go for a jog before the heat got fierce. After all it was June, and temperatures could get well into the nineties. Several days later after our first encounter with Mr X, sorry I cannot for the life of me remember his name, I was just returning from my jog and was looking forward to jumping into the hotel pool, before doing my cool down routine, when I saw him walking around the pool. It was probably about 0730, breakfast being from 0800. Yes, you've guessed, if I was to jump into the pool, I would have to avoid all these towels that had mysteriously arrived there. Priceless, I loved the guy, in my eyes he was my hero, a star. Second only to Clint Eastwood for sorting out the bad guys. I only ever saw one altercation with a hotel guest that he appeared to 'win', and Lynn and I were party to a heated discussion he was having one day with the hotel management. During which he was reported as saying, "What was the f...ing point in having all the signs around the place, about leaving towels on sunbeds, when nobody gave a flying f..k about enforcing the rule." Or something similar. He informed them that they should be paying him, because he was doing their job. **In today's selfish, arrogant society he would no doubt have a nervous breakdown.** Ever since that holiday, I have always wanted to have the balls to do what he did, but have never summoned up the courage. Mainly, because I would not class my demeanour as intimidating. During one holiday alone to Tenerife, Playa de Las Americas, 2013, I was sorely tempted to follow the example of the ex-railway man when I stayed at the Hotel Columbus, in Playa de Las Americas, where the area around the swimming pool was adjourned with a myriad signs, asking guests not to leave towels on sun beds. **NO ESTA PERMITIDO RESERVAR HAMACUS. IT IS FORBIDDEN TO RESERVE SUN-BEDS.** Needless to say, every sunbed had a towel draped on, long before breakfast and certainly before many went off into town or to the beach. Selfish and arrogant springs to mind, or should that be illiterate. But to be fair to the alcohol dependents, who rarely if ever, left the bar area for the two weeks of their holiday, they did need somewhere to sleep before embarking on their next, 'heavy session'. During my stay, I only heard several Eastern European accents, apart from Spanish of course, the rest of the time it was English. Previously, when discussing Brits Abroad, I've pontificated about the towels on sunbeds scenario, and what I predict will be its conclusion, and so I think it's time I put the topic to bed, if you'll pardon the pun.

After my initial enthusiasm for beach holidays, I started looking at tours and City Breaks, and today very few of my holidays are purely beach holidays. I also try to avoid travelling between June and September, during school holidays. I wonder why, and it's not purely and simply to do with cost or children? Perhaps, Reality TV programmes, might have something to do with it.

The things I enjoyed most about my travels, especially after retirement, was planning, organising, researching, and booking holidays on my computer. I would plan every aspect of the trip, so that the trip itself was as stress free as was possible, and all my energies could be channelled into enjoying the experience of not only travelling, but also upon reaching my destination. I also loved planning trips in advance, so that as and when time and money permitted, I could fine-tune the arrangements with actual dates and personnel. These could range from long distant walks, city breaks to long haul travel. However, the more I travelled, the more I realised I'd done very little, but compared to many I had done much. My list would never be completely exhausted, but as I got older and aging took its toll, I knew there would come a time when I would be more than happy and satisfied with my achievements and travel-log. I desperately missed sharing my holidays with others, especially when we both shared a common goal. I've often thought of calculating how many holidays I'd actually taken alone, but quickly dismissed the idea after asking myself, why? After my East Coast Canadian trip in May/June 2016, I was so drained after the break-up of another relationship and finding myself once again alone, I arrived home and for the first time since retirement in 2006, I hadn't planned any more trips. I had lost my buzz to travel. However, I was chuffed by the number of things on my bucket list, that I had ticked off. However, by mid-July, 2016, I was slowly getting my motivation back and planned trips to Edinburgh, with my niece Claire, and Madeira, alone, both in September, 2016. In November 2016, I travelled to Tasmania with stopovers in Singapore and Hong Kong, on the way out and back. However, by now I was resigning myself to the fact, that travelling alone was just no fun anymore. In fact, it felt as though I was running away, and trying to hide from my depression. But in spite of the lonely moments I experienced, and there were many, I still had several things on my bucket list that I wanted to do, and it was annoying me. So, summoning up my final reserves of energy, I arranged trips touring Scotland by train in August, 2017, and travelling on the Pacific Coast Highway 1 from Los Angeles to San Francisco, in September, 2017, both alone. Unfortunately, during my Pacific Coast Highway trip one night, alone in my room, I suffered a 4-hour transient memory loss, very scary, and after recovering, spent the rest of the trip coming to terms with the fact, that my travelling alone days were perhaps, coming to an end. My final long-haul trips on my travel bucket list were planned for April 2018 to South America, visiting Rio de Janeiro, Brazil and then returning to the Pacific Coast in September, 2018, to travel the northern leg of the Pacific Coast Highway from Seattle to San Francisco, via Portland, but this time on Amtrak. In 2019, I visited Nice and Rio, but this time with my younger brother, Stephen, who had just lost his partner Denise. During the Rio trip, I suffered a further transient memory loss, but this time I was with my brother. As I proof this chapter, I am planning further trips with my brother Stephen, in 2020, to Nice, Lisbon, Madrid and a visit to Switzerland, to travel on the Bernini and Glacial Express routes through the Alps. I've enjoyed my recent, brotherly bonding trips, for more than just the obvious reasons but unfortunately, Covid-19 has put a stop to all that. What will happen after Covid I'm not sure. As I write this section of my autobiography, I realise I could write another book based on my travel exploits and experiences. Is that another two or three more books after this? Over the years, my travels have given me such varied experiences of life in the real world, with these people in particular, giving me hours of sadness, anger and enjoyment, such is the roller coaster of their existence. And, to re-iterate, it also gave me an insight of what other nationalities thought about the Brits. As a distraught teenager, I ran away from home and ended up sat on a bench in Hayle, Cornwall, wondering what life was about. 60 years later, I'm still running away, but this time so I could hear English being spoken correctly by non-Brits, who had learnt it as a second language. But before getting to my destination, the Brits could ensure that even this experience could be seriously marred because of their obsession with alcohol, and how some passengers blatantly plan how to flout the drinking rules and regulations, both in the airport and on the plane, so they can fuel their obsession. Whilst not needing research evidence for my personal experiences in this regard to be confirmed, in 2024, Michael O'Leary, CEO of Ryanair, together with experienced airline staff, including the captain, whilst talking to the Telegraph newspaper gave an insight of male and female behaviour on planes **with British passengers being cited as the worst offenders.** Acts of loud, aggressive, behaviour, via physical and verbal abuse, horrendous fights with some passengers even vomiting on staff if they tried to, 'calm the situation'. Whilst reading the catalogue of disgraceful incidents I was thinking, what next, breathalysing passengers before boarding the plane? I also didn't need to confirm, which tribe these people belonged to. **But this is the reality of life in 2025 under the guise of progress.**

My Retired Job Portfolio and Job Seekers' Allowance: 56 plus years.

By retiring from full time employment, I assumed I had to all intents and purposes, terminated my educational journey, but the task of finding a part time job soon showed this assumption was misplaced. Don't forget that, 'to assume makes an ass of you and me.' The number of application forms, letters and CVs, I forwarded to potential employers was numerous. As I had never been out of work since leaving school at 16, the process of applying for work, as opposed to promotion, was not so much alien to me in the sense of what needed to be done, but to the fact that I was unaware of how the work place functioned in the year 2006. **Heather and I were appalled, to say the least, as to the way prospective employers treated applicants, to such an extent that I came to understand how many gave up trying to find employment, and decided to just live off the State. A massive turnaround of mindset for me.** For a person who had never voted in his life, I nevertheless agreed with Norman Tebbit's philosophy of, get up off your arse and find a job. Yes, I know he said get on your bike, but let's not be pedantic, the sentiment is still the same. Don't forget, I didn't need a job to survive and my motives for wanting to work for only 16 or so hours a week, were not driven by financial necessity. But it was soul destroying, time consuming and came as a big shock to me to find that, time after time employers did not even have the courtesy to say, "Thank you, but no thank you." Spending many hours filling in application forms, getting CRB checks, aligning my letters of application to suit the job description and specification, and then getting absolutely no response to all my efforts, as though such preparation to detail had ever taken place, made me very, very angry. When did this almost total disregard for job applicants start? After all, I was only applying sometimes, to put tins of beans on a shelf. No disrespect to people who do that job, but this was not something I expected, now that I'd decided to leave the stressful world of full-time employment. I can remember contacting one personnel officer to ask why I had not been contacted to say that they had at least received my application, and was given the excuse that they received so many applications, it was not practical to do so. When I pointed out I had enclosed a stamped addressed envelope, for the sole purpose of knowing my application had at least been received, the Human Resources Officer still stuck to her original mantra. As she was obviously unaware of the content of my CV, she was ignorant of the fact that I used to lecture on communication and so, I informed her that I thought that the policy they adopted was disrespectful, arrogant and just plain rude to the applicants, and was surprised by her intransigence. I also said, that I was surprised that anyone would want to work for a company with such a policy. I suggested perhaps, they might consider me for the post of replying to the thousands of applications they got for each job. If they got as many as she claimed, I thought that would be equivalent to 16 hours of, 'Thank you but no, thank yous'. Sadly, her reply was short, curt and dismissive, as by now she had decided I was an arrogant tosser. When I've watched TV programmes explaining the plight of the unemployed and heard of other people who had applied for hundreds of jobs, with many never even getting an interview, made me ask myself once again, **how had society plummeted to such a depth that even people who wanted to work, were treated with such disdain and disrespect.** Even when I dubbed down my application to stack shelves in Asda, taking my application into the personnel office myself, the result was just the same, **FUCK OFF, WE DON'T WANT YOU, you're too educated, don't speak with the correct accent, whatever that was, and if we employed you, we probably wouldn't be able to talk to you like Gordon Ramsey talks to potential chefs on his TV programmes.** How had some of these existing employers achieved their positions? I fully appreciated that by offering a job to a 56-year-old guy that didn't desperately need the money, was perhaps depriving a 'more deserving' applicant, but no such explanation was ever offered, probably because they would have been accused of some 'ism, 'ist or 'ic'. By the way, just in case you are wondering, I didn't tell them I didn't need the money, just the company of people that would keep me in touch with the sadly declining, face to face communicating world. With my isolation from my previous life and then this treatment, I seriously, was becoming paranoid as to what I had done to deserve such treatment. But all was not doom and gloom, as I was invited for an interview for a job working in regional passport offices, that were soon to be set up throughout the country, to deal with the constant flood of passport applications, and the flood of people entering the country for a whole raft of reasons. This appearing to be one of the main reasons, the country decided to leave the EEU in 2016. This was right up my street as it was part time, involved interviewing people and communication. I felt I more than satisfied all the 7 criteria on the job specification, which was to be used as the basis for the interviews, to be held in a posh hotel at Manchester airport. My interview was for 4 pm in the afternoon and arriving in my best, 'bib and tucker', I was informed the interviews were running late. No worries, but what ensued was a catalogue of all things I used to lecture on related to poor communication and, 'you don't get a second chance to make a first impression'. This isn't sour grapes, because I was not offered a position, but a statement of fact. It was like one of the John Cleese, of Monty Python and Faulty Tower's Fame, management videos that I watched in the mid-80s when I was studying for my management qualifications. Without boring the reader with all the details, it was obvious that both interviewers, one male and one female, were knackered, sorry tired, and just wanted to go home. I thought at one point, they were going to fall asleep on me. I know Heather became bored with me, but that took 12 plus years, not twelve minutes. They were going through the motions, watching my lips move, but not listening to what I was saying. I thanked them for their time, shook hands and left, but I was not a happy bunny. They were obviously not aware of the work of Albert Mehrabian on communication or the world of kinetics. By now, you will realise that there was a recurring theme to my personal contacts, just before and after retirement. I was becoming a very disgruntled bunny! When I received the letter telling me that, on this particular occasion I had not been successful, I immediately phoned them up, and asked if I could speak to someone in Human Resources for feedback, as to why they didn't think I was suitable for the position. When I was an interviewer, examiner feedback was standard procedure for anyone who has not reached the required grade. They informed me they couldn't divulge, why I was not suitable over the phone. No problems, I've plenty of time on my hands, when and where do you want me to give me such information face to face, now known as, 'face time'? Silence. Hello, is there anybody out there? sang Pink Floyd. That would not be possible, Mr Briggs, we are far too busy. It would appear the world was far too busy to speak to anyone. Perhaps, the phrase, 'face to face', had thrown her, but she didn't even offer to send me a text or acknowledge my existence on facebook. There was, however, some respite to all this doom and gloom, brought about by my weekly visits to Preston Job Plus Centre. I was not sure what the plus signified, and I never asked because when I was a lad it used to be the dole office. Every week, I would bring home part time jobs for Heather to look at over our evening meal. These were presented, tongue in cheek, for her thoughts as to my suitability for the position. It also sometimes, took the form of a quiz as to what the job actually was. In my many years of absence from the Job Centre and highlighted in Chapter 1, Setting The Scene, I was not familiar with the changes that had occurred, 'to sell jobs', to potential applicants by giving them 'new titles'. Did I want to be **AN AMBIENT REPLENISHMENT OPERATIVE, A SANDWICH ARTIST, A HOMICIDAL PERPETRATION AND PREVENTION OFFICER?** Sometimes, it was simply that Preston College wanted a life model for a few hours a week in the Arts and Media Department. I'm not at liberty to divulge personal details, as to whether Heather thought I was suitable to get my kit off in front of students at Preston College, but it was paying £12 per hour. She did mention though, that I wouldn't be able to sit still for more than five minutes. Not long after this, I did work with such students as part of their final year studying film making, when I became involved in making training videos for the Countryside Ranger service, as part of a new recruits' induction training programme. Yes, I did manage to secure several starring roles, but never told the students that many years earlier they may have seen a totally different side to Mr James Briggs. The reader can choose which side. It was amazing to find out the lengths employers would go, to re-label what were to all intents and purposes, fairly mundane jobs to appeal to applicants, who they would then disrespect by not acknowledging their applications or that they even existed. I must admit, I found this re-labelling quite amusing but sometimes, wondered how this form of advertising passed the trade descriptions act. However, sifting my way through all the dross, I did manage to secure a steady mix of voluntary and paid positions, that not only provided me with extra funds to tick off more things from my travel bucket list, but also restored my self-esteem, which had taken quite a bashing. For varying lengths of time during 2006 to 2008, I signed up and worked for:

Store checkers, Mystery Shopping, which I really enjoyed, but by the time I took into consideration travel time, the time it took to visit the stores, and the time it took to write up and forward the reports, I realised, it almost equated to me actually paying them for my time. Even after my supervisor frequently praised me for the quality of my reports, which prompted me to ask for a pay rise, the situation didn't improve, and so I had to say goodbye.

TNT and DEYA, which basically involved book and leaflet deliveries. Again, I enjoyed the work as I saw it as basically being paid to go for a walk, carrying a heavy bag or pushing a trolley. Peter Kay pointed out in his first autobiography, The Sound of Laughter, that when he delivered leaflets and post, he sometimes threw them into the canal or re-posted stuff, as he couldn't be bothered to deliver them. Perhaps, I was doing something wrong, if I wanted to be successful. Deya was responsible for Yellow Pages and as a result of this, I also delivered The Phone Book and Thomsons. Again, I really enjoyed the work, as the books were only once a year in the Preston area, and the leaflets were spasmodic as and when you were available. Can leaflets be spasmodic I wonder? After the first year they even asked me, if I wanted to become a supervisor and although, it was nice to be asked I wasn't looking for more responsibility, and politely declined. In the end, after several years, my back started to remind me that my L4/L5 disc bulging was not getting any better, and so reluctantly, I stopped delivering the books.

Ipsos Mori, Market Research, was the national company that carried out market research and after spending a day's training at the Leyland Hotel, and a few days out tramping the streets with a supervisor, I was deemed capable enough to be let out on my own. The work involved interviewing people on the doorstep, or in their homes, putting the data onto a laptop, and then downloading the stuff, via the telephone, once you got home. Each week there were different topics to get feedback about. I enjoyed the work, it was flexible, the pay was good but as time went on, they kept asking me to do more. I'd explained I wasn't looking for full time work, and a few days a week was all I was prepared to do. Unfortunately, I was guilty of my own success, because they appreciated my work ethic, and wanted to train me up to be a supervisor. **Again, I'm not trying to massage my ego, but this was a time when for some, getting up, going to work on time and putting in a decent day's work for a decent wage, was not top priority. Drinking coffee, having a fag, sending texts, getting drunk, watching Jeremy Kyle, and throwing a sickie, was more the order of the day.** This attitude was totally alien to me and my generation, and so I was seen as someone worth cultivating. Unfortunately, cultivation was not what I was looking for, and being given more money to try and get some lazy sod, who was addicted to their mobile, to put in a decent day's work, without a sickie every several weeks, was not what I was looking for, and so reluctantly, I stopped asking for surveys. **Apologies to all the hard-working individuals, who don't fall into the above categories.** One day when I was visiting the Job Plus Centre in Preston, I was approached by a female member of the staff, who asked if I was on Job Seekers' Allowance. Having voluntarily resigned from UCLAN, I said no, as I thought I was not entitled to any. She then explained, that as I had worked full time in university and paid tax and a Class 1 stamp, as well as being self-employed, paying a class 2 stamp, I was entitled to it. Incidentally, paying two lots of NI stamps for years, didn't entitle me to two lots of OAP and so folks, it wasn't alright for me! She explained I would have a telephone interview of about 30 minutes, followed by a face-to-face interview, based on an application form I would be asked to fill out. Face to face, not an impersonal, text tennis rally? OK. I would then be passed to another person, who would try and find me some work. If successful, I would be entitled to the allowance, which as I recall was then just under £70 pw, as long as I could prove I was regularly seeking employment at my weekly appointment at the Job Plus Centre, in Preston. This seemed a lot of trouble for £70, but what the hell, I had paid my National Insurance for 40 years and even two lots since 1988, when I also became self-employed, so I thought, let's go for it. She arranged for my first telephone interview, and gave me the relevant paper work to take with me. The telephone interview went fine, but my face-to-face with Mr X, was not a roaring success when he found out how much money I used to earn, and couldn't quite understand why I had given up all that money, to end up applying for Job Seekers' Allowance. I could see his point of view, but when I glibly answered that there was more to life than money, he looked at me as though I was stark, raving mad. Yes, I know it could be argued, money gives you more choices, but in my experience, it definitely doesn't bring you happiness, just a better quality of misery, said Spike Milligan. It was also becoming apparent to me that in today's society people never seemed to have enough materialism, no matter how much they already had. He also couldn't understand, why I would consider working for minimal wage, or as it had now been re-branded, national working wage, when I could go back to teaching for over a hundred pounds a day, and then rest. Remaining calm, I pointed out that it was one of his colleagues who had persuaded me to apply, telling me that I was entitled to it, so please don't shoot the messenger. He eventually passed me over to his colleague, who was sat in the desk next to him, and would see if he could find me suitable employment. The body language between the two was, that they felt I had no place being there. I personally felt they were not used to interviewing people, who only had had 1 week off work in 10 plus years, and that was just for an operation to remove their appendix, even complimenting me on this fact, who spoke good English, and didn't threaten or spoke to them with foul language. When I first started visiting the centre, I was surprised how many security personnel there were, but soon realised that at any moment in time they may be called into action. Visiting an Afro Caribbean lady, can I say that or have they also been re-branded? The following Tuesday at 1330, my allotted, 'signing in slot', I immediately wanted to give her a hug. Now I definitely couldn't do that. She seemed totally and utterly dejected with her lot in life, which is not how I had come to see the Afro Caribbean community. To me they were happy, cheerful, laid-back people. Perhaps, she had been in the UK too long, or was it too long in her present situation? No matter, how many smiles I gave her or how much I tried to win her over with my charm, wit and repartee, she would not be moved. Perhaps she thought I was being patronising, I hope not, as that was the last thing I wanted to be. At times I thought she was going to burst into tears, which would have meant the security springing into action, and wrestling me to the ground for giving her abuse. To say the place was depressing, was a gross distortion of the facts. Why would anyone want to work there? Surely, not for the money or the prestige. Perhaps, their personality was bordering on finding pleasure in S and M. I was informed I was entitled to 3 months' allowance before being signed off, but after only half that time I voluntarily signed myself off. They never found me a job, I found my own, and as fast as they sent me confirmation in the post as to my entitlement, they would send me another a few days later, because I had delivered a few leaflets, or conducted a few interviews. It was costing them over £70 a week in postage, just to communicate with me.

Some 10 plus years later, post Brexit, which my mum would have thought was a new breakfast cereal, the debate about employment, or should I say lack of, was still a main topic of conversation. So, to re-iterate a situation pointed out in the early pages of this book, that highlighted the fact that unfortunately, the bigoted, racist, sexist, misogynistic, chauvinists in defence of their extreme views, showed their true colours by spinning the argument that, if we got rid of, 'all these bloody foreigners taking our jobs', they could work. As most of them had carved out a nice little life style having regular sex, to produce children, sorry baby goats, each worth a small fortune in benefits, creating sham illnesses, known as, 'a sickie', whilst living off the state, the thought of working to earn a living, was totally and utterly alien to them. In honest truth, these migrant workers were doing jobs many of the Brits didn't want to do, and who could earn far more staying on benefits. The effects of Brexit are already being realised, but if many jobs are created, after ethnic cleansing has been performed, I bet many who voted yes will panic as they would have no one to blame for being bone idle, shiftless g..., with no jobs, would now have to look forward to the prospect of having to work. Which in itself would probably see them rushing to the doctors, suffering from stress. It's interesting post Brexit/Pandemic that in 2025, trains are regularly cancelled because of, 'shortage of staff' and the rail and postal workers aware that we are in yet another recession, decide to go on strike. The results of which are causing many companies to now look to Europe, to employ staff to try and run their businesses. FARCICAL, IF NOT TRUE. Perhaps they, whoever they are, can blame poor A Level results on Brexit or the Pandemic, and not on the fact that some students didn't study long and intensive enough. Or they couldn't use their smartphones to find the answer. I make no apologies for my honesty, whilst appreciating the fact I am generalising, and not all out of work people and students are like that. But in my experience, and referring to the research, the work ethic of many Eastern Europeans is far, far superior to their English counterparts. **My top five in terms of a positive work ethic are Polish, Rumanians, other Eastern Europeans, Chinese and last young, white English.** Finally, and again to remind the reader, on the issue of progress and wanting to get rid of certain elements in society, because they didn't belong to the, 'correct tribe', didn't a small German gentleman become a significant part of history by also wanting to ethnic cleanse? I often wonder every year on Poppy Day, what the veterans, who sacrificed their lives for their country, think when they see and hear, on a regular basis, the things I see and hear. **Because in 2025, the UK is certainly not a far more tolerant, compassionate, harmonious country to live in.**

CTS Travel and Transport.

As part of my routine, of being on the lookout for part time work, I answered an advertisement for traffic data enumerators, carrying out surveys, with a company called CTS Traffic and Transport in Preston, and was put on their data base to be offered work, as and when surveys became available. Most surveys consisted of starting at 0700 and finishing at 1900, so data could be collected before and after the, 'rush hours'. Enumerators had to meet at a designated place, sometimes an hour before the survey started, to be briefed by the supervisor, and then taken to the site where each survey was to be conducted. This meant leaving home very early, and returning quite late. You were paid a mileage, travel allowance, and a fixed sum of money for collecting the data. This was dependent on the type of survey, and sometimes there were extra monetary incentives for meeting certain targets, i.e. a certain minimum number of interviews during the survey. Supervisors got more money, as theoretically they were more experienced. However, I soon realised that this was not always the case. One big drawback to the work was that it was mainly outdoors, and so was dependent on the weather as to how cold, wet and miserable you became as the day progressed. If it was just a count, you could sit in your car as long as you could park legally near to the site, but this was not possible with face-to-face interviews. The biggest headache was keeping your paperwork dry. I also appreciated that for the HR girls in the office, staff recruitment was very difficult and sometimes Talony Williams and her assistant, Adele Williams, had to recruit within days, which made quality control extremely difficult. **And the recurring theme of the work ethic of some young white males, once again reared its ugly head.** But once I started to become a regular on the CTS road-show, people such as David Woolham, Paul Broadbent, his mate Bob and myself, all with backgrounds in management and could be classed as elderly, started to enjoy each other's company. After my first survey, which I enjoyed, I was offered various jobs and started to get familiar with not only CTS traffic and its personnel, but also the differing types of survey. The surveys could be, Manual Traffic Counts, Journey Time Studies, ATC Installations, Speed Surveys, Manual Occupancy and Duration Surveys, Q Lengths, Parking Inventories, Interviews and data collection for Sustrans, (Sustainable transport).

For several months, after some short training, I worked in the office inputting data onto the computers. This meant that I was now being offered work, both in and out of the office. I was enjoying the variety of work, being paid and meeting some interesting characters. Apart from the HR girls in the office, there was Jeremy Rowlands, Jed, the boss, Joe Maclaren, who was in charge of organising the surveys, together with Ashley. Jeremy also owned the Continental pub in Penwortham, which was just over the River Ribble from where I now live. Then there was Noel Murphy, from Blackburn, who worked on data input. Finally, there was Lisa, Jeremy's sister, who did the wages, but who eventually, ended up working at the Continental, where she was put in charge of the restaurant. A dear old guy called Michael took over from Lisa, to do the wages and pay the bills but unfortunately, his efforts went unappreciated and unrewarded, and I suspect he eventually, would leave or have a breakdown. Supervisors out on site initially consisted of Dave Woolham, and ex-employee of a famous cruise company; Dave Clarke, an ex-copper, and Emma Watson, who had known 'Jed' a long time. I got along really well with all of them, but Emma was dipsy and the girls in the office started putting me with her to, 'look after her'. But it was Dave Woolham, whom I worked with the most as he would always ask for me, when he was offered work. Thank you, David. He always gave me high ratings, and had on more than one occasion recommended me for a supervisor's job, after I had worked there about three months. I declined telling the girls I was not interested in having to put up with crap from enumerators, who just didn't turn up or wanted to spend a day on their mobiles and get paid for it. Eventually, I did become a supervisor, as I was getting tired of having different supervisors who had been given the job purely, because the girls in the office became desperate and couldn't find anyone more suitable. When I took the girls in the office to task on this issue they said, "Well Brigadier, you know how you can rectify it." Brigadier, being Talony's nickname for me. I finally agreed to supervise, but only if I could pick my team and whilst this was not always possible, most times I ended up with who I wanted. People such as Dee Gull, Paul Broadbent and Bob, his mate from Warrington, Simon Howarth, a driving instructor, Angela Scott, a retired secondary teacher, Heath from Liverpool, and Dave Mc Cluskey, to name a few. As mentioned, the problem for Talony and Adele was, that they frequently had to recruit staff at short notice, and so ended up at times getting desperate, recruiting students who really were only interested in the money, and not getting up early or collecting accurate data. As the University of Central Lancashire was virtually on the doorstep from CTS Traffic, word amongst the students travelled fast. That is not to say all the students had a bad work ethic, but many just could not be bothered to get up early to get on site, even when lifts had been arranged for them. I also managed to secure a supervisor's job for my then mate Tim Kinder, after he left the bank to set up his own courier business, but then became the subject of criminal proceedings, which eventually led to the breakdown of our 20 plusyear friendship. As a result of his, 'bad behaviour', I went to see Joe, Jeremy and Talony, and Mr Kinder was, 'frozen out', of being offered further work. When I became a Countryside Ranger, and met Donna Parkinson, on a training weekend, I recruited her for CTS traffic. She was a young girl who, at the time, was on temporary contracts with various companies, and was always looking to supplement her income. Even after I'd left CTS, I used to see Donna for lunch occasionally and we'd catch up on gossip. Unfortunately, as time went by, and Donna became involved in a relationship, our lunch dates ceased. I enjoyed working at CTS traffic for several years, because they basically left me alone to get on with it, and occasionally massaged my ego. During a year, I could earn several thousands of pounds, which for me meant more travelling, but it was never a happy place to work, and there was always bitching and backstabbing, which was a shame, because with the correct leadership it could have been a great business. The management style, if you could call it management, was reactive rather than pro-active and even then, issues were not fully addressed. Quality control was non-existent, staff recruitment was haphazard, leadership was by e-mail, and staff motivation was non-existent. Need I say more? In fact, people such as Dave Woolham, Paul Broadbent and Bob from Warrington, who in the past had high profile positions in commerce and industry, would discuss with me, what we would do if we ever bought the business off Jeremy. We always agreed that only a few of the staff would be retained, and neither Joe nor Jeremy would be amongst them. Eventually, I left not long after Dave Woolham fell out with them, and went to go and live in Tenerife.

The Ranger Service: 2007-2012.

Becoming a Volunteer Countryside Ranger happened purely as a result of reading an article in a free Lancashire County Council community newspaper, whilst living in Leyland. In letters to the editor, there was one about a girl whose mother had just retired, and she said her mum was at a loss as to how to occupy her time, away from being a mum and housekeeper. There was no mention of dad. She pointed out, that as her mum loved being outdoors, if anyone could suggest any voluntary work she could do along those lines, and that something to do with the countryside would be ideal. The reply to the letter included details of how to become a volunteer Countryside Ranger. This piqued my curiosity, and so I filled out my details online, and was asked to attend for an informal, introductory interview at Spring Wood picnic site, Whalley, Lancashire. At the interview there was also a lady, called Marilyn, and myself. The lady turned out to be the lady referred to in the article. The interview was conducted by a Mr Paul Shoreman, who showed us around the site at Spring Wood, explained the role of a Ranger and said we would soon be contacted, furnishing us with details of the two training weekends, that all volunteers had to attend. In the meantime, if we wished to attend any of the sites at weekend, and spend the day with full time and qualified volunteer rangers, who had completed their training, to get some practical experience of what the role entailed, that would be beneficial. Although the role was purely voluntary, Lancashire CC would pay £10 per duty to help with travel costs and a yearly fee, equal to a proportion of the number of duties carried out, to help with incidental costs such as clothing and kit. Once qualified, every Ranger was presented with a woven and metal badge and T shirt. As I didn't expect anything at all, I considered this a bonus. All I had to do now was find a local site, and attend the training sessions, which then were held at Wycoller Country Park, Trawden, Colne, and run by Paul Shoreman and Paul Greenhall. There were a small group of us at Wycoller for the first training weekend, including Marilyn and a guy called Graham Cooper. Graham was a very clever man with a passion for the countryside, and a brilliant amateur photographer with his own website. Graham had previously worked, 'for the government', and although we became mates, I never actually found out the specifics of what that entailed, but he joked that if he told me he would also have to kill me. Sometimes, he would tell me he'd recently visited the naval dockyard in Portsmouth on business, but that was as much information as he would share. The Ranger service was full of people like Graham who had interesting former lives as well as present ones. Peter P, who had a permanent tan, not as orange as Mr Trump, used to be part of the Maxwell newspaper empire. Steve Plummer, Plum to his friends, helped build planes for British Aerospace, at Salmesbury. In fact, quite a few ex and present employees worked for BAE. Little did the public know what dark secrets the Countryside Rangers Service held.

The basic training was over two weekends and covered such topics as The Structure of Countryside Services, Policies and Strategies, The Role of the Ranger, Wildlife and Countryside Acts, Visitor Management and Emergency Procedures, Basic Navigation, Fell Craft and Site Familiarisation. The sites and full time Rangers being:

Wycoller, Peter Short.

Widdop and South Pennines, Peter Greenhall.

Healey Nab, Crook of Lune, Clougha and Condor Green, Nick Haigh.

Lytham, Sarah Dornan.

Central, (Pendle and the Ribble Valley), and Rossendale, Paul Shoreman.

Beacon Fell and all other sites, Andy Greenwood, Head Ranger. Better known as Father Christmas as Andy was a big guy with an equivalent beard. Sadly, he passed away in early 2019.

I had to miss a portion of my basic training due to a long-standing prior engagement, but Paul Shoreman invited me to Spring Wood, Whalley, for 1:1 tuition during the following week to complete my training. A gesture I really appreciated and the sort of thing Rangers were renowned for. Hopefully I later repaid that gesture by joining the basic training programme, and doing a session at the start of day one, on Communication and Control. Which was an ice breaker session, combined with theoretical and practical help on dealing with people. When I left the service, I gave Paul permission to use my material and do the session himself. Memories of leaving the University of North London, in 1997, came flooding back. Once qualified I told Christine, in the office, what my preferences regarding the sites were. This was not to say I couldn't work at other sites, but it just made the job of sorting out weekly weekend rotas, mainly Sundays, so much easier. You could elect to do a two, three or a four-week rota depending on how much time you wanted to devote to the job. A day rota would consist of meet 0930, for a briefing and job allocation by the duty Ranger; out on site by ten and returning, depending on the time of the year, by 1530 to 1700. After passing basic qualification, you were encouraged to attend the Advanced Navigation course over 6 weeks and the Rescue and Emergency Care course over several weekends. Without the Advanced Navigation qualification, Rangers were not allowed out on the open moor alone. What I particularly appreciated about rangering was, that if you had a particular interest in a subject, that would enhance the service provided by Countryside Services, the full time, paid rangers would try and accommodate your wishes, and provide training for you. Lancashire CC often used Graham Cooper's photographs for promotional material. During the following years, I not only passed my Advanced Navigation and Rescue and Emergency Care courses, but also passed my Guided Walk Leadership, leading walks on my own and with other Rangers, as not only part of the Rangers and local Walking Festival programme, but also part of the county's social Inclusion policy, to encourage minority groups to visit the local countryside. I found the Disabled Ramblers Walking weekend particularly rewarding. To see people with various disabilities, zooming around the countryside in their Trampers, which were motorised wheelchairs adapted to be used in the countryside on specially constructed paths and walkways, and then to watch these people get out and walk and stand at famous landmarks, brought tears to my eyes. One such weekend included visits to Holcombe Moor, Rivington Pike and 'The Rocket'/Darwen Tower. These people were fiercely independent and didn't want your sympathy, but I will never forget the 70-year-old lady who asked me if I would help her just to negotiate the steps up to Darwen Tower itself. She walked with a pair of crutches, and had been disabled since childhood. As she reached her goal, I watched her lean against the wall to admire the view, and at which point I said, "I'll leave you alone for a moment to admire the view." "No," she replied, "please stay," and as I stood next to her against the wall, she reached out and held my hand and said to me, "Thank you, Jim, I've wanted to do this since I was a little girl, but was never allowed as my parents couldn't get me here. I can now die a happy bunny." I had to turn away as the tears streamed down my face. Seeing this, she told me not to be so silly and to pull myself together. "Men, what are you like?" It's a crazy experience laughing and crying at the same time. Another time, I provided back up on one of Graham Cooper's, 'Historical Walks around Pendle', providing commentary on the history of dry stone walls, and frequently accompanied other Rangers when they led walks. Their knowledge was incredible, and I frequently took notes. I was also only one of three volunteers to be sent on a 5-day, Dry Stone Walling Course, after which I spent many a day repairing, re-building and building dry stone walls with fellow rangers. I wanted to attend a Hedge laying course, but never got around to it. I also helped Paul Shoreman work in local schools and with the local community to build bird and bat boxes, as well as tree and flower planting sessions. I sometimes, attended sessions at Lee Quarry, in Rawtenstall, marshalling on cross country cycling events, and having starring roles in training videos. When people asked me, if I had ever been in amateur dramatics, I could now tell them I'd had major starring roles in real life action movies on Beacon Fell.

My first Ranger session was at Spring Wood, and Paul took me around many of the sites in the white Ranger, 4x4, truck, explaining what to expect on duty as a Ranger. There were over several hundred sites on Paul's patch, some of which were used for purposes, where the aim of encouraging people to enjoy the countryside was interpreted quite literally. At that time, I was only aware of dogging sites via the internet, and certainly didn't expect them to be part of the role of the Countryside Ranger. But yes, Central area, which included Pendle and the Ribble Valley, had three sites where boys met to entertain each other. Why only boys I never found out, but the topic was the butt of many a joke by the Rangers, if you'll excuse the pun. For me, it proved the point that you never stop learning. There I was a biologist, with a keen interest in human behaviour, having just retired with a wealth of experience, knowledge, skill and expertise, and a CV I was extremely proud of, totally unaware of what was happening down at my local Country Park. Paul soon put me in the picture as to the lengths these people would go, to avoid being troubled by the local police and Rangers. To enhance my learning experience further, he then took me to visit the three sites to see if there was any, 'activity', that Sunday afternoon. Approaching one of the sites in the distinctly recognisable white, Countryside Ranger truck Paul parked near to a blacked out windowed 4x4, and told me to just follow his lead once we got out. We took two black litter bags out of the back of the truck and two litter pickers, and proceeded to pick up litter in the car park, getting nearer and nearer to the car in question. Suddenly, a guy jumped out of the 4x4 and proceeded to shout at us, asking what we were doing. Considering our truck was a give-away, we were both wearing high viz jackets and Paul had his uniform on, this seemed a strange question. You don't have to study human behaviour to recognise guilt on someone's face. At this juncture, I need to point out that Paul Shoreman was not a big guy and didn't create a, 'don't mess with me' aura, but he was very good at dealing with and diffusing situations. Years later, he became a Senior Officer in the Community police force. The guy mincing across the car park looked physically intimidating, to say the least, but as soon as he opened his mouth, the effeminate tone to his voice rather shattered the initial illusion.

"Good afternoon, Sir, having a good day?" said Paul.

"No, I'm not, no thanks to you two."

"I'm sorry to hear that, sir, what's the problem?" During this initial encounter, the gentleman was obviously trying to stop us litter picking around his vehicle, but following Paul's lead we continued with our task whilst Paul held the conversation. As we got nearer, we could detect activity, from the noise coming from the back of their 4x4.

"I'm fucking sick of this, that's what," said the guy, "I'm up here trying to do a spot of bird watching and working on my computer, and you people keep fucking disturbing me."

"I'm sorry to hear that, sir, but there's no need to use that language," as another condom and drinks can was put in the black bin bag. "We are just doing our job."

"Well, can't you do it someplace else?"

"Sorry, sir, no can do," said Paul, by which time we had reached the black 4x4, and suddenly a second male came mincing out of the car, looking even prettier, but less dishevelled than his mate. Now I know, these descriptions sound very politically incorrect, and could land me in a lot of trouble with some greedy solicitor in a court of law, but this is my autobiography and so I don't give a shit, back to the plot. Paul immediately decided to engage his, 'travel companion', and asked him, if he was also doing a spot of bird watching and working on his computer. "Oh yes," came the hurried reply and before any of them could add to this, Paul asked if they did this on a regular basis and, if so, had they spotted the golden eagles that nested nearby?

"Yes," was the quick reply, "will you be long?"

"Why do you ask, we have a job to do, which involves ensuring the countryside is a safe and clean place for the public to visit and enjoy," replied Mr Shoreman.

"No reason, we'd just like to get on with what we're doing," came the response.

"I bet you would, but not on my watch, there isn't a golden eagle within fifty miles of here, so if you don't leave the site immediately, I will contact my colleagues in the police force and ask them to remove you."

"What do you mean?" asked miscreant number one with a flick of his head.

"Please don't keep insulting our intelligence, sir, you know perfectly well what I mean. What you do in your own home, has nothing to do with us, but what you do in the countryside, where families come with their children, is, now please would you leave?"

"You can't make us; we'll stay as long as we want."

"Fair enough," said Paul, "I have asked kindly, and will put that in my report, I have your vehicle registration, but would you be so kind as to give me your names? According to the Countryside Act of 2004, and the Pendle bye laws pertaining to parking, I can ask you to leave, if I suspect you are contravening such laws, which I do."

"Fuck off," came the reply. Again, following Paul's lead, we finished picking litter and returned to our vehicle, where Paul asked me to make a note of the vehicle registration. He then said it seemed a good time and place to have a spot of lunch, and taking his flask and sandwiches proceeded to go and sit at one of the picnic tables in the car park. I followed suit. Within minutes, the car departed but then another 4x4 entered the car park, but left almost immediately, when it realised there were Rangers having lunch. I'd only been a volunteer Ranger for five minutes, and already I'd been thrown into the murky underground world of crime and buggery in Pendle Witch Country. If this was to be a taste of things to come, I had better increase my personal health liability insurance. Over lunch, Paul said that the police had bigger fish to fry, and were not particularly interested if guys wanted to rodger each other in a car park on a Sunday afternoon, but as Rangers we couldn't ignore their activity and had policies in place to deal with it. If we reported more than 3 incidents, the police had to act upon such information. Apart from being very impressed with Paul, he wasn't Head Ranger at Central for nothing, I never parked my car in a car park again, without being suspicious of any male sitting alone admiring the view, and if there were two of them, they obviously had to be up to no good. Talk about guilty, before being proven innocent. After lunch, Paul took me to another site that the boys frequented, and explained how they used the root cover of a fallen down tree to build a, 'nest', with blankets and how, if there were a few of them, they posted lookouts so they wouldn't be disturbed. Why did they never include situations like these in the story lines of television programmes like Heartbeat, The Bill or Countryfile? Although many years later, Peter Kay, the Bolton comedian, and Sian Gibson, his work colleague, made dogging an issue, in an episode of their hilarious TV programme, Car Share. Many months later, when I was on duty again in the truck with Paul, he decided we should re-visit the car park, where I had experienced my first taste of male dogging. Just before arriving on site, we came across some elderly gentlemen aptly nicknamed by Paul, 'the last of the summer wine boys'. As a Ranger, you built up a rapport with the local countryside fraternity; walkers, farmers, cyclists etc. and these were your eyes and ears as to what was going on in your patch, i. e. stolen cars dumped, dead foxes on the road, signage that needed replacing, walls and fences in disrepair, etc. The last of the summer wine boys were 3-4 male dog walkers in the Pendle area who, like their name suggests, wandered around the countryside, and had their fingers on the pulse for everything that went on within 5 miles of their houses. I say 5, but it could have been 55, needless to say you always stopped to have a word with the locals. Upon stopping the truck and getting out, Paul had no sooner introduced me to them, than they started complaining about a dry stone wall that had needed to be repaired, and why nothing was being done about it. Now at the time I hadn't done any courses or training on dry stone walling, otherwise I could have stepped in and responded, but as that was to come later in my ranger training, I just smiled. Giving them some excuse, Paul then asked, if they had anything else to report and quick as a flash one of them said, "What do you mean, have we seen any young men buggering each other in the car park, no not recently?" Priceless- you just had to smile, it's what made the day.

The Ranger Service also had a quarterly newsletter which relied on contributions from those involved directly, or indirectly and needless to say I offered many articles for inclusion. At one point, they were looking for a new editor and I was asked if I would be interested. Again, nice to be considered, but no, thank you. There was also the Annual Ranger Seminar, held in Downham Community Hall, which was an opportunity for the service to say thank you to the volunteers, and to meet up with fellow Rangers and enjoy a very nice buffet lunch. There was a timetable of guest speakers, who talked about all things green and pleasant. This was usually organised by Paul Shoreman with Andy Greenwood, overseeing proceedings and in 2010, appreciating how difficult it was to get articulate, interesting speakers, asked Paul if I could help organise the speakers and timetable for the next seminar. That day, apart from organising the speakers, I also arranged a stand to display my sister Janet's card and craft business. She had created some cards specifically of the countryside around Beacon Fell. Heather was persuaded to be one of the guest speakers, talking about 'tics'. Denzil Broadbent, a member of Oldham Mountain Rescue, talked about working at altitude, after visiting Everest. Yes, of course, I had a guest spot and talked about when Heather and I visited Kariega Wildlife Safari Park in South Africa. Unfortunately, Andy G at the last minute invited some fly by night councillor, without informing me, who wanted to come and prattle on about how much LCC valued the Ranger Countryside services, and so the timetable was changed. Although Andy was the big cheese, I nevertheless was very annoyed, and being a volunteer, was not worried about any serious fallout. Telling Andy that the only reason the councillor wanted to come was, because there was a local election pending, and I strongly objected to my seminar being used for political gain. Needless to say, 12 months later this very important individual was nowhere to be seen and in 2017, the Ranger Countryside Services was rumoured to be getting axed. By 2019, it had well and truly been dissipated.

When I first joined the rangers there were 9 full time rangers who appreciated the input and help provided by the Volunteers, which totalled approximately 130. By the time I left the full-time numbers had been culled down to 6. In 2016, I met Brian the longest serving volunteer whilst shopping in Morrisons, and he informed me that LCC had just employed another guru, on an astronomical salary, whose mission statement was to steer the county through a very difficult period of further job losses and cuts, into the next era but it was looking like the Countryside Services would be disbanded, or was that re-branded, in 2017/2018? In 2017, I bumped into another long-standing volunteer, Margaret Corless, well not literally, outside Booth's Supermarket, (can you recognise a pattern to my everyday movements here?), who brought me up to speed with what was going to happen to the Countryside Rangers. The deadline for its demise was 2018, but already some of the full-time Rangers were trying to secure other positions, whilst the longer serving ones were looking for severance pay. Nick Hague, who was recruited when I was a volunteer, was first out and had moved to Cuerden Country Park. It was rumoured the volunteers could, 'take up the slack', of the work the paid Rangers did. No, not a joke but a serious consideration from a brain-dead bureaucrat.

I loved being a Ranger if for no other reason, than working with people who wanted to be there, rather than having to be there. Come rain or shine, hail or thunder they met for their briefing every Sunday morning, and just got on with their duties and dealt with whatever came their way. OK, when you get a group of people who have to work together, you will always have personality clashes, givers and takers, talkers and doers and yes, the Ranger service was not alone in that respect, because everyone who was a volunteer, had a voice and had choices. The rule for me was to try and avoid people I had issues with, or who had issues with me, it was that simple. But in my years of rangering, making sure I spell that correctly with an's and not od's, fall outs and disagreements were few and far between. Sadly, with the recession, endless restructuring with suggestions as to, 'the way forward', with politics and religion constantly interfering, I decided it was time after nearly 6 years, to move on.

St. Catherine's Hospice, 2009-2015.

St. Catherine's was a local hospice in Lostock Hall, Preston, providing long term health care for basically terminally ill patients. It needed £5million per annum to stand still and relied on an army of approximately 500 volunteers to help with its fund raising. Whilst it received lottery funding and various grants from various sources, as a charity the bulk of its income was self-generated. I started working for St Catherine's when Heather decided she wanted to do the, Midnight and Memories Walk, and raise some money for the hospice. I accepted a volunteer job, on registration, in the Sports Hall at the Police Headquarters, Hutton. The HQ was a huge place with playing fields, ample parking and ideal for starting a sporting, fund raising event that annually attracted over a thousand entrants. OK, it wasn't on the scale of the London Marathon but for the hospice, was a massive fund raiser. For me the bacon butty and cup of tea we could have during the evening/morning. was more than recompense for my labours. The walk was 13.1 miles starting at midnight and finishing in the early hours of the morning at the Police Headquarters in Longton, Preston. It passed through the Hospice after 8/9 miles. During its heyday this initially was an only women fund-raising event that attracted several thousand women and raised thousands of pounds for the Hospice. It was one of several high-profile events that Catherine's organised. Bike rides, pop and classical concerts at Hoghton Tower, with the obligatory firework finale, bucket collections, fairs in the grounds of the hospice itself, corporate events, sky diving, abseiling and a whole raft of events that were organised by the fund-raising team, headed by Lorainne Charlesworth, Andrew Bennison and Norman Cutler, to name but a few of the dedicated staff. I particularly was involved in a lot of local events organised by Emma Jacovelli, who was responsible for many events within the local community, such as bucket collections at Asda, Tesco and Morrisons, and running a stall at local fetes in Leyland, Lostock Hall and Penwortham. I also liked travelling to Blackpool, to give out medals to the cyclists finishing the annual bike fund raiser from Manchester to Blackpool, or the local bike fund raiser finishing at the rugby ground in Fulwood.

I also enjoyed being involved in the annual Classical Concert and Firework display held at Hoghton Tower, not far from where Heather and I used to live. The annual concert was a long-standing event so much so that when Heather and I moved to Preston, we attended it with family and friends. In previous years, there were no major problems at the entrance or in the parking area, which was all staffed by the police and volunteers, and the events were deemed a success. Obviously, its success or failure was very much dependent on the weather, and because the previous year the event had to be cancelled because of bad weather, losing Catherine's thousands of pounds in revenue, it was decided by the powers that be that a pop event on a Friday, as well as the Saturday, Classical and Firework night would be trialled. **It was also decided to employ the services of an Events Company to WORK WITH the volunteers.** What was obvious to me after the first pop evening, which attracted a much younger clientele than the Saturday crowd, was that the Friday audience was much more alcohol fuelled than the Saturday one. Large groups arriving, many hours before the event started, very inebriated. Arriving early, once the gates opened at 4 pm was not the issue, as families arrived to have BBQs prior to the classical concert. In fact, pitches and gazebos could be booked around the perimeter of the field. What was the issue was, the state of the people arriving as many of the Friday crowd, just thinking it was another pop concert, had obviously been drinking many hours before arriving, whereas the Saturday crowd, which was generally much older, because it was a classical concert, usually arrived relatively sober. **Again, when did the Brits, especially the younger element, but not entirely, become obsessed with and** dependent upon alcohol, and couldn't attend any social occasion or entertainment event, be it inside or outside, without a can or bottle in their hands?

To allow for this, at each event many volunteers arrived on site at around 3pm, and didn't leave until after midnight. The first time I attended, the musicians were doing sound checks and rehearsals, resulting in me hearing many of the tunes hours before the actual start. 'Don't you want me, baby?' sang Human League, which proved to be an apt tune as I exited the site many hours later. It is also worth reminding the reader, that volunteers are people who give of their time **FREELY**, apart from a free drink of tea, coffee or a soft drink and a burger, and hopefully a thank you. So, you can imagine my indignation when a power crazed, events' organiser, still in diapers, told myself and my colleagues, we were spending too much time talking to the paying customers, and not enough time getting their money off them to park. Now I know I can talk too much, and some people might think the rebuke was justified, but our spiel consisted of, **"Hi, thanks for coming. £3 please, follow the track up and please park where the marshalls in high viz jackets tell you to park, as we're expecting a large crowd tonight. Thanks for supporting St. Catherine's and have a great night."** When I asked the young lad, because that's all he was, and who incidentally, was being paid for his efforts, if he could take over and show my colleagues and me what we should be doing, he informed me he was far too busy and didn't have time. Pointing out that he had worked at a Kylie Minogue concert. What Kylie had to do with anything, other than she'd had cancer, I wasn't sure. Neither were my colleagues. He then contacted his boss, via his walkie talkie, asking him to come to the entrance to deal with a trouble causer, namely Mr B. Incidentally, I was stone cold sober.

POWER YOU CAN TAKE BUT RESPECT YOU HAVE TO EARN.

I and my colleagues temporarily carried on to avoid long Qs developing, but when 'the boss' arrived and he also was not prepared to spend some time showing us how it should be done, I and my team decided to give the event workers no choice, and left our pitches to go and inform Andrew Bennison, my immediate boss, why there could be chaos at the entrance to the site. Again, whilst sad, the voice inside my head told me, yet again, the world was and is changing, Jim and not for the better. Time to say goodbye once again. I worked for Catherine's for 4 plus years and thoroughly enjoyed my time with them and would have carried on, if only someone from Catherine's hierarchy had intervened and pointed out that the volunteers were doing their best, which in the past had always been more than good enough. Also, this was a St Catherine's Cancer fund raising event not an AC/DC concert at the Manchester Evening News Arena, and people had paid good money to attend, and so the least Catherine's could give them was the time of day. For the record, I subsequently sent St. Catherine's a letter explaining my version of events, prior to my departure and the reasons for my actions. I subsequently found out, that this was the subject of much heated discussion at St Catherine's. Andrew Bennison tried very hard to make me change my mind, and said he could only apologise for the way I and others were treated. I told Andy that once I had made my decision, it was extremely unlikely I would change my mind, and that St. Catherine's, by employing such power crazed, testosterone fuelled youngsters, had to accept some responsibility. Sorry, Andy. Only Lorainne Charlesworth didn't respond to the letter. Why ever not, Lorainne? Was it due to the fact that my two P, Principle was not the same as hers, because I saw people not pounds in front of me? She obviously saw things the other way round. Many months later, I met Andy B at another fund raiser in Bamber Bridge and again he apologised, and said I would be welcomed back. I also met up with Emma J at the Leyland Festival, and we exchanged hugs and smiles. She said she missed me! Thanks, Emma. Thanks, Andy. Keep counting the pennies, Lorainne.

Penwortham Racing Park: 2012 plus, Which Tribe Do You Belong To? Tickle-tackle and Playground Syndrome.

Returning to some of the themes raised in previous chapters such as, 'Driving a Licence to Kill', our Residential Park apart from having postage stamp signs saying, Speed Limit 10 mph, also has signs such as, Keep dogs on leads and No Cycling. Unfortunately, most people, including visitors and residents, choose to ignore these, and so it's no wonder I get annoyed, frustrated and at times depressed.

It has been established that my personality was such, that from being a teenager I seem to have suffered from mood swings, periods of depression and experienced panic attacks, usually triggered by disappointment or rejection. My earliest recollection being, during my teenage years, when I left home after being rejected by a girl named Hilary. But doesn't every teenager suffer from hormonal angst, social and emotional immaturity? From September, 1987 to February, 1988, after the breakdown of my marriage, I found solace in the mood enhancing, anti-depressant drug, Mogadon, to which I became highly addicted. Immersed in mood enhancers, sleeping pills, and wallowing in self-pity, my depression was certainly ruling the roost. Little knowing it would return with a vengeance in 1999, 2012 and 2016. Winston Churchill, who also suffered from such, referring to depression as, 'My Black Dog'. **Black dog: melancholy, depression of spirits, ill humour. In some places when a child is sulking, it is said, 'the black dog is on his back.'** Oxford Popular English Dictionary.

A huge, dark blanket wraps around you making you feel sad, angry and hopeless, and prevents normal interaction with society. With depression there's a difference between perception and reality. It's an illness, that doesn't stop people getting on with their lives, and one that many people live with, all their lives. In fact, many high-profile celebrities, especially those with reputations for making people laugh, I don't think that included Churchill, **appearing externally as very confident extroverts, but internally suffer from the depressive malady**. With many actors finding solace and a comfort zone hiding behind, 'the role', which masked reality. This being one reason why actors and performers don't actually retire, because they need their comfort blanket, some becoming more depressive as the roles dry up. As the adulation, the fix, the comfort blanket becomes less and less and returning to 'normality' becomes greater and greater, the person can sometimes resort to drastic measures, with sometimes tragic consequences. For me, experiencing my life going from appreciation, sometimes adulation, to almost total isolation was a bitter pill to swallow. Other high-profile figures, including Stephen Fry, finding their depression just too much, sought solace by trying to end their lives. Then there were people such as Marilyn Munroe, Brian Epstein, the famous Beatles manager, and more recently Caroline Flack, in 2020, being more successful than others, by overdosing. Michael Caine in his autobiography, 'From the Elephant and Castle to Hollywood', said that you accumulated regrets, that ate away at you. When playing the role of Clarence, an aging magician being forced through circumstance to live in a retirement home, in the film, 'Is Anybody Out There?' he qualified this by saying, **"You accumulate regrets, that stick to you like bruises."** During my life, I have had a few bruises and regrets as these memoirs have shown. David Walliams, christened Williams, in his autobiography, 'Camp David', said there were times in his life when, **"light became dark, colour faded and all that was beautiful, became ugly,"** (p130). Going on to say,

"What is so pernicious about depression is that you lose all perspective, and all past happiness seems false."

A classic symptom of depression is detaching from friends and family, when in actual fact being alone makes it worse, because there is a need to belong somewhere, which makes people vulnerable. Suicidal patients try to convince themselves, that society would be better off without them. I'm not medically trained but, in my case, there appeared to be a combination of 2 types of depression:

Reactive - to a life event. As I discovered in my teens when I realised, I didn't handle rejection very well.

Endogenous – was something that came from the inside, could not be explained by outside forces and seemed to be caused by biochemical imbalance in the brain.

On the 27th July, 2012, Heather loaded up a transit with Paul, her son, and set off to drive back south to be nearer her family. Twenty-four hours previously I had left Claughton Avenue for 4, Park Rd, Preston, PR1 9YD. I'd moved myself with a local one-man-and-his van, well two actually, with Heather helping me to settle in, before returning to Claughton to prepare for her move back, down to the West Midlands. To say I was very emotional would be an understatement, but managed not to show myself up in front of the removal guys. The actual day was somewhat of a blur, because this was not part of my retirement plan, but having a roof over my head was top priority, and 4 Park Road fitted the bill. It was ironic that I had moved back to being around the corner from Park Way, where it had all started some 62 years before, albeit the two were some 40 miles apart. To be honest I was also a little relieved, to say the least, as at one stage, once Heather was adamant she wanted to move, it looked like I wasn't going to find anywhere suitable to live, and would have to rent. Financially, I couldn't afford to buy Heather out so, when I secured this Park Home, I decided I would immerse myself into putting my own stamp on it, which was not too difficult as John and Gladys, the couple I had purchased it from, were old, partially blind, suffered from osteoarthritis and were partially deaf, and as a result their home was in need of tender loving care. In that respect, it meant I could just shut myself away, and systematically DIY my way through my new home, mixing paint with tears. I also set about tidying up the brook and its bank between Hazel and Derek, my new neighbours on that side of my new home. Technically, the riverbank was the responsibility of the Environmental Agency and the Park owners, and before I arrived on the scene Julio Bassa, would periodically spray the area with weed killer. And that was only because my neighbour Hazel used to pester him to do so. After having words with Julio, I decided to take on the challenge to, 'tidy it up', as opposed to just having weed killer sprayed on it periodically.
Whilst I've previously alluded to self-induced illnesses and the fact that it was people's choice, as to how they wanted to ruin their own lives, and kill themselves, but what has always angered me is these people don't seem to care about what impact their selfish and delusional behaviour, can have on others, sometimes under the guise of being pet lovers. The research evidence for the effects of passive smoking on pets is well documented, with some scientists finding, **'Pets at more risk from passive smoking than humans'**, **(Sarah Knapton, Science Editor, 29/12/2015).** As nicotine junkies, were they aware that they were subjecting their pets to respiratory problems, certain allergies, nasal and lung cancer, as a result of the dog having to breathe in all the carcinogenic pollutants that existed in their property, via cigarettes or fancy tasting vapes? And if so, did they bother? Are these people also aware that cruelty to animals is punishable by an unlimited fine and/or 5 years in prison? Once the veterinary service and RSPCA get involved, to decide if the home environment provides a suitable environment in which to have pets, that's when things become interesting. In 2023, John, my chain-smoking neighbour, was diagnosed with lung cancer but still continued to smoke- 'vape' whilst having chemotherapy treatment, and sadly passed away not long after. If such drug addicts, also suffered from playground syndrome

and were part of the dog mafia, then beware if you wanted to confront them with the facts and truth. I used to be a senior lecturer on communication, and still smile, when I'm accused of talking too much. I only remind the reader of this because I often wondered if these pet lovers considered that, although their dog's constant barking was the dog's way of communicating as to their plight, the dogs were also guilty of the same crime? **After all, someone has to speak up and represent the dogs.** Or was it simply that their owners were not very good at controlling their pet's behaviour? Giving them a reward every 30 seconds, because they haven't attacked an innocent passer- by, may convey to others that they are responsible owners, but I wonder what Barbara Woodhouse, Dog Trainer, of 'walkies' fame, 9/5/1910- 9/7/1988, would have to say on the matter. **The term rescue dogs is another interesting one, as it involves deciding who needs rescuing from whom? At this juncture, I would like to repeat, to ASSUME makes an ass of you and me. Just as people who pay scant regard to family planning, have sex and get pregnant, suddenly become experts on parenting and child care, and those who have family planned, studied human behaviour, child development and child care, and wanted children but sadly didn't or couldn't, don't know what they are talking about. So is the assumption that you have to have a pet to be a pet lover, and if you don't you are not. In my 30s time spent with Doogle, Sian and Wendy's dog, was enjoyable and much later my time with Fritz, the German shepherd dog, that materialised when I first moved into Penwortham Residential Park, and lasted 18 months, was equally so. Fritz resided at a lady's house I was in a relationship with, but because when I first moved I was told that large dogs were not allowed, and so Denise and I never brought him to 4 Park Rd. However, some residents now flout that rule, because that's why we have rules, so arrogant, ignorant people can ignore them.** At times, living at 4 Park Rd was like living in a dog compound, which held daily dog yapping and talking competitions, as there appeared to be more dogs than people and where many owners had substituted talking to, 'the wall', as did Shirley Valentine, or their partner, with talking to the dog, as though they were actual children. **"Come on do a lickle wee wee, Should I cook you some little sausages. Have you missed me my children?"** No doubt, my psychology colleagues would have much to say on the subject. I know the animal rights activists will quote, 'a dog is a man's best friend,' which today is probably an unacceptable sexist expression, but dogs don't appear to be best friends with their fellow dogs, as I frequently see them wanting to 'do battle' outside my property. Can dogs be a woman's best friend? For a single, lonely person I totally understand the companionship argument, but for people in relationships, I wonder. The comedy, crime movie, Keeping Mum, 2005, involved a very annoying, yappy dog that more than upset the neighbours, until suddenly it yapped no more. Watch the film. **Question: Do yappy dogs suffer from tonsillitis and sore throats?**

In 2023, another yappy dog arrived after Shiela, another neighbour, who lived on Park View, sold her property to, 'a character', after her husband, Mervyn, had sadly passed away. I say character, because from day one she systematically upset and offended the neighbours with her wild accusations and rude behaviour. You could hear her saying to her dog, **"O' Right darling,"** on a regular basis, accompanied by her loud rendition of some obscure pop song. Her daily DIY projects included erecting flags, cameras, illuminations, offensive signs and extra fencing. One neighbour Jack, who lived on Park View, was frequently accused of untold sexual misconduct towards her because, according to Jack, he looked at her. Then there was Jimmy, the post man of 14 plus years who was accused of, 'flicking elastic bands at her', and so she complained to his boss at the Post Office, suggesting he be sacked. In view of what the Post Office was going through at the time with Paula Vennels et al, I would think this was the least of their worries. Both my neighbours Carol, John and I, had been totally ignored upon saying, Good Morning to her. You didn't have to be a psychologist to realise she had personality and psychological issues, such as paranoia, and I don't know how many complaints had been made to Wyldecrest about her behaviour, but again did the site owners not at least interview her before allowing her onto the site, or was it a case of, as long as she pays her site fee, all is forgiven? There was a rumour that social services had helped pay for her to move onto the site, so they could tick the box that she had been re-housed as she was proving to be a nuisance wherever she lived. Before I first moved onto the site, I visited Mr Campbell the site owner at the time, as he wanted to know who was moving into one of his homes. Having attended three Tribunals involving Wyldecrest, I wasn't going to waste my time complaining to Wyldecrest as I knew nothing would get done. Another neighbour, upon moving in after the previous one had lost her husband and moved out, together with her two yappy dogs, held up his yappy dog at our first meeting, giving me the impression he wanted me to give it a kiss, before it approved of my existence. Incidentally, this was an ex-SAS man. No comment.

I nicknamed these dog owners as**, 'the dog mafia',** as they could be seen and heard, on a daily basis, huddled together outside various properties, putting the world to rights, or should I say for some, engaging in tickle -tackle? In fact, I nicknamed two new residents, Tickle and Tackle, as they strolled around the park, trying to ingratiate themselves with the residents but in actual fact, were trying to accumulate as much gossip as possible to be further relayed onto others who would care to listen. In much the same way as data is collected and sold on. Did these people watch the soaps? I found it all hilarious, annoying and sometimes, sad. I say sad because many of these people had human partners at home. But then again you can be lonely in a crowded room. I've decided to dedicate the song, Walking The Dog, by Rufus Thomas, in 1964, to these people. Of course, as I've said, you also had your quota of insecure residents who suffered from, **'playground syndrome'.** My house cost more money than your house, guess how much I paid for my car? My television is the latest 200-inch model, our garden furniture cost over £1,000, and my neighbour only paid £75 for theirs. Our Christmas decorations are better than yours, and we pay more money for our garden plants than you do. Not forgetting to remind other people how much money they earned or could earn by returning to work. I am proud of my achievements and the sacrifices I made to attain them and am not afraid to let people know. But teenagers are supposed to grow out of their insecurities as they acquire more experience and life skills getting into adulthood. But some, because of possible insecurity, self-delusion or arrogance, instead of growing out of the syndrome take it with them as they get older. Luckily these people were in a minority compared to the many 'good eggs' that resided on the Park. **"Being rich was all a matter of relativity. They might be big fishes in a small pond, but out in the ocean, the whales wouldn't even contemplate putting them in the peanut bowl."** (James P, 1983. Billionaire, PB 15:156).

I've been asked on several occasions, since finding myself alone and depressed, did I fancy getting a dog for company, not knowing I had previous experiences of dogs being part of my life. But I'd always preferred the company of humans, especially the female gender, who didn't always want to talk about football, booze, busts and bottoms. Let alone give a dog a kiss. Some may argue I had difficulty looking after myself, let alone having a pet dog that I would have to stalk and pick up its shit. Also, perhaps I was too selfish, as having a pet is restrictive and would prohibit me from impulsively going to the airport to catch a plane. If I had a dog, would it laugh at my jokes, help me with house work etc? However, I do now realise that if you don't have humans in your locker, then to turn to a dog's companionship can offer an alternative to contemplating suicide. I am also aware that there are many people, even those in relationships, who shy away from human company, preferring the company of animals instead. A member of my extended family is one such person. Whilst finding lots of positives about living on Penwortham Residential Park, as time went on more issues started to irritate me, no matter how patient I was or how much I tried to put things into perspective. **The tipping point, according to the author, Gerald Seymour, is when what had meandered took on a new momentum. The day of reckoning would involve giving some of the residents their knives back, that they had decided to lodge in my back for what I could only assume was because I was a chatterbox. I personally didn't think I was that important to warrant such attention. Knowing which knives belonged to whom would be easy as the more expensive ones would belong to the, 'Playground Syndrome Brigade'. Did I consider a, 'Keeping Mum', solution, as it did cross my mind on more than one occasion?** When I initially moved into the Park in July 2012, it was a relatively harmonious place with Mr Campbell, the site owner, 'The Big Bad Wolf' but once he sold the site to Alfie Best's Wyldecrest, in 2019, more things took on a decidedly negative perspective and Mr Campbell was seen in a totally different light. The residents, after seeking advice, decided to form a Resident's Association so it could question Wyldecrest's questionable practices. But some residents decided not to join the fight and the Park became a divided one which may or may not degenerate into tribal warfare. I named it the Trump Park in that some believed the lies and bullshit pedalled by Best's Wyldecrest and Mr Bassa, and those who didn't. In much the same way that America had become a divided country because of Trump. A special mention to John and Jacky, Arthur and Carol, Peter and Brenda, Jadwiga, Stuart and Jean, Liz and 'Jock', Hazel, Dorothy, Alan and Dee who doggedly stood up to be counted, whilst being stabbed in the back by some of the on-looking residents. As mentioned, there are always more talkers than doers and takers than givers. **As Julio B, the self-proclaimed, 'site maintenance man', although it was a long time before residents were actually informed as to what his job title was, but never found out what his job description or job specification was and/or what qualifications he held to carry certain roles, was the face of Wyldecrest, he was also the target for justified scrutiny. Did he even have a current First Aid Qualification to save an elderly resident's life, after all residents had to be over 55 to live there? Or would he phone up Craig Johnson or David Sunderland in Essex to ask them what to do as he watched them die? Perhaps number 22 Park Rd. could advise him whilst they were drinking coffee.** To repeat, I am very proud of my knowledge, skills, expertise, experience and qualifications and am not ashamed to tell people what they are. All under the guise of just being a chatter box, which some sad people think is a contagious disease that should be avoided and treated. Some even putting a time limit on how long a conversation should take, and if it is seen as this was over-running, then a snide comment could be made to raise a laugh. So sad or is that amusing? Perhaps they are jealous, I don't know, or do I? After Mr Bassa had his employment terminated by Campbells, when they sold to Wyldecrest, the residents decided to pass around the hat and give him a leaving do. However, a short while later he returned to the Park, as he'd been re-instated by Wyldecrest. **Had he re-applied for his old job? Had he attended an interview? What criteria had Wyldecrest applied to decide, other than time spent on PRP, as the most suitable person for the post? Who knows? Did he return his monetary leaving present, and did he now have a job title, description or job specification, outlining SPECIFICALLY WHAT HE WAS PAID TO DO? Had he attended courses on current Park Home legislation etc to update his CV and experience portfolio? Being the, 'maintenance man', was he allowed to charge the residents a fee, extra to his wage/salary, to do maintenance work for them? Or ask for a payment if a resident wanted to use discarded items left lying around, before he himself decided to put them in his** personal storage or take them home. If he did no one was informed. **Was he allowed to remove items for himself when clearing a site plot?** He was always quick to point out that he'd been attached to the site for many, many years and appeared to have a rather inflated opinion of what his role was. **He obviously didn't know the difference between experience and duplication.** But we soon realised his new role involved denying any problems created since Wyldecrest took over the site, and brought to his attention was anything to do with him. Even blaming his previous employer Mr Campbell in a written submission to a judicial enquiry, as being the culprit for the problems. **Is that not libel?** Or carrying out some dubious duties which some would argue, he was not qualified or legally allowed to do. Such as **entering residents' properties, without permission, known as trespass,** to try and persuade them to pay their site fees which they were withholding, until the result of an Industrial tribunal was known and telling them they could be evicted, **known as verbal harassment.** I personally have evidence of at least 4 residents who were subjected to such, and was also aware of others. **In August 2024, Mr Bassa was reported to Wyldecrest for breaking data protection laws by spitefully posting everyone's electricity bills in the 'office window' just to try and prove he'd actually read the meters, after all the bills, 28/7/2024, had been estimated. The breaches included display of personal and individual data, unauthorised access to personal data and lack of consent. To date Wyldecrest, have not responded and the case has been reported to the relevant authority. Although the offending information was removed, unfortunately for Mr Bassa, it was not before photographic evidence was taken to support the resident's claim in anticipation of future denials.** As for the details of the tribunal case, these were outlined in a **98 page, A4 document** which could provide enough material for a book in its own right as, to date, there is more evidence that was not included, but which may yet emerge at a later date. Some evidence being provided by a Lancashire Evening Post journalist, Catherine Musgrove, citing Mr Best as her source, after she had phoned him up to enquire about a banking collapse caused by Wyldecrest bulldozers trying to create more space to fit more units onto the Park, as more units related to more money. When I contacted Catherine Musgrove about the article mentioning issues such as due diligence, authenticating facts, proper research, personally visiting the site etc., she said she found my communication patronising but never rebutted my claim that it was inaccurate. Was she persuaded by Best because he was a 'budding billionaire', with access to an expensive legal team? Although, after our initial spat, we did exchange a few e-mails but since then she has been conspicuous by her absence. Surprising as journalists usually pursue topics of local community interest. Since Wyldecrest arrived in Preston, she would have enough articles to present a monthly up-date diary, that the readers could skim and scan. But perhaps she has other crooks to catch, or fish to fry. After 18 months, the residents won their case but Wyldecrest, as expected, appealed. The appeal was refused, but was then referred to a 2nd Tier Tribunal case that was heard on 16th February, 2024, in Liverpool. In June 2024, the Judicial System again made its 3rd and final judgement, with PRP again winning its argument. Incidentally, Penwortham Residential Park was not the only site in the UK that had taken, or was taking, Mr A Best, affectionately known as 'Helicopter Man', as he frequently used such to portray the image of a very busy successful entrepreneur, travelling the globe, 'doing good'. Or as Private Eye referred to them, as, 'sharp practices'. **Even Mr Best at a Select Committee in March 2012, admitted there was no such thing as a Rogue Park Owner-they were all criminals.** Is that why in 2024, he abandoned the UK to go abroad leaving family and the day-to-day practices to be dealt with by a Mr D Sunderland, Estates Manager, and a Craig Johnson, the Assistant Director /Customer Relations Officer, affectionately known as, 'The Enforcers'. However, as I write this section, I am led to believe Sunderland is under investigation as, **not a fit and proper person to manage a site.** Well, there's a surprise, as we already know he has no formal qualifications that allow him to attend tribunals, masquerading as a legal bod. I've been informed he's a Scottish salesperson. Sadly, as mentioned, the dispute split the once relatively harmonious Park into those who were happy to massage Mr Bassa's ego by believing the words coming out of his mouth, (only worth 7% according to Albert Mehrabian), and his pathetic protestations as to his innocence. Such people preferring not to hear the facts, attend meetings or tribunals, or include themselves in the fight for justice, but would be more than happy to share the spoils others fought to get. In 2024, one new resident, who had only recently joined the Resident's Association, decided to help Mr Bassa carry out, 'his duties', by leaf blowing and spraying weed killer, after Mr Bassa had recently come out of hospital. I am led to believe that the person was paid £100 a day for his services. What price loyalty, I ask? To me, it was obvious which tribe/gang this resident wanted to belong to, and it wasn't the Resident's Association. **I have no respect for such people and as for Mr Bassa, I chose not to speak to him, long before Mr Craig Johnson instructed us not to do so.** We have in the past been informed, but were not party to the 'sick note',' Mr Bassa had given, to take time off work suffering from stress, because people kept asking him too many pertinent questions as to what he actually did. Ah, bless! Forget the pot holes, virtually non-existent lighting, very, very limited car parking space and other loss of amenities, he must not be asked to do anything other than **WHAT HE HAS BEEN INSTRUCTED TO DO, OR NOT DO.** Such requests being directed to Mr Craig Johnson. 13/10/2023. However, again to be fair to Mr Bassa, he excelled in either sitting on the steps outside the office, or walking up and down Park Road, outside my property, talking as loudly as he could on his mobile. Or talking to anyone that would listen to his excuses of why certain jobs were NOT done, and **slandering certain residents** who didn't like him. Have I evidence that he has slandered me, and two other residents? Watch this space for future updates. With reference to the once non-existent, park-lighting, this situation was resolved after South Ribble Council at their own Industrial Tribunal insisted, that unless most of the resident's grievances were resolved, the council wouldn't renew Wyldecrest's site licence. Suddenly Mr Bassa was called into action, the speed **depending on which dignitaries were due to visit the site and see for themselves, such as say the Tribunal Judge.** Mr Bassa earned a reputation for frequently and especially, when a gale force weather forecast was given, he would take out his leaf blower and blow the leaves to one side of the road. Only for them to return several hours later, when the wind force increased. Or, as mentioned, he would get out his wheelbarrow, fill it with a bit of black stuff, and partially fill in a few pot holes, so the visitors wouldn't fall down them, possibly breaking their ankles, and sue Wyldecrest, easily done if half the park was in darkness. As for the residents who he considered not as important, he only filled in a few holes a few times a year, but only if heavy rain was forecast, so the fill would be washed away after 24 hours. I gave him the rap-nickname, 'The Phantom Leaf Blower and Part Time Hole Filler', **"Anyhow, all the best, O'right, Ye know what I'm saying, See you in a bit, That's Nothin to do with me."** That's the chorus to be sung after each verse. **But which tribe does Mr Bassa actually belong to: maintenance man, CHIS, gopher, rap artist, road sweeper, delusional park operator/visitor?** On the 5th August, 2021, 9 pm 'Undercover Boss', he gained television notoriety after a television crew visited the Park, from which Mr Best got some free publicity, and as a result Mr Bassa was invited to one of Mr Best's properties, for another subtle PR exercise by the site owner. Mr Bassa was subsequently given a £5,000 bonus, less tax of course, a pay rise and a company van, by his employer after he had spent, what one could only call, a relatively short amount of time in Mr Bassa's company. At the time of writing this book, I had spent 13 plus years observing JB. Many viewed the payments and 'sweeteners' to Mr Bassa with suspicion, not least as a possible bribe to ensure loyalty. Ironically, his company van has the logo,

Wyldecrest: Live Your Dream on the side. But many residents feel, the word dream should be replaced with nightmare. After his TV appearance, he took on a persona that was not apparent, when he worked for Mr Campbell. A persona that gave JB a false sense of security working for a site owner that was no stranger to controversy, and had a reputation for creating an image that didn't always stand up to close scrutiny and involved, according to Private Eye, 'sharp practices'. (Alfie Best- Saint or Sinner? Private Eye, 26/7/2018). Was Mr Bassa frightened of his new employer and his team, as this might account for his change of behaviour? As alluded to previously, Mr Best was like many who had money, power and influence who had a reputation for not taking kindly to criticism, true or otherwise, and appeared to be quick in taking, amongst other forms of retribution, legal action against those that questioned the way he operated. A bit like an infamous American President or Russian Oligarch. So, look out, Mr Briggs. Will I still be around to write a follow up to this book? But as far as I'm aware, he hasn't yet tried to sue Ian Hislop and Private Eye for publishing less than flattering remarks about him in its articles, of which there have been several. I wonder why? Was Mr Bassa now a CHIS, (Covert Human Information Source), under the guise of having the label, 'site maintenance man'? In the police force, these were once known as snouts but in today's, re-branded world are now known as intelligence sources but I find intelligence a difficult concept to apply to a person, who blows leaves just before high winds are forecast, and loosely fills in a few holes in the road, hours before torrential rain is forecast. At the end of 2024, Mr Bassa spent weeks trying to put up several pieces of guttering around, 'his office', but never succeeded, because as soon as anyone passed by, he would down tools and talk. 6 months into 2025, there is still no guttering. Regarding the tribunal, he had given written evidence that stated, **he was more than happy with the improvements that Wyldecrest had made since taking over the Park.** In stark contrast to the Resident Association's grievances. It was also worth noting that during this period Mr Bassa was given another site to, 'look after', which meant he was only seen at Penwortham Residential Park at certain times. Why was he being sidelined? One could only presume that JB was bored sitting in his site office, or on its steps, rapping most days as he hadn't enough work. Or perhaps he was developing bladder problems drinking so much coffee with his most ardent supporter, Francis, at 22, Park Rd. who had ambitions of being a councillor. Who knows? To reiterate, **certain residents after being reported by Mr Bassa were, 'put on the naughty step', (flashbacks to my time as a primary school teacher), and even told by Mr Johnson not to speak to Mr Bassa, as he had time off work with stress because, 'he had to answer some questions about site issues and what his job involved.' Mr Bassa making some outrageous claims, as to the intimidation and harassment he was subjected to. No mention being made of Mr Bassa's aggressive behaviour towards the white residents, which some could argue was bordering on racist, as he frequently gave them 'black looks'. And as a result of which, such residents were told to address their concerns to Mr Johnson so he could speak to Mr Bassa and rectify the situation. I'm not sure what Wyldecrest's definition of rectify is, as since they have taken over the Park, many complaints to Mr Johnson have been ignored. POWER YOU CAN TAKE, RESPECT YOU HAVE TO EARN. It's ironic that when Mr Johnson came to speak to the residents, not long after Wyldecrest took over the site, HE ACTUALLY SAID THIS SITUATION COULD HAPPEN. Does he do the lottery, I wonder? The words democracy and dictatorship immediately spring to mind or perhaps its abdication, not delegation of responsibilities.** As said, I personally lost all respect for Mr Bassa, after I'd decided which tribe he belonged to. He'd helped divide a once relatively harmonious park into two camps. Those who were frightened of reprisals, and believed the bullshit that some were pedalling, many of whom lived on, 'Wisteria Drive', and stroked Mr Bassa's very insecure ego, and those who were fighting to see what they were getting for their site fee, worth a minimum of £100,000 plus pa to Wyldecrest. **POWER plus GREED IS TOXIC.** Not forgetting the side issues of fuel and water bills. **In February 2021, Private Eye reported that Wyldecrest Parks had lost a third appeal in a legal battle with a 77-year-old, over inflated, site charges for electricity, where it was claimed that the company was charging over three times the average daily domestic tariff. At this juncture, the film, Erin Brockovich, springs to mind and a recap of the issues concerning, Aging and the Elderly. Enter Mr Bates v The Post Office, 2023. Late in 2024, Wyldecrest, without any consultation, said they were going to install smart meters, and were going to increase site fees to pay for them. Not a one-off fee but, a monthly one. How much does it cost to install a smart meter?** My legacy when I leave Penwortham Residential Park, is the brook at the side of my property, what will be JB's? An arrogant person that didn't realise how well off he was, but who was prepared to be bought for 40 pieces of silver, or is that gold? I've tried to add a biblical reference, because Mr B, I am told, attends church. Or at least that is where I think he is going, when he is frequently picked up from 'the office' by Francis of 22 Park Rd. fame at 0930 on some Sunday mornings. Why not his home I ask? Perhaps when she regularly visits him in his little office, as a change of venue to drink coffee, they are also planning the next sermon, thou shalt not lie, bear false witness, covet thy neighbour. Have we not come across others like those found at Wyldecrest, during the writing of this book? According to Paterson J and Holmes A, 2018, there are two types of people in the workplace. There are the bosses and there are those who have bosses. Some of the former answer to no one and nothing, not even the law and it is their attacks of pride, tantrums and whims to which the latter must attend. **POWER YOU CAN TAKE BUT RESPECT YOU HAVE TO EARN.** Whilst immersing myself in giving lots of TLC to my property, I also found that I had plenty of time to reflect on how I had arrived at my present situation. With time on my hands, this also gave me the motivation to write my autobiography, something that was on my to-do list. **"It's when you reach the end of things, that you want to go back."** (Connolly M, 2016, The Wrong Side of Goodbye, PB, 3:31). It's ironic that I finally ended up living in my wished for detached property, at a time when I became detached from the rest of society. On the 27th July, 2012, why had I single handedly chosen to say goodbye to my soul mate, friend, travel companion and confidant? I was struggling to understand how I had chosen to return to being on my own again and, although I didn't know it at the time, a return to the Black Dog. **At 62 years of age, my WORST-CASE SCENARIO was being on my own. Had I self-destructed, had I imploded? After all I was a people person, but some people thought I should be avoided at all costs, because I could make people's ears bleed.** From then on, my only recourse was to embark on a damage limitation exercise. **"Although I'm broken, I'm still breathing."** (Wadge A, 2018. Faith's Song).

Some 13 years previously, when Heather and I decided to set up house and live together in Houghton, I vowed that I never, ever again wanted to return to a life of solitude, loneliness and depression, with no one to share my life with. So, what was I playing at? Being in a state of perpetual loneliness, was to me a terrible way to try and live your life. It was such a futile existence. **"When everyone has left you behind, you are alone. When you have left everyone behind, there is solitude."** Schiller. On one of the last weekend away trips to the Mercure Hotel, Chester, Little Sutton, March 2012, I had been informed by Heather, that I had become boring. **"...a bore is a person who deprives you of solitude, without providing you with company,"** (James P, 2011, Dead Man's Grip, P308, quoting Gian Vincenzo Gravino an Italian author). What would Paul Shoreman have thought, knowing Heather called me boring? Especially, as not many months previously we had wined, dined, laughed and joked together at a dinner evening at Claughton Avenue with Paul, his wife Jenni and Donna Parkinson, a young ranger. **I know, they say what people think of you has nothing to do with you, but it affects you nonetheless, once you find out.** This was not the first indication that Heather wanted out and that she had grown tired of the travel and lifestyle, but it was the most significant. I continued to function, don't forget, as a teacher I was good at role play, but not really living, just treading water all the time, preparing to face the inevitable by simply letting go. Since that moment, every day was about dealing with this constant feeling of nausea and isolation with this heavy, leaded aching in the chest, that felt as though I might at any moment have a heart attack. Not to mention the sudden, panic attacks, and having to deal with the depression and the fact that at any moment in time I could become very emotional. Coming to terms with the negativity of self-pity, knowing that everybody had their own problems, and certainly didn't want to be bored with mine, let alone be able to offer solutions as to how to rid myself of the nightmare, was very difficult. Reality was a bitter pill to swallow. **"If someone is lonely when they are on their own, then they are keeping bad company."** (James P, 2009. Dead Tomorrow, p428). I hated it and never found a permanent solution of how to cope. **"He listened to the silence and the silence listened back."** (Connolly J, 2011. The Whisperers, p84). At times, adopting the strategy of, 'talking to the wall', made famous in the Willy Russell film, Shirley Valentine, released in 1989, helped. At least no one answered back, and your opinion was never challenged. But deploying words isn't always the same as talking. **But how do you gauge, qualify or quantify happiness when you are on your own, lonely and depressed?** On the issue of me being labelled a chatterbox, who would you rather be associated with, someone who is trying to address his loneliness and depression, and had earned a living by communicating and wanted to be sociable by spending time talking, or with someone wanting to be anti-social, who avoided eye contact and didn't want to verbally communicate by tapping, scrolling and swiping? Psychologists talk about **reframing** by looking at things in a positive rather than negative manner and, **"Deflecting an undesirable emotion with a series of routine actions."** (Booth S, 2010. The Kill Call, PB page 81). There are different kinds of courage, but overcoming being alone at three o'clock in the morning, when everything was dark, cold and all seemed lost, must be one of the most courageous. In September, 2013, David Threlfall, played Len, a retired Police Officer who had lost his wife, in a four part TV drama entitled, 'What Remains'. Apart from being a brilliant murder mystery, for me, it was more significant for not only its portrayal of relationships with people finding themselves alone, for a variety of reasons, and the coping mechanisms they adopted, but also a very poignant reminder of the destructive power of loneliness on people. During the drama, Len replaced, 'the Shirley Valentine wall', with his wife's grave stone, telling it, "I can't do this for the next 20 years." Or was it a case of I don't want to do it rather than I can't? **On the 7th January, 2016 a BBC documentary titled, The Age of Loneliness, was a mix of statistics and real people in life suffering from, 'The Silent Epidemic', claiming there were 7.6 million single households in the country and blamed social media, or should we say anti-social media for their isolation? Again, claiming over 1 million older people had not physically spoken to anyone in the last month.** One participant, when asked to describe loneliness, said that it was something you couldn't see, smell or touch, you could only feel it. Another 72-year-old had donated her body to medical science, because she couldn't bear the thought of no one turning up at her funeral, after being indirectly labelled of having no further use. For me, having no one in situ to share a hug and cuddle with was terrible, and I always looked forward to getting a heart to heart, once every six weeks, when I drove over to Rawtenstall to see my friend Beryl Harper. Communication on the Park initially with passers-by and other residents was a life line for me to escape the loneliness, but sadly, some decided to put a time limit on conversations, perhaps because they were too busy stabbing others in the back. Thank goodness, there were some genuine, lovely people who were quite happy to share. Thank you, Claire and family, Lesley and family, Lesley and Mark and Carol to name but a few.

Escaping further and further into my books and autobiography, my life escaped into a dream world of fiction, mixed with reality. I had three lives, one in the past, when I was writing my autobiography, one that was escaping into my fictional books and the third was the reality of the here and now. Reality was solitude and loneliness, which I tried to avoid at all costs. A fate I think that happens to all aging people. This is not to slight my family or friends for neglect, but just the fact that you can be lonely in a crowded room. Steve Coogan referred to this in his autobiography as, **"The reality of age, the acceptance of our mortality."** (Coogan S, 2015, Easily Distracted, 12:69). Spike Milligan, whom many referred to as a comic genius, frequently suffered from depression and in a BBC4 documentary titled, Love, Light and Peace, shown on 30/07/2016, talked frankly about his illness. **"Mental pain is worse than any physical pain. It's invisible, that's the awful part of it. Invisible pain ingresses you all the time, versatility your moods. Crying itself is a relief but people say, snap out of it –that's silly. It's like saying to someone who has a broken leg, come on walk, you're alright."**

For me, after 37 years, and then again after 75 years of existence, I contemplated a solution. **It's not unusual for people at some stage in their lives, to contemplate suicide. As youngsters it's usually to do with a cry for help, or to seek attention, but as we get older it's called the euthanasia debate.** Then it's about reality, reasoning and conviction. It's about acceptance, that the life they have lived is over in a quality sense. Family and friends just take you for granted, and to all intents and purposes, have faded away. There is nothing to look forward to. There are no achievable goals or dreams, and if there are they just seem to be pointless, if you cannot share them. Knowing that the rest of their remaining lives will be plagued with questions and why, with the past coming back with frequent regularity, at the most unexpected, inconvenient times. David Hosp, in his book, Innocence, 2007 p187, referred to this as, **"Geriatric delusions fed by loneliness."** At that stage, death seems a very peaceful solution. It also seems such an injustice, **"the inability of the deceased to prepare to say goodbye to loved ones and make their peace,"** (Hall, MR, 2011, The Redeemed, 9:133).

I wasn't going to let that happen to me, and decided I would say my goodbyes in this autobiography. I had always said I wanted a quick, sudden death, and was not at all frightened by the prospect of having one, as long as my solution to ending my life did the job, and did not leave me a vegetable. I was thinking of putting such a scenario into my will, but decided to spare the solicitor a moral/ethical dilemma. **Over the years, I had constantly questioned the meaning of and futility of life, and had long ago agreed that other than to continue the survival of the species by having children, sorry baby goats/kids, it was purely and simply an emotional roller coaster ride, interspersed with physical and psychological bouts of activity, replicating and duplicating what others had done before.** It had taken me a long time to realise, that unless you share your experiences, what good were they? It was all well and good having been on the beach at Camps Bay, just outside Cape Town, in South Africa, on Christmas Day, along with the bronzed bodies wearing Christmas hats, to appreciate what Christmas day meant to different cultures, unless you had someone by your side to share it with and discuss its significance. What is the purpose of walking along Waikiki Beach, in Hawaii, unless you had someone to feel the sand between their toes with you? To have witnessed, in Kariega Game Reserve, South Africa, two charging rhinos, weighing 2 tonnes each, coming towards you, unless there was someone else there, to experience the adrenaline rush at that moment. To watch a brilliantly written play/film, brilliantly acted, that moved you to tears, unless you had someone there to offer you a Kleenex tissue. In all of these scenarios, I had Heather. Or to have had the aeroplane you were travelling in struck by lightning upon leaving Auckland airport and survived, unless there was someone with you to verify the story. In this case, it was the personnel on the 1993, Australian rugby tour. How can you have good sex on your own? I don't know who said it, but you don't always travel fastest when you are alone. So here I was at 75 plus years of age with no desires whatsoever, to prolong the journey. Let alone have some medical practitioner decide for me, that in order to support the pharmaceutical industry in its never-ending pursuit of profits, that keeping me alive with the drugs and their side effects, was a humanitarian, ethical and moral thing to do. Give me a break! Come on, how many times can you tolerate the John Major, Spitting Image, Eating Peas Sketch? 4, Park Road had been bought to put a roof over my head, but more so, for the fact that it gave me a project to distract me from the inevitability, that I would probably end my life still trying to come to terms with what I had achieved, and how I had arrived at such a destination. **"Some people slipped from this world without protest, glad to be free of its troubles; others fought to the last moment, resisting the inexorable tides of death until the waters closed over their heads."** (Hall MR, 2012, The Flight, p416). **"Death didn't frighten me, but dying petrified me."** (Booth S, 2004, 'One Last Breath,' p46). **"In fact, he wasn't afraid of death at all. It was the thought of living that caused him pain." "I used to fear the progression of old age, and I was scared of dying. I imagined turning into first my dad, then my grandad, seeing that as the most depressing descent into oblivion. The thought of seeing my children turn into adolescents, then adults, then become middle aged –peak and decline."** (Bruce A, Cambridge Blue, 2008, p170). Luckily, I didn't have any children of my own, but had witnessed others degenerate and so at times in my adulthood, felt relieved that I wasn't a dad. And so, when Heather, after succumbing to the psychological and emotional blackmailing that her children subjected her to, decided she wanted to return to the Midlands to be with her family, the stark realisation that I would be in my worst-case scenario and return to the blanket of solitude and loneliness, with no hugs, cuddles, verbal sparring, sharing or caring, filled me with trepidation. Such loneliness and solitude ate away at me, like a malignant cancer taking away my resolve, fortitude and identity. Some people worry and wonder what will eventually kill them, but I knew that returning to such loneliness and emptiness would eventually lead to my demise. Whenever I had resigned from positions in the past, it was because I'd stopped believing in the product. I now have stopped believing in life, and that any remaining dreams would not become reality. Heather said she was still very fond of me, which seemed a long way from when Jay, years previously, announced at his wedding on a gullet in Turkey, "I've never seen Heather looking so happy, and I think that has a lot to do with Jim." A statement that some 4 years later, was attached to a picture of Heather with her new man Roger, on Facebook, but this time her happiness was not attributed to me. It's a fickle, funny, revolving door world. The truth was when Heather decided to call it a day, she had become bored and the novelty of me being her partner, had worn off. The travel, whilst exciting at the time, had outlived its usefulness, or so I thought. My jokes, repartee and constant fights for justice, had become repetitive. The tactile bonding had become fractious. She appeared to have lost that sparkle in her eyes. She wanted to return to her roots and her families' needs and expectations. I respected and accepted such. We had had 12 plus fabulous years together, but that didn't ignore the fact, that I still wanted someone to share my needs and expectations. As mentioned, years previously when Heather and I decided to buy a house together, she informed me that her 3 children were grown up, and were now big enough to look after themselves and that her middle son, Paul, who was still living with her, would have to find a place of his own. She wanted some me time. As it turned out, the expression, "As long as mum's happy that's all that matters," were just words uttered under the influence of alcohol, which wasn't uncommon for Mark and Charlotte. It became apparent they didn't like mum having me time, were jealous and didn't like the fact she was 2 hours up the road being independent, enjoying and being successful in her job, travelling the world, meeting lots of new people, being an integral part of the Briggs extended family, making new friends, and having fun and frivolity, or was she just role playing? For me as a 16-year-old, I thought the solution to personal devastation was to run away but at 74, with a lifetime of experiences, some things are just so obvious, you had to accept reality. Running away and not facing reality solved nothing. In the end even if I did run, I felt I had nowhere left to go. Travelling took over to fill the void. Imposed loneliness was numbing, and a complete and utter waste of space, time and energy. It was a private emptiness that could not be filled. I'd been there in 1987. It was a dark place to be, when you experienced, but couldn't share. **It's all in the state of mind. If you think you are beaten, you are. If you think you dare not, you don't. If you like to win, but think you can't, it's almost sure you won't. If you think you'll lose, you've lost. For out in the world, you'll find it's all in the state of mind.** (Source Unknown). For me, it was not only my state of mind but an acceptance of the reality of my situation. It's a terrible thing, when someone or something takes away your smile, and you return to a dark place. To become religious, and for the first time ever to quote a proverb, **'Without a vision people perish.'** A happy ending always depends on where you stop the story. Once Heather and I had cancelled an impending trip to Canada, because we needed the money to move house, I stopped dreaming –Not good. During our final times together at Claughton, Heather and I had calmness, respect and smiles. There was an empathy, because neither of us was deriving any pleasure from what was happening. Although I could tell that Heather was relieved that the deed had been done, she had no desires to rub my nose in it, and comforted herself in the Bird time honoured tradition of, "Oh, for goodness' sake, pull yourself together, it's your own fault, if you just come and live with me in Bedworth, you won't be on your own." But as Lady Di found out, there were more than two people in the relationship. Certain members of Heather's family were uncomfortable with sharing, and definitely didn't like seeing her happy in her new home in Lancashire. So, as I've said on the 26th July, 2012, I moved out of Claughton Avenue. Prior to that, there were slivers of light that brightened the darkness with Heather and I visiting or attending social functions together, but for me the upset and heartache that each of those visits and trips caused, I knew that once I found the strength and modus operandi to end the journey, I would. Hilary Minev would say I was being melodramatic again, but now at 70 with 20 more years of life experiences, the drama was not a role play exercise to attract attention, but serious business. On each occasion Heather and I got together, after we had moved into separate abodes, her body language didn't match the words coming out of her mouth. I was certainly getting the verbal and nonverbal messages. She was going through the motions, and in a masochistic way I wanted to get back to my own space and loneliness, to deal with such motions. Which were to get the new accommodation in order, write my autobiography, apologise for past indiscretions, spend any superfluous savings on remaining travel plans, alter my will, plan my funeral and tie up any financial issues, and my demise would just come as a natural progression after that. Having decided on my course of action, I knew that I would see it through because to me there was no viable alternative. It would not be a cry for help, or an attention seeking act, or to make people feel guilty, but of addressing the issue of my worst-case scenario versus best case scenario. With each passing day, I found accepting what I was hoping to achieve, quite therapeutic. At this stage, I reminded myself of the Vocational Service Motto, that had guided me thus far: **I have to live with myself and so I want to be fit for myself to know; I want to be able as days go by, always to look myself straight in the** eye. I don't want to stand with the setting sun and hate myself for the things I've done. I want to go out with my head erect. I want to deserve all men's respect. For here in the struggle for fame and self, I want to be able to like myself. I don't want to look at myself, and know that I'm bluster and bluff and an empty show. I can never hide myself from me; I see what others may never see. I know what others will never know; I can never fool myself, and so, whatever happens I want to be free. (Edward A. Guest). I certainly felt, I could go out with my head held high. I'm not boasting or expecting a reward, but to highlight the irony that I accepted that in the past I was guilty of some indiscretions, but later realised that even doing the right thing doesn't necessarily guarantee things will work out. I had done what I felt was the right thing to do at the time. Yes, I had regrets and wanted to try and make amends, before I left my personal space but I also knew I wanted to be free from the solitude and loneliness, because I had been there and promised myself, I'd do everything possible in my life to avoid returning. As Mary Jo Blithe said, "You need someone to love, hug and ...." You have to play the hand that you are dealt and unlike, Who Wants to be A Millionaire, you can't ask Chris Tarrant or Jeremy Clarkson to swop the question, ask the audience, take 50:50 or phone a friend. Oliver Stark used phrases such as **"various shades of lonely"** and went on to say, **"The horrible fact of being alone was that you went home feeling dog tired, but as soon as you were through the door the bright lights in your heart flickered on, and you were trapped with your own carousel of memories. Home was a place you sometimes didn't want to get to." "He missed the rhythm of being two. Beating a drum with one stick had no rhythm at all."** (p22). Referring to love he said, "Perhaps it was just a fantasy, that kept emerging from the deep to ruin your life." And that it sometimes, "stopped in the station for a day or two." "It was never easy to open the door to need, ... **what he wanted was nothing more than to hug up close to someone and let the world drift away."** (Stark O, 2010, The American Devil, 52:297/8   0.

Although in theory, Heather and I had agreed to be friends from afar, and continue to travel together as and when the opportunity arose, I was too cynical and experienced to accept it was going to be that simple, the longer the situation continued. She'd already informed me she didn't want to go to Canada, but was considering instead going to Thailand with Beth, her friend. Did that materialise, I never found out, but suspected it was more to do with showing me that there were others, that she could call upon to travel with. When Roger entered her life, she was quick to inform me, she was off to Canada to meet his family and relatives. We did however, attend Warners for one last time with the family, in early 2013, and also managed a weekend in London, to support our friend Natalie in the World Triathlon championships, before having our final cruise to Venice, along the Adriatic coast followed by a week in Corfu. But upon returning from that in October 2013, we both went our separate ways. Strange though it may seem, I became very much at ease with what I wanted to do. In the beginning, the job description for Heather and me was about sharing, helping, enjoying, advising, supporting and trying to improve the quality of our lives. In part, we had both reciprocally achieved that, but for me I felt that I could no longer live the dream, once she returned home. The family commitment would prohibit that. I've been informed that blood comes before everything and would change Heather, or should I say, return her to destined, genotypical behaviour. Heather would be and was a different animal in West Midlands than she was in Lancashire, and would display her mother's, at times harsh, aloof and matter-of-fact remoteness, to deal with my obvious pain and her own demons. My frequent bouts of emotion, prior and shortly after we separated, bore testament to that and made me resolve not to openly show my true feelings to Heather again. It was in fact true, that I had a choice and to the general observer it was quite a simple one, but the reality for me was much more complex. Going with her to Bedworth and being unhappy, or staying in Preston and being unhappy. I wanted to come out of it with some of my dignity intact. Grovelling in the gutter was not what I had come to accept as a solution to any problem. Self-pity may be, grovelling, no. I had stooped that low in prior situations, and found the whole experience totally demeaning. As for moving to Bedworth with her, let's be honest, the family for one reason or another, didn't want me there, I was a boring, opinionated, old fart. **Let's not forget the vast majority of people don't like and can't deal with honesty.** Also, I didn't want to go to a place I didn't really enjoy visiting; with people whose destructive and selfish life styles were at odds with my generation, and whose philosophies, ethics and morals were being shaped by what was on their smartphones, which I found difficult to comprehend. Most of these people were decent people, but belonged to an era that was at odds with mine. They communicated differently to me, via text, mobile, facebook, etc. I liked to communicate verbally with a smile, and eye to eye contact. They visited people's houses and rudely sat there texting and playing games on their latest piece of technology, with very little respect for their host or hostess. I was aware that respect had to be earned, but always felt that no matter which male entered Heather's personal space, would not be given the opportunity to earn it. Glib expressions such as, **'As long as mum's happy that's all that matters,'** sounded fine but the reality of the situation was that, apart from Melanie, her family and so-called friends forgot to qualify that with, 'as long as she doesn't move more than a mile away from where we live.' If they did believe their own press, why didn't they ever phone to ask if she was in fact, happy when she lived in Preston? Or physically visit to personally ask her. **What most people really appreciate is a social visit or call BEFORE, not a sympathy visit or call AFTER.** The selfish, emotional and psychological blackmail they subjected her to when **HEATHER DECIDED** to move to Lancashire, made me very angry. Was this something to do with the fact that she had been married and divorced twice, before we met and **they were sceptical of all things male entering Heather Anne's life**? The children's biological father was very rarely, if ever, mentioned. Even when Heather informed them of his death, the response was minimal to say the least. It didn't take me long to realise that although, I was perceived as perhaps an improvement on Heather's previous male relationships, because I appeared to care, this didn't extend to taking her away, so she could become happy at home, work and play, and certainly not to display behaviour that meant she had a life of her own, that was independent of their needs. Selfish and unreliable Mark certainly didn't like the idea of being ousted from number one alpha male in Heather's life. The irony was that, according to Heather, Mark was just like his father and although, I never met him, his legacy caused me a lot of heartache. Could it be that both her boys were in denial as to their true identity? Oh yes, they had Heather's competitiveness, but displayed only a few of her more favourable traits. According to Heather, Mark certainly had his father's liking for alcohol dependency, with Paul full of his father's bigoted bullshit. I always found it strange that Heather's two previous marriages were never, 'brought to the table', and even when the two gentlemen passed away, there was only a fleeting mention and certainly no mention of attendance at the funeral. It was as though their involvement in Heather and her children's life was a non- event. Were these people's participation in Heather's life so terrible, that their demise should be treated with such disdain? Heather must have loved her partners in the beginning. It did, however, give me another insight into how the Bird/Sutton dynasty viewed outsiders. Her daughter Melanie, whom I got to like immensely, was not blameless but she at least, did embrace the fact that communication was a two-way process and frequently visited, talked and phoned. Once Mel had forgiven me for taking her mum away, we eventually got around to the occasional hug, which was a revelation for Mel because at first, she had great difficulty understanding my open, chatty, tactile nature. Why do you always shake hands with Jim and exchange hugs, she used to ask Jason, her boyfriend at the time? It's a Northern thing, would have been my reply. After all, I was a physical therapist and earned a living from a hands-on approach to treatment. Even after Heather and I split up, and Heather had found someone called Roger to share her life with, Mel **initially,** still found time to e-mail me and ask as to my welfare. This meant a lot to me. She once reduced me to tears, when she said she and Macey missed me. Thanks, Mel. I know I never knowingly made Heather unhappy, but significant others in her life did, with their indifference to her happiness when she moved to Preston. She couldn't understand why her so-called friends and sons never wanted to visit her in Hoghton, or Leyland. Perhaps Paul, her bigoted, racist son, may have felt there were just too many coloured people there, he referring to them as coons, and that visiting would somehow have intimidated him or worse still, given him some foreign disease. Years later, I suspect he was a BNP and Brexiteer. **Why, oh why, do some people think they are superior to someone else because of race, colour, creed, political persuasion or money? Is it just downright ignorance, arrogance or insecurity, as to their position in the animal world?** Do they not realise that there's a before and after to their lives? This was a person, who had caused Heather endless, sleepless nights in his youth, because of his wayward, criminal behaviour and for me, was the nearest thing to Andy out of the TV hit show, 'Little Britain', starring Matt Lucas and David Walliams.

"Yea, I know," was Paul's mantra, even before the words had left your lips. You couldn't tell Paul anything. He knew and probably, still thinks he knows it all. This fact being based on only one actual fact, as previously alluded to, "The boys are just like their father." Was Heather also in denial because she recognised and resented the fact, that they were more like their dad than her? Having said that, although Paul frustrated me, I got to like him because he appeared to have 'grown out of his bad boy phase'. Sadly his bigoted, 'Yea I know' side, still resided.

Unfortunately, Mark and I, although civil to one another, never did find any common ground. Ironic, as my background was football and sport, having spent 12 months training at Old Trafford, the ground of his favourite team, but a place when I first met him, he had never even visited. Also, I wasn't opposed to a few lagers. I suppose the issue for Mark was, I only liked a few lagers and knew when I'd had enough and didn't masturbate when I watched men's football. The very first time I met him socially, in his local pub, he wanted to get me drunk, and I realised then all was not well with the boy's world. Heather assured me he was trying to grow up but to me he had a long way to go. His reputation by several observers was one of being a very selfish, piss artist that never did seem to leave him. He seemed incapable of communication, unless it involved football or he was under the influence of alcohol. Did Heather worry, of course she did, but he was family so, like his sister Melanie, they chose to look the other way! As for Charlotte well, yea, like, ye know, like what I mean, like, babes, cool? Love Island, Rules OK! Were Mark and Charlotte aware that I was not alone in my evaluation of their relationship and personalities, or was I the only honest one to bring this to one's attention? Or perhaps they were and adopted the attitude of, hey, we have had x thousand hits on the like button, and just as many followers on face book, so people must like us. Yea right! OK, Babes.

Early on, when Heather and I discussed why the family and her so called friends never wanted to visit Lancashire, I instinctively thought it must have been me that they wanted to avoid, but soon realised using me as an excuse was a cheap shot, and was a cop-out as to the real reason. A clear example of insincerity in disguise. Personally, for me initially it was a case of, 'Mum, you have made your bed, lie on it, but we are not going to be seen to overtly support you.' At least Charlotte was honest enough to berate Heather for seeking a better quality of life up North, because she told Heather she was not happy as she was losing a baby sitter. This being the person that openly admitted, on my 60th birthday, to not being able to live with a man, in this case Mark, that didn't drink copious amounts of alcohol and was a nicotine junkie. Words that sprung to mind were dependency and addiction, because her father had lived most of his life, 'down at the club', and was living proof of how alcohol was an essential part of a full life. What harm can the odd cigarette with its 32 chemicals have? Perhaps, she had some inside knowledge as to the state of people's lungs, liver and kidneys that the rest of us mere mortals were not party to. **Don't forget, these people are supposed to be the highest form of intelligence in the animal kingdom.** Returning from the Warner's family get together in March, 2013, was very difficult for me, as it was the last that Heather was to attend. Upon arriving home, I was immediately thrust into my Churchillian, 'black dog', with a vengeance, the darkness getting murkier with each passing day. The weekend was such a happy, if not emotional occasion, with truckloads of genuine 'belly laughs' and laughter. Seeing our Lilian and Jack jiving, playing Mr and Mrs, and then winning the bingo was magic. Unfortunately, prior to Heather's journey south, she had wanted to clarify our relationship, because I had sent her an inappropriate Valentine's card and bought her a box of chocolates. She needed to establish, that we were now just good friends. No more, no less. For me, the card was a way of saying I was missing her terribly, but I suppose because we didn't share a house anymore, she felt we had to renegotiate the contract. For a very brief time, after I'd found out about Roger's existence, I wondered what contract she had negotiated with Roger. But as I had never met him, I in spirit wished him all the best with her family, and realised it had f..k all to do with me.   As highlighted, earlier in my literal journey, I have never understood the feminine mind, but still love most of them dearly. Returning to the German philosopher, Nietzsche, **"If you look long enough into the void, the void would look back into you."**

    In spite of all my personal, inward turmoil and some of my neighbour's attitude to life's realities, most of the time I have loved living at 4 Park Rd. If only for the fact that it's been my first experience of living in a community environment with all its interactive anomalies. It's mostly a peaceful place because the people who lived there, were all from a previous generation and many shared many of the old morals and values, that I was brought up with. There's no f..ing or geffing, unless you were one of those who strutted around the park kicking a football at the end of a piece of string, or shadow boxed in the garden. No football flags, no Radio 1 blaring out, and no children crying or screaming, apart from those visiting and doing, 'sleep-overs'. Unfortunately, we did have the yapping dogs that frequently disturbed the reverie. After John died, Carol, my neighbour, decided to sell her property and at the end of 2024, I had new neighbours, Ian and Susan, who had a dog called Honey. No comment. I also frequently wondered if the Lewis Hamilton impersonators on the park, which also included the visitors, because there were no speed bumps or non-smiley emojis, just pot holes, ever consider the error of their ways. After all, residents were over 55 and many had physical mobility issues, and therefore could not suddenly jump out the way of these petrol heads. **WHAT'S THE RUSH, FOLKS?** Anyhow back to the positives, the park's position and locality meant that everything was on my doorstep, travel, walks, shopping etc. It was 25 minutes' walk into the centre of Preston and to the railway station, from where I could catch a train and be in Manchester airport within just over an hour. The people who lived on the Residential Park were, as one would expect, a mixed bunch, but amongst the few grumpy, miserable, selfish sods, there were many good eggs. I include myself in that summation. I have tried to avoid listing those, whose company I enjoyed, and those whose I didn't. As stated previously, they know who they are, because I have told them. My favourites usually stopping for a quick chat, if they were passing my property and finding me in the front garden working, reading or sipping some fluid or another. I also appreciate that many people would not put quick and chat together, when referring to Jim Briggs. There has never been a time when I've seriously regretted living at 4 Park Rd. Even when one dog loving, alcohol dependent neighbour, who struggled with role definition, regarding job sharing, was replaced by another. But it's ironically the place, where I have suffered most from loneliness and depression.

The sad thing is no one ever really knows how much somebody else is hurting. We could be standing next to somebody, who is completely broken and we wouldn't even know it. (Sun Gazing. com)

According to Silverline, 29/11/17, the UK was in the grip of a loneliness epidemic. In 2025, the situation had deteriorated even more.

I can't end this section without wondering how much time in my 75 years of existence, I had spent alone. **What I did know for certain was, that I missed what I used to do and who I used to be. Loneliness isn't reserved for the elderly at Christmas, it's about not being truly seen as connected to another.** As I write these thoughts on my retirement, apart from having to adjust and accept the loss of 'friends', it started off brilliantly with Rangers, CTS Traffic and the other part time jobs. Not forgetting the trips around the world, and subsequent journeys with Heather, but once Heather left, it was a rapid slide down the slippery pole to obscurity. There was, however, an upside to being and living on my own, because in the past I'd been accused of only loving myself. But imagine, if you lived on your own and didn't love yourself. Being in denial and pretending to love, but in actual fact sometimes despised and sometimes hated? What had these people to look forward to?

8.
THE END IS IN SIGHT:

Funerals, Death, Hindsight, Regrets and the Euthanasia Debate.

"**On the day of my birth, my death began its walk. It's walking towards me now, without hurrying.**" Jean Cocteau. As for life, "**We are all just walking each other home.**" (Man Up, BBC Drama, 29/12/23). We're all, irrespective of race, colour, creed or political persuasion, fellow travellers on the road to the coffin.

A philosopher was once asked, "**What's the best fate that can befall a man?**" and he answered, "**First, not to have been born, and failing that, to die early.**" (Hopkins B, 1998. Our Kid, HB. 28:320). "**Growing old is not for cowards. What scares me, is getting to the end before I finish.**" W. Churchill. "**So, this is old age, a heavy chair near the television and panic buttons everywhere. Handles around the bath and piss-soaked knickers in the sink. A woman popping round twice a day to see if you're dead yet. Which is preferable? A good brain and a body that was fucked? Or hale and hearty flesh and bone, with nothing left up top?**" (Billingham M, 2002, Scaredy Cat, 14: 226/7). "**Be aware, every morning that you may not last the day, and every evening that you may not last the night.**". (Gerritsen T, 2004. Body Double, p27). How do you know when the time comes? You don't, it just does. Is it fate, circumstance or by design? "**Maybe he had finally had enough of his own company.**" (Pobi R, 2012. Bloodman, p8). **Some people say that you know when you are getting to the end of your life, because strangely you want to go back. You also realise that all the materialism becomes meaningless.** I started this autobiography by stating that death, no matter what your station in life, would eventually come to you in some guise or another, early, late, natural, by violence, via crime, disease or aging. For many years I had also believed, after attending funerals, nursing homes and talking to many elderly people, that there comes a point in many people's lives, when they realise that they find it difficult to relate to anything anymore, '**the tipping point**'. The values, morals and standards of behaviour that they had been brought up with were being eroded, and superseded by others, such as materialistic greed, in the name of progress. But this so-called progress was one of the things that was making them depressed. "**What is life all about, if there's no love at the end of it?**" (Call The Midwife, BBC 1, 25/12/25).

"**When I look around me today nothing works.** (And if we do work, 'the sickie' ensures we don't have to work for long). **We don't want anything to work and it's never changed. We don't like each other. We don't respect each other. We talk about compassion, but there is none. Hundreds and thousands of years of Christianity, and the preaching of gospels, and the bringing of the word of God and kindness and humanity to the world, and it hasn't worked. There are more people than ever desolate and lost.**" (The Ghost of Richard Harris, Sky Arts, Samson Films, 2022). **I now am in a society where selfishness, greed and hate are prized attributes. Where people prefer to talk to Alexa, or a smartphone, rather than make eye to eye contact with a human being and speak the truth. Where the most popular tribute is to try and copy Hitler, not by gassing the Jews and creating a blue-eyed race, but by getting rid of all the foreigners, the coloured people and LGBT community, because they are a disease, a 'blot on the landscape', but more importantly, they don't** belong to our tribe of white supremists. "I don't care if God saves our gracious Queen or not, I'm tired of the whole rotten lot." (Woodruff W, 2006, Nab End and Beyond, 4:79). And that was 19 years ago. On July 19th. 2024, the Daily Mail included an article by Tom Utley titled, 'Why would I want a new wonder drug, that would let me live long enough to see my grandkids grow up.' The articles gave many reasons why he asked the question, but for me the most significant, in relation to the title of this book, was his summation. **"The fact is that when I look at our country today, I see a civilisation in decline, barely recognisable as the Britain I grew up to love."** Mr Utley was born in 1953, 3 years after me. What was even more significant was, the fact that I came across this article after I had just returned from a city break to Dubai, which claimed to be the cleanest city in the world. After the visit, I decided that in comparison the UK was becoming a third world country. As I got older, I personally had a sense of being deserted. I'd become a nuisance that no one wanted to be associated with. Most if not all of my family and friends had departed, or chosen for a variety of reasons not to stay in touch. Perhaps they hadn't downloaded the app that told them to phone a sad, lonely, aging relative or friend, because there was no cash back. Or was it just that, for one reason or another, they'd been driven away? Had I self-destructed or imploded with my behaviour and intransigence? Would Hilary still think I was just being melodramatic? During my journey it has been unsettling and at times confusing, before finally realising that life cannot be managed and organised via lists. In the end, I also realised that no one wanted to listen anymore. People would ask me a question, but their body language was such that it was blatantly obvious, they didn't want to listen to my reply, no matter how brief. Or was it because they didn't want to hear the truth? Perhaps they were being patronising, or condescending, or perhaps they were just being rude. **And in the history of civilisation, this was a bad time for the truth.** If you are informed that your conversation is considered boring, and you are aware that no one is interested in what you have to say, the answer is very simple, isolate and stop conversing. I also surmised, that I must have been too honest. But how can you be too honest? You are either honest or not. In my life, I'd been accused of being resistant to change, but if one is eventually going to die no matter how, when or where or how does Darwin's theory of survival, 'Adapt or die', stand up to close scrutiny? It doesn't, because you don't necessarily have to adapt or change to NOT end up dead. On the 26th June, 2021, during a visit to see Alex, one of my neighbours when I lived on Alandale Drive, Royton, he suddenly and very angrily told me, I was pissing him off with my rudeness, by interrupting conversations to just talk about myself, as though I didn't want to hear what anyone else had to say. I was shocked, to say the least, as it was him who had invited me in to his house with a smile, asked his wife Anne to make me a cup of tea and asked me what had I been up to since I last saw him. His 40-year-old daughter, Gemma, who now had a child, was also present. I wondered, if this was something he'd been psyching himself up to say for a long time, at the first opportunity that presented itself. Was he carrying the anger from past interactions? Did his Catholicism object to my divorce and Godless lifestyle? Whatever the f..k that means. Or was it just early signs of Dementia? I just stared at him, and quietly and calmly asked, if he wanted me to leave? He said, he thought that would be a good idea. I pleaded no mitigating circumstances, thanked his wife Anne for the tea, apologised to Gemma, and left. Walking calmly across to Haydn's house, my other neighbour, who I had just been informed by Alex, had lost his partner Joan, a few years earlier, to cancer. I spent the rest of my visit in a dazed state. Ironically Haydn, the master of joke telling, used to always tell everyone, with a glint in his eye, that I was a boring bastard who you couldn't shut up. Did I really make people's ears bleed? It was at that moment I recalled what Heather had said, when she left me all those years ago, I'd become boring. **I thought only the young got bored with the elderly becoming lonely. Had I become boring because, "I thought too much,** analysed too much, and agonised too much?" (Keane J, 2009. Scarlet Woman, 36:369). And once you realise that you'd become boring, then surely it was time to consider leaving the party. Or was it that my personality meant, **"You let things bruise your soul, and question what is wrong with humanity."** (Rowbotham M, 2013, Watching You, PB, p143). And yes, as a result of all my studies and life experiences I had developed, to put it mildly, a pessimistic view, or was it a distorted perception, of human nature? I was finding it more and more difficult to find people to communicate with; to find positivity, empathy and compassion; to find happiness and enjoyment in others. And more and more difficult to motivate myself into finding reasons to continue. **"If it is so hard to find the perfect place to live –how difficult do you think it is, to find the perfect place to die?"** (Booth S, 2003, Blood on the Tongue, 13:216). In August 2024, a famous, ex England cricketer, who suffered from depression, asked his wife to help him end his life before later being hit by a train at Esher train station.

It's accepted, and quite rightly so, that most individuals think they are important, unique and special and that they imagine their lives to be like a journey, and talk about finding themselves whilst on it and gain closure at the end. But despite what the religious zealots, soothsayers, politicians and bull-shitters want you to believe, what they fail to realise is, that there is very little to find, as their genetic, DNA make-up has been defined at birth, and **the only closure that is guaranteed is death. Also, if anyone wants to know how significant the majority of most people's lives is, just visit the local crematorium and see how much time has been allotted to celebrate it on the daily funeral timetable. The last time I looked, it was 30 minutes. Not forgetting that local councils view dead bodies as clinical waste.**

As the aging process started to take its toll, and pessimism and cynicism became rife, I became less tolerant to certain people's behaviour and my biggest worry was mental illness. That's when I started to consider if it was possible to 'switch it off'. 24/7 the thoughts became a never-ending loop of mainly negative, annoying, angry emotions. The issue of 'flat lining' and the euthanasia debate took on more serious proportions, and the stark realisation that the only way to 'switch it off' was to end one's life. Suicide, the act of a coward or a brave person? People either willingly embraced the prospect of death, and prepared for the inevitable, by going through their bucket list, deciding on a box or a vase, drafting a will and sorting out a funeral plan, or went into denial, and tried to convince themselves that death was for everyone else but, themselves. **For many talking about death and euthanasia, let alone embracing it, was a no-no, which is crazy, even accepting that beliefs about death and how bodies are dealt with, can vary tremendously.** With no permitted cremations in Islam, to many now addressing their loved ones via anti-social media as if they had spent their time in the here-after with them. But there are few absolutes in life, and death is one of them with change being the other. **Don't forget, we are supposed to be the highest form of intelligence in the animal kingdom, so why do many people not want to accept the facts, or in many cases not even want to discuss, accepting responsibility for their own lives, bodies and eventual demise?** Personally, I've never been into this aging business. Dribbling everywhere, pissing everywhere, aching everywhere and defecating everywhere, and not being able to remember how many times you were guilty of such actions. Rob George, Professor of Palliative Care, King's College, London, in the TV programme, 'We Need to Talk about Death', 2/1/19, said that **dying should be about quality of life not quantity.** Neither should the final years be seen as a trade-off, one against the other but about living the best life a person can, right up to the last moment. **He said that in today's world for many, their final years meant spending half their time in hospital and the other half recovering from the after effects of such hospital** interventions. He called this, 'death by a thousand cuts', involving drugs, organ failure, as a result of interventions, blood tests, IVs and losing hair. What kind of living is that, or put another way, what kind of dying? The lingering death, or as the Chinese call it, Li Chi. The programme argued that Palliative Care worked best, when **it was not just tagged on at the end when all treatments had finished.** During the programme, it was argued that by reclaiming the narrative to the ending of life, a person can live it right up to the last moment, by enjoying the time that's left, by doing the things that make them human, rather than making their blood tests better. With reference to the research, the programme also argued that by putting money into early intervention Palliative Care, in specialist care homes and hospices, it was considerably less expensive than the conventional methods, which exerted a considerable strain on hospitals, not only financially, but also on the human and material resources needed to cater for the elderly. **Again, if the politicians, pharmaceutical industry and purse holders had the best interests of the elderly populace at the forefront of their NHS narrative, why has this path to improving and updating the NHS, by directing more resources into early, Palliative Care never seriously been pursued? The emphasis here being on seriously.** Personally, I hadn't reached the stage where intervention was necessary, but for me life was no fun anymore. The fact was nothing changed and being in a recurring loop of nostalgia just overwhelmed me, and was akin to being trapped in a washing machine on a slow spin cycle. Not that I had first-hand experience of such. When you are lonely, a day is too long and a week is a lifetime. People tell you to, 'snap out of it,' but, **"That's like telling me to make up my mind to give up cancer,"** (Trump ML, 2020. Too Much and Never Enough, 7:92). It had become debilitating waking up every day devoid of dreams, hope and trying to overcome the negativity by what psychologists call **reframing,** by looking at things in a positive, rather than a negative light. Jo Nesbo in, The Thirst, 2017, talks about 5 Kinds of awakening, (6:80), with waking up alone being number 2. The outcomes of this being either a sweet sensation of freedom or, at other times, melancholy. I was certainly entrenched in the latter, and as Peter Laws in his book, Unleashed, 2017, 25:211, reminds us, **"melancholy people are a turn-off."** Was this another reason I had become boring? I'd reached a point when I was tired of being surrounded by, at times, the obese, alcohol obsessed, techno zombies, dog mafia, grunting Neolithic man, and all the jealousy, envy, lies, deceit, sexism, racism, two faced, back stabbing, smiling and bullshit. I was struggling to find what was real and truthful. **Honesty and the truth were rarely on the agenda, and being in denial and delusion was commonplace, and an essential fact of life for many.** At the end of the day, if you'll pardon the pun, I realised that to rely on the medical profession I would be left in the clutches of pharmacology or technology, where the quality of life was determined by lots of wires attached to a blinking machine, a dribbling mouth, a blinking eye, screaming, shouting, paranoia, shit in the diaper and resentful visits from very busy relatives, and the odd friend. I am not denigrating the wonderful, hardworking personnel working in the NHS, but as I considered earlier, seriously questioned the system they had to work in. **In a democracy, where people theoretically have choices, who then has the right to TELL THEM how they are going to die?** Let alone condemn others, who love them and agonisingly want to respect their wishes, with a possible 14 years in prison. **Is that not a dictatorship?** Who decided and when was an act of love deemed a criminal offence, citing coercion and possible greed as ulterior motives for their actions? Who decided, and when was a person's decision to die with dignity taken out of their hands by a total stranger, or a pharmaceutical industry that has an invested interest in keeping them alive? Parliament debating changing the law 4 times in the last 10 plus years, with the last in 2024 ending in a more favourable outcome than those previously. The irony being, that during the writing of this book I have shown that many of the people making such decisions, have been shown to not be the most honest characters in society. On the 13/11/23, ITV screened the documentary, A Time to Die, pointing out that 425M people worldwide have the right to medically assisted suicide. With nearly 650 Brits travelling to Switzerland, so their wishes, for a price, would be honoured. The Islam religion forbids its followers to even think of it or the culprit will be banished to hell. Hopefully, the trains, buses, boats, planes and French Air Traffic Control won't be on strike that day and if not, will those people be able to use their bus passes and senior rail cards?

It's an indescribable feeling and quite empowering, accepting responsibility for one's own demise. But sometimes, because of circumstance, people are forced into having to make that decision. It was no consolation to me when I discovered the American actor, Robin Williams took his own life because he suffered from Dementia with Lewy Bodies, something mum suffered from. In January 2018, the TV programme, '24 hours in Accident and Emergency', followed the fate of an 84-year-old lady. She was already on chemotherapy, but was admitted with serious sepsis, and was then diagnosed with pneumonia. This was treated aggressively, but as she was very ill the doctor asked her to consider her final wishes, if her heart stopped. After a tearful discussion with her daughter and son, she decided that she didn't want to be resuscitated and then having made the decision, she told them they didn't need to wait around and could go home. Sadly, she passed away 5 months later. The Indian faith sees death as a family occasion, when everyone gathers to be with their loved ones **before** the dying person passes away and who, incidentally, has decided for themselves it's time to go, not an unknown member of the medical profession or judiciary. The euthanasia debate seriously entered my thought processes whilst dealing with elderly patients at my Eaves Lane clinic in the 1990s. Several of whom would hint at the idea of ending their own lives, as if they wanted my blessing or opinions on the subject. At the time, did they realise that they were planting the seed that would grow and germinate in my thought processes, and become a central issue when my mother became ill with dementia and Parkinson's disease, and her quality of life became virtually non-existent? When she died in 2010, at the age of 90, 24 members of my family, who were by her bedside, were relieved that her suffering and misery had ended. I also believed that her paranoia, hallucinations and distress, were in many respects, due to the side effects of the drugs that were designed to alleviate her condition. **But then again, where would the pharmaceutical industry be if it did produce any drugs, that cured anything with one magic pill? Bankrupt. "We need drug trials. We need new medicine and new breakthroughs, but the pharmaceutical companies are corporations with shareholders and CEOs who like to get paid. There's more money in finding the next Viagra than curing cancer." "Last year, the top ten pharmaceutical companies spent seventy-three billion dollars on advertising and less than twenty-nine billion on research. Tell me where their focus is?" "The ethics committee gets paid by the drugs company too. Everybody gets paid by the drug company."** (Slaughter k, 2010. Blindsighted, PB, 18: 360-365). The drugs are developed to control and create dependency, with their side effects, which require more drugs to control. This prolonging dependency on the drugs to satisfy the shareholders, investors and fund managers, who would like to recoup the vast amounts of money they have spent on Research and Development. I can accept that but, **"As I see it, we are faced with an increasingly worrying, incalculable and unanswerable problem," says Dr Ed. "In as much as we are keeping people alive for much longer than is good for either them or the rest of the world. Yet no one has the balls to ask why. And I furthermore suggest, we would be much better off letting nature take its course a little more."** (Evans C, 2015. Call the Midlife, Health, 1;26). Having lived a life full of dreams and aspirations, and had a career I was immensely proud of, with many acquaintances, colleagues, friends and travels, but by the end I'd decided to keep myself to myself, withdrawing more into my dark and confused world of just me and my memories. When you are bruised, you circle the wagons and shut down. **"But no friends travelled with him. His life was now no more than existence and sometimes he felt so cold, he cried out for comfort."** (McAuliffe N, 2003. The Crime Tsar, PB p399). **"He ached in his heart and in his soul…awash with his gnawing emptiness."**

(Alison Bruce, The Calling, 2011, P 227).

"…one of the hazards of a solitary life. You run the risk of becoming tangled in the hair of memory." (Griffiths E, 2022. The Locked Room, PB, 23:182).

As Dido sang on her No Angels album in 2000, 'I'm so lonely I don't want to be with myself anymore.' And when there's just you and you've decided you don't like just you, it can be a problem. As Val McDermid wrote, **"alone with the nuttersphere,"** (Splinter The Silence, 2017, 12:91).

That's what happens when the wonderment goes. I missed the physicality that loneliness deprived you of. The horrible feeling of desperation, that suddenly smacked you in the face when you realised, you had no more doors to knock on, or go through, and no more paths to explore. The silence was very oppressive. As George Ezra sang on his 2022 album, 'Gold Rush Kid', "Is there anybody out there in the silence?" He also sang about, "Giving up on myself." Alan Bennet, the playwright, once said, **"If you have a partner, you can stop talking to yourself."**

"The disease is relentless. It doesn't let go. There's no respite. And one day the patient wakes up and believes a different narrative, one where fighting makes no odds, because there's no light at the end of the tunnel." (McDermid V, 2015. Splinter the Silence, 4:28).

Whilst greatly saddened, I took some comfort from the 2016 Para Olympic, wheelchair, ex world champion athlete, who had decided it would be her last Olympics and had therefore signed euthanasia forms, prior to travelling to Rio de Janeiro, stating that without her sport, carrying on living just seemed a pointless exercise. After all, life shouldn't be about survival, it should be about enjoyment. **Great things can happen when we share life. Life's better when we share. I was alone and in an abyss.** In the David Baldacci novel, Memory Man, 2015, colours were significant for one of the leading characters Decker, with white representing despair and blue death. For me, being overwhelmed with isolation and loneliness there were times when I was whiter than white, as depression engulfed me, and knew that eventually I would embrace blue. The problem with carrying on when you are lonely and isolated is, that unless you decide to show yourself, by leaving your house, nobody knows for certain you're there. You are to all intents and purposes, invisible. In much the same way as you can become, when you retire. Knowing that if you suffered a heart attack, stroke, slip or fall, it could be hours, days or weeks before being discovered. That's presuming you wanted to be discovered. You then realise that if you decide not to carry on and end your life, still nobody would know, because you now can't show yourself. It's ironic that when you don't need anything, life offers you plenty but as you get older and need something, life deprives you. **"Harry had heard about people wanting to die, and had never understood it. To Harry, life had always been sweet, to be savoured. But now he understood those old people: infirm, filled with pain, just downright, bloody tired. Life got thin, he could see that now. Life became too much. And then ….well, was death so terrible, really?"** (Keane J, 2011. The Make, p371). My brother Stephen thinks that people who commit suicide are selfish, because they don't consider those they have left behind, and what impact taking their own lives will have on them.

But does he not consider, that many of those that are left behind, never considered the person who committed suicide enough, and if they did, only patronised them and viewed them as cash cows or baby sitters? Who's having his record collection, it must be worth a few bobs? they ask. Also, by ending their lives, rather than being selfish and prolonging it, many feel they are doing their family and friends, well the few that have stayed in touch, a favour as they would be better off, when they'd gone. When did a right to die become a duty? Life is about choice. **"Don't judge anyone's choice. Not until you know what options they had to choose from."** (Booth S, 2017, Secrets of Death, PB, 10:139).

As a person, who was a strong advocate of self-analysis, I frequently didn't like who I'd become. Which didn't help with my depression. I wished I hadn't become boring. I wish I didn't talk too much. I wish I didn't know what I knew about human behaviour, so that I didn't despair about what was happening around me on a daily basis. I wish I didn't feel all this anger and angst, against certain tribes in society. But at the end of the day, an ironic pun, I had to arrive at these points to decide when it was time to leave the scene.

John Steinbeck said, **"Death was a friend and sleep was Death's brother."** The choice could simply be, the finality of death as opposed to the uncertainty of life.

"Was it cowardly to plan your own death, to face up to that final unknown prospect and meet it without flinching." (Booth S, 2017, Secrets of Death, PB, 10:34).

There's another argument that individuals who commit suicide are not thinking rationally. Ironically one of the side effects of anti-depressants is suicidal thoughts. Whilst others argue: **"We often forget that the decision to commit suicide tends to be taken by rationally thinking, sane people who no longer consider that life has anything left to offer," Aune said, "Old people who have lost their life's companion or whose health is failing, for example."..."First of all, you have to define the meaning of rational. When someone who is depressed opts to escape from the pain by taking their own life, you have to assume the distressed party has weighed up both sides. On the other hand, it is difficult to see suicide as rational in the typical scenario, where the sufferer is on their way out of a trough, and only then finds the energy to perform the active deed which suicide is. Can suicide be a completely spontaneous act? Of course, it can. It is usual, however, for there to be attempts first, especially amongst women. In the USA, there are calculated to be ten pseudo – suicide attempts amongst women for every one suicide. Pseudo? Taking five sleeping tablets is a cry for help, serious enough it's true, but I don't include it as a suicide attempt when half a bottle of pills is still on the bedside table."... "Men are 3 times more likely to commit suicide than women and are more successful because they choose more aggressive, lethal methods than women. Guns and tall buildings, instead of cutting their wrists or taking an overdose. It is very unusual for a woman to shoot herself."** (Nesbo J, 2002. Nemesis, p134-5).

Although Roxy Music's Brian Ferry's ex-wife, Lucy Birley, would disagree because in July, 2018, she shot herself. The programme, 'How to Die', BBC 2, 10/02/2016, was a true, brilliant, if very sad, insight into a very intelligent, fun-loving guy called Simon, who ran his own company, but as life was going along swimmingly was diagnosed with Motor Neurone's Disease and given a timetable of how his body would eventually shut down, rendering him a virtual cabbage. Before the disease started to affect his mental and physical capabilities, he decided that he was going to travel to Basel, in Switzerland, on his next birthday, and pay for assisted suicide, as the courts would not accept assisted suicide in the UK. Switzerland, Luxembourg and Belgium are countries where anyone, who so wished, subject to stringent checks, could ask another to administer saline solution to open and flush out the veins; then sodium thiopental, which quickly knocked you out and rendered you unconscious; then pancuronium bromide, a muscle relaxant which stopped the breathing and finally, the lethal dose of 50-400 ccs of potassium chloride, that stopped the heart. For me, this course of action would be so much easier for all concerned than enduring all the heartache and upset caused by preserving life, not to mention the cost savings. Apart from those methods previously alluded to, Carbon Monoxide poisoning used to be the traditional method amongst depressed middle –aged men, with a pipe from the exhaust into the car. However, the design of modern more eco –friendly cars has stymied that. **As mentioned previously, surely the Health Minister had been advised, that euthanasia was a brilliant cost cutting exercise, by allowing people, who so wished, to die in a dignified fashion.** But both assisted suicides, an offence under the 1961 Suicide Act, punishable by 14 years in prison, and Active Euthanasia, which is treated as either murder or manslaughter, are illegal under British Law. **But is assisted suicide wrong? 14 years in prison for showing love and compassion by carrying out someone's wishes by helping them out of their misery, so they did not have to endure their own suffering. Who decided mercy was a crime? What a crazy world we live in. Is this because we are the highest form of intelligence in the animal kingdom?** Or is it, as I suspect over the years, the greedy pharmaceutical industry has had a say, using the moral and ethical arguments, to put a stop to that idea. **Keep them alive, they're worth more I hear them shout, or should that be whisper? Profits before people.** Also care packages are big business for many. All the talk about the ethics of dying is really a question of who takes charge of the process- and why should it only be the doctors or politicians? When, as we know, the latter have difficulty looking after themselves, never mind others in distress. The 'right to die groups' argue there's always a right time and a place to die. Whilst the Greek philosophers thought every person should choose for themselves when they die. Nietzsche, a German philosopher, also considered that the individual had a full moral right to take his/her own life. He used the word *freitod* or voluntary death. Simon's story was all about how he persuaded his family to comply with his wishes. In January 2018, a similar case to Simon's, but this time related to a gentleman named Noel, who also had been diagnosed with Motor Neurone's Disease, was challenging the courts arguing that the Suicide Act, 1961, was incompatible with parts of European Convention on Human Rights, that protect against discrimination and guaranteed respect for private and family life. In another TV episode of, 24 hours in Accident and Emergency, Channel 4, 8/1/2019, David's wife Jill, aged 40, having been diagnosed with ME repeatedly informed her husband that she wanted to end her own life. Her third attempt was when he returned home to find her with a plastic bag over her head, with a string tied around her throat. She was barely alive but pleaded with him to help her. He tightened the string until he knew she was dead, and then phoned 999. He said his actions were humane and it was what his wife, who he dearly loved, had begged him to do. He was charged with murder, but his sentence was later reduced to assisted suicide and was given a 9 months', suspended prison sentence. **It's crazy that we can take our pets to the vets to be put down, to save them further distress but such acts of kindness are frowned upon when it involves a human being. And we pontificate about compassion and being intelligent.** For me, suicide was all about choice and the motivation, maybe destiny, but certainly not to seek attention or sympathy and more to do with mental peace and tranquillity. **"A death faced with forethought and a clear conscience was a privilege granted only to a few."** (Hall MR, 2011. The Redeemed, 9:133).

In January, 2024, C4 screened, Truelove, about a group of old friends who, after a drinking session after attending another friend's funeral, came to an agreement to help, as and when the time arose, each other to end their lives all in the name of true love. Sometime later when such became a reality, the moral dilemmas and implications of what they had previously agreed to, became the essence of the drama.

As I've said I wasn't a religious person and a non–believer in an afterlife, even though studies have suggested that we, as the highest form of intelligence in the animal kingdom, are actually hardwired to believe in a creator, a controlling creative force we pay homage to, through ritualistic acts. As Marx pointed out religion was the people's opium. But for me, as a biologist, life was a balance between nature, nurture, conditioning and circumstance. I believed in the capacity of people, in particular religious zealots, to do terrible things, and conversely for other people to do good deeds. As for me, I knew **I was not a bad person,** full of anger and frustration when I'd been let down or disappointed, or just dismissed as though I was an insignificant entity, but does that make someone bad? Derek Smallwood, a PE advisor, said at times I was like a red rag to a bull when I came across injustice. I just thought I was honest and wanted to try and put things right. **After all what is diplomacy but insincerity in disguise? Why can't people be more honest, at least then everyone would know where they stood, instead of believing they were in a better place than they actually were, with several knives anchored in their backs? People do not like honesty. In a democracy, what is the point of being asked your opinion, knowing that your honest answer may be ignored or cause offence, or you may become an ic, ist, or an ism? Or is it that in the year 2023, you run the risk of being sued or trolled?** Money, money, money sang the pop group Abba. For me, this literal journey of writing my autobiography had been a roller coaster of highs and lows, but was very necessary. Not to get into someone's Top 10 of books to read, although that would be appreciated, but to give substance and meaning to **my life**. The escape it afforded me was, at times, quite therapeutic and cathartic, but there were other times when I had to distance myself from it, because the memories were too raw and the facts too depressing. **"People want to avoid the past, I suppose that's natural. When we tally up all we've said and done over the years, despite the wonderful memories, the regrets may be fewer but stand out more prominently, glowing coals that we never quite extinguish, try though we might."** (Deaver J, 2010. Edge, p276).

So here I was, a communication and people person with no people to communicate with, apart from my six house mates, mum, Maurice, Elliot, Leo, the wall and Dee. That's not being disrespectful to my sister Lillian, brothers Jack and Stephen, niece Claire, Laura and the children, cousin Amy and the few friends I had dotted around the world, but I couldn't expect them to be on call 24/7 just because I was lonely and depressed. Michael Palin, of travelogue and Monty Python fame, once remarked that he just wanted to grow old with his mates. Sadly, for me my mates, for one reason or another, were in short supply. Being a social animal, to be deprived of company and conversation was not good, and so as I've said there came a time when I reached **the TIPPING POINT**, when decisions had to be made and actions had to be taken. As Neil White pointed out in his 2010 novel, Dead Silent, page 162, **"… northern men, you just keep it all in, hold everything back, until it turns into a poison and eats away at you."** Not forgetting, **"Little girls grow up to be women, little boys grow up to be little boys."** (Fry S, The Liar, 1991. PB, 13:357). For me, problems were a question of ownership, and don't forget for many years I'd been guided by the mantra, **you do people a great service, if you don't bore them with your problems because they have enough of their own.** A problem shared was not a problem halved, it just meant two people were now aware of the same problem.

For me, **the cold reality of death was a checklist of questions and tasks:**

After the body was discovered it had to be disposed of fairly quickly, first, if no autopsy was required, to the undertakers/Chapel of Rest, and then the church or crematorium. If no post mortem was required a week of frenzied activity ensued, where the body was the focus of attention to address the issues of:

Who needs to be informed? Should the corpse be buried or cremated? What kind of service did the deceased want? What should we dress them in, tracksuit or dress suit? What about the order of service, music to be played, songs to be sung, verses to be read? Who is the chosen one to read the eulogy, and does anyone want to read a verse or poem?

What nice things should be said about the corpse? Although, many funerals are doused with hypocrisy and insincerity, where lies are spouted and told. Also, it's not really the acceptable thing to slander the dead but for many two faced, back stabbers why change the habit of a lifetime? Also, certain people only want to know how old he/she was so they can then decide if they've had 'a good run'.

Where should the wake be held, and should the sandwich fillings be salmon paste or cheese? Neither of which the pasty faced, microbiotic, seaweed eaters will want.

At the funeral, some will openly cry, whilst others will stoically remain dry eyed. **Of course, many of the techno, addicted zombies will crave a glance at their smartphone because even the dead cannot be spared 30 minutes.** Others will no doubt think of the will, and what possessions he/she has left behind that maybe are, 'up for grabs', once the funeral is over.

"Like piranha fish coming off hunger strike." (Harvey, J, 2001. "In a true Light," PB, 1:13). Why else had the takers in the family and so-called friends come to pay their respects? Having not seen them for years, it couldn't be because they cared. As Vanessa Redgrave reminds us, in the 2006 film, Venus, **"When you die, everyone wants to be your friend."**

"She wondered who would turn up at her own funeral. That you had to be dead to have one was annoying. There should be pre-death wakes, so people could celebrate their life with others of their choosing. No hangers-on, no one turning up for the sake of appearances. No unwanted colleagues expressing insincere sympathy; just people who really cared."

(Fox K, 2007. Skin and Bone, p208). You would think as the highest form of intelligence in the animal kingdom, this idea should at least be considered. I personally think it's a great idea. Just like 'un-birthdays', in Alice in Wonderland. Anyhow, back to the funeral. As mentioned, there will be always be the threat of a mobile, smart phone, sounding off and once the culprit was identified, a steel bar should be crashed against their knee caps and groin. They should then be quietly removed from the premises and dropped on the compost heap with the dead flowers. Disrespectful, rude bastards. **No, you're not that important and if you think you are, don't forget it could be your turn next, and for everyone there's always a before and after.**

At the wake, the chosen few will laugh and reminisce, trying to remember the last time they could be arsed to phone or visit. With these people providing more evidence of the fact that they chose to ignore the fact that communication was a two-way process, by adopting the attitude, 'How dare you die without letting us know?' The diatribe of reasons given for their intransigence would at times border on downright lies. **"Lesley had received a lot of sympathy at first, but now her friends were finding** other claims on their time and compassion; there was always someone needing attention." (Yorke M, 1996. A Question of Belief, p170).

Food would be consumed, and drinks taken. Goodbyes and thank yous would follow, until the next time. Who will it be next time?

"In the end there's never any point dwelling on the past, nor spending too much time mourning the dead." (Kernick S, 2011. Payback, p463). And that's it, your life in a few hours, if people can be bothered to stay until the end, because they had to get back to attend a very important meeting. Was it worth it? Did it matter?

"We're born, we live, we die, we're dust." (Nail J, 2004. A Northern Soul, HB. 23:390). Death is like the tide, it goes out slowly but it can't be stopped, wrote Miss Alcott in Little Women. The sheer insignificance of it all! In the words of the Beatles and Marmalade, 1996, 'Oh, blah dee, Oh, blah dah, Life goes on.' As the final piece of music was playing and the curtain was closing, someone else would be doing your old job. Another funeral would be slowly creeping down the driveway. People might even stop to ask,

"WHAT's APP ENED OR WHAT THE F… WAS THAT ALL ABOUT?"

Most people go through their lives, not recognising the utter meaningless of most of it, whilst accepting the gloss. Guided by the M mentality of me, me, me, money, money, money. What kind of car they drive, the postcode they live in, the supermarket they shop at, the brand of clothes they wore. Max Wall, who during the pre and post war years was one of, if not the top highest paid performers in the entertainment industry, but whose private life left plenty to be desired and eventually he ended up bankrupt. He was considered a very clever wordsmith, as he wrote his own scripts, based on observations of human behaviour. He said the problem with people was that they thought they were happy going to a football match, getting drunk or taking a ride on a fairground. He believed this was false happiness, and that real happiness was being at peace with oneself without all the materialism. I personally realised that the longer my life was prolonged, the more chance I'd end up totally devoid of emotion and quite possibly with a mental illness. I was certainly becoming less tolerant and grumpier. I was also experiencing occasional, transient memory loss and confusion, not the senior moment, jokey stuff but actual, where am I, what am I doing, etc? Scary business and to date I've had 3 episodes, lasting from 30 minutes to several hours. Two of which have been whilst abroad, not with a broad I might add. As mentioned, on 24.9.2017, aged 67, at the Victoria Inn in Monterey, California, I did suffer transient memory loss for several hours. Another was in the presence of my younger brother, Stephen, whilst I was abroad in Rio de Janeiro, Brazil. This one lasted about 20 to 30 minutes. The condition can affect the recipient verbally, visually or informationally.

My conscience was clear. During my life I had done the best that I could. My head was held high. **"One shouldn't leave this life, without a sense of completion."** (McKellen I, 2015. Mr Holmes). For me, I hoped I hadn't left a trail of devastation in my wake. I also hoped that the few people I genuinely cared about, respected and loved, were in a good place. I could leave in the knowledge, that in my life I had done what I genuinely thought was the best at that moment in time. Knowing what I know now would I do it all again, because I still didn't know who was telling the truth? The journey has been a fascinating and insightful study into human behaviour. **In the cold light of day, what is anyone's life worth other than to say they existed for x number of years duplicating, replicating or devising a variation of, what others had done before? Other than reproduction to perpetuate the** species, what was the other stuff about? So, for me not having produced children meant, my life had achieved zero and therefore it could be argued, a waste of time. After all, is that not the reality of life, as one life begins another comes to an end? But although, I had failed to reproduce was that such a bad thing, when I see what has been produced by others? Also, hindsight is a wonderful thing.

"If only I'd have known how very dangerous love was, I wouldn't have loved. If only I had known how very deep the sea was, I wouldn't have set sail. If only I had known my very own ending, I wouldn't have begun. – (Nizar Qabban.** Alanea R, Girls of Riyadh, 2005. PB 49:271). But that's life, so full of 'If onlys'. As the psychoanalysts say, there is a moment when all hope disappears, all pride is gone, all expectations have receded and all faith is shattered, but other lives go on, until someone else starts to wonder and asks, **"WHAT's APP ENED OR WHAT THE F… WAS THAT ALL ABOUT?"** Again the irony at the end of my life was, that for someone who in the beginning lived in a council house with 8 other people, and as he grew up sought the limelight, the attention, the applause, the adulation, the adrenaline rush and, in simplicity, just wanted acceptance and a hug, I spent my final hours totally alone, no partner, no children and no one sitting by my side holding my hand. Just like Mrs Merton, aka Caroline Aherne. Life for me had come down to a series of daily tasks, that I would or wouldn't complete. Had I managed to drive everyone away? It would appear to be the case, and a bitter pill for me to swallow. In the state of California, a prisoner on Death Row is allowed 5 people to witness their death. I would have none. But as I hated goodbyes was that such a bad thing? **"It's not about love, it's about being forgotten. We only exist, if others think about us. It is like the tree that falls in the forest, with nobody around to hear it. Who the fuck cares?"** (Rowbotham M, 2011, Shatter, p106). **To re-emphasise, the greatest sadness about old age applies to most, if not all, elderly people, is that during life you meet, converse with, interact, conspire with, sleep, argue etc. with many, many people but at the end, there's just you and you are left with this aching hollowness, wondering what has happened to all those people. Where have they all gone? It's as though that for any given life x number of people have been tasked with being part of that person's life on the understanding that, at various stages they have to 'drop out' of existence.** Yes, 2016 to 2025 were definitely the worst times of my life even taking into consideration the effects that the global pandemic had on people's lives. I've since wondered, if lockdown made adultery that much harder? It would be interesting to see if the separation, divorce statistics were drastically altered as a result of Covid as excuses such as 'working late' became redundant. Sometimes, I felt so alone the hollowness frightened me. Other times, I was consumed with despair. Solitude only allows you to wallow in your memories. The irony of loneliness is that you are **not alone,** as there are millions of other people in the same situation. **The only time in my life when I was truly happy was when I was communicating face to face with people, but because society had become addicted to the technology it meant very few individuals looked you in the eyes and spoke directly to you. If they did, there appeared to be a time limit on how long they could spare to talk to you. East Enders await. 'Will you excuse me I have to take this.' So not only did I have no one to share with, but also no one to talk to. The most I could hope for was to become a swipe, scroll and a tap on the like button on someone's smartphone. Gee, thanks.**

At the end of the day, I'm very proud of my achievements. Lucky, yes, extremely grateful, yes, but not a bad person. I know everything in life is relative and open to different interpretations, but I'd enough knowledge, skills, expertise and experience to arrive at that conclusion**.** But during my life I'd doubted that, and wondered if I was in denial, after all humans are all about self-delusion. Had I suffered from Imposter Syndrome? As Phil Collins sang in 1984, 'Take a look at me now, there's just an empty space.' **As I saw it, the question that adults should repeatedly ask themselves during their lives and certainly at the end is, how good have I been at being a human being, because as you enter adulthood you are given plenty of labels and titles, but not given a job description or job specification?** But as I was coming to the end of my journey I couldn't for the life of me understand **how I had arrived at my worst-case scenario, being over 65, living alone, grossly cynical, boring, sad, lonely, lugubrious, isolated, tearful on a daily basis, depressed and desperate for a cuddle and a hug.** I didn't blame anyone but myself, for ending up boring and alone at the age of 65 plus, at 4 Park Road, how could I? Like the drug addict and alcohol dependent person, who during their lives systematically aimed to implode, lie and self-destruct, did I spend my life, because of the decisions I made, aiming for my worst-case scenario and ultimately self-destruction? Had I like them been in denial during my life as to the reality of my actions, or was it bad luck, poor judgement, naivety, inexperience, fate or destiny? Was it final payback for my early errant ways? **I was hoping that by putting down my memories in print I would find the answers but sadly I didn't find them all.** "There comes a time in man's search for meaning when one realises that there are no answers and when you come to that horrible, unavoidable realisation you accept it or you kill yourself. Or you simply stop searching." (John Hurt in the Film, Jackie, 2016).

But like Celia Imrie in the film, The Best Exotic Marigold Hotel, I didn't want to be marginalised, ignored and condescended to by not only society, but also members of my own family just because I was over 65, lonely and depressed. The silence in my life was deafening and the plan was to finish this piece of writing and consider saying a silent goodbye. **I would hopefully determine when and how my life would end,** not because I'd lost all perspective and was not thinking rationally, quite the opposite. By putting things into perspective, I'd come to the conclusion that although I still had some dreams, for one reason or another, I could not share them with the people I wanted to. I could carry on travelling alone, or running away, if that's how it could be perceived, but without someone to spark off and share the exercise, it was just that, an exercise and a devalued one to boot. When I was a teenager, I ran away to Cornwall after Hilary Mather had, 'chucked me', or should I say, 'dispensed with my services', to escape the hurt? Now at the age of 74, I dealt with the hurt by travelling, escaping into books, playing my music, gardening, writing and questioning, watching TV dramas and daily exercise. But the day comes when you have to face reality and act accordingly. Why is it some people say, 'You're not going to do anything stupid are you?' If a decision is based on fact and reasoning and is made by a lucid, reasonably intelligent, articulate person, who is mentally competent and used to making his own decisions, how can such a decision be stupid? There's a difference between giving up trying, and coming to terms with what life has thrown at you. One is fatalistic, whilst the other is realistic. In fact, the more I reasoned the more acceptable I was as to my destiny. **1 person dies by suicide every 40 seconds and this number is the highest in countries with relatively high incomes. (World Health Organisation, 2019).** Admittedly, I would have liked my sojourn to have gone on a little longer and perhaps not a fitting end for a person who had a reputation for giving others a smile, in case they didn't have one of their own but sadly, that's the reality of life. I grew up proud of my academic achievements and that I always made my own decisions, rightly or wrongly. During the journey, I'd had some wonderful people to help, advise and guide me, but the final decision would be mine and mine alone. **"Not you, not him, not her, not them. In the end we're all alone. Whatever needs to get done, I can do it on my own."** (Deaver J, 2012. XO, PB 38:237). As Frank Sinatra and Matt Munroe used to sing, 'Regrets

I've had a few but then again too few to mention.......I did it my way.' Regrets you can't undo what's been done. You can't live your life full of what ifs, only what is. **Also, I have never heard anyone say, 'I wish I'd have let myself be happier.'** Once I realised that I didn't handle rejection very well, but loved the attention that being centre stage gave me, the reason for my subsequent behaviour during my life was obvious to explain. That's not to endorse my actions or give credence to them, but I realised why I eventually ended up on my own, alone and depressed. Pay back, call it what you want, but that's what happened. **"I am going out on my own terms, whilst I can still make the choice."** (Gimenez M, 2013. Con Law, p265).

"Say goodbye to the life you've known, to your friends and lovers and family home. Run and hide as best you can. There's no escaping the Whispering Man. Now, die with dignity...." (Deaver J, 2019. The Never Game, PB, 44:268). To determine your own destiny, by knowing when and how you are to terminate your life, with just a penny left, now that's clever and the icing on the cake. **"Happy is he who is forever faced with the hour of his death, and prepares himself for the end every day."** (Gerritsen T, 2004. Body Double, p29).

The film, Get Low, in 2009, was a true story of Felix Bush, a hermit, starring, Robert Duvall, Sissy Spacek and Bill Murray, who planned his own funeral and who he wanted to attend it, whilst he was still alive, so he could enjoy it.

Alex Scott, the ex-England, women's footballer and now television presenter, upon being eliminated from, Strictly Come Dancing, 1/12/2019, said, **"Don't cry because it's over. Smile because it happened."** Possible source, Bobby Ball, a welder and entertainer from Oldham. Rock on, Tommy. William Shakespeare, King Lear, Act 5, **HE DIES.** Or as the Spanish say, **Nada Mas,** it's over. To coin a cliché, **'He died a very sad, very lonely man.'** Who realised late on in life NOT to fill the silence, but let it continue. Silence is Golden, Golden, sang the Tremeloes, in 1964.

I can't end this sojourn without leaving the reader with my final thoughts to consider, whilst you're waiting to die. To die takes 4 minutes for all the vital organs to shut down, and at the point of flat-lining the body loses 21 grams.

So, there you have it, my life to date. The fact that during my life, I was not only an active person, but also at times, by being honest, a confrontational one. Sometimes in my life I felt doing my best was not always appreciated and good enough, but then again everyone has their own agenda. **"Perfection is not human."** (Gerritsen T, 2004. Body Double, PB, p106). **I may not have been a high-profile celeb or superstar, but who is to say that just because of personal choice, decisions at the time and circumstance, I could have trodden a different path. Life is all about 'trade-offs'. Death is an open door, yet society informs us we mustn't go through it without another's permission. Why didn't I become a professional footballer? Why didn't I stay and work in computers? Why didn't I go and live in Jersey? Why didn't I become a fulltime writer? Why didn't I become a cabinet maker, as I loved creating things? Why didn't I become a DJ as music was highly significant in my life? Why didn't I choose a career treading the boards, as I clearly enjoyed being centre stage playing a role, craving attention and acceptance?** Having experienced varying levels of success and enjoyment in all of these things, making what I thought would be lifetime friendships in all of them, my reply is, **no one asked, or should I say very few asked.** Or was the truth that it was not on my radar and if it was, no one pointed me in the right direction? Or was it just the vicissitudes of life? I'll let the reader decide. Having read many biographies and autobiographies my journey with all its snapshots, episodes and their significance, like many, was similar to others, but without the aid of the paparazzi and modern technology to record and distort the events at the time. I lived in 6 houses and this made me realise, that it is not as easy to empty your memories, pleasant and painful, from your mind, as it was to empty the furniture from such houses. Not forgetting we cannot live without memories, just as we cannot live within them. Also, you can't ever un-know something. If someone puts some knowledge in your head, you can't just get rid of it unless trauma, accident or mental illness intervenes. So, what of the future, my destiny, what do I see? Was it more transient memory loss and confusion? **No, thank you.**

In 2004, Lynne Truss in her book, Talking To The Hand, gave 6 good reasons to stay home and bolt the door, as she was struggling coming to terms with what was happening in society. 20 years later, yours truly was going through the same emotional turmoil. At this juncture, can I thank Lindsay Bainbridge at Teesside University for introducing me to Talk To The Hand. "**I do not claim to have uttered all of the truth here, but I hope that everything I have said is true.**" Ghali Al-Qsaibi.

"**I don't fear death, but Oh God, I'd have liked to have fixed some of this before I go. Close the book with a flourish.**" Christopher Plummer in the film, Knives Out, 2019. But sadly, I couldn't. In the 1930s Mae West said, "**You only live once, but if you do it right, once is enough.**" Sky Arts, 17/0/2024, Dirty Blonde. I like the quote by Stan Laurel of Laurel and Hardy fame, "**If anyone at my funeral has a long face, I will never speak to them again.**"

I'd like my final words to be those of the great actress, Dame Maggie Smith, who sadly passed away in September, 2024, spoken in the 2015 film, The 2nd Best Exotic Marigold Hotel, "**There's no such thing as an ending, just a place where you leave the story.**" I hope you've enjoyed mine, as I've found it quite cathartic writing it all down. I started writing this book by making a section titled, Dreams and Aspirations. Now I'm at the end, I hope to get it published just like at the ending to Greta Gerwig's, 2019, Oscar winning film, Little Women.

James Briggs, July, 2025.

What's App Ened? Or What The F... Was All That About?

Author Biography

James Briggs, Cert Ed., ACP., B.Ed.(Hons), DO., FADip.(TOI), PgCLTHE and a Fellow of the Higher Education Academy, was a successful schoolboy footballer and athlete. Turning down a professional football apprenticeship with Oldham Athletic FC he trained as a Biology/PE teacher in the late 60's and 70's, and spent 17 years in Primary Education before re-training to become an Osteopath/Sports Therapist. In 1991/2 he was the Sports Therapist on the NW Counties Junior Rugby League Tour to Australia, Fiji and New Zealand. He's a non-fictional, published author, who has also written and had published several articles related to his work in health, exercise and sport. Returning to full time teaching in 1996/7, but this time in Higher Education, meant he spent 35 years in education and over 18 years in health care. But most importantly 75 years experiencing life.

www.ingramcontent.com/pod-product-compliance
Lightning Source LLC
Chambersburg PA
CBHW061123070526
44584CB00033B/4204